Interstate Classics Series

CLASSICS
OF
ORGANIZATIONAL
BEHAVIOR

Second Edition

CLASSICS
OF
ORGANIZATIONAL
BEHAVIOR

Edited by

Walter E. Natemeyer, Ph.D.

Jay S. Gilberg, Ph.D.

THE INTERSTATE
Printers & Publishers, Inc.

Danville, Illinois

CLASSICS OF ORGANIZATIONAL BEHAVIOR, Second Edition. Copyright © 1989 by The Interstate Printers & Publishers, Inc. All rights reserved. First edition, 1978. Printed in the United States of America.

Library of Congress Catalog Card No. 88-80497

1 2 3
4 5 6
7 8 9

ISBN 0-8134-2814-9

Topical Contents

III. INTERPERSONAL AND GROUP BEHAVIOR

IV. LEADERSHIP AND POWER

V. ORGANIZATIONAL CHANGE AND DEVELOPMENT

VI. EMERGING CLASSICS

Chronological Contents

Preface

"Management" is frequently defined as the process of utilizing numerous resources (personnel, materials, physical plant, equipment, information, time, and money) in order to accomplish organizational goals. Maximum organizational effectiveness clearly requires competent management of all resources. None, however, is more important in determining the long-term effectiveness of an organization than its people, for they control how well all of the other resources are managed. If an organization utilizes its human resources effectively, the successful management of all of the organization's other resources becomes much more feasible. The importance of the human element in the practice of management has been increasingly recognized since the pioneering Hawthorne experiments more than 60 years ago. Since that time the behavioral sciences have become an integral part of the field of management, and the professional literature of organizational behavior has proliferated. Within this now immense body of knowledge, certain works stand out as more important than others, as "classics." The purpose of this book is to familiarize the reader with some of the outstanding contributions to the knowledge and literature of organizational behavior.

Selecting this set of "classics" has not been an easy task. Not only is there no consensus on just what constitutes the "classics" of organizational behavior, but the limitations of space and balance necessitated that many excellent articles be omitted. While the editors fully expect to be criticized for these exclusions, it should be considerably more difficult to challenge their inclusions. For what remains is a collection of readable, time-tested, and oft-referenced readings from many of the most important writers in the field.

Ten years have passed since *Classics of Organizational Behavior* was first published. Of the 32 readings in the first edition, 21 have been retained in the second edition. Eleven articles are entirely new, including four "emerging classics." "Classic" implies recognized and enduring worth. The editors believe that the selections contained herein have each achieved such recognition.

The book is organized into six sections, each beginning with a brief introduction. Within each section, the selections are typically presented in chronological order so that the reader may gain a sense of the evolution of thought in the field of organizational behavior. Section I provides an overview of management and the behavioral sciences. Section II deals with individual behavior, and motivation. In Section III, the readings focus on interpersonal and group behavior, while Section IV contains selections on leadership and power. Section V addresses organizational change and development, and Section VI concludes with recent "emerging classics."

Classics of Organizational Behavior, 2nd ed., could not have been published without the help of numerous others. We wish to thank the authors and publishers of these "classics" for permission to reproduce their work. The suggestions and comments of colleagues Paul Hersey, John M. Ivancevich, J. Timothy McMahon, and Richard L. Schott were much appreciated. The assistance from Ronald L. McDaniel and others at The Interstate Printers & Publishers, Inc., was very helpful. Finally, we would like to thank our wives, Carolann and Lucy, for their support and encouragement throughout this project.

Walter E. Natemeyer

Jay S. Gilberg

February 1988

OUR CONTRIBUTORS

J. Stacy Adams

Clayton P. Alderfer

Chris Argyris

Warren G. Bennis

Robert R. Blake

Kenneth H. Blanchard

John P. Campbell

Dorwin Cartwright

Lester Coch

Marvin D. Dunnette

Fred E. Fiedler

John R. P. French, Jr.

Wendell French

J. Richard Hackman

Paul Hersey

Frederick Herzberg

Robert J. House

Irving L. Janis

Rosabeth Moss Kanter

Edward E. Lawler III

Rensis Likert

Jay W. Lorsch

Joseph Luft

Norman R. F. Maier

Abraham H. Maslow

David C. McClelland

Douglas M. McGregor

Terence R. Mitchell

Jane S. Mouton

John Naisbitt

Walter E. Natemeyer

Greg R. Oldham

Thomas J. Peters

Jeffrey Pfeffer

Bertram Raven

Fritz J. Roethlisberger

Harold M. F. Rush

Gerald R. Salancik

Edgar H. Schein

Warren H. Schmidt

Robert Tannenbaum

Robert H. Waterman, Jr.

Karl E. Weick, Jr.

Alvin Zander

About the Editors

Walter E. Natemeyer received his B.B.A. and M.B.A. from Ohio University and his Ph.D. in Organizational Behavior from The University of Houston. He has taught at Ohio University (1970-71), The University of Houston (1972-75), and The University of Houston-Clear Lake (1975-83). In addition to occasionally serving as an adjunct professor, Dr. Natemeyer is president of North American Training and Development, Inc., a Houston-based management consulting firm. He has served as consultant to more than 100 major organizations in the United States and abroad.

Jay S. Gilberg received his B.A. and M.A. from Ohio University and his Ph.D. in Government from The University of Texas. He has taught at Ohio University (1978-79), The University of Texas (1979-84), and The University of Texas at Dallas (1984-87). In addition to serving as an adjunct professor, Dr. Gilberg manages the San Diego operations of a personnel consulting firm.

I

Management and the Behavioral Sciences

Introduction. Organizational behavior as an academic discipline consists of those aspects of the behavioral sciences that focus on the understanding of human behavior in organizations. The Hawthorne experiments are generally considered to be the genesis of the application of the behavioral sciences to influence organizational behavior and management. The famous experiments—conducted at the Western Electric Company's plant in Cicero, Illinois—began in the late 1920s as an attempt to determine the impact of working conditions on employee productivity. However, what evolved during nearly a decade of research was the scientifically based realization that the effects of psychological and social factors on the work behavior of employees were as significant as the more traditional physiological factors. A definitive account of these experiments is contained in *Management and the Worker* (1939), by Fritz J. Roethlisberger and William J. Dickson. Reprinted here is the more concise description of the studies as given by Roethlisberger in a chapter from his book *Management and Morale* (1941).

Thirty years after the Hawthorne studies began, Douglas M. McGregor published his article "The Human Side of Enterprise." No author has done more to popularize the notion of industrial humanism. McGregor contrasts the more traditional view of the worker as lazy and resistant (Theory X) with a more positive and humanistic view (Theory Y). He contends that significant increases in human effort will result in organizational settings that create opportunities, remove obstacles, encourage growth, and provide guidance. McGregor's 1957 article presents the main themes of his more famous 1960 book of the same title.

Chris Argyris, in "The Individual and the Organization," contends that the requirements of the formal structure of organizations are often incompatible with the development or maturation of the human personality. He argues that the various aspects of formal organizations (such as task specialization, unity of direction, chain of command, and span of control) tend to inhibit the development of psychologically healthy, mature

1

adults. This failure to integrate the individual and the organization results in negative consequences for both the organization and its employees. The article reprinted here summarized his landmark 1957 book, *Personality and Organization*.

The fourth selection is "The World of Work and the Behavioral Sciences: A Perspective and an Overview," by Harold M. F. Rush. Rush defines behavioral science as the systematic study of behavior and provides an overview of its role in the field of management from both historical and contemporary perspectives. The work of pioneering researchers, such as Elton Mayo and Kurt Lewin, is briefly reviewed and interpreted. Contemporary behavioral science is seen as an applied, normative, and humanistic science that views the organization as a total system and focuses upon the improvement of interpersonal and group dynamics within that system.

The final article in this section is "Making Behavioral Science More Useful," by Jay W. Lorsch. The appeal of simple cures to complex management problems is discussed. Lorsch argues, however, that "universal" theories of behavior may not apply to specific managerial situations. He believes that there is great potential for the behavioral sciences to develop "situational" theories that can improve a manager's ability to analyze, understand, and deal with the complex social and human issues he or she faces.

1. The Hawthorne Experiments*

FRITZ J. ROETHLISBERGER

At a recent meeting the researches in personnel at the Hawthorne plant of the Western Electric Company were mentioned by both a management man and a union man. There seemed to be no difference of opinion between the two regarding the importance or relevance of these research findings for effective management-employee relations. This seemed to me interesting because it suggested that the labor situation can be discussed at a level where both sides can roughly agree. The question of what this level is can be answered only after closer examination of these studies.

In the February, 1941, issue of the *Reader's Digest* there appeared a summary statement of these researches by Stuart Chase, under the title, "What Makes the Worker Like to Work?" At the conclusion of his article, Stuart Chase said, "There is an idea here so big that it leaves one gasping." Just what Mr. Chase meant by this statement is not explained, but to find out one can go back to the actual studies and see what was learned from them. In my opinion, the results were very simple and obvious—as Sherlock Holmes used to say to Dr. Watson, "Elementary, my dear Watson." Now this is what may have left Stuart Chase "gasping"—the systematic exploitation of the simple and the obvious which these studies represent.

There seems to be an assumption today that we need a complex set of

ideas to handle the complex problems of this complex world in which we live. We assume that a big problem needs a big idea; a complex problem needs a complex idea for its solution. As a result, our thinking tends to become more and more tortuous and muddled. Nowhere is this more true than in matters of human behavior. It seems to me that the road back to sanity—and here is where my title comes in—lies

(1) In having a few simple and clear ideas about the world in which we live.

(2) In complicating our ideas, not in a vacuum, but only in reference to things we can observe, see, feel, hear, and touch. Let us not generalize from verbal definitions; let us know in fact what we are talking about.

(3) In having a very simple method by means of which we can explore our complex world. We need a tool which will allow us to get the data from which our generalizations are to be drawn. We need a simple skill to keep us in touch with what is sometimes referred to as "reality."

(4) In being "tough-minded," i.e., in not letting ourselves be too disappointed because the complex world never quite fulfills our most cherished expectations of it. Let us remember that the concrete phenomena will always elude any set of abstractions that we can make of them.

(5) In knowing very clearly the class of phenomena to which our ideas and methods relate. Now, this is merely a way of saying, "Do not use a saw as a hammer." A saw is a useful tool precisely because it is limited and designed for a certain purpose. Do not criticize the use-

*Source: From Fritz J. Roethlisberger, *Management and Morale* (Cambridge, Mass.: Harvard University Press). Copyright © 1941 by the President and Fellows of Harvard College; copyright © 1969 by Fritz J. Roethlisberger. Selection has been retitled and originally appeared as Chapter II, "The Road Back to Sanity," pp. 7-26. Reprinted by permission of the publishers.

fulness of a saw because it does not make a good hammer.

Although this last statement is obvious with regard to such things as "saws" and "hammers," it is less well understood in the area of human relations. Too often we try to solve human problems with nonhuman tools and, what is still more extraordinary, in terms of nonhuman data. We take data from which all human meaning has been deleted and then are surprised to find that we reach conclusions which have no human significance.

It is my simple thesis that a human problem requires a human solution. First, we have to learn to recognize a human problem when we see one; and, second, upon recognizing it, we have to learn to deal with it as such and not as if it were something else. Too often at the verbal level we talk glibly about the importance of the human factor; and too seldom at the concrete level of behavior do we recognize a human problem for what it is and deal with it as such. *A human problem to be brought to a human solution requires human data and human tools.* It is my purpose to use the Western Electric researches as an illustration of what I mean by this statement, because, if they deserve the publicity and acclaim which they have received, it is because, in my opinion, they have so conclusively demonstrated this point. In this sense they are the road back to sanity in management-employee relations.

EXPERIMENTS IN ILLUMINATION

The Western Electric researches started about sixteen years ago, in the Hawthorne plant, with a series of experiments on illumination. The purpose was to find out the relation of the quality and quantity of illumination to the efficiency of industrial workers. These studies lasted several years, and I shall not describe them in detail. It will suffice to point out that the results were quite different from what had been expected.

In one experiment the workers were divided into two groups. One group, called the "test group," was to work under different illumination intensities. The other group, called the "control group," was to work under an intensity of illumination as nearly constant as possible. During the first experiment, the test group was submitted to three different intensities of illumination of increasing magnitude, 24, 46, and 70 foot candles. What were the results of this early experiment? Production increased in both rooms—in both the test group and the control group—and the rise in output was roughly of the same magnitude in both cases.

In another experiment, the light under which the test group worked was decreased from 10 to 3 foot candles, while the control group worked, as before, under a constant level of illumination intensity. In this case the output rate in the test group went up instead of down. It also went up in the control group.

In still another experiment, the workers were allowed to believe that the illumination was being increased, although, in fact, no change in intensity was made. The workers commented favorably on the improved lighting condition, but there was no appreciable change in output. At another time, the workers were allowed to believe that the intensity of illumination was being decreased, although again, in fact, no actual change was made. The workers complained somewhat about the poorer lighting, but again there was no appreciable effect on output.

And finally, in another experiment, the intensity of illumination was decreased to .06 of a foot candle, which is the intensity of illumination approximately equivalent to that of ordinary moonlight. Not until this point was reached was there any appreciable decline in the output rate.

What did the experimenters learn? Obviously, as Stuart Chase said, there was something "screwy," but the experimenters were not quite sure who or what was screwy—they themselves, the subjects, or the results. One thing was clear: the results were negative. Nothing of a positive nature had been learned about the relation of illumination to industrial efficiency. If the results were to be taken at their face value, it would appear that there was no relation between illumination and industrial efficiency. However, the investigators were not yet quite willing to draw this conclusion. They realized the difficulty of testing for the effect of a single variable in a situation where there were many uncontrolled variables. It was thought therefore that another experiment should be devised in which other variables affecting the output of workers could be better controlled.

A few of the tough-minded experimenters already were beginning to suspect their basic ideas and assumptions with regard to human motivation. It occurred to them that the trouble was not so much with the results or with the subjects as it was with their notion regarding the way their subjects were supposed to behave—the notion of a simple cause-and-effect, direct relationship between certain physical changes in the workers' environment and the responses of the workers to these changes. Such a notion completely ignored the human meaning of these changes to the people who were subjected to them.

In the illumination experiments, therefore, we have a classic example of trying to deal with a human situation in nonhuman terms. The experimenters had obtained no human data; they had been handling electric-light bulbs and plotting average output curves. Hence their results had no human significance. That is why they seemed screwy. Let me suggest here, however, that the results were not screwy, but the experimenters were—a "screwy" person being by def-inition one who is not acting in accordance with the customary human values of the situation in which he finds himself.

THE RELAY ASSEMBLY TEST ROOM

Another experiment was framed, in which it was planned to submit a segregated group of workers to different kinds of working conditions. The idea was very simple: A group of five girls were placed in a separate room where their conditions of work could be carefully controlled, where their output could be measured, and where they could be closely observed. It was decided to introduce at specified intervals different changes in working conditions and to see what effect these innovations had on output. Also, records were kept, such as the temperature and humidity of the room, the number of hours each girl slept at night, the kind and amount of food she ate for breakfast, lunch, and dinner. Output was carefully measured, the time it took each girl to assemble a telephone relay of approximately forty parts (roughly a minute) being automatically recorded each time; quality records were kept; each girl had a physical examination at regular intervals. Under these conditions of close observation the girls were studied for a period of five years. Literally tons of material were collected. Probably nowhere in the world has so much material been collected about a small group of workers for such a long period of time.

But what about the results? They can be stated very briefly. When all is said and done, they amount roughly to this: A skillful statistician spent several years trying to relate variations in output with variations in the physical circumstances of these five operators. For example, he correlated the hours that each girl spent in bed the night before with variations in output the following day. Inasmuch as some people said that the effect of being out late one night was not felt the following day but the day after that, he correlated variations in output with the amount of rest the operators had had two nights before. I mention this just to point out the fact that he missed no obvious tricks and that he did a careful job and a thorough one, and it took him many years to do it. The attempt to relate changes in physical circumstances to variations in output resulted in not a single correlation of enough statistical significance to be recognized by any competent statistician as having any meaning.

Now, of course, it would be misleading to say that this negative result was the only conclusion reached. There were positive conclusions, and it did not take the experimenters more than two years to find out that they had missed the boat. After two years of work, certain things happened which made them sit up and take notice. Different experimental conditions of work, in the nature of changes in the number and duration of rest pauses and differences in the length of the working day and week, had been introduced in this Relay Assembly Test Room. For example, the investigators first introduced two five-minute rests, one in the morning and one in the afternoon. Then they increased the length of these rests, and after that they introduced the rests at different times of the day. During one experimental period they served the operators a specially prepared lunch during the rest. In the later periods, they decreased the length of the working day by one-half hour and then by one hour. They gave the operators Saturday morning off for a while. Altogether, thirteen such periods of different working conditions were introduced in the first two years.

During the first year and a half of the experiment, everybody was happy, both the investigators and the operators. The investigators were happy because as conditions of work improved the output

rate rose steadily. Here, it appeared, was strong evidence in favor of their preconceived hypothesis that fatigue was the major factor limiting output. The operators were happy because their conditions of work were being improved, they were earning more money, and they were objects of considerable attention from top management. But then one investigator—one of those tough-minded fellows—suggested that they restore the original conditions of work, that is, go back to a full forty-eight-hour week without rests, lunches and what not. This was Period XII. Then the happy state of affairs, when everything was going along as it theoretically should, went sour. Output, instead of taking the expected nose dive, maintained its high level.

Again the investigators were forcibly reminded that human situations are likely to be complex. In any human situation, whenever a simple change is introduced—a rest pause, for example—other changes, unwanted and unanticipated, may also be brought about. What I am saying here is very simple. If one experiments on a stone, the stone does not know it is being experimented upon—all of which makes it simple for people experimenting on stones. But if a human being is being experimented upon, he is likely to know it. Therefore, his attitudes toward the experiment and toward the experimenters become very important factors in determining his responses to the situation.

Now that is what happened in the Relay Assembly Test Room. To the investigators, it was essential that the workers give their full and wholehearted coöperation to the experiment. They did not want the operators to work harder or easier depending upon their attitude toward the conditions that were imposed. They wanted them to work as they felt, so that they could be sure that the different physical conditions of work were solely responsible for the variations in output. For each of the experimental changes, they wanted subjects whose responses would be uninfluenced by so-called "psychological factors."

In order to bring this about, the investigators did everything in their power to secure the complete coöperation of their subjects, with the result that almost all the practices common to the shop were altered. The operators were consulted about the changes to be made, and, indeed, several plans were abandoned because they met with the disapproval of the girls. They were questioned sympathetically about their reactions to the conditions imposed, and many of these conferences took place in the office of the superintendent. The girls were allowed to talk at work; their "bogey" was eliminated. Their physical health and well-being became matters of great concern. Their opinions, hopes, and fears were eagerly sought. What happened was that in the very process of setting the conditions for the test—a so-called "controlled" experiment—the experimenters had completely altered the social situation of the room. Inadvertently a change had been introduced which was far more important than the planned experimental innovations: the customary supervision in the room had been revolutionized. This accounted for the better attitudes of the girls and their improved rate of work.

THE DEVELOPMENT OF A NEW AND MORE FRUITFUL POINT OF VIEW

After Period XII in the Relay Assembly Test Room, the investigators decided to change their ideas radically. What all their experiments had dramatically and conclusively demonstrated was the importance of employee attitudes and sentiments. It was clear that the responses of workers to what was happening about them were dependent upon the significance these events had for them.

In most work situations the meaning of a change is likely to be as important, if not more so, than the change itself. This was the great *éclaircissement*, the new illumination, that came from the research. It was an illumination quite different from what they had expected from the illumination studies. Curiously enough, this discovery is nothing very new or startling. It is something which anyone who has had some concrete experience in handling other people intuitively recognizes and practices. Whether or not a person is going to give his services whole-heartedly to a group depends, in good part, on the way he feels about his job, his fellow workers, and supervisors—the meaning for him of what is happening about him.

However, when the experimenters began to tackle the problem of employee attitudes and the factors determining such attitudes—when they began to tackle the problem of "meaning"—they entered a sort of twilight zone where things are never quite what they seem. Moreover, overnight, as it were, they were robbed of all the tools they had so carefully forged; for all their previous tools were nonhuman tools concerned with the measurement of output, temperature, humidity, etc., and these were no longer useful for the human data that they now wanted to obtain. What the experimenters now wanted to know was how a person felt, what his intimate thinking, reflections, and preoccupations were, and what he liked and disliked about his work environment. In short, what did the whole blooming business—his job, his supervision, his working conditions—mean to him? Now this was human stuff, and there were no tools, or at least the experimenters knew of none, for obtaining and evaluating this kind of material.

Fortunately, there were a few courageous souls among the experimenters. These men were not metaphysicians, psychologists, academicians, professors, intellectuals, or what have you. They were men of common sense and of practical affairs. They were not driven by any great heroic desire to change the world. They were true experimenters, that is, men compelled to follow the implications of their own monkey business. All the evidence of their studies was pointing in one direction. Would they take the jump? They did.

EXPERIMENTS IN INTERVIEWING WORKERS

A few tough-minded experimenters decided to go into the shops and—completely disarmed and denuded of their elaborate logical equipment and in all humility—to see if they could learn how to get the workers to talk about things that were important to them and could learn to understand what the workers were trying to tell them. This was a revolutionary idea in the year 1928, when this interviewing program started—the idea of getting a worker to talk to you and to listen sympathetically, but intelligently, to what he had to say. In that year a new era of personnel relations began. It was the first real attempt to get human data and to forge human tools to get them. In that year a novel idea was born; dimly the experimenters perceived a new method of human control. In that year the Rubicon was crossed from which there could be no return to the "good old days." Not that the experimenters ever wanted to return, because they now entered a world so exciting, so intriguing, and so full of promise that it made the "good old days" seem like the prattle and play of children.

When these experimenters decided to enter the world of "meaning," with very few tools, but with a strong sense of curiosity and a willingness to learn, they had many interesting adventures. It would be too long a story to tell all of them, or even a small part of them.

They made plenty of mistakes, but they were not afraid to learn.

At first, they found it difficult to learn to give full and complete attention to what a person had to say without interrupting him before he was through. They found it difficult to learn not to give advice, not to make or imply moral judgments about the speaker, not to argue, not to be too clever, not to dominate the conversation, not to ask leading questions. They found it difficult to get the person to talk about matters which were important to him and not to the interviewer. But, most important of all, they found it difficult to learn that perhaps the thing most significant to a person was not something in his immediate work situation.

Gradually, however, they learned these things. They discovered that sooner or later a person tends to talk about what is uppermost in his mind to a sympathetic and skillful listener, and they became more proficient in interpreting what a person is saying or trying to say. Of course they protected the confidences given to them and made absolutely sure that nothing an employee said could ever be used against him. Slowly they began to forge a simple human tool—imperfect, to be sure—to get the kind of data they wanted. They called this method "interviewing." I would hesitate to say the number of manhours of labor which went into the forging of this tool. There followed from studies made through its use a gradually changing conception of the worker and his behavior.

A NEW WAY OF VIEWING EMPLOYEE SATISFACTION AND DISSATISFACTION

When the experimenters started to study employee likes and dislikes, they assumed, at first, that they would find a simple and logical relation between a person's likes or dislikes and certain items and events in his immediate work situation. They expected to find a simple connection, for example, between a person's complaint and the object about which he was complaining. Hence, the solution would be easy: correct the object of the complaint, if possible, and presto! the complaint would disappear. Unfortunately, however, the world of human behavior is not so simple as this conception of it; and it took the investigators several arduous and painful years to find this out. I will mention only a few interesting experiences they had.

Several times they changed the objects of the complaint only to find that the attitudes of the complainants remained unchanged. In these cases, correcting the object of the complaint did not remedy the complaint or the attitude of the person expressing it. A certain complaint might disappear, to be sure, only to have another one arise. Here the investigators were running into so-called "chronic kickers," people whose dissatisfactions were more deeply rooted in factors relating to their personal histories. For such people the simple remedy of changing the object of the complaint was not enough.

Several times they did absolutely nothing about the object of the complaint, but after the interview, curiously enough, the complaint disappeared. A typical example of this was that of a woman who complained at great length and with considerable feeling about the poor food being served in the company restaurant. When, a few days later, she chanced to meet the interviewer, she commented with great enthusiasm upon the improved food and thanked the interviewer for communicating her grievance to management and for securing such prompt action. Here no change had been made in the thing criticized; yet the employee felt that something had been done.

Many times they found that people did not really want anything done about the things of which they were complaining. What they did want was an opportunity to talk about their troubles to a sympathetic listener. It was astonishing to find the number of instances in which workers complained about things which had happened many, many years ago, but which they described as vividly as if they had happened just a day before.

Here again, something was "screwy," but this time the experimenters realized that it was their assumptions which were screwy. They were assuming that the meanings which people assign to their experience are essentially logical. They were carrying in their heads the notion of the "economic man," a man primarily motivated by economic interest, whose logical capacities were being used in the service of this self-interest.

Gradually and painfully in the light of the evidence, which was overwhelming, the experimenters had been forced to abandon this conception of the worker and his behavior. Only with a new working hypothesis could they make sense of the data they had collected. The conception of the worker which they developed is actually nothing very new or startling; it is one which any effective administrator intuitively recognizes and practices in handling human beings.

First, they found that the behavior of workers could not be understood apart from their feelings or sentiments. I shall use the word "sentiment" hereafter to refer not only to such things as feelings and emotions, but also to a much wider range of phenomena which may not be expressed in violent feelings or emotions—phenomena that are referred to by such words as "loyalty," "integrity," "solidarity."

Secondly, they found that sentiments are easily disguised, and hence are difficult to recognize and to study. Manifestations of sentiment take a number of different forms. Feelings of personal integrity, for example, can be expressed by a handshake; they can also be expressed, when violated, by a sitdown strike. Moreover, people like to rationalize their sentiments and to objectify them. We are not so likely to say "I feel bad," as to say "The world is bad." In other words, we like to endow the world with those attributes and qualities which will justify and account for the feelings and sentiments we have toward it; we tend to project our sentiments on the outside world.

Thirdly, they found that manifestations of sentiment could not be understood as things in and by themselves, but only in terms of the total situation of the person. To comprehend why a person felt the way he did, a wider range of phenomena had to be explored. The following three diagrams illustrate roughly the development of this point of view.

It will be remembered that at first the investigators assumed a simple and direct relation between certain physical changes in the worker's environment and his responses to them. This simple state of mind is illustrated in diagram I. But all the evidence of the early experiments showed that the responses of employees to changes in their immediate working environment can be understood only in terms of their attitudes—the "meaning" these changes have for them. This point of view is represented in diagram II. However, the "meaning" which these changes have for the worker is not strictly and primarily logical, for they are fraught with human feelings and values. The "meaning," therefore, which any individual worker assigns to a particular change depends upon (1) his social "conditioning," or what sentiments (values, hopes, fears, expectations, etc.) he is bringing to the work situation because of his previous family and group associations, and hence the relation of the change to these sentiments; and (2) the kind of human satisfactions he is deriving from his social participation with other workers and supervisors in the immediate work group of which he is a member, and hence the effect of the change on

his customary interpersonal relations. This way of regarding the responses of workers (both verbal and overt) is represented in diagram III. It says briefly: Sentiments do not appear in a vacuum; they do not come out of the blue; they appear in a social context. They have to be considered in terms of that context, and apart from it they are likely to be misunderstood.

One further point should be made about that aspect of the worker's environment designated "Social Situation at Work" in diagram III. What is meant is that the worker is not an isolated, atomic individual; he is a member of a group, or of groups. Within each of these groups the individuals have feelings and sentiments toward each other, which bind them together in collaborative effort. Moreover, these collective sentiments can, and do, become attached to every item and object in the industrial environment—even to output. Material goods, output, wages, hours of work, and so on, cannot be treated as things in themselves. Instead, they must be interpreted as carriers of social value.

OUTPUT AS A FORM OF SOCIAL BEHAVIOR

That output is a form of social behavior was well illustrated in a study made by the Hawthorne experimenters, called the Bank Wiring Observation Room. This room contained fourteen workmen representing three occupational groups—wiremen, soldermen, and inspectors. These men were on group piecework, where the more they turned out the more they earned. In such a situation one might have expected that they would have been interested in maintaining total output and that the faster workers would have put pressure on the slower workers to improve their efficiency. But this was not the case. Operating within this group were four basic sentiments, which can be expressed briefly as follows: (1) You should not turn out too much work; if you do, you are a "rate buster." (2) You should not turn out too little work; if you do, you are a "chiseler." (3) You should not say anything to a supervisor which would react to the detriment of one of your associates; if you do, you are a "squealer." (4) You should not be too officious; that is, if you are an inspector you should not act like one.

To be an accepted member of the group a man had to act in accordance with these social standards. One man in this group exceeded the group standard of what constituted a fair day's work. Social pressure was put on him to conform, but without avail, since he enjoyed doing things the others disliked. The best-liked person in the group was the one who kept his output exactly where the group agreed it should be.

Inasmuch as the operators were agreed as to what constituted a day's work, one might have expected rate of output to be about the same for each member of the group. This was by no means the case; there were marked differences. At first the experimenters thought that the differences in individual performance were related to differences in ability, so they compared each worker's relative rank in output with his relative rank in intelligence and dexterity as measured by certain tests. The results were interesting: the lowest

producer in the room ranked first in intelligence and third in dexterity; the highest producer in the room was seventh in dexterity and lowest in intelligence. Here surely was a situation in which the native capacities of the men were not finding expression. From the viewpoint of logical, economic behavior, this room did not make sense. Only in terms of powerful sentiments could these individual differences in output level be explained. Each worker's level of output reflected his position in the informal organization of the group.

WHAT MAKES THE WORKER NOT WANT TO COOPERATE?

As a result of the Bank Wiring Observation Room, the Hawthorne researchers became more and more interested in the informal employee groups which tend to form within the formal organization of the company, and which are not likely to be represented in the organization chart. They became interested in the beliefs and creeds which have the effect of making each individual feel an integral part of the group and which make the group appear as a single unit, in the social codes and norms of behavior by means of which employees automatically work together in a group without any conscious choice as to whether they will or will not coöperate. They studied the important social functions these groups perform for their members, the histories of these informal work groups, how they spontaneously appear, how they tend to perpetuate themselves, multiply, and disappear, how they are in constant jeopardy from technical change, and hence how they tend to resist innovation. In particular, they became interested in those groups whose norms and codes of behavior are at variance with the technical and economic objectives of the company as a whole. They examined the social conditions under which it is more likely for the employee group to separate itself out in opposition to the remainder of the groups which make up the total organization. In such phenomena they felt that they had at last arrived at the heart of the problem of effective collaboration. They obtained a new enlightenment of the present industrial scene; from this point of view, many perplexing problems became more intelligible.

Some people claim, for example, that the size of the pay envelope is the major demand which the employee is making of his job. All the worker wants is to be told what to do and to get paid for doing it. If we look at him and his job in terms of sentiments, this is far from being as generally true as we would like to believe. Most of us want the satisfaction that comes from being accepted and recognized as people of worth by our friends and work associates. Money is only a small part of this social recognition. The way we are greeted by our boss, being asked to help a newcomer, being asked to keep an eye on a difficult operation, being given a job requiring special skill—all of these are acts of social recognition. They tell us how we stand in our work group. We all want tangible evidence of our social importance. We want to have a skill that is socially recognized as useful. We want the feeling of security that comes not so much from the amount of money we have in the bank as from being an accepted member of a group. A man whose job is without social function is like a man without a country; the activity to which he has to give the major portion of his life is robbed of all human meaning and significance.

If this is true—and all the evidence of the Western Electric researches points in this direction—have we not a clue as to the possible basis for labor unrest and disputes? Granted that these disputes are often stated in terms of wages, hours of work, and physical conditions of work, is it not possible that these demands are disguising, or in part are the symptomatic expression of, much more deeply rooted human situations which we have not as yet learned to recognize, to understand, or to control? It has been said there is an irresistible urge on the part of workers to tell the boss off, to tell the boss to go to hell. For some workers this generalization may hold, and I have no reason to believe it does not. But, in those situations where it does, it is telling us something very important about these particular workers and their work situations. Workers who want to tell their boss to go to hell sound to me like people whose feelings of personal integrity have been seriously injured. What in their work situations has shattered their feelings of personal integrity? Until we understand better the answer to this question, we cannot handle effectively people who manifest such sentiments. Without such understanding we are dealing only with words and not with human situations—as I fear our over-logicized machinery for handling employee grievances sometimes does.

The matters of importance to workers which the Hawthorne researches disclosed are not settled primarily by negotiating contracts. If industry today is filled with people living in a social void and without social function, a labor contract can do little to make coöperation possible. If, on the other hand, the workers are an integral part of the social situations in which they work, a legal contract is not of the first importance. Too many of us are more interested in getting our words legally straight than in getting our situations humanly straight.

In summary, therefore, the Western Electric researches seem to me like a beginning on the road back to sanity in employee relations because (1) they offer a fruitful working hypothesis, a few simple and relatively clear ideas for the study and understanding of human situations in business; (2) they offer a simple method by means of which we can explore and deal with the complex human problems in a business organization—this method is a human method: it deals with things which are important to people; and (3) they throw a new light on the precondition for effective collaboration. Too often we think of collaboration as something which can be logically or legally contrived. The Western Electric studies indicate that it is far more a matter of sentiment than a matter of logic. Workers are not isolated, unrelated individuals; they are social animals and should be treated as such.

This statement—the worker is a social animal and should be treated as such—is simple, but the systematic and consistent practice of this point of view is not. If it were systematically practiced, it would revolutionize present-day personnel work. Our technological development in the past hundred years has been tremendous. Our methods of handling people are still archaic. If this civilization is to survive, we must obtain a new understanding of human motivation and behavior in business organizations—an understanding which can be simply but effectively practiced. The Western Electric researches contribute a first step in this direction.

2. The Human Side of Enterprise*

DOUGLAS M. McGREGOR

It has become trite to say that industry has the fundamental know-how to utilize physical science and technology for the material benefit of mankind, and that we must now learn how to utilize the social sciences to make our human organizations truly effective.

To a degree, the social sciences today are in a position like that of the physical sciences with respect to atomic energy in the thirties. We know that past conceptions of the nature of man are inadequate and, in many ways, incorrect. We are becoming quite certain that, under proper conditions, unimagined resources of creative human energy could become available within the organizational setting.

We cannot tell industrial management how to apply this new knowledge in simple, economic ways. We know it will require years of exploration, much costly development research, and a substantial amount of creative imagination on the part of management to discover how to apply this growing knowledge to the organization of human effort in industry.

MANAGEMENT'S TASK: THE CONVENTIONAL VIEW

The conventional conception of management's task in harnessing human energy to organizational requirements can be stated broadly in terms of three propositions. In order to avoid the complications introduced by a label, let us call this set of propositions "Theory X":

1. Management is responsible for organizing the elements of productive enterprise—money, materials, equipment, people—in the interest of economic ends.

2. With respect to people, this is a process of directing their efforts, motivating them, controlling their actions, modifying their behavior to fit the needs of the organization.

3. Without this active intervention by management, people would be passive—even resistant—to organizational needs. They must therefore be persuaded, rewarded, punished, controlled—their activities must be directed. This is management's task. We often sum it up by saying that management consists of getting things done through other people.

Behind this conventional theory there are several additional beliefs—less explicit, but widespread:

4. The average man is by nature indolent—he works as little as possible.

5. He lacks ambition, dislikes responsibility, prefers to be led.

6. He is inherently self-centered, indifferent to organizational needs.

7. He is by nature resistant to change.

8. He is gullible, not very bright, the ready dupe of the charlatan and the demagogue.

The human side of economic enterprise today is fashioned from propositions and beliefs such as these. Conventional organization structures and managerial policies, practices, and programs reflect these assumptions.

In accomplishing its task—with these assumptions as guides—management has conceived of a range of possibilities.

At one extreme, management can be "hard" or "strong." The methods for directing behavior involve coercion and

*Source: From Management Review (November 1957). Copyright © 1957 by American Management Association, Inc., Reprinted by permission of the publisher. All rights reserved.

threat (usually disguised), close supervision, tight controls over behavior. At the other extreme, management can be "soft" or "weak." The methods for directing behavior involve being permissive, satisfying people's demands, achieving harmony. Then they will be tractable, accept direction.

This range has been fairly completely explored during the past half century, and management has learned some things from the exploration. There are difficulties in the "hard" approach. Force breeds counter-forces: Restriction of output, antagonism, militant unionism, subtle but effective sabotage of management objectives. This "hard" approach is especially difficult during times of full employment.

There are also difficulties in the "soft" approach. It leads frequently to the abdication of management—to harmony, perhaps, but to indifferent performance. People take advantage of the soft approach. They continually expect more, but they give less and less.

Currently, the popular theme is "firm but fair." This is an attempt to gain the advantages of both the hard and the soft approaches. It is reminiscent of Teddy Roosevelt's "speak softly and carry a big stick."

IS THE CONVENTIONAL VIEW CORRECT?

The findings which are beginning to emerge from the social sciences challenge this whole set of beliefs about man and human nature and about the task of management. The evidence is far from conclusive, certainly, but it is suggestive. It comes from the laboratory, the clinic, the schoolroom, the home, and even to a limited extent from industry itself.

The social scientist does not deny that human behavior in industrial organization today is approximately what management perceives it to be. He has, in fact, observed it and studied it fairly extensively. But he is pretty sure that this behavior is *not* a consequence of man's inherent nature. It is a consequence rather of the nature of industrial organizations, of management philosophy, policy, and practice. The conventional approach of Theory X is based on mistaken notions of what is cause and what is effect.

Perhaps the best way to indicate why the conventional approach of management is inadequate is to consider the subject of motivation.

PHYSIOLOGICAL NEEDS

Man is a wanting animal—as soon as one of his needs is satisfied, another appears in its place. This process is unending. It continues from birth to death.

Man's needs are organized in a series of levels—a hierarchy of importance. At the lowest level, but pre-eminent in importance when they are thwarted, are his *physiological needs*. Man lives for bread alone, when there is no bread. Unless the circumstances are unusual, his needs for love, for status, for recognition are inoperative when his stomach has been empty for a while. But when he eats regularly and adequately, hunger ceases to be an important motivation. The same is true of the other physiological needs of man—for rest, exercise, shelter, protection from the elements.

A satisfied need is not a motivator of behavior! This is a fact of profound significance that is regularly ignored in the conventional approach to the management of people. Consider your own need for air. Except as you are deprived of it, it has no appreciable motivating effect upon your behavior.

SAFETY NEEDS

When the physiological needs are reasonably satisfied, needs at the next higher level begin to dominate man's behavior—to motivate him. These are called *safety needs*. They are needs for protection against danger, threat, deprivation. Some people mistakenly refer to these as needs for security. However, unless man is in a dependent relationship where he fears arbitrary deprivation, he does not demand security. The need is for the "fairest possible break." When he is confident of this, he is more than willing to take risks. But when he feels threatened or dependent, his greatest need is for guarantees, for protection, for security.

The fact needs little emphasis that, since every industrial employee is in a dependent relationship, safety needs may assume considerable importance. Arbitrary management actions, behavior which arouses uncertainty with respect to continued employment or which reflects favoritism or discrimination, unpredictable administration of policy—these can be powerful motivators of the safety needs in the employment relationship *at every level*, from worker to vice president.

SOCIAL NEEDS

When man's physiological needs are satisfied and he is no longer fearful about his physical welfare, his *social needs* become important motivators of his behavior—needs for belonging, for association, for acceptance by his fellows, for giving and receiving friendship and love.

Management knows today of the existence of these needs, but it often assumes quite wrongly that they represent a threat to the organization. Many studies have demonstrated that the tightly knit, cohesive work group may, under proper conditions, be far more effective than an equal number of separate individuals in achieving organizational goals.

Yet management, fearing group hostility to its own objectives, often goes to considerable lengths to control and direct human efforts in ways that are inimical to the natural "groupiness" of human beings. When man's social needs—and perhaps his safety needs, too—are thus thwarted, he behaves in ways which tend to defeat organizational objectives. He becomes resistant, antagonistic, uncooperative. But this behavior is a consequence, not a cause.

EGO NEEDS

Above the social needs—in the sense that they do not become motivators until lower needs are reasonably satisfied—are the needs of greatest significance to management and to man himself. They are the *egoistic needs*, and they are of two kinds:

1. Those needs that relate to one's self-esteem—needs for self-confidence, for independence, for achievement, for competence, for knowledge.
2. Those needs that relate to one's reputation—needs for status, for recognition, for appreciation, for the deserved respect of one's fellows.

Unlike the lower needs, these are rarely satisfied; man seeks indefinitely for more satisfaction of these needs once they have become important to him. But they do not appear in any significant way until physiological, safety, and social needs are all reasonably satisfied.

The typical industrial organization offers few opportunities for the satisfaction of these egoistic needs to people at lower levels in the hierarchy. The conventional methods of organizing work, particularly in mass-production industries, give little heed to these aspects of human motivation. If the practices of scientific management were deliberately calculated to thwart these needs, they could hardly accomplish this purpose better than they do.

SELF-FULFILLMENT NEEDS

Finally—a capstone, as it were, on the hierarchy of man's needs—there are what we may call the *needs for self-*

fulfillment. These are the needs for realizing one's own potentialities, for continued self-development, for being creative in the broadest sense of that term.

It is clear that the conditions of modern life give only limited opportunity for these relatively weak needs to obtain expression. The deprivation most people experience with respect to other lower-level needs diverts their energies into the struggle to satisfy *those* needs, and the needs for self-fulfillment remain dormant.

MANAGEMENT AND MOTIVATION

We recognize readily enough that a man suffering from a severe dietary deficiency is sick. The deprivation of physiological needs has behavioral consequences. The same is true—although less well recognized—of deprivation of higher-level needs. The man whose needs for safety, association, independence, or status are thwarted is sick just as surely as the man who has rickets. And his sickness will have behavioral consequences. We will be mistaken if we attribute his resultant passivity, his hostility, his refusal to accept responsibility to his inherent "human nature." These forms of behavior are *symptoms* of illness—of deprivation of his social and egoistic needs.

The man whose lower-level needs are satisfied is not motivated to satisfy those needs any longer. For practical purposes they exist no longer. Management often asks, "Why aren't people more productive? We pay good wages, provide good working conditions, have excellent fringe benefits and steady employment. Yet people do not seem to be willing to put forth more than minimum effort."

The fact that management has provided for these physiological and safety needs has shifted the motivational emphasis to the social and perhaps to the egoistic needs. Unless there are opportunities *at work* to satisfy these higher-level needs, people will be deprived; and their behavior will reflect this deprivation. Under such conditions, if management continues to focus its attention on physiological needs, its efforts are bound to be ineffective.

People *will* make insistent demands for more money under these conditions. It becomes more important than ever to buy the material goods and services which can provide limited satisfaction of the thwarted needs. Although money has only limited value in satisfying many higher-level needs, it can become the focus of interest if it is the *only* means available.

THE CARROT-AND-STICK APPROACH

The carrot-and-stick theory of motivation (like Newtonian physical theory) works reasonably well under certain circumstances. The *means* for satisfying man's physiological and (within limits) his safety needs can be provided or withheld by management. Employment itself is such a means, and so are wages, working conditions, and benefits. By these means the individual can be controlled so long as he is struggling for subsistence.

But the carrot-and-stick theory does not work at all once man has reached an adequate subsistence level and is motivated primarily by higher needs. Management cannot provide a man with self-respect, or with the respect of his fellows, or with the satisfaction of needs for self-fulfillment. It can create such conditions that he is encouraged and enabled to seek such satisfactions for *himself*, or it can thwart him by failing to create those conditions.

But this creation of conditions is not "control." It is not a good device for directing behavior. And so management finds itself in an odd position. The high standard of living created by our modern technological know-how provides quite adequately for the satisfaction of physiological and safety needs. The only significant exception is where management practices have not created confidence in a "fair break"—and thus where safety needs are thwarted. But by making possible the satisfaction of low-level needs, management has deprived itself of the ability to use as motivators the devices on which conventional theory has taught it to rely—rewards, promises, incentives, or threats and other coercive devices.

The philosophy of management by direction and control—*regardless of whether it is hard or soft*—is inadequate to motivate because the human needs on which this approach relies are today unimportant motivators of behavior. Direction and control are essentially useless in motivating people whose important needs are social and egoistic. Both the hard and the soft approach fail today because they are simply irrelevant to the situation.

People, deprived of opportunities to satisfy at work the needs which are now important to them, behave exactly as we might predict—with indolence, passivity, resistance to change, lack of responsibility, willingness to follow the demagogue, unreasonable demands for economic benefits. It would seem that we are caught in a web of our own weaving.

A NEW THEORY OF MANAGEMENT

For these and many other reasons, we require a different theory of the task of managing people based on more adequate assumptions about human nature and human motivation. I am going to be so bold as to suggest the broad dimensions of such a theory. Call it "Theory Y," if you will.

1. Management is responsible for organizing the elements of productive enterprise—money, materials, equipment, people—in the interest of economic ends.

2. People are *not* by nature passive or resistant to organizational needs. They have become so as a result of experience in organizations.

3. The motivation, the potential for development, the capacity for assuming responsibility, the readiness to direct behavior toward organizational goals are all present in people. Management does not put them there. It is a responsibility of management to make it possible for people to recognize and develop these human characteristics for themselves.

4. The essential task of management is to arrange organizational conditions and methods of operation so that people can achieve their own goals *best* by directing *their own* efforts toward organizational objectives.

This is a process primarily of creating opportunities, releasing potential, removing obstacles, encouraging growth, providing guidance. It is what Peter Drucker has called "management by objectives" in contrast to "management by control." It does *not* involve the abdication of management, the absence of leadership, the lowering of standards, or the other characteristics usually associated with the "soft" approach under Theory X.

SOME DIFFICULTIES

It is no more possible to create an organization today which will be a full, effective application of this theory than it was to build an atomic power plant in 1945. There are many formidable obstacles to overcome.

The conditions imposed by conventional organization theory and by the approach of scientific management for the past half century have tied men to limited jobs which do not utilize their capabilities, have discouraged the acceptance of responsibility, have encouraged passivity, have eliminated meaning from work. Man's habits, attitudes, expectations—his whole conception of membership in an industrial organization—have been conditioned by his experience under these circumstances.

People today are accustomed to being directed, manipulated, controlled in industrial organizations and to finding satisfaction for their social, egoistic, and self-fulfillment needs away from the job. This is true of much of management as well as of workers. Genuine "industrial citizenship"—to borrow again a term from Drucker—is a remote and unrealistic idea, the meaning of which has not even been considered by most members of industrial organizations.

Another way of saying this is that Theory X places exclusive reliance upon external control of human behavior, while Theory Y relies heavily on self-control and self-direction. It is worth noting that this difference is the difference between treating people as children and treating them as mature adults. After generations of the former, we cannot expect to shift to the latter overnight.

STEPS IN THE RIGHT DIRECTION

Before we are overwhelmed by the obstacles, let us remember that the application of theory is always slow. Progress is usually achieved in small steps. Some innovative ideas which are entirely consistent with Theory Y are today being applied with some success.

DECENTRALIZATION AND DELEGATION

These are ways of freeing people from the too-close control of conventional organization, giving them a degree of freedom to direct their own activities, to assume responsibility, and, importantly, to satisfy their egoistic needs. In this connection, the flat organization of Sears, Roebuck and Company provides an interesting example. It forces "management by objectives," since it enlarges the number of people reporting to a manager until he cannot direct and control them in the conventional manner.

JOB ENLARGEMENT

This concept, pioneered by I.B.M. and Detroit Edison, is quite consistent with Theory Y. It encourages the acceptance of responsibility at the bottom or the organization; it provides opportunities for satisfying social and egoistic needs. In fact, the reorganization of work at the factory level offers one of the more challenging opportunities for innovation consistent with Theory Y.

PARTICIPATION AND CONSULTATIVE MANAGEMENT

Under proper conditions, participation and consultative management provide encouragement to people to direct their creative energies toward organizational objectives, give them some voice in decisions that affect them, provide significant opportunities for the satisfaction of social and egoistic needs. The Scanlon Plan is the outstanding embodiment of these ideas in practice.

PERFORMANCE APPRAISAL

Even a cursory examination of conventional programs of performance appraisal within the ranks of management will reveal how completely consistent they are with Theory X. In fact, most such programs tend to treat the individual as though he were a product under inspection on the assembly line.

A few companies—among them General Mills, Ansul Chemical, and General Electric—have been experimenting with approaches which involve the individual in setting "targets" or objectives *for himself* and in a *self-*evaluation of performance semiannually or annually. Of course, the superior plays an important leadership role in this process—one, in fact, which demands substantially more competence than the conventional approach. The role is, however, considerably more congenial to many managers than the role of "judge" or "inspector" which is usually forced upon them. Above all, the individual is encouraged to take a greater responsibility for planning and appraising his own contribution to organizational objectives; and the accompanying effects on egoistic and self-fulfillment needs are substantial.

APPLYING THE IDEAS

The not infrequent failure of such ideas as these to work as well as expected is often attributable to the fact that a management has "bought the idea" but applied it within the framework of Theory X and its assumptions.

Delegation is not an effective way of exercising management by control. Participation becomes a farce when it is applied as a sales gimmick or a device for kidding people into thinking they are important. Only the management that has confidence in human capacities and is itself directed toward organizational objectives rather than toward the preservation of personal power can grasp the implications of this emerging theory. Such management will find and apply successfully other innovative ideas as we move slowly toward the full implementation of a theory like Y.

THE HUMAN SIDE OF ENTERPRISE

It is quite possible for us to realize substantial improvements in the effectiveness of industrial organizations during the next decade or two. The social sciences can contribute much to such developments; we are only beginning to grasp the implications of the growing body of knowledge in these fields. But if this conviction is to become a reality instead of a pious hope, we will need to view the process much as we view the process of releasing the energy of the atom for constructive human ends—as a slow, costly, sometimes discouraging approach toward a goal which would seem to many to be quite unrealistic.

The ingenuity and the perseverance of industrial management in the pursuit of economic ends have changed many scientific and technological dreams into commonplace realities. It is now becoming clear that the application of these same talents to the human side of enterprise will not only enhance substantially these materialistic achievements, but will bring us one step closer to "the good society."

3. The Individual and the Organization*

CHRIS ARGYRIS

It is a fact that most industrial organizations have some sort of formal structure within which individuals must work to achieve the organization's objectives.[1] Each of these basic components of organization (the formal structure and the individuals) has been and continues to be the subject of much research, discussion, and writing. An extensive search of the literature leads us to conclude, however, that most of these inquiries are conducted by persons typically interested in one or the other of the basic components. Few focus on both the individual and the organization.

Since in real life the formal structure and the individuals are continuously interacting and transacting, it seems useful to consider a study of their simultaneous impact upon each other. It is the purpose of this paper to outline the beginnings of a systematic framework by which to analyze the nature of the relationship between formal organization and individuals and from which to derive specific hypotheses regarding their mutual impact.[2] Although a much more detailed definition of formal organization will be given later, it is important to emphasize that this analysis is limited to those organizations whose original formal structure is defined by such traditional principles of organization as "chain of command," "task specialization," "span of control," and so forth. Another limitation is that since the nature of individuals varies from culture to

culture, the conclusions of this paper are also limited to those cultures wherein the proposed model of personality applies (primarily American and some Western European cultures).

The method used is a simple one designed to take advantage of the existing research on each component. The first objective is to ascertain the basic properties of each component. Exactly what is known and agreed upon by the experts about each of the components? Once this information has been collected, the second objective follows logically. When the basic properties of each of these components are known, what predictions can be made regarding their impact upon one another once they are brought together?

SOME PROPERTIES OF HUMAN PERSONALITY

The research on the human personality is so great and voluminous that it is indeed difficult to find agreement regarding its basic properties.[3] It is even more difficult to summarize the agreements once they are inferred from the existing literature. Because of space limitations it is only possible to discuss in detail one of several agreements which seems to the writer to be the most relevant to the problem at hand. The others may be summarized briefly as follows. Personality is conceptualized as (1) being an organization of parts where the parts maintain the whole and the whole

*Source: From Chris Argyris, "The Individual and the Organization: Some Problems of Mutual Adjustment," *Administrative Science Quarterly*, Vol. 2, No. 1 (June 1957), pp. 1-24. Copyright © 1957 *The Administrative Science Quarterly*. Reprinted by permission of *The Administrative Science Quarterly*.

maintains the parts; (2) seeking internal balance (usually called adjustment) and external balance (usually called adaptation); (3) being propelled by psychological (as well as physical) energy; (4) located in the need systems; and (5) expressed through the abilities. (6) The personality organization may be called "the self" which (7) acts to color all the individual's experiences, thereby causing him to live in "private worlds," and which (8) is capable of defending (maintaining) itself against threats of all types.

The self, in this culture, tends to develop along specific trends which are operationally definable and empirically observable. The basic developmental trends may be described as follows. The human being, in our culture:

1. tends to develop from a state of being passive as an infant to a state of increasing activity as an adult. (This is what E. H. Erikson has called self-initiative and Urie Bronfenbrenner has called self-determination.[4])

2. tends to develop from a state of dependence upon others as an infant to a state of relative independence as an adult. Relative independence is the ability to "stand on one's own two feet" and simultaneously to acknowledge healthy dependencies.[5] It is characterized by the individual's freeing himself from his childhood determiners of behavior (e.g., the family) and developing his own set of behavioral determiners. The individual does not tend to react to others (e.g., the boss) in terms of patterns learned during childhood.[6]

3. tends to develop from being capable of behaving in only a few ways as an infant to being capable of behaving in many different ways as an adult.[7]

4. tends to develop from having erratic, casual, shallow, quickly dropped interests as an infant to possessing a deepening of interests as an adult. The mature state is characterized by an endless series of challenges where the reward comes from doing something for its own sake. The tendency is to analyze and study phenomena in their full-blown wholeness, complexity, and depth.[8]

5. tends to develop from having a short-time perspective (i.e., the present largely determines behavior) as an infant to having a much longer time perspective as an adult (i.e., the individual's behavior is more affected by the past and the future).[9]

6. tends to develop from being in a subordinate position in the family and society as an infant to aspiring to occupy at least an equal and/or superordinate position relative to his peers.

7. tends to develop from having a lack of awareness of the self as an infant to having an awareness of and control over the self as an adult. The adult who experiences adequate and successful control over his own behavior develops a sense of integrity (Erikson) and feelings of self-worth (Carl R. Rogers).[10]

These characteristics are postulated as being descriptive of a basic multidimensional developmental process along which the growth of individuals in our culture may be measured. Presumably every individual, at any given moment in time, could have his degree of development plotted along these dimensions. The exact location on each dimension will probably vary with each individual and even with the same individual at different times. Self-actualization may now be defined more precisely as the individual's plotted scores (or profile) along the above dimensions.[11]

A few words of explanation may be given concerning these dimensions of personality development:

1. They are only one aspect of the total personality. All the properties of personality mentioned above must be used in trying to understand the behavior of a particular individual. For example, much depends upon the individual's self-concept, his degree of adaptation and adjustment, and the way he perceives his private world.

2. The dimensions are continua, where the growth to be measured is assumed to be continuously changing in degree. An individual is presumed to develop continuously in degree from infancy to adulthood.

3. The only characteristic assumed to hold for all individuals is that, barring unhealthy personality development, they will

move from the infant toward the adult end of each continuum. This description is a model outlining the basic growth trends. As such, it does not make any predictions about any specific individual. It does, however, presume to supply the researcher with basic developmental continua along which the growth of any individual in our culture may be described and measured.

4. It is postulated that no individual will ever obtain maximum expression of all these developmental trends. Clearly all individuals cannot be maximally independent, active, and so forth all the time and still maintain an organized society. It is the function of culture (e.g., norms, mores, and so forth) to inhibit maximum expression and to help an individual adjust and adapt by finding his optimum expression.

A second factor that prevents maximum expression and fosters optimum expression are the limits set by the individual's own personality. For example, some people fear the same amount of independence and activity that others desire, and some people do not have the necessary abilities to perform certain tasks. No given individual is known to have developed all known abilities to their full maturity.

5. The dimensions described above are constructed in terms of latent or genotypical characteristics. If one states that an individual needs to be dependent, this need may be ascertained by clinical inference, because it is one that individuals are not usually aware of. Thus one may observe an employee acting as if he were independent, but it is possible that if one goes below the behavioral surface the individual may be quite dependent. The obvious example is the employee who always seems to behave in a manner contrary to that desired by management. Although this behavior may look as if he is independent, his contrariness may be due to his great need to be dependent upon management which he dislikes to admit to himself and to others.

One might say that an independent person is one whose behavior is not caused by the influence others have over him. Of course, no individual is completely independent. All of us have our healthy dependencies (i.e., those which help us to be creative and to develop). One operational criteria to ascertain whether an individual's desire to be, let us say, independent

and active is truly a mature manifestation is to ascertain the extent to which he permits others to express the same needs. Thus an autocratic leader may say that he needs to be active and independent; he may also say that he wants subordinates who are the same. There is ample research to suggest, however, that his leadership pattern only makes him and his subordinates more dependence-ridden.

SOME BASIC PROPERTIES OF FORMAL ORGANIZATION

The next step is to focus the analytic spotlight on the formal organization. What are its properties? What are its basic "givens"? What probable impact will they have upon the human personality? How will the human personality tend to react to this impact? What sorts of chain reactions are probable when these two basic components are brought together?

FORMAL ORGANIZATIONS AS RATIONAL ORGANIZATIONS

Probably the most basic property of formal organization is its logical foundation or, as it has been called by students of administration, its essential rationality. It is the planners' conception of how the intended consequences of the organization may best be achieved. The underlying assumptions made by the creators of formal organization is that within respectable tolerances man will behave rationally, that is, as the formal plan requires him to behave. Organizations are formed with particular objectives in mind, and their structures mirror these objectives. Although man may not follow the prescribed paths, and consequently the objectives may never be achieved, Herbert A. Simon suggests that by and large man does follow these prescribed paths:

> Organizations are formed with the intention and design of accomplishing goals; and the people who work in organizations believe, at least part of the time, that they are striving toward these same goals. We must not lose sight of the fact that however

far organizations may depart from the traditional description . . . nevertheless most behavior in organizations is intendedly rational behavior. By "intended rationality" I mean the kind of adjustment of behavior to goals of which humans are capable—a very incomplete and imperfect adjustment, to be sure, but one which nevertheless does accomplish purposes and does carry out programs.[12]

In an illuminating book, L. Urwick eloquently describes this underlying characteristic.[13] He insists that the creation of a formal organization requires a logical "drawing-office" approach. Although he admits that "nine times out of ten it is impossible to start with a clean sheet," the organizer should sit down and in a "cold-blooded, detached spirit . . . draw an ideal structure." The section from which I quote begins with Urwick's description of how the formal structure should be planned. He then continues:

Manifestly that is a drawing-office job. It is a designing process. And it may be objected with a great deal of experience to support the contention that organization is never done that way . . . human organization. Nine times out of ten it is impossible to start with a clean sheet. The organizer has to make the best possible use of the human material that is already available. And in 89 out of those 90 percent of cases he has to adjust jobs around to fit the man; he can't change the man to fit the job. He can't sit down in a cold-blooded, detached spirit and draw an ideal structure, an optimum distribution of duties and responsibilities and relationships, and then expect the infinite variety of human nature to fit into it.

To which the reply is that he can and he should. If he has not got a clean sheet, that is no earthly reason why he should not make the slight effort of imagination required to assume that he has a clean sheet. It is not impossible to forget provisionally the personal facts—that old Brown is admirably methodical but wanting in initiative, that young Smith got into a mess with Robinson's wife and that the two men must be kept at opposite ends of the building, that Jones is one of those creatures who can think like a Wrangler about other people's duties but is given to periodic amnesia about certain aspects of his own.[14]

The task of the organizer, therefore, is to create a logically ordered world where, as Fayol suggests, there is a "proper order" and in which there is a "place for everything (everyone)."[15]

The possibility that the formal organization can be altered by personalities, as found by Conrad M. Arensberg and Douglas McGregor[16] and Ralph M. Stogdill and Katheleen Koehler,[17] is not denied by formal organizational experts. Urwick, for example, states in the passage below that the planner must take into account the human element. But it is interesting to note that he perceives these adjustments as "temporary deviations from the pattern in order to deal with idiosyncrasy of personality." If possible, these deviations should be minimized by careful preplanning.

He [the planner] should never for a moment pretend that these (human) difficulties don't exist. They do exist; they are realities. Nor, when he has drawn up an ideal plan of organization, is it likely that he will be able to fit in all the existing human material perfectly. There will be small adjustments of the job to the man in all kinds of directions. But those adjustments are deliberate and temporary deviations from the pattern in order to deal with idiosyncrasy. There is a world of difference between such modification and drifting into an unworkable organization because Green has a fancy for combining bits of two incompatible functions, or White is "empire-building" . . . or Black has always looked after the canteen, so when he is promoted to Sales Manager, he might as well continue to sell buns internally, though the main product of the business happens to be battleships.

What is suggested is that problems of organization should be handled in the right order. Personal adjustments must be made, insofar as they are necessary. But fewer of them will be necessary and they will present fewer deviations from what is logical and simple, if the organizer first makes a plan, a design—to which he would work if he had the ideal human material. He should expect to be driven from it here and there. But he will be driven from it far less and his machine will work much more smoothly if he *starts* with a plan. If he starts with a motley collection of human oddities and tries to organize to fit them all in, thinking first of their various shapes and sizes and colors, he may have a patchwork quilt; he will not have an organization.[18]

The majority of experts on formal organization agree with Urwick. Most of them emphasize that no organizational structure will be ideal. None will exemplify the maximum expression of the principles of formal organization. A satisfactory aspiration is for optimum expression, which means modifying the ideal structure to take into account the individual (and any environmental) conditions. Moreover, they urge that the people must be loyal to the formal structure if it is to work effectively. Thus Taylor emphasizes that scientific management would never succeed without a "mental revolution."[19] Fayol has the same problem in mind when he emphasizes the importance of *esprit de corps*.

It is also true, however, that these experts have provided little insight into *why* they believe that people should undergo a "mental revolution," or why an *esprit de corps* is necessary if the principles are to succeed. The only hints found in the literature are that resistance to scientific management occurs because human beings "are what they are" or "because it's human nature." But *why* does "human nature" resist formal organizational principles? Perhaps there is something inherent in the principles which causes human resistance. Unfortunately too little research specifically assesses the impact of formal organizational principles upon human beings.

Another argument for planning offered by the formal organizational experts is that the organization created by logical, rational design, in the long run, is more human than one created haphazardly. They argue that it is illogical, cruel, wasteful, and inefficient not to have a logical design. It is illogical because design must come first. It does not make sense to pay a large salary to an individual without clearly defining his position and its relationship to the whole. It is cruel because, in the long run, the participants suffer when no clear organizational structure exists. It is wasteful because, unless jobs are clearly predefined, it is impossible to plan logical training, promotion, resigning, and retiring policies. It is inefficient because the organization becomes dependent upon personalities. The personal touch leads to playing politics, which Mary Follett has described as a "deplorable form of coercion."[20]

Unfortunately, the validity of these arguments tends to be obscured in the eyes of the behavioral scientist because they imply that the only choice left, if the formal, rational, predesigned structure is not accepted, is to have no organizational structure at all, with the organizational structure left to the whims, pushes, and pulls of human beings. Some human-relations researchers, on the other hand, have unfortunately given the impression that formal structures are "bad" and that the needs of the individual participants should be paramount in creating and administering an organization. A recent analysis of the existing research, however, points up quite clearly that the importance of of the organization is being recognized by those who in the past have focused largely upon the individual.[21]

In the past, and for the most part in the present, the traditional organizational experts based their "human architectural creation" upon certain basic principles or assumptions about the nature of organization. These principles have been described by such people as Urwick,[22] Mooney, Holden *et al.*, Fayol, Dennison, Brown, Gulick, White, Gaus, Stene, Hopf, and Taylor. Although these principles have been attacked by behavioral scientists, the assumption is made in this paper that to date no one has defined a more useful set of formal organization principles. Therefore the principles are accepted as givens. This frees us to inquire about their probable impact upon people, *if they are used as defined.*

TASK (WORK) SPECIALIZATION

As James J. Gillespie suggests, the roots of these principles of organization may be traced back to certain principles of industrial economics, the most important of which is the basic economic assumption held by builders of the industrial revolution that "the concentration of effort on a limited field of endeavor increases quality and quantity of output."[23] It follows from the above that the necessity for specialization should increase as the quantity of similar things to be done increases.

If concentrating effort on a limited field of endeavor increases the quality and quantity of output, it follows that organizational and administrative efficiency is increased by the specialization of tasks assigned to the participants of the organization.[24] Inherent in this assumption are three others. The first is that the human personality will behave more efficiently as the task that it is to perform becomes specialized. Second is the assumption that there can be found a one best way to define the job so that it is performed at greater speed.[25] Third is the assumption that any individual differences in the human personality may be ignored by transferring more skill and thought to machines.[26]

A number of difficulties arise concerning these assumptions when the properties of the human personality are recalled. First, the human personality we have seen is always attempting to actualize its unique organization of parts resulting from a continuous, emotionally laden, ego-involving process of growth. It is difficult, if not impossible, to assume that this process can be choked off and the resultant unique differences of individuals ignored. This is tantamount to saying that self-actualization can be ignored. The second difficulty is that task specialization requires the individual to use only a few of his abilities. Moreover, as specialization increases, the less complex motor abilities are used more frequently. These, research suggests, tend to be of lesser psychological importance to the individual. Thus the principle violates two basic givens of the healthy adult human personality. It inhibits self-actualization and provides expression for few, shallow, superficial abilities that do not provide the "endless challenge" desired by the healthy personality.

Harold L. Wilensky and Charles N. Lebeaux correctly point out that task specialization causes what little skill is left in a job to become very important.[27] Now small differences in ability may make enormous differences in output. Thus two machine-shovel operators or two drill-press operators of different degrees of skill can produce dramatically different outputs. Ironically, the increasing importance of this type of skill for the healthy, mature worker means that he should feel he is performing self-satisfying work while using a small number of psychologically unchallenging abilities, when in actuality he may be predisposed to feel otherwise. Task specialization, therefore, requires a healthy adult to behave in a less mature manner, but it also requires that he feel good about it!

Not only is the individual affected, but the social structure as well is modified as a result of the situation described above. Wilensky and Lebeaux, in the same analysis, point out that placing a great emphasis on ability makes "Who you are" become less important that "What you can do." Thus the culture begins to reward relatively superficial, materialistic characteristics.

CHAIN OF COMMAND

The principle of task specialization creates an aggregate of parts, each performing a highly specialized task. An aggregate of parts, each busily performing its particular objective, does not form an organization, however. A pattern of parts must be formed so that the interrelationships among the parts create the organization. Following the logic of specialization, the planners create a new function (leadership) the primary responsibility of which is to control, direct, and coordinate the interrelationships of the parts and to make certain that each part performs its objective adequately. Thus the planner makes the assumption that administrative and organizational efficiency is increased by arranging the parts in a determinate hierarchy of authority in which the part on top can direct and control the part on the bottom.

If the parts being considered are individuals, then they must be motivated to accept direction, control, and coordination of their behavior. The leader, therefore, is assigned formal power to hire, discharge, reward, and penalize the individuals in order to mold their behavior in the pattern of the organization's objectives.

The impact of such a state of affairs is to make the individuals dependent upon, passive, and subordinate to the leader. As a result, the individuals have little control over their working environment. At the same time their time perspective is shortened because they do not control the information necessary to predict their futures. These requirements of formal organization act to inhibit four of the growth trends of the personality, because to be passive, subordinate, and to have little control and a short time perspective exemplify in adults the dimensions of immaturity, not adulthood.

The planners of formal organization suggest three basic ways to minimize this admittedly difficult position. First, ample rewards should be given to those who perform well and who do not permit their dependence, subordination, passivity, and so forth to influence them in a negative manner. The rewards should be material and psychological. Because of the specialized nature of the worker's job, however, few psychological rewards are possible. It becomes important, therefore, that adequate material rewards are made available to the productive employee. This practice can lead to new difficulties, since the solution is, by its nature, not to do anything about the on-the-job situation (which is what is causing the difficulties) but to pay the individual for the dissatisfactions he experiences. The result is that the employee is paid for his dissatisfaction while at work and his wages are given to him to gain satisfactions outside his work environment.

Thus the management helps to create a psychological set which leads the employees to feel that basic causes of dissatisfaction are built into industrial life, that the rewards they receive are wages for dissatisfaction, and that if satisfaction is to be gained, the employee must seek it outside the organization.

To make matters more difficult, there are three assumptions inherent in the above solution that also violate the basic givens of human personality. First, the solution assumes that a whole human being can split his personality so that he will feel satisfied in knowing that the wages for his dissatisfaction will buy him satisfaction outside the plant. Second, it assumes that the employee is primarily interested in maximizing his economic gains. Third, it assumes that the employee is best rewarded as an individual producer. The work group in which he belongs is not viewed as a relevant factor. If he produces well, he should be rewarded. If he does not, he should be penalized even though he may be restricting production because of informal group sanctions.

The second solution suggested by the planners of formal organization is to have technically competent, objective, rational, loyal leaders. The assumption is made that if the leaders are technically competent presumably they cannot have "the wool pulled over their eyes" and that therefore the employees will have a high respect for them. The leaders should be objective and rational and personify the rationality inherent in the formal structure. Being rational means that they must avoid becoming emotionally involved. As one executive states, "We try to keep our personality out of the job." The leader must also be impartial; he must not permit his feelings to operate when he is evaluating others. Finally, the leader must be loyal to the organization so that he can inculcate the loyalty in the employees that Taylor, Fayol, and others believe is so important.

Admirable as this solution may be, it also violates several of the basic properties of personality. If the employees are to respect an individual for what he does rather than for who he is, the sense of integrity based upon evaluation of the total self which is developed in people is lost. Moreover, to ask the leader to keep his personality out of his job is to ask him to stop actualizing himself. This is not possible as long as he is alive. Of course, the executive may want to feel that he is not involved, but it is a basic given that the human personality is an organism always actualizing itself. The same problem arises with impartiality. No one can be completely impartial. As has been shown, the self concept always operates when we are making judgments. In fact, as Rollo May has pointed out, the best way to be impartial is to be as partial as one's needs predispose one to be but to be aware of this partiality in order to correct for it at the moment of decision.[28] Finally, if a leader can be loyal to an organization under these conditions, there may be adequate grounds for questioning the health of his personality make-up.

The third solution suggested by many

adherents to formal organizational principles is to motivate the subordinates to have more initiative and to be more creative by placing them in competition with one another for the positions of power that lie above them in the organizational ladder. This solution is traditionally called "the rabble hypothesis." Acting under the assumption that employees will be motivated to advance upward, the adherents of formal organizations further assume that competition for the increasingly (as one goes up the ladder) scarcer positions will increase the effectiveness of the participants. D. C. S. Williams, conducting some controlled experiments, shows that the latter assumption is not necessarily valid. People placed in competitive situations are not necessarily better learners than those placed in noncompetitive situations.[29] M. Deutsch, as a result of extensive controlled experimental research, supports Williams' results and goes much further to suggest that competitive situations tend to lead to an increase in tension and conflict and a decrease in human effectiveness.[30]

UNITY OF DIRECTION

If the tasks of everyone in a unit are specialized, then it follows that the objective or purpose of the unit must be specialized. The principle of unity of direction states that organizational efficiency increases if each unit has a single activity (or homogeneous set of activities) that are planned and directed by the leader.[31]

This means that the goal toward which the employees are working, the path toward the goal, and the strength of the barriers they must overcome to achieve the goal are defined and controlled by the leader. Assuming that the work goals do not involve the egos of the employees, (i.e., they are related to peripheral, superficial needs), then ideal conditions for psychological failure have been created. The reader may recall that a basic given of a healthy personality is the aspiration for psychological success. Psychological success is achieved when each individual is able to define his own goals, in relation to his inner needs and the strength of the barriers to be overcome in order to reach these goals. Repetitive as it may sound, it is nevertheless true that the principle of unity of direction also violates a basic given of personality.

SPAN OF CONTROL

The principle of span of control[32] states that administrative efficiency is increased by limiting the span of control of a leader to no more than five or six subordinates whose work interlocks.[33]

It is interesting to note that Ernest Dale, in an extensive study of organizational principles and practices in one hundred large organizations, concludes that the actual limits of the executive span of control are more often violated than not,[34] while in a recent study James H. Healey arrives at the opposite conclusion.[35] James C. Worthy reports that it is formal policy in his organization to extend the span of control of the top management much further than is theoretically suggested.[36] Finally, W. W. Suojanen, in a review of the current literature on the concept of span of control, concludes that it is no longer valid, particularly as applied to the larger government agencies and business corporations.[37]

In a recent article, however, Urwick criticizes the critics of the span-of-control principle.[38] For example, he notes that in the case described by Worthy, the superior has a large span of control over subordinates whose jobs do not interlock. The buyers in Worthy's organization purchase a clearly defined range of articles; therefore they find no reason to interlock with others.

Simon criticizes the span-of-control principle on the grounds that it increases the "administrative distance" between individuals. An increase in administrative distance violates, in turn, another formal organizational principle that administrative efficiency is enhanced by keeping at a minimum the number of organizational levels through which a matter must pass before it is acted on.[39] Span of control, continues Simon, inevitably increases red tape, since each contact between agents must be carried upward until a common superior is found. Needless waste of time and energy result. Also, since the solution of the problem depends upon the superior, the subordinate is in a position of having less control over his own work situation. This places the subordinate in a work situation in which he is less mature.

Although the distance between individuals in different units increases (because they have to find a common superior), the administrative distance between superior and subordinate within a given unit decreases. As Whyte correctly points out, the principle of span of control, by keeping the number of subordinates at a minimum, places great emphasis on close supervision.[40] Close supervision leads the subordinates to become dependent upon, passive toward, and subordinate to, the leader. Close supervision also tends to place the control in the superior. Thus we must conclude that span of control, if used correctly, will tend to increase the subordinate's feelings of dependence, submissiveness, passivity, and so on. In short, it will tend to create a work situation which requires immature, rather than mature, participants.

AN INCONGRUENCY BETWEEN THE NEEDS OF A MATURE PERSONALITY AND OF FORMAL ORGANIZATION

Bringing together the evidence regarding the impact of formal organizational principles upon the individual, we must conclude that there are some basic incongruencies between the growth trends of a healthy personality in our culture and the requirements of formal organization. If the principles of formal organization are used as ideally defined, then the employees will tend to work in an environment where (1) they are provided minimal control over their work-a-day world, (2) they are expected to be passive, dependent, subordinate, (3) they are expected to have a short-time perspective, (4) they are induced to perfect and value the frequent use of a few superficial abilities, and (5) they are expected to produce under conditions leading to psychological failure.

All of these characteristics are incongruent to the ones healthy human beings are postulated to desire. They are much more congruent with the needs of infants in our culture. In effect, therefore, formal organizations are willing to pay high wages and provide adequate seniority if mature adults will, for eight hours a day, behave in a less mature manner. If this analysis is correct, this inevitable incongruency increases (1) as the employees are of increasing maturity, (2) as the formal structure (based upon the above principles) is made more clear-cut and logically tight for maximum formal organizational effectiveness, (3) as one goes down the line of command, and (4) as the jobs become more and more mechanized (i.e., take on assembly-line characteristics).

As in the case of the personality developmental trends, this picture of formal organization is also a model. Clearly, no company actually uses the formal principles of organization exactly as stated by their creators. There is ample evidence to suggest that they are being modified constantly in actual situations. Those who expound these principles, however, probably would be willing to defend their position that this is the reason that human-relations problems exist; the principles are not followed as they should be.

In the model of the personality and the formal organization, we are assuming the extreme of each in order that the analysis and its results can be highlighted. Speaking in terms of extremes helps us to make the position sharper. In doing this, we make no assumption that all situations in real life are extreme (i.e., that the individuals will always want to be more mature and that the formal organization will always tend to make people more dependent, passive, and so forth, all the time).[41] The model ought to be useful, however, to plot the degree to which each component tends toward extremes and then to predict the problems that will tend to arise.

Returning to the analysis, it is not difficult to see why some students of organization suggest that immature and even mentally retarded individuals probably would make excellent employees in certain jobs. There is very little documented experience to support such a hypothesis. One reason for this lack of information is probably the delicacy of the subject. Examples of what might be obtained if a systematic study were made may be found in a recent work by Mal Brennan.[42] He cites the Utica Knitting Mill, which made arrangements during 1917 with the Rome Institution for Mentally Defective Girls to employ twenty-four girls whose mental age ranged from six to ten years of age. The girls were such excellent workers that they were employed after the war emergency ended. In fact, the company added forty more in another of their plants. It is interesting to note that the managers praised the subnormal girls highly. According to Brennan, in several important reports they said that:

> when business conditions required a reduction of the working staff, the hostel girls were never "laid off" in disproportion to the normal girls; that they were more punctual, more regular in their habits, and did not indulge in as much "gossip and levity." They received the same rate of pay, and they had been employed successfully at almost every process carried out in the workshops.

In another experiment reported by Brennan, the Works Manager of the Radio Corporation, Ltd., reported that of five young morons employed, "the three girls compared very favourably with the normal class of employee in that age group. The boy employed in the store performed his work with satisfaction. . . . Although there was some doubt about the fifth child, it was felt that getting the most out of him was just a matter of right placement." In each of the five cases, the morons were reported to be quiet, respectful, well behaved, and very obedient. The Works Manager was especially impressed by their truthfulness. A year later the same Works Manager was still able to advise that "in every case, the girls proved to be exceptionally well-behaved, particularly obedient, and strictly honest and trustworthy. They carried out work required of them to such a degree of efficiency that *we were surprised they were classed as subnormals for their age.*"[43]

SUMMARY OF FINDINGS

If one were to put these basic findings in terms of propositions, one could state:

Proposition I. *There Is a Lack of Congruency between the Needs of Healthy Individuals and the Demands of the Formal Organization.*

If one uses the traditional formal principles of organization (*i.e.*, chain of command, task specialization, and so on) to create a social organization, and if one uses as an input agents who tend toward mature psychological development (*i.e.*, who are predisposed toward relative independence, activeness, use of important abilities, and so on), then one creates a disturbance, because the needs of healthy individuals listed above are not congruent with the requirements of formal organization, which tends to require the agents to work in situations where they are dependent, passive, use few and unimpor-

tant abilities, and so forth.

Corollary 1. The disturbance will vary in proportion to the degree of incongruency between the needs of the individuals and the requirements of formal organization.[44]

An administrator, therefore, is always faced with a tendency toward continual disturbance inherent in the work situation of the individuals over whom he is in charge.

Drawing on the existing knowledge of the human personality, a second proposition can be stated.

Proposition II. *The Results of This Disturbance Are Frustration, Failure, Short-Time Perspective, and Conflict.*[45]

If the agents are predisposed to a healthy, mature self-actualization, the following results will occur:

1. They will tend to experience frustration because their self-actualization will be blocked.

2. They will tend to experience failure because they will not be permitted to define their own goals in relation to their central needs, the paths to these goals, and so on.

3. They will tend to experience short-time perspective, because they have no control over the clarity and stability of their future.

4. They will tend to experience conflict, because, as healthy agents, they will dislike the frustration, failure, and short-time perspective which is characteristic of their present jobs. If they leave, however, they may not find new jobs easily, and even if new jobs are found, they may not be much different.[46]

Based upon the analysis of the nature of formal organization, one may state a third proposition.

Proposition III. *The Nature of the Formal Principles of Organization Cause the Subordinate, at Any Given Level, to Experience Competition, Rivalry, Intersubordinate Hostility, and to Develop a Focus toward the Parts Rather than the Whole.*

1. Because of the degree of dependence, subordination, and so on of the subordinates upon the leader, and because the

number of positions above any given level always tends to decrease, the subordinates aspiring to perform effectively and to advance will tend to find themselves in competition with, and receiving hostility from, each other.[47]

2. Because, according to the formal principles, the subordinate is directed toward and rewarded for performing his own task well, the subordinate tends to develop an orientation toward his own particular part rather than toward the whole.

3. This part-orientation increases the need for the leader to coordinate the activity among the parts in order to maintain the whole. This need for the leader, in turn, increases the subordinates' degree of dependence, subordination, and so forth. This is a circular process whose impact is to maintain and/or increase the degree of dependence, subordination, and so on, as well as to stimulate rivalry and competition for the leader's favor.

A BIRD'S-EYE, CURSORY PICTURE OF SOME OTHER RELATED FINDINGS

It is impossible in the short space available to present all of the results obtained from the analysis of the literature. For example, it can be shown that employees tend to adapt to the frustration, failure, short-time perspective, and conflict involved in their work situations by any one or a combination of the following acts:

1. Leaving the organization.
2. Climbing the organizational ladder.
3. Manifesting defense reactions such as daydreaming, aggression, ambivalence, regression, projection, and so forth.
4. Becoming apathetic and disinterested toward the organization, its make-up, and its goals. This leads to such phenomena as: (a) employees reducing the number and potency of the needs they expect to fulfill while at work; (b) employees goldbricking, setting rates, restricting quotas, making errors, cheating, slowing down, and so on.
5. Creating informal groups to sanction the defense reactions and the apathy, disinterest, and lack of self-involvement.
6. Formalizing the informal group.
7. Evolving group norms that perpetuate

the behavior outlined in (3), (4), (5), and (6) above.

8. Evolving a psychological set in which human or nonmaterial factors become increasingly unimportant while material factors become increasingly important.

9. Acculturating youth to accept the norms outlined in (7) and (8).

Furthermore, it can also be shown that many managements tend to respond to the employees' behavior by:

1. Increasing the degree of their pressure-oriented leadership.
2. Increasing the degree of their use of management controls.
3. Increasing the number of "pseudo"-participation and communication programs.

These three reactions by management actually compound the dependence, subordination, and so on that the employees experience, which in turn cause the employees to increase their adaptive behavior, the very behavior management desired to curtail in the first place.

Is there a way out of this circular process? The basic problem is the reduction in the degree of dependency, subordination, submissiveness, and so on experienced by the employee in his work situation. It can be shown that job enlargement and employee-centered (or democratic or participative) leadership are elements which, if used correctly, can go a long way toward ameliorating the situation. These are limited, however, because their success depends upon having employees who are ego-involved and highly interested in the organization. This dilemma between individual needs and organization demands is a basic, continual problem posing an eternal challenge to the leader. How is it possible to create an organization in which the individuals may obtain optimum expression and, simultaneously, in which the organization itself may obtain optimum satisfaction of its demands? Here lies a fertile field for future research in organizational behavior.

NOTES

1. Temporarily, "formal structure" is defined as that which may be found on the organization charts and in the standard operating procedures of an organization.

2. This analysis is part of a larger project whose objectives are to integrate by the use of a systematic framework much of the existing behavioral-science research related to organization. The total report will be published by Harper & Brothers as a book, tentatively entitled *The Behavioral Sciences and Organization*. The project has been supported by a grant from the Foundation for Research on Human Behavior, Ann Arbor, Michigan, for whose generous support the writer is extremely grateful.

3. The relevant literature in clinical, abnormal, child, and social psychology, and in personality theory, sociology, and anthropology was investigated. The basic agreements inferred regarding the properties of personality are assumed to be valid for most contemporary points of view. Allport's "trait theory," Cattell's factor analytic approach, and Kretschmer's somatotype framework are not included. For lay description see the author's *Personality Fundamentals for Administrators*, rev. ed. (New Haven, 1954).

4. E. H. Erikson, *Childhood and Society* (New York, 1950); Urie Bronfenbrenner, "Toward an Integrated Theory of Personality," in Robert R. Blake and Glenn V. Ramsey, *Perception* (New York, 1951), pp. 206-257. See also R. Kotinsky, *Personality in the Making* (New York, 1952), pp. 8-25.

5. This is similar to Erikson's sense of autonomy and Bronfenbrenner's state of creative interdependence.

6. Robert W. White, *Lives in Progress* (New York, 1952), pp. 339 ff.

7. Lewin and Kounin believe that as the individual develops needs and abilities the boundaries between them become more rigid. This explains why an adult is better able than a child to be frustrated in one activity and behave constructively in another. See Kurt Lewin, *A Dynamic Theory of Personality* (New York, 1935) and Jacob S. Kounin, "Intellectual Development and Rigidity," in R. Barker, J. Kounin, and H. R. Wright, eds., *Child Behavior and Development* (New York, 1943), pp. 179-198.

8. Robert White, *op. cit.*, pp. 347 ff.

9. Lewin reminds those who may believe that a long-time perspective is not characteristic of the majority of individuals of the billions of dollars that are invested in insurance policies. Kurt Lewin, *Resolving Social Conflicts* (New York, 1948), p. 105.

10. Carl R. Rogers, *Client-Centered Therapy* (New York, 1951).

11. Another related but discrete set of developmental dimensions may be constructed to measure the protective (defense) mechanisms individuals tend to create as they develop from infancy to adulthood. Exactly how these would be related to the above model is not clear.

12. Herbert A. Simon, *Research Frontiers in Politics and Government* (Washington, D.C., 1955), ch. ii, p. 30.

13. L. Urwick, *The Elements of Administration* (New York, 1944).

14. *Ibid.*, pp. 36-39; quoted by permission of Harper & Brothers.

15. Cited in Harold Koontz and Cyril O'Donnell, *Principles of Management* (New York, 1955), p. 24.

16. Conrad M. Arensberg and Douglas McGregor, Determination of Morale in an Industrial Company, *Applied Anthropology*, Vol. 1 (Jan.-March 1942), 12-34.

17. Ralph M. Stogdill and Katheleen Koehler, *Measures of Leadership Structure and Organization Change* (Columbus, O., 1952).

18. *Ibid.*, pp. 36-39; quoted by permission of Harper & Brothers.

19 For a provocative discussion of Taylor's philosophy, see Reinhard Bendix, *Work and Authority in Industry* (New York, 1956), pp. 274-319.

20. Quoted in *ibid.*, pp. 36-39.

21. Chris Argyris, *The Present State of Research in Human Relations* (New Haven, 1954), ch. i.

22. Urwick, *op. cit.*

23. James J. Gillespie, *Free Expression in Industry* (London, 1948), pp. 34-37.

24. Herbert A. Simon, *Administrative Behavior* (New York, 1947), pp. 80-81.

25. For an interesting discussion see Georges Friedman, *Industrial Society* (Glencoe, Ill., 1955), pp. 54 ff.

26. *Ibid.*, p. 20. Friedman reports that 79 percent of Ford employees had jobs for which they could be trained in one week.

27. Harold L. Wilensky and Charles N.

Lebeaux, *Industrialization and Social Welfare* (New York, 1955), p. 43.

28. Rollo May, "Historical and Philosophical Presuppositions for Understanding Therapy," in O. H. Mowrer, *Psychotherapy Theory and Research* (New York, 1953), pp. 38-39.

29. D. C. S. Williams, Effects of Competition between Groups in a Training Situation, *Occupational Psychology*, Vol. 30 (April 1956), 85-93.

30. M. Deutsch, An Experimental Study of the Effects of Cooperation and Competition upon Group Process, *Human Relations*, Vol. 2 (1949), 199-231.

31. The sacredness of these principles is questioned by a recent study. Gunnar Heckscher concludes that the principles of unity of command and unity of direction are formally violated in Sweden: "A fundamental principle of public administration in Sweden is the duty of all public agencies to cooperate directly without necessarily passing through a common superior. This principle is even embodied in the constitution itself, and in actual fact it is being employed daily. It is traditionally one of the most important characteristics of Swedish administration that especially central agencies, but also central and local agencies of different levels, cooperate freely and that this is being regarded as a perfectly normal procedure" *(Swedish Public Administration at Work* [Stockholm, 1955], p. 12).

32. First defined by V. A. Graicunas in an article entitled "Relationship in Organization," in L. Gulick and L. Urwick, eds., *Papers on the Science of Administration*, 2d ed. (New York, 1947), pp. 183-187.

33. L. Urwick, *Scientific Principles and Organization* (New York, 1938), p. 8.

34. Ernest Dale, *Planning and Developing the Company Organization Structure* (New York, 1952), ch. xx.

35. James H. Healey, Coordination and Control of Executive Functions, *Personnel*, Vol. 33 (Sept. 1956), 106-117.

36. James C. Worthy, Organizational Structure and Employee Morale, *American Sociological Review*, Vol. 15 (April 1950), 169-179.

37. W. W. Suojanen, The Span of Control—Fact or Fable?, *Advanced Management*, Vol. 20 (1955), 5-13.

38. L. Urwick, The Manager's Span of Control, *Harvard Business Review*, Vol. 34 (May-June 1956), 39-47.

39. Simon, *op. cit.*, pp. 26-28.

40. William Whyte, "On the Evolution of Industrial Sociology" (mimeographed paper presented at the 1956 meeting of the American Sociological Society).

41. In fact, much evidence is presented in the book from which this article is drawn to support contrary tendencies.

42. Mal Brennan, *The Making of a Moron* (New York, 1953), pp. 13-18.

43. Mr. Brennan's emphasis.

44. This proposition does not hold under certain conditions.

45. In the full analysis, specific conditions are derived under which the basic incongruency increases or decreases.

46. These points are taken, in order, from: Roger G. Barker, T. Dembo, and K. Lewin, "Frustration and Regression: An Experiment with Young Children," *Studies in Child Welfare*, Vol. XVIII, No. 2 (Iowa City, Ia., 1941); John Dollard et al., *Frustration and Aggression* (New Haven, 1939); Kurt Lewin et al., "Level of Aspiration," in J. McV. Hunt, ed., *Personality and the Behavior Disorders* (New York, 1944), pp. 333-378; Ronald Lippitt and Leland Bradford, Employee Success in Work Groups, *Personnel Administration*, Vol. 8 (Dec. 1945), 6-10; Kurt Lewin, "Time Perspective and Morale," in Gertrud Weiss Lewin, ed., *Resolving Social Conflicts* (New York, 1948), pp. 103-124; and Theodore M. Newcomb, *Social Psychology* (New York, 1950), pp. 361-373.

47. These problems may not arise for the subordinate who becomes apathetic, disinterested, and so on.

4. The World of Work and the Behavioral Sciences: A Perspective and an Overview*

HAROLD M. F. RUSH

"Man does not live by bread alone . . .," so the Bible says. A lot of businessmen today are adding, "Nor does he *work* for bread alone, at least not anymore!"

There is a growing realization that the employee today is, indeed, a new breed. He appears to have different values, different needs, different motivations than his predecessor. He is better educated, he is a product of the knowledge explosion, he is more aware politically, socially, and economically, he is more demanding, he is less easily managed by traditional controls, and he is generally more sophisticated.

Managing the "new man" has become an increasingly difficult job. The once-proven incentives don't seem quite so effective. At least they don't result in the spark of creativity and dedication to the job that management wants. Many of management's attempts to provide adequate incentives have ended in frustration. The motivation it seeks is still lacking.

FOCUS ON MOTIVATION

Motivation, that ubiquitous theme in contemporary management literature, seems to be the prime concern of the manager who is trying, not just to turn out a product, but to gain a competitive edge in the marketplace. Despite all the talk about motivation today, it isn't a new concern of businessmen. They al-

ways have been, and probably always will be, interested in motivation. But only secondarily. Their *real* concern is productivity. Managers have always known that there is some connection between motivation and productivity, but in recent years, these two concepts appear as twins. There seems to be an inextricable link. What that link represents involves a set of highly complex notions about the nature of people and what motivates them to greater productivity.

There is evidence that management is trying hard to understand the new work force's motivations and behavior. To gain insight, business is increasingly turning to the field whose prime concern is human behavior: behavioral science.

WHAT IS BEHAVIORAL SCIENCE?

Reduced to its essential properties, behavioral science is the systematic study of behavior. Broadly speaking, behavioral science is one of the three commonly accepted divisions of continuing scientific inquiry, along with the physical and biological sciences. As a field with scientific standing, behavioral science is less mature than the biological and physical sciences, and its scope of inquiry and resulting body of knowledge is considerably less clearly defined than those of its sister sciences.

*Source: From Harold M. F. Rush, *Behavioral Science: Concepts and Management Application* (1969), Chapter 1, pp. 1-8. Copyright © 1969 The National Industrial Conference Board. Reprinted by permission. Footnotes omitted.

For example, the term "behavioral sciences" has been used to encompass all facets of the study of behavior, including those affected or caused by biological processes. It has also been used to denote the study of behavior of any type, including animal behavior. However, it is usually used to describe the study of *human* behavior. Furthermore, popular usage restricts the term to *human social sciences*, or the study of men in social settings.

Sometimes the behavioral sciences are spoken of as "social sciences," an older term, but many professionals in the field prefer "behavioral science" to "social science," since the newer term is felt to be more descriptive. Also, some laymen tend to confuse social science with the political and economic systems called "socialism."

Although "behavioral science" may be a more descriptive appellation than "social science," there is still the possibility that the generic term "behavioral science" causes some laymen to equate it with a school of psychology known as "behaviorism"—the "stimulus-response" school.

While behavior science encompasses this approach to studying behavior, its field is much larger, embracing many schools of thought and several academic disciplines, including psychology, sociology, anthropology, socioeconomics, political science, linguistics, and education. The field has consistency only in terms of its unifying concern: the study of behavior in social or cultural settings.

TRANSACTIONALISM

The social setting is the environment in which the behavior occurs, and as the various academic disciplines approach their study of behavior in this context, the result is called "transactionalism," connoting the full interaction of the various behavioral sciences, including the processes and the connections between these processes. In other words, sepa-

rate entities are not assumed, nor are events or phenomena having an effect on behavior seen as isolated factors. Rather they are viewed as part of the total environment in relation to the organism's (man's) behavior.

The unifying concern of the various behavioral sciences might imply agreement among them on theory and methodology; however, this is clearly not the case. There is no single, commonly accepted theory of human nature. In fact, there is widespread disagreement about the nature of the problem, and there are widely varying methodologies, even within one given academic discipline. Therefore, behavioral science is seen as an *approach*, as contrasted with a neatly defined theory of human behavior, that places equal emphasis on behavior and science. Generally, the study of behavior follows the outline of scientific method which implies the development of a systematic theory and an experimental plan for testing the theory. As these tests or investigations are carried out, new hypotheses are evolved, and these, in turn, are tested under controlled conditions. Furthermore, the behavioral sciences, in their investigations, generally follow the three fundamental steps of scientific method: research, development, and application. Unlike the biological and physical sciences, the behavioral sciences have a more difficult time in following rigidly the rules of scientific method because the subject of their inquiry is more variable. Simply, people and their environment are forever changing.

PREDICTABILITY OF BEHAVIOR

While people and the environment do change, the behavioral sciences seek to predict how most people are *likely* to behave under a given set of conditions as opposed to certainty. The predictive nature of the inquiry is underscored by experimental manipulation of the environment in order to create conditions under which men are likely to respond in a given fashion.

Because of this predictive emphasis, business has in recent years turned increasingly to the behavioral sciences for insight and assistance in dealing with "people problems." Industry attempts to understand the processes and nuances of behavior in order to create environmental conditions under which certain kinds of behavior are most likely to take place. In business terms this usually translates into a desire for greater productivity.

Many of the component "behavioral sciences" are about the same age as the industrial economy and there are many areas of common concern. However, the interest of business in behavioral science and that of behavioral science in business are fairly recent developments. This may be understood in terms of mutual need, with many factors contributing to the convergence, including a tremendous change in the nature of business and of the behavioral sciences. A complete marriage of the two hasn't resulted, yet there is evidence of increasing mutual interest.

THREE PHASES OF
BEHAVIORAL SCIENCE

The Conference Board surveyed a cross section of business firms and found that most had some interest in the work of behavioral science; and a majority of those firms indicating interest reported some behavioral science activity within their companies. Furthermore, all three phases of research, development, and application of behavioral science were to be found in industry.

This would not have been the case even a couple of decades ago, for a number of reasons. The behavioral sciences evidenced little interest in business or the relation of man to his work, and business paid little attention to the systematic study of behavior.

GENESIS: HAWTHORNE STUDIES

It is usually agreed that historically, the merger of industry and the behavioral sciences in their current form began with the research conducted by Elton Mayo and his colleagues in the Hawthorne plant of Western Electric Company. This pioneering industrial behavioral research has taken on the stature of a classic milestone study, and the work of the Mayo group is widely referred to as the "Hawthorne Studies." The studies, begun in 1927, are generally held to be the precursors of the behavioral science movement in industry. They were among the first to illustrate the effect of group pressures and norms of individual behavior within the work-group setting.

Among other findings related to the individual and the group, the Hawthorne researchers found that employees would sacrifice greater production (and correspondingly greater pay on a piece-work basis), rather than risk the displeasure or ostracism of their fellow workers. Management today is all too familiar with the nature of group pressures against "rate busters." In the late 1920s, however, this finding upset a lot of previously accepted notions about the economic motivations of workers.

INFLUENCE AND IMPLICATIONS OF GROUPS

The implication that workers could influence the behavior of fellow workers on a significant level was surprising even to the researchers. The studies were originally designed to investigate the relationship of fatigue and monotony to conditions of work. The researchers did, indeed, demonstrate a relationship here, and their findings resulted in shorter work weeks and the institution of regular rest periods during the workday, both of which appeared to increase worker productivity. But with each experimental investigation of environmental or external factors (rest, light, temperature, etc.), the researchers uncovered evidence of behavioral patterns that were not dependent upon the physical environment. For example, they found that people in the factory were not just a collection of individuals who worked in physical proximity to each other. Instead, there was an observable pattern of interpersonal interaction among the workers that followed the now widely accepted definition of a group: common purposes or interests; interdependent status and psychological awareness of each other; interdependent roles and relationships; and norms or values, created by the group, which regulate the behavior of members.

As the studies evolved, it was dramatically demonstrated that the workers *perceived themselves as a group*. As a result, the Hawthorne research took on three additional characteristics which were not a part of the original research design. The impact of physical or external factors on productivity among the work force became peripheral to the study. Rather the investigators refocused their research to concentrate on the work force in terms of (a) the individual workers with attitudes and motives, (b) the relationship of the individual to his work group, and (c) the role of the work group as an entity.

Observations in these areas had special significance for management, for it was demonstrated that supervisors were not dealing with isolated individuals on a one-to-one basis; instead, the supervisor was dealing with a group. Moreover, this group had interpersonal values that took precedence over individual considerations or management's imposed values, including compensation incentives and production standards.

CAUSES OF TIME LAG

The Hawthorne Studies formed the groundwork for, and influenced, subsequent studies of man and his work, but interest in them was not widespread at first. Economic conditions, particularly the Great Depression, caused

management to feel no compelling need to concern itself with worker motivation and group interaction. It has been said that one of the most significant things about the Hawthorne studies was their appearance "twenty years ahead of their time."

At that time the behavioral sciences themselves showed little interest in investigating groups, as such, within industry—or, indeed, groups anywhere. In psychology, there appeared to be a feeling that to study groups was somehow "unscientific," since it was widely believed that groups did not have "personalities" that could be studied in operational terms. Even in sociology and anthropology, by definition disciplines concerned with social units, there was little concern with the group as an entity with a "life" of its own. The interest was in the individual's relationship to his "membership" or "reference" group, as well as in the study of one group's observable interaction with another.

Even within the existing field of industrial psychology there was little attention directed toward the interaction, motivation, and productivity of groups. Industry has used psychologists for a long time–even before the Hawthorne studies–and the field of industrial psychology is still a significant contributor to the growing body of knowledge about human behavior in relation to work. However, through the work of industrial psychologists in selection and placement, human engineering, attitude measurement, personal counseling and assessment, the field of inquiry remains the individual, as opposed to the group.

SCIENTIFIC BASIS FOR STUDY OF GROUPS

In the late 1930s there arose a movement within psychology that provided a basis for the scientific study of groups. The social psychologist Kurt Lewin and his colleagues, applying Gestalt principles, demonstrated that groups, through the perceptions and interactions of their members, have a personality of their own that is observable in terms of cohesiveness, motivations, beliefs, goals, values, actions, and purposive direction. These group forces are seen as superseding consideration of individuals in the group; the group assumes a personality that is more than a composite of the members' individual personalities. "That the whole is greater than the sum of its parts" is the rudimentary principle of the Gestalt. Furthermore, many of the qualities and characteristics of individual human personality can be observed in groups, as dynamic, interacting forces. By demonstrating that groups, like individuals, are "living systems," Lewin provided a theoretical base for further study of groups as distinct entities with cohesiveness as an experimental variable.

From the foundations laid by the Hawthorne Studies and supported by subsequent research on group and individual behavior, as championed by Lewin and his colleagues, there has arisen a relatively new field within social psychology known as organizational psychology. Paralleling this development, the field of sociology has also applied itself to the study of groups as living systems, and recently there has arisen a field within the behavioral sciences known as "organizational behavior." This newest specialty is actually an interdisciplinary one that encompasses social psychological and sociological approaches, and in many instances it also includes economics, because the field of interest is mainly groups *within industry*.

EVOLUTION OF BEHAVIORAL SCIENCES

The coming-together of industry and the behavioral sciences may be explained in terms of the evolution of the culture in which both the behavioral sciences and industry exist, and especially in the pattern of evolution of industry itself. Even more germane is the evolution of management style and technology.

Organization theorists see distinct stages of organizational growth and styles of management. These changes are viewed as attempts to maintain a balance of concern for the economic objectives and concern for the human factors through which the objectives are realized. These two concerns appear to be central, yet with each stage of evolution the pendulum swings too far one way or the other. In moving from one phase to another, there is a tendency to overcompensate with each swing; too much informality is compensated for by too much stress on rules and regulations.

GROWTH OF "SCIENTIFIC MANAGEMENT"

The small entrepreneurial organization was typical of industry at first. As the handicraft economy grew into a factory economy of mass production, industry felt a need to standardize. This stage of growth is often called the "scientific management" stage, championed by F. W. Taylor, whose philosophy was "The basic objective of management is to provide maximum prosperity for the employer, coupled with maximum prosperity for the employee." However, "scientific management" assumed that the goals of the individual and the organization are the same. The movement emphasized time-and-motion studies and other aspects of "efficiency"; it called for standards of performance and for regulations and procedures for each job; and it emphasized organization structures and lines of authority and responsibility. It has been criticized for ignoring the needs of people, despite Taylor's statement that "maximum prosperity for the employee" was one of its aims.

HUMAN RELATIONS

Following this stage there came the

period characterized by the "human relations" movement in industry. Here the emphasis was on creating a work force with high morale. It represented an attempt to break down formal or arbitrary boundaries that are part of the fabric of a stratified and bureaucratic organizational structure. Managers trained in "human relations" learned to be "friendly" toward their subordinates, to call them by their first names, and generally to try to keep people content as a part of "one big happy family." The attempt to democratize the organization found expression in company-sponsored recreational activities, and in increased emphasis on fringe benefits.

The "human relations" movement (the one most often confused with the current behavioral science movement) has been criticized widely as manipulative, insincere, and, most importantly, as ignoring the reality of economic variables. It is accused of equating high morale with high productivity. To some organization theorists, this represents a naive and simplistic view of the nature of man. They hold that, on the contrary, "there are a lot of happy but unproductive workers."

The contemporary behavioral science movement in industry is synonymous with none of its predecessor movements, though it has something in common with each of them. For example, it is concerned with increased efficiency of the work force, as was "scientific management"; it puts strong emphasis upon relations among people in the work setting, as did the "human relations" movement; it seeks to build an environment in which individual talents can be expressed and in which informal communication takes place, conditions akin to those in the entrepreneurial atmosphere. But behavioral science's definitions of these variables are different from those of preceding movements, and the conditions that make their realization possible are viewed in a different light.

CHARACTERISTICS OF CONTEMPORARY BEHAVIORAL SCIENCE

While it is difficult to generalize about so diverse a movement, there are nevertheless several common traits relative to industrial application:

1. It is an applied science.
2. It is normative and value centered.
3. It is humanistic and optimistic.
4. It is oriented toward economic objectives.
5. It is concerned with the total climate or milieu.
6. It stresses the use of groups.
7. It is aimed at participation.
8. It is concerned with development of interpersonal competence.
9. It views the organization as a total system.
10. It is an ongoing process to manage change.

AN APPLIED SCIENCE

The intent of the behavioral sciences as they address themselves to modern business is to provide insights into human behavior as it relates to the work force. While the premises of the behavioral sciences usually are tested under controlled or laboratory conditions, and there usually is developmental or middle phase research to validate initial hypotheses, the purpose of the research is to find *application* in industry's practices.

NORMATIVE AND VALUE CENTERED

Rather than being purely descriptive of the how and why of human behavior, the behavioral sciences in industry are aimed at bringing about change in a predetermined direction. That change is usually interpreted as increased concern with the human side of the management process, on the assumption that both the organization and the individual benefit thereby. The normative nature of the behavioral sciences is underscored by the proliferation of theories about management style, ranging from "how-to" prescriptions to polemics about change in basic practices. There is implicit a value judgement of the behavioral approach's superiority to other approaches.

HUMANISTIC AND OPTIMISTIC

The behavioral sciences are grounded in a belief that the needs and motivations of people are a prime concern. Furthermore, there is an acceptance of the value of the individual as a thinking, feeling organism, and of the fact that without these considerations the organization that does not take this into account falls short of its purpose as a social entity.

There is optimism about the innate potential of man to be independent, creative, productive, and capable of contributing positively to the objectives of the organization. There is an assumption that man not only has these potentialities, but, under the proper conditions, will actualize them. These "proper conditions" are based on the application of the fundamental concept of the dignity of the individual.

ORIENTED TOWARD ECONOMIC OBJECTIVES

Coupled with the humanistic and optimistic concerns is an emphasis on utilizing man's potential to reach organizational goals. Indeed, it is widely held that optimum utilization of man's potential actually results in increased productivity and profit for the firm. The needs of individuals and the needs of organizations are seen as consonant, rather than opposing, variables. Regardless of the form that humane management takes, there is the underlying aim of meeting the organization's objectives through the commitment and involvement of the work force.

TOTAL CLIMATE OR MILIEU

The approach is to change the total environment rather than to try to improve only the physical conditions or to increase employee satisfactions by changing isolated work processes.

Satisfactory working conditions, adequate compensation, and the necessary equipment for the job are viewed as only a small part of the requirements for a motivational climate. Of greater importance are the creation of an atmosphere of effective supervision, the opportunity for the realization of personal goals, congenial relations with others at the place of work, and a sense of accomplishment. In other words, the aim is to change the psychological environment in terms of what the behavioral sciences have discovered about man's personal needs.

THE USE OF GROUPS

Building upon research which demonstrates that groups do exist as social units within industry, the current emphasis is on effective use of group effort and interaction. Especially in the realm of supervisor-subordinate relations, the group theory of organization stresses the effectiveness of cohesive groups in carrying out organizational objectives. The relationship of the boss to the work group is seen as having crucial import, for research has shown that group norms may take precedence over supervisory directives unless the group has confidence in and respect for the boss.

Not only are large companies trying to capitalize on the advantages of concerted effort, but there is a realization that the larger organization is, in fact, a collection of overlapping formal and informal groups. Effective supervision is equated with optimal use of these groups, as contrasted with the earlier one-to-one approach to supervising employees.

AIM FOR PARTICIPATION

Research has shown repeatedly that people are more deeply committed to a course of action if they have had a voice in planning it. In industry there has been a growing realization that the most effective means of gaining commitment and involvement is to obtain the participation of the work force in reaching decisions and plans of action that effect them. The use of participation as a management tool is one of the cardinal principles of the contemporary behavioral science movement; in fact, "behavioral science management" and "participative management" are often used as interchangeable terms.

Participation in this sense is not the brand of "consultative supervision," often identified with the human relations movement, under which a manager, who has already decided upon a course of action, asks the opinion of subordinates merely to give them a *sense* of participation. The use of participation implies that the supervisor really *wants* the opinion of the employees and that he is willing to be influenced by their feelings and ideas.

Another consideration in applying the principle of participation is the relative import of the decision being evolved. Behavioral scientists insist that the degree of influence employees have on their superior's decision, and the corresponding influence that decision will have on the work force, is related greatly to the impact of the decision in terms of matters that *really* affect the *job*, as contrasted with company recreational activities, for example.

DEVELOPMENT OF INTERPERSONAL COMPETENCE

Interpersonal relations refers to everything that transpires between one person and another, or between an individual and a group. This seemingly simple definition is deceptive, however, for the concept encompasses one person's perception of others, his evaluation and understanding of them, and his mode of reacting, inwardly and outwardly, to others—all in relation to the center of his particular universe: himself.

"Interpersonal competence" implies a facility in dealing with others in a face-to-face relationship. The term also connotes what is referred to as "authenticity" in interaction with others. It implies an atmosphere of trust and openness in order for effective communication to take place between individuals and between groups. A key word is "leveling," or straightforward, honest, and candid communication, coupled with "feedback" given in equally candid terms. Both words imply authenticity in expressing one's own feelings and ideas as well as in responding to others.

Special attention is directed to the role of conflict in interpersonal competence. Conflict is viewed as a natural result of the interaction of people and groups. More traditional management approaches have stressed the need to avoid conflict or to smooth it over should it arise. Behavioral science theory recognizes the existence of conflict and views it as healthy and even creative, provided it is dealt with openly. Conflict is approached, ideally, as a problem-solving matter between parties in disagreement. Within a framework of authenticity, the energy involved in the conflict can be directed toward constructive purposes.

The opposite of the problem-solving approach is called "win-lose," a term which usually implies that if a matter is decided in favor of one position, the opposing position loses. "Win-lose" equates with entrenched hostility or unnecessary competition between individuals or between groups. The "win-lose" complex implies perpetration of unresolved conflict, which tends to grow so long as it remains unresolved. The behavioral science approach to abatement of "win-lose" is not to create an atmosphere in which everyone reaches a compromise and ends up liking each other. Harmony is sought, but personal differences are held to be natural in face-to-face groups. The optimum resolution of "win-lose" is the creation of an atmosphere that is problem-solving and in which conflicting parties deal objectively with the conflict over ideas, instead of attacking the person holding an opposing viewpoint.

A TOTAL SYSTEM

The "living system" of an organization is viewed as an enlarged version of man. The organization is believed to have, on a large scale, all the qualities of the individual, including beliefs, mode of behaving, objectives, personality, and motivations. It has inputs, interaction, responses, and outputs. This theory assumes that all behavior is goal seeking, in individuals and in organizations. Improvement of the system, therefore, is aimed at increasing its effectiveness, as a totality, in order that it may reach its goals.

Because of the overlapping, reinforcing, and interrelated nature of the system's components, development or improvement of the organization is geared to improve all parts of the system.

To the behaviorally oriented thinker, dealing with isolated factors in organization improvement results in minimal pay-off. For example:

- New machines are of little value unless people are trained to operate them. Long-range economic planning is unidimensional unless manpower planning is integrated with it.
- Open communication is dependent upon trust among people.
- Individual objectives cannot be meshed with organizational objectives unless the organizational objectives are clearly defined and communicated.
- An atmosphere of candor and interpersonal authenticity can be disastrous unless

there is generally a condition of mental health among the work force.
- Manager development is of little value unless the manager understands its objectives and identifies with them.
- Striving for good human relations is a waste of time and a misdirection of effort unless the end result is the economic advancement of the firm.
- Asking for participation on the part of employees is pointless unless they are committed to the objective being sought.

AN ONGOING PROCESS TO MANAGE CHANGE

Organizations as dynamic entities are characterized by pervasive change. The management of change is seen as the real job of the manager. Managing change takes two forms (1) acclimating the work force to externally and internally created change, and (2) building an atmosphere in which change is not only welcomed but created by the work force.

The "ongoing process" is a goal of behavioral science management. It also is, by definition, the essence of managing change. For this reason, managing change is seen as a self-perpetuating, ever-evolving phenomenon. As an organization reaches one plateau of effectiveness, and as societal and internal changes are introduced and assimulated, new goals are established. Working toward these goals is viewed as an ongoing process of actualizing the organization's potential; therefore the "stop-and-start" times of a "program" are replaced by change as a way of life.

5. Making Behavioral Science More Useful*

JAY W. LORSCH

Since World War II management thought and practice have undergone great change. The computer has revolutionized information processing and, along with operations research and other quantitative techniques, has improved management decision making. New methods of market and consumer research also provide better information on which to base decisions. All these developments mean better tools for obtaining and analyzing information for more effective management.

During the same period the behavioral sciences—anthropology, psychology, social psychology, and sociology—have also contributed many potential ideas and theories to management. Unlike the first set of management tools, these ideas have focused not only on how decisions are made, but also on how employees from top management levels to the factory floor implement them. Thus these ideas should be of use to every manager: how to communicate effectively; how to give performance evaluations to employees; how to resolve conflicts between individuals or between one department and another; how to design organization structures, measurement systems, and compensation packages; how to introduce changes in organization, procedures, and strategy.

In spite of their potential for wide application, however, these ideas have been only sparingly used. Surely, General Foods, Volvo, and Procter & Gamble have introduced innovations in some factory

organizations, and some management organizations have done so as well, but how many other company managements have failed to use the available knowledge? Further, why have the companies that have claimed success in one location or division been so reluctant to apply the ideas in other appropriate places?

One obvious reason seems to be the confusion, skepticism, and controversy about the relevance of these ideas in the minds of many managers. For example: Is participative management a suitable style for all managers? Can job enrichment be applied in a unionized factory? Will managers set realistic goals with a management by objectives program? Has laboratory training improved managerial effectiveness? And, ultimately, some hardheaded manager always asks, "What does all this psychological mumbo-jumbo contribute to the bottom line?" The list of such questions may seem endless, but, equally discouraging, the answers the experts provide often seem unpersuasive and even contradictory.

Another facet of the situation, however, concerns me even more. The behavioral sciences occasionally burst with enthusiasm about certain ideas. Job enlargement, T-Groups, creative thinking, participative leadership, and management by objectives are cases in point. Each set of ideas or each technique becomes almost a fad with strong advocates who tout its early successes. Then, as a growing number of companies try the ideas or

*Source: Jay W. Lorsch, "Making Behavioral Science More Useful," *Harvard Business Review* (March-April 1979). Copyright © 1979 by the President and Fellows of Harvard College. Reprinted by permission of *Harvard Business Review*. All rights reserved.

techniques and as reports of failure and disappointment mount, the fad quickly dies. This often repeated pattern has caused many managers to lose interest in trying other behavioral science ideas which could help them.

In this article, I explore why so much heat and confusion have arisen around these behavioral science ideas and why, consequently, they have had such a limited impact on management practice. Because this is a matter of applying knowledge developed in the academic world to the problems of practicing managers, I am addressing both managers and academics. What can managers do themselves to make better use of the behavioral sciences? What can they demand from academics to get more practical knowledge? What can the academics working in this field do to provide more knowledge practitioners can use?

LURE OF THE UNIVERSAL THEORY

One major reason for the difficulties in applying behavioral science knowledge has been the interpretation that such ideas are applicable to all situations. From their earliest attempts to apply these ideas, both behavioral scientists developing the knowledge and managers applying it have at one time or another maintained the universality of the ideas. For example, Rensis Likert's participative-management ("Systems 4" Management) model was a call by a behavioral scientist for a universal application of ideas regardless of industry, company size, or geographic location.[1]

Over the past few years, Likert's voice has been joined by many other behavioral scientists who assume that their theories are also universally appropriate. Many of these theories were derived from studies carried out during and after World War II. The data from these studies were interpreted as supporting, for example, the notion that all employees have strong needs for group membership at work and, consequently, the universal superiority of

participative management. Researchers were not concerned whether these ideas were more appropriate in one setting than in another, with different groups of employees, with different jobs, and so forth.

Along with this search for the universal went a tendency to invent specific techniques for applying the theories, which it was argued would lead to improved results in all situations. Examples are management by objectives, autonomous work groups, laboratory training, job enrichment, and participative leadership.

By now many managers have tried these techniques, and their attempts have led to numerous difficulties stemming from the variable conditions existing in different companies. For example, a basic premise underlying management by objectives is that if people set their own goals, they will be committed to them. Because of the nature of the business or of the technology, however, in some situations employees can have little or no real voice in setting goals.

To illustrate, consider the case of the back office of a large bank, where managers down to first-line supervisors were directed to become involved in an MBO program. The quantity, schedule, and quality of their work, however, were imposed on them by the work flow from other groups in the bank and by their customers' requests, rather than being set by the managers themselves. Moreover, upper managers trying to meet strategic goals set their cost targets. These lower-level managers had little or no leeway in which to choose their own goals. As a result, they soon saw the management by objectives program as a sham.

Another example of a situation not fitting a theory occurs when a manager's personality is not consistent with what is demanded of a participative leader. As Harry Levinson and Abraham Zaleznik, among others, have indicated, although personality development is a life-long process, a 35-year-old's character is generally stable and is unlikely to change in radically new directions.[2] Since one's style of dealing with others is closely linked to one's personality makeup, it is not surprising that some managers are comfortable with one way of managing subordinates and some with another.

To illustrate my point: Companies have faced a major difficulty in introducing autonomous work groups and similar techniques. These techniques require supervisors to involve their subordinates more heavily in decision making, and many of these managers find it difficult to adjust to this new "participative" style. Not only have they spent many years managing in a different way, but also they consciously or unconsciously chose to be foremen because their personalities were suited to the traditional, more directive role.

Such situational problems are a primary reason that so many of these techniques are flashes in the pan. They are applied successfully in a few companies where conditions are right and receive attention and publicity. Without considering the differences, managers, consultants, and academics alike decide the technique can be applied to other situations. Because conditions are not right, the second-generation attempts are often failures, and the enthusiasm dies.

EACH SITUATION IS UNIQUE

Neither universal theories nor the resulting techniques have been the only behavioral science ideas available to managers. Another set of ideas is built on the premise that the organization can be viewed as a social system. This approach developed out of the Hawthorne studies by Elton Mayo, F. J. Roethlisberger, and William Dickson.[3]

In this well-known study, it was learned that worker behavior is the result of a complex system of forces including the personalities of the workers, the nature of their jobs, and the formal measurement and reward practices of the organization. Workers behave in ways that management

does not intend, not because they are irresponsible or lazy but because they need to cope with their work situation in a way that is satisfying and meaningful to them. From this perspective, what is effective management behavior and action depends on the specifics in each situation.

Although many scholars, including Roethlisberger and Mayo themselves, elaborated on these ideas and taught them at many business schools, managers never gave them the attention they gave to the universal ideas. Interestingly enough, many saw the central significance of the Hawthorne studies as being either the *universal* importance of effective interpersonal communication between supervisors and workers or the so-called "Hawthorne Effect." The latter is the notion that any change in practice will *always* lead to positive results in the short run simply because of the novelty of the new practice.

In essence, this world-renowned study, which its authors saw as proving that human issues need to be viewed from a "social system," or situational perspective, was interpreted by others as a call for universal techniques of "good human relations." (For Roethlisberger's comments on this, see *The Elusive Phenomena*.[4])

Of course, stating that one should *always* take a situational perspective could be seen as a universal prescription itself. My concern is not with universal ideas, such as this and others which I shall mention shortly, which seem to hold generally true. Rather, it is with techniques invented under a specific set of conditions, which have not been' more widely tried but which their advocates argue have universal application.

Why these social-system concepts did not catch on is a matter of conjecture, but one reasonable explanation is that managers naturally prefer the simplest apparent approach to a problem. When faced with the choice between the complex and time-consuming analysis required to apply such situational ideas and the simpler, quicker prescriptions of universal theories and techniques, most managers seem to prefer the simpler universal approach. The human tendency to follow the fads and fashions also adds to the appeal of these techniques. If competitors are trying T-groups for management development, shouldn't we? If the company across the industrial park is using MBO, shouldn't we as well?

In spite of the rush to simple popular solutions in the last decade, some behavioral scientists have become aware that the universal theories and the techniques they spawned have failed in many situations where they were inappropriate. These scholars are trying to understand situational complexity and to provide managers with tools to analyze the complex issues in each specific situation and to decide on appropriate action. Examples of these efforts are listed in *Exhibit 5-1.*

These behavioral scientists do not all agree on what variables are important to understand. At this stage, people conceptualize the issues and define the variables and the important relationships among them in many different ways. Also, the "theories" they have developed often throw light on a limited set of applications.

All these behavioral scientists focusing on situational theories, however, share two fundamental assumptions. First, the proper target of behavioral science knowledge is the complex interrelationships that shape the behavior with which all managers must deal. Harold J. Leavitt, in his well-known text *Managerial Psychology,* presents a diagram (see *Exhibit 5-2)* that illustrates clearly the basic set of relationships.[5] Behavior in an organization results, he writes, from the interaction of people's needs, their task requirements, and the organization's characteristics. He uses two-headed arrows to both suggest this complex interdependence and indicate that behavior itself can influence the other forces over time.

Although Leavitt's was an early and, from today's perspective, a simplified view of the relationships involved, it captures the essential issues in situational theories

and is very close to the Roethlisberger and Dickson conception.

The second assumption that behavioral scientists focusing on situational theories seem to share is that, at this juncture, they cannot hope to provide a grand and general theory of human behavior in organizations. Rather, what the behavioral sciences can, and should, provide are what L. J. Henderson called "walking sticks" to guide the managers along complex decison-making paths about human affairs.[6] In this case, by walking sticks I mean conceptual models for understanding the complexity of the human issues a manager faces.

Such models represent the product these scholars have to offer managers. Universal prescriptions or techniques are like a mirage. Each situation is unique and the manager must use these conceptual models to diagnose it. With an understanding of the complex and interrelated causes of behavior in the organization, the manager can use his or her intellect and creative ability to invent a new solution or to judge what existing solutions might fit the situation.

AN APPLIED EXAMPLE

The case of a major insurance company illustrates how a situational walking stick can help managers. Like many of its competitors, the top management of this company was concerned about the high rate of turnover among its younger professional staff. The managers felt that they did not understand the causes of this turnover and were unwilling to accept the conclusion that their competitors reached— namely, that the basic cause was low pay. Instead, they used an in-house consultant to help them diagnose the causes of their problem.

This consultant used a relatively simple situational model—the concept of the psychological contract as a framework for diagnosing the causes of the problem.[7] From this perspective, the relationship between a group of employees and the

Exhibit 5-1

EXAMPLES OF SITUATIONAL FRAMEWORKS

Author	Publication	Major focus
Fred E. Fiedler	*A Theory of Leadership Effectiveness* (New York: McGraw-Hill, 1967).	Leadership of a work unit
John P. Kotter	*Organizational Dynamics* (Reading, Mass.: Addison-Wesley, 1978).	Organizational change
Edward E. Lawler	*Pay and Organizational Effectiveness: A Psychological View* (New York: McGraw-Hill, 1971).	Employee motivation
Paul R. Lawrence and Jay W. Lorsch	*Organization and Environment* (Division of Research, Harvard Business School, Harvard University, 1967).	Organizational arrangements to fit environmental requirements
Harry Levinson	*Men, Management and Mental Health* (Harvard University Press, 1962).	Employee motivation
Jay W. Lorsch and John Morse	*Organizations and Their Members* (New York: Harper and Row, 1975).	Organizational arrangements and leadership in functional units
Edgar H. Schein	*Career Dynamics: Matching Individual and Organizational Needs* (Reading, Mass.: Addison-Wesley, 1978).	Life stage careers, and organizational requirements
Robert Tannenbaum and Warren H. Schmidt	*"How To Choose A Leadership Pattern"* (HBR May-June 1973).	Leadership
Victor H. Vroom and Philip W. Yetton	*Leadership and Decision-Making* (University of Pittsburgh Press, 1973).	Leadership behavior for different types of decisions
Joan Woodward	*Industrial Organization: Theory and Practice* (Oxford University Press, 1965).	Organizational design

company is seen as an implicit, as well as explicit, contract.

While this contract is not binding in the legal sense, it is of psychological importance. Employees have certain expectations about what they are to get from their work in the company—both economically and psychologically. If these expectations are not met, the employees become dissatisfied, and ultimately can express themselves by walking out the door.

With these ideas in mind, the consultant, through a series of interviews in offices that had varying levels of turnover, sought the answers to two basic questions: What did the employees expect from the company? And how well were these expectations being met?

He learned that these young employees considered their current salary level relatively unimportant. More important to them were future career opportunities, the chance to do their jobs with minimum interference from above, and immediate supervisors who cared about their progress and tried to facilitate their learning. Furthermore, the consultant found that staff turnover was much lower in offices where managers were meeting expectations than where they were not.

From this diagnosis, top management developed an approach to improve the skills of its middle managers in meeting the expectations of its younger staff. By discovering the basic causes of its turnover problem, the company avoided the trap its competitors with identical problems fell in of mistakenly relying on salary increases as a way of trying to buy the loyalty of its younger staff.

POTENTIAL OF SITUATIONAL THEORIES

The insurance company case illustrates the greatest potential the behavioral sciences have for managers at present. They can provide situational theories to analyze, order, understand, and deal with the complex social and human issues managers face. By their nature the universal theories make simplified assumptions about the

human and business factors involved in a situation.

For example, many universal theories do not recognize that not all employees have the same career expectations. Yet we now know that while older managers may be more interested in jobs that enable them to develop subordinates and build the organization for the future, younger persons, such as the professionals just mentioned, are at a stage of life where advancement is usually critical.[8]

Similarly, different business tasks do not all lend themselves to similar leadership styles or reward schemes; running a production shop may require directive leadership, but managing a group of professional underwriters for an insurance company may require employee involvement in decisions.

Even though they neither provide ready-made solutions nor solve all classes of human problems, the situational theories are tools to understand the variety and complexity of these problems. The manager has to select the theory that seems most relevant to his or her specific problem, analyze the situation according to it, develop his or her own action alternatives, and choose among them.

A hospital laboratory provides a useful analogy. It is full of diagnostic tools, but the doctor has to make the choice of the appropriate ones. Then, he makes a diagnosis and decides on the appropriate treatment. So it will be for managers. The behavioral sciences can provide conceptual frameworks for analyzing problems. They will indicate what data are required, in some cases how best to collect them, how the problem areas are related to each other, and the outcomes with which the managers will be concerned. With this analysis the managers can then use their experience, intuition, and intellect to decide which actions make sense.

From this description, the analytical process may seem difficult and time-consuming. How true this is will depend to some extent on the complexity of the problem and the experience that a manager has in applying these tools. A man-

Exhibit 5-2

BASIC FORCES SHAPING BEHAVIOR

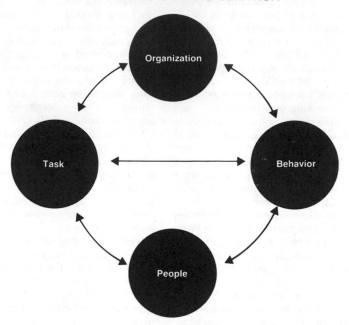

ager with experience can apply them with the same ease and skill a physician displays in using his diagnostic tools. Applying these tools to complex and infrequently encountered issues, however, may require some expertise beyond the scope of a typical line manager—a problem I shall deal with shortly.

The trend toward more situational theories signifies only a decline in emphasis on universal theories and the techniques they have spawned, not that these theories and techniques should or will disappear. Undoubtedly, on a limited number of issues, such generalizations are useful guides to actions. The problem for a manager is to identify those issues where a universal theory is helpful, and not confuse them with issues where the solution depends on the situation.

For example, certain maxims about interpersonal communication seem to be generally useful in conducting perfor-

mance appraisal interviews. And it seems clear that it is absolutely necessary for the top management of a unit undergoing a change to be committed to the process for it to be successful. Use of such valid generalizations from the behavioral sciences should continue and expand.

But the application of techniques and universal principles that are inappropriate in a variety of situations must decline. Because of the tendency toward fads in both managers and academics, I am not naive enough to think that the misapplications of universal theories will suddenly end. My hope is that the increasing availability and use of situational theories will gradually make universal ideas less attractive. As managers become more sophisticated diagnosticians, they will be less likely to try an idea or a technique simply because it is a fad.

Managers need also to recognize a number of current difficulties in using situational theories and must, with the help of those who are developing these ideas, seek solutions to them. In essence, in the behavioral science market they must act as consumers who influence the end product, and in their companies they must, among other things, act as teachers so that they and their associates are prepared to use these tools.

THE MANAGER AS A CONSUMER

If a manager, acting as a consumer, begins to explore the relevant literature, what is he likely to find? To what extent are the situational theories in a useful, usable form? Unfortunately, much needs to be done to make many of these tools more widely applicable. As managers become informed and demanding consumers, I hope they can influence behavioral scientists to take steps to overcome the current problems.

THE TOWER OF BABEL

One difficulty with today's situational tools is that each scholar (or group of scholars) has developed his or her own language and methods and makes interpretations based on his or her values, assumptions, and research about individual behavior. Also, in the same way physical scientists and engineers have done, each set of scholars, not surprisingly, prefers its own ideas and rejects those "not invented here." Understandably, communication among behavioral scientists and their communication with managers is confused. Different scholars use different labels to mean the same thing. Because no one relates his ideas to those of others, an academic Tower of Babel develops.

Managers and scholars alike find it difficult to understand what one label means in one model as compared to another or how the ideas developed by one group relate to those developed elsewhere. Clearly, what managers and academics can and must do is judge future studies more carefully and explicitly to determine whether they are related to each other. In this way, we will be able to see the parallels and differences in various theories and will be able to make more informed decisions about their relevance to particular problems. Similarly, such action should gradually reduce much of the variation in language and terminology that characterizes the behavioral sciences.

LACK OF PARSIMONY

Many of these concepts are so complex that managers need to learn how to define the concepts and their relationships before they can apply them. All this takes time and, naturally, makes these ideas less appealing to the busy line executive. By their preference for complex and elegant theories that greatly exceed the needs of most managers, academics have compounded the problem. Rather than worrying about how to help managers, many academics seem preoccupied with impressing their colleagues. In my own experience, moreover, it is the relatively simple concepts that managers find most useful.

As consumers of knowledge, managers can and should reject those theories that are too complex and seek those simple enough to be understood and implemented by intelligent managers. But academics must strive to develop such theories, what Sheldon has called "friendly" models.[9] By this, he means theories that are not so complex as to intimidate potential users, yet are complete enough to enable them to deal with the real human complexities they face.

One way to ensure such a balance is for managers to encourage and for academics to conduct more research focusing on managerial issues. Experience in medicine and space technology, for example, has demonstrated anew the axiom that research leading to a productive and practical payout will also likely lead to important theoretical results. Certainly, encouraging the design of research programs that tie real managerial concerns to theoretical behavioral science issues should also lead to gains in knowledge complete enough to be useful and simple enough to use.

Managers should also look for research that clarifies the conditions where findings are relevant and where they are not. In this manner, the distinction between situationally relevant ideas and universally applicable ones should be clearer. This, in turn, should reduce some of the misuses of behavioral science and also discourage academics from developing techniques in a vacuum.

AN ASIDE TO ACADEMICS

Although HBR readers are primarily practitioners, much of my preceding argument has particular relevance to my academic colleagues. Managers can only influence us indirectly by their reactions as consumers. The responsibility for the changes in the development of knowledge for which I am calling lies directly with academics. Yet, in many centers of behavioral science research, researchers are more concerned with proving a minor but neat conceptual point or resolving a measurement issue than with tackling issues that have clear practical application.

Disciplinary traditions, the promotion criteria in most universities, and the acceptance standard for most relevant publications place more emphasis on theoretical elegance and methodological perfection than on practical use of knowledge.

It will, therefore, require more than just pressure from consumers to make the necessary changes in our approach to knowledge-building. It is going to require dedication and courage from the behavioral scientists who believe, as I do, that our tools are still too little used.

THE MANAGER AS MANAGER

If academics can be encouraged to move in such directions, the manager's job will be easier. He or she will gradually acquire simpler conceptual tools that are relevant to real problems, specific about the range of situations to which they apply, and related to each other.

Even today, however, a few such conceptual tools exist. The issue for managers is how to select the specific set of tools relevant to a particular type of problem. To help in this regard, in Exhibit 5-3 I compare the conceptual tools from Exhibit 5-1 as to their major focus, the type of management or organizational issues for which they are most relevant, and some of the key questions managers must be able to answer to use these tools.

In examining Exhibit 5-3, bear in mind some caveats. First, the list represents my personal choices. It is not exhaustive. It is based on my own and some of my colleagues' experiences in helping managers deal with these problems. Second, many of these tools are relatively new and still somewhat crude. Although. in some cases, fairly sophisticated and validated techniques have been developed for answering the key questions, in others the manager will have to rely on his or her own knowledge and judgment of the situation. Third, in such a compact article, it is obviously not possible to define the variables in each conceptual framework or state the relationships among them. For this the reader will have to refer to the original works listed in Exhibit 5-1.

By using tools such as these, managers will be forced to be more diagnostic. They will have to approach human problems with the same analytical rigor they devote to marketing or financial issues. This approach means less acceptance of the latest fad in management practice, whether it be management by objective, job enrichment, office of the president, sensitivity training, or whatever. Instead, managers can use these tools to identify problems and diagnose their causes. Then they can invent their own solutions or even examine what other companies are doing to see what might be relevant to their situation. In this process, managers should not ignore their intuitive hunches and past experience. Accord-

Exhibit 5-3

SITUATIONAL FRAMEWORKS AND THEIR APPLICATIONS

Framework	Major focus	Issues	Leadership	Management selection	Career planning	Measurement and performance feedback	Compensation	Job Design	Division and coordination of activities	Organizational change	Diagnostic questions
Fiedler	Leadership of a work unit		●				●				What is the preferred leadership style of the relevant manager(s) on a continuum from permissive, passive, considerate, to controlling, active, and structuring? What is the quality of leader relations with the members of the subordinate group(s)? How well-defined and structured are the activities being performed by subordinates? How much positional authority does the leader(s) have?
Kotter	Organizational change					●		●	●		Is management concerned with short-term, moderate-term, or long-term change? If *short-term*, what is the current state of the organization's human and financial resources, its organization process and structure, its technology, and its external environment? If *moderate-term*, how well are the organization's resources, structure, and process aligned with each other and the external environment and the goals of management? If these are not well aligned, what changes have caused this? If *long-term*, are major changes likely in top management, in the organization's human and financial resources, its structure and processes, or its technology and external environment, which would make one or two of these elements out of line with the other? How maleable are the other elements so that a new alignment can be created? Is the organization inventing resources to achieve sufficient flexibility to adapt to such major changes?

(Continued)

Exhibit 5-3 (Continued)

Framework	Major focus	Issues									Diagnostic questions
		Leadership	Management selection	Career planning	Measurement and performance feedback	Compensation	Job Design	Division and coordination of activities	Organizational change		
Lorsch and Morse	Organizational arrangements and leadership in functional units	●			●	●	●				What is the nature of the unit's tasks? How certain are they? What goals do members have to work toward? How quickly is feedback about results available? What are members' shared psychological predispositions in terms of working together versus alone, preference for close supervision or not, preference for clear and predictable activities or for ambiguous ones? How well does existing leadership style, unit structure, measurement, and job design fit the unit task and members' predisposition?
Schein	Life stage, careers, and organizational requirements	●	●								At what stage of life is (are) the relevant individual(s)? Where are these people in their careers? What are their underlying career interests? What are the key dimensions of jobs available now and in the future? What are future personnel requirements for these jobs?
Vroom and Yetton	Leadership behavior for different types of decisions	●									Who among the boss and his subordinates has information to make a high-quality decision? Is the problem well-defined or not? Is acceptance of decisions by subordinates critical to implementation? Do subordinates share the organizational goals to be attained in making these decisions? Is conflict among subordinates likely in seeking solutions?

(Continued)

Exhibit 5-3 (Continued)

Framework	Major focus	Leadership	Management selection	Career planning	Measurement and performance feedback	Compensation	Job Design	Division and coordination of activities	Organizational change	Diagnostic questions
Lawler	Employee Motivation			●	●	●				What do the relevant individuals expect to get as rewards for their behavior on the job? How valuable are these rewards to these individuals? How hard do these individuals believe it will be to achieve the results expected of them?
Lawrence and Lorsch	Organizational arrangements to fit environmental requirements			●			●			How different are the organizational practices, traditions, and the goals and time horizons of members of various organization units? To what extent are these differences consistent with the different activities each unit is performing (e.g., selling products versus manufacturing them, versus designing them)? To what extent is it necessary for these units to work collaboratively and to what extent can they perform activities independent of each other? Do the existing mechanisms for dividing and coordinating work (e.g., authority structure, coordinating rules, cross-unit committees, rewards, and measurement) facilitate the necessary division of work and coordination?
Levinson et al.	Employee motivation		●	●	●	●				What is the psychological contract between the relevant individuals and the company? What does each party expect to receive from the other? How well is each party living up to its part of the contract?

ingly, this more rigorous analysis should be compared with such insights to arrive at the best possible judgments.

NEED FOR EDUCATION

Because these situational tools require more skill, knowledge, and time, line managers may need help and support in the longer run to realize their full potential. Education and training, in both university courses and company management-development programs, can and should aim at giving managers knowledge about these tools and the skills necessary to apply them. Such programs will have to provide not only content, but also, and equally important, practice in using these tools for analysis and problem solving.

In calling for management education, I am not suggesting that line managers can or should develop knowledge of or skill in applying a broad range of these ideas. Rather, as Exhibit 5-1 shows, they should gain understanding about those concepts which are relevant to the problems they regularly encounter. For example, concepts that focus on understanding leadership issues with a small group of workers (e.g., Fiedler's) would be of value to first-level supervisors.

At the general manager level, concepts that enhance understanding of multiple-unit organizations would be more relevant (e.g., Lawrence and Lorsch). This is not to say that some of these tools will not have utility at many organizational levels. For example, managers concerned with compensation issues might find Lawler's ideas useful whether their subordinates are salesmen, blue collar workers, or general managers.

ROLE OF STAFF

In the long run, along with educational programs, corporations will need to develop staff specialists with a broader range of knowledge about the behavioral sciences. These specialists, whatever their titles—organization development agent, human resources expert, organization designer, behavioral scientist—should be able to apply their wider and deeper behavioral science knowledge to a broader range of issues.

Their role would be analogous to what market research analysts, cost analysts, and so on, perform. Their job should be first to help managers decide what concepts will be most useful in understanding the problems they face, to design studies to gather data, to analyze them, and to work with their line colleagues to develop solutions. Again, academics have an important contribution to make. They can develop courses and programs to educate the professionals to staff these functions.

AWARENESS OF ONE'S VALUES AND STYLE

To use these tools effectively, both line and staff managers will need to be aware of their own values and their own preferred management styles. Without such awareness, one can easily and unwittingly confuse one's own sense of what is right or appropriate with what the situation seems to require and objective analysis seems to suggest. With self-knowledge about one's values and preferences, one can at least be explicit when making choices between what a situation requires and one's own preferences.

Achieving such self-awareness is not easy. It requires a willingness to be introspective and cognizant of one's limits as well as one's strengths, one's preferences as well as one's dislikes. Such probing is difficult for many managers; yet it is something that a number of seasoned, mature, and successful managers achieve. With this self-understanding, they are better able to comprehend their relationships with others around them. These same qualities must also be put to work to apply behavioral science knowledge effectively.

TOOLS ARE AVAILABLE NOW

Based on what you have read here, you may conclude that it is better to defer trying these situational tools until they have been improved, expanded, and refined. No doubt such improvements are needed. But if managers use the best of the existing situational tools now, in spite of their shortcomings, they will no doubt achieve improved effectiveness in dealing with the complex human problems of management.

The need for solving these human problems has never been more pressing. The increased size of organizations makes this so, as do the inflationary pressures on personnel costs and the rate of change in the environment of many companies. Additionally, demands from many employees for a more rewarding organizational life are growing. These situational tools offer a virtually untapped resource to provide more effective management of the human assets of most companies.

To use these tools will not be easy, and managers will have to make efforts at many levels: to be more critical consumers of behavioral science knowledge; to become more analytic and diagnostic; to gradually build educational programs and staff resources for developing skill and knowledge in using these tools; and, finally, to become more self-aware, so they can discriminate between their own preferences, current fads, and what will be most effective in their particular situations.

These efforts will be difficult, but to defer doing these things is to neglect these new and valuable tools that the behavioral sciences are making available, and this would be a tragic waste.

NOTES

1. Rensis Likert, *New Patterns of Management* (New York: McGraw-Hill, 1961).

2. Harry Levinson, *The Exceptional Executive* (Cambridge, Mass.: Harvard University Press, 1968); Abraham Zaleznik, *Human Dilemmas of Leadership* (New York: Harper & Row, 1966).

3. Elton Mayo, *The Human Problems of an Industrial Civilization* (New York: Viking Press, 1960); Fritz J. Roethlisberger and William Dickson, *Management and the Worker* (Cambridge, Mass.: Harvard University Press, 1939).

4. Fritz J. Roethlisberger, *The Elusive Phenomena*, ed. George F. F. Lombard (Boston: Division of Research, Harvard Business School, 1977).

5. Harold J. Leavitt, *Managerial Psychology* (Chicago: University of Chicago Press, 1958), p. 286.

6. L. J. Henderson, *On the Social System: Selected Writings* (Chicago: University of Chicago Press, 1970).

7. The concept of the psychological contract was first developed by Harry Levinson et al. in *Men, Management and Mental Health* (Cambridge, Mass: Harvard University Press, 1966).

8. See Daniel Levinson et al., *The Seasons of a Man's Life* (New York: Alfred Knopf, 1978); or Edgar H. Schein, *Career Dynamics* (Reading, Mass.: Addison-Wesley, 1978).

9. Alan Sheldon, "Friendly Models," *Science, Medicine, and Man*, Vol. 1, 1973, p. 49.

II

Individual Behavior
and Motivation

Introduction. An understanding of human behavior is obviously imperative if managers are to improve the performance of their organization's human resources. This section reviews some of the major theories of individual behavior and motivation. The first of these is probably the best known—Abraham H. Maslow's "A Theory of Human Motivation." It was in this article that Maslow originally set forth his famous "hierarchy of needs," which classifies all human needs into five categories—physiological, safety, love, esteem, and self-actualization. He contends that these needs are arranged in a hierarchy of prepotency, such that needs at the lowest level (physiological) must be at least minimally satisfied before the next higher level of needs (safety) will become the primary determinant of behavior. In turn, the safety needs must be satisfied before the love needs become prepotent, and so on. Maslow's theory also holds that a satisfied need is no longer a motivator, and this concept has enlightened many managers of the fact that continued emphasis on the satisfaction of lower-level needs is likely to result in diminishing returns.

J. Stacy Adams' "Toward an Understanding of Inequity" is premised upon Leon Festinger's theory of cognitive dissonance. Adams' "Theory of Inequity" holds that inequity exists for Worker A whenever his or her perceived job inputs and outcomes are inconsistent with Worker B's job inputs and outcomes. For example, inequity would exist if a person perceived that he or she was working much harder than another person who received the same pay. Adams suggests that the presence of inequity creates tension within Person A to reduce the inequity. Numerous examples of how inequity may be reduced are presented, such as increasing (or decreasing) one's effort if it is perceived to be low (or high) relative to others' work effort. Adams concludes by reviewing four experiments that provide evidence in support of his theory.

David C. McClelland, in "Achievement Motivation," sugggests that people can be divided into two groups: (1) a minority that is challenged by opportunity and willing to work hard to achieve, and (2) a majority that really does not care all that much about achievement. Focusing on this first group, those people who possess a high degree of "achievement motivation," McClelland cites several characteristics of such individuals: (1) they set challenging but attainable goals for themselves; (2) they prefer to work at a problem, thus influencing the outcome, rather than leaving the outcome to chance or to others; (3) they are more concerned with personal achievement than with the rewards of success; and (4) they prefer concrete feedback on how well they are doing. McClelland concludes by suggesting that achievement motivation can be developed within individuals, if the environment in which they live and work is supportive of such change.

Frederick Herzberg's "One More Time: How Do You Motivate Employees?" originally appeared in the *Harvard Business Review* in 1968 and earned the distinction of being that journal's all-time best-selling reprint. In it, Herzberg recounts his famous "hygiene-motivation theory," which suggests that while the "hygiene" factors (such as company policies and administration, supervision, working conditions, interpersonal relations, salary, status, and security) are important (poor hygiene factors cause job dissatisfaction), it is the growth or "motivation" factors (such as achievement, recognition, interesting work, increased responsibility, promotion) that lead to improved job satisfaction and performance. Thus, the only way to motivate an employee is with challenging work in which responsibility can be assumed. This is typically done by means of job enrichment. Herzberg cautions the reader not to confuse job enrichment with job enlargement, which is the process of merely increasing the number of meaningless tasks performed by a worker. Job enrichment, in marked contrast, is the deliberate upgrading of the scope, challenge, and responsibility of a job. Herzberg cites an example of a successful job-enrichment experiment and concludes by providing a step-by-step guide to job enrichment.

"Expectancy Theory," written by John P. Campbell, Marvin D. Dunnette, Edward E. Lawler III, and Karl E. Weick, Jr., holds that individuals have cognitive "expectancies" regarding outcomes that are likely to occur as a result of what they do and that individuals have preferences among these various outcomes. Consequently, motivation occurs on the basis of what the individual expects to occur as a result of what he or she chooses to do. The authors review the evolution of expectancy theories of motivation and then focus on their "hybrid expectancy model," which views the motivation to work as the end result of a complex perceptual process that includes: (1) Expectancy I (the perceived probability that an individual can do the job); (2) the nature of the task goals (categorized as external or internal); (3) Expectancy II (the perceived probability of receiving a reward given achievement of the task goal); (4) the nature of the rewards that can be obtained for achieving the task goal; (5) the instrumentality or importance of the rewards to the satisfaction of the individual's needs;

and (6) the needs of the individual. While this theory is clearly more complex than most other motivation theories, it provides managers with a comprehensive checklist of factors that affect the motivation to work. An improvement in any of the elements of the expectancy theory model should result in a corresponding improvement in motivation and performance.

The final selection in this section is "Existence, Relatedness and Growth Theory," by Clayton P. Alderfer. The author contends that human needs can be divided into three categories: existence, relatedness, and growth. "Existence" needs include all the various forms of material and physiological desires. "Relatedness" needs involve relationships with significant others, including family, friends, and co-workers. "Growth" needs relate to the inner desire to utilize one's capacities more fully and to grow and develop as a human being. Alderfer sets forth 10 propositions relating to how the satisfaction of one need affects the intensity of the others.

6. A Theory of Human Motivation*

ABRAHAM H. MASLOW

I. INTRODUCTION

In a previous paper[1] various propositions were presented which would have to be included in any theory of human motivation that could lay claim to being definitive. These conclusions may be briefly summarized as follows:

1. The integrated wholeness of the organism must be one of the foundation stones of motivation theory.

2. The hunger drive (or any other physiological drive) was rejected as a centering point or model for a definitive theory of motivation. Any drive that is somatically based and localizable was shown to be atypical rather than typical in human motivation.

3. Such a theory should stress and center itself upon ultimate or basic goals rather than partial or superficial ones, upon ends rather than means to these ends. Such a stress would imply a more central place for unconscious than for conscious motivations.

4. There are usually available various cultural paths to the same goal. Therefore conscious, specific, local-cultural desires are not as fundamental in motivation theory as the more basic, unconscious goals.

5. Any motivated behavior, either preparatory or consummatory, must be understood to be a channel through which many basic needs may be simultaneously expressed or satisfied. Typically an act has *more* than one motivation.

6. Practically all organismic states are to be understood as motivated and as motivating.

7. Human needs arrange themselves in hierarchies of prepotency. That is to say, the appearance of one need usually rests on the prior satisfaction of another, more pre-potent need. Man is a perpetually wanting animal. Also no need or drive can be treated as if it were isolated or discrete; every drive is related to the state of satisfaction or dissatisfaction of other drives.

8. *Lists* of drives will get us nowhere for various theoretical and practical reasons. Furthermore any classification of motivations must deal with the problem of levels of specificity or generalization of the motives to be classified.

9. Classifications of motivations must be based upon goals rather than upon instigating drives or motivated behavior.

10. Motivation theory should be human-centered rather than animal-centered.

11. The situation or the field in which the organism reacts must be taken into account but the field alone can rarely serve as an exclusive explanation for behavior. Furthermore the field itself must be interpreted in terms of the organism. Field theory cannot be a substitute for motivation theory.

12. Not only the integration of the organism must be taken into account, but also the possibility of isolated, specific, partial or segmental reactions.

It has since become necessary to add to these another affirmation.

13. Motivations theory is not synonymous with behavior theory. The motivations are only one class of determinants of behavior. While behavior is almost always motivated, it is also almost always biologically, culturally and situationally determined as well.

The present paper is an attempt to formulate a positive theory of motiva-

*Source: From *Psychological Review*, Vol. 50 (July 1943), pp. 370-396. Footnotes and pertinent references combined and renumbered; references not appearing in text have been omitted.

tion which will satisfy these theoretical demands and at the same time conform to the known facts, clinical and observational as well as experimental. It derives most directly, however, from clinical experience. This theory is, I think, in the functionalist tradition of James and Dewey, and is fused with the holism of Wertheimer,[2] Goldstein,[3] and Gestalt Psychology, and with the dynamicism of Freud[4] and Adler.[5] This fusion or synthesis may arbitrarily be called a "general-dynamic" theory.

It is far easier to perceive and to criticize the aspects in motivation theory than to remedy them. Mostly this is because of the very serious lack of sound data in this area. I conceive this lack of sound facts to be due primarily to the absence of a valid theory of motivation. The present theory then must be considered to be a suggested program or framework for future research and must stand or fall, not so much on facts available or evidence presented, as upon researches yet to be done, researches suggested perhaps, by the questions raised in this paper.

II. THE BASIC NEEDS

The "physiological" needs.—The needs that are usually taken as the starting point for motivation theory are the so-called physiological drives. Two recent lines of research make it necessary to revise our customary notions about these needs, first, the development of the concept of homeostasis, and second, the finding that appetites (preferential choices among foods) are a fairly efficient indication of actual needs or lacks in the body.

Homeostasis refers to the body's automatic efforts to maintain a constant, normal state of the blood stream. Cannon[6] has described this process for (1) the water content of the blood, (2) salt content, (3) sugar content, (4) protein content, (5) fat content, (6) calcium content, (7) oxygen content, (8) constant hydrogen-ion level (acid-base balance) and (9) constant temperature of the blood. Obviously this list can be extended to include other minerals, the hormones, vitamins, etc.

Young in a recent article[7] has summarized the work on appetite in its relation to body needs. If the body lacks some chemical, the individual will tend to develop a specific appetite or partial hunger for that food element.

Thus it seems impossible as well as useless to make any list of fundamental physiological needs for they can come to almost any number one might wish, depending on the degree of specificity of description. We can not identify all physiological needs as homeostatic. That sexual desire, sleepiness, sheer activity and maternal behavior in animals, are homeostatic, has not yet been demonstrated. Furthermore, this list would not include the various sensory pleasures (tastes, smells, tickling, stroking) which are probably physiological and which may become the goals of motivated behavior.

In a previous paper[8] it has been pointed out that these physiological drives or needs are to be considered unusual rather than typical because they are isolable, and because they are localizable somatically. That is to say, they are relatively independent of each other, of other motivations and of the organism as a whole, and secondly, in many cases, it is possible to demonstrate a localized, underlying somatic base for the drive. This is true less generally than has been thought (exceptions are fatigue, sleepiness, maternal responses) but it is till true in the classic instances of hunger, sex, and thirst.

It should be pointed out again that any of the physiological needs and the consummatory behavior involved with them serve as channels for all sorts of other needs as well. That is to say, the person who thinks he is hungry may actually be seeking more for comfort, or dependence, than for vitamins or proteins. Conversely, it is possible to satisfy the hunger need in part by other activities such as drinking water or smoking cigarettes. In other words, relatively isolable as these physiological needs are, they are not completely so.

Undoubtedly these physiological needs are the most prepotent of all needs. What this means specifically is, that in the human being who is missing everything in life in an extreme fashion, it is most likely that the major motivation would be the physiological needs rather than any others. A person who is lacking food, safety, love, and esteem would most probably hunger for food more strongly than for anything else.

If all the needs are unsatisfied, and the organism is then dominated by the physiological needs, all other needs may become simply non-existent or be pushed into the background. It is then fair to characterize the whole organism by saying simply that it is hungry, for consciousness is almost completely preempted by hunger. All capacities are put into the service of hunger-satisfaction, and the organization of these capacities is almost entirely determined by the one purpose of satisfying hunger. The receptors and effectors, the intelligence, memory, habits, all may now be defined simply as hunger-gratifying tools. Capacities that are not useful for this purpose lie dormant, or are pushed into the background. The urge to write poetry, the desire to acquire an automobile, the interest in American history, the desire for a new pair of shoes are, in the extreme case, forgotten or become of secondary importance. For the man who is extremely and dangerously hungry, no other interests exist but food. He dreams food, he remembers food, he thinks about food, he emotes only about food, he perceives only food and he wants only food. The more subtle determinants that ordinarily fuse with the physiological drives in organizing even feeding, drinking or sexual behavior, may now be so completely overwhelmed as to allow us to speak at this time (but *only* at this time) of pure hunger drive and behavior, with the one unqualified aim of relief.

Another peculiar characteristic of the human organism when it is dominated by a certain need is that the whole philosophy of the future tends also to change. For our chronically and extremely hungry man, Utopia can be defined very simply as a place where there is plenty of food. He tends to think that, if only he is guaranteed food for the rest of his life, he will be perfectly happy and will never want anything more. Life itself tends to be defined in terms of eating. Anything else will be defined as unimportant. Freedom, love, community feeling, respect, philosophy, may all be waved aside as fripperies which are useless since they fail to fill the stomach. Such a man may fairly be said to live by bread alone.

It cannot possibly be denied that such things are true but their *generality* can be denied. Emergency conditions are, almost by definition, rare in the normally functioning peaceful society. That this truism can be forgotten is due mainly to two reasons. First, rats have few motivations other than physiological ones, and since so much of the research upon motivation has been made with these animals, it is easy to carry the rat-picture over to the human being. Secondly, it is too often not realized that culture itself is an adaptive tool, one of whose main functions is to make the physiological emergencies come less and less often. In most of the known societies, chronic extreme hunger of the emergency type is rare, rather than common. In any case, this is still true in the United States. The average American citizen is experiencing appetite rather than hunger when he says "I am hungry." He is apt to experience sheer life-and-death hunger only by accident and then only a few times through his entire life.

Obviously a good way to obscure the "higher" motivations, and to get a lopsided view of human capacities and human nature, is to make the organism extremely and chronically hungry or thirsty. Anyone who attempts to make an emergency picture into a typical one, and who will measure all of man's goals and desires by his behavior during extreme physiological deprivation is certainly being blind to many things. It is quite true that man lives by bread alone—when there is no bread. But what happens to man's desires when there *is* plenty of bread and when his belly is chronically filled?

At once other (and "higher") needs emerge and these, rather than physiological hungers, dominate the organism. And when these in turn are satisfied, again new (and still "higher") needs emerge and so on. This is what we mean by saying that the basic human needs are organized into a hierarchy of relative prepotency.

One main implication of this phrasing is that gratification becomes as important a concept as deprivation in motivation theory, for it releases the organism from the domination of a relatively more physiological need, permitting thereby the emergence of other more social goals. The physiological needs, along with their partial goals, when chronically gratified cease to exist as active determinants or organizers of behavior. They now exist only in a potential fashion in the sense that they may emerge again to dominate the organism if they are thwarted. But a want that is satisfied is no longer a want. The organism is dominated and its behavior organized only by unsatisfied needs. If hunger is satisfied, it becomes unimportant in the current dynamics of the individual.

This statement is somewhat qualified by a hypothesis to be discussed more fully later, namely that it is precisely those individuals in whom a certain need has always been satisfied who are best equipped to tolerate deprivation of that need in the future, and that furthermore, those who have been de-prived in the past will react differently to current satisfactions than the one who has never been deprived.

The safety needs.—If the physiological needs are relatively well gratified, there then emerges a new set of needs, which we may categorize roughly as the safety needs. All that has been said of the physiological needs is equally true, although in lesser degree, of these desires. The organism may equally well be wholly dominated by them. They may serve as the almost exclusive organizers of behavior, recruiting all the capacities of the organism in their service, and we may then fairly describe the whole organism as a safety-seeking mechanism. Again we may say of the receptors, the effectors, of the intellect and the other capacities that they are primarily safety-seeking tools. Again, as in the hungry man, we find that the dominating goal is a strong determinant not only of his current world-outlook and philosophy but also of his philosophy of the future. Practically everything looks less important than safety, (even sometimes the physiological needs which being satisfied, are now underestimated). A man, in this state, if it is extreme enough and chronic enough, may be characterized as living almost for safety alone.

Although in this paper we are interested primarily in the needs of the adult, we can approach an understanding of his safety needs perhaps more efficiently by observation of infants and children, in whom these needs are much more simple and obvious. One reason for the clearer appearance of the threat or danger reaction in infants, is that they do not inhibit this reaction at all, whereas adults in our society have been taught to inhibit it at all costs. Thus even when adults do feel their safety to be threatened we may not be able to see this on the surface. Infants will react in a total fashion and as if they were endangered, if they are disturbed or dropped suddenly, startled by loud noises, flashing light, or other un-usual sensory stimulation, by rough handling, by general loss of support in the mother's arms, or by inadequate support.[9]

In infants we can also see a much more direct reaction to bodily illnesses of various kinds. Sometimes these illnesses seem to be immediately and *per se* threatening and seem to make the child feel unsafe. For instance, vomit-ing, colic or other sharp pains seem to make the child look at the whole world in a different way. At such a moment of pain, it may be postulated that, for the child, the appearance of the whole world suddenly changes from sunniness to darkness, so to speak, and becomes a place in which anything at all might happen, in which previously stable things have suddenly become unstable. Thus a child who because of some bad food is taken ill may, for a day or two, develop fear, nightmares, and a need for protection and reassurance never seen in him before his illness.

Another indication of the child's need for safety is his preference for some kind of undisrupted routine or rhythm. He seems to want a predictable, orderly world. For instance, injustice, unfair-ness, or inconsistency in the parents seems to make a child feel anxious and unsafe. This attitude may be not so much because of the injustice *per se* or any particular pains involved, but rather because this treatment threatens to make the world look unreliable, or un-safe, or unpredictable. Young children seem to thrive better under a system which has at least a skeletal outline of rigidity, in which there is a schedule of a kind, some sort of routine, something that can be counted upon, not only for the present but also far into the future. Perhaps one could express this more accurately by saying that the child needs an organized world rather than an unorganized or unstructured one.

The central role of the parents and the normal family setup are indisputable.

Quarreling, physical assault, separation, divorce or death within the family may be particularly terrifying. Also parental outbursts of rage or threats of punish-ment directed to the child, calling him names, speaking to him harshly, shaking him, handling him roughly, or actual physical punishment sometimes elicit such total panic and terror in the child that we must assume more is involved than the physical pain alone. While it is true that in some children this terror may represent also a fear of loss of par-ental love, it can also occur in com-pletely rejected children, who seem to cling to the hating parents more for sheer safety and protection than be-cause of hope of love.

Confronting the average child with new, unfamiliar, strange, unmanageable stimuli or situations will too frequently elicit the danger or terror reaction, as for example, getting lost or even being separated from the parents for a short time, being confronted with new faces, new situations or new tasks, the sight of strange, unfamiliar or uncontrollable ob-jects, illness or death. Particularly at such times, the child's frantic clinging to his parents is eloquent testimony to their role as protectors (quite apart from their roles as food-givers and love-givers).

From these and similar observations, we may generalize and say that the av-erage child in our society generally pre-fers a safe, orderly, predictable, or-ganized world, which he can count on, and in which unexpected, unmanage-able or other dangerous things do not happen, and in which, in any case, he has all-powerful parents who protect and shield him from harm.

That these reactions may so easily be observed in children is in a way a proof of the fact that children in our society, feel too unsafe (or, in a word, are badly brought up). Children who are reared in an unthreatening, loving family do *not* ordinarily react as we have described above.[10] In such children the danger reactions are apt to come mostly to objects or situations that adults too would consider dangerous.[11]

The healthy, normal, fortunate adult in our culture is largely satisfied in his safety needs. The peaceful, smoothly running, "good" society ordinarily makes its members feel safe enough from wild animals, extremes of temperature, criminals, assault and murder, tyranny, etc. Therefore, in a very real sense, he no longer has any safety needs as active motivators. Just as a sated man no longer feels hungry, a safe man no longer feels endangered. If we wish to see these needs directly and clearly we must turn to neurotic or near-neurotic individuals, and to the economic and social underdogs. In between these extremes, we can perceive the expressions of safety needs only in such phenomena as, for instance, the common preference for a job with tenure and protection, the desire for a savings account, and for insurance of various kinds (medical, dental, unemployment, disability, old age).

Other broader aspects of the attempt to seek safety and stability in the world are seen in the very common preference for familiar rather than unfamiliar things, or for the known rather than the unknown. The tendency to have some religion or world-philosophy that organizes the universe and the men in it into some sort of satisfactorily coherent, meaningful whole is also in part motivated by safety-seeking. Here too we may list science and philosophy in general as partially motivated by the safety needs (we shall see later that there are also other motivations to scientific, philosophical or religious endeavor).

Otherwise the need for safety is seen as an active and dominant mobilizer of the organism's resources only in emergencies, e.g., war, disease, natural catastrophes, crime waves, societal disorganization, neurosis, brain injury, chronically bad situation.

Some neurotic adults in our society are, in many ways, like the unsafe child in their desire for safety, although in the former it takes on a somewhat special appearance. Their reaction is often to unknown, psychological dangers in a world that is perceived to be hostile, overwhelming and threatening. Such a person behaves as if a great catastrophe were almost always impending, i.e., he is usually responding as if to an emergency. His safety needs often find specific expression in a search for a protector, or a stronger person on whom he may depend, or perhaps, a Fuehrer.

The neurotic individual may be described in a slightly different way with some usefulness as a grown-up person who retains his childish attitudes toward the world. That is to say, a neurotic adult may be said to behave "as if" he were actually afraid of a spanking, or of his mother's disapproval, or of being abandoned by his parents, or having his food taken away from him. It is as if his childish attitudes of fear and threat reaction to a dangerous world had gone underground, and untouched by the growing up and learning processes, were now ready to be called out by any stimulus that would make a child feel endangered and threatened.[12]

The neurosis in which the search for safety takes its clearest form is in the compulsive-obsessive neurosis. Compulsive-obsessives try frantically to order and stabilize the world so that no unmanageable, unexpected or unfamiliar dangers will ever appear.[13] They hedge themselves about with all sorts of ceremonials, rules and formulas so that every possible contingency may be provided for and so that no new contingencies may appear. They are much like the brain injured cases, described by Goldstein,[14] who manage to maintain their equilibrium by avoiding everything unfamiliar and strange and by ordering their restricted world in such a neat, disciplined, orderly fashion that everything in the world can be counted upon. They try to arrange the world so that anything unexpected (dangers) cannot possibly occur. If, through no fault of their own, something unexpected does occur, they go into a panic reaction as if this unexpected occurrence constituted a grave danger. What we can see only as a none-too-strong preference in the healthy person, e.g., preference for the familiar, becomes a life-and-death necessity in abnormal cases.

The love needs.—If both the physiological and the safety needs are fairly well gratified, then there will emerge the love and affection and be-longingness needs, and the whole cycle already described will repeat itself with this new center. Now the person will feel keenly, as never before, the absence of friends, or a sweetheart, or a wife, or children. He will hunger for affectionate relations with people in general, namely, for a place in his group, and he will strive with great intensity to achieve this goal. He will want to attain such a place more than anything else in the world and may even forget that once, when he was hungry, he sneered at love.

In our society the thwarting of these needs is the most commonly found core in cases of maladjustment and more severe psychopathology. Love and affection, as well as their possible expression in sexuality, are generally looked upon with ambivalence and are customarily hedged about with many restrictions and inhibitions. Practically all theorists of psychopathology have stressed thwarting of the love needs as basic in the picture of maladjustment. Many clinical studies have therefore been made of this need and we know more about it perhaps than any of the other needs except the physiological ones.[15]

One thing that must be stressed at this point is that love is not synonymous with sex. Sex may be studied as a purely physiological need. Ordinarily sexual behavior is multi-determined, that is to say, determined not only by sexual but also by other needs, chief among which are the love and affection needs. Also not to be overlooked is the fact that the

love needs involve both giving *and* receiving love.[16]

The esteem needs.—All people in our society (with a few pathological exceptions) have a need or desire for a stable, firmly based, (usually) high evaluation of themselves, for self-respect, or self-esteem, and for the esteem of others. By firmly based self-esteem, we mean that which is soundly based upon real capacity, achievement and respect from others. These needs may be classified into two subsidiary sets. These are, first, the desire for strength, for achievement, for adequacy, for confidence in the face of the world, and for independence and freedom.[17] Secondly, we have what we may call the desire for reputation or prestige (defining it as respect or esteem from other people), recognition, attention, importance or appreciation.[18] These needs have been relatively stressed by Alfred Adler and his followers, and have been relatively neglected by Freud and the psychoanalysts. More and more today however there is appearing widespread appreciation of their central importance.

Satisfaction of the self-esteem need leads to feelings of self-confidence, worth, strength, capability and adequacy of being useful and necessary in the world. But thwarting of these needs produces feelings of inferiority, of weakness and of helplessness. These feelings in turn give rise to either basic discouragement or else compensatory or neurotic trends. An appreciation of the necessity of basic self-confidence and an understanding of how helpless people are without it, can be easily gained from a study of severe traumatic neurosis.[19]

The need for self-actualization.—Even if all these needs are satisfied, we may still often (if not always) expect that a new discontent and restlessness will soon develop, unless the individual is doing what he is fitted for. A musician must make music, an artist must paint, a poet must write, if he is to be ultimately happy. What a man *can* be, he *must* be. This need we may call self-actualization.

This term, first coined by Kurt Goldstein, is being used in this paper in a much more specific and limited fashion. It refers to the desire for self-fulfillment, namely, to the tendency for him to become actualized in what he is potentially. This tendency might be phrased as the desire to become more and more what one is, to become everything that one is capable of becoming.

The specific form that these needs will take will of course vary greatly from person to person. In one individual it may take the form of the desire to be an ideal mother, in another it may be expressed athletically, and in still another it may be expressed in painting pictures or in inventions. It is not necessarily a creative urge although in people who have any capacities for creation it will take this form.

The clear emergence of these needs rests upon prior satisfaction of the physiological, safety, love and esteem needs. We shall call people who are satisfied in these needs, basically satisfied people, and it is from these that we may expect the fullest (and healthiest) creativeness.[20] Since, in our society, basically satisfied people are the exception, we do not know much about self-actualization, either experimentally or clinically. It remains a challenging problem for research.

The preconditions for the basic need satisfactions.—There are certain conditions which are immediate prerequisites for the basic need satisfactions. Danger to these is reacted to almost as if it were a direct danger to the basic needs themselves. Such conditions as freedom to speak, freedom to do what one wishes so long as no harm is done to others, freedom to express one's self, freedom to investigate and seek for information, freedom to defend one's self, justice, fairness, honesty, orderliness in the group are examples of such preconditions for basic need satisfactions. Thwarting in these freedoms will be reacted to with a threat or emergency response. These conditions are not ends in themselves but they are *almost* so since they are so closely related to the basic needs, which are apparently the only ends in themselves. These conditions are defended because without them the basic satisfactions are quite impossible, or at least, very severely endangered.

If we remember that the cognitive capacities (perceptual, intellectual, learning) are a set of adjustive tools, which have, among other functions, that of satisfaction of our basic needs, then it is clear that any danger to them, any deprivation or blocking of their free use, must also be indirectly threatening to the basic needs themselves. Such a statement is a partial solution of the general problems of curiosity, the search for knowledge, truth and wisdom, and the ever-persistent urge to solve the cosmic mysteries.

We must therefore introduce another hypothesis and speak of degrees of closeness to the basic needs, for we have already pointed out that *any* conscious desires (partial goals) are more or less important as they are more or less close to the basic needs. The same statement may be made for various behavior acts. An act is psychologically important if it contributes directly to satisfaction of basic needs. The less directly it so contributes, or the weaker this contribution is, the less important this act must be conceived to be from the point of view of dynamic psychology. A similar statement may be made for the various defense or coping mechanisms. Some are very directly related to the protection or attainment of the basic needs, others are only weakly and distantly related. Indeed if we wished, we could speak of more basic and less basic defense mechanisms, and then affirm that danger to the more basic defenses is more threatening than danger to less basic defenses (always remembering that this is so only because of their relationship to the basic needs).

The desires to know and to understand.—So far, we have mentioned the cognitive needs only in passing. Acquiring knowledge and systematizing the universe have been considered as, in part, techniques for the achievement of basic safety in the world, or, for the intelligent man, expressions of self-actualization. Also freedom of inquiry and expression have been discussed as preconditions of satisfactions of the basic needs. True though these formulations may be, they do not constitute definitive answers to the question as to the motivation role of curiosity, learning, philosophizing, experimenting, etc. They are, at best, no more than partial answers.

This question is especially difficult because we know so little about the facts. Curiosity, exploration, desire for the facts, desire to know may certainly be observed easily enough. The fact that they often are pursued even at great cost to the individual's safety is an earnest of the partial character of our previous discussion. In addition, the writer must admit that, though he has sufficient clinical evidence to postulate the desire to know as a very strong drive in intelligent people, no data are available for unintelligent people. It may then be largely a function of relatively high intelligence. Rather tentatively, then, and largely in the hope of stimulating discussion and research, we shall postulate a basic desire to know, to be aware of reality, to get the facts, to satisfy curiosity, or as Wertheimer phrases it, to see rather than to be blind.

This postulation, however, is not enough. Even after we know, we are impelled to know more and more minutely and microscopically on the one hand, and on the other, more and more extensively in the direction of world philosophy, religion, etc. The facts that we acquire, if they are isolated or atomistic, inevitably get theorized about, and either analyzed or organized or both. This process has been phrased by some as the search for "meaning." We shall then postulate a desire to understand, to systematize, to organize, to analyze, to look for relations and meanings.

Once these desires are accepted for discussion, we see that they too form themselves into a small hierarchy in which the desire to know is prepotent over the desire to understand. All the characteristics of a hierarchy of prepotency that we have described above, seem to hold for this one as well.

We must guard ourselves against the too easy tendency to separate these desires from the basic needs we have discussed above, *i.e.*, to make a sharp dichotomy between "cognitive" and "conative" needs. The desire to know and to understand are themselves conative, *i.e.*, have a striving character, and are as much personality needs as the "basic needs" we have already discussed.[21]

III. FURTHER CHARACTERISTICS OF THE BASIC NEEDS

The degree of fixity of the hierarchy of basic needs.—We have spoken so far as if this hierarchy were a fixed order but actually it is not nearly as rigid as we may have implied. It is true that most of the people with whom we have worked have seemed to have these basic needs in about the order that has been indicated. However, there have been a number of exceptions.

(1) There are some people in whom, for instance, self-esteem seems to be more important than love. This most common reversal in the hierarchy is usually due to the development of the notion that the person who is most likely to be loved is a strong or powerful person, one who inspires respect or fear, and who is self confident or aggressive. Therefore such people who

lack love and seek it, may try hard to put on a front of aggressive, confident behavior. But essentially they seek high self-esteem and its behavior expressions more as a means-to-an-end than for its own sake; they seek self-assertion for the sake of love rather than for self-esteem itself.

(2) There are other, apparently innately creative people in whom the drive to creativeness seems to be more important than any other counter-determinant. Their creativeness might appear not as self-actualization released by basic satisfaction, but in spite of lack of basic satisfaction.

(3) In certain people the level of aspiration may be permanently deadened or lowered. That is to say, the less prepotent goals may simply be lost, and may disappear forever, so that the person who has experienced life at a very low level, i.e., chronic unemployment, may continue to be satisfied for the rest of his life if only he can get enough food.

(4) The so-called "psychopathic personality" is another example of permanent loss of the love needs. These are people who, according to the best data available,[22] have been starved for love in the earliest months of their lives and have simply lost forever the desire and the ability to give and to receive affection (as animals lose sucking or pecking reflexes that are not exercised soon enough after birth).

(5) Another cause of reversal of the hierarchy is that when a need has been satisfied for a long time, this need may be underevaluated. People who have never experienced chronic hunger are apt to underestimate its effects and to look upon food as a rather unimportant thing. If they are dominated by a higher need, this higher need will seem to be the most important of all. It then becomes possible, and indeed does actually happen, that they may, for the sake of this higher need, put themselves into the position of being deprived in a more basic need. We may expect that after a long-time deprivation of the more basic need there will be a tendency to reevaluate both needs so that the more prepotent need will actually become consciously prepotent for the individual who may have given it up very lightly. Thus, a man who has given up his job rather than lose his self-respect, and who then starves for six months or so, may be willing to take his job back even at the price of losing his self-respect.

(6) Another partial explanation of *apparent* reversals is seen in the fact that we have been talking about the hierarchy of prepotency in terms of consciously felt wants or desires rather than of behavior. Looking at behavior itself may give us the wrong impression. What we have claimed is that the person will *want* the more basic of two needs when deprived in both. There is no necessary implication here that he will act upon his desires. Let us say again that there are many determinants of behavior other than the needs and desires.

(7) Perhaps more important than all these exceptions are the ones that involve ideals, high social standards, high values and the like. With such values people become martyrs; they will give up everything for the sake of a particular ideal, or value. These people may be understood, at least in part, by reference to one basic concept (or hypothesis) which may be called "increased frustration-tolerance through early gratification." People who have been satisfied in their basic needs throughout their lives, particularly in their earlier years, seem to develop exceptional power to withstand present or future thwarting of these needs simply because they have strong, healthy character structure as a result of basic satisfaction. They are the "strong" people who can easily weather disagreement or opposition, who can swim against the stream of public opinion and who can stand up for the truth at great personal cost. It is just the ones who have loved and been well loved, and who have had many deep friendships who can hold out

against hatred, rejection or persecution.

I say all this in spite of the fact that there is a certain amount of sheer habituation which is also involved in any full discussion of frustration tolerance. For instance, it is likely that those persons who have been accustomed to relative starvation for a long time, are partially enabled thereby to withstand food deprivation. What sort of balance must be made between these two tendencies, of habituation on the one hand, and of past satisfaction breeding present frustration tolerance on the other hand, remains to be worked out by further research. Meanwhile we may assume that they are both operative, side by side, since they do not contradict each other. In respect to this phenomenon of increased frustration tolerance, it seems probable that the most important gratifications come in the first two years of life. That is to say, people who have been made secure and strong in the earliest years, tend to remain secure and strong thereafter in the face of whatever threatens.

Degrees of relative satisfaction.—So far, our theoretical discussion may have given the impression that these five sets of needs are somehow in a step-wise, all-or-none relationship to each other. We have spoken in such terms as the following: "If one need is satisfied, then another emerges." This statement might give the false impression that a need must be satisfied 100 per cent before the next need emerges. In actual fact, most members of our society who are normal, are partially satisfied in all their basic needs and partially unsatisfied in all their basic needs at the same time. A more realistic description of the hierarchy would be in terms of decreasing percentages of satisfaction as we go up the hierarchy of prepotency. For instance, if I may assign arbitrary figures for the sake of illustration, it is as if the average citizen is satisfied perhaps 85 per cent in his physiological needs, 70 per cent in his safety needs, 50 per cent in his love needs, 40 per cent in his self-

esteem needs, and 10 per cent in his self-actualization needs.

As for the concept of emergence of a new need after satisfaction of the prepotent need, this emergence is not a sudden, saltatory phenomenon but rather a gradual emergence by slow degrees from nothingness. For instance, if prepotent need A is satisfied only 10 per cent then need B may not be visible at all. However, as this need A becomes satisfied 25 per cent, need B may emerge 5 per cent, as need A becomes satisfied 75 per cent need B may emerge 90 per cent, and so on.

Unconscious character of needs.— These needs are neither necessarily conscious nor unconscious. On the whole, however, in the average person, they are more often unconscious rather than conscious. It is not necessary at this point to overhaul the tremendous mass of evidence which indicates the crucial importance of unconscious motivation. It would by now be expected, on a priori grounds alone, that unconscious motivations would on the whole be rather more important than the conscious motivations. What we have called the basic needs are very often largely unconscious although they may, with suitable techniques, and with sophisticated people become conscious.

Cultural specificity and generality of needs.—This classification of basic needs makes some attempt to take account of the relative unity behind the superficial differences in specific desires from one culture to another. Certainly in any particular culture an individual's conscious motivational content will usually be extremely different from the conscious motivational content of an individual in another society. However, it is the common experience of anthropologists that people, even in different societies, are much more alike than we would think from our first contact with them, and that as we know them better we seem to find more and more of this commonness. We then recognize the most startling differences to be superficial rather than basic, e.g., differences in style of hairdress, clothes, tastes in food, etc. Our classification of basic needs is in part an attempt to account for this unity behind the apparent diversity from culture to culture. No claim is made that it is ultimate or universal for all cultures. The claim is made only that it is relatively *more* ultimate, more universal, more basic, than the superficial conscious desires from culture to culture, and makes a somewhat closer approach to common-human characteristics. Basic needs are *more* common-human than superficial desires or behaviors.

Multiple motivations of behavior.— These needs must be understood *not* to be *exclusive* or single determiners of certain kinds of behavior. An example may be found in any behavior that seems to be physiologically motivated, such as eating, or sexual play or the like. The clinical psychologists have long since found that any behavior may be a channel through which flow various determinants. Or to say it in another way, most behavior is multi-motivated. Within the sphere of motivational determinants any behavior tends to be determined by several or *all* of the basic needs simultaneously rather than by only one of them. The latter would be more an exception than the former. Eating may be partially for the sake of filling the stomach, and partially for the sake of comfort and amelioration of other needs. One may make love not only for pure sexual release, but also to convince one's self of one's masculinity, or to make a conquest, to feel powerful, or to win more basic affection. As an illustration, I may point out that it would be possible (theoretically if not practically) to analyze a single act of an individual and see in it the expression of his physiological needs, his safety needs, his love needs, his esteem needs and self-actualization. This contrasts sharply with the more naive brand of trait psychology in which one trait or one motive accounts for a certain kind of

act, *i.e.*, an aggressive act is traced solely to a trait of aggressiveness.

Multiple determinants of behavior.—Not all behavior is determined by the basic needs. We might even say that not all behavior is motivated. There are many determinants of behavior other than motives.[23] For instance, one other important class of determinants is the so-called "field" determinants. Theoretically, at least, behavior may be determined completely by the field, or even by specific isolated external stimuli, as in association of ideas, or certain conditioned reflexes. If in response to the stimulus word "table," I immediately perceive a memory image of a table, this response certainly has nothing to do with my basic needs.

Secondly, we may call attention again to the concept of "degree of closeness to the basic needs" or "degree of motivation." Some behavior is highly motivated, other behavior is only weakly motivated. Some is not motivated at all (but all behavior is determined).

Another important point[24] is that there is a basic difference between expressive behavior and coping behavior (functional striving, purposive goal seeking). An expressive behavior does not try to do anything; it is simply a reflection of the personality. A stupid man behaves stupidly, not because he wants to, or tries to, or is motivated to, but simply because he *is* what he is. The same is true when I speak in a bass voice rather than tenor or soprano. The random movements of a healthy child, the smile on the face of a happy man even when he is alone, the springiness of the healthy man's walk, and the erectness of his carriage are other examples of expressive, non-functional behavior. Also the *style* in which a man carries out almost all his behavior, motivated as well as unmotivated, is often expressive.

We may then ask, is *all* behavior expressive or reflective of the character structure? The answer is "No." Rote, habitual, automatized, or conventional behavior may or may not be expressive. The same is true for most "stimulus-bound" behaviors.

It is finally necessary to stress that expressiveness of behavior, and goal-directedness of behavior are not mutually exclusive categories. Average behavior is usually both.

Goals as centering principle in motivation theory.—It will be observed that the basic principle in our classification has been neither the instigation nor the motivated behavior but rather the functions, effects, purposes, or goals of the behavior. It has been proven sufficiently by various people that this is the most suitable point for centering in any motivation theory.[25]

Animal- and human-centering.—This theory starts with the human being rather than any lower and presumably "simpler" animal. Too many of the findings that have been made in animals have been proven to be true for animals but not for the human being. There is no reason whatsoever why we should start with animals in order to study human motivation. The logic or rather illogic behind this general fallacy of "pseudo-simplicity" has been exposed often enough by philosophers and logicians as well as by scientists in each of the various fields. It is no more necessary to study animals before one can study man than it is to study mathematics before one can study geology or psychology or biology.

We may also reject the old, naive, behaviorism which assumed that it was somehow necessary, or at least more "scientific" to judge human beings by animal standards. One consequence of this belief was that the whole notion of purpose and goal was excluded from motivational psychology simply because one could not ask a white rat about his purposes. Tolman[26] has long since proven in animal studies themselves that this exclusion was not necessary.

Motivation and the theory of psychopathogenesis.—The conscious motivational content of everyday life has, according to the foregoing, been conceived to be relatively important or unimportant accordingly as it is more or less closely related to the basic goals. A desire for an ice cream cone might actually be an indirect expression of a desire for love. If it is, then this desire for the ice cream cone becomes extremely important motivation. If however the ice cream is simply something to cool the mouth with, or a casual appetitive reaction, then the desire is relatively unimportant. Everyday conscious desires are to be regarded as symptoms, as *surface indicators of more basic needs*. If we were to take these superficial desires at their face value we would find ourselves in a state of complete confusion which could never be resolved, since we would be dealing seriously with symptoms rather than with what lay behind the symptoms.

Thwarting of unimportant desires produces no psychopathological results; thwarting of a basically important need does produce such results. Any theory of psychopathogenesis must then be based on a sound theory of motivation. A conflict or a frustration is not necessarily pathogenic. It becomes so only when it threatens or thwarts the basic needs, or partial needs that are closely related to the basic needs.[27]

The role of gratified needs.—It has been pointed out above several times that our needs usually emerge only when more prepotent needs have been gratified. Thus gratification has an important role in motivation theory. Apart from this, however, needs cease to play an active determining or organizing role as soon as they are gratified.

What this means is that, e.g., a basically satisfied person no longer has the needs for esteem, love, safety, etc. The only sense in which he might be said to have them is in the almost metaphysical sense that a sated man has hunger, or a filled bottle has emptiness. If we are interested in what *actually* motivates us, and not in what has, will, or might motivate us, then a satisfied need is not a motivator. It must be considered for all practical purposes simply not to exist, to have disappeared. This point should be emphasized because it has been either overlooked or contradicted in every theory of motivation I know.[28] The perfectly healthy, normal, fortunate man has no sex needs or hunger needs, or needs for safety, or for love, or for prestige, or self-esteem, except in stray moments of quickly passing threat. If we were to say otherwise, we should also have to aver that every man had all the pathological reflexes, e.g., Babinski, etc., because if his nervous system were damaged, these would appear.

It is such considerations as these that suggest the bold postulation that a man who is thwarted in any of his basic needs may fairly be envisaged simply as a sick man. This is a fair parallel to our designation as "sick" of the man who lacks vitamins or minerals. Who is to say that a lack of love is less important than a lack of vitamins? Since we know the pathogenic effects of love starvation, who is to say that we are invoking value-questions in an unscientific or illegitimate way, any more than the physician does who diagnoses and treats pellagra or scurvy? If I were permitted this usage, I should then say simply that a healthy man is primarily motivated by his needs to develop and actualize his fullest potentialities and capacities. If a man has any other basic needs in any active, chronic sense, then he is simply an unhealthy man. He is as surely sick as if he had suddenly developed a strong salt-hunger or calcium hunger.[29]

If this statement seems unusual or paradoxical the reader may be assured that this is only one among many such paradoxes that will appear as we revise our ways of looking at man's deeper motivations. When we ask what man wants of life, we deal with his very essence.

IV. SUMMARY

(1) *There are at least five sets of goals, which we may call basic needs.* These are briefly physiological, safety, love, esteem, and self-actualization. In addition, we are motivated by the desire to achieve or maintain the various conditions upon which these basic satisfactions rest and by certain more intellectual desires.

(2) *These basic goals are related to each other, being arranged in a hierarchy of prepotency.* This means that the most prepotent goal will monopolize consciousness and will tend of itself to organize the recruitment of the various capacities of the organism. The less prepotent needs are minimized, even forgotten or denied. But when a need is fairly well satisfied, the next prepotent ("higher") need emerges, in turn to dominate the conscious life and to serve as the center of organization of behavior, since gratified needs are not active motivators.

Thus man is a perpetually wanting animal. Ordinarily the satisfaction of these wants is not altogether mutually exclusive, but only tends to be. The average member of our society is most often partially satisfied and partially unsatisfied in all of his wants. The hierarchy principle is usually empirically observed in terms of increasing percentages of non-satisfaction as we go up the hierarchy. Reversals of the average order of the hierarchy are sometimes observed. Also it has been observed that an individual may permanently lose the higher wants in the hierarchy under special conditions. There are not only ordinarily multiple motivations for usual behavior, but in addition many determinants other than motives.

(3) *Any thwarting or possibility of thwarting of these basic human goals, or*

danger to the defenses which protect them, or to the conditions upon which they rest, is considered to be a psychological threat. With a few exceptions, all psychopathology may be partially traced to such threats. A basically thwarted man may actually be defined as a "sick" man, if we wish.

(4) It is such basic threats which bring about the general emergency reactions.

✱ (5) Certain other basic problems have not been dealt with because of limitations of space. Among these are (a) the problem of values in any definitive motivation theory, (b) the relation between appetites, desires, needs and what is "good" for the organism, (c) the etiology of the basic needs and their possible derivation in early childhood, (d) redefinition of motivational concepts, i.e., drive, desire, wish, need, goal, (e) implication of our theory for hedonistic theory, (f) the nature of the uncompleted act, or success and failure, and of aspiration-level, (g) the role of association, habit and conditioning, (h) relation to the theory of inter-personal relations, (i) implications for psychotherapy, (j) implication for theory of society, (k) the theory of selfishness, (l) the relation between needs and cultural patterns, (m) the relation between this theory and Allport's theory of functional autonomy. These as well as certain other less important questions must be considered as motivation theory attempts to become definitive.

NOTES

1. Maslow, A. H. A preface to motivation theory. Psychosomatic Med., 1943, 5, 85-92.
2. Wertheimer, M. Unpublished lectures at the New School for Social Research.
3. Goldstein, K. The organism. New York: American Book Co., 1939.
4. Freud, S. New introductory lectures on psychoanalysis. New York: Norton, 1933.
5. Adler, A. Social interest. London: Faber & Faber, 1938.
6. Cannon, W. B. Wisdom of the body. New York: Norton, 1932.
7. Young, P. T. The experimental analysis of appetite. Psychol. Bull., 1941, 38, 129-164.
8. Maslow, A preface to motivation theory, op cit.
9. As the child grows up, sheer knowledge and familiarity as well as better motor development make these "dangers" less and less dangerous and more and more manageable. Throughout life it may be said that one of the main cognative functions of education is this neutralizing of apparent dangers through knowledge, e.g., I am not afraid of thunder because I know something about it.
10. Shirley, M. Children's adjustments to a strange situation. J. Abnorm. (soc.) Psychol., 1942, 37, 201-217.
11. A "test battery" for safety might be confronting the child with a small exploding firecracker, or with a bewhiskered face, having the mother leave the room, putting him upon a high ladder, a hypodermic injection, having a mouse crawl up to him, etc. Of course I cannot seriously recommend the deliberate use of such "tests" for they might very well harm the child being tested. But these and similar situations come up by the score in the child's ordinary day-to-day living and may be observed. There is no reason why these stimuli should not be used with, for example, young chimpanzees.
12. Not all neurotic individuals feel unsafe. Neurosis may have at its core a thwarting of the affection and esteem needs in a person who is generally safe.
13. Maslow, A. H., & Mittelmann, B. Principles of abnormal psychology. New York: Harper & Bros., 1941.
14. Goldstein, op cit.
15. Maslow & Mittelmann, op cit.
16. For further details see Maslow, A. H. The dynamics of psychological security-insecurity. Character & Pers., 1942, 10, 331-344 and Plant, J. Personality and the cultural pattern. New York: Commonwealth Fund, 1937, Chapter 5.
17. Whether or not this particular desire is universal we do not know. The crucial question, especially important today, is "Will men who are enslaved and dominated, inevitably feel dissatisfied and rebellious?" We

may assume on the basis of commonly known clinical data that a man who has known true freedom (not paid for by giving up safety and security but rather built on the basis of adequate safety and security) will not willingly or easily allow his freedom to be taken away from him. But we do not know that this is true for the person born into slavery. The events of the next decade should give us our answer. See discussion of this problem in Fromm, E. *Escape from freedom*. New York: Farrar and Rinehart, 1941.

18. Perhaps the desire for prestige and respect from others is subsidiary to the desire for self-esteem or confidence in oneself. Observation of children seems to indicate that this is so, but clinical data give no clear support for such a conclusion.

19. Kardiner, A. *The traumatic neuroses of our time*. New York: Hoeber, 1941. For more extensive discussion of normal self-esteem, as well as for reports of various researchers, see Maslow, A. H., Dominance, personality and social behavior in women. *J. soc. Psychol.*, 1939, 10, 3-39.

20. Clearly creative behavior, like painting, is like any other behavior in having multiple determinants. It may be seen in "innately creative" people whether they are satisfied or not, happy or unhappy, hungry or sated. Also it is clear that creative activity may be compensatory, ameliorative or purely economic. It is my impression (as yet unconfirmed) that it is possible to distinguish the artistic and intellectual products of basically satisfied people from those of basically unsatisfied people by inspection alone. In any case, here too we must distinguish, in a dynamic fashion, the overt behavior itself from its various motivations or purposes.

21. Wertheimer, *op cit.*

22. Levy, D. M. Primary affect hunger. *Amer. J. Psychiat.*, 1937, 94, 643-652.

23. I am aware that many psychologists and psychoanalysts use the term "motivated" and "determined" synonymously, e.g., Freud. But I consider this an obfuscating usage. Sharp distinctions are necessary for clarity of thought, and precision in experimentation.

24. To be discussed fully in a subsequent publication.

25. The interested reader is referred to the very excellent discussion of this point in Murray, H. A., *et al. Explorations in personality*. New York: Oxford University Press, 1938.

26. Tolman, E. C. *Purposive behavior in animals and men*. New York: Century, 1932.

27. Maslow, A. H. Conflict, frustration, and the theory of threat. *J. abnorm. (soc.) Psychol.*, 1943, 38, 81-86.

28. Note that acceptance of this theory necessitates basic revision of the Freudian theory.

29. If we were to use the word "sick" in this way, we should then also have to face squarely the relations of man to his society. One clear implication of our definition would be that (1) since a man is to be called sick who is basically thwarted, and (2) since such basic thwarting is made possible ultimately only by forces outside the individual, then (3) sickness in the individual must come ultimately from a sickness in the society. The "good" or healthy society would then be defined as one that permitted man's highest purposes to emerge by satisfying all his prepotent basic needs.

7. Toward an Understanding of Inequity*

J. STACY ADAMS

Equity, or more precisely, inequity, is a pervasive concern of industry, labor, and government. Yet its psychological basis is probably not fully understood. Evidence suggests that equity is not merely a matter of getting "a fair day's pay for a fair day's work," nor is inequity simply a matter of being underpaid. The fairness of an exchange between employee and employer is not usually perceived by the former purely and simply as an economic matter. There is an element of relative justice involved that supervenes economics and underlies perceptions of equity or inequity.[1]

The purpose of this paper is to present a theory of inequity, leading toward an understanding of the phenomenon and, hopefully, resulting in its control.[2] Whether one wishes to promote social justice or merely to reduce economically disadvantageous industrial unrest, an understanding of inequity is important. In developing the theory of inequity, which is based upon Festinger's theory of cognitive dissonance[3] and is, therefore, a special case of it, we shall describe major variables involved in an employee-employer exchange, before we proceed to define inequity formally. Having defined it, we shall analyze its effects. Finally, such evidence as is available will be presented in support of the theory. Throughout we shall emphasize some of the simpler aspects of inequity and try to refrain from speculating about many of the engaging, often complex, relationships between in-equity and other phenomena, and about what might be termed "higher order" inequities. In the exposition that follows we shall also refer principally to wage inequities, in part because of their importance and in part because of the availability of methods to measure the marginal utility of wages.[4] It should be evident, however, that the theoretical notions advanced are relevant to any social situation in which an exchange takes place, whether the exchange be of the type taking place between man and wife, between football teammates, between teacher and student, or even, between Man and his God.

Whenever two individuals exchange anything, there is the possibility that one or both of them will feel that the exchange was inequitable. Such is frequently the case when a man exchanges his services for pay. On the man's side of the exchange are his education, intelligence, experience, training, skill, seniority, age, sex, ethnic background, social status, and, very importantly, the effort he expends on the job. Under special circumstances other attributes will be relevant: personal appearance or attractiveness, health, possession of an automobile, the characteristics of one's spouse, and so on. They are what he perceives are his contributions to the exchange, for which he expects a just return. Homans calls them "investments."[5] These variables are brought by him to the job. Henceforth they will be referred to as his *inputs*. These inputs, let us emphasize, are as *perceived by*

*Source: From Journal of Abnormal Psychology, Vol. 67, No. 5 (1963), pp. 422-436. Copyright © 1963 by the American Psychological Association. Reprinted by permission. References and footnotes combined.

their contributor and are not *necessarily* isomorphic with those of the other party to the exchange. This suggests two conceptually distinct characteristics of inputs, *recognition* and *relevance*.

The possessor of an attribute, or the other party to the exchange, or both, may recognize the existence of the attribute in the possessor. If either the possessor or both members of the exchange recognize its existence, the attribute has the potentiality of being an input. If only the nonpossessor recognizes its existence it cannot be considered psychologically an input so far as the possessor is concerned. Whether or not an attribute having the potential of being an input is an input, is contingent upon the possessor's perception of its relevance to the exchange. If he perceives it to be relevant, if he expects a just return for it, it is an input. Problems of inequity arise if only the possessor of the attribute considers it relevant in the exchange. Crozier relates an observation that is apropos.[6] Paris-born bank clerks worked side by side with other clerks who did identical work and earned identical wages, but were born in the Provinces. The Parisians were dissatisfied with their wages, for they considered that Parisian breeding was an input deserving monetary compensation. The bank management, while recognizing that place of birth distinguished the two groups, did not, of course, consider birthplace relevant in the exchange of services for pay.

The principal inputs listed earlier vary in type and in their degree of relationship to one another. Some variables, such as age, are clearly continuous; others, such as sex and ethnicity, are not. Some are intercorrelated, seniority and age, for example; sex, on the other hand, is largely independent of the other variables, with the possible exception of education and some kinds of effort. Although these intercorrelations, or the lack of them, exist in a state of nature, it is probable that the individual cognitively treats all input variables as independent. Thus, for example, if he were assessing the sum of his inputs, he might well "score" age and seniority separately.

On the other side of the exchange are the rewards received by an individual for his services. These *outcomes*, as they will be termed, include pay, rewards intrinsic to the job, seniority benefits, fringe benefits, job status and status symbols, and a variety of formally and informally sanctioned perquisites. An example of the latter is the right of higher status persons to park their cars in priviliged locations, or the right to have a walnut rather than a metal desk. Seniority, mentioned as an input variable, has associated with it a number of benefits such as job security, "bumping" privileges, greater fringe benefits, and so on. These benefits are outcomes and are distinguished from the temporal aspects of seniority (that is, longevity), which are properly inputs. As in the case of job inputs, job outcomes are often intercorrelated. For example, greater pay and higher job status are likely to go hand in hand.

In a manner analogous to inputs, outcomes are as *perceived*, and, again, we should characterize them in terms of recognition and relevance. If the recipient or both the recipient and giver of an outcome in an exchange recognize its existence, it has the potentiality of being an outcome psychologically. If the recipient considers it relevant to the exchange and it has some marginal utility for him, it *is* an outcome. Not infrequently the giver or "buyer," to use economic terms, may give or yield something which, perhaps at some cost to him, is either irrelevant or of no marginal utility to the recipient. An employer may give an employee a carpet for his office in lieu, say, of a salary increment and find that the employee is dissatisfied, perhaps because in the subculture of that office a rug has no meaning, no psychological utility. Conversely, a salary increment may be inadequate, if formalized status recognition was what was wanted and was what had greater utility.

In classifying some variables as inputs and others as outcomes, it is not implied that they are independent, except conceptually. Job inputs and outcomes are, in fact, intercorrelated, but imperfectly so. Indeed, it is because they are imperfectly correlated that we need at all be concerned with job inequity. There exist normative expectations of what constitute "fair" correlations between inputs and outcomes. The bases of the expectations are the correlations obtaining for a reference person or group—a co-worker or colleague, a relative or neighbor, a group of co-workers, a craft group, an industry-wide pattern. A bank clerk, for example, may determine whether her inputs and outcomes are fairly correlated—in balance, so to speak—by comparing them with the relationship between the inputs and outcomes of other female clerks in her section. The sole punch press operator in a manufacturing plant may base his judgement on what he believes are the inputs and outcomes of other operators in the community or region. For a particular physicist the relevant reference person may be an organic chemist of the same academic "vintage." While it is clearly important to be able to specify the appropriate reference person or group, it represents a distinct theoretical area in which work has begun[7] but which would take this paper too far afield. For the purposes of this paper, it will be assumed that the reference person or group will be one comparable to the comparer on one or more attributes, usually a co-worker.[8]

When the normative expectations of the person making social comparisons are violated—when he finds his inputs and outcomes are not in balance in relation to those of others—feelings of inequity result.

INEQUITY DEFINED

Although it has been suggested how inequity arises, a rigorous definition must be formulated. But we introduce first two references terms, Person and Other. Person is any individual for whom equity or inequity exists. Other is any individual or group used by Person as a referent when he makes social comparisons of his inputs and outcomes. Other is usually a different individual, but may be Person in another job, or even in another social role. Thus, for example, Other might be Person in the job he held six months earlier, in which case he might compare his present and past inputs and outcomes. Or, as Patchen has suggested, Other might be Person in a future job to which he aspires.[9] In such an instance he would make a comparison of his present inputs and outcomes to his estimates of those in the future. The terms Person and Other may also refer to groups rather than to individuals, as for example when a class of jobs (for example, toolmakers) is out of line with another class (for example, maintenance men). In such cases, it is convenient to deal with the class as a whole rather than with individual members of the class. This is essentially what is done when the relative ranking of jobs is evaluated in the process of devising an equitable wage or salary structure.

Using the theoretical model introduced by Festinger,[10] inequity is defined as follows: Inequity exists for Person whenever his perceived job inputs and/or outcomes stand psychologically in an obverse relation to what he perceives are the inputs and/or outcomes of Other. The first point to note about the definition is that it is the perception by Person of his and Other's inputs and outcomes that must be dealt with, not necessarily the actual inputs and outcomes. The point is important, for while perception and reality may be and often are in close accord, wage administrators are likely to assume an identity of the two. Second, if we let A designate Person's inputs and outcomes and let B designate Other's, by "obverse relation" we mean that not A follows from B. But we emphasize that the relation necessary for inequity to exist is psychological in character, not logical. Thus, there is no logical obversion in male Person's being subordinate to female Other, but, as Clark has observed, the inputs of Person and Other in such a situation may be dissonant, with the consequence that inequity is felt by Person.[11]

As was previously suggested, the dissonant relation of an individual's inputs and outcomes in comparison to another's is historically and culturally determined. This is why we insist that the incongruity is primarily psychological, even though it might, in addition, have a logical character. Each individual has a different history of learning, but to the extent that he learns from people sharing similar values, social norms, and language that is, the extent to which he shares the same culture, his psychological reactions will be similar to theirs. The larger the cultural group, the greater will be the number of individuals who perceive similarly and react similarly to a given set of relations between input and outcomes. In the United States there is a strong, but perhaps weakening, predilection for the belief that effort and reward must be positively correlated. Considering the population at large, this belief has the status of a cultural norm and partially explains rather uniform reactions toward certain kinds of inequity—toward "featherbedding," for example.

It is interesting to note that the American attitude toward work and reward is by no means universal. In highly industrialized Japan, for example, there is little relationship between the kind and amount of work an employee does and the monetary reward he receives. Pay is largely determined by age, education, length of service, and family size, and very little, if at all, by productivity. In his study of Japanese factories, Abegglen states:

It is not at all difficult to find situations where workers doing identical work at an identical pace receive markedly different salaries, or where a skilled workman is paid at a rate below that of a sweeper or doorman. The position occupied and the amount produced do not determine the reward provided.[12]

This, of course, is not to suggest that inequity is nonexistent for Japanese workers. They and their employers enter into an exchange just as Americans, but the terms of the exchange are quite different. Hence, the basis for inequity is different.

In order to predict when an individual will experience inequity under given conditions of inputs and outcomes, it is necessary to know something of the values and norms to which he subscribes—with what culture or subculture he is associated. Granted this knowledge, it is then possible to specify what constitutes an obverse relation of input and outcomes for Person. In a given society, even ours, there is usually enough invariance in fundamental beliefs and attitudes to make reasonably accurate, general predictions.

It is shown in Table 7-1 how inequity results whenever the inputs or outcomes, or both, of Person stand in an obverse relation to either the inputs or outcomes, or both, of Other. Though inputs and outcomes may in most cases be measured continuously (ethnicity and sex are obvious exceptions), we have dichotomized them into "high" and "low" for the purpose of simplicity. The entries in the table are relative rather than absolute quantities. Thus, 1 indicates more felt inequity than 0, and 2 indicates more felt inequity than 1. But before pursuing the implications of Table 7-1 and of the definition of inequity, let us agree to use amount of effort as an instance of inputs and pay as an instance of outcomes. Any other input and outcome would do as well; we wish merely to use constant instances for the illustrations that will follow.

The first important consequence to

Table 7-1

AMOUNT OF INEQUITY FOR PERSON AS A RESULT OF DIFFERENT INPUTS
AND OUTCOMES FOR PERSON AND OTHER

Person	Inputs-Outcomes			
	Other			
	Low-High	High-Low	Low-Low	High-High
Low-High	0	2	1	1
High-Low	2	0	1	1
Low-Low	1	1	0	0
High-High	1	1	0	0

Note. The first member of the pair indicates inputs and the second member, outcomes.

observe from the definition is that in-equity results for Person not only when he is relatively underpaid, but also when he is relatively overpaid. Person will, for example, feel inequity exists not only when his effort is high and his pay low, while Other's effort and pay are high, but also when his effort is low and his pay high, while Other's effort and pay are low.

Although there is not direct, reliable evidence on this point, it is probable that the thresholds for inequity are different (in absolute terms from a base of equity) in cases of under- and overcompensation. The threshold would be greater presumably in cases of over-compensation, for a certain amount of incongruity in these cases can be ac-ceptably rationalized as "good fortune." In his work on pay differentials Jaques notes that in instances of undercompen-sation British workers paid 10 percent less than the equitable level show:

an active sense of grievance, complaints or the desire to complain, and, if no redress is given, an active desire to change jobs, or to take action. . . .[13]

In cases of overcompensation, he ob-serves that at the 10–15 percent level above equity:

there is a strong sense of receiving prefer-ential treatment, which may harden into

bravado, with underlying feelings of un-ease. . . .[14]

He states further:

The results suggest that it is not necessarily the case that each one is simply out to get as much as he can for his work. There ap-pear to be equally strong desires that each one should earn the right amount—a fair and reasonable amount relative to others.[15]

While Jagues' conceptualization of inequity is quite different from that ad-vanced in this paper, his observations lend credence to the hypothesis that overcompensation results in feelings of inequity and that the threshold for these feelings is higher than in the case of un-dercompensation.

From the definition and Table 7-1, we may observe as a second consequence that when Person's and Other's inputs and outcomes are analogous, equity is assumed to exist, and that when their inputs and outcomes are discrepant in any way inequity will exist. We assume that it is not the absolute magnitude of perceived inputs and outcomes that results in ineq-uity, but rather the relative magnitudes pertaining to Person and Other. For exam-ple, there will be no inequity if both Per-son and Other expend much effort in their jobs and both obtain low pay. The 0 entries in the main diagonal of Table 7-1 reflect the fact that when the inputs and outcomes of Person and Other are matched, no inequity exists. It is further assumed, and shown in Table 7-1, that no inequity will result if both the inputs and outcomes of Person are matched and those of Other are matched, but are different for Person and for Other. To illustrate: if Person expends low effort and receives low pay, while Other expends high effort and receives high pay, equity rather than inequity will result. The converse also holds true.

With regard to the amount of inequity that exists, we have assumed that greater inequity results when both inputs and outcomes are discrepant than when only inputs or outcomes are discrepant. This signifies, for example, that Person will experience more inequity when his effort is high and pay low, while Other's effort is low and pay high, than when Person's effort is high and pay low, while Other's effort and pay are both high. In Table 7-1 only three relative magnitudes of inequity, ranging from 0 to 2, are shown. In reality, of course, many more degrees could be distinguished, especially with variables such as effort and pay which are theoretically continuous. The point to be emphasized is that equity-inequity is not an all-or-none phenomenon.

It will be noted that in the definition of inequity and Table 7-1, inputs have not been differentiated nor have outcomes. There are two reasons for this. First, the processes that govern inequity are applicable irrespective of the specific inputs and outcomes obtaining in a particular situation. For example, inequity may result whether low inputs are in the form of low effort or of poor education, or whether high outcomes stem from high pay or from great rewards intrinsic to the job. Second, there is a degree of interchangeability between different inputs and between different outcomes; furthermore inputs are additive, as are outcomes. It is implied, therefore, that a given total of Person's inputs may be achieved by increasing or decreasing any one or more separate inputs; similarly, a given total of Person's outcomes may result from increasing or decreasing one or more separate outcomes. For example, if Person found it necessary to increase his inputs in order to reduce inequity, he could do so not only by increasing his effort, but also by acquiring additional training or education. If, on the other hand, greater outcomes were required to achieve equity, obtaining new status symbols might be equivalent to an increase in compensation, or a combination of improved job environment and increased discretionary content of the job might be.

The question of the interchangeability and additivity of different inputs on the one hand, and of different outcomes on the other is an important one. Does a man evaluating his job inputs give the same weight to formal education as he does to on-the-job experience? If he has completed high school and has held his job two years, and a co-worker, whom he uses as a comparison person, completed the ninth grade only and has been on the job four years, will he judge their inputs as equivalent or not? Is the frequently used practice of giving a man a prestigeful title an effective substitute for greater monetary outcomes? Definitive answers to such questions await research. However, this much may be hypothesized: Within certain limits of inequity there will be a tendency on the part of Person to manipulate and weigh cognitively his own inputs and outcomes and those of Other in such a manner as to minimize the degree of felt inequity. Beyond these limits of inequity the tendency will be to manipulate and weigh inputs and outcomes so as to maximize the inequity, because as will be discussed later, this will increase the motivation to adopt behavior that will eliminate the inequity entirely.[16] In both processes it is assumed that normal men are limited by reality in the amount of cognitive manipulation and weighing of inputs and outcomes they can perform. Except, perhaps, in the case of very small degrees of inequity such manipulation and weighing could not serve by themselves to achieve equity.

In discussing inequity, the focus has been exclusively on Person. In so doing, however, we have failed to consider that whenever inequity exists for Person, it will also exist for Other, provided their perceptions of inputs and outcomes are isomorphic or nearly so. A glance at Table 7-1 will make this apparent, and we may predict from the table the inequity for Other as well as for Person. Only when the perceptions of Person and Other do not agree, would the inequity be different for each. In such a case, one would enter Table 7-1 twice, once for Person and once for Other. It is sufficient at this point merely to note that inequity is bilateral or multilateral, and symmetric under some conditions. Later we shall consider the implications of this in greater detail.

EFFECTS OF INEQUITY

Having defined inequity and specified its antecedents, we may next attend to its effects. First, two general postulates, closely following dissonance theory:[17] (a) The presence of inequity in Person creates tension in him. The tension is proportional to the magnitude of inequity present. (b) The tension created in Person will drive him to reduce it. The strength of the drive is proportional to the tension created; *ergo*, it is proportional to the magnitude of inequity present. In short, the presence of inequity will motivate Person to achieve equity or reduce inequity, and the strength of motivation to do so will vary directly with the amount of inequity. The question, then, is *how* may Person reduce inequity? The following actions enumerate and illustrate the means available to Person when reducing inequity. [*Italics in following list not in original.*]

1. *Person may increase his inputs if they are low relative to Other's inputs and to his own outcomes.* If, for example, Person's effort were low compared to Other's and to his own pay, he could reduce inequity by increasing his effort

on the job. This might take the form of Person's increasing his productivity, as will be shown in experiments described later, or enhancing the quality of his work. If inputs other than effort were involved, he could increase his training or education. Some inputs cannot, of course, be altered easily—sex and ethnicity, for instance. When such inputs are involved, other means of reducing inequity must be adopted.

2. *Person may decrease his inputs if they are high relative to Other's inputs and to his own outcomes.* If Person's effort were high compared to Other's and to his own pay, he might reduce his effort and productivity, as is illustrated later in a study of grocery clerks. It is interesting to note that effort is the principal input susceptible to reduction; education, training, experience, intelligence, skill, seniority, age, sex, ethnicity, and so on are not readily decreased or devalued realistically, though they may be distorted psychologically within limits. They are givens; their acquisition is not reversible. The implication is that when inequity results from inputs being too high, decreases in productivity are especially likely to be observed. One may speculate that restrictive production practices often observed are in fact attempts at reducing inequity.

There exists in industry a tendency to select and hire personnel with education, intellect, and training which are often greater than that required by the job in which they are placed. Since it is likely that in many instances the comparison persons for these individuals will have lesser inputs and, perhaps, greater outcomes, it is evident that some of the newly hired will experience feelings of inequity. In consequence, education, intellect, and training not being readily modified, lowered productivity may be predicted.

3. *Person may increase his outcomes if they are low relative to Other's outcomes and to his own inputs.* When Person's pay is low compared to Other's

and to his expended effort, he may reduce inequity by obtaining a wage increase. Evidence of this is given later in a study of clerical workers. He could also, if appropriate, acquire additional benefits, perquisites, or status. An increase in status, however, might create new problems, for the acquisition of higher status without higher pay would of itself create dissonance, particularly if the new status of Person placed him in a superordinate position vis-à-vis Other.

4. *Person may decrease his outcomes if they are high relative to Other's outcomes and to his own inputs.* This might take the form of Person's lowering his pay. Though an improbable mode of reducing inequity, it is nevertheless theoretically possible. Although it is usually assumed that persons with very high personal incomes are motivated by tax laws to donate much to charitable and educational institutions, it is not improbable that this behavior on the part of some is motivated as well by feelings of inequity.

5. *Person may "leave the field" when he experiences inequity of any type.* This may take the form of quitting his job or obtaining a transfer or reassignment, or of absenteeism. In a study by Patchen it was observed that men who said their pay should be higher had more absences than men who said the pay for their jobs was fair.[18] Although the author did not conceptualize "fair pay" as in the present paper, it is clear at least that "fair" was defined by respondents in relational terms, for he states:

> The data show also that the actual amount of a man's pay has, in itself, little effect on how often he is absent. The important question regardless of how much he is getting, is whether he thinks the rate is fair.[19]

Leaving the field is perhaps a more radical means of coping with inequity and its adoption will vary not only with the magnitude of inequity present, but also with Person's tolerance of inequity and his ability to cope with it flexibly.

Though it has not been demonstrated, there are probably individual differences in tolerance and flexibility.

6. *Person may psychologically distort his inputs and outcomes, increasing or decreasing them as required.* Since most individuals are heavily influenced by reality, distortion is generally difficult. It is pretty difficult to distort to oneself that one has a BA degree, that one has been an accountant for seven years, and that one's salary is $500 per month, for example. However, it is possible to alter the utility of these. For example, State College is a small backwoods school with no reputation, or, conversely, State College has one of the best Business Schools in the state and the Dean is an adviser to the Bureau of the Budget. Or, one can consider the fact that $500 per month will buy all of the essential things of life and quite a few luxuries, or, conversely, that it will never permit one to purchase period furniture or a power cruiser.

7. *Person may increase, decrease, or distort the inputs and outcomes of Others, or force Other to leave the field.* Basically, these means are the same as discussed above, but applied to Other. The direction of change in inputs and outcomes would, however, be precisely opposite to changes effected in Person. Thus, for example, if Person's effort were too low compared to Other's and to his own pay, he might induce Other to decrease his effort instead of increasing his own effort. Or, if he were comparatively poorly qualified for his job, he might try to have his better qualified colleague fired or transferred.

8. *Person may change his referent Other when inequity exists.* If Person were a draftsman working harder, doing better quality work, and being paid less than Other at the next board, he might eschew further comparisons with Other and pick someone with more nearly the same capability and pay. The ease of doing this would vary considerably with the ubiquity of Other and with the

availability of a substitute having some attributes in common with Person.

Not all the means of reducing inequity that have been listed will be equally satisfactory, and the adoption of some may result in very unsteady states. The nature of the input and outcome discrepencies and environmental circumstances may render some means more available than others as may personality characteristics of Person and Other. To illustrate this we may consider a Person whose effort is high and whose pay is low, and an Other whose effort and pay are low. If Person acts to increase his pay and is successful, he will effectively reduce the inequity; but if he is unsuccessful, as well he might be, given rigid job and wage structures, inequity will continue. Person might, on the other hand, try to reduce his productivity. This, however, might be quite risky if minimal production standards were maintained and unsatisfactory productivity were penalized. There is the further consideration that if Person and Other are both on the same production line, a decrease in effort by Person might affect Other's production and pay, with the result that Other would object to Person's behavior. Another means for Person to reduce his inequity is to try to have Other increase his effort. If Other perceives his and Person's inputs and outcomes in the same way as Person, he might, indeed, accede to this influence and raise his effort. If, to the contrary, he perceives no discrepancy between his and Person's inputs, he may be expected to resist Person strongly. Alternatively, Person could resort to leaving the field, or to distortion, as discussed earlier. If distortion is unilateral on Person's part, it may resolve his inequity, though not Other's. This leads into another interesting aspect of inequity.

Person and Other may or may not constitute a social system, that is, Person may be to Other what Other is to Person, so that they are referents for one another. Or, Other's referent may be someone other than Person, say, an individual X, who is quite irrelevant to Person's social comparisons. When Person and Other do not form a social system, the way in which Person reduces his inequity will have no effect on Other and there will, therefore, be no feedback effects upon Person. When the two do constitute a social system, the interaction that may take place is of considerable interest. Considering only those instances when Person and Other have identical perceptions of their inputs and outcomes it is a truism that when inequity exists for Person it also exists for Other (though probably not in the same amount since one will be overpaid and the other underpaid). Hence, both will be motivated to reduce the inequity; but it does not follow that they will adopt compatible means. If compatible means are adopted, both will achieve equity. For example, if Person expended little effort and received high pay, while Other's effort and pay were both high, a state of equity could be achieved by Person's increasing his effort somewhat and by Other's reducing his a bit. Or, the two could agree that the easiest solution was for Other to reduce his effort to Person's level. However, this solution might prove inadequate, for other reasons; for example, this might endanger their jobs by reducing production to an economically unprofitable level.

Many possibilities of incompatible solutions exist for Person and Other. Continuing with the preceding example, Person could increase his effort and Other could decrease his. From the point of view of each considered alone, these actions should reduce inequity. When considered simultaneously, however, it is apparent that now Person's effort and pay will be high, whereas Other will expend low effort and receive high pay. A new state of inequity has been created! As a further example, if Person's effort were high and his pay low, while Other's effort were low and his pay high, Person might reduce his own effort while Other was trying to induce the supervisor to increase Person's salary. If Other were unsuccessful in his attempt, a new, but reduced, state of inequity would result. If, on the other hand Other were successful in obtaining a raise for Person, equity might be established, but a new situation, hardly more comfortable than inequity, would result: Person would have received a pay increment for a decrement in effort.

Private, psychological distortion of one's inputs and outcomes is especially likely to result in unsuccessful reduction of inequity, if done by only one party. For instance, if Person is overcompensated and manages to convince himself that he is not, it will be extremely difficult for Other to convince him, say, that he should work harder. Or, if Other were to convince himself that he was working just as hard as Person, Person could not effectively convince Other to increase his productivity or to take a cut in pay. The very fact that one of the parties is operating at a private, covert level makes it nearly impossible to communicate. The perceptions of the two parties being now different, the fundamental premises that must underlie joint action cannot be agreed upon. Distortion by one party in effect breaks the social system that had previously existed.

SUPPORTING EVIDENCE

The evidence in direct support of the theory of inequity will now be considered. The data that are available may be divided grossly into two types, observational and experimental. Directly supporting evidence is, on the whole, somewhat meager for the reason that little research has been focused on the specific question of job inequity. The work of Zaleznik et al.,[20] Homans,[21] and Patchen,[22] has dealt with significant aspects of the problem, but, with the exception of Homans' study of clerical

employees,[23] the data collected by these researchers are difficult to relate to the present theory.

A CASE OF PAY INEQUITY AMONG CLERICAL WORKERS[24]

Rather than dealing with two individuals, we are here concerned with two groups of female clerical workers, cash posters and ledger clerks, in one division of a utilities company. Both groups worked in the same large room. Cash posting consisted of recording daily the amounts customers paid on their bills, and management insisted that posting be precisely up to date. It required that cash posters pull customer cards from the many files and make appropriate entries on them. The job, therefore, was highly repetitive and comparatively monotonous, and required little thought but a good deal of physical mobility. Ledger clerks, in contrast, performed a variety of tasks on customer accounts, such as recording address changes, making breakdowns of over- and underpayments, and supplying information on accounts to customers or company people on the telephone. In addition, toward the end of the day, they were required by their supervisor to assist with "cleaning up" cash posting in order that it be current. Compared to the cash posters, "ledger clerks had to do a number of nonrepetitive clerical jobs . . . requiring some thought but little physical mobility." They had a more responsible job.

Ledger clerks were considered to be of higher status than cash posters, since promotion took place from cash poster to ledger clerk. Their weekly pay, however, was identical. In comparison to cash posters, ledger clerks were older and had more seniority and experience.

These are the facts of the situation. In terms of the theory, the following may be stated:

1. The cash posters had lower inputs than the ledger clerks: They were younger, had less seniority and experience, and had

less responsible jobs. Their outcomes were in some respect lower than the ledger clerks': Their job had less variety, was more monotonous, required greater physical effort, and had less intrinsic interest. Very importantly, however, their pay was equal to the ledger clerks'.

2. The ledger clerks had higher inputs than the cash posters: They were older, had more seniority and experience, and had more responsible positions. Their outcomes were higher on several counts: Their status was higher, their job had greater variety and interest, and physical effort required was low. Their pay, nonetheless, was the same as the cash posters'. The requirement that they help "clean up" (note the connotation) posting each day introduced ambiguity in their inputs and outcomes. On the one hand, this required greater inputs—that is, having to know two jobs—and, on the other hand, lowered their outcomes by having to do "dirty work" and deflating their self-esteem.

It is clear from the discrepancies between inputs and outcomes that inequities existed. In capsule form, the outcomes of ledger clerks were too low compared to their own inputs and to the inputs and outcomes of cash posters. The evidence is strong that the ledger clerks at least, felt the inequity. They felt that they ought to get a few dollars more per week to show that their job was more important—in our terms, their greater inputs ought to be paralleled by greater outcomes. On the whole, these clerks did not do much to reduce inequity, though a few complained to their union representative, with, apparently, little effect. However, the workers in this division voted to abandon their independent union for the CIO, and Homans intimates that the reason may have been the independent union's inability to force a resolution of the inequity.[25] He further implies that had management perceived and resolved the inequity, the representative function of a union would have been quite superfluous.

A CASE OF STATUS INEQUITY IN SUPERMARKETS[26]

We shall be concerned here with the checkout counters in a chain of supermarkets, which are manned by a "ringer" and a "bundler." Ringers are the cashiers who add on the register the sum due from the customer, take his payment, and make change. Bundlers take goods out of the cart and put them in bags to be taken out. Under normal conditions, ringing was a higher status, better paid job, handled by a permanent, full-time employee. Bundling was of lower status and lower pay, and was usually done by part-time employees, frequently youngsters. Furthermore, psychologically, bundlers were perceived as working for ringers.

Because customer flow in supermarkets varies markedly from day to day, a preponderance of employees were part-timers. This same fact required that many employees be assigned to checkout counters during rush hours. When this occurred, many ringer-bundler teams were formed and it is this that resulted in the creation of status inequity for employees differed considerably in a number of input variables, notably sex, age, and education. Not infrequently, then, a bundler would be directed to work for a ringer whose status (determined by sex, age, education, etc.) was lower. For example, a college male 21 years of age would be ordered to work for a high school girl ringer of 17. Or a college girl would be assigned as a bundler for an older woman with only a grade school education. The resulting status inequities may be described as follows in our theoretical terms: A bundler with higher inputs than a ringer had lower outcomes.

When interviewed by the investigator, the store employees were quite explicit about the inequities that existed. Furthermore, this was true of ringers, as well as bundlers, showing that inequities were felt bilaterally in these cooperative jobs. To restore equity it would have been necessary to form teams such that inputs and outcomes were matched. Clark had stated the principle in the following manner:

> A person's job status (which is determined by the amount of pay, responsibility, variety and absence from interference his job has) should be in line with his social status (which is determined by his sex, age, education, and seniority.)[27]

That store employees attempted to reduce existing inequities is evident from the data. The principal means of doing so appeared to be by the bundlers reducing their work speed—that is, by reducing their inputs, which would have effectively decreased inequity since some of their other inputs were too high relative to their own outcomes and to the inputs of the ringers. One girl explicitly stated to the investigator that when she was ordered to bundle for a ringer of lower social status than hers, she deliberately slowed up bundling.

Interestingly, this behavior is nicely reflected in the financial operation of the stores. A substantial part of the total labor cost of operating a supermarket is the cost of manning checkout counters. It follows, therefore, that one should be able to observe a correlation between the incidence of inequities among ringer-bundler teams and the cost of store operations, since the inequity reduction took the form of lowered productivity. This is indeed what was found. When the eight supermarkets were ranked on labor efficiency[28] and "social ease,"[29] the two measures correlated almost perfectly—that is, the greater the inequity, the greater the cost of operating the stores. To give an example, one of the two stores studied most intensively ranked high in inequity and had a cost of 3.85 man-hours per $100 of sales, whereas the other which ranked low in inequity, had cost of only 3.04 per $100 of sales. Thus, it cost approximately 27 percent more to operate the store in which inequities were higher.

A further finding of Clark's is worth reporting, for it gives one confidence that the relative inefficiency of the one store was indeed due to the presence of relatively more inequity. This store went through a period of considerable labor turnover (perhaps as a result of employees leaving the field to reduce inequity), and associated with this was an increase in labor efficiency and an increase in the social ease index. There is, therefore, quasi-experimental evidence that when inequities are reduced, individual productivity increases, with the result that operating costs decrease.

EXPERIMENT I[30]

One of the more interesting hypotheses derivable from the theory of inequity is that when Person is overpaid in relation to Other, he may reduce the inequity by increasing his inputs. Therefore, an experiment was designed in which one group of subjects was overcompensated and one was equitably compensated—that is, one group in which outcomes were too great and one in which outcomes were equitable, given certain inputs, relative to some generalized Other.

The task chosen was a one page controlled association public opinion interview (for example, "Which of these five automobiles do you associate with a rising young junior executive?"), which subjects were to administer in equal numbers to male and female members of the general public. The subjects were under the impression that they were being hired for a real task and that their employment would continue for several months. In actuality, however, they conducted interviews for 2.5 hours only, after which time they were told about the experiment and were paid for their participation.

Two groups of 11 male university students, hired through the college employment office, were used as subjects. Each was paid $3.50 per hour—an amount large enough so that a feeling of overcompensation could be induced, but not so large that it could not also be made to appear equitable. In one group (E), subjects were made to feel quite unqualified to earn $3.50 per hour, because of lack of interviewer training and experience. The other group of subjects (C) were made to feel fully qualified to earn $3.50 per hour, by being informed that they were far better educated than census takers and that education and intelligence were the prime requisites of interviewing. It may be noted that the referent Others for all subjects were trained interviewers at large, not a specific, known person. The complete instructions to the groups were, of course, much more elaborate, but details need not be given here. The critical point is that the E group felt overcompensated, whereas the C group felt fairly paid.

From the theory, it was predicted that the E group would attempt to increase their inputs so as to bring them in line with their outcomes and with the alleged inputs of trained interviewers. Since there was little they could do to increase their training and experience, this left productivity as the principal means of altering inputs. Theoretically, E group subjects could also have tried to reduce their outcomes; this, however, was impossible since the pay was fixed. In sum, then, it was predicted that the E group would obtain more interviews per unit time than the C group. This is what the results demonstrated. Whereas the C group obtained an average of only .1899 interviews per minute, the E group obtained a significantly greater average of .2694, or an average of 42 percent more ($x^2 = 4.55$, $df = 1$, $p <$ .05).

Results comparable to these have been obtained by Day in a laboratory experiment with children who were given training trials in which they pushed a plunger mechanism to obtain M&M candies.[31] The number of candies received varied between 1 and 6 and was directly depend-

ent upon the magnitude of pressure exerted on the plunger. After responses had been stabilized, 25 M&Ms were received by each subject on each of five trials regardless of the pressure exerted. Day's data show that a significant number of subjects respond to the increased reward by increased pressure on the over-rewarded trials. In terms of our theoretical model, the children in Day's study are comparing their input (pressure) and outcomes (M&Ms) during the over-rewarded trials with those during the training trials. The latter trials establish a base upon which to determine what constitutes "equity." The "overpayment" of 25 M&M candies results in inequity, which may be reduced by increasing pressure inputs.

EXPERIMENT II[32]

If it is reasonable to suppose that the results of the previously described experiment by Adams and Rosenbaum[33] were a result of the E subjects' working harder to protect their jobs because they were insecure in the face of their "employer's" low regard for their qualifications, it is reasonable to suppose that the same results would not obtain if subjects were convinced that their "employer" would have no knowledge of their productivity. Conversely, if the theory we have offered is valid, overpaid subjects should produce more than controls, whether they thought the "employer" knew the results of their work or whether they thought he did not.

Following this reasoning, Arrowood designed a factorial experiment in which subjects from Minneapolis were either overpaid or equitably paid and performed their work under either public or private conditions.[34] The first two conditions were similar to those in Experiment I: Subjects were hired at $3.50 per hour to conduct interviews and were made to feel unqualified or qualified for the job. The public-private distinction was achieved by having subjects either submit their work to the "employer" (the experimenter) or mail it in pre-addressed envelopes to New York. In the latter case, subjects were under the impression that the experimenter would never see their work.

The results, shown in Table 7-2, validate the hypothesis tested in Experiment I and permit one to reject the alternative hypothesis. In both the Public and Private conditions, overpaid subjects produced significantly more than equitably paid subjects. The fact that mean production in the Public conditions was significantly greater than in the Private conditions is irrelevant to the hypothesis since there was no significant interaction between the inequity-equity and public-private dimensions.

EXPERIMENT III[35]

Since the results of the two previous experiments strongly corroborated a derivation from the theory, it was decided to test a further, but related, derivation. The hypothesis was that whereas subjects overpaid *by the hour* would produce more than equitably paid controls, subjects overpaid *on a piecework basis* would produce less than equitably paid controls. The rationale for the latter half of the hypothesis was that because inequity was associated with each *unit* produced, inequity would increase as work proceeded; hence, subjects would strive not so much to *reduce* inequity as to avoid increasing it. In other words, because inequity would mount as more units were produced, overpaid piecework subjects would tend to restrict production.

Nine subjects were assigned to each of the following groups: Overpaid $3.50 per hour ($H_e$) equitably paid $3.50 per

hour (H_c), overpaid $.30 per unit ($P_e$), equitably paid $.30 per unit ($P_c$). In all major respects, the task and instructions were identical to those in Experiment I.

As may be seen in Table 7-3, the hypothesis received unequivocal support. Overpaid hourly subjects produced more than their controls and overpaid piecework subjects produced less than their controls. The interaction between the inequity-equity and hourly-piecework dimensions is highly significant ($x^2 = 7.11$, $df = 1$, $p < .01$).

EXPERIMENT IV[36]

The prediction that piecework subjects experiencing wage inequity would have a lower productivity than subjects perceiving their wages as fair was supported by the previous experiment. The rationale for the prediction was that because dissonance is linked with units of production, dissonance would increase as more units were produced, and, consequently, subjects would attempt to avoid increasing dissonance by restricting production. There is, however, an alternative explanation that would account for the same manifest behavior. It is entirely possible for subjects to *reduce* dissonance by increasing their effort on the production of each unit, for example, by increasing the quality of their work, which would have the effect of increasing the production time per unit and, therefore, have the consequence of reducing productivity. In terms of the theoretical framework presented earlier, this explanation assumes that pieceworkers would reduce their dissonance by increasing their inputs,

Table 7-2

PRODUCTION SCORES OF SUBJECTS IN EXPERIMENT II

	Public	Private
Overpaid	67.20	52.43
Equitably paid	59.33	41.50

Table 7-3

MEAN PRODUCTIVITY AND MEDIAN DISTRIBUTION OF HOURLY AND
PIECEWORK EXPERIMENTAL AND CONTROL SUBJECTS IN EXPERIMENT III

	Condition			
	H_e	H_c	P_e	P_c
Mean productivity	.2723	.2275	.1493	.1961
Cases above median	8	4	1	5
Cases below median	1	5	8	4

very much as the hourly workers. Only the mode of increasing inputs varies: Whereas hourly workers increase inputs on a *quantitative* dimension, pieceworkers increase them on a *qualitative* dimension.

Unfortunately, the task used in Experiment III did not lend itself to measuring quality of work. In the present experiment the work performed by subjects was so designed as to permit measurement of both amount of work and quality of work. The specific hypothesis tested is: Pieceworkers who perceive that they are inequitably overpaid will perform better quality work and have lower productivity than pieceworkers who are paid the same rate and perceive they are equitably paid.

The interviewing task used in the previous experiments was modified so as to permit the measurement of quality. The modification consisted of making the three principal questions open-end questions. As an example, one question was "Does a man who owns a shelter have the moral right to exclude others from it, if they have no shelter?" (Yes or No), which was followed by, "What are your reasons for feeling that way?" The subjects task was to obtain as much information as possible from a respondent on the latter part of the question. The measure of work quality thus was the amount of recorded information elicited from respondents. More specifically, the dependent measure of quality was the number of words per interview recorded

in the blank spaces following the three open-end questions. As before, the measure of productivity was the number of interviews obtained per minute during a total period of approximately two hours.

Twenty-eight subjects were used, half randomly assigned to a condition in which they were made to feel overpaid, half to a condition in which the identical piecework rate was made to appear equitable. The results supported the hypothesis. First, as in the previous experiment, the productivity of subjects in whom feelings of inequitable overpayment were induced was significantly lower than that of control subjects. Productivity rates for these groups were .0976 and .1506, respectively ($t = 1.82$, $p < .05$, one-tailed test). Second, work quality was significantly higher among overpaid subjects than among controls (69.7 versus 45.3, $t = 2.48$, $p < .02$, two-tailed test).

These quality and productivity data support the hypothesis that under piecework conditions subjects who perceive that they are overpaid will tend to reduce dissonance by increasing their inputs on each unit so as to improve its quality and, as a result, will decrease their productivity. Thus, the alternative explanation for the results obtained with pieceworkers in Experiment III has some validity. This is not to say that the dissonance avoiding hypothesis originally offered is invalid, for if a job does not permit an increase of work input *per unit produced*, dissonance avoidance may well occur. This, however, remains to be demonstrated; the fact that we were unable to measure quality of work in Experiment III does not mean that subjects did not reduce dissonance by some means, including the improvement of quality on each unit produced.

CONCLUSIONS

We have offered a general theory of inequity, reviewed its implications, and presented evidence in support of it. Although the support given the theory is gratifying, additional data are required to test particular aspects of it. In addition, research is needed to determine what variables guide the choice of comparison persons. While this is a theoretical and research endeavor in its own right, it would contribute much to the understanding of inequity.

The analysis of inequity in terms of discrepancies between a man's job inputs and job outcomes, and the behavior that may result from these discrepancies, should result in a better understanding of one aspect of social conflict and should increase the degree of control that may be exercised over it. In moving toward an understanding of inequity, we increase our knowledge of our most basic productive resource, the human organism.

NOTES

1. G. C. Homans, *Social Behavior: Its Elementary Forms* (New York: Harcourt, Brace, & World, 1961). E. Jacques, *Measurement of Responsibility* (London: Tavistock, 1956). E. Jaques, *Equitable Payment* (New York: Wiley, 1961). E. Jaques, "An Objective Approach to Pay Differentials," *Time Motion Stud.* 10 (1961): 25-28. M. Patchen, *The Choice of Wage Comparisons* (Englewood Cliffs, N.J.: Prentice-Hall, 1961). S. A. Stouffer, et al., *The American Soldier: Adjustment during Army Life* (Princeton:

Princeton Univer. Press, 1949). A. Zaleznik, C. R. Christensen, and F. J. Roethlisberger, *The Motivation, Productivity and Satisfaction of Workers* (Boston: Harvard University, Graduate School of Business Administration, 1958).

2. This paper and some of the experimental work reported in it are part of a program of theory development and research on wages and productivity undertaken by the author at the Behavioral Research Service, General Electric Company. The author wished to acknowledge his indebtedness to Leon Festinger for his work on cognitive dissonance and to George C. Homans for his ideas on distributive justice, which stimulated much of the present essay. He is also grateful to A. J. Arrowood, W. B. Rosenbaum, F. Tweed, and Patricia Jacobsen for assistance in conducting experiments.

3. L. A. Festinger, "A Theory of Social Comparison Processes," *Hum. Relat.* 7 (1954): 117-40.

4. J. S. Adams, "The Measurement of Perceived Equity in Pay Differentials" (Unpublished manuscript, General Electric Company, Behavioral Research Service, 1961). T. E. Jeffery and L. V. Jones, *Compensation-Plan Preferences: An Application of Psychometric Scaling* (Chapel Hill, N.C.: University of North Carolina, Psychometric Laboratory, 1961).

5. Homans, *Social Behavior. . . , op. cit.*

6. M. Crozier, personal communication, 1960.

7. R. K. Merton and Alice S. Kitt, "Contributions to the Theory of Reference Group Behavior," in *Studies in the Scope and Method of "The American Soldier,"* eds. R. K. Merton and P. F. Lazarsfeld (Glencoe, Ill.: Free Press, 1950), pp. 40-105. Patchen, *The Choice, op. cit.* Stouffer, et al., *American Soldier . . . , op. cit.*

8. This assumption follows Festinger, *'A Theory of Social. . . ,"* *op.cit.* who states: "Given a range of possible persons for comparison, someone close to one's own ability or opinion will be chosen for comparison (p. 121)." Generally, co-workers will more nearly fit this criterion than will other persons.

9. Patchen, *The Choice . . . , op. cit.*

10. L. A. Festinger, *A Theory of Cognitive Dissonance* (Evanston, Ill.: Row, Peterson, 1957).

11. J. V. Clark, "A Preliminary Investigation

of Some Unconscious Assumptions Affecting Labor Efficiency in Eight Supermarkets" (Ph.D. diss., Harvard Graduate School of Business Administration, 1958).

12. J. G. Abegglen, *The Japanese Factory* (Glencoe, Ill.: Free Press, 1958), p. 68.

13. Jaques, *Equitable Payment, op. cit.*, p. 26.

14. *Ibid.*, p. 26.

15. *Ibid.*, p. 26.

16. This process is analogous to that postulated by Festinger, *A Theory of Cognitive . . . , op. cit.*, when he discusses the relation of magnitude of cognitive dissonance to seeking information that will increase dissonance. He hypothesizes that at high levels of dissonance increasing information may be sought, with the result that the person will change his opinion and thus reduce dissonance.

17. Festinger, *A Theory of Cognitive . . . , op. cit.*

18. M. Patchen, *Study of Work and Life Satisfaction; Report II. Absences and Attitudes Toward Work Experiences* (Ann Arbor, Mich.: Institute for Social Research, 1959).

19. *Ibid.*, p. 12.

20. Zaleznik, et al., *op. cit.*

21. G. C. Homans, "Status among Clerical Workers," *Hum. Organiz.* 12 (1953): 5-10. Homans, *Social Behavior.*

22. Patchen, *Study of Work . . . , op. cit.* Patchen, *The Choice . . ., op. cit.*

23. Homans, "Status . . . ," *op. cit.*

24. *Ibid.*

25. *Ibid.*

26. Clark, *op. cit.*

27. *Ibid.*

28. As an index of labor efficiency, Clark used the number of man-hours per $100 of sales.

29. "Social ease" is a complex index, devised by Clark, the value of which is basically the number of pairs of part-time employees, out of all possible pairs, whose inputs and outcomes were "in line," according to the definition given in the quotation from Clark.

30. J. S. Adams and W. B. Rosenbaum, "The Relationship of Worker Productivity to Cognitive Dissonance about Wage Inequities," *J. Appl. Psychol.* 46 (1962): 161-64.

31. C. R. Day, "Some Consequences of Increased Reward Following Establishment of Output-Reward Expectation Level" (Master's thesis, Duke University, 1961).

32. A. J. Arrowood, "Some Effects on Productivity of Justified and Unjustified Levels of Reward Under Public and Private Conditions" (Unpublished doctoral dissertation, University of Minnesota, Department of Psychology, 1961).

33. Adams and Rosenbaum, *op. cit.*

34. Arrowood, *op. cit.*

35. Adams and Rosenbaum, *op. cit.*

36. J. S. Adams, "Productivity and Work Quality as a Function of Wage Inequities," *Industrial Relations* (1963).

8. Achievement Motivation*

DAVID C. McCLELLAND

Most people in this world, psychologically, can be divided into two broad groups. There is that minority which is challenged by opportunity and willing to work hard to achieve something, and the majority which really does not care all that much.

For nearly twenty years now, psychologists have tried to penetrate the mystery of this curious dichotomy. Is the need to achieve (or the absence of it) an accident, is it hereditary, or is it the result of environment? Is it a single, isolatable human motive, or a combination of motives—the desire to accumulate wealth, power, fame? Most important of all, is there some technique that could give this will to achieve to people, even whole societies, who do not now have it?

While we do not yet have complete answers for any of these questions, years of work have given us partial answers to most of them and insights into all of them. There is a distinct human motive, distinguishable from others. It can be found, in fact tested for, in any group.

Let me give you one example. Several years ago, a careful study was made of 450 workers who had been thrown out of work by a plant shutdown in Erie, Pennsylvania. Most of the unemployed workers stayed home for a while and then checked back with the United States Employment Service to see if their old jobs or similar ones were available. But a small minority among them behaved differently: the day they were laid off, they started job-hunting.

They checked both the United States and the Pennsylvania Employment Office; they studied the "Help Wanted" sections of the papers; they checked through their union, their church, and various fraternal organizations; they looked into training courses to learn a new skill; they even left town to look for work, while the majority when questioned said they would not under any circumstances move away from Erie to obtain a job. Obviously the members of that active minority were differently motivated. All the men were more or less in the same situation objectively: they needed work, money, food, shelter, job security. Yet only a minority showed initiative and enterprise in finding what they needed. Why? Psychologists, after years of research, now believe they can answer that question. They have demonstrated that these men possessed in greater degree a specific type of human motivation. For the moment let us refer to this personality characteristic as "Motive A" and review some of the other characteristics of the men who have more of the motive than other men.

Suppose they are confronted by a work situation in which they can set their own goals as to how difficult a task they will undertake. In the psychological laboratory, such a situation is very simply created by asking them to throw rings over a peg from any distance they may choose. Most men throw more or less randomly, standing now close, now far away, but those with Motive A seem to calculate carefully where they are most likely to get a sense of mastery.

*Source: Originally entitled "That Urge to Achieve." From Think magazine, pp. 82-89, published by IBM. Copyright © 1966 by International Business Machines Corporation. Reprinted by permission.

They stand nearly always at moderate distances, not so close as to make the task ridiculously easy, nor so far away as to make it impossible. They set moderately difficult, but potentially achievable goals for themselves, where they objectively have only about a one-in-three chance of succeeding. In other words, they are always setting challenges for themselves, tasks to make them stretch themselves a little.

But they behave like this only if *they* can influence the outcome by performing the work themselves. They prefer not to gamble at all. Say they are given a choice between rolling dice with one in three chances of winning and working on a problem with a one-in-three chance of solving in the time allotted, they choose to work on the problem even though rolling the dice is obviously less work and the odds of winning are the same. They prefer to work at a problem rather than leave the outcome to chance or to others.

Obviously they are concerned with personal achievement rather than with the rewards of success *per se*, since they stand just as much chance of getting those rewards by throwing the dice. This leads to another characteristic the Motive A men show—namely, a strong preference for work situations in which they get concrete feedback on how well they are doing, as one does, say in playing golf, or in being a salesman, but as one does not in teaching, or in personnel counseling. A golfer always knows his score and can compare how well he is doing with par or with his own performance yesterday or last week. A teacher has no such concrete feedback on how well he is doing in "getting across" to his students.

THE *n* ACH MEN

But why do certain men behave like this? At one level the reply is simple: because they habitually spend their time thinking about doing things better. In fact, psychologists typically measure the strength of Motive A by taking samples of a man's spontaneous thoughts (such as making up a story about a picture they have been shown) and counting the frequency with which he mentions doing things better. The count is objective and can even be made these days with the help of a computer program for content analysis. It yields what is referred to technically as an individual's *n* Ach score (for "need for Achievement"). It is not difficult to understand why people who think constantly about "doing better" are more apt to do better at job-hunting, to set moderate, achievable goals for themselves, to dislike gambling (because they get no achievement satisfaction from success), and to prefer work situations where they can tell easily whether they are improving or not. But why some people and not others come to think this way is another question. The evidence suggests it is not because of special training they get in the home from parents who set moderately high achievement goals but who are warm, encouraging, and nonauthoritarian in helping their children reach these goals.

Such detailed knowledge about one motive helps correct a lot of common sense ideas about human motivation. For example, much public policy (and much business policy) is based on the simple-minded notion that people will work harder "if they have to." As a first approximation, the idea isn't totally wrong, but it is only a half-truth. The majority of unemployed workers in Erie "had to" find work as much as those with higher *n* Ach but they certainly didn't work as hard at it. Or again, it is frequently assumed that *any* strong motive will lead to doing things better. Wouldn't it be fair to say that most of the Erie workers were just "unmotivated"? But our detailed knowledge of various human motives shows that each one leads a person to behave in *dif-*

ferent ways. The contrast is not between being "motivated" or "unmotivated" but between being motivated toward A or toward B or C, etc.

A simple experiment makes the point nicely: subjects were told that they could choose as a working partner either a close friend or a stranger who was known to be an expert on the problem to be solved. Those with higher *n* Ach (more "need to achieve") chose the experts over their friends, whereas those with more *n* Aff (the "need to affiliate with others") chose friends over experts. The latter were not "unmotivated"; their desire to be with someone they liked was simply a stronger motive than their desire to excel at the task. Other such needs have been studied by psychologists. For instance, the need for Power is often confused with the need for Achievement because both may lead to "outstanding" activities. There is a distinct difference. People with a strong need for Power want to command attention, get recognition, and control others. They are more active in political life and tend to busy themselves primarily with controlling the channels of communication both up to the top and down to the people so that they are more "in charge." Those with high *n* Power are not as concerned with improving their work performance daily as those with high *n* Ach.

It follows, from what we have been able to learn, that not all "great achievers" score high in *n* Ach. Many generals, outstanding politicians, great research scientists do not, for instance, because their work requires other personality characteristics, other motives. A general or a politician must be more concerned with power relationships, a research scientist must be able to go for long periods without the immediate feedback the person with high *n* Ach requires, etc. On the other hand, business executives, particularly if they are in positions of real responsibility or if they are salesmen, tend to score high in *n* Ach. This is true even in a Communist country like Poland: apparently there,

as well as in a private economy, a manager succeeds if he is concerned about improving all the time, setting moderate goals, keeping track of his or the company's performance, etc.

MOTIVATION AND HALF-TRUTHS

Since careful study has shown that common sense notions about motivation are at best half-truths, it also follows that you cannot trust what people tell you about their motives. After all, they often get their ideas about their own motives from common sense. Thus a general may say he is interested in achievement (because he has obviously achieved), or a businessman that he is interested only in making money (because he has made money), or one of the majority of unemployed in Erie that he desperately wants a job (because he knows he needs one); but a careful check of what each one thinks about and how he spends his time may show that each is concerned about quite different things. It requires special measurement techniques to identify the presence of *n* Ach and other such motives. Thus what people say and believe is not very closely related to these "hidden" motives which seem to affect a person's "style of life" more than his political, religious or social attitudes. Thus *n* Ach produces enterprising men among labor leaders or managers, Republicans or Democrats, Catholics or Protestants, capitalists or Communists.

Wherever people begin to think often in *n* Ach terms, things begin to move. Men with high *n* Ach get more raises and are promoted more rapidly, because they keep actively seeking ways to do a better job. Companies with many such men grow faster. In one comparison of two firms in Mexico, it was discovered that all but one of the top executives of a fast growing firm had higher *n* Ach scores than the highest scoring executive in an equally large but slow-growing firm. Countries with many such rapidly growing firms tend to show above average rates of national economic growth. This appears to be the reason why correlations have regularly been found between the n Ach content in popular literature (such as popular songs or stories in children's textbooks) and subsequent rates of national economic growth. A nation which is thinking about doing better all the time (as shown in its popular literature) actually does do better economically speaking. Careful quantitative studies have shown this to be true in Ancient Greece, in Spain in the Middle Ages, in England from 1400-1800, as well as among contemporary nations, whether capitalist or Communist, developed or underdeveloped.

Contrast these two stories for example. Which one contains more n Ach? Which one reflects a state of mind which ought to lead to harder striving to improve the way things are?

• **Excerpt from story A (4th grade reader):** "Don't Ever Owe a Man—The world is an illusion. Wife, children, horses, and cows are all just ties of fate. They are ephemeral. Each after fulfilling his part in life disappears. So we should not clamour after riches which are not permanent. As long as we live it is wise not to have any attachments and just think of God. We have to spend our lives without trouble, for is it not time that there is an end to grievances? So it is better to live knowing the real state of affairs. Don't get entangled in the meshes of family life."

• **Excerpt from story B (4th grade reader):** "How I Do Like to Learn—I was sent to an accelerated technical high school. I was so happy I cried. Learning is not very easy. In the beginning I couldn't understand what the teacher taught us. I always got a red cross mark on my papers. The boy sitting next to me was very enthusiastic and also an outstanding student. When he found I couldn't do the problems he offered to show me how he had done them. I could not copy his work. I must learn through my own reasoning. I gave his paper back and explained I had to do it myself. Sometimes I worked on a problem until midnight. If I couldn't finish, I started early in the morning. The red cross marks on my work were getting less common. I conquered my difficulties. My marks rose. I graduated and went on to college."

Most readers would agree, without any special knowledge of the n Ach coding system, that the second story shows more concern with improvement than the first, which comes from a contemporary reader used in Indian public schools. In fact the latter has a certain Horatio Alger quality that is reminiscent of our own McGuffey readers of several generations ago. It appears today in the textbooks of Communist China. It should not, therefore, come as a surprise if a nation like Communist China, obsessed as it is with improvement, tended in the long run to outproduce a nation like India, which appears to be more fatalistic.

The n Ach level is obviously important for statesmen to watch and in many instances to try to do something about, particularly if a nation's economy is lagging. Take Britain, for example. A generation ago (around 1925) it ranked fifth among 25 countries where children's readers were scored for n Ach—and its economy was doing well. By 1950 the n Ach level had dropped to 27th out of 39 countries—well below the world average—and today, its leaders are feeling the severe economic effects of this loss in the spirit of enterprise.

ECONOMICS AND n ACH

If psychologists can detect n Ach levels in individuals or nations, particularly before their effects are widespread, can't the knowledge somehow be put to use to foster economic development? Obviously detection or diagnosis is not enough.

What good is it to tell Britain (or India for that matter) that it needs more *n* Ach, a greater spirit of enterprise? In most such cases, informed observers of the local scene know very well that such a need exists, though they may be slower to discover it than the psychologist hovering over *n* Ach scores. What is needed is some method of developing *n* Ach in individuals or nations.

Since about 1960, psychologists in my research group at Harvard have been experimenting with techniques designed to accomplish this goal, chiefly among business executives whose work requires the action characteristics of people with high *n* Ach. Initially, we had real doubts as to whether we could succeed, partly because like most American psychologists we had been strongly influenced by the psychoanalytic view that basic motives are laid down in childhood and cannot really be changed later, and partly because many studies of intensive psychotherapy and counseling have shown minor if any long-term personality effects. On the other hand we were encouraged by the nonprofessionals: those enthusiasts like Dale Carnegie, the Communist idealogue or the Church missionary, who felt they could change adults and in fact seemed to be doing so. At any rate we ran some brief (7 to 10 days) "total push" training courses for businessmen designed to increase their *n* Ach.

FOUR MAIN GOALS

In broad outline the courses had four main goals: (1) They were designed to teach the participants how to think, talk, and act like a person with high *n* Ach, based on our knowledge of such people gained through 17 years of research. For instance, men learned how to make up stories that would code high in *n* Ach (i.e., how to think in *n* Ach terms), how to set moderate goals for themselves in the ring toss game (and in life). (2) The courses stimulated the participants to set higher but carefully planned and realistic work goals for themselves over the next two years. Then we checked back with them every six months to see how well they were doing in terms of their own objectives. (3) The courses also utilized techniques for giving the participants knowledge about themselves. For instance, in playing the ring toss game, they could observe that they behaved differently from others—perhaps in refusing to adjust a goal downward after failure. This would then become a matter for group discussion and the man would have to explain what he had in mind in setting such unrealistic goals. Discussion could then lead on to what a man's ultimate goals in life were, how much he cared about actually improving performance v. making a good impression or having many friends. In this way the participants would be freer to realize their achievement goals without being blocked by old habits and attitudes. (4) The courses also usually created a group *esprit de corps* from learning about each other's hopes and fears, successes and failures, and from going through an emotional experience together, away from everyday life, in a retreat setting. This membership in a new group helps a man achieve his goals, partly because he knows he has their sympathy and support and partly because he knows they will be watching to see how well he does. The same effect has been noted in other therapy groups like Alcoholics Anonymous. We are not sure which of these course "inputs" is really absolutely essential—that remains a research question—but we were taking no chances at the outset in view of the general pessimism about such efforts, and we wanted to include any and all techniques that were thought to change people.

The courses have been given: to executives in a large American firm, and in several Mexican firms, to underachieving high school boys; and to businessmen in India from Bombay and from a small city—Kakinada in the state of Andhra Pradesh. In every instance save one (the Mexican case), it was possible to demonstrate statistically, some two years later, that the men who took the course had done better (made more money, got promoted faster, expanded their businesses faster) than comparable men who did not take the course or who took some other management course.

Consider the Kakinada results, for example. In the two years preceding the course 9 men, 18 percent of the 52 participants, had shown "unusual" enterprise in their businesses. In the 18 months following the course 25 of the men, in other words nearly 50 percent, were unusually active. And this was not due to a general upturn of business in India. Data from a control city, some forty-five miles away, show the same base rate of "unusually active" men as in Kakinada before the course—namely, about 20 percent. Something clearly happened in Kakinada: the owner of a small radio shop started a chemical plant; a banker was so successful in making commercial loans in an enterprising way that he was promoted to a much larger branch of his bank in Calcutta; the local political leader accomplished his goal (it was set in the course) to get the federal government to deepen the harbor and make it into an all-weather port; plans are far along for establishing a steel rolling mill, etc. All this took place without any substantial capital from the outside. In fact, the only costs were for our 10-day courses plus some brief follow-up visits every six months. The men are raising their own capital and using their own resources for getting business and industry moving in a city that had been considered stagnant and unenterprising.

The promise of such a method of developing achievement motivation seems very great. It has obvious applications in helping underdeveloped countries, or "pockets of poverty" in the United States, to move faster economically. It has great potential for businesses that need to "turn around" and take a more enterprising approach toward their growth and development. It may even be helpful in developing more n Ach among low-income groups. For instance, data show that lower-class Negro Americans have a very low level of n Ach. This is not surprising. Society has systematically discouraged and blocked their achievement striving. But as the barriers to upward mobility are broken down, it will be necessary to help stimulate the motivation that will lead them to take advantage of new opportunities opening up.

EXTREME REACTIONS

But a word of caution: Whenever I speak of this research and its great potential, audience reaction tends to go to opposite extremes. Either people remain skeptical and argue that motives can't really be changed, that all we are doing is dressing Dale Carnegie up in fancy "psychologese," or they become converts and want instant course descriptions by a return mail to solve their local motivation problems. Either response is unjustified. What I have described here in a few pages has taken 20 years of patient research effort, and hundreds of thousands of dollars in basic research costs. What remains to be done will involve even larger sums and more time for development to turn a promising idea into something of wide practical utility.

ENCOURAGEMENT NEEDED

To take only one example, we have not yet learned how to develop n Ach really well among low-income groups. In our first effort—a summer course for bright underachieving 14-year-olds—we found that boys from the middle class improved steadily in grades in school over a two-year period, but boys from the lower class showed an improvement after the first year followed by a drop back to their beginning low grade average. (See Figure 8-1.) Why? We speculated that it was

Figure 8-1

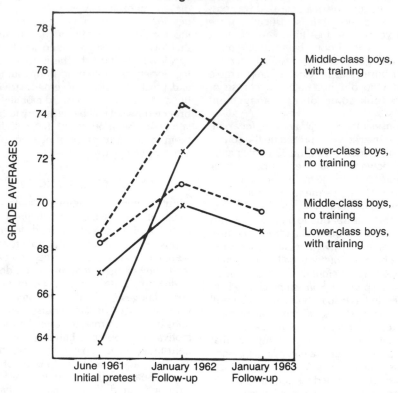

In a Harvard study, a group of underachieving 14-year-olds was given a six-week's course designed to help them do better in school. Some of the boys were also given training in achievement motivation, or n Ach (solid lines). As graph reveals, the only boys who continued to improve after a two-year period were the middle-class boys with the special n Ach training. Psychologists suspect the lower-class boys dropped back, even with n Ach training, because they returned to an environment in which neither parents nor friends encouraged achievement.

because they moved back into an environment in which neither parents nor friends encouraged achievement or upward mobility. In other words, it isn't enough to change a man's motivation if the environment in which he lives doesn't support at least to some degree his new efforts. Negroes striving to rise out of the ghetto frequently confront this problem: they are often faced by skepticism at home and suspicion on the job, so that even if their n Ach is raised, it can be lowered

again by the heavy odds against their success. We must learn not only to raise n Ach but also to find methods of instructing people in how to manage it, to create a favorable environment in which it can flourish.

Many of these training techniques are now only in the pilot testing stage. It will take time and money to perfect them, but society should be willing to invest heavily in view of their tremendous potential for contributing to human betterment.

9. One More Time: How Do You Motivate Employees?*

FREDERICK HERZBERG

How many articles, books, speeches, and workshops have pleaded plaintively, "How do I get an employee to do what I want him to do?"

The psychology of motivation is tremendously complex, and what has been unraveled with any degree of assurance is small indeed. But the dismal ratio of knowledge to speculation has not dampened the enthusiasm for new forms of snake oil that are constantly coming on the market, many of them with academic testimonials. Doubtless this article will have no depressing impact on the market for snake oil, but since the ideas expressed in it have been tested in many corporations and other organizations, it will help—I hope—to redress the imbalance in the aforementioned ratio.

"MOTIVATING" WITH KITA

In lectures to industry on the problem, I have found that the audiences are anxious for quick and practical answers, so I will begin with a straightforward, practical formula for moving people.

What is the simplest, surest, and most direct way of getting someone to do something? Ask him? But if he responds that he does not want to do it, then that calls for a psychological consultation to determine the reason for his obstinancy. Tell him? His response shows that he does not understand you, and now an expert in communication methods has to be brought in to show you how to get

through to him. Give him a monetary incentive? I do not need to remind the reader of the complexity and difficulty involved in setting up and administering an incentive system. Show him? This means a costly training program. We need a simple way.

Every audience contains the "direct action" manager who shouts, "Kick him!" And this type of manager is right. The surest and least circumlocuted way of getting someone to do something is to kick him in the pants—give him what might be called the KITA.

There are various forms of KITA, and here are some of them.

NEGATIVE PHYSICAL KITA

This is a literal application of the term and was frequently used in the past. It has, however, three major drawbacks: (1) it is inelegant; (2) it contradicts the precious image of benevolence that most organizations cherish; and (3) since it is a physical attack, it directly stimulates the autonomic nervous system, and this often results in negative feedback—the employee may just kick you in return. These factors give rise to certain taboos against negative physical KITA.

The psychologist has come to the rescue of those who are no longer permitted to use negative physical KITA. He has uncovered infinite sources of psychological vulnerabilities and the appropriate methods to play tunes on them. "He took my rug away"; "I wonder what he meant by that''; ''The boss is always going around me''—these symptomatic expressions of ego sores that have been rubbed raw are the result of application of:

NEGATIVE PSYCHOLOGICAL KITA

This has several advantages over negative physical KITA. First, the cruelty is not visible; the bleeding is internal and comes much later. Second, since it affects the higher cortical centers of the brain with its inhibitory powers, it reduces the possibility of physical backlash. Third, since the number of psychological pains that a person can feel is almost infinite, the direction and site possibilities of the KITA are increased many times. Fourth, the person administering the kick can manage to be above it all and let the system accomplish the dirty work. Fifth, those who practice it receive some ego satisfaction (one-upmanship), whereas they would find drawing blood abhorrent. Finally, if the employee does complain, he can always be accused of being paranoid, since there is no tangible evidence of an actual attack.

Now, what does negative KITA accomplish? If I kick you in the rear (physically or psychologically), who is motivated? *I* am motivated; *you* move! Negative KITA does not lead to motivation, but to movement. So:

POSITIVE KITA

Let us consider motivation. If I say to you, ''Do this for me or the company, and in return I will give you a reward, an incentive, more status, a promotion, all the quid pro quos that exist in the industrial organization,'' am I motivating you? The overwhelming opinion I receive from management people is, ''Yes, this is motivation.''

I have a year-old Schnauzer. When it was a small puppy and I wanted it to move, I kicked it in the rear and it moved. Now that I have finished its obedience training, I hold up a dog biscuit when I want the Schnauzer to move. In this instance, who is motivated—I or the dog? The dog wants the biscuit, but it is I who want it to move. Again, I am the one who is motivated, and the dog is the one who moves. In this instance all I did was apply KITA frontally; I exerted a pull instead of a push. When industry wishes to use such positive KITAs, it has available an incredible number and variety of dog biscuits (jelly beans for humans) to wave in front of the employee to get him to jump.

Why is it that managerial audiences are quick to see that negative KITA is *not* motivation, while they are almost unanimous in their judgment that positive KITA *is* motivation? It is because negative KITA is rape, and positive KITA is seduction. But it is infinitely worse to be seduced than to be raped; the latter is an unfortunate occurrence, while the former signifies that you were a party to your own downfall. This is why positive KITA is so popular; it is a tradition; it is in the American way. The organization does not have to kick you; you kick yourself.

MYTHS ABOUT MOTIVATION

Why is KITA not motivation? If I kick my dog (from the front or the back), he will move. And when I want him to move again, what must I do? I must kick him again. Similarly, I can charge a man's battery, and then recharge it, and recharge it again. But it is only when he has his own generator that we can talk about motivation. He then needs no outside stimulation. He *wants* to do it.

With this in mind, we can review some positive KITA personnel practices that were developed as attempts to instill ''motivation.''

1. REDUCING TIME SPENT AT WORK

This represents a marvelous way of motivating people to work—getting them off the job! We have reduced (formally and informally) the time spent on the job over the last 50 or 60 years until we are finally on the way to the "6½-day weekend." An interesting variant of this approach is the development of off-hour recreation programs. The philosophy here seems to be that those who play together, work together. The fact is that motivated people seek more hours of work, not fewer.

2. SPIRALING WAGES

Have these motivated people? Yes, to seek the next wage increase. Some medievalists still can be heard to say that a good depression will get employees moving. They feel that if rising wages don't or won't do the job, perhaps reducing them will.

3. FRINGE BENEFITS

Industry has outdone the most welfare-minded of welfare states in dispensing cradle-to-the-grave succor. One company I know of had an informal "fringe benefit of the month club" going for a while. The cost of fringe benefits in this country has reached approximately 25 percent of the wage dollar, and we still cry for motivation.

People spend less time working for more money and more security than ever before, and the trend cannot be reversed. These benefits are no longer rewards; they are rights. A 6-day week is inhuman, a 10-hour day is exploitation, extended medical coverage is a basic decency; and stock options are the salvation of American initiative. Unless the ante is continuously raised, the psychological reaction of employees is that the company is turning back the clock.

When industry began to realize that both the economic nerve and the lazy nerve of their employees had insatiable appetites, it started to listen to the behavioral scientists who, more out of a humanist tradition than from scientific study, criticized management for not knowing how to deal with people. The next KITA easily followed.

4. HUMAN RELATIONS TRAINING

Over 30 years of teaching and, in many instances, of practicing psychological approaches to handling people have resulted in costly human relations programs and, in the end, the same question: How do you motivate workers? Here, too, escalations have taken place. Thirty years ago it was necessary to request "Please don't spit on the floor." Today the same admonition requires three "pleases" before the employee feels that his superior has demonstrated the psychologically proper attitudes toward him.

The failure of human relations training to produce motivation led to the conclusion that the supervisor or manager himself was not psychologically true to himself in his practice of interpersonal decency. So an advanced form of human relations KITA, sensitivity training, was unfolded.

5. SENSITIVITY TRAINING

Do you really, really understand yourself? Do you really, really, really trust the other man? Do you really, really, really, really cooperate? The failure of sensitivity training is now being explained, by those who have become opportunistic exploiters of the technique, as a failure to really (five times) conduct proper sensitivity training courses.

With the realization that there are only temporary gains from comfort and economic and interpersonal KITA, personnel managers concluded that the fault lay not in what they were doing, but in the employee's failure to appreciate what they were doing. This opened up the field of communications, a whole new area of "scientifically" sanctioned KITA.

6. COMMUNICATIONS

The professor of communications was invited to join the faculty of management training programs and help in making employees understand what management was doing for them. House organs, briefing sessions, supervisory instruction on the importance of communication, and all sorts of propaganda have proliferated until today there is even an International Council of Industrial Editors. But no motivation resulted, and the obvious thought occurred that perhaps management was not hearing what the employees were saying. That led to the next KITA.

7. TWO-WAY COMMUNICATION

Management ordered morale surveys, suggestion plans, and group participation programs. Then both employees and management were communicating and listening to each other more than ever, but without much improvement in motivation.

The behavioral scientists began to take another look at their conceptions and their data, and they took human relations one step further. A glimmer of truth was beginning to show through in the writings of the so-called higher-order–need psychologists. People, so they said, want to actualize themselves. Unfortunately, the "actualizing" psychologists got mixed up with the human relations psychologists, and a new KITA emerged.

8. JOB PARTICIPATION

Though it may not have been the theoretical intention, job participation often became a "give them the big picture" approach. For example, if a man is tightening 10,000 nuts a day on an assembly line with a torque wrench, tell him he is building a Chevrolet. Another approach had the goal of giving the employee a *feeling* that he is determining, in some measure, what he does on his job. The goal was to provide a *sense* of achievement rather than a substantive achievement in his task. Real achievement, of course, requires a task that makes it possible.

But still there was no motivation. This led to the inevitable conclusion that the employees must be sick, and therefore to the next KITA.

9. EMPLOYEE COUNSELING

The initial use of this form of KITA in a systematic fashion can be credited to the Hawthorne experiment of the Western Electric Company during the early 1930s. At that time, it was found that the employees harbored irrational feelings that were interfering with the rational operation of the factory. Counseling in this instance was a means of letting the employees unburden themselves by talking to someone about their problems. Although the counseling techniques were primitive, the program was large indeed.

The counseling approach suffered as a result of experiences during World War II, when the programs themselves were found to be interfering with the operation of the organizations; the counselors had forgotten their role of benevolent listeners and were attempting to do something about the problems that they heard about. Psychological counseling, however, has managed to survive the negative impact of World War II experiences and today is beginning to flourish with renewed sophistication. But, alas, many of these programs, like all the others, do not seem to have lessened the pressure of demands to find out how to motivate workers.

Since KITA results only in short-term movement, it is safe to predict that the cost of these programs will increase steadily and new varieties will be developed as old positive KITAs reach their satiation points.

HYGIENE VS. MOTIVATORS

Let me rephrase the perennial question this way: How do you install a generator in an employee? A brief review of my motivation-hygiene theory of job attitudes is required before theoretical and practical suggestions can be offered. The theory was first drawn from an examination of events in the lives of engineers and accountants. At least 16 other investigations, using a wide variety of populations (including some in the Communist countries), have since been completed, making the original research one of the most replicated studies in the field of job attitudes.

The findings of these studies, along with corroboration from many other investigations using different procedures, suggest that the factors involved in producing job satisfaction (and motivation) are separate and distinct from the factors that lead to job dissatisfaction. Since separate factors need to be considered, depending on whether job satisfaction or job dissatisfaction is being examined, it follows that these two feelings are not opposites of each other. The opposite of job satisfaction is not job dissatisfaction but, rather, *no* job satisfaction; and, similarly, the opposite of job dissatisfaction is not job satisfaction, but *no* job dissatisfaction.

Stating the concept presents a problem in semantics, for we normally think of satisfaction and dissatisfaction as opposites—*i.e.,* what is not satisfying must be dissatisfying, and vice versa. But when it comes to understanding the behavior of people in their jobs, more than a play on words is involved.

Two different needs of man are involved here. One set of needs can be thought of as stemming from his animal nature—the built-in drive to avoid pain from the environment, plus all the learned drives which become conditioned to the basic biological needs. For example, hunger, a basic biological drive, makes it necessary to earn money, and then money becomes a specific drive. The other set of needs relates to that unique human characteristic, the ability to achieve and, through achievement, to experience psychological growth. The stimuli for the growth needs are tasks that induce growth; in the industrial setting, they are the *job content.* Contrariwise, the stimuli induc-

ing pain-avoidance behavior are found in the *job environment.*

The growth or *motivator* factors that are intrinsic to the job are: achievement, recognition for achievement, the work itself, responsibility, and growth or advancement. The dissatisfaction-avoidance or *hygiene* (KITA) factors that are extrinsic to the job include: company policy and administration, supervision, interpersonal relationships, working conditions, salary, status, and security.

A composite of the factors that are involved in causing job satisfaction and job dissatisfaction, drawn from samples of 1,685 employees, is shown in Figure 9-1. The results indicate that motivators were the primary cause of satisfaction, and hygiene factors the primary cause of unhappiness on the job. The employees, studied in 12 different investigations, included lower-level supervisors, professional women, agricultural administrators, men about to retire from management positions, hospital maintenance personnel, manufacturing supervisors, nurses, food handlers, military officers, engineers, scientists, housekeepers, teachers, technicians, female assemblers, accountants, Finnish foremen, and Hungarian engineers.

They were asked what job events had occurred in their work that had led to extreme satisfaction or extreme dissatisfaction on their part. Their responses are broken down in the exhibit into percentages of total "positive" job events and total "negative" job events. (The figures total more than 100 percent on both the "hygiene" and "motivators" sides because often at least two factors can be attributed to a single event; advancement, for instance, often accompanies assumption of responsibility.)

To illustrate, a typical response involving achievement that had a negative effect for the employee was, "I was unhappy because I didn't do the job successfully." A typical response in the small number of positive job events in

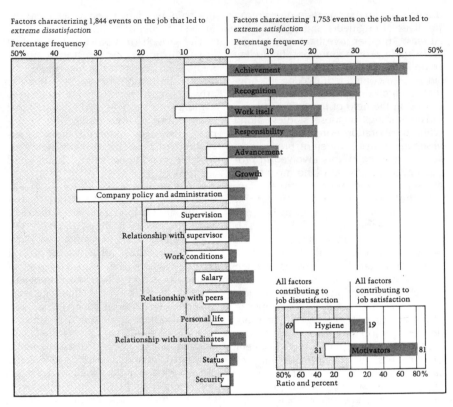

Figure 9-1

**FACTORS AFFECTING JOB ATTITUDES, AS REPORTED IN
12 INVESTIGATIONS**

the Company Policy and Administration grouping was, "I was happy because the company reorganized the section so that I didn't report any longer to the guy I didn't get along with."

As the lower right-hand part of the exhibit shows, of all the factors contributing to job satisfaction, 81 percent were motivators. And of all the factors contributing to the employees' dissatisfaction over their work, 69 percent involved hygiene elements.

ETERNAL TRIANGLE

There are three general philosophies of personnel management. The first is based on organizational theory, the second on industrial engineering, and the third on behavioral science.

The organizational theorist believes that human needs are either so irrational or so varied and adjustable to specific situations that the major function of personnel management is to be as pragmatic as the occasion demands. If jobs are organized in a proper manner, he reasons the result will be the most efficient job structure, and the most favorable job attitudes will follow as a matter of course.

The industrial engineer holds that man is mechanistically oriented and economically motivated and his needs are best met by attuning the individual to the most efficient work process. The goal of personnel management therefore should be to concoct the most appropriate incentive system and to design the specific working conditions in a way that facilitates the most efficient use of the human machine. By structuring jobs in a manner that leads to the most efficient operation, the engineer believes that he can obtain the optimal organization of work and the proper work attitudes.

The behavioral scientist focuses on group sentiments, attitudes of individual employees, and the organization's social and psychological climate. According to his persuasion, he emphasizes one or more of the various hygiene and motivator needs. His approach to personnel management generally emphasizes some form of human relations education, in the hope of instilling healthy employee attitudes and an organizational climate which he considers to be felicitous to human values. He believes that proper attitudes will lead to efficient job and organizational structure.

There is always a lively debate as to the overall effectiveness of the approaches of the organizational theorist and the industrial engineer. Manifestly they have achieved much. But the nagging question for the behavioral scientist has been: What is the cost in human problems that eventually cause more expense to the organization—for instance, turnover, absenteeism, errors, violation of safety rules, strikes, restriction of output, higher wages, and greater fringe benefits? On the other hand, the behavioral scientist is hard put to document much manifest improvement in personnel management, using his approach.

The three philosophies can be depicted as a triangle, as is done in Figure 9-2, with

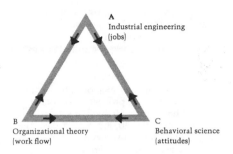

A
Industrial engineering
(jobs)

B
Organizational theory
(work flow)

C
Behavioral science
(attitudes)

Figure 9-2

"TRIANGLE" OF PHILOSOPHIES
OF PERSONNEL MANAGEMENT

each persuasion claiming the apex angle. The motivation-hygiene theory claims the same angle as industrial engineering, but for opposite goals. Rather than rationalizing the work to increase efficiency, the theory suggests that work be *enriched* to bring about effective utilization of personnel. Such a systematic attempt to motivate employees by manipulating the motivator factors is just beginning.

The term *job enrichment* describes this embryonic movement. An older term, job enlargement, should be avoided because it is associated with past failures stemming from a misunderstanding of the problem. Job enrichment provides the opportunity for the employee's psychological growth, while job enlargement merely makes a job structurally bigger. Since scientific job enrichment is very new, this article only suggests the principles and practical steps that have recently emerged from several successful experiments in industry.

JOB LOADING

In attempting to enrich an employee's job, management often succeeds in reducing the man's personal contribution, rather than giving him an opportunity for growth in his accustomed job. Such an endeavor, which I shall call horizontal job loading (as opposed to vertical loading, or providing motivator factors), has been the problem of earlier job enlargement programs. This activity merely enlarges the meaninglessness of the job. Some examples of this approach, and their effect are:

• Challenging the employee by increasing the amount of production expected of him. If he tightens 10,000 bolts a day, see if he can tighten 20,000 bolts a day. The arithmetic involved shows that multiplying zero by zero still equals zero.

• Adding another meaningless task to the existing one, usually some routine clerical activity. The arithmetic here is adding zero to zero.

• Rotating the assignments of a number of jobs that need to be enriched. This means washing dishes for a while, then washing silverware. The arithmetic is substituting one zero for another zero.

• Removing the most difficult parts of the assignment in order to free the worker to accomplish more of the less challenging assignments. This traditional industrial engineering approach amounts to subtraction in the hope of accomplishing addition.

These are common forms of horizontal loading that frequently come up in preliminary brainstorming sessions on job enrichment. The principles of vertical loading have not all been worked out as yet, and they remain rather general, but I have furnished seven useful starting points for consideration in Table 9-1.

A SUCCESSFUL APPLICATION

An example from a highly successful job enrichment experiment can illustrate the distinction between horizontal and vertical loading of a job. The subjects of this study were the stockholder correspondents employed by a very large corporation. Seemingly, the task required of these carefully selected and highly trained correspondents was quite complex and challenging. But almost all indexes of performance and job attitudes were low, and exit interviewing confirmed that the challenge of the job existed merely as words.

A job enrichment project was initiated in the form of an experiment with one group, designated as an achieving unit, having its job enriched by the principles described in Table 9-1. A control group continued to do its job in the traditional way. (There were also two "uncommitted" groups of correspondents formed to measure the so-called Hawthorne Effect—that

Table 9-1

PRINCIPLES OF VERTICAL JOB LOADING

Principle	Motivators involved
A. Removing some controls while retaining accountability	Responsibility and personal achievement
B. Increasing the accountability of individuals for own work	Responsibility and recognition
C. Giving a person a complete natural unit of work (module, division, area, and so on)	Responsibility, achievement, and recognition
D. Granting additional authority to an employee in his activity; job freedom	Responsibility, achievement, and recognition
E. Making periodic reports directly available to the worker himself rather than to the supervisor	Internal recognition
F. Introducing new and more difficult tasks not previously handled	Growth and learning
G. Assigning individuals specific or specialized tasks, enabling them to become experts	Responsibility, growth and advancement

is, to gauge whether productivity and attitudes toward the job changed artificially merely because employees sensed that the company was paying more attention to them in doing something different or novel. The results for these groups were substantially the same as for the control group, and for the sake of simplicity I do not deal with them in this summary.) No changes in hygiene were introduced for either group other than those that would have been made anyway, such as normal pay increases.

The changes for the achieving unit were introduced in the first two months, averaging one per week of the seven motivators listed in Table 9-1. At the end of six months the members of the achieving unit were found to be outperforming their counterparts in the control group, and in addition indicated a marked increase in their liking for their jobs. Other results

showed that the achieving group had lower absenteeism and, subsequently, a much higher rate of promotion.

Figure 9-3 illustrates the changes in performance, measured in February and March, before the study period began, and at the end of each month of the study period. The shareholder service index represents quality of letters, including accuracy of information, and speed of response to stockholders' letters of inquiry. The index of a current month was averaged into the average of the two prior months, which means that improvement was harder to obtain if the indexes of the previous months were low. The "achievers" were performing less well before the six-month period started, and their performance service index continued to decline after the introduction of the motivators, evidently because of uncertainty over their newly granted responsibilities. In the third month, however, performance improved, and soon the members of this group had reached a high level of accomplishment.

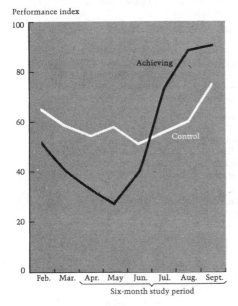

Performance index

Feb. Mar. Apr. May Jun. Jul. Aug. Sept.

Six-month study period

Figure 9-3
SHAREHOLDER SERVICE INDEX
IN COMPANY EXPERIMENT
(Three-month cumulative average)

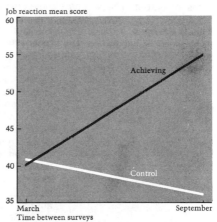

Job reaction mean score

March   September
Time between surveys

Figure 9-4
CHANGES IN ATTITUDES TOWARD
TASKS IN COMPANY EXPERIMENT
(Changes in mean scores over
six-month period)

Figure 9-4 shows the two groups' attitudes toward their job, measured at the end of March, just before the first motivator was introduced, and again at the end of September. The correspondents were asked 16 questions, all involving motivation. A typical one was, "As you see it, how many opportunities do you feel that you have in your job for making worthwhile contributions?" The answers were scaled from 1 to 5, with 80 as the maximum possible score. The achievers became much more positive about their job, while the attitude of the control unit remained about the same (the drop is not statistically significant).

How was the job of these correspondents restructured? Table 9-2 lists the sug-

Table 9-2

ENLARGEMENT VS. ENRICHMENT OF CORRESPONDENTS' TASKS IN COMPANY EXPERIMENT

Horizontal loading suggestions (rejected)	Vertical loading suggestions (adopted)	Principle
Firm quotas could be set for letters to be answered each day, using a rate which would be hard to reach.	Subject matter experts were appointed within each unit for other members of the unit to consult with before seeking supervisory help. (The supervisor had been answering all specialized and difficult questions.)	G
The women could type the letters themselves, as well as compose them, or take on any other clerical functions.	Correspondents signed their own names on letters (The supervisor had been signing all letters.)	B
All difficult or complex inquiries could be channeled to a few women so that the remainder could achieve high rates of output. These jobs could be exchanged from time to time.	The work of the more experienced correspondents was proofread less frequently by supervisors and was done at the correspondents' desks, dropping verification from 100% to 10%. (Previously, all correspondents' letters had been checked by the supervisor.)	A
The women could be rotated through units handling different customers, and then sent back to their own units.	Production was discussed, but only in terms such as "a full day's work is expected." As time went on, this was no longer mentioned. (Before, the group had been constantly reminded of the number of letters that needed to be answered.)	D
	Outgoing mail went directly to the mailroom without going over supervisors' desks. (The letters had always been routed through the supervisors.)	A
	Correspondents were encouraged to answer letters in a more personalized way. (Reliance on the form-letter approach had been standard practice.)	C
	Each correspondent was held personally responsible for the quality and accuracy of letters. (This responsibility had been the province of the supervisor and the verifier.)	B, E

gestions made that were deemed to be horizontal loading, and the actual vertical loading changes that were incorporated in the job of the achieving unit. The capital letters under "Principle" after "Vertical loading" refer to the corresponding letters in Table 9-1. The reader will note that the rejected forms of horizontal loading correspond closely to the list of common manifestations of the phenomenon [under the subheading "JOB LOADING"].

STEPS TO JOB ENRICHMENT

Now that motivator idea has been described in practice, here are the steps that managers should take in instituting the principle with their employees [*italic first sentences not in original*]:

1. *Select those jobs in which (a) the investment in industrial engineering does not make changes too costly, (b) attitudes are poor, (c) hygiene is becoming very costly, and (d) motivation will make a difference in performance.*

2. *Approach these jobs with the conviction that they can be changed.* Years of tradition have led managers to believe that the content of the jobs is sacrosanct and the only scope of action that they have is in ways of stimulating people.

3. *Brainstorm a list of changes that may enrich the jobs, without concern for their practicality.*

4. *Screen the list to eliminate suggestions that involve hygiene, rather than actual motivation.*

5. *Screen the list for generalities, such as "give them more responsibility," that are rarely followed in practice.* This might seem obvious, but the motivator words have never left industry; the substance has just been rationalized and organized out. Words like "responsibility," "growth," "achievement," and "challenge," for example, have been elevated to the lyrics of the patriotic anthem for all organizations. It is the old problem typified by the pledge of allegiance to

the flag being more important than contributions to the country—of following the form, rather than the substance.

6. *Screen the list to eliminate any* horizontal [*emphasis in original*] *loading suggestions.*

7. *Avoid direct participation by the employees whose jobs are to be enriched.* Ideas they have expressed previously certainly constitute a valuable source for recommended changes, but their direct involvement contaminates the process with human relations hygiene and, more specifically, gives them only a *sense* of making a contribution. The job is to be changed, and it is the content that will produce the motivation, not attitudes about being involved or the challenge inherent in setting up a job. The process will be over shortly, and it is what the employees will be doing from then on that will determine their motivation. A sense of participation will result only in short-term movement.

8. *In the initial attempts at job enrichment, set up a controlled experiment.* At least two equivalent groups should be chosen, one an experimental unit in which the motivators are systematically introduced over a period of time, and the other one a control group in which no changes are made. For both groups, hygiene should be allowed to follow its natural course for the duration of the experiment. Pre- and post-installation tests of performance and job attitudes are necessary to evaluate the effectiveness of the job enrichment program. The attitude test must be limited to motivator items in order to divorce the employee's view of the job he is given from all the surrounding hygiene feelings that he might have.

9. *Be prepared for a drop in performance in the experimental group the first few weeks.* The changeover to a new job may lead to a temporary reduction in efficiency.

10. *Expect your first-line supervisors to experience some anxiety and hostility*

over the changes you are making. The anxiety comes from their fear that the changes will result in poorer performance for their unit. Hostility will arise when the employees start assuming what the supervisors regard as their own responsibility for performance. The supervisor without checking duties to perform may then be left with little to do.

After a successful experiment, however, the supervisor usually discovers the supervisory and managerial functions he has neglected, or which were never his because all his time was given over to checking the work of his subordinates. For example, in the R&D division of one large chemical company I know of, the supervisors of the laboratory assistants were theoretically responsible for their training and evaluation. These functions, however, had come to be performed in a routine, unsubstantial fashion. After the job enrichment program, during which the supervisors were not merely passive observers of the assistants' performance, the supervisors actually were devoting their time to reviewing performance and administering thorough training.

What has been called an employee-centered style of supervision will come about not through education of supervisors, but by changing the jobs that they do.

CONCLUDING NOTE

Job enrichment will not be a one-time proposition, but a continuous management function. The initial changes, however, should last for a very long period of time. There are a number of reasons for this:

- The changes should bring the job up to the level of challenge commensurate with the skill that was hired.
- Those who have still more ability eventually will be able to demonstrate it better and win promotion to higher-level jobs.
- The very nature of motivators, as opposed to hygiene factors, is that they have a much longer-term effect on employees' attitudes. Perhaps the job will have to be enriched again, but this will not occur as frequently as the need for hygiene.

Not all jobs can be enriched, nor do all jobs need to be enriched. If only a small percentage of the time and money that is now devoted to hygiene, however, were given to job enrichment efforts, the return in human satisfaction and economic gain would be one of the largest dividends that industry and society have ever reaped through their efforts at better personnel management.

The argument for job enrichment can be summed up quite simply: If you have someone on a job, use him. If you can't use him on the job, get rid of him, either via automation or by selecting someone with lesser ability. If you can't use him and you can't get rid of him, you will have a motivation problem.

10. Expectancy Theory*

JOHN P. CAMPBELL

MARVIN D. DUNNETTE

EDWARD E. LAWLER III

KARL E. WEICK, JR.

Expectancy theory, because of its greater potential relevance to managerial behavior, will be discussed more fully.

EARLY COGNITIVE THEORIES

Concomitant with the development of drive x habit theory, Lewin[1] and Tolman[2] developed and investigated cognitive, or expectancy, theories of motivation. Even though Lewin was concerned with human subjects and Tolman worked largely with animals, much of their respective theorizing contained common elements. Basic to the cognitive view of motivation is the notion that individuals have cognitive *expectancies* concerning the outcomes that are likely to occur as the result of what they do and that individuals have preferences among outcomes. That is, an individual has an "idea" about possible consequences of his acts, and he makes conscious choices among consequences according to their probability of occurence and their value to him.

Thus for the cognitive theorist it is the anticipation of reward that energizes behavior and the perceived value of various outcomes that gives behavior its direction. Tolman spoke of a *belief-value* matrix that specifies for each individual the value he places on particular outcomes and his belief that they can be attained.

Atkinson[3] has compared drive theory and expectancy theory. Although he points out some differences, he emphasizes that both theories are actually quite similar and contain many of the same concepts. Both include the notion of a reward or favorable outcome that is desired, and both postulate a learned connection contained within the organism. For expectancy theory this learned connection is a behavior-outcome expectancy, and for drive theory it is an *S-R* habit strength.

However, the theories differ in two ways which are important for research on motivation in an organizational setting. For example, they differ in what they state is activated by the anticipation of reward. Expectancy theory sees the anticipation of a reward as functioning selectively on actions expected to lead to it. Drive theory views the magnitude of the anticipated goals as a source of general excitement—a nonselective influence on performance.

Expectancy theory is also much looser in specifying how expectancy-outcome connections are built up. Drive theory postulates that *S-R* habit strengths are built up through repeated associations of stimulus and response; that is, the reward or outcome must ac-

---

*Source: From John P. Campbell et al., *Managerial Behavior, Performance, and Effectiveness,* pp. 343-348. Copyright © 1970 by McGraw-Hill, Inc. Used with permission of McGraw-Hill Book Company. References converted to footnotes.

tually have followed the response to a particular stimulus in order for the *S-R* connection to operate in future choice behavior. Such a process is sufficient but not necessary for forming expectancy-outcome relationships. An individual may form expectancies vicariously (someone may tell him that complimenting the boss's wife leads to a promotion, for example) or by other symbolic means. This last point is crucial since the symbolic (cognitive) manipulation of various *S-R* situations seems quite descriptive of a great deal of human behavior.

These two differences make the cognitive or expectancy point of view much more useful for studying human motivation in an organizational setting. In fact, it is the one which has been given the most attention by theorists concerned with behavior in organizations.

INSTRUMENTALITY-VALENCE THEORY

Building on expectancy theory and its later amplifications by Atkinson,[4] W. Edwards,[5] Peak,[6] and Rotter,[7] Vroom[8] has presented a process theory of work motivation that he calls *instrumentality theory*. His basic classes of variables are expectancies, valences, choices, outcomes, and instrumentalities.

Expectancy is defined as a belief concerning the likelihood that a particular act will be followed by a particular outcome. Presumably, the degree of belief can vary between 0 (complete lack of belief that it will follow) and 1 (complete certainty that it will). Note that it is the perception of the individual that is important, not the objective reality. This same concept has been referred to as *subjective probability* by others (e.g., W. Edwards).

Valence refers to the strength of an individual's preference for a particular outcome. An individual may have either a positive or a negative preference for an outcome; presumably, outcomes gain their valence as a function of the degree to which they are seen to be related to the needs of the individual. However, this last point is not dealt with concretely in Vroom's formulation. As an example of these two concepts, one might consider an increase in pay to be a possible outcome of a particular act. The theory would then deal with the valence of a wage increase for an individual and his expectancy that particular behaviors will be followed by a wage increase outcome. Again, valence refers to the perceived or expected value of an outcome, not its real or eventual value.

According to Vroom, outcomes take on a valence value because of their *instrumentality* for achieving other outcomes. Thus he is really postulating two classes of outcomes. In the organizational setting, the first class of outcomes might include such things as money, promotion, recognition, etc. Supposedly, these outcomes are directly linked to behavior. However, as Vroom implicitly suggests, wage increases or promotion may have no value by themselves. They are valuable in terms of their instrumental role in securing second level outcomes such as food, clothing, shelter, entertainment, and status, which are not obtained as the direct result of a particular action.

According to Vroom, instrumentality, like correlation, varies between $+1.0$ and -1.0. Thus a first level outcome may be seen as always leading to some desired second level outcome ($+1.0$) or as never leading to the second level outcome (-1.0). In Vroom's theory the formal definition of valence for a first level outcome is the sum of the products between its instrumentalities for all possible second level outcomes and their respective valences.

To sum up, Vroom's formulation postulates that the motivational force, or effort, an individual exerts is a function of (1) his expectancy that certain outcomes will result from his behavior (e.g., a raise in pay for increased effort) and (2) the valence, for him, of those outcomes. The valence of an outcome is in turn a function of its instrumentality for obtaining other outcomes and the valence of these other outcomes.

A HYBRID EXPECTANCY MODEL

Since his formulation first appeared, a number of investigators have attempted to extend Vroom's model to make it more explicit and more inclusive in terms of relevant variables (Graen;[9] L. W. Porter and Lawler[10]). Although we shall not discuss the contributions of these writers in detail, we would like to incorporate a number of their ideas in our own composite picture of an expanded expectancy model. However, any imperfections in what follows should be ascribed to us and not to them.

One major addition to Vroom's model is the necessity for a more concrete specification of the task or performance goals toward which work behavior is directed. Graen[11] refers to this class of variables as *work roles*, but we prefer to retain the notion of *task goals*. Task goals may be specified externally by the organization or the work group, or internally by the individual's own value system. Examples of task goals include such things as production quotas, time limits for projects, quality standards, showing a certain amount of loyalty to the organization, exhibiting the right set of attitudes, etc.

We would also like to make more explicit a distinction between first and second level outcomes. First level outcomes are outcomes contingent on achieving the task goal or set of task goals. A potential first level outcome is synonymous with the term "incentive," and an outcome which is actually realized is synonymous with the term "reward." The distinction is temporal. Like task goals, first level outcomes may be external or internal. Some examples of external first level outcomes granted by the organization are job security, pay, promotions, recognition, and increased autonomy. An individual may also set up his own internal incentives or reward himself with internally mediated outcomes such as ego satisfaction.

As pointed out in the discussion of Vroom's model first level outcomes may or may not be associated with a plethora of second level outcomes; that is, the externally or internally mediated rewards are instrumental in varying degrees for obtaining second level outcomes, such as food, housing, material goods, community status, and freedom from anxiety.

The concepts of valence for first and second level outcomes and the instrumentality of first for second level outcomes are defined as before, but the notion of expectancy decomposes into two different variables. First, individuals may have expectancies concerning whether or not they will actually accomplish the task goal if they expend effort (expectancy I); that is, an individual makes a subjective probability estimate concerning his chances for reaching a particular goal, given a particular situation. For example, a manufacturing manager may think the odds of his getting a new product into production by the first of the year are about 3 to 1 (*i.e.,* expectancy I = 0.75). Perhaps the primary determiner of expectancy I is how the individual perceives his own job skills in the context of what is specified as his task goals and the various difficulties and external constraints standing in the way of accomplishing them. Certainly, then, an employee's perceptions of his own talents determine to a large degree the direction and intensity of his job behavior. This first kind of expectancy should be more salient for more complex and higher level tasks such as those involved in managing.

Second, individuals possess expectancies concerning whether or not achievement of specified task goals will actually be followed by the first level outcome (expectancy II). In other words, they form subjective probability estimates of the degree to which rewards are *contingent* on achieving task goals. The individual must ask himself what the probability is that his achievement of the goal will be rewarded by the organization. For example, the manufacturing manager may be virtually certain (expectancy II = 1.0) that if he does get the new product into production by the first of the year, he will receive a promotion and a substantial salary increase. Or, and this may be the more usual case, he may see no relationship at all between meeting the objective and getting a promotion and salary increase.

None of the authors cited so far have explicitly labeled these two kinds of expectancies. Indeed, in a laboratory or other experimental setting the distinction may not be necessary since the task may be so easy that accomplishing the goal is always a certainty (*i.e.,* expectancy I is 1.0 for everybody) or the contingency of reward on behavior may be certain and easily verified by the subject (*i.e.,* expectancy II is 1.0 for everybody). Vroom[12] defines expectancy as an action-outcome relationship which is represented by an individual's subjective probability estimate that a particular set of behaviors will be followed by a particular outcome. Since Vroom presents no concrete definitions for the terms "action" and "outcome," his notion of expectancy could include both expectancy I and expectancy II as defined above. Thus effort expenditure could be regarded as an action, and goal performance as an outcome; or performance could be considered behavior, and money an outcome. Vroom uses both kinds of examples to illustrate the expectancy variable and makes no conceptual distinction between them. However, in the organizational setting, the distinction seems quite necessary. Rewards may or may not be contingent on goal accomplishment, and the individual may or may not believe he has

the wherewithal to reach the goal. A schematic representation of this hybrid is shown in Figure 10-1.

We have purposely been rather vague concerning the exact form of the relationships between these different classes of variables. This schematic model is no way meant to be formal theory. To propose explicit multiplicative combinations or other configural or higher order functions is going a bit too far beyond our present measurement capability. Rather, we shall sum up the relationships contained in our expanded model as follows:

1. The valence of a first level outcome (incentive or reward) is a function of the instrumentality of that outcome for obtaining second level outcomes (need satisfactions) and the valences of the relevant second level outcomes.

2. The decision by an individual to work on a particular task and expend a certain amount of effort in that direction is a function of (a) his personal probability estimate that he can accomplish the task (expectancy I), (b) his personal probability estimate that his accomplishment of the task goal will be followed by certain first level outcomes or rewards (expectancy II), and (c) the valence of the first level outcomes.

3. The distinction between external and internal goals and rewards leads to a number of potential conflict situations for the individual. For example, an individual might estimate his chances for accomplishing a particular task is virtually certain (*i.e.,* expectancy = 1.0). However, the internal rewards which are virtually certain to follow (*i.e.,* expectancy = 1.0) may have a very low or even negative valence (e.g., feelings of extreme boredom or distants). If external rewards, such as a lot of money, have a very high valence, a serious stress situation could result from outcomes which have conflicting valences. It would be to an organization's advantage to ensure positive valences for both internal and external rewards. Other conflict situations could be produced by high positive valences for outcomes and low estimates of type I expectancies (*i.e.,* the individual does not think he can actually do the job).

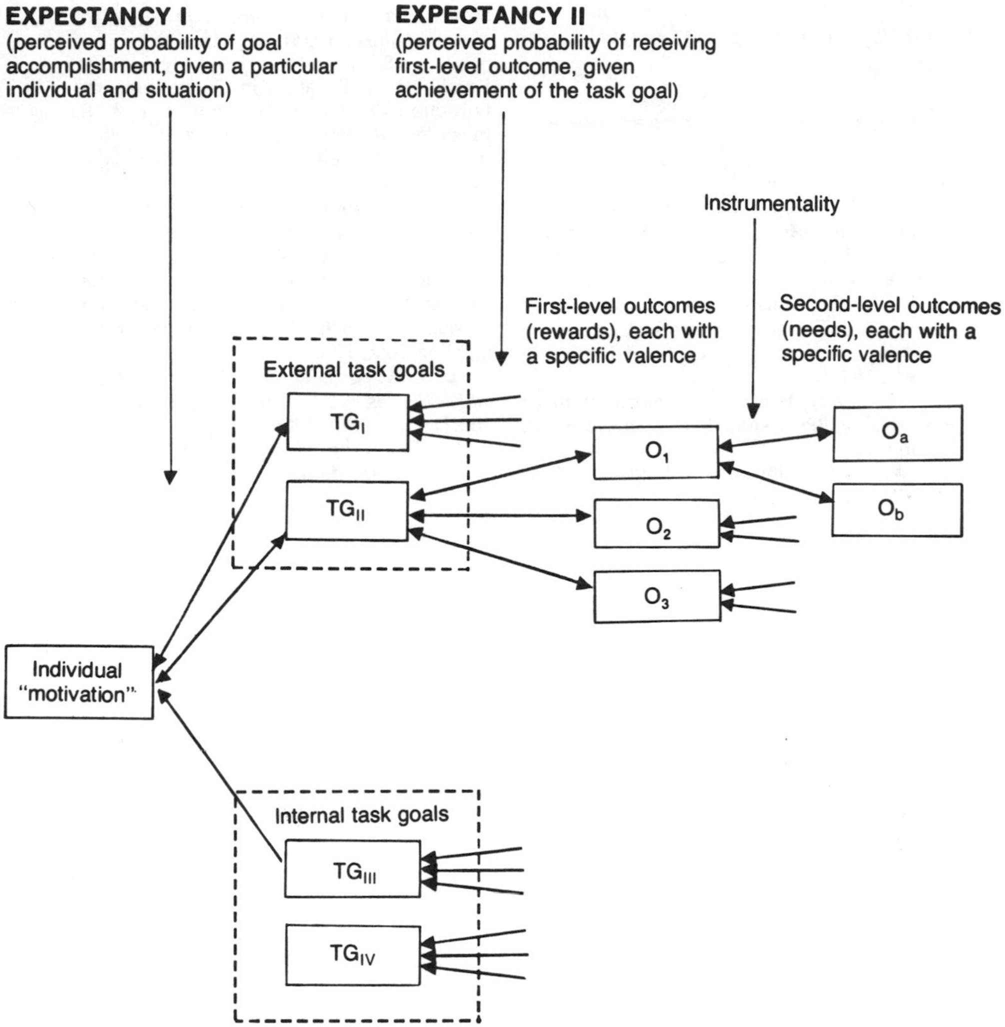

EXPECTANCY I
(perceived probability of goal accomplishment, given a particular individual and situation)

EXPECTANCY II
(perceived probability of receiving first-level outcome, given achievement of the task goal)

Instrumentality

First-level outcomes (rewards), each with a specific valence

Second-level outcomes (needs), each with a specific valence

External task goals

TG_I

TG_{II}

O_1

O_2

O_3

O_a

O_b

Individual "motivation"

Internal task goals

TG_{III}

TG_{IV}

Figure 10-1

SCHEMATIC REPRESENTATION OF HYBRID EXPECTANCY MODEL OF
WORK MOTIVATION OUTLINING DETERMINANTS OF DIRECTION,
AMPLITUDE, AND PERSISTENCE OF INDIVIDUAL EFFORT

Even though this kind of hybrid expectancy model seems to be a useful way of looking at organizational behavior and even though we have devoted more space to it, the reader should keep in mind that it is not the only process theory that one could use. Equity theory is its major competitor. . . .

NOTES

1. K. Lewin, The Conceptual Representation and the Measurement of Psychological Forces (Durham, N.C.: Duke University Press, 1938).

2. E. C. Tolman, Purposive Behavior in Animals and Men (New York: Century. By permission of the University of California Press, 1932).

3. J. W. Atkinson, An Introduction to Motivation (Princeton, N.J.: Van Nostrand, 1964).

4. J. W. Atkinson (ed.), Motives in Fantasy, Action and Society (Princeton, N.J.: Van Nostrand, 1958).

5. W. Edwards, "The Theory of Decision Making," Psychological Bulletin, Vol. 51 (1954), pp. 380-417.

6. H. Peak, "Attitude and Motivation," in M. R. Jones (ed.) Nebraska Symposium on Motivation (Lincoln, Nebr.: University of Nebraska Press, 1955), pp. 149-188.

7. J. B. Rotter, "The Role of the Psychological Situation in Determining the Direction of Human Behavior," in M. R. Jones (ed.) Nebraska Symposium on Motivation (Lincoln, Nebr.: University of Nebraksa Press, 1955).

8. V. H. Vroom, Work and Motivation (New York: Wiley, 1964).

9. G. B. Graen, Work Motivation: The Behavioral Effects of Job Content and Job Context Factors in an Employment Situation. Unpublished doctoral dissertation (University of Minnesota, 1967).

10. L. W. Porter and E. E. Lawler, Managerial Attitudes and Performance (Homewood, Ill.: Dorsey-Irwin, 1968).

11. Graen, op. cit.

12. Vroom, op. cit.

11. Existence, Relatedness and Growth Theory*

CLAYTON P. ALDERFER

The purpose of this chapter is to present E.R.G. theory and show how it is similar to and different from related viewpoints.

The theory deals primarily with two classes of variables—satisfactions and desires. It postulates three basic need categories which provide the basis for enumerating specific satisfactions and desires. It contains propositions which predict how satisfaction relates to desire, and it deals with the question of how chronic desires relate to satisfaction.

E.R.G. THEORY

BASIC CONCEPTS

The definition of terms such as "need," "drive," "instinct," and "motive" has been a point of controversy for some time among students of motivation. Some have actively advocated the abandonment of some or all of such terms. Others have avoided a firm position in the discussion. And still others have continued to struggle with the numerous conceptual problems associated with the terms. For the purposes of presenting E.R.G. theory, a number of distinctions should be made so that the scope and purpose of the theory can be clarified.

A common distinction used by those who are willing to utilize need-like concepts is that between primary and secondary motives. Primary needs refer to innate tendencies which an organism possesses by the nature of being the type of creature it is. Sometimes this distinction also includes the notion that primary needs are biologically or physiologically rooted. E.R.G. theory holds the view that existence, relatedness, and growth needs are primary needs in the sense of their being innate, but holds open the question of whether all three are biologically based. Secondary needs refer to acquired or learned tendencies to respond. E.R.G. needs can be increased in strength by learning processes but they do not come into being as a result of learning.

E.R.G. is *not* intended to be a theory to explain how people learn, make choices, or perform. It is a theory about the subjective states of satisfaction and desire. Campbell, Dunnette, Lawler, and Weick have made a useful distinction between two types of motivation theory. One type they term "mechanical" or "process" theories, while the other type is called "substantive" or "content" theories. The first type attempts to define major classes of variables that are important for explaining motivated behavior. The second type are more concerned with what it is within an individual or his environment that energizes and sustains behavior. E.R.G. theory is a content theory.

Although both satisfaction and desire are subjective states of a person, they differ in the degree of subjectivity. Satisfac-

*Source: From Clayton P. Alderfer, *Existence, Relatedness and Growth* (New York: The Free Press, 1972), pp. 6-21. Copyright © by The Free Press. Reprinted by permission. Adapted from Clayton P. Alderfer, "An Empirical Test of a New Theory of Human Needs," *Organizational Behavior and Human Performance*, Vol. 4 (1969), pp. 142-175. Copyright © 1969 by the Academic Press, Inc. References have been omitted.

tion concerns the outcome of an event between a person and his environment. It refers to the internal state of a person who has obtained what he was seeking and is synonymous with getting and fulfilling. Because satisfaction involves interaction with a person's environment, its assessment (for both the person and a researcher) hinges in part on the objective nature of a person's external world. Satisfaction depends both upon the way the world "actually" is and how this reality is perceived by the person.

Frustration is the opposite condition from satisfaction. For some operational purposes, one might wish to distinguish between satisfaction and frustration. If one produced an experimental manipulation which attempted to *increase* the gratification of subjects he would call this satisfaction, but if he attempted to *decrease* the gratification of subjects he would call this frustration. A similar point has been made by Rosenzweig, who made a distinction between primary and secondary frustration. In his view, "primary frustration involves the sheer existence of an active need. . . . Secondary frustration more strictly embraces the definition given above, emphasis being placed upon supervenient obstacles or obstructions in the path of the active need."

Compared to satisfaction, desire is even more subjective, for it does not have a necessary external referent. The term refers exclusively to an internal state of a person which may be synonymous with concepts, such as want, preference, need strength, need intensity, and motive. There is no necessary parallel external state for a desire as there is for a satisfaction. Consequently measurement of desires is more difficult. A person may have defenses which prohibit his own awareness of his desires. Even if he is aware of his desires, he may not choose to report them because he doubts if he would benefit from doing so. Fundamentally, a person is alone with his desires. He cannot rely on a shared consensus of

social reality to find out what he wants.

A further distinction may be made between *episodic* and *chronic* desires. *Episodic* desires tend to be situation specific, and they change in response to relevant changes in the situation. Statements about episodic changes in desires are intended to apply across people, without regard for individual differences. *Chronic* desires, on the other hand, reflect more or less enduring states of a person. They are seen as being a consequence both of episodic desires and of learning. To partial out the effects of chronic and episodic desires would require a study which, to some degree, was longitudinal.

According to this definitional system, the term "need" is a concept subsuming both desires and satisfactions (frustrations). For example, when a statement contains the words "existence needs," it includes both existence desires and existence satisfactions (frustrations). Depending on one's theory, there may be no reason to distinguish between the terms "desire," "satisfaction," and "need." If there were always a correspondence between lack of satisfaction (or frustration) and desire, one might abandon these terms and simply refer to "need" as the presence of a deficiency or excess which, if not altered, would impair the health of the organism.

In recent years, there has been an increasing tendency to make use of open-systems concepts for understanding the human personality. This approach offers the possibility of bridging the gap between those views of man which tend to view him primarily in reactive, tension-producing ways and those orientations which tend to focus on his proactive, stimulus-seeking qualities. Acting as a metatheory or broader framework, open-systems theory stands behind E.R.G. theory. All the major concepts and propositions of E.R.G. should be consistent with the logic of open-systems theory. In a loose sense, E.R.G. theory is derived from an open-systems view of man.

The primary categories of human needs follow from the criteria of personality as an open system outlined by Allport. Existence needs reflect a person's requirement for material and energy exchange and for the need to reach and maintain a homeostatic equilibrium with regard to the provision of certain material substances. Relatedness needs acknowledge that a person is not a self-contained unit but must engage in transactions with his human environment. Growth needs emerge from the tendency of open systems to increase in internal order and differentiation over time as a consequence of going beyond steady states and interacting with the environment.

Existence needs include all the various forms of material and physiological desires. Hunger and thirst represent deficiencies in existence needs. Pay, fringe benefits, and physical working conditions are other types of existence needs. One of the basic characteristics of existence needs is that they can be divided among people in such a way that one person's gain is another's loss when resources are limited. If two people are hungry, for example, the food eaten by one is not available to the other. When a salary decision is made that provides one person or group of people with more pay, it eliminates the possibility of some other person or group getting extra money. This property of existence needs frequently means that a person's (or group's) satisfaction, beyond a bare minimum, depends upon the comparison of what he gets with what others get in the same situation.

However, this comparison is not "interpersonal" in the sense of necessitating comparison with known significant others. The interpersonal aspect of equity is not an issue for existence needs. The comparison process for material goods is simply among piles of goods, without necessarily attaching the added dimension of knowing who the others are who would obtain smaller or larger shares. It turns out in our society that people have learned to state such comparisons in interpersonal terms. Consequently, in developing operational definitions, some existence-need comparisons were stated as interpersonal comparisons. However, this reflects a realistic limitation of the measures, stemming from certain aspects of our culture for which the theory, not being a learning theory, does not account.

Relatedness needs involve relationships with significant other people. Family members are usually significant others, as are superiors, coworkers, subordinates, friends, and enemies. One of the basic characteristics of relatedness needs is that their satisfaction depends on a process of sharing or mutuality. People are assumed to satisfy relatedness needs by mutually sharing their thoughts and feelings. Acceptance, confirmation, understanding, and influence are elements of the relatedness process. Significant others include groups as well as individuals. Any human unit can become a significant other for a person if he has sustained interaction with this person either by virtue of his own choice or because of the setting in which he is located. Families, work groups, friendship groups, and professional groups are examples of significant groups with which a person might have a relationship and therefore relatedness needs.

The theoretical roots of the relatedness concept are two-fold. One set of theorists have focussed primarily on what occurs between persons when they relate to each other. Out of this work has come Rogers' theory of interpersonal relationships and Argyris' concepts of authentic relationships and interpersonal competence. Complementary to the emphasis on what happens between the parties is the attention to what happens within each person. Freudian and neo-Freudian theorists such as Sullivan, Horney, and Klein have given particular attention to how significant others may be represented intrapsychically and what emotions these representations may carry.

This conception of relatedness needs

does not necessitate equal formal power between (or among) people for satisfaction to occur, although for some emotions, such as anger, power equalization tends to aid authentic expression. The essential conditions involve the willingness of both (or all) persons to share their thoughts and feelings as fully as possible while trying to enable the other(s) to do the same thing. Certainly not all interpersonal relationships are characterized by the mutual sharing and concern implied by this definition. However, I wish to suggest that this is the direction toward which relationships move when people wish to be meaningfully related to each other and when the relationship is not marred by defensiveness or lack of commitment by one or more of the parties.

Furthermore, the outcome of satisfying relatedness needs need not always be a positive affectual state for both or either person. The exchange or expression of anger and hostility is a very important part of meaningful interpersonal relationships, just as is the expression of warmth and closeness. Thus, the opposite of relatedness satisfaction is not necessarily anger, but it is a sense of distance or lack of connection.

A major difference between relatedness and existence needs arises under conditions of scarcity with respect to either satisfaction. For existence needs, a limited supply of material goods can result in one party being highly satisfied if, for example, he obtains all or nearly all of the scarce supply. However, for relatedness satisfaction a scarce supply is hypothesized to affect both parties in similar ways. That is to say, if a relationship is not working, both (or all) parties suffer. This is not to say that the parties suffer equally. The relationship may be more central for one of the parties than for the other. However, the degree of suffering or satisfaction among the parties always tends to be positively correlated for relatedness needs. For existence needs, however, the degree of suffering among parties tends to be inversely related when there is scarcity and

uncorrelated when there is no scarcity.

Growth needs impel a person to make creative or productive effects on himself and the environment. Satisfaction of growth needs comes from a person engaging problems which call upon him to utilize his capacities fully and may include requiring him to develop additional capacities. A person experiences a greater sense of wholeness and fullness as a human being by satisfying growth needs. Thus, satisfaction of growth needs depends on a person finding the opportunities to be what he is most fully and to become what he can. This concept owes much to the existential psychologists, such as Maslow, Allport, and Rogers; the ego-oriented psycho-analysts such as Fromm and White; and the laboratory psychologists concerned with a varied experience, curiosity, and activation.

Specific growth needs are defined in terms of environmental settings with which a person contends. Barker's work on the ecological environment offers a relatively precise definition of what is meant here by environmental settings.

> The ecological environment of a person's molar behavior, the molar environment, consists of bounded, physical-temporal locales and variegated but stable patterns in the behavior of people en masse.

Most people's lives contain several environmental settings in the form of organizational roles and leisure-time activities. Some of the settings studied in this research include jobs, college fraternity life, academic work, and extracurricular activities.

E.R.G. theory assumes that these broad categories of needs are active in all living persons. How strong each need is is one question the theory addresses. All people are alike in that they possess some degree of each need, but they differ in the strength of their needs. There is no postulate of strict prepotency as Maslow has offered, but there are propositions relating lower-level need satisfaction to higher-level desires.

Summary.—Each of the three basic needs in E.R.G. theory were defined in terms of a target toward which efforts at gratification were aimed and in terms of a process through which, and only through which, satisfaction could be obtained. For existence needs, the targets were material substances, and the process was simply getting enough. When the substances are scarce, the process quickly becomes "win-lose," and one person's gain is correlated with another's loss. For relatedness needs, the targets were significant others (persons or groups) and the process was mutual sharing of thoughts and feelings. For growth needs, the targets were environmental settings, and there were joint processes of a person becoming more differentiated and integrated as a human being.

PROPOSITIONS RELATING SATISFACTION TO DESIRE

Seven major propositions in the E.R.G. theory provide a basis from which empirically testable hypotheses relating satisfaction to desire can be logically derived. The form of this derivation is as follows. If *A* is an operational indicator of an E., an R., or a G. satisfaction and *B* is an operational indicator of an E., an R., or a G. desire, then *A* should show an empirically verifiable relationship to *B* in such a way as predicted by one of the E.R.G. propositions. If empirical results provide support for the *A* to *B* relationship, one would have more confidence in the theory. If the empirical results do not provide support for the *A* to *B* relationship, then one can have less confidence in the theory. The structure of this theory is such that the results can provide support for some propositions while not for others.

The major propositions in E.R.G. theory are as follows:

P1. The less existence needs are satisfied, the more they will be desired.

P2. The less relatedness needs are satisfied, the more existence needs will be desired.

P3. The more existence needs are satisfied, the more relatedness needs will be desired.

P4. The less relatedness needs are satisfied, the more they will be desired.

P5. The less growth needs are satisfied, the more relatedness needs will be desired.

P6. The more relatedness needs are satisfied, the more growth needs will be desired.

P7. The more growth needs are satisfied, the more they will be desired.

These propositions indicate that any desire can have several types of satisfaction (including some outside its particular category) affecting its strength. Any satisfaction also affects more than one type of desire (including some outside its particular category). This multiple determination property is shown in Figure 11-1 which gives a summary of the propositions in diagrammatic form.

An additional aspect of the theory, however, concerns providing explanatory concepts or mechanisms which lie behind the various propositions. These explanatory concepts are intended to help answer the "why" questions for the various propositions. As such, they add richness to the theoretical framework. They may be seen as analogous to axioms which provide a basis from which the main propositions can be derived.

Within need categories.—Proposition 1, which deals with the impact of the existence need satisfaction on existence desires, has an assumption of the *interchangeability* of various satisfiers of existence needs. Pay and fringe benefits are obvious examples where an organization actually makes choices about how to compensate its employees. The investigations of Nealey and others have been based on this assumption. Where the interchangeability assumption may not be as obvious is with such things as physical working conditions or physical demands of the job. However, most job-evaluation systems contain provisions where an employee is paid more because he has dirty, hazard-

Figure 11-1
SATISFACTION TO DESIRE PROPOSITIONS FROM E.R.G. THEORY*

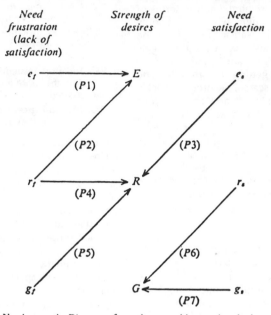

* Numbers on the Diagram refer to the proposition numbers in the text.

ous, or physically taxing duties in his job. Moreover, Jacques has formulated a view of payment based upon the time span of discretion. According to his view, there is a correspondence between equitable payment and discretion. He reported that there is evidence to support the view that the length of discretionary time span corresponds with the financial loss which would be caused by sub-standard discretion.

Dunnette and Lawler and Porter have argued that pay can stimulate and satisfy needs other than for material goods. Lawler and Porter showed correlations between managers' pay and their esteem and autonomy satisfaction. Reasoning from expectancy theory, Dunnette suggested that pay can be used as a reward for those who seek power, status, and achievement. His view was that pay could be instrumental for satisfying these other needs.

Some of the implications of these views conflict with E.R.G. theory while others do not. According to the E.R.G. definitional system, pay is an existence need; it is a material substance which can be scarce and thereby promote a win-lose orientation among people who do not have enough. Pay *per se* cannot satisfy relatedness or growth needs but could be part of a process which results in these needs being satisfied. Giving a person a raise, for example, might be a way of communicating a feeling of esteem for him. It might also be a tactic for "keeping him quiet." Additional pay might be a way for a person to obtain greater autonomy but only if he is able to use the money to create an environmental setting conducive to his being independent and self-directive. The discussion of $P2$ will deal further with this issue.

The structure of $P4$ is similar to that of $P1$ when it states that lack of satisfaction of relatedness needs leads to higher relatedness desires. The explanatory mechanism in this proposition is *transferability* of significant others. Persons who lack a basic scheme of connectedness and sharing in their emotional lives with significant others will seek to obtain that need satisfaction. If they are unable to obtain the satisfaction with the original person where the satisfaction is missing, they will tend to transfer the desire to others. Some of the earliest clues about the operation of this process are found in Freud's work on transference.

Expectant libidinal impulses will inevitably be roused, in anyone whose need for love is not being satisfactorily gratified in reality, by each new person coming upon the scene, and it is more than probable that both parts of the libido, the conscious and the unconscious, will participate in this attitude.

Proposition 7 is like *P1* and *P4* in that it implies that satisfaction of growth needs in one environmental setting affects a person's desires in other settings. But it is also different because the sign of the relationship between satisfaction and desire is positive rather than negative. The explanatory mechanism in this proposition is the notion of *expanding* environments. Persons who experience growth in one setting tend not only to seek more opportunities in that setting but also seek more settings in which to rise and develop their talents.

Downward and upward movement in the hierarchy.—The concepts of existence, relatedness, and growth needs were presented as separate and distinct categories. One of the ways in which the needs can be ordered, however, is on a continuum in terms of their concreteness. Existence needs are the most concrete. Their presence or absence is the easiest for the person to verify due to the fact that they can be reduced to material substances. Relatedness needs are less concrete than existence needs. Their presence

or absence depends on the state of a relationship between two or more people. To verify the state of relatedness needs depends on the consensual validation of the people involved in the relationship. Finally, growth needs are the least concrete. Ultimately, their specific objectives depend on the uniqueness of each person. At the most precise level, the state of a person's growth can be fully known only to him and only when he is not deluding himself. The continuum from more to less concreteness is also a continuum from more to less verifiability and from less to more potential uncertainty for the person.

Propositions 2 and 5 follow from the concept of *frustration-regression* which played such an important part in Lewinian field theory. Regression meant a more primitive, less mature way of behaving, not necessarily behavior that had been produced earlier in life. Frustration-regression is employed in E.R.G. theory to identify one motivational basis for explaining primitivity of some desires.

The sense in which *frustration-regression* is employed in E.R.G. theory concerns the tendency of persons to desire more concrete ends as a consequence of being unable to obtain more differentiated, less concrete ends. Thus, a person wants material substances when his relatedness needs are not satisfied because he is using them as a more concrete way of establishing his connectedness with other people. He wants relationships with significant others when his growth needs are not being met because he is using them for alternative sources of stimulation. In neither case will substitute gratification satisfy the original desire, but rationality is only part of the picture in understanding motivation.

It is in this sense that a person may use the size of his pay check as an indicator of the esteem in which he is held by his boss, colleagues, or organization. At the cultural level, Fromm has called this kind of phenomenon the "market orientation." From her work with psychiatric patients, Horney proposed that the neurotic quest for material possessions not only followed from anxiety about interpersonal relationships but also served as an indirect way of expressing hostility.

Propositions 3 and 6 follow from the concept of *satisfaction-progression* which played an important part in Maslow's original concept of the need hierarchy. In the case of E.R.G. theory, however, the movement up the hierarchy from relatedness satisfaction to growth desires does not presume satisfaction of existence needs. The assumption implied in the satisfaction-progression mechanism is that a person has more energy available for the more personal and less certain aspects of living if he has obtained gratification in the more concrete areas. Movement from existence satisfaction to relatedness desires is possible because a person fears others as competitors for scarce material goods less as he satisfies his existence needs. Satisfaction of relatedness needs provides a source of social support for persons seeking to develop and use their skills and talents. As his relatedness needs become satisfied, a person is freed to want to grow by a sense of greater authenticity in his relations with others.

PROPOSITIONS RELATING DESIRES TO SATISFACTION

Any theory that takes a position by stating that certain human characteristics (such as needs) apply to all people must also deal with the fact that people are different. Assuming that all persons have existence, relatedness, and growth needs is not the same as assuming that all people have these needs in the same degree. E.R.G. theory does not assume that all people have the same chronic strength of the various needs. However, the theory does assume that to *some* degree all people do have all three broad categories of needs.

The relationship between chronic desires and satisfaction in E.R.G. theory depends both on the particular need in question and on the nature of the material, interpersonal, and ecological conditions facing the person. The var-

ious needs and relevant conditions will be taken up according to need category. Each of the following propositions is based on the conceptual definitions of the needs, both the targets and the processes for obtaining need satisfaction.

Existence needs.—Satisfaction of existence needs depends on a person's getting enough of the various material substances that he wants. When there is scarcity (as is most often the case), a person with high needs will be able to obtain a lower proportion of his desires than a person with low needs. When there is no scarcity, then everyone can get what he wants, and there would be no difference in degree of satisfaction between those with different chronic existence needs. An example can be taken from the case of oxygen, an existence need that is normally but not always in very abundant supply. When there is no shortage of oxygen, then everyone can get all he needs. People rarely express much dissatisfaction under these conditions. However, when oxygen exists in limited supply, as is true in a submarine, then those people with higher needs, such as a person with a heart condition, would suffer more as the amount available diminished than those with lower needs. To summarize:

P8a. When existence materials are scarce, then the higher chronic existence desires are, the less existence satisfaction.

P8b. When existence materials are not scarce, then there will be no differential existence satisfaction as a function of chronic existence desires.

Relatedness needs.—Satisfaction of relatedness needs depends on people establishing relationships in which they can mutually share their relevant thoughts and feelings. Most people are to some degree responsive to the thoughts and feelings of others with whom they interact. Consequently, persons with varying needs almost always have the possibility of increasing the amount of mutual exchange that occurs by being more empathic and sharing more of themselves. At the same time, people differ in the degree of exchange that they want or can tolerate comfortably. These preferences set limits on the satisfaction they can obtain and also on the satisfaction others who interact with them can obtain.

In the optimally satisfying relationship, a person is able to share and be heard on all relevant matters to him. In a highly dissatisfying relationship, a person is able to share and be heard on a very small proportion of relevant issues. Persons who are very high on chronic relatedness needs may find it more difficult to achieve satisfaction under normal conditions because they may be perceived as overwhelming others with their thoughts and feelings, while persons very low on chronic relatedness needs may find it difficult to achieve satisfaction under normal conditions because they do not invest enough of themselves in the relationship for it to become very satisfying. In a very satisfying relationship, the degree of chronic relatedness needs may have no impact on satisfaction because a person is able to establish conditions which permit him to share and be heard as much as he wants, however much that is. In a very dissatisfying relationship, a person with very high relatedness needs may be able to get more satisfaction because he is more willing to invest himself, and even the most deteriorating relationship can benefit by the efforts of one party.

In order to state these ideas in propositional form, a distinction among the three kinds of interpersonal states is employed as a moderating variable between chronic relatedness desires and relatedness satisfaction. The terms "highly satisfying," "normal," and "highly dissatisfying" are loosely defined at this point, but they do provide a point from which to begin research.

P9a. In highly satisfying relationships, there is no differential relatedness satisfaction as a function of chronic relatedness desires.

P9b. In normal relationships, persons very high and very low on chronic relatedness desires tend to obtain lower satisfaction than persons with moderate desires.

P9c. In highly dissatisfying relationships, then, the higher chronic relatedness desires, the more relatedness satisfaction.

Growth needs.—Satisfaction of growth needs depends on a person's being able to find ways to utilize his capabilities and to develop new talents. Ecological environments vary in the degree to which they permit or encourage the use of a person's full capabilities. Some settings contain very little opportunity for discretion and offer little stimulation or challenge. A prototypic example of this kind of setting would be an assembly-line job. Other settings offer a high degree of stimulation and choice to persons. The job of a high level executive might be a case of this type of setting. Growth satisfaction depends on a person's taking a proactive stance toward his environment, but if the setting is unresponsive, it matters little if the person wants to produce effects because he cannot. Thus, the major mediating effect of the environment concerns whether the setting offers challenge and choice.

P10a. In challenging discretionary settings, then, the higher chronic growth desires, the more growth satisfaction.

P10b. In nonchallenging, nondiscretionary settings, there will be no differential growth satisfaction as a function of chronic growth desires.

Summary and implications.—By combining propositions 1 to 7 with 8 to 10, one obtains a set of answers to the questions of how need satisfaction relates to desire and how chronic desires relate to need satisfaction. According to this view, the relationship between satisfaction and desire is essentially instantaneous. As soon as a person is aware of whether his needs are being satisfied, his desires change according to the propositions outlined above. But the relationships between chronic desires and satisfaction are not instantaneous. Because of the mediating effects of external conditions, there is a time delay (of unknown degree at this time) between how quickly a person of given chronic desires obtains the possible satisfactions available to him.

The impact of combining propositions 1 and 8a is to define an existence-need deficiency cycle: Under scarcity, the less a person is satisfied the more he desires, and the more he desires the less he is satisfied. As a result a person could become fixated on material needs.

The impact of combining propositions 7 and 10a is to define a growth-need enrichment cycle: In challenging discretionary settings, the more a person is satisfied the more he desires, and the more he desires the more he is satisfied. As a result, a person who is already growth oriented is likely to become increasingly so.

Although relatedness satisfactions do not play a direct role in either of these cycles, they can play a supporting or suppressing part in both. If relatedness satisfaction decreases, then the existence desires tend to increase while growth desires tend to decrease, thereby supporting the growth enrichment cycle while suppressing the existence deficiency cycle.

III

Interpersonal and Group Behavior

Introduction. Ever since the Hawthorne experiments formally "discovered" the impact of social and psychological factors on work behavior, managers have been "on notice" that groups can have negative as well as positive consequences for the organizations in which they exist. For this reason there has been ever-increasing interest in the nature and implications of group behavior in organizations. The transition from individual to group behavior is aptly accomplished by this section's first selection, for it focuses on the conceptual midpoint—interpersonal behavior. "The Johari Window," which originally appeared as a chapter in Joseph Luft's book, *Group Processes: An Introduction to Group Dynamics,* describes four categories of interpersonal awareness. Quadrant 1 focuses on that which is "known to self" and "known to others" and is labeled as "Open." Quadrant 2, referred to as "Blind," relates to "not known to self" but "known to others." Quadrant 3, the "Hidden" category, deals with situations "known to self" but "not known to others." And quadrant 4, called "Unknown," refers to aspects of interpersonal relations that are "not known to self" and "not known to others." Luft points out how a change in one's awareness level impacts numerous aspects of intragroup and intergroup behavior.

It is generally accepted that Kurt Lewin "invented" the field of group dynamics—that is, he was responsible, either directly or indirectly, for most of the pioneering research on group dynamics. Two of Lewin's close associates, Dorwin Cartwright and Alvin Zander, went on to produce what was for many years the standard text on the subject, *Group Dynamics.* They defined "group dynamics" as the field of inquiry dedicated to advancing knowledge about the nature of groups, how they develop, and their relationships to individuals, other groups, and larger institutions. The first chapter of their text, "Origins of Group Dynamics," traces the evolution of the field of group dynamics and reviews several of the more significant pioneering research studies on group behavior.

Although the utilization of groups as decisionmaking entities in organizations has multiplied in recent decades—due primarily to the realization that groups that receive greater support within the organization often make better decisions—there are potential hazards in group decisionmaking. Norman R. F. Maier, in "Assets and Liabilities in Group Problem Solving: The Need for an Integrative Function," assesses both the assets (greater sum total of knowledge and information, greater number of approaches to a problem, participation in problem solving increases acceptance, better comprehension of the decision) and the liabilities (social pressure, can be swayed by vocal minority, individual domination, conflicting secondary goals) of group problem solving. Maier finds that several factors can serve as assets *or* liabilities and concludes by examining the role of the group leader in capitalizing on group assets and avoiding group liabilities.

"Groups and Intergroup Relationships," a selection from Edgar H. Schein's 1970 book, *Organizational Psychology,* focuses on the nature of groups in organizations. After defining a group as any number of people who interact with one another, are aware of one another, and perceive themselves to be a group, Schein examines the nature of formal and informal groups in organizations, as well as the functions fulfilled by organizational groups. A variety of factors that determine the kinds of groups that will exist in an organization are discussed, and the questions of whether these groups will fulfill organizational functions, personal functions, or both are analyzed.

While groupthink—the psychological drive for consensus at any cost that suppresses dissent and appraisal of alternatives in cohesive decisionmaking groups—has always been with us, the conceptualization of the phenomenon is credited to Irving L. Janis. In the preface to his 1972 book, *Victims of Groupthink,* Janis says the basic idea occurred to him while he was reading an account of the ill-fated Bay of Pigs Invasion of Cuba in a biography of President John F. Kennedy. Janis asked himself, "How could bright, shrewd men like John F. Kennedy and his advisors be taken in by the CIA's stupid patchwork plan?" In an article, "Groupthink," which was published one year before his book, Janis discusses the main symptoms of groupthink, using the Bay of Pigs Invasion, Vietnam, and Pearl Harbor as examples of the dire consequences that can occur when groupthink stalks the corridors of power. He concludes by citing a list of remedies drawn from two highly successful group decisionmaking examples—the formulation of the Marshall Plan during President Truman's Administration and the handling of the Cuban Missile Crisis by President Kennedy and his advisors. Given the current popularity of "cooperative," or "consensus," approaches to group decisionmaking, the chance that a group will deteriorate into "groupthink" is significant. Unlike the true "consensus" approach, however, groupthink suppresses conflict and independent critical thinking, which results in a deterioration of mental efficiency, reality testing, and moral judgment.

12. The Johari Window*

JOSEPH LUFT

When Luft and Ingham (1955) first presented the Johari Window to illustrate relationships in terms of awareness, they were surprised to find so many people, academicians and nonprofessionals alike, using and tinkering with the model. It seems to lend itself as a heuristic device to speculating about human relations. It is simple to visualize the four quadrants of the model:

Quadrant 1, the area of free activity, or open area, refers to behavior and motivation known to self and known to others.

Quadrant 2, the blind area, is where others can see things in ourselves of which we are unaware.

Quadrant 3, the avoided or hidden area, represents things we know but do not reveal to others (e.g., a hidden agenda or matters about which we have sensitive feelings).

Quadrant 4, the area of unknown activity, points to the area where neither the individual nor others are aware of certain behaviors or motives. Yet we can assume their existence because eventually some of these things become known, and we

Figure 12-1

THE JOHARI WINDOW

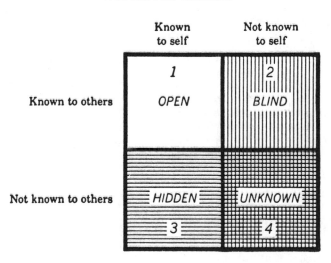

*Source: From Joseph Luft, *Group Processes: An Introduction to Group Dynamics,* 2nd Ed. (Palo Alto, Calif.: Mayfield Publishing Company, 1970), Chapter 3, "The Johari Window: A Graphic Model of Awareness in Interpersonal Relations," pp. 11-20. Copyright © 1963 Mayfield Publishing Company. Reprinted by permission. Footnotes omitted.

Figure 12-2

DEGREES OF OPENNESS

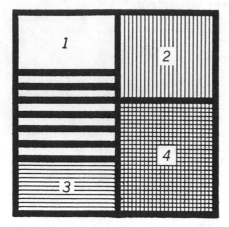

then realize that these unknown behaviors and motives were influencing relationships all along.

In a new group, Q1 is very small; there is not much free and spontaneous interaction. As the group grows and matures, Q1 expands in size, and this usually means we are freer to be more like ourselves and to perceive others as they really are. Quadrant 3 shrinks in area as Q1 grows larger. We find it less necessary to hide or deny things we know or feel. In an atmosphere of growing mutual trust, there is less need for hiding pertinent thoughts or feelings. It takes longer for Q2 to reduce in size because usually there are "good" reasons of a psychological nature to blind ourselves to certain things we feel or do. Quadrant 4 changes somewhat during a learning laboratory, but we can assume that such changes occur even more slowly than shifts in Q2. At any rate, Q4 is undoubtedly far larger and more influential in an individual's relationships than the hypothetical sketch illustrates. [Figure 12-4]

The Johari Window may be applied to *intergroup* relations. Quadrant 1 then means behavior and motivation known to the group and also known to other groups. Quadrant 2 signifies an area of behavior to which a group is blind, but other groups are aware of the behavior, e.g., cultism or prejudice. Quadrant 3, the hidden area, refers to things a group knows about itself, but which are kept from other groups. Quadrant 4, the unknown area, means a group is unaware of some aspects of its own behavior, and other groups are also unaware of this behavior. Later, as the group learns new things about itself, there is a shift from Q4 to one of the other quadrants.

PRINCIPLES OF CHANGE

1. A change in any one quadrant will affect all other quadrants.
2. It takes energy to hide, deny, or be blind to behavior which is involved in interaction.
3. Threat tends to decrease awareness; mutual trust tends to increase awareness.
4. Forced awareness (exposure) is undesirable and usually ineffective.
5. Interpersonal learning means a change has taken place so that Q1 is larger and one or more of the other quadrants has grown smaller.
6. Working with others is facilitated by a large enough area of free activity. An increased Q1 means more of the resources and skills in the membership can be applied to a task.
7. The smaller the first quadrant, the poorer the communication.
8. There is universal curiosity about the unknown area, but this is held in check by custom, social training, and diverse fears.
9. Sensitivity means appreciating the covert aspects of behavior, in quadrants 2, 3, and 4, and respecting the desire of others to keep them so.
10. Learning about group processes as they are being experienced helps to increase awareness (enlarge Q1) for the group as a whole as well as for individual members.
11. The value system of a group and its membership may be noted in the way *unknowns* in the life of the group are confronted.

Figure 12-3

INTERACTION BETWEEN TWO PERSONS

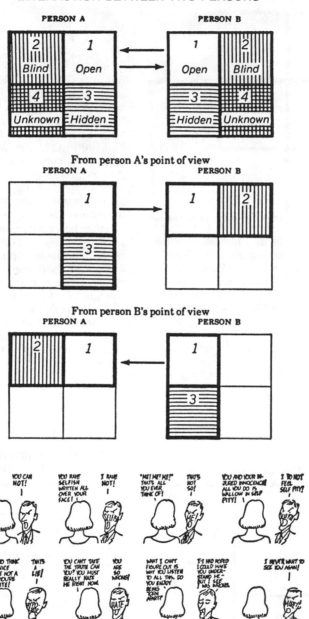

From person A's point of view

From person B's point of view

Figure 12-4

THE RELATIVE SIZE OF Q4

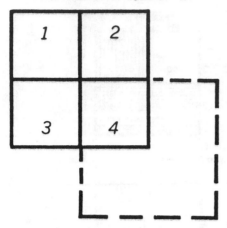

Having familiarized himself with this outline, a group member might learn to use it to help himself to a clearer understanding of the significant events in a group. Furthermore, the outline is sufficiently broad and loose so that it may have heuristic value in stimulating the identification and elaboration of problems in new ways. Several illustrations of different kinds of intergroup and intragroup behavior are given below.

THE OBJECTIVES OF A GROUP DYNAMICS LABORATORY

Using the model, we may illustrate one of the general objectives of the laboratory, namely, to increase the area of free activity (Q1) so that more of the relationships in the group are free and open. It follows, therefore, that the work of the laboratory is to increase the area of Q1 while reducing the area of quadrants 2, 3, and 4. The largest reduction in area would be in Q3, then in Q2, and the smallest reduction would be in Q4.

An enlarged area of free activity among the group members implies less threat or fear and greater probability that the skills and resources of group members can be brought to bear on the work of the group. The enlarged area suggests greater openness to information, opinions, and new ideas about each member as well as about specific group processes. Since the hidden or avoided area, Q3, is reduced, less energy is tied up in defending this area. Since more of one's needs are unbound, there is greater likelihood of satisfaction with the work and more involvement with what the group is doing.

Figure 12-5

LABORATORY OBJECTIVES

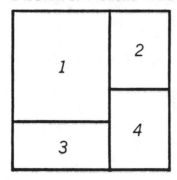

Figure 12-6

BEGINNING INTERACTION IN A NEW GROUP

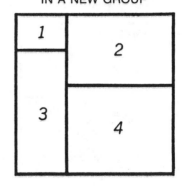

THE INITIAL PHASE OF GROUP INTERACTION

Applying the model to a typical meeting of most groups, we can recognize that interaction is relatively superficial, that anxiety or threat is fairly large, that interchange is stilted and unspontaneous. We also may note that ideas or suggestions are not followed through and are usually left undeveloped, that individuals seem to hear and see relatively little of what is really going on.

THE MODEL MAY DEPICT INTERGROUP PROCESSES AS WELL AS INTRAGROUP PROCESSES

The group may be treated as an entity or unit. Cattell, for instance, uses the term "syntality" to mean the quality of a group analogous to the personality of an individual. Lewin conceives of the group as an organized field of forces, a structured whole. In this model, a group may relate to other groups in a manner similar to the relationship between individuals. The first quadrant (Fig. 12-8) represents behavior and motivation of a group which is known to group members and also known to others. A college seminar, for instance, may share certain knowledge and behavior about itself with other classes on campus, such as requirements for the course, subject matter of the seminar, or the amount of work it sets out to do. However, many things occur in a seminar that are known to its members, but not known to outside groups (quadrant 3).

An illustration of an area of avoided behavior might be the students' feeling that their seminar is very special or quite superior to other classes. Or they might feel the course is a waste of time, but for some reason they do not share this attitude with outsiders. Or sometimes a special event occurs, and this is kept from outsiders.

Quadrant 2, the blind area, is characteristic of certain cults that are unaware of some aspects of their own behavior, though outsiders are able to discern the cultish qualities. Or the prejudices of a certain group may be perfectly apparent to outsiders but not to the group members themselves.

Quadrant 4 applies to attitudes and behavior that exist in the group but for some reason remain unknown to the group and to outsiders. An illustration of this might be an unresolved problem with regard to over-all goals of the group. If the group is covertly split and some members want to go off in

Figure 12-7

ONE WAY OF LOOKING AT A GROUP

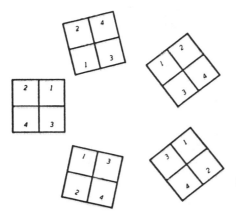

Figure 12-8

A GROUP AS A WHOLE

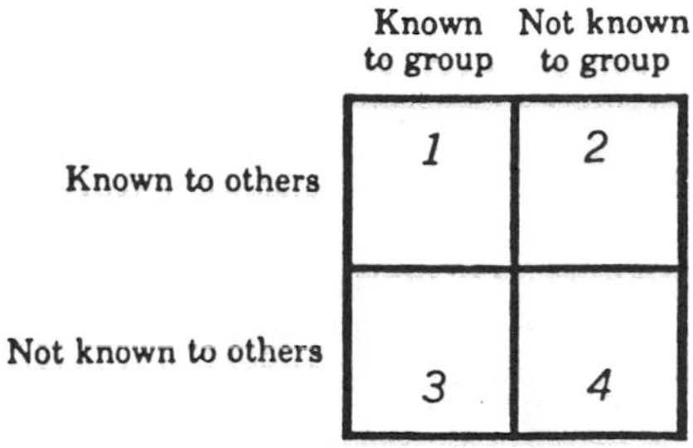

	Known to group	Not known to group
Known to others	1	2
Not known to others	3	4

Figure 12-9
INTERACTION BETWEEN TWO GROUPS

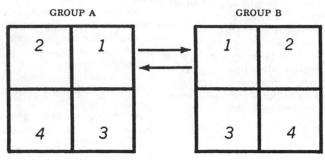

different directions—and if this fact has never been recognized or brought out in the open—then we could see the development of difficulties which remain unknown to the group members and unknown to the members of other groups. For example, in a large scientific enterprise, the physicists and engineers were having great difficulty with the machinists. Only after a long period of investigation did it become apparent that the question of status and privilege was producing bitter feelings between groups, yet the members of the various groups were unaware of the ramifications of this problem.

REPRESENTATIONS OF INTERACTION

Another way of representing a relationship is shown in Fig. 12-10, where all the information bearing on the relationship is contained in the matrix. Each person in the relationship has blind spots in areas open to the other person, and both are blind or lack awareness with respect

Figure 12-10

A MODEL OF PERSON-TO-PERSON INTERACTION: EMPLOYEE-SUPERVISOR

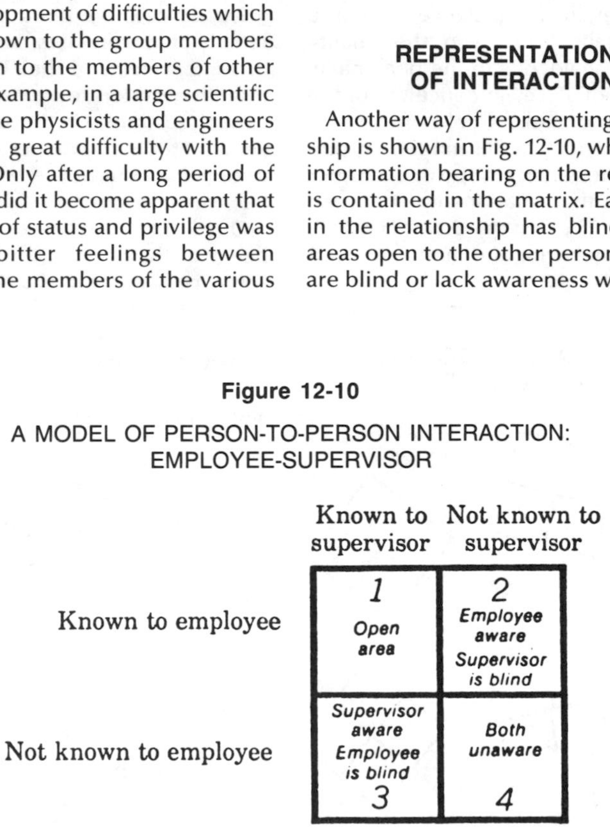

	Known to supervisor	Not known to supervisor
Known to employee	*1* *Open area*	*2* *Employee aware Supervisor is blind*
Not known to employee	*Supervisor aware Employee is blind* *3*	*Both unaware* *4*

to certain aspects of their relationship, as represented by quadrant 4. A critical factor in the relationship is the manner in which the unknowns are dealt with; recurring interaction patterns establish the style or quality of the interpersonal tie. Every relationship can be characterized by the constraint inherent in the relationship.

The persons represented are interdependent in Q1, and each is both independent and dependent in Q2 and Q3. Independence is defined here as awareness which is exclusive; the dependent one lacks awareness of an interpersonally relevant matter of which the other *is* aware. Withholding information or feelings which are interpersonally relevant is therefore a way of controlling or manipulating the other. Both persons are dependent where both are unaware, in Q4.

13. Origins of Group Dynamics*

DORWIN CARTWRIGHT

ALVIN ZANDER

If it were possible for the overworked hypothetical man from Mars to take a fresh view of the people of Earth, he would probably be impressed by the amount of time they spend doing things together in groups. He would note that most people cluster into relatively small groups, with the members residing together in the same dwelling, satisfying their basic biological needs within the group, depending upon the same source for economic support, rearing children, and mutually caring for the health of one another. He would observe that the education and socialization of children tend to occur in other, usually larger, groups in churches, schools, or other social institutions. He would see that much of the work of the world is carried out by people who perform their activities in close interdependence within relatively enduring associations. He would perhaps be saddened to find groups of men engaged in warfare, gaining courage and morale from pride in their unit and a knowledge that they can depend upon their buddies. He might be gladdened to see groups of people enjoying themselves in recreations and sports of various kinds. Finally he might be puzzled why so many people spend so much time in little groups talking, planning, and being "in conference." Surely he would conclude that if he wanted to understand much about what is happening on Earth he would have to examine rather carefully the ways in which groups form, function, and dissolve.

Now if we turn to a more customary perspective and view our society through the eyes of Earth's inhabitants, we discover that the functioning or malfunctioning of groups is recognized increasingly as one of society's major problems. In business, government, and the military, there is great interest in improving the productivity of groups. Many thoughtful people are alarmed by the apparent weakening and disintegration of the family. Educators are coming to believe that they cannot carry out their responsibilities fully unless they understand better how the classroom functions as a social group. Those concerned with social welfare are diligently seeking ways to reduce intergroup conflicts between labor and management. The operation of juvenile gangs is a most troublesome obstacle in attempts to prevent crime. It is becoming clear that much mental illness derives in some way from the individual's relations with groups and that groups may be used effectively in mental therapy.

Whether one wishes to understand or to improve human behavior, it is necessary to know a great deal about the nature of groups. Neither a coherent view of man nor an advanced social technology is possible without dependable answers to a host of questions concerning the operation of groups, how individuals relate to groups, and how groups relate to larger society. When, and under what conditions, do groups form? What conditions are necessary for their growth and effective functioning? What

*Source: From Dorwin Cartwright and Alvin Zander, Group Dynamics, 3rd Ed., pp. 3-21. Copyright © 1968 by Dorwin Cartwright and Alvin Zander. Reprinted by permission of Harper & Row, Publishers, Inc. References and footnotes combined and renumbered.

factors foster the decline and disintegration of groups? How do groups affect the behavior, thinking, motivation, and adjustment of individuals? What makes some groups have powerful influence over members while other groups exert little or none? What characteristics of individuals are important determinants of the properties of groups? What determines the nature of relations between groups? When groups are part of a larger social system, what circumstances make them strengthen or weaken the more inclusive organization? How does the social environment of a group affect its properties? Questions like these must be answered before we will have a real understanding of human nature and human behavior. They must be answered, too, before we can hope to design an optimal society and bring it into being.

The student of group dynamics is interested in acquiring knowledge about the nature of groups and especially about the psychological and social forces associated with groups. Such an interest has, of course, motivated intellectual activities of thoughtful people for centuries. The earliest recorded philosophical literature contains a great deal of wisdom about the nature of groups and the relations between individuals and groups. It also contains a variety of specifications concerning the "best" ways of managing group life. During the period from the sixteenth through the nineteenth centuries there was created in Europe an impressive literature dealing with the nature of man and his place in society. In this literature one can find most of the major orientations, or "basic assumptions," which guide current research and thinking about groups. It is evident that the modern student of group dynamics is not essentially different in his interests from scholars writing at various times over the centuries. And yet, it is equally clear that the approach to the study of groups known as "group dynamics" is strictly a twentieth-century development; it is significantly different from that of preceding centuries.

What, then, is group dynamics? The phrase has gained popular familiarity since World War II but, unfortunately, with its increasing circulation its meaning has become imprecise. According to one rather frequent usage, group dynamics refers to a sort of political ideology concerning the ways in which groups should be organized and managed. This ideology emphasizes the importance of democratic leadership, the participation of members in decisions, and the gains both to society and to individuals to be obtained through cooperative activities in groups. The critics of this view have sometimes caricatured it as making "togetherness" the supreme virtue, advocating that everything be done jointly in groups that have and need no leader because everyone participates fully and equally. A second popular usage of the term group dynamics has it refer to a set of techniques, such as role playing, buzz-sessions, observation and feedback of group process, and group decision, which have been employed widely during the past decade or two in training programs designed to improve skill in human relations and in the management of conferences and committees. These techniques have been identified most closely with the National Training Laboratories whose annual training programs at Bethel, Maine, have become widely known. According to the third usage of the term group dynamics, it refers to a field of inquiry dedicated to achieving knowledge about the nature of groups, the laws of their development, and their interrelations with individuals, other groups, and larger institutions.

It is not possible, of course, to legislate how terms are to be used in a language. Nevertheless, it is important for clarity of thinking and communication to distinguish among these three quite distinct things which have been given the same label in popular discussions. Everyone has an ideology, even though he may not be able to state it very explicitly, concerning the ways in which group life should be organized. Those responsible for the management of groups and the training of people for participation in groups can fulfill their responsibilities only by the use of techniques of one sort or another. But there is no rigidly fixed correspondence between a particular ideology about the "ideal" nature of groups and the use of particular techniques of management and training. And it should be obvious that the search for a better understanding of the nature of group life need not be linked to a particular ideology or adherence to certain techniques of management. In this book we shall limit our usage of the term group dynamics to refer to the field of inquiry dedicated to advancing knowledge about the nature of group life.

Group dynamics, in this sense, is a branch of knowledge or an intellectual specialization. Being concerned with human behavior and social relationships, it can be located within the social sciences. And yet it cannot be identified readily as a subpart of any of the traditional academic disciplines. In order to gain a better understanding of how group dynamics differs from other familiar fields, let us consider briefly some of its distinguishing characteristics. [*Initial sentences in following list not italic in original.*]

1. *Emphasis on theoretically significant empirical research.* We noted above that an interest in groups can be found throughout history and that such an interest cannot, therefore, distinguish group dynamics from its predecessors. The difference lies, rather, in the way this interest is exploited. Until the beginning of the present century those who were curious about the nature of groups relied primarily upon personal experience and historical records to provide answers to their questions. Not being burdened by the necessity of accounting for an accumulation of carefully gathered empirical data, writers in this speculative era devoted their energies to the creation of comprehensive theoretical treatments of groups. These theoretical systems, especially the ones produced during the nineteenth century, were elaborate and widely inclusive, having been created by men of outstanding intellectual ability. The list of names from this era contains such impressive thinkers as Cooley, Durkheim, Freud, Giddings, LeBon, McDougall, Ross, Tarde, Tönnies, and Wundt. Their ideas can still be seen in contemporary discussions of group life.

By the second decade of this century an empiricist rebellion had begun in social science, principally in the United States and especially in psychology and sociology. Instead of being content with speculation about the nature of groups, a few people began to seek out facts and to attempt to distinguish between objective data and subjective impression. Although rather simple empirical questions initally guided this research, a fundamentally new criterion for evaluating knowledge about groups was established. Instead of asking merely whether some proposition about the nature of groups is plausible and logically consistent, those interested in groups began to demand that the proposition be supported by reliable data that can be reproduced by an independent investigator. Major effort went into the devising and improving of techniques of empirical research that would provide reliability of measurement, standardization of observation, effective experimental design, and the statistical analysis of data. When, in the late 1930s, group dynamics began to emerge as an identifiable field the empiricist rebellion was well along in social psychology and sociology, and from the outset group dynamics could employ the research methods characteristic of an empirical science. In fact, group dynamics is to be distinguished from its intellectual predecessors primarily by its basic reliance on careful observation, quantification, measurement, and experimentation.

But one should not identify group dynamics too closely with extreme empiricism. Even in its earliest days, work in group dynamics displayed an interest in the construction of theory and the derivation of testable hypotheses from theory, and it has come progressively to maintain a close interplay between data collection and the advancement of theory.

2. *Interest in dynamics and interdependence of phenomena.* Although the phrase group dynamics specifies groups as the object of study, it also focuses attention more sharply on questions about the dynamics of group life. The student of group dynamics is not satisfied with just a description of the properties of groups or of events associated with groups. Nor is he content with a classification of types of groups or of forms of group behavior. He wants to know how the phenomena he observes depend on one another and what new phenomena might result from the creation of conditions never before observed. In short, he seeks to discover general principles concerning what conditions produce what effects.

This search requires the asking of many detailed questions about the interdependence among specific phenomena. If a change of membership occurs in a group, which other features of the group will change and which will remain stable? Under what conditions does a group tend to undergo a change of leadership? What are the pressures in a group which bring about uniformity of thinking among its members? What conditions inhibit creativity among group members? What changes in a group will heighten productivity, lower it, or not affect it at all? If the cohesiveness of a group is raised, which other of its features will change? Answers to

questions like these reveal how certain properties and processes depend on others.

Theories of group dynamics attempt to formulate lawful relations among phenomena such as these. As these theories have been elaborated, they have guided work in group dynamics toward the intensive investigation of such things as change, resistance to change, social pressures, influence, coercion, power, cohesion, attraction, rejection, interdependence, equilibrium, and instability. Terms like these, by suggesting the operation of psychological and social forces, refer to the dynamic aspects of groups and play an important role in theories of group dynamics.

3. *Interdisciplinary relevance.* It is important to recognize that research on the dynamics of groups has not been associated exclusively with any one of the social science disciplines. Sociologists have, of course, devoted great energy to the study of groups, as illustrated by investigations of the family, gangs, work groups, military units, and voluntary associations. Psychologists have directed their attention to many of the same kinds of groups, concentrating for the most part on the ways groups influence the behavior, attitudes, and personalities of individuals and the effects of characteristics of individuals on group functioning. Cultural anthropologists, while investigating many of the same topics as sociologists and psychologists, have contributed data on groups living under conditions quite different from those of modern industrial society. Political scientists have extended their traditional interest in large institutions to include studies of the functioning of legislative groups, pressure groups, and the effects of group membership on voting. And economists have come increasingly to collect data on the way decisions to spend or save money are made in the family, how family needs and relationships affect the size of the labor force,

how goals of unions affect policies in business, and how decisions having economic consequences are reached in businesses of various kinds. Since an interest in groups is shared by the various social science disciplines, it is clear that any general knowledge about the dynamics of groups has significance widely throughout the social sciences.

4. *Potential applicability of findings to social practice.* Everyone who feels a responsibility for improving the functioning of groups and the quality of their consequences for individuals and society must base his actions upon some more or less explicit view of the effects that will be produced by different conditions and procedures. Anyone who is concerned with improving the quality of work in a research team, the effectiveness of a Sunday school class, the morale of a military unit, with decreasing the destructive consequences of intergroup conflict, or with attaining any socially desirable objective through groups, can make his efforts more effective by basing them on a firm knowledge of the laws governing group life.

The various professions that specialize in dealing with particular needs of individuals and of society have much to gain from advances in the scientific study of groups. One outstanding development in the more advanced societies during the past century has been the increasing differentiation undergone by the traditional professions of medicine, law, education, and theology. Today there are people who receive extensive training and devote their lives to such professional specialties as labor-management mediation, public health education, marriage counseling, human relations training, intergroup relations, social group work, pastoral counseling, hospital administration, adult education, public administration, psychiatry, and clinical psychology— just to mention a few. The professionalization of practice in these many areas has brought about a self-conscious desire to improve standards and the establishment of requirements for proper training. The major universities now have professional schools in many of these fields to provide such training. As this training has been extended and rationalized, members of these professions have become increasingly aware of the need for knowledge of the basic findings and principles produced in the social sciences. All of these professions must work with people, not simply as individuals but in groups and through social institutions. It should not be surprising, therefore, to find that courses in group dynamics are becoming more and more common in the professional schools, that people trained in group dynamics are being employed by agencies concerned with professional practice, and that group dynamics research is often carried out in connection with the work of such agencies.

In summary, then, we have proposed that group dynamics should be defined as a field of inquiry dedicated to advancing knowledge about the nature of groups, the laws of their development, and their interrelations with individuals, other groups, and larger institutions. It may be identified by four distinguishing characteristics (a) an emphasis on theoretically significant empirical research, (b) an interest in dynamics and the interdependence among phenomena, (c) a broad relevance to all the social sciences, and (d) the potential applicability of its findings in efforts to improve the functioning of groups and their consequences on individuals and society. Thus conceived, group dynamics need not be associated with any particular ideology concerning the ways in which groups should be organized and managed nor with the use of any particular techniques of group management. In fact, it is a basic objective of group dynamics to provide a better scientific basis for ideology and practice.

CONDITIONS FOSTERING THE RISE OF GROUP DYNAMICS

Group dynamics began, as an identifiable field of inquiry, in the United States toward the end of the 1930s. Its origination as a distinct specialty is associated primarily with Kurt Lewin (1890-1947) who popularized the term group dynamics, made significant contributions to both research and theory in group dynamics, and in 1945 established the first organization devoted explicitly to research on group dynamics. Lewin's contribution was of great importance, but, as we shall see in detail, group dynamics was not the creation of just one person. It was, in fact, the result of many developments that occurred over a period of several years and in several different disciplines and professions. Viewed in historical perspective, group dynamics can be seen as the convergence of certain trends within the social sciences and, more broadly, as the product of the particular society in which it arose.

The time and place of the rise of group dynamics were, of course, not accidental. American society in the 1930s provided the kind of conditions required for the emergence of such an intellectual movement. And, over the years since that time, only certain countries have afforded a favorable environment for its growth. To date, group dynamics has taken root primarily in the United States and the countries of northwestern Europe, although there have also been important developments in Israel, Japan, and India. Three major conditions seem to have been required for its rise and subsequent growth.

A SUPPORTIVE SOCIETY

If any field of inquiry is to prosper, it must exist in a surrounding society which is sufficiently supportive to provide the institutional resources required. By the end of the 1930s cultural and economic conditions in the United States were favorable for the emergence and growth of group dynamics. Great value was placed on science, technology, rational problem-solving, and progress. There was a fundamental conviction that in a democracy human nature and society can be deliberately improved by education, religion, legislation, and hard work. American industry had grown so rapidly, it was believed, not only because of abundant natural resources but especially because it had acquired technological and administrative "know how." The heros of American progress were inventors, like Bell, Edison, Franklin, Fulton, and Whitney, and industrialists who fashioned new social organizations for efficient mass production. Although there had grown up a myth about the inventor as a lone wolf working in his own tool shed, research was already becoming a large-scale operation—just how big may be seen in the fact that private and public expenditures for research in the United States in 1930 amounted to more than $160,000,000 and increased, even during the depression years, to nearly $350,000,000 by 1940.

Most of this research was, of course, in the natural and biological sciences and in engineering and medicine. The idea that research could be directed profitably to the solution of social problems gained acceptance much more slowly. But even in the 1930s significant resources were being allotted to the social sciences. The dramatic use of intelligence testing during World War I had stimulated research on human abilities and the application of testing procedures in school systems, industry, and government. "Scientific management," though slow to recognize the importance of social factors, was laying the groundwork for a scientific approach to the management of organizations. The belief that the solution of "social problems" could be facilitated by systematic fact-finding was gaining acceptance.

Thomas and Znaniecki had, by 1920, demonstrated that the difficulties accompanying the absorption of immigrants into American society could be investigated systematically;[1] several research centers had been created to advance knowledge and to improve practice with respect to the welfare of children; by the early 1930s practices in social work and juvenile courts were being modified on the basis of findings from an impressive series of studies on juvenile gangs in Chicago that had been conducted by Thrasher[2] and Shaw;[3] and, enough research had been completed on intergroup relations by 1939 so that Myrdal could write a comprehensive treatment of the "Negro problem" in America.[4] Symptomatic of the belief in the feasibility of empirical research on social problems was the establishment in 1936 of the Society for the Psychological Study of Social Issues with 333 charter members. Thus, when the rapid expansion of group dynamics began after World War II, there were important segments of American society prepared to provide financial support for such research. Support came not only from academic institutions and foundations but also from business, the federal government, and various organizations concerned with improving human relations.

DEVELOPED PROFESSIONS

The attempt to formulate a coherent view of the nature of group life may be motivated by intellectual curiosity or by the desire to improve social practice. A study of the conditions bringing the field of group dynamics into existence reveals that both of these motivations played an important role. Interest in groups and a recognition of their importance in society were apparent early among social scientists, who according to a common stereotype are motivated by idle curiosity. But it should be also noted that some of the most influential early systematic writing about the nature of groups came from the pens of

people working in the professions, people whose motivation has often been said to be purely practical. Before considering the social scientific background of group dynamics, we will describe briefly some of the developments within the professions that facilitated its rise.

By the 1930s a large number of distinct professions had come into existence in the United States, probably more than in any other country. Many of these worked directly with groups of people, and as they became concerned with improving the quality of their practice they undertook to codify procedures and to discover general principles for dealing with groups. It gradually became evident, more quickly in some professions than in others, that generalizations from experience can go only so far and that systematic research is required to produce a deeper understanding of group life. Thus, when group dynamics began to emerge as a distinct field, the leaders of some of the professions were well prepared to foster the idea that systematic research on group life could make a significant contribution to their professions. As a result, several professions helped to create a favorable atmosphere for the financing of group dynamics research, provided from their accumulated experience a broad systematic conception of group functioning from which hypotheses for research could be drawn, afforded facilities in which research could be conducted, and furnished the beginnings of a technology for creating and manipulating variables in experimentation on groups. Four professions played an especially important part in the origin and growth of group dynamics.

● *Social Group Work.* This profession should be mentioned first because it was one of the earliest to recognize explicitly that groups can be managed so as to bring about desired changes in members. Being responsible for the operation of clubs, recreational groups, camps and athletic teams, group workers came to realize that their techniques of dealing with groups had important effects on group processes and on the behaviors, attitudes, and personalities of those participating in these groups. Although the objective of group work included such diverse purposes as "character building," "providing constructive recreation," "keeping the kids off the street and out of trouble," and, later, "psychotherapy," it gradually became evident that, whatever the objective, some techniques of group management were more successful than others. One of the earliest experimental studies of groups concerned the effects of several leadership practices on the adjustment of boys in their summer camp cabins.[5] The wealth of experience acquired by group workers has been systemized by Busch,[6] Coyle,[7] and Wilson and Ryland.[8] Group dynamics drew heavily on this experience at the outset, and group dynamicists have continued to collaborate with group workers on various research projects.

• *Group Psychotherapy.* Although group psychotherapy is commonly considered a branch of psychiatry, the use of groups for psychotherapeutic purposes has grown up in other than strictly medical settings, the Alcoholics Anonymous movement being one outstanding example. In the development of a professional approach to psychotherapeutic work with groups, psychoanalytic theory has exerted the major, though not exclusive, influence. Freud's writing (especially his *Group Psychology and the Analysis of the Ego*) has set the tone, but many of the techniques for dealing with groups and much of the emphasis upon group processes have been contributed by people drawing from the field of group work—see, for example, the writings of Redl,[9] Scheidlinger,[10] and Slavson.[11] A rather different tradition, although strongly psychoanalytic in its orientation, has grown up in England under the influence of Bion[12] and a group of people associated with the Tavistock

Institute of Human Relations.[13] An important feature of this approach is the application of psychoanalytic group work to "natural" groups in the military establishment, industry, and the community. Still another approach in group psychotherapy was established by the unusually creative and pioneering work of Moreno.[14] His techniques of role-playing (more precisely, psychodrama and sociodrama) and sociometry were among the earliest contributions to the field and have been of great value both in group psychotherapy and in research on group dynamics. Although many of the developments in group psychotherapy and in group dynamics have been simultaneous, the early work in group psychotherapy had a clear and distinct influence on the initial work in group dynamics. And the two lines of endeavor have continued to influence each other, as can be seen, for example, in the systematic treatment of group psychotherapy by Bach.[15]

• *Education.* The revolution in American public education that occurred in the first quarter of this century, influenced strongly by the writings of Dewey, broadened the conception of both the purposes and the procedures of education. The goal of education in the public schools became the preparation of children for life in society rather than merely the transmission of knowledge. "Learning by doing" became a popular slogan and was implemented by such things as group projects, extracurricular activities, and student government. Teachers became interested in installing skills of leadership, cooperation, responsible membership, and human relations. It gradually became apparent that teachers, like group workers, were having to take actions affecting the course of events in children's groups and needed principles to guide these events toward constructive ends. A similar trend was developing simultaneously in adult education, where the problems were made even more apparent by the voluntary nature of participation in adult-education programs. There began to emerge the conception of the teacher as a group leader who affects his students' learning not merely by his subject-matter competence but also by his ability to heighten motivation, stimulate participation, and generate morale. Although controversy over this general approach to education has persisted up to the present time, the education profession had, by the late 1930s, accumulated a considerable fund of knowledge about group life. Group dynamics drew upon this experience in formulating hypotheses for research, and group dynamicsists established close working relations with educators and schools of education. Both educational practice and research in group dynamics have benefited from this association.

• *Administration.* Under this label is a whole cluster of specialties, all concerned with the management of large organizations. Included are such specific professions as business administration, public administration, hospital administration, and educational administration. Although each of these must develop expertise in its particular sphere of operation, all share the necessity of designing effective procedures for coordinating the behavior of people. For this reason, they share a common interest in the findings of social science. It might be expected, therefore, that systematic treatments of management would early come to a recognition of the importance of groups in large enterprises and that management practices for dealing with groups would become highly developed. Actually, the historical facts are rather different. Until the 1930s efforts to develop principles of management were remarkably blind to the existence of groups. One noteworthy exception is found in the writings of Mary P. Follett,[16] who after World War I attempted to construct a systematic approach to administration, and more generally to government, in which groups were recognized as important

elements. Her ideas, however, gained little acceptance.

In fact, the individualistic orientation held sway until about 1933 when the first of several books by Mayo and his associates[17] made its appearance. These publications reported an extensive program of research begun in 1927 at the Hawthorne plant of the Western Electric Company. The initial objective of this research was to study the relation between conditions of work and the incidence of fatigue among workers. A variety of experimental variations was introduced—frequency of rest pauses, length of working hours, nature of wage incentives—with the intention of discovering their influence on fatigue and productivity. It is to the great credit of these investigators that they were alert to the existence of effects not anticipated, for the important changes actually produced by their experiments turned out to be in interpersonal relations among workers and between workers and management. The results of this program of research led Mayo and his associates to place major emphasis on the social organization of the work group, on the social relations between the supervisor and his subordinates, on informal standards governing the behavior of members of the work group, and on the attitudes and motives of workers existing in a group context.

The impact of this research upon all branches of administration can hardly be exaggerated. Haire has described it in the following way:

After the publication of these researches, thinking about industrial problems was radically and irrevocably changed. It was no longer possible to see a decrement in productivity simply as a function of changes in illumination, physical fatigue, and the like. It was no longer possible to look for explanation of turnover simply in terms of an economic man maximizing dollar income. The role of the leader began to shift from one who directed work to one who enlisted co-operation. The incentive to work was no longer seen as simple and unitary but rather infinitely varied, complex, and changing. The new view opened the way for, and demanded, more research and new conceptualizations to handle the problems.[18]

Another important contribution to this new view of management was the systematic theory of management published in 1938 by Barnard,[19] which was the product of his many years of experience as a business executive. Although this book did not put primary stress on groups as such, it placed human needs and social processes in the forefront of consideration. Barnard made it clear that management practice can be satisfactorily understood and effectively fashioned only if large organizations are conceived as social institutions composed of people in social interrelations.

The emergence of group dynamics in the late 1930s came, then, at the very time when administrators and organization theorists were beginning to emphasize the importance of groups and of "human relations" in administration. In subsequent years the findings from research in group dynamics have been incorporated increasingly into systematic treatments of administration and a growing number of administrators have supported group dynamics research in various ways.

Before leaving the discussion of the role of the professions in the origin and growth of group dynamics, we should note that the developments reported here had counterparts to varying degrees in other areas of social practice, many of which were not highly professionalized. Special mention should be made of the support that has come from those concerned with providing a scientific basis for work in intergroup relations, public health, the military, religious education, community organization, and speech.[20]

DEVELOPED SOCIAL SCIENCE

In considering the conditions that stimulated the present approach to group dynamics within the social sciences, it is essential to recognize that this approach could originate only because certain advances had been accomplished in the social sciences at large. Thus, the rise of group dynamics required not only a supportive society and developed professions but also developed social sciences.

A basic premise of group dynamics is that the methods of science can be employed in the study of groups. This assumption could be entertained seriously only after the more general belief had gained acceptance that man, his behavior, and his social relations can be properly subjected to scientific investigation. And, any question about the utilization of scientific methods for learning about human behavior and social relations could not rise, of course, before the methods of science were well developed. It was only in the nineteenth century that serious discussions of this possibility occurred. Comte's extensive treatment of positivism in 1830 provided a major advance in the self-conscious examination of basic assumptions about the possibility of subjecting human and social phenomena to scientific investigation; and the controversies over evolutionary theories of man in the last half of the century resulted in a drastically new view of the possibility of extending the scientific enterprise to human behavior. Not until the last decades of the nineteenth century were there many people actually observing, measuring, or conducting experiments on human behavior. The first psychological laboratory was established only in 1879.

One can hardly imagine how group dynamics could have come into existence before the belief had taken root that empirical research can be conducted on groups of people, that important social phenomena can be measured, that group variables can be manipulated for experimental purposes, and that laws governing group life can be discovered. These beliefs gained acceptance only in recent years, though they had been advocated now and then by writers since the seventeenth century, and they are not universally held even today. There remain those who assert that human behavior does not operate according to laws, that important social phenomena cannot be quantified, and that experimentation on groups is impossible or immoral, or even both. William H. Whyte, Jr., in his attack on "the organization man," has spoken most eloquently for those who remain skeptical about the applicability of the methods of science to the study of man.[21] He defines *scientism* as "the promise that with the same techniques that have worked in the physical sciences we can eventually create an exact science of man." He identifies scientism as a major component of the Social Ethic which, in his opinion, is weakening American society. And, the tragedy of scientism, he maintains, is that it is based on an illusion, for "a 'science of man' cannot work in the way its believers think it can." Were such views to prevail, group dynamics could not thrive.

• *The Reality of Groups.* An important part of the early progress in social science consisted in clarifying certain basic assumptions about the reality of social phenomena. The first extensions of the scientific method of human behavior occurred in close proximity to biology. Techniques of experimentation and measurement were first applied to investigations of the responses of organisms to stimulation of the sense organs and to modification of responses due to repeated stimulation. There was never much doubt about the "existence" of individual organisms, but when attention turned to groups of people and to social institutions, a great confusion arose. Discussion of these matters invoked terms like "group mind," "collective representations," "collective unconscious," and "culture." And people

argued heatedly as to whether such terms refer to any real phenomena or whether they are mere "abstractions" or "analogies." On the whole, the disciplines concerned with institutions (anthropology, economics, political science, and sociology) have freely attributed concrete reality to supra-individual entities, whereas psychology, with its interest in the physiological bases of behavior, has been reluctant to admit existence to anything other than the behavior of organisms. But in all these disciplines there have been conflicts between "institutionalists" and "behavioral scientists."

The sharpest cleavage occurred in the early days of social psychology, naturally enough since it is a discipline concerned directly with the relations between the individual and society. Here the great debate over the "group mind" reached its climax in the 1920s. Although many people took part, the names of William McDougall and Floyd Allport are most closely associated with this controversy. At one extreme was the position that groups, institutions, and culture have reality quite apart from the particular individuals who participate in them. It was maintained that a group may continue to exist even after there has been a complete turnover of membership, that it has properties, such as a division of labor, a system of values, and a role structure, that cannot be conceived as properties of individuals, and that laws governing these group-level properties must be stated at the group level. A slogan reflecting this approach is the statement, attributed to Durkheim, that "every time a social phenomenon is directly explained by a psychological phenomenon, we may be sure that the explanation is false." In strong reaction to all this was the view, advanced most effectively by Allport, that only individuals are real and that groups or institutions are "sets of ideals, thoughts, and habits repeated in each individual mind and existing only in those minds."[22] Groups, then, are abstractions from collections of individual organisms. "Group mind" refers to nothing but similarities among individual minds, and individuals cannot be parts of groups, for groups exist only in the minds of men.

It may appear strange that social scientists should get involved in philosophical considerations about the nature of reality. As a matter of fact, however, the social scientist's view of reality makes a great deal of difference to his scientific behavior. In the first place, it determines what things he is prepared to subject to empirical investigation. Lewin pointed out this fact succinctly in the following statement:

Labeling something as "nonexistent" is equivalent to declaring it "out of bounds" for the scientist. Attributing "existence" to an item automatically makes it a duty of the scientist to consider this item as an object of research; it includes the necessity of considering its properties as "facts" which cannot be neglected in the total system of theories; finally, it implies that the terms with which one refers to the item are acceptable as scientific "concepts" (rather than as "mere words").[23]

Secondly, the history of science shows a close interaction between the techniques of research which at any time are available and the prevailing assumptions about reality. Insistence on the existence of phenomena that cannot at that time be objectively observed, measured, or experimentally manipulated accomplishes little scientific value if it does not lead to the invention of appropriate techniques of empirical research. As a practical matter, the scientist is justified in excluding from consideration allegedly real entities whose empirical investigation appears impossible. And yet, as soon as a new technique makes it possible to treat empirically some new entity, this entity immediately acquires "reality" for the scientist. As Lewin noted, "The taboo against believing in the existence of a social entity is probably most effectively broken by handling this entity experimentally."[24]

The history of the "group mind" controversy well illustrates these points. The early insistence on the reality of the "group mind," before techniques for investigating such phenomena were developed, contributed little to their scientific study. Allport's denial of the reality of the group actually had a strongly liberating influence on social psychologists, for he was saying, in effect, "Let us not be immobilized by insisting on the reality of things which we cannot now deal with by means of existing techniques of research." He, and like-minded psychologists, were then able to embark upon a remarkably fruitful program of research on the attitudes of individuals toward institutions and on the behavior of individuals in social settings. Although this view of reality was too limited to encourage the empirical study of properties of groups, it did stimulate the development of research techniques that subsequently made a broader view of reality scientifically feasible. Until these techniques were in existence those who persisted in attributing reality to groups and institutions were forced to rely on purely descriptive studies or armchair speculation from personal experience, and such work was legitimately criticized as being "subjective" since the objective techniques of science were rarely applied to such phenomena.

● *Development of Techniques of Research.* Of extreme importance for the origin of group dynamics, then, was the shaping of research techniques that could be extended to research on groups. This process, of course, took time. It began in the last half of the nineteenth century with the rise of experimental psychology. Over the subsequent years more and more aspects of human experience and behavior were subjected to techniques of measurement and experimentation. Thus, for example, during the first third of this century impressive gains were made in the measurement of attitudes. Noteworthy among these were the scale of "social distance" developed by Bogardus,[25] the comprehensive treatment of problems of scaling by Thurstone[26] and Thurstone and Chave,[27] and the much simpler scaling technique of Likert.[28] Parallel to these developments, and interacting with them, were major advances in statistics. By the late 1930s powerful statistical methods had been fashioned, which made possible efficient experimental designs and the evaluation of the significance of quantitative findings. These advances were important, of course, not only for the rise of group dynamics but for progress in all the behavioral sciences.

Within this general development we may note three methodological gains contributing specifically to the rise of group dynamics. [Initial sentences in following list not italic in original.]

1. Experiments on individual behavior in groups. As noted above, research in group dynamics is deeply indebted to experimental psychology for the invention of techniques for conducting experiments on the conditions affecting human behavior. But experimental psychology did not concern itself at first with social variables; it was only toward the beginning of the present century that a few investigators embarked upon experimental research designed to investigate the effects of social variables upon the behavior of individuals. The nature of this early experimental social psychology has been described by G. W. Allport this way:

> The first experimental problem—indeed the only problem for the first three decades of experimental research—was formulated as follows: What change in an individual's normal solitary performance occurs when other people are present?[29]

And according to Allport, the first laboratory answer to this question came from Triplett, who compared the performance of children in winding fishing reels when working alone and when working together with other children.[30]

Triplett concluded from this experience that the group situation tended to generate an increase in output of energy and achievement.

Of greater significance for the development of experimental social psychology was the work of Moede, begun at Leipzig in 1913, in which he undertook a systematic investigation of the effects of having several people take part simultaneously in a variety of the then standard psychological experiments.[31] This work was influential in the development of social psychology primarily because Münsterberg called it to the attention of F. H. Allport and encouraged him to repeat and extend it. Allport not only conducted several impressive experiments but also provided a theoretical framework for interpreting the findings.[32] By 1935 Dashiell was able to write a long summary of the work comparing behavior elicited when the subject was working in isolation and in the presence of others.[33] Another important study of this era was that conducted by Moore in which he experimentally demonstrated the influence of "expert" and "majority" opinion upon the moral and aesthetic judgments of individuals.[34] These early experiments not only demonstrated the feasibility of conducting experiments on the influence of groups upon individual behavior; they also developed techniques that are still in use.

A somewhat different but closely related line of research attempted to compare the performance of individuals and of groups. In these studies, as illustrated by the work of Gordon,[35] Watson,[36] and Shaw,[37] tasks were employed that could be performed either by individuals or by groups of people, and the question was asked whether individuals or groups did the better job. As it turned out, this question is unanswerable unless the conditions are further specified, but much was learned in seeking an answer.

All this work made it much more

likely that such a field as group dynamics could develop by bringing groups into the laboratory. Although these early experiments did not, strictly speaking, deal with properties of groups, they made it evident that the influence of groups upon individuals could be studied experimentally, and they made it much easier to conceive of the idea of varying group properties experimentally in the laboratory.

2. *Controlled observation of social interaction.* One might think that the most obvious device for learning about the nature of group functioning would be simply to watch groups in action. Indeed, this procedure has been employed by chroniclers and reporters throughout history and has continued to be a source of data, perhaps most impressively as employed by social anthropologists in their reports of the behavior, culture, and social structure of primitive societies. The major drawback of the procedure as a scientific technique is that the reports given by observers (the scientific data) depend to such a high degree upon the skill, sensitivity, and interpretive predilections of the observer. The first serious attempts to refine methods of observation, so that objective and quantitative data might be obtained, occurred around 1930 in the field of child psychology. A great amount of effort went into the construction of categories of observation that would permit an observer simply to indicate the presence or absence of a particular kind of behavior or social interaction during the period of observation. Typically, reliability was heightened by restricting observation to rather overt interactions whose "meaning" could be revealed in a short span of time and whose classification required little interpretation by the observer. Methods were also developed for sampling the interactions of a large group of people over a long time so that efficient estimates of the total interaction could be made on the basis of more limited observations. By use of such procedures and by careful training of observers quantitative data of high reliability were obtained. The principal researchers responsible for these important advances were Goodenough,[38] Jack,[39] Olson,[40] Parten,[41] and Thomas.[42]

3. *Sociometry.* A somewhat different approach to the study of groups is to ask questions of the members. Data obtained in this manner can, of course, reflect only those things the individual is able, and willing, to report. Nevertheless such subjective reports from the members of a group might be expected to add valuable information to the more objective observations of behavior. Of the many devices for obtaining information from group members one of the earliest and most commonly used is the sociometric test, which was invented by Moreno.[43] During World War I, Moreno had administrative responsibility for a camp of Tyrolese displaced persons, and he observed that the adjustment of people seemed to be better when they were allowed to form their own groups within the camp. Later, in the United States, he undertook to check this insight by more systematic research on groups of people in such institutions as schools and reformatories. For this purpose, he constructed a simple questionnaire on which each person was to indicate those other people with whom he would prefer to share some specified activity. It quickly became apparent that his device, and modifications of it, could provide valuable information about interpersonal attractions and repulsions among any collection of people. The data concerning "who chooses whom" could be converted into a "sociogram," or a picture in which individuals are represented by circles and choices by lines. Inspection of such sociograms revealed that some groups were more tightly knit than others, that individuals varied greatly in their social expansiveness and in the number of choices they received, and

that cliques formed on the basis of characteristics such as age, sex, and race. In short, the sociometric test promised to yield valuable information about both individuals and interpersonal relations in groups. Although based essentially on subjective reports of individuals, the sociometric test provides quantifiable data about patterns of attractions and repulsions existing in a group. The publication by Moreno[44] in 1934 of a major book based on experience with the test and the establishment in 1937 of a journal, *Sociometry*, ushered in a prodigious amount of research employing the sociometric test and numerous variations of it.

The significance of sociometry for group dynamics lay both in the provision of a useful technique for research on groups and in the attention it directed to such features of groups as social position, patterns of friendship, sub-group information, and, more generally, informal structure.

BEGINNINGS OF GROUP DYNAMICS

By the mid-1930s conditions were ripe within the social sciences for a rapid advance in empirical research on groups. And, in fact, a great burst of such activity did take place in America just prior to the entry of the United States into World War II. This research, moreover, began to display quite clearly the characteristics that are now associated with work in group dynamics. Within a period of approximately five years several important research projects were undertaken, more or less independently of one another but all sharing these distinctive features. We now briefly consider four of the more influential of these.

EXPERIMENTAL CREATION OF SOCIAL NORMS

In 1936 Sherif published a book containing a systematic theoretical analysis of the concept *social norm* and an in-

genious experimental investigation of the origin of social norms among groups of people.[45] Probably the most important feature of this book was its bringing together of ideas and observations from sociology and anthropology and techniques of laboratory experimentation from experimental psychology. Sherif began by accepting the existence of customs, traditions, standards, rules, values, fashions, and other criteria of conduct (which he subsumed under the general label, social norm). Further, he agreed with Durkheim that such "collective representations" have, from the point of view of the individual, the properties of exteriority and constraint. At the same time, however, he agreed with F. H. Allport that social norms have been too often treated as something mystical and that scientific progress can be achieved only by subjecting phenomena to acceptable techniques of empirical research. He proposed that social norms should be viewed simultaneously in two ways: *(a)* as the product of social interaction and *(b)* as social stimuli which impinge upon any given individual who is a member of a group having these norms. Conceived in this way, it would be possible to study experimentally the origin of social norms and their influence on individuals.

In formulating his research problem, Sherif drew heavily upon the findings of Gestalt psychology in the field of perception. He noted that this work had established that there need not necessarily be a fixed point-to-point correlation between the physical stimulus and the experience and behavior it arouses. The frame of reference a person brings to a situation influences in no small way how he sees that situation. Sherif proposed that psychologically a social norm functions as such a frame of reference. Thus, if two people with different norms face the same situation (for example, a Mohammedan and a Christian confront a meal of pork chops), they will see it and react to it in widely different ways. For each, however, the norm serves to give meaning and to provide a stable way of reacting to the environment.

Having thus related social norms to the psychology of perception, Sherif proceeded to ask how norms arise. It occured to him that he might gain insight into this problem by placing people in a situation that had no clear structure and in which they would not be able to bring to bear any previously acquired frame of reference or social norm. Sherif stated the general objective of his research as follows:

> ... What will an individual do when he is placed in an objectively unstable situation in which all basis of comparison, as far as the external field of stimulation is concerned, is absent? In other words, what will he do when the external frame of reference is eliminated, in so far as the aspect in which we are interested is concerned? Will he give a hodgepodge of erratic judgments? Or will he establish a point of reference of his own? *Consistent* results in this situation may be taken as the index of a subjectively evolved frame of reference. . . .
>
> Coming to the social level we can push our problem further. What will a group of people do in the same unstable situation? Will the different individuals in the group give a hodgepodge of judgments? Or will there be established a common norm peculiar to the particular group situation and depending upon the presence of these individuals together and their influence upon one another? If they in time come to perceive the uncertain and unstable situation which they face in common in such a way as to give it some sort of order, perceiving it as ordered by a frame of reference developed among them in the course of the experiment, and if this frame of reference is peculiar to the group, then we may say that we have at least the prototype of the psychological process involved in the formation of a norm in a group.[46]

In order to subject these questions to experimental investigation, Sherif made use of what is known in psychology as the autokinetic effect. It had previously

been shown in perceptual research that if a subject looks at a stationary point of light in an otherwise dark room he will soon see it as moving. Furthermore, there are considerable individual differences in the extent of perceived motion. Sherif's experiment consisted of placing subjects individually in the darkened room and getting judgments of the extent of apparent motion. He found that upon repeated test the subject establishes a range within which his judgments fall and that this range is peculiar to each individual. Sherif then repeated the experiment, but this time having groups of subjects observe the light and report aloud their judgments. Now he found that the individual ranges of judgment converged to a group range that was peculiar to the group. In additional variations Sherif was able to show that.

> When the individual, in whom a range and a norm within that range are first developed in the individual situation, is put into a group situation, together with other individuals who also come into the situation with their own ranges and norms established in their own individual sessions, the ranges and norms tend to converge.[47]

Moreover, "when a member of a group faces the same situation subsequently *alone*, after once the range and norm of his group have been established, he perceives the situation in terms of the range and norm that he brings from the situation."[48]

Sherif's study did much to establish the feasibility of subjecting group phenomena to experimental investigation. It should be noted that he did not choose to study social norms existing in any natural group. Instead, he formed new groups in the laboratory and observed the development of an entirely new social norm. Although Sherif's experimental situation might seem artificial, and even trivial, to the anthropologist or sociologist, this very artificiality gave the findings a generality not ordinarily achieved by naturalistic research. By subjecting a group-level concept, like social norm, to psychological analysis, Sherif helped obliterate what he considered to be the unfortunate categorical separation of individual and group. And his research helped establish among psychologists the view that certain properties of groups have reality, for, as he concluded, "the fact that the norm thus established is peculiar to the group suggests that there is a factual psychological basis in the contentions of social psychologists and sociologists who maintain that new and supra-individual qualities arise in the group situations."[49]

SOCIAL ANCHORAGE OF ATTITUDES

During the years 1935–39, Newcomb was conducting an intensive investigation of the same general kind of problem that interested Sherif but with quite different methods.[50] Newcomb selected a "natural" rather than a "laboratory" setting in which to study the operation of social norms and social influence processes, and he relied primarily upon techniques of attitude measurement, sociometry, and interviewing to obtain his data. Bennington College was the site of his study, the entire student body were his subjects, and attitudes toward political affairs provided the content of the social norms.

It was first established that the prevailing political atmosphere of the campus was "liberal" and that entering students, who came predominantly from "conservative" homes, brought with them attitudes that deviated from the college culture. The power of the college community to change attitudes of students was demonstrated by the fact that each year senior students were more liberal than freshmen. The most significant feature of this study, however, was its careful documentation of the ways in which these influences operated. Newcomb showed for example, how the community "rewarded" students for adopting the approved attitudes. Thus, a sociometric-like test, in which students

chose those "most worthy to represent the College at an intercollegiate gathering," revealed that the students thus chosen in each class were distinctly less conservative than those not so chosen. And, those students enjoying a reputation for having a close identification with the college, for being "good citizens," were also relatively more liberal in their political attitudes. By means of several ingenious devices Newcomb was able to discover the student's "subjective role," or self-view of his own relationship to the student community. Analysis of these data revealed several different ways in which students accommodated to the social pressures of the community. Of particular interest in this analysis was the evidence of conflicting group loyalties between membership in the college community and membership in the family group and some of the conditions determining the relative influence of each.

Newcomb's study showed that the attitudes of individuals are strongly rooted in the groups to which people belong, that the influence of a group upon an individual's attitudes depends upon the nature of the relationship between the individual and the group, and that groups evaluate members, partially at least, on the basis of their conformity to group norms. Although most of these points had been made in one form or another by writers in the speculative era of social science, this study was especially significant because it provided detailed objective, and quantitative evidence. It thereby demonstrated, as Sherif's study did in a different way, the feasibility of conducting scientific research on important features of group life.

GROUPS IN STREET CORNER SOCIETY

The sociological and anthropological background of group dynamics is most apparent in the third important study of this era. In 1937 W. F. Whyte moved into one of the slums of Boston to begin a three and one-half year study of social clubs, political organizations, and racketeering. His method was that of "the participant observer," which had been most highly developed in anthropological research. More specifically, he drew upon the experience of Warner and Arensberg which was derived from the "Yankee City" studies. In various ways he gained admittance to the social and political life of the community and faithfully kept notes of the various happenings that he observed or heard about. In the resulting book, Whyte reported in vivid detail on the structure, culture, and functioning of the Norton Street gang and the Italian Community Club.[51] The importance of these social groups in the life of their members and in the political structure of the larger society was extensively documented.

In the interpretation and systematization of his findings, Whyte was greatly influenced by the "interactionist" point of view that was then being developed by Arensberg and Chapple, and that was subsequently presented by such writers as Chapple,[52] Bales,[53] and Homans.[54] The orientation derived by Mayo and his colleagues from the Western Electric studies is also evident in Whyte's analysis of his data. Although he made no effort to quantify the interactions he observed, Whyte's great care for detail lent a strong flavor of objectivity to his account of the interactions among the people he observed. His "higher order" concepts, like social structure, cohesion, leadership, and status, were clearly related to the more directly observable interactions among people, thus giving them a close tie with empirical reality.

The major importance of this study for subsequent work in group dynamics was threefold: (a) It dramatized, and described in painstaking detail, the great significance of groups in the lives of individuals and in the functioning of larger social systems. (b) It gave impetus to the interpretation of group properties and processes in terms of interactions among individuals. (c) It generated a number of hypotheses concerning the relations among such variables as initiation of interaction, leadership, status, mutual obligations, and group cohesion. These hypotheses have served to guide much of Whyte's later work on groups as well as the research of many others.

EXPERIMENTAL MANIPULATION OF GROUP ATMOSPHERE

By far the most influential work in the emerging study of group dynamics was that of Lewin, Lippitt, and White.[55] Conducted at the Iowa Child Welfare Research Station between 1937 and 1940, these investigations of group atmosphere and styles of leadership accomplished a creative synthesis of the various trends and developments considered above. In describing the background of this research, Lippitt noted that the issue of what constitutes "good" leadership had come to the fore in the professions of social group work, education, and administration, and he observed that, with the exception of the Western Electric studies, remarkably little research had been conducted to help guide practice in these professions. In setting up his theoretical problem, he drew explicitly on the previous work in social, clinical, and child psychology, sociology, cultural anthropology, and political science. And in designing his research, he made use with important modifications, of the available techniques of experimental psychology, controlled observation, and sociometry. This work, then, relied heavily upon previous advances in social science and the professions, but it had an originality and significance which immediately produced a marked impact on all these fields.

The basic objective of this research was to study the influences upon the group as a whole and upon individual members of certain experimentally induced "group atmospheres," or "styles of leadership." Groups of ten- and eleven-year-old children were formed to meet regularly over a period of several weeks under the leadership of an adult, who induced the different group atmospheres. In creating these groups care was taken to assure their initial comparability; by utilizing the sociometric test, playground observations, and teacher interviews, the structural properties of the various groups were made as similar as possible; on the basis of school records and interviews with the children, the backgrounds and individual characteristics of the members were equated for all the groups; and the same group activities and physical setting were employed in every group.

The experimental manipulation consisted of having the adult leaders behave in a prescribed fashion in each experimental treatment, and in order to rule out the differential effects of the personalities of the leaders, each one led a group under each of the experimental conditions. Three types of leadership, or group atmosphere, were investigated: democratic, autocratic, and laissez faire.

In the light of present-day knowledge it is clear that a considerable number of separable variables were combined within each style of leadership. Perhaps for this very reason, however, the effects produced in the behavior of the group members were large and dramatic. For example, rather severe forms of scapegoating occurred in the autocratic groups, and at the end of the experiment the children in some of the autocratic groups proceeded to destroy the things they had constructed. Each group, moreover, developed a characteristic level of aggressiveness, and it was demonstrated that when individual members were transferred from one group to another their aggressiveness changed to approach the new group level. An interesting insight into the dynamics of aggression was provided by the rather violent emotional "explo-

sion" which took place when some of the groups that had reacted submissively to autocratic leadership were given a new, more permissive leader.

As might be expected from the fact that this research was both original and concerned with emotionally loaded matters of political ideology, it was immediately subjected to criticism, both justified and unjustified. But the major effect on the social sciences and relevant professions was to open up new vistas and to raise the level of aspiration. The creation of "miniature political systems" in the laboratory and the demonstration of their power to influence the behavior and social relations of people made it clear that practical problems of group management could be subjected to the experimental method and that social scientists could employ the methods of science to solve problems of vital significance to society.

Of major importance for subsequent research in group dynamics was the way in which Lewin formulated the essential purpose of these experiments. The problem of leadership was chosen for investigation, in part, because of its practical importance in education, social group work, administration, and political affairs. Nevertheless, in creating the different types of leadership in the laboratory the intention was not to mirror or to simulate any "pure types" that might exist in society. The purpose was rather to lay bare some of the more important ways in which leader behavior may vary and to discover how various styles of leadership influence the properties of groups and the behavior of members. As Lewin put it, the purpose "was not to duplicate any given autocracy or democracy or to study an 'ideal' autocracy or democracy, but to create set-ups which would give insight into the underlying group dynamics."[56] This statement, published in 1939, appears to be the earliest use by Lewin of the phrase group dynamics.

It is important to note rather carefully how Lewin generalized the research problem. He might have viewed this research primarily as a contribution to the technology of group management in social work or education. Or he might have placed it in the context of research on leadership. Actually, however, he stated the problem in a most abstract way as one of learning about the underlying dynamics of group life. He believed that it was possible to construct a coherent body of empirical knowledge about the nature of group life that would be meaningful when specified for any particular kind of group. Thus, he envisioned a general theory of groups that could be brought to bear on such apparently diverse matters as family life, work groups, classrooms, committees, military units, and the community. Furthermore, he saw such specific problems as leadership, status, communication, social norms, group atmosphere, and intergroup relations as part of the general problem of understanding the nature of group dynamics. Almost immediately, Lewin and those associated with him began various research projects designed to contribute information relevant to a general theory of group dynamics. Thus, French conducted a laboratory experiment designed to compare the effects of fear and frustration on organized versus unorganized groups. Bavelas undertook an experiment to determine whether the actual behavior of leaders of youth groups could be significantly modified through training.[57] Later, Bavelas suggested to Lewin the cluster of ideas that became known as "group decision." With America's entry into the war, he and French, in association with Marrow, explored group decision and related techniques as a means of improving industrial production;[58] and Margaret Mead interested Lewin in studying problems related to wartime food shortages, with the result that Radke together with others[59] conducted experiments on group decision as a means of changing food habits.

SUMMARY

Group dynamics is a field of inquiry dedicated to advancing knowledge about the nature of groups, the laws of their development, and their interrelations with individuals, other groups, and larger institutions. It may be identified by its reliance upon empirical research for obtaining data of theoretical significance, its emphasis in research and theory upon the dynamic aspects of group life, its broad relevance to all the social sciences, and the potential applicability of its findings to the improvement of social practice.

It became an identifiable field toward the end of the 1930s in the United States and has experienced a rapid growth since that time. Its rise was fostered by certain conditions that were particularly favorable in the United States just prior to World War II. These same conditions have facilitated its growth here and in certain other countries since that time. Of particular importance among these has been the acceptance by significant segments of society of the belief that research on groups is feasible and ultimately useful. This belief was initially encouraged by a strong interest in groups among such professions as social group work, group psychotherapy, education, and administration. It was made feasible because the social sciences had attained sufficient progress, by clarifying basic assumptions about the reality of groups and by designing research techniques for the study of groups, to permit empirical research on the functioning of groups.

By the end of the 1930s several trends converged with the result that a new field of group dynamics began to take shape. The practical and theoretical importance of groups was by then documented empirically. The feasibility of conducting objective and quantitative research on the dynamics of group life was no longer debatable. And the reality of groups had been removed from the realm of mysticism and placed squarely within the domain of empirical social science. Group norms could be objectively measured, even created experimentally in the laboratory, and some of the processes by which they influence the behavior and attitudes of individuals had been determined. The dependence of certain emotional states of individuals upon the prevailing group atmosphere had been established. And different styles of leadership had been created experimentally and shown to produce marked consequences on the functioning of groups. After the interruption imposed by World War II, rapid advances were made in constructing a systematic, and empirically based, body of knowledge concerning the dynamics of group life.

NOTES

1. W. I. Thomas and F. Znaniecki, *The Polish Peasant in Europe and America* (Boston: Badger, 1918).

2. F. Thrasher, *The Gang* (Chicago: University of Chicago Press, 1927).

3. C. R. Shaw, *The Jack Roller* (Chicago: University of Chicago Press, 1939).

4. G. Myrdal, *An American Dilemma* (New York: Harper, 1944).

5. W. Newstetter, M. Feldstein, and T. M. Newcomb, *Group Adjustment, A Study in Experimental Sociology* (Cleveland: Western Reserve University, School of Applied Social Sciences, 1938).

6. H. M. Busch, *Leadership in Group Work* (New York: Association Press, 1934).

7. G. L. Coyle, *Social Process in Organized Groups* (New York: Rinehart, 1930).

8. G. Wilson and G. Ryland, *Social Group Work Practice* (Boston: Houghton Mifflin, 1949).

9. F. Redl and D. Wineman, *Children Who Hate* (Glencoe, Ill.: Free Press, 1951).

10. S. Scheidlinger, *Psychoanalysis and Group Behavior* (New York: Norton, 1952).

11. S. R. Slavson, *Analytic Group Psychotherapy* (New York: Columbia University Press, 1950).

12. W. R. Bion, "Experiences in Groups, I-VI," *Human Relations*, Vol. 1 (1948): 314-20, 487-96; 2 (1949): 13-22, 295-303; 3 (1950): 3-14, 395-402.

13. A. T. M. Wilson, "Some Aspects of Social Process," *Journal of Social Issues* (1951, Suppl. Series 5).

14. J. L. Moreno, *Who Shall Survive?* (Washington, D.C.: Nervous and Mental Diseases Publishing Co., 1934).

15. G. R. Bach, *Intensive Group Psychotherapy* (New York: Ronald Press, 1954).

16. M. P. Follett, *The New State: Group Organization the Solution of Popular Government* (New York: Longmans, Green, 1918). M. P. Follett, *Creative Experience* (New York: Longmans, Green, 1924).

17. E. Mayo, *The Human Problems of an Industrial Civilization* (New York: Macmillan, 1933). F. J. Roethlisberger and W. J. Dickson, *Management and the Worker* (Cambridge, Mass.: Harvard University Press, 1939).

18. M. Haire, "Group Dynamics in the Industrial Situation," in *Industrial Conflict*, eds. A. Kornhauser, R. Dubin, and A. M. Ross (New York: McGraw-Hill, 1954) p. 376.

19. C. I. Barnard, *The Functions of the Executive* (Cambridge, Mass.: Harvard University Press, 1938).

20. For example, at the time Lewin established the Research Center for Group Dynamics at M.I.T., the American Jewish Congress created a related organization known as the Commission on Community Interrelations to undertake "action research" on problems of intergroup relations. And heavy financial support for research in group dynamics has come from the National Institute of Mental Health, the United States Navy and Air Force, and several large business organizations.

21. W. H. Whyte, Jr., *The Organization Man* (New York: Simon and Schuster, 1956).

22. F. H. Allport, *Social Psychology* (Boston: Houghton Mifflin, 1924), p. 9.

23. K. Lewin, *Field Theory in Social Science* (New York: Harper, 1951), p. 190.

24. *Ibid.*, p. 193.

25. E. S. Bogardus, "Measuring Social Distance," *Journal of Applied Sociology*, Vol. 9 (1925): 299-308.

26. L. L. Thurstone, "Attitudes Can Be Measured," *Journal of Sociology*, Vol. 33 (1928): 529-54.

27. L. L. Thurstone and E. J. Chave, *The*

Measurement of Attitude (Chicago: University of Chicago Press, 1929).

28. R. Likert, "A Technique for the Measurement of Attitudes," *Archives of Psychology* No. 140 (1932).

29. G. W. Allport, "The Historical Background of Modern Social Psychology," in *Handbook of Social Psychology*, ed. G. Lindzey (Cambridge, Mass.: Addison-Wesley, 1954), p.46.

30. N. Triplett, "The Dynamogenic Factors in Pacemaking and Competition," *American Journal of Psychology*, Vol. 9 (1897): 507-33.

31. W. Moede, *Experimentelle massenpsychologie* (Leipzig: S. Hirzel, 1920).

32. F. H. Allport, *op. cit.*

33. J. F. Dashiell, "Experimental Studies of the Influence of Social Situations on the Behavior of Individual Human Adults," in *Handbook of Social Psychology*, ed. C. C. Murchison (Worcester, Mass.: Clark University Press, 1935), pp. 1097-1158.

34. H. T. Moore, "The Comparative Influence of Majority and Expert Opinion," *American Journal of Psychology*, Vol. 32 (1921): 16-20.

35. K. Gordon, "Group Judgments in the Field of Lifted Weights," *Journal of Experimental Psychology*, Vol. 7 (1924): 398-400.

36. G. B. Watson, "Do Groups Think More Effectively than Individuals?," *Journal of Abnormal and Social Psychology*, Vol. 23 (1928): 328-36.

37. M. E. Shaw, "A Comparison of Individuals and Small Groups in the Rational Solution of Complex Problems," *American Journal of Psychology*, Vol. 44 (1932): 491-504.

38. F. L. Goodenough, "Measuring Behavior Traits by Means of Repeated Short Samples," *Journal of Juvenile Research*, Vol. 12 (1928): 230-35.

39. L. M. Jack, "An Experimental Study of Ascendent Behavior in Preschool Children," *Univ. of Iowa Studies in Child Welfare*, Vol. 9, no. 3 (1934).

40. W. C. Olson and E. M. Cunningham, "Time-Sampling Techniques," *Child Development*, Vol. 5 (1934): 41-58.

41. M. B. Parten, "Social Participation among Preschool Children," *Journal of Abnormal and Social Psychology*, Vol. 27 (1932): 243-69.

42. D. S. Thomas, "An Attempt to Develop Precise Measurement in the Social Behavior Field," *Sociologus*, Vol. 9 (1933): 1-21.

43. Moreno, *op. cit.*

44. *Ibid.*

45. M. Sherif, *The Psychology of Social Norms* (New York: Harper, 1936).

46. *Ibid.*, pp. 90-91.

47. *Ibid.*, p. 104.

48. *Ibid.*, p. 105.

49. *Ibid.*

50. T. M. Newcomb, *Personality and Social Change* (New York: Dryden, 1943).

51. W. F. Whyte, Jr., *Street Corner Society* (Chicago: University of Chicago Press, 1943).

52. E. D. Chapple, "Measuring Human Relations: An Introduction to the Study of Interaction of Individuals," *Genetic Psychology Monographs*, Vol. 22 (1940): 3-147.

53. R. F. Bales, *Interaction Process Analysis* (Cambridge, Mass.: Addison-Wesley, 1950).

54. G. C. Homans, *The Human Group* (New York: Harcourt, Brace, 1950).

55. K. Lewin, R. Lippitt, and R. White, "Patterns of Aggressive Behavior in Experimentally Created 'Social Climates'," *Journal of Social Psychology* 10 (1939): 271-99. R. Lippitt, "An Experimental Study of Authoritarian and Democratic Group Atmospheres," *Univ. of Iowa Studies in Child Welfare*, Vol. 16, No. 3 (1940): 43-195.

56. K. Lewin, *Resolving Social Conflicts* (New York: Harper, 1948), p. 74.

57. A. Bavelas, "Morale and Training of Leaders," in *Civilian Morale*, ed. G. Watson (Boston: Houghton Mifflin, 1942).

58. A. J. Marrow, *Making Management Human* (New York: McGraw-Hill, 1957).

59. K. Lewin, "Forces Behind Food Habits and Methods of Change," *Bulletin of the National Research Council*, Vol. 108 (1943): 35-65. M. Radke and D. Klisurich, "Experiments in Changing Food Habits," *Journal of the American Dietetics Association*, Vol. 23 (1947): 403-09.

14. Assets and Liabilities in Group Problem Solving: The Need for an Integrative Function*

NORMAN R. F. MAIER

A number of investigations have raised the question of whether group problem solving is superior, inferior, or equal to individual problem solving. Evidence can be cited in support of each position so that the answer to this question remains ambiguous. Rather than pursue this generalized approach to the question, it seems more fruitful to explore the forces that influence problem solving under the two conditions.[1] It is hoped that a better recognition of these forces will permit clarification of the varied dimensions of the problem-solving process, especially in groups.

The forces operating in such groups include some that are assets, some that are liabilities, and some that can be either assets or liabilities, depending upon the skills of the members, especially those of the discussion leader. Let us examine these three sets of forces.[2]

GROUP ASSETS

GREATER SUM TOTAL OF KNOWLEDGE AND INFORMATION

There is more information in a group than in any of its members. Thus problems that require the utilization of knowledge should give groups an advantage over individuals. Even if one member of the group (e.g., the leader) knows much more than anyone else, the limited unique knowledge of lesser-informed individuals could serve to fill in some gaps in knowledge. For example, a skilled machinist might contribute to an engineer's problem solving and an ordinary workman might supply information on how a new machine might be received by workers.

GREATER NUMBER OF APPROACHES TO A PROBLEM

It has been shown that individuals get into ruts in their thinking.[3] Many obstacles stand in the way of achieving a goal, and a solution must circumvent these. The individual is handicapped in that he tends to persist in his approach and thus fails to find another approach that might solve the problem in a simpler manner. Individuals in a group have the same failing, but the approaches in which they are persisting may be different. For example, one researcher may try to prevent the spread of a disease by making man immune to the germ, another by finding and destroying the carrier of the germ, and still another by altering the environment so as to kill the germ before it reaches man. There is no way of determining which approach will best achieve the desired goal, but undue persistence in any one will stifle new discoveries. Since group members do not have identical approaches, each can contribute by knocking others out of ruts in thinking.

PARTICIPATION IN PROBLEM SOLVING INCREASES ACCEPTANCE

Many problems require solutions that

*Source: From Psychological Review, Vol. 74, No. 4 (July 1967), pp. 239-249. Copyright © 1967 by the American Psychological Association. Reprinted by permission.

depend upon the support of others to be effective. Insofar as group problem solving permits participation and influence, it follows that more individuals accept solutions when a group solves the problem than when one person solves it. When one individual solves a problem he still has the task of persuading others. It follows, therefore, that when groups solve such problems, a greater number of persons accept and feel responsible for making the solution work. A low-quality solution that has good acceptance can be more effective than a higher-quality solution that lacks acceptance.

BETTER COMPREHENSION OF THE DECISION

Decisions made by an individual, which are to be carried out by others, must be communicated from the decision-maker to the decision-executors. Thus individual problem solving often requires an additional stage—that of relaying the decision reached. Failures in this communication process detract from the merits of the decision and can even cause its failure or create a problem of greater magnitude than the initial problem that was solved. Many organizational problems can be traced to inadequate communication of decisions made by superiors and transmitted to subordinates, who have the task of implementing the decision.

The chances for communication failures are greatly reduced when the individuals who must work together in executing the decision have participated in making it. They not only understand the solution because they saw it develop, but they are also aware of the several other alternatives that were considered and the reasons why they were discarded. The common assumption that decisions supplied by superiors are arbitrarily reached therefore disappears. A full knowledge of goals, obstacles, alternatives, and factual information is essential to communication, and this

communication is maximized when the total problem-solving process is shared.

GROUP LIABILITIES

SOCIAL PRESSURE

Social pressure is a major force making for conformity. The desire to be a good group member and to be accepted tends to silence disagreement and favors consensus. Majority opinions tend to be accepted regardless of whether or not their objective quality is logically and scientifically sound. Problems requiring solutions based upon facts, regardless of feelings and wishes, can suffer in group problem-solving situations.

It has been shown that minority opinions in leaderless groups have little influence on the solution reached, even when these opinions are the correct ones.[4] Reaching agreement in a group often is confused with finding the right answer, and it is for this reason that the dimensions of a decision's acceptance and its objective quality must be distinguished.[5]

VALENCE OF SOLUTIONS

When leaderless groups (made up of three or four persons) engage in problem solving, they propose a variety of solutions. Each solution may receive both critical and supportive comments, as well as descriptive and explorative comments from other participants. If the number of negative and positive comments for each solution are algebraically summed, each may be given a valence index.[6] The first solution that receives a positive valence value of 15 tends to be adopted to the satisfaction of all participants about 85 percent of the time, regardless of its quality. Higher quality solutions introduced after the critical value for one of the solutions has been reached have little chance of achieving real consideration. Once some degree of consensus is reached, the jelling process seems to proceed rather rapidly.

The critical valence value of 15 appears not to be greatly altered by the nature of the problem or the exact size of the group. Rather, it seems to designate a turning point between the idea-getting process and the decision-making process (idea evaluation). A solution's valence index is not a measure of the number of persons supporting the solution, since a vocal minority can build up a solution's valence by actively pushing it. In this sense, valence becomes an influence in addition to social pressure in determining an outcome.

Since a solution's valence is independent to its objective quality, this group factor becomes an important liability in group problem solving, even when the value of a decision depends upon objective criteria (facts and logic). It becomes a means whereby skilled manipulators can have more influence over the group process than their proportion of membership deserves.

INDIVIDUAL DOMINATION

In most leaderless groups a dominant individual emerges and captures more than his share of influence on the outcome. He can achieve this end through a greater degree of participation (valence), persuasive ability, or stubborn persistence (fatiguing the opposition). None of these factors is related to problem-solving ability, so that the best problem solver in the group may not have the influence to upgrade the quality of the group's solution (which he would have had if left to solve the problem by himself).

Hoffman and Maier found that the mere fact of appointing a leader causes this person to dominate a discussion.[7] Thus, regardless of his problem-solving ability a leader tends to exert a major influence on the outcome of a decision.

CONFLICTING SECONDARY GOAL. WINNING THE ARGUMENT

When groups are confronted with a problem, the initial goal is to obtain a solution. However, the appearance of several alternatives causes individuals to have preferences and once these emerge the desire to support a position is created. Converting those with neutral viewpoints and refuting those with opposed viewpoints now enters into the problem-solving process. More and more the goal becomes that of winning the decision rather than finding the best solution. This new goal is unrelated to the quality of the problem's solution and therefore can result in lowering the quality of the decision [*footnote omitted*].

FACTORS THAT SERVE AS ASSETS OR LIABILITIES, DEPENDING LARGELY UPON THE SKILL OF THE DISCUSSION LEADER

DISAGREEMENT

The fact that discussion may lead to disagreement can serve either to create hard feelings among members or lead to a resolution of conflict and hence to an innovative solution.[9] The first of these outcomes of disagreement is a liability, especially with regard to the acceptance of solutions; while the second is an asset, particularly where innovation is desired. A leader can treat disagreement as undesirable and thereby reduce the probability of both hard feelings and innovation, or he can maximize disagreement and risk hard feelings in his attempts to achieve innovation. The skill of a leader requires his ability to create a climate for disagreement which will permit innovation without risking hard feelings. The leader's perception of disagreement is one of the critical factors in this skill area.[10] Others involve permissiveness,[11] delaying the reaching of a solution,[12] techniques for processing information and opinions,[13] and techniques for separating idea-getting from idea-evaluation.[14]

CONFLICTING INTERESTS VERSUS MUTUAL INTERESTS

Disagreement in discussion may take many forms. Often participants disagree with one another with regard to solutions, but when issues are explored one finds that these conflicting solutions are designed to solve different problems. Before one can rightly expect agreement on a solution, there should be agreement on the nature of the problem. Even before this, there should be agreement on the goal, as well as on the various obstacles that prevent the goal from being reached. Once distinctions are made between goals, obstacles, and solutions (which represent ways of overcoming obstacles), one finds increased opportunities for cooperative problem solving and less conflict.[15]

Often there is also disagreement regarding whether the objective of a solution is to achieve quality or acceptance,[16] and frequently a stated problem reveals a complex of separate problems, each having separate solutions so that a search for a single solution is impossible.[17] Communications often are inadequate because the discussion is not synchronized and each person is engaged in discussing a different aspect. Organizing discussion to synchronize the exploration of different aspects of the problem and to follow a systematic procedure increases solution quality.[18] The leadership function of influence discussion procedure is quite distinct from the function of evaluating or contributing ideas.[19]

When the discussion leader aids in the separation of the several aspects of the problem-solving process and delays the solution-mindedness of the group,[20] both solution quality and acceptance improve; when he hinders or fails to facilitate the isolation of these varied processes, he risks a deterioration in the group process.[21] His skill thus determines whether a discussion drifts toward conflicting interests or whether mutual interests are located. Coopera-

tive problem solving can only occur after the mutual interests have been established and it is surprising how often they can be found when the discussion leader makes this his task.[22]

RISK TAKING

Groups are more willing than individuals to reach decisions involving risks.[23] Taking risks is a factor in acceptance of change, but change may either represent a gain or a loss. The best guard against the latter outcome seems to be primarily a matter of a decision's quality. In a group situation this depends upon the leader's skill in utilizing the factors that represent group assets and avoiding those that make for liabilities.

TIME REQUIREMENTS

In general, more time is required for a group to reach a decision than for a single individual to reach one. Insofar as some problems require quick decisions, individual decisions are favored. In other situations acceptance and quality are requirements, but excessive time without sufficient returns also represents a loss. On the other hand, discussion can resolve conflicts, whereas reaching consensus has limited value.[24] The practice of hastening a meeting can prevent full discussion, but failure to move a discussion forward can lead to boredom and fatigue-type solutions, in which members agree merely to get out of the meeting. The effective utilization of discussion time (a delicate balance between permissiveness and control on the part of the leader), therefore, is needed to make the time factor an asset rather than a liability. Unskilled leaders tend to be too concerned with reaching a solution and therefore terminate a discussion before the group potential is achieved.[25]

WHO CHANGES

In reaching consensus or agreement, some members of a group must change. Persuasive forces do not operate in individual problem solving in the same way they operate in a group situation; hence, the changing of someone's mind is not an issue. In group situations, however, who changes can be an asset or a liability. If persons with the most constructive views are induced to change the end-product suffers; whereas if persons with the least constructive points of view change the end-product is upgraded.. The leader can upgrade the quality of a decision because his position permits him to protect the person with a minority view and increase his opportunity to influence the majority position. This protection is a constructive factor because a minority viewpoint influences only when facts favor it.[26]

The leader also plays a constructive role insofar as he can facilitate communications and thereby reduce misunderstandings.[27] The leader has an adverse effect on the end-product when he supresses minority views by holding a contrary position and when he uses his office to promote his own views.[28] In many problem-solving discussions, the untrained leader plays a dominant role in influencing the outcome, and when he is more resistant to changing his views than are the other participants, the quality of the outcome tends to be lowered. This negative leader-influence was demonstrated by experiments in which untrained leaders were asked to obtain a second solution to a problem after they had obtained their first one.[29] It was found that the second solution tended to be superior to the first. Since the dominant individual had influenced the first solution, he had won his point and therefore ceased to dominate the subsequent discussion which led to the second solution. Acceptance of a solution also increases as the leader sees disagreement as idea-producing rather than as a source of difficulty or trouble.[30] Leaders who see some of their participants as trouble-makers obtain fewer innovative solutions and gain less

acceptance of decisions made than leaders who see disagreeing members as persons with ideas.

THE LEADER'S ROLE FOR INTEGRATED GROUPS

TWO DIFFERING TYPES OF GROUP PROCESS

In observing group problem solving under various conditions it is rather easy to distinguish between cooperative problem-solving activity and persuasion or selling approaches. Problem-solving activity includes searching, trying out ideas on one another, listening to understand rather than to refute, making relatively short speeches, and reacting to differences in opinion as stimulating. The general pattern is one of rather complete participation, involvement, and interest. Persuasion activity includes the selling of opinions already formed, defending a position held, either not listening at all or listening in order to be able to refute, talking dominated by a few members, unfavorable reactions to disagreement, and a lack of involvement of some members. During problem solving the behavior observed seems to be that of members interacting as segments of a group. The interaction pattern is not between certain individual members, but with the group as a whole. Sometimes it is difficult to determine who should be credited with an idea. "It just developed," is a response often used to describe the solution reached. In contrast, discussions involving selling or persuasive behavior seem to consist of a series of interpersonal interactions with each individual retaining his identity. Such groups do not function as integrated units but as separate individuals, each with an agenda. In one situation the solution is unknown and is sought; in the other, several solutions exist and conflict occurs because commitments have been made.

THE STARFISH ANALOGY

The analysis of these two group processes suggests an analogy with the behavior of the rays of a starfish under two conditions; one with the nerve ring intact, the other with the nerve ring sectioned.[31] In the intact condition, locomotion and righting behavior reveal that the behavior of each ray is not merely a function of local stimulation. Locomotion and righting behavior reveal a degree of coordination and interdependence that is centrally controlled. However, when the nerve ring is sectioned, the behavior of one ray still can influence others, but internal coordination is lacking. For example, if one ray is stimulated, it may step forward, thereby exerting pressure on the sides of the other four rays. In response to these external pressures (tactile stimulation), these rays show stepping responses on the stimulated side so that locomotion successfully occurs without the aid of neural coordination. Thus integrated behavior can occur on the basis of external control. If, however, stimulation is applied to opposite rays, the specimen may be "locked" for a time, and in some species the conflicting locomotions may divide the animal, thus destroying it.[32]

Each of the rays of the starfish can show stepping responses even when sectioned and removed from the animal. Thus each may be regarded as an individual. In a starfish with a sectioned nerve ring the five rays become members of a group. They can successfully work together for locomotion purposes by being controlled by the dominant ray. Thus if uniformity of action is desired, the group of five rays can sometimes be more effective than the individual ray in moving the group toward a source of stimulation. However, if "locking" or the division of the organism occurs, the group action becomes less effective than individual action. External control, through the influence of a dominant ray, therefore can lead to adaptive behavior for the starfish as a whole, but it can also result in a conflict that destroys the organism. Something more than external influence is needed.

In the animal with an intact nerve ring, the function of the rays is coordinated by the nerve ring. With this type of internal organization the group is always superior to that of the individual actions. When the rays function as a part of an organized unit, rather than as a group that is physically together, they become a higher type of organization—a single intact organism. This is accomplished by the nerve ring, which in itself does not do the behaving. Rather, it receives and processes the data which the rays relay to it. Through this central organization, the responses of the rays become part of a larger pattern so that together they constitute a single coordinated total response rather than a group of individual responses.

THE LEADER AS THE GROUP'S CENTRAL NERVOUS SYSTEM

If we now examine what goes on in a discussion group we find that members can problem-solve as individuals, they can influence others by external pushes and pulls, or they can function as a group with varying degrees of unity. In order for the latter function to be maximized, however, something must be introduced to serve the function of the nerve ring. In our conceptualization of group problem solving and group decision,[33] we see this as the function of the leader. Thus the leader does not serve as a dominant ray and produce the solution. Rather, his function is to receive information, facilitate communications between the individuals, relay messages, and integrate the incoming responses so that a single unified response occurs.

Solutions that are the product of good group discussions often come as surprises to discussion leaders. One of these is unexpected generosity. If there is a weak member, this member is given less to do, in much the same way as an organism adapts to an injured limb and alters the function of other limbs to keep locomotion on course. Experimental evidence supports the point that group decisions award special consideration to needy members of groups.[34] Group decisions in industrial groups often give smaller assignments to the less gifted.[35] A leader could not effectually impose such differential treatment on group members without being charged with discriminatory practices.

Another unique aspect of group discussion is the way fairness is resolved. In a simulated problem situation involving the problem of how to introduce a new truck into a group of drivers, the typical group solution involves a trading of trucks so that several or all members stand to profit. If the leader makes the decision the number of persons who profit is often confined to one.[36] In industrial practice, supervisors assign a new truck to an individual member of a crew after careful evaluation of needs. This practice results in dissatisfaction, with the charge of *unfair* being leveled at him. Despite these repeated attempts to do justice, supervisors in the telephone industry never hit upon the notion of a general reallocation of trucks, a solution that crews invariably reach when the decision is theirs to make.

In experiments involving the introduction of change, the use of group discussion tends to lead to decisions that resolve differences.[37] Such decisions tend to be different from decisions reached by individuals because of the very fact that disagreement is common in group problem solving and rare in individual problem solving. The process of resolving difference in a constructive setting causes the exploration of additional areas and leads to solutions that are integrative rather than compromises.

Finally, group solutions tend to be tailored to fit the interests and personalities of the participants; thus group solutions to problems involving fairness, fears, face-saving, etc., tend to vary from one group to another. An outsider cannot process these variables because they are not subject to logical treatment.

If we think of the leader as serving a function in the group different from that of its membership, we might be able to create a group that can function as an intact organism. For a leader, such functions as rejecting or promoting ideas according to his personal needs are out of bounds. He must be receptive to information contributed, accept contributions without evaluating them (posting contributions on a chalk board to keep them alive). Summarize information to facilitate integration, stimulate exploratory behavior, create awareness of problems of one member by others, and detect when the group is ready to resolve differences and agree to a unified solution.

Since higher organisms have more than a nerve ring and can store information, a leader might appropriately supply information, but according to our model of a leader's role, he must clearly distinguish between supplying information and promoting a solution. If his knowledge indicates the desirability of a particular solution, sharing this knowledge might lead the group to find this solution, but the solution should be the group's discovery. A leader's contributions do not receive the same treatment as those of a member of the group. Whether he likes it or not, his position is different. According to our conception of the leader's contribution to discussion, his role not only differs in influence, but gives him an entirely different function. He is to serve much as the nerve ring in the starfish and to further refine this function so as to make it a higher type of nerve ring.

This model of a leader's role in group process has served as a guide for many of our studies in group problem solving. It is not our claim that this will lead to the best possible group function under all conditions. In sharing it we hope to indicate the nature of our guidelines in exploring group leadership as a function quite different and apart from group membership. Thus the model serves as a stimulant for research problems and as a guide for our analyses of leadership skills and principles.

CONCLUSIONS

On the basis of our analysis, it follows that the comparison of the merits of group versus individual problem solving depends on the nature of the problem, the goal to be achieved (high quality solution, highly accepted solution, effective communication and understanding of the solution, innovation, a quickly reached solution, or satisfaction), and the skill of the discussion leader. If liabilities inherent in groups are avoided, assets capitalized upon, and conditions that can serve either favorable or unfavorable outcomes are effectively used, it follows that groups have a potential which in many instances can exceed that of a superior individual functioning alone, even with respect to creativity.

This goal was nicely stated by Thibaut and Kelley when they

> wonder whether it may not be possible for a rather small, intimate group to establish a problem solving process that capitalizes upon the total pool of information and provides for great interstimulation of ideas without any loss of innovative creativity due to social restraints.[38]

In order to accomplish this high level of achievement, however, a leader is needed who plays a role quite different from that of the members. His role is analogous to that of the nerve ring in the starfish which permits the rays to execute a unified response. If the leader can contribute the integrative requirement, group problem solving may emerge as a unique type of group function. This type of approach to group processes places the leader in a particular role in which he must cease to contribute, avoid evaluation, and refrain from thinking about solutions or group *products*. Instead he must concentrate on the group *process*, listen in order to understand rather than to appraise or refute, assume responsibility for accurate communication between members, be sensitive to unexpressed feelings, protect minority points of view, keep the discussion moving, and develop skills in summarizing.

NOTES

1. L. R. Hoffman, "Group Problem Solving," in *Advances in Experimental Social Psychology*, vol. 2, ed. L. Berkowitz (New York: Academic Press, 1965), pp. 99-132. H. H. Kelley and J. W. Thibaut, "Experimental Studies of Group Problem Solving and Process," in *Handbook of Social Psychology*, ed. G. Lindzey, (Cambridge, Mass.: Addison-Wesley, 1954), pp. 735-85.

2. The research reported here was supported by Grant No. MH-02704 from the United States Public Health Service. Grateful acknowledgment is made for the constructive criticism of Melba Colgrove, Junie Janzen, Mara Julius, and James Thurber.

3. K. Duncker, "On Problem Solving," *Psychological Monographs*, 1945, 58 (5, Whole No. 270). N. R. F. Maier, "Reasoning in Humans. I. On Direction," *Journal of Comparative Psychology* 10 (1930): 115-43. M. Wertheimer, *Productive Thinking* (New York: Harper, 1959).

4. N. R. F. Maier and A. R. Solem, "The Contribution of a Discussion Leader to the Quality of Group Thinking: The Effective Use of Minority Opinions," *Human Relations* 5 (1952): 277-88.

5. N. R. F. Maier, *Problem Solving Discussions and Conferences: Leadership Methods and Skills* (New York: McGraw-Hill, 1963).

6. L. R. Hoffman and N. R. F. Maier, "Valence in the Adoption of Solutions by Problem-Solving Groups: Concept, Method, and Results," *Journal of Abnormal and Social Psychology* 69 (1964): 264-71.

7. L. R. Hoffman and N. R. F. Maier, "Valence in the Adoption of Solutions by

Problem-Solving Groups: II. Quality and Acceptance as Goals of Leaders and Members," mimeographed (1967).

8. Footnote omitted; unclear reference in original.

9. L. R. Hoffman, "Conditions for Creative Problem Solving," *Journal of Psychology* 52 (1961): 429-44. L. R. Hoffman, E. Harburg, and N. R. F. Maier, "Differences and Disagreement as Factors in Creative Group Problem Solving," *Journal of Abnormal and Social Psychology* 64 (1962): 206-14. L. R. Hoffman and N. R. F. Maier, "Quality and Acceptance of Problem Solutions by Members of Homogeneous and Heterogeneous Groups," *Journal of Abnormal and Social Psychology* 62 (1961): 401-07. N. R. F. Maier, *The Appraisal Review* (New York: Wiley, 1958). Maier, *Problem* . . . (1963). N. R. F. Maier and L. R. Hoffman, "Acceptance and Quality of Solutions as Related to Leaders' Attitudes toward Disagreement in Group Problem Solving," *Journal of Applied Behavioral Science* 1 (1965): 373-86.

10. *Ibid.*

11. N. R. F. Maier, "An Experimental Test of the Effect of Training on Discussion Leadership," *Human Relations* 6 (1953): 161-73.

12. N. R. F. Maier and L. R. Hoffman, "Quality of First and Second Solutions in Group Problem Solving," *Journal of Applied Psychology* 44 (1960): 278-83. N. R. F. Maier and A. R. Solem, "Improving Solutions by Turning Choice Situations into Problems," *Personnel Psychology* 15 (1962): 151-57.

13. Maier, *Problem* . . . (1963). N. R. F. Maier and L. R. Hoffman, "Using Trained 'Developmental' Discussion Leaders to Improve Further the Quality of Group Decisions," *Journal of Applied Psychology* 44 (1960): 247-51. N. R. F. Maier and R. A. Maier, "An Experimental Test of the Effects of 'Developmental' vs. 'Free' Discussions on the Quality of Group Decisions," *Journal of Applied Psychology* 41 (1957): 320-23.

14. N. R. F. Maier, "Screening Solutions to Upgrade Quality: A New Approach to Problem Solving Under Conditions of Uncertainty," *Journal of Psychology* 49 (1960): 217-31. Maier, *Problem . . . (1963). A. F. Osborn, Applied Imagination* (New York: Scribner's, 1953).

15. L. R. Hoffman and N. R. F. Maier, "The Use of Group Decision to Resolve a Problem of Fairness," *Personnel Psychology* 12 (1959): 545-59. Maier, "Screening . . ." (1960). Maier, *Problem* . . . (1963). Maier

and Solem, "Improving . . ." (1962). A. R. Solem, "1965: Almost Anything I Can Do, We Can Do Better," *Personnel Administration* 28 (1965): 6-16.

16. N. R. F. Maier and L. R. Hoffman, "Types of Problems Confronting Managers," *Personnel Psychology* 17 (1964): 261-69.

17. Maier, *Problem* . . . (1963).

18. Maier and Hoffman, "Using . . ." (1960). Maier and Maier, "An Experimental . . ." (1957).

19. N. R. F. Maier, "The Quality of Group Decisions as Influenced by the Discussion Leader," *Human Relations* 3 (1950): 155-74. Maier, "An Experimental . . ." (1953).

20. Maier, "The Appraisal . . ." (1958). Maier, *Problem* . . . (1963). Maier and Solem, "Improving . . ." (1962).

21. Solem, "Almost . . ." (1965).

22. N. R. F. Maier, *Principles of Human Relations* (New York: Wiley, 1952). Maier, *Problem* . . . (1963). N. R. F. Maier and J. J. Hayes, *Creative Management* (New York: Wiley, 1962).

23. M. A. Wallach and N. Kogan, "The Roles of Information, Discussion and Concensus in Group Risk Taking," *Journal of Experimental and Social Psychology* 1 (1965): 1-19. M. A. Wallach, N. Kogan, and D. J. Bem, "Group Influence on Individual Risk Taking," *Journal of Abnormal and Social Psychology* 65 (1962): 75-86.

24. Wallach and Kogan, "The Roles . . ." (1965).

25. Maier and Hoffman, "Quality . . ." (1960).

26. Maier, "The Quality . . ." (1950). Maier, *Principles* . . . (1952). Maier and Solem, "The Contribution . . ." (1952).

27. Maier, *Principles* . . . (1952). Solem, *1965. . . .*

28. Maier and Hoffman, "Quality . . ." (1960). N. R. F. Maier and L. R. Hoffman, "Group Decision in England and the United States," *Personnel Psychology* 15 (1962): 75-87. Maier and Solem, "The Contribution . . ." (1952).

29. Maier and Hoffman, "Using . . ." (1960).

30. Maier and Hoffman, "Acceptance . . ." (1965).

31. W. F. Hamilton, "Coordination in the Starfish. III. The Righting Reaction as a Phase of Locomotion (Righting and Locomotion)," *Journal of Comparative Psychology* 2 (1922): 81-94. A. R. Moore, "The Nervous Mechanism of Coordination in the Crinoid *Antedon*

rosaceus," *Journal of Genetic Psychology* 6 (1924): 281-88. A. R. Moore and M. Doudoroff, "Injury, Recovery and Function in an Aganglionic Central Nervous System," *Journal of Comparative Psychology* 28 (1939): 313-28. T. C. Schneirla and N. R. F. Maier, "Concerning the Status of the Starfish," *Journal of Comparative Psychology* 30 (1940): 103-10.

32. W. J. Crozier, "Notes on Some Problems of Adaptation," *Biological Bulletin* 39 (1920): 116-29. Moore and Doudoroff, "Injury . . ." (1939).

33. Maier, *Problem* . . . (1963).

34. Hoffman and Maier, "The Use . . ." (1959).

35. Maier, *Principles* . . . (1952).

36. Maier and Hoffman, "Group . . ." (1962). N. R. F. Maier and L. F. Zerfoss, "MRP: A Technique for Training Large Groups of Supervisors and Its Potential Use in Social Research," *Human Relations* 5 (1952): 177-86.

37. Maier, *Principles* . . . (1952). Maier, "An Experimental . . ." (1953). N. R. F. Maier and L. R. Hoffman, "Organization and Creative Problem Solving," *Journal of Applied Psychology* 45 (1961): 277-80. N. R. F. Maier and L. R. Hoffman, "Financial Incentives and Group Decision in Motivating Change," *Journal of Social Psychology* 64 (1964): 369-78. N. R. F. Maier and L. R. Hoffman, "Types of Problems Confronting Managers," *Personnel Psychology* 17 (1964): 261-69.

38. J. W. Thibaut and H. H. Kelley, *The Social Psychology of Groups* (New York: Wiley, 1961), p. 268.

15. Groups and Intergroup Relationships*

EDGAR H. SCHEIN

Groups in organizations have become the subject of much mythology and the target for strong feelings. Though groups are nearly universal in organizations, some managers who have little faith in teamwork and committees pride themselves on running an operation in which things are done only by individuals, not by groups. Elsewhere, one finds managers saying with equal pride that they make all their major decisions in groups and rely heavily on teamwork. People differ greatly in their stereotypes of what a group is, what a group can and cannot do, and how effective a group can be. A classic joke told by those who are against the use of groups is that "a camel is a horse which was put together by a committee."

What, then, is the "truth" about groups? Why do they exist? What functions do groups fulfill for the organization and for their members? How should one conceptualize a group, and how does one judge the goodness or effectiveness of a group? What kinds of things can groups do and what can they not do? What impact do groups have on their members, on each other, and on the organization within which they exist? What are the pro's and con's of intergroup cooperation and intergroup competition? How does one manage and influence groups? These are some of the questions we will discuss in this chapter.

The reason for devoting an entire chapter to groups is that there is ample evidence that they do have a major impact on their members, on other groups, and on the host organization. Their existence ultimately is stimulated by the very concept of organization. An organization divides up its ultimate task into subtasks which are assigned to various subunits. These subunits in turn may divide the task and pass it down further, until a level is reached where several people take a subgoal and divide it among themselves as individuals, but no longer create units. At this level of formal organization, we have the basis for group formation along functional lines. The sales department or some part thereof may come to be a group; the production department may be a single group or a set of groups; and so on. What basically breaks an organization into groups, therefore, is division of labor. The organization itself generates forces toward the formation of various smaller functional task groups within itself.

DEFINITION OF A GROUP

How big is a group and what characterizes it? It has generally been difficult to define a group, independent of some specific purpose or frame of reference. Since we are examining psychological problems in organizations, it would appear most appropriate to define the group in psychological terms.

● *A psychological group is any number of people who (1) interact with one another, (2) are psychologically aware*

*Source: From Edgar H. Schein, *Organizational Psychology*, 2nd Ed., pp. 80-89. Copyright © 1970. Reprinted by permission of Prentice-Hall, Inc., Englewood Cliffs, New Jersey.

*of one another, and (3) perceive them-
selves to be a group.*

The size of a group is thus limited by
the possibilities of mutual interaction
and mutual awareness. Mere aggregates
of people do not fit this definition because they do not interact and do not
perceive themselves to be a group even
if they are aware of each other as, for
instance, a crowd on a street corner
watching some event. A total department, a union, or a whole organization
would not be a group in spite of thinking of themselves as "we," because
they generally do not all interact and
are not all aware of each other. Work
teams, committees, subparts of departments, cliques, and various other informal associations among organizational
members would fit this definition of a
group.

Having defined a group, and having
indicated that the basic force toward
group formation arises out of the organizational process itself, let us now
examine the kinds of groups which are
actually found in organizations and the
functions which such groups appear to
fulfill for the organization and for its
members.

TYPES OF GROUPS
IN ORGANIZATIONS

FORMAL GROUPS

Formal groups are created in order to
fulfill specific goals and carry on
specific tasks which are clearly related
to the total organizational mission. Formal groups can be of two types, based
on their duration. *Permanent* formal
groups are bodies such as the top management team, work units in the various
departments of the organization, staff
groups providing specialized services to
the work organization, permanent
committees, and so on. *Temporary* formal groups are committees or task
forces which may be created to carry
out a particular job but which, once the
job is carried out, cease to exist unless

some other task is found for them or unless they take on informal functions.
Thus, an organization may create a
committee or study group to review salary policies, to study the relationship
between the organization and the
community, to try to invent some proposals for improving relations between
the union and management, to think of
new products and services, and so on.
Temporary formal groups may exist for
a long time. What makes them temporary is that they are defined as such by
the organization and that the members
feel themselves to be a part of a group
which may at any time go out of existence.

INFORMAL GROUPS

As I have pointed out, the members of
organizations are formally called upon
to provide only certain activities to fulfill their organizational role. But, because the whole man actually reports
for work or joins the organization and
because man has needs beyond the
minimum ones of doing his job, he will
seek fulfillment of some of these needs
through developing a variety of relationships with other members of the organization. If the ecology of the work area
and the time schedule of the work permit, these informal relationships will
develop into informal groups. In other
words, the *tendency* toward informal
groups can almost always be assumed
to exist because of the nature of man.
How this tendency works itself out in
the actual creation of groups, however,
depends very much on the physical location of people, the nature of their
work, their time schedules, and so on.
Informal groups therefore arise out of
the particular combination of "formal"
factors and human needs.

Some examples may help to clarify
this important point. It has been found
in a number of studies of friendship and
informal association that such relationships can be predicted to a large degree
simply from the probability of who

would meet whom in the day-to-day routine. In a housing project, this likelihood was largely determined by the actual location and direction of doorways.[1] Those people who met because their doorways faced were more likely to become friends than those whose doorways made meeting less likely. In the bank-wiring room of the Hawthorne studies, the two major informal cliques were the "group in the front" and the "group in the back," this pattern arising out of actual job-related interactions as well as slight differences in the work performed in the two parts of the room. The reason why the men in front considered themselves to be superior was that they were doing more difficult work, though they were not actually paid more for it. Thus, informal groups tend to arise partly out of the formal features of the organization.

If the organization sets itself to *prevent* informal group formation, it can do so by designing the work and its physical layout in such a way that no opportunities for interaction arise, as in the case of the assembly line, or it can systematically rotate leaders and key members to prevent any stable group structure from emerging, as the Chinese Communists did in handling American prisoners of war in Korea.[2]

Assuming that the organization does not set out to limit informal group formation, and that the nature of the work permits it, what kinds of informal groups do we find in organizations? The commonest kinds can be called, to follow Dalton's terminology, *horizontal cliques*.[3] By this, he means an informal association of workers, managers, or organizational members who are more or less of the same rank, and work in more or less the same area. The bank-wiring room had two such cliques in it. Most organizations that have been studied, regardless of their basic function (that is, mutual benefit, business, commonweal, or service), have an extensive informal organization consisting of many such cliques.

A second type, which can be called a *vertical clique*, is a group composed of members from different levels within a given department. For example, in several organizations that Dalton studied, he found groups that consisted of a number of workers, one or two foremen, and one or more higher-level managers. Some of the members were actually in superior-subordinate relationships to one another. A group such as this apparently comes into being because of earlier acquaintance of the members or because they need each other to accomplish their goals. For example, such groups often serve a key communication function both upward and downward.

A third type of clique can be called a *mixed clique*.[4] This will have in it members of different ranks, from different departments, and from different physical locations. Such cliques may arise to serve common interests or to fulfill functional needs that are not taken care of by the organization. For example, the head of manufacturing may cultivate a relationship with the best worker in the maintenance department in order to be able to short-circuit formal communication channels when a machine breaks down and he needs immediate maintenance work. On the college campus we have seen the growth of informal groups which consist of students, faculty, and high level administrators to work on problems that the formal committee structure cannot handle. Relationships outside of the organizational context may be an important basis for the formation of such cliques. For example, a number of members may live in the same part of town, or attend the same church, or belong to the same social club.

FUNCTIONS FULFILLED BY GROUPS

FORMAL, ORGANIZATIONAL FUNCTIONS

By formal, organizational functions, I

mean those which pertain to the accomplishment of the organization's basic mission. Thus, by definition, formal groups serve certain formal functions such as getting work out, generating ideas, or serving as liaison. The formal functions are the tasks that are assigned to the group and for which it is officially held responsible.

PSYCHOLOGICAL, PERSONAL FUNCTIONS

Because organizational members bring with them a variety of needs, and because group formation can fulfill many of these needs, we can list a number of psychological functions which groups fulfill for their members. Groups can provide:

a. An outlet for *affiliation needs*, that is, needs for friendship, support, and love.

b. A means of *developing, enhancing, or confirming a sense of identity and maintaining self-esteem.* Through group membership a person can develop or confirm some feelings of who he is, can gain some status, and thereby enhance his sense of self-esteem.

c. A means of *establishing and testing reality.* Through developing consensus among group members, uncertain parts of the social environment can be made "real" and stable, as when several workers agree that their boss is a slave-driver or when, by mutual agreement, they establish the reality that if they work harder, management will cut the piece rate of whatever they are making. Each person can validate his own perceptions and feelings best by checking them with others.

d. A means of *increasing security and a sense of power* in coping with a common and powerful enemy or threat. Through banding together into bargaining units such as unions or through agreeing to restrict output, groups can offset some of the power that management has over members individually.

e. A means of *getting some job done that members need to have done,* such as gathering information, or helping out when some are sick or tired, or avoiding boredom and providing stimulation to one another, or bringing new members of the

organization quickly into the informal structure, and so on.

MULTIPLE OR MIXED FUNCTIONS

One of the commonest findings that comes from the study of groups in oranizations—and which incidentally, is a reason why organizations are so much more complex than traditional organization theory envisioned—is that most groups turn out to have both formal and informal functions; they serve the needs of both the organization and the individual members. Psychological groups, therefore, may well be the key unit for facilitating the integration of organizational goals and personal needs.

For example, a formal work crew such as is found in industry or in the Army (say, a platoon) often becomes a psychological group that meets a variety of the psychological needs mentioned. If this process occurs, it often becomes the source of much higher levels of loyalty, commitment, and energy in the service of organizational goals than would be possible if the psychological needs were met in informal groups that did not coincide with the formal one. One key issue for research and for management practice, therefore, is the determination of the conditions which will facilitate the fulfillment of psychological needs in *formal* work groups.

An example of an informal group that begins to serve formal, organizational functions would be the kind of grouping, found by Dalton, that enables top management to use informal channels of communication to obtain information quickly on conditions in various parts of the organization, and which also enables line operators to determine quickly what changes in production policy are in the offing and prepare for them long before they are formally announced. The actual mechanism might be the exchange of information at lunch, at the local meeting of the Rotary Club, over golf at the country club, or through an informal telephone conversation. According to Dalton, these contacts not only meet many psychological needs, but they are clearly *necessary* for the maintenance of organizational effectiveness.

VARIABLES AFFECTING THE INTEGRATION IN GROUPS OF ORGANIZATIONAL GOALS AND PERSONAL NEEDS

There are a variety of factors that will determine the kinds of groups which will tend to exist in an organization and whether such groups will tend to fulfill both organizational and personal functions or only one or the other. These variables can be divided up into three classes: environmental factors—the cultural, social, and technological climate in which the group exists; membership factors—the kinds of people, categorized in terms of personal background, values, relative status, and so on, who are in the group; and dynamic factors—how the group is organized, the manner in which the group is led or managed, the amount of training members have received in leadership and membership skills, the kinds of tasks given to the group, its prior history of success or failure, and so on.

ENVIRONMENTAL FACTORS

Environmental factors such as the organization of the work, the physical location of workers, and the time schedule imposed will determine who will interact with whom and therefore which people are likely to form into groups in the first place. If groups are to be encouraged to fulfill organizational tasks, it obviously follows that the work environment must permit and, in fact, promote the emergence of "logical" groups. This end can be accomplished by actually designating certain groups as work teams, or allowing groups to emerge by facilitating interaction and allowing enough free time for it to occur.

In many cases, the nature or location of

a job itself requires effective group action, as in bomber, tank, or submarine crews, in groups who work in isolation for long periods of time (say, in a radar station), or in medical teams or ward personnel in a hospital. In other cases, even though the technical requirements do not demand it, an organization often encourages group formation. For example, the Army, rather than replace soldiers one at a time, has begun to use four-man groups who go through basic training together as combat replacements. In the hotel industry, where it is crucial that the top management of a given hotel work well together, one company has begun a conscious program of training the top team together before they take charge of a hotel in order to insure good working relations.

The degree to which such logically designed groups come to serve psychological needs will depend to a large extent on another environmental factor—the managerial climate. The managerial climate is determined primarily by the prevailing assumptions in the organization about the nature of man. If assumptions of *rational-economic man* are favored, it is unlikely that groups will be rationally utilized in the first place. According to those assumptions, groups are at most to be tolerated or, preferably, destroyed in the interest of maximizing individual efficiency. If coordination is required, it is to be supplied by the assembly line or some other mechanical means. Consequently, a climate based on assumptions of rational-economic man is most likely to produce defensive antimanagement groups. Such groups will arise to give their members the sense of self-esteem and security that the formal organization denies them.

An organization built on the assumptions and values of *social man* will encourage and foster the growth of groups, but may err in not being logical in creating groupings that will facilitate task performance. This kind of organization often maintains a philosophy of job design and job allocation built on the assumptions of rational-economic man, but then attempts to meet man's affiliative needs by creating various social groups for him extrinsic to the immediate work organization—company bowling leagues, baseball teams, picnics, and social activities. The organizational logic then dictates that in exchange for the fulfillment of his social needs, a man should work harder on his individually designed job. This logic does not permit the integration of formal and informal group forces, because the groups have no intrinsic task function in the first place.

An organization built on the assumptions and values of self-actualizing man is more likely to create a climate conducive to the emergence of psychologically meaningful groups because of the organization's concern with the meaningfulness of work. However, such organizations—for example, research divisions of industrial concerns or university departments—often fail to see the importance of groups as a means for individual self-actualization. So much emphasis is given to challenging each individual and so little emphasis is given to collective effort in which individual contributions are difficult to judge, that groups are not likely to be encouraged to develop.

The effective integration of organizational and personal needs probably requires a climate based on the assumptions of complex man because groups are not the right answer to all problems at all times. Those organizations which are able to use groups effectively tend to be very careful in deciding when to make use of a work team or a committee and when to set up conditions which promote or discourage group formation. There are no easy generalizations in this area, hence a diagnostic approach may be the most likely to pay off. The type of task involved, the past history of the organization with regard to the use of groups, the people available and their ability to be effective group members, the kind of group leadership available—these are all critical.

MEMBERSHIP FACTORS

Whether a group will work effectively on an organizational task and at the same time become psychologically satisfying to its members depends in part on the group composition. For any effective work to occur, there must be a certain amount of consensus on basic values and on a medium of communication. If personal backgrounds, values, or status differentials prevent communication, the group cannot perform well. It is particularly important that relative status be carefully assessed in order to avoid the fairly common situation where a lower-ranking member will not give accurate information to a higher-ranking member because he does not wish to be punished for saying possibly unpleasant things or things he believes the other does not wish to hear.

The commonest example is the department staff meeting in which the boss asks his various subordinates how things are going in their units. Often subordinates will respond only with vague statements that everything is all right because they know that the boss wants and expects things that way, and because they do not wish to be embarrassed in front of their peers by admitting failures. Consequently, for problem-solving, such a group is very ineffective.

Another typically difficult group is a committee composed of representatives of various departments of the organization. Each person is likely to be so concerned about the group he came from, wishing to uphold its interests as its representative, that it becomes difficult for the members to become identified with the new committee.

A third kind of problem group, illustrating conflict of values, is the typical labor–management bargaining committee. Even though the mission of the group may be to invent new solutions to chronic problems, the labor members typically cannot establish good communications with the management members because they feel that the latter look down upon them, devalue them as human beings, and do not respect them. These attitudes may be communicated in subtle ways, such as by asking that the meetings be held in management's meeting rooms rather than offering to meet on neutral territory or in a place suggested by the labor group.

For each of the above problems, the only remedy is to provide the group enough common experience to permit a communication system and a climate of trust to emerge. Such common experience can be obtained by holding long meetings away from the place of work, thereby encouraging members to get to know each other in more informal settings, or by going through some common training experience. Thus experience-based training exercises or workshops serve not only to educate people about groups, but also to provide group members a common base of experience from which to build better working relationships.

An inadequate distribution of relevant abilities and skills may be another important membership problem. For any work group to be effective, it must have within it the resources to fulfill the task it is given. If the group fails in accomplishing its task

because of lack of resources and thereby develops a psychological sense of failure, it can hardly develop the strength and cohesiveness to serve other psychological needs for its members. All of these points indicate that just bringing a collection of people into interaction does not insure a good working group. It is important to consider the characteristics of the members and to assess the likelihood of their being able to work with one another and serve one another's needs.[5]

NOTES

1. L. Festinger, S. Schachter, and K. Back, *Social Pressures in Informal Groups: A Study of a Housing Project* (New York: Harper & Row, 1950).

2. E. H. Schein, "The Chinese Indoctrination Program for Prisoners of War," *Psychiatry* 19 (1956): 149-72.

3. M. Dalton, *Men Who Manage* (New York: John Wiley, 1959).

4. Dalton has called these "random" cliques.

5. A number of research studies have attempted to determine whether group effectiveness could be predicted from personality variables. Among these the best example is William Schutz' work reported in *FIRO: A Three-dimensional Theory of Interpersonal Behavior* (New York: Holt, Rinehart, and Winston, 1958).

16. Groupthink*

IRVING L. JANIS

"How could we have been so stupid?" President John F. Kennedy asked after he and a close group of advisers had blundered into the Bay of Pigs invasion. For the last two years I have been studying that question, as it applies not only to the Bay of Pigs decision-makers but also to those who led the United States into such other major fiascos as the failure to be prepared for the attack on Pearl Harbor, the Korean War stalemate and the escalation of the Vietnam War.

Stupidity certainly is not the explanation. The men who participated in making the Bay of Pigs decision, for instance, comprised one of the greatest arrays of intellectual talent in the history of American Government—Dean Rusk, Robert McNamara, Douglas Dillon, Robert Kennedy, McGeorge Bundy, Arthur Schlesinger, Jr., Allen Dulles and others.

It also seemed to me that explanations were incomplete if they concentrated only on disturbances in the behavior of each individual within a decision-making body: temporary emotional states of elation, fear, or anger that reduce a man's mental efficiency, for example, or chronic blind spots arising from a man's social prejudices or idiosyncratic biases.

I preferred to broaden the picture by looking at the fiascos from the standpoint of group dynamics as it has been explored over the past three decades, first by the great social psychologist Kurt Lewin and later in many experimental situations by myself and other behavioral scientists. My conclu-

sion after poring over hundreds of relevant documents—historical reports about formal group meetings and informal conversations among the members—is that the groups that committed the fiascos were victims of what I call "groupthink."

"GROUPY"

In each case study, I was surprised to discover the extent to which each group displayed the typical phenomena of social conformity that are regularly encountered in studies of group dynamics among ordinary citizens. For example, some of the phenomena appear to be completely in line with findings from social-psychological experiments showing that powerful social pressures are brought to bear by the members of a cohesive group whenever a dissident begins to voice his objections to a group consensus. Other phenomena are reminiscent of the shared illusions observed in encounter groups and friendship cliques when the members simultaneously reach a peak of "groupy" feelings.

Above all, there are numerous indications pointing to the development of group norms that bolster morale at the expense of critical thinking. One of the most common norms appears to be that of remaining loyal to the group by sticking with the policies to which the group has already committed itself, even when those policies are obviously working out badly and have unintended consequences that disturb the conscience of each member. This is one of the key characteristics of groupthink.

*Source: From Psychology Today Magazine (November 1971), pp. 43-46, 74-76. Copyright © 1971 Ziff-Davis Publishing Company.

1984

I use the term groupthink as a quick and easy way to refer to the mode of thinking that persons engage in when *concurrence-seeking* becomes so dominant in a cohesive ingroup that it tends to override realistic appraisal of alternative courses of action. Groupthink is a term of the same order as the words in the newspeak vocabulary George Orwell used in his dismaying world of *1984*. In that context, groupthink takes on an invidious connotation. Exactly such a connotation is intended, since the term refers to a deterioration in mental efficiency, reality testing and moral judgments as a result of group pressures.

The symptoms of groupthink arise when the members of decision-making groups become motivated to avoid being too harsh in their judgments of their leaders' or their colleagues' ideas. They adopt a soft line of criticism, even in their own thinking. At their meetings, all the members are amiable and seek complete concurrence on every important issue, with no bickering or conflict to spoil the cozy, "we-feeling" atmosphere.

KILL

Paradoxically, soft-headed groups are often hard-hearted when it comes to dealing with outgroups or enemies. They find it relatively easy to resort to dehumanizing solutions—they will readily authorize bombing attacks that kill large numbers of civilians in the name of the noble cause of persuading an unfriendly government to negotiate at the peace table. They are unlikely to pursue the more difficult and controversial issues that arise when alternatives to a harsh military solution come up for discussion. Nor are they inclined to raise ethical issues that carry the implication that *this fine group of ours, with its humanitarianism and its high-minded principles, might be capable of adopting* a course of action that is inhumane and immoral.

NORMS

There is evidence from a number of social-psychological studies that as the members of a group feel more accepted by the others, which is a central feature of increased group cohesiveness, they display less overt conformity to group norms. Thus we would expect that the more cohesive a group becomes, the less the members will feel constrained to censor what they say out of fear of being socially punished for antagonizing the leader or any of their fellow members.

In contrast, the groupthink type of conformity tends to increase as group cohesiveness increases. Groupthink involves nondeliberate suppression of critical thoughts as a result of internalization of the group's norms, which is quite different from deliberate suppression on the basis of external threats of social punishment. The more cohesive the group, the greater the inner compulsion on the part of each member to avoid creating disunity, which inclines him to believe in the soundness of whatever proposals are promoted by the leader or by a majority of the group's members.

In a cohesive group, the danger is not so much that each individual will fail to reveal his objections to what the others propose but that he will think the proposal is a good one, without attempting to carry out a careful, critical scrutiny of the pros and cons of the alternatives. When groupthink becomes dominant, there also is considerable suppression of deviant thoughts, but it takes the form of each person's deciding that his misgivings are not relevant and should be set aside, that the benefit of the doubt regarding any lingering uncertainties should be given to the group consensus.

STRESS

I do not mean to imply that all cohesive groups necessarily suffer from groupthink. All ingroups may have a mild tendency toward groupthink, displaying one or another of the symptoms from time to time, but it need not be so dominant as to influence the quality of the group's final decision. Neither do I mean to imply that there is anything necessarily inefficient or harmful about group decisions in general. On the contrary, a group whose members have properly defined roles, with traditions concerning the procedures to follow in pursuing a critical inquiry, probably is capable of making better decisions than any individual group member working alone.

The problem is that the advantages of having decisions made by groups are often lost because of powerful psychological pressures that arise when the members work closely together, share the same set of values and, above all, face a crisis situation that puts everyone under intense stress.

The main principle of groupthink, which I offer in the spirit of Parkinson's Law, is this:

The more amiability and esprit de corps there is among the members of a policy-making ingroup, the greater the danger that independent critical thinking will be replaced by groupthink, which is likely to result in irrational and dehumanizing actions directed against outgroups.

SYMPTOMS

In my studies of high-level governmental decision-makers, both civilian and military, I have found eight main symptoms of groupthink.

1. INVULNERABILITY

Most or all of the members of the ingroup share an *illusion* of invulnerability that provides for them some degree of reassurance about obvious dangers and leads them to become over-optimistic and willing to take extraordinary risks. It also causes them to fail to respond to clear warnings of danger.

The Kennedy ingroup, which uncritically accepted the Central Intelligence Agency's disastrous Bay of Pigs plan, operated on the false assumption that they could keep secret the fact that the United States was responsible for the invasion of Cuba. Even after news of the plan began to leak out, their belief remained unshaken. They failed even to consider the danger that awaited them: a worldwide revulsion against the U.S.

A similar attitude appeared among the members of President Lyndon B. Johnson's ingroup, the "Tuesday Cabinet," which kept escalating the Vietnam War despite repeated setbacks and failures. "There was a belief," Bill Moyers commented after he resigned, "that if we indicated a willingness to use our power, they [the North Vietnamese] would get the message and back away from an all-out confrontation. . . . There was a confidence—it was never bragged about, it was just there—that when the chips were really down, the other people would fold."

A most poignant example of an illusion of invulnerability involves the ingroup around Admiral H. E. Kimmel, which failed to prepare for the possibility of a Japanese attack on Pearl Harbor despite repeated warnings. Informed by his intelligence chief that radio contact with Japanese aircraft carriers had been lost, Kimmel joked about it: "What, you don't know where the carriers are? Do you mean to say that they could be rounding Diamond Head (at Honolulu) and you wouldn't know it?" The carriers were in fact moving full-steam toward Kimmel's command post at the time. Laughing together about a danger signal, which labels it as a purely laughing matter, is a characteristic manifestation of groupthink.

2. RATIONALE

As we see, victims of groupthink ignore warnings; they also collectively construct rationalizations in order to discount warnings and other forms of negative feedback that, taken seriously, might lead the group members to reconsider their assumptions each time they recommit themselves to past decisions. Why did the Johnson ingroup avoid reconsidering its escalation policy when time and again the expectations on which they based their decisions turned out to be wrong? James C. Thompson, Jr., a Harvard historian who spent five years as an observing participant in both the State Department and the White House, tells us that the policymakers avoided critical discussion of their prior decisions and continually invented new rationalizations so that they could sincerely recommit themselves to defeating the North Vietnamese.

In the fall of 1964, before the bombing of North Vietnam began, some of the policymakers predicted that six weeks of air strikes would induce the North Vietnamese to seek peace talks. When someone asked, "What if they don't?" the answer was that another four weeks certainly would do the trick.

Later, after each setback, the ingroup agreed that by investing just a bit more effort (by stepping up the bomb tonnage a bit, for instance), their course of action would prove to be right. *The Pentagon Papers* bear out these observations.

In *The Limits of Intervention*, Townsend Hoopes, who was acting Secretary of the Air Force under Johnson, says that Walt W. Rostow in particular showed a remarkable capacity for what has been called "instant rationalization." According to Hoopes, Rostow buttressed the group's optimism about being on the road to victory by culling selected scraps of evidence from news reports or, if necessary, by inventing "plausible" forecasts that had no basis in evidence at all.

Admiral Kimmel's group rationalized away their warnings, too. Right up to December 7, 1941, they convinced themselves that the Japanese would never dare attempt a full-scale surprise assault against Hawaii because Japan's leaders would realize that it would precipitate an all-out war which the United States would surely win. They made no attempt to look at the situation through the eyes of the Japanese leaders— another manifestation of groupthink.

3. MORALITY

Victims of groupthink believe unquestioningly in the inherent morality of their ingroup; this belief inclines the members to ignore the ethical or moral consequences of their decisions.

Evidence that this symptom is at work usually is of a negative kind—the things that are left unsaid in group meetings. At least two influential persons had doubts about the morality of the Bay of Pigs adventure. One of them, Arthur Schlesinger Jr., presented his strong objections in a memorandum to President Kennedy and Secretary of State Rusk but suppressed them when he attended meetings of the Kennedy team. The other, Senator J. William Fulbright, was not a member of the group, but the President invited him to express his misgivings in a speech to the policymakers. However, when Fulbright finished speaking the President moved on to other agenda items without asking for reactions of the group.

David Kraslow and Stuart H. Loory, in *The Secret Search for Peace in Vietnam*, report that during 1966 President Johnson's ingroup was concerned primarily with selecting bomb targets in North Vietnam. They based their selections on four factors—the military advantage, the risk to American aircraft and pilots, the danger of forcing other countries into the fighting, and the danger of heavy civilian casualties. At their regular Tuesday luncheons, they weighed these factors the way school teachers grade examination papers, averaging them out. Though evidence on this point is scant, I suspect that the group's ritualistic adherence to a standardized procedure induced the members to feel morally justified in their destructive way of dealing with the Vietnamese people—after all, the danger of heavy civilian casualties from U.S. air strikes was taken into account on their checklists.

4. STEREOTYPES

Victims of groupthink hold stereotyped views of the leaders of enemy groups: they are so evil that genuine attempts at negotiating differences with them are unwarranted, or they are too weak or too stupid to deal effectively with whatever attempts the ingroup makes to defeat their purposes, no matter how risky the attempts are.

Kennedy's groupthinkers believed that Premier Fidel Castro's air force was so ineffectual that obsolete B-26s could knock it out completely in a surprise attack before the invasion began. They also believed that Castro's army was so weak that a small Cuban-exile brigade could establish a well-protected beachhead at the Bay of Pigs. In addition, they believed that Castro was not smart enough to put down any possible internal uprisings in support of the exiles. They were wrong on all three assumptions. Though much of the blame was attributable to faulty intelligence, the point is that none of Kennedy's advisers even questioned the CIA planners about these assumptions.

The Johnson advisers' sloganistic thinking about "the Communist apparatus" that was "working all around the world" (as Dean Rusk put it) led them to overlook the powerful nationalistic strivings of the North Vietnamese government and its efforts to ward off Chinese domination. The crudest of all stereotypes used by Johnson's inner circle to justify their policies was the domino theory ("If we don't stop the Reds in South Vietnam, tomorrow they will be in Hawaii and next week they will be in San Francisco," Johnson once said). The group so firmly accepted this stereotype that it became almost impossible for any adviser to introduce a more sophisticated viewpoint.

In the documents on Pearl Harbor, it is clear to see that the Navy commanders stationed in Hawaii had a naive image of Japan as a midget that would not dare to strike a blow against a powerful giant.

5. PRESSURE

Victims of groupthink apply direct pressure to any individual who momentarily expresses doubts about any of the group's shared illusions or who questions the validity of the arguments supporting a policy alternative favored by the majority. This gambit reinforces the concurrence-seeking norm that loyal members are expected to maintain.

President Kennedy probably was more active than anyone else in raising skeptical questions during the Bay of Pigs meetings, and yet he seems to have encouraged the group's docile, uncritical acceptance of defective arguments in favor of the CIA's plan. At every meeting, he allowed the CIA representatives to dominate the discussion. He permitted them to give their immediate refutations in response to each tentative doubt that one of the others expressed, instead of asking whether anyone shared the doubt or wanted to pursue the implications of the new worrisome issue that had just been raised. And at the most crucial meeting, when he was calling on each member to give his vote for or against the plan, he did not call on Arthur Schlesinger, the one man there who was known by the President to have serious misgivings.

Historian Thomson informs us that whenever a member of Johnson's ingroup began to express doubts, the group used subtle social pressures to "domesticate" him. To start with, the dissenter was made to feel at home, provided that he lived up to two restrictions: 1) that he did not voice his doubts to outsiders, which would play into the hands of the opposition; and 2) that he kept his criticisms within the bounds of acceptable deviation, which meant not challenging any of the fundamental assumptions that went into the group's prior commitments. One such "domesticated dissenter" was Bill Moyers. When Moyers arrived at a meeting, Thomson tells us, the President greeted him with, "Well, here comes Mr. Stop-the-Bombing."

6. SELF-CENSORSHIP

Victims of groupthink avoid deviating from what appears to be group consensus; they keep silent about their misgivings and even minimize to themselves the importance of their doubts.

As we have seen, Schlesinger was not at all hesitant about presenting his strong objections to the Bay of Pigs plan in a memorandum to the President and the Secretary of State. But he became keenly aware of his tendency to suppress objections at the White House meetings. "In the months after the Bay of Pigs I bitterly reproached myself for having kept so silent during those crucial discussions in the cabinet room," Schlesinger writes in *A Thousand Days*. "I can only explain my failure to do more than raise a few timid questions by reporting that one's impulse to blow the whistle on this nonsense was simply undone by the circumstances of the discussion."

7. UNANIMITY

Victims of groupthink share an *illusion* of unanimity within the group concerning all judgments expressed by members who speak in favor of the majority view. This symptom results partly from the preceding one, whose effects are augmented by the false assumption that any individual who remains silent during any part of the discussion is in full accord with what the others are saying.

When a group of persons who respect each other's opinions arrives at a unanimous view, each member is likely to feel that the belief must be true. This reliance on consensual validation within the group tends to replace individual critical thinking and reality testing unless there are clear-cut disagreements among the members. In contemplating a course of action such as the invasion of Cuba, it is painful for the members to confront disagreements within their group, particularly if it becomes apparent that there are widely divergent views about whether the preferred course of action is too risky to undertake at all. Such disagreements are likely to arouse anxieties about making a serious error. Once the sense of unanimity is shattered, the members no longer can feel complacently confident about the decision they are inclined to make. Each man must then face the annoying realization that there are troublesome uncertainties and he must diligently seek out the best information he can get in order to decide for himself exactly how serious the risks might be. This is one of the unpleasant consequences of being in a group of hard-headed, critical thinkers.

To avoid such an unpleasant state, the members often become inclined, without quite realizing it, to prevent latent disagreements from surfacing when they are about to initiate a risky course of action. The group leader and the members support each other in playing up the areas of convergence in their thinking, at the expense of fully exploring divergencies that might reveal unsettled issues.

"Our meetings took place in a curious atmosphere of assumed consensus," Schlesinger writes. His additional comments clearly show that, curiously, the consensus was an illusion—an illusion that could be maintained only because the major participants did not reveal their own reasoning or discuss their idiosyncratic assumptions and vague reservations. Evidence from several sources makes it clear that even the three principals—President Kennedy, Rusk and McNamara—had widely differing assumptions about the invasion plan.

8. MINDGUARDS

Victims of groupthink sometimes appoint themselves as mindguards to protect the leader and fellow members from adverse information that might break the complacency they shared about the effectiveness and morality of past decisions. At a large birthday party for his wife, Attorney General Robert F. Kennedy, who had been constantly informed about the Cuban invasion plan, took Schlesinger aside and asked him why he was opposed. Kennedy listened coldly and said, "You may be right or you may be wrong, but the President has made his mind up. Don't push it any further. Now is the time for everyone to help him all they can."

Rusk also functioned as a highly effective mindguard by failing to transmit to the group the strong objections of three "outsiders" who had learned of the invasion plan—Undersecretary of State Chester Bowles, USIA Director Edward R. Murrow, and Rusk's intelligence chief, Roger Hilsman. Had Rusk done so, their warnings might have reinforced Schlesinger's memorandum and jolted some of Kennedy's ingroup, if not the President himself, into reconsidering the decision.

PRODUCTS

When a group of executives frequently displays most or all of these interrelated symptoms, a detailed study of their deliberations is likely to reveal a number of immediate consequences. These consequences are, in effect, products of poor decision-making practices because they lead to inadequate solutions to the problems under discussion.

First, the group limits its discussions to a few alternative courses of action (often only two) without an initial survey of all the alternatives that might be worthy of consideration.

Second, the group fails to reexamine the course of action initially preferred by the majority after they learn of risks and drawbacks they had not considered originally.

Third, the members spend little or no time discussing whether there are no obvious gains they may have overlooked or ways of reducing the seemingly prohibitive costs that made rejected alternatives appear undesirable to them.

Fourth, members make little or no attempt to obtain information from experts within their own organizations who might be able to supply more precise estimates of potential losses and gains.

Fifth, members show positive interest in facts and opinions that support their preferred policy; they tend to ignore facts and opinions that do not.

Sixth, members spend little time deliberating about how the chosen policy might be hindered by bureaucratic inertia, sabotaged by political opponents, or temporarily derailed by common accidents. Consequently, they fail to work out contingency plans to cope with foreseeable setbacks that could endanger the overall success of their chosen course.

SUPPORT

The search for an explanation of why groupthink occurs has led me through a quagmire of complicated theoretical issues in the murky area of human motivation. My belief, based on recent social psychological research, is that we can best understand the various symptoms of groupthink as a mutual effort among the group members to maintain self-esteem and emotional equanimity by providing social support to each other, especially at times when they share responsibility for making vital decisions.

Even when no important decision is pending, the typical administrator will begin to doubt the wisdom and morality of his past decisions each time he receives information about setbacks, particularly if the information is accompanied by negative feedback from prominent men who originally had been his supporters. It should not be surprising, therefore, to find that individual members strive to develop unanimity and esprit de corps that will help bolster each other's morale, to create an optimistic outlook about the success of pending decisions, and to reaffirm the positive value of past policies to which all of them are committed.

PRIDE

Shared illusions of invulnerability, for example, can reduce anxiety about taking risks. Rationalizations help members believe that the risks are really not so bad after all. The assumption of inherent morality helps the members to avoid feelings of shame or guilt. Negative stereotypes function as stress-reducing devices to enhance a sense of moral righteousness as well as pride in a lofty mission.

The mutual enhancement of self-esteem and morale may have functional value in enabling the members to maintain their capacity to take action, but it has maladaptive consequences insofar as concurrence-seeking tendencies interfere with critical, rational capacities and lead to serious errors of judgment.

While I have limited my study to decision-making bodies in Government, groupthink symptoms appear in business, industry and any other field where small, cohesive groups make the decisions. It is vital, then, for all sorts of people—and especially group leaders—to know what steps they can take to prevent groupthink.

REMEDIES

To counterpoint my case studies of the major fiascos, I have also investi-gated two highly successful group enterprises, the formulation of the Marshall Plan in the Truman Administration and the handling of the Cuban missile crisis by President Kennedy and his advisers. I have found it instructive to examine the steps Kennedy took to change his group's decision-making processes. These changes ensured that the mistakes made by his Bay of Pigs ingroup were not repeated by the missile-crisis ingroup, even though the membership of both groups was essentially the same.

The following recommendations for preventing groupthink incorporate many of the good practices I discovered to be characteristic of the Marshall Plan and missile-crisis groups:

1. The leader of a policy-forming group should assign the role of critical evaluator to each member, encouraging the group to give high priority to open airing of objections and doubts. This practice needs to be reinforced by the leader's acceptance of criticism of his own judgments in order to discourage members from soft-pedaling their disagreements and from allowing their striving for concurrence to inhibit critical thinking.

2. When the key members of a hierarchy assign a policy-planning mission to any group within their organization, they should adopt an impartial stance instead of stating preferences and expectations at the beginning. This will encourage open inquiry and impartial probing of a wide range of policy alternatives.

3. The organization routinely should set up several outside policy-planning and evaluation groups to work on the same policy question, each deliberating under a different leader. This can prevent the insulation of an ingroup.

4. At intervals before the group reaches a final consensus, the leader should require each member to discuss the group's deliberations with associates in his own unit of the organization—assuming that those associates can be trusted to adhere to the same security regulations that govern the policy-makers—and then to report back their reactions to the group.

5. The group should invite one or more outside experts to each meeting on a staggered basis and encourage the experts to challenge the views of the core members.

6. At every general meeting of the group, whenever the agenda calls for an evaluation of policy alternatives, at least one member should play devil's advocate, functioning as a good lawyer in challenging the testimony of those who advocate the majority position.

7. Whenever the policy issue involves relations with a rival nation or organization, the group should devote a sizable block of time, perhaps an entire session, to a survey of all warning signals from the rivals and should write alternative scenarios on the rivals' intentions.

8. When the group is surveying policy alternatives for feasibility and effectiveness, it should from time to time divide into two or more subgroups to meet separately under different chairmen, and then come back together to hammer out differences.

9. After reaching a preliminary consensus about what seems to be the best policy, the group should hold a "second-chance" meeting at which every member expresses as vividly as he can all his residual doubts, and rethinks the entire issue before making a definitive choice.

HOW

These recommendations have their disadvantages. To encourage the open airing of objections, for instance, might lead to prolonged and costly debates when a rapidly growing crisis requires immediate solution. It also could cause rejection, depression and anger. A leader's failure to set a norm might create cleavage between leader and members that could develop into a disruptive power struggle if the leader looks on the emerging consensus as anathema. Setting up outside evaluation groups might increase the risk of security leakage. Still, inventive executives who know their way around the organizational maze probably can figure out how to apply one or another of the prescriptions successfully, without harmful side effects.

They also could benefit from the advice of outside experts in the administrative and behavioral sciences. Though these experts have much to offer, they have had few chances to work on policy-making machinery within large organizations. As matters now stand, executives innovate only when they need new procedures to avoid repeating serious errors that have deflated their self-images.

In this era of atomic warheads, urban disorganization and ecocatastrophes, it seems to me that policymakers should collaborate with behavioral scientists and give top priority to preventing groupthink and its attendant fiascos.

IV

Leadership and Power

Introduction. Leadership is generally defined as the process of influencing the activities of others toward the accomplishment of organizational goals, whereas power is the resource that enables a leader to actually influence others. For centuries, people have sought the valid prescription for effective leadership, and the literature of organizational behavior is rich with theories of leadership and power. This section reviews some of the better-known theoretical models.

Power enables leaders to exercise influence over other people. John R. P. French, Jr., and Bertram Raven, in "The Bases of Social Power," suggest that there are five major bases of power: (1) *expert power,* which is based on the perception that the leader possesses some special knowledge or expertise; (2) *referent power,* which is based on the follower's liking, admiring, or identifying with the leader; (3) *reward power,* which is based on the leader's ability to mediate rewards for the follower; (4) *legitimate power,* which is based on the follower's perception that the leader has the legitimate right or authority to exercise influence over him or her; and (5) *coercive power,* which is based on the follower's fear that noncompliance with the leader's wishes will lead to punishment. Subsequent research on these power bases has indicated that emphasis on expert and referent power are more positively related to subordinate performance and satisfaction than utilization of reward, legitimate, or coercive power.

Fred E. Fiedler's article, "Style or Circumstance: The Leadership Enigma," begins by asking, "What is it that makes a person an effective leader?" The author suggests that the answer lies in the prescriptions of his contingency theory of leadership, which was popularized in his 1967 book, *A Theory of Leadership Effectiveness.* According to Fiedler's theory, the appropriate leadership style is determined by three critical elements in the leader's situation: (1) the power position of the leader; (2) the task structure; and (3) the leader-member personal relationships. The nature of these three factors determines the "favorableness" of the situation for the leader, which in turn requires a particular leadership style. Fiedler views leader behavior as a single dimension ranging from "task-oriented" to "relationship-oriented." He contends that task-oriented leaders perform

189

best in very favorable or very unfavorable situations, whereas relationship-oriented leaders are best in mixed situations. Fiedler concludes by suggesting that it may be to an organization's advantage to try to design jobs to fit leaders' styles rather than attempting to change leaders' behavior to fit the situation.

In their 1973 article, "How to Choose a Leadership Pattern," Robert Tannenbaum and Warren H. Schmidt view leader behavior on a continuum ranging from authoritarian (boss-centered) to democratic (subordinate-centered) and discuss numerous behavior points occurring along this spectrum. The problem facing managers is how to be "democratic" in relations with subordinates while maintaining adequate authority and control within the organization. In making this decision, managers are asked to examine various forces in themselves, forces in their subordinates, and forces inherent in the situation. The unique circumstances of the situation then determines the appropriate pattern of leader behavior. It is important to note the "situational" nature of their analysis, which was written some 15 years before the approach became popular.

Robert J. House and Terence R. Mitchell's article, "Path-Goal Theory of Leadership," presents a theory similar to the expectancy theory of motivation, in that it focuses upon the leader's impact on the motivation, performance, and satisfaction of his or her subordinates. The theory is called "Path-Goal" because it is primarily concerned with how the leader influences the subordinates' perceptions of their task goals and the paths to goal attainment. House and Mitchell espouse two general propositions: (1) that leader behavior is acceptable and satisfying to subordinates to the extent that the subordinates see such behavior as a source of immediate or future satisfaction, and (2) that the leader's behavior will increase subordinates' effort to the extent that such behavior makes satisfaction of subordinates' needs dependent on effective performance and that such behavior provides the guidance, support, and rewards necessary for effective performance. The means by which leaders can enhance subordinates' motivation to perform are discussed, as are a number of studies that have provided empirical support for the theory. The authors conclude by suggesting that the conceptual nature of path-goal theory and its relative infancy are likely to make it more useful as a means of stimulating insight into the leadership process than as a proven guide for managerial action.

Gerald R. Salancik and Jeffrey Pfeffer advance a model of power which contends that power is one of the few institutional mechanisms capable of reforming organizations to successfully cope with a changing environment. In the selection "Who Gets Power—and How They Hold on to It," Salancik and Pfeffer argue that power helps organizations become "aligned" with external realities to the extent that power is acquired by those subunits of the organization most able to cope with the organization's current critical problems and uncertainties. These critical "contingencies" in the external environment change over time.

Hence, organizations with mechanisms for sharing and redistributing power in a timely fashion have an increased capacity to be attuned with the needs and demands emanating from their environment.

Paul Hersey and Kenneth H. Blanchard are noted for their conceptualization of "Situational Leadership," which was originally called the "life cycle theory of leadership." In their updated and expanded article, "Situational Leadership and Power," Hersey, Blanchard, and Walter E. Natemeyer suggest that the appropriate leadership style and power bases for a particular situation are primarily dependent upon the task-maturity level of the follower(s). "Maturity" is defined as a function of task-relevant education and experience, achievement motivation, and willingness and ability to accept responsibility. Leadership is seen as a combination of two types of behavior—"task behavior" (directive) and "relationship behavior" (supportive). Seven power bases are also discussed—coercive, connection, reward, legitimate, referent, information, and expert. The authors suggest that as a follower matures in his or her work situation, the leader should decrease emphasis on "direction" and use of "position power" and evolve into more of a participative-delegative style supported by "personal power."

17. The Bases of Social Power*

JOHN R. P. FRENCH, JR.

BERTRAM RAVEN

The processes of power are pervasive, complex, and often disguised in our society. Accordingly one finds in political science, in sociology, and in social psychology a variety of distinctions among different types of social power or among qualitatively different processes of social influence.[1] Our main purpose is to identify the major types of power and to define them systematically so that we may compare them according to the changes which they produce and the other effects which accompany the use of power. The phenomena of power and influence involve a dyadic relation between two agents which may be viewed from two points of view: (a) What determines the behavior of the agent who exerts power? (b) What determines the reactions of the recipient of this behavior? We take this second point of view and formulate our theory in terms of the life space of P, the person upon whom the power is exerted. In this way we hope to define basic concepts of power which will be adequate to explain many of the phenomena of social influence, including some which have been described in other less genotypic terms.

Recent empirical work, especially on small groups, has demonstrated the necessity of distinguishing different types of power in order to account for the different effects found in studies of social influence. Yet there is no doubt that more empirical knowledge will be needed to make final decisions concerning the necessary differentiations, but this knowledge will be obtained only by research based on some preliminary theoretical distinctions. We present such preliminary concepts and some of the hypotheses they suggest.

POWER, INFLUENCE, AND CHANGE

PSYCHOLOGICAL CHANGE

Since we shall define power in terms of influence, and influence in terms of psychological change, we begin with a discussion of change. We want to define change at a level of generality which includes changes in behavior, opinions, attitudes, goals, needs, values and all other aspects of the person's psychological field. We shall use the word "system" to refer to any such part of the life space.[2] Following Lewin the state of a system at time 1 will be denoted $s_1(a)$.[3]

Psychological change is defined as any alteration of the state of some system a over time. The amount of change is measured by the size of the difference between the states of the system a at time 1 and at time 2: $ch(a) = s_2(a) - s_1(a)$.

Change in any psychological system may be conceptualized in terms of psychological forces. But it is important to note that the change must be coordinated to the resultant force of all the

*Source: From Dorwin Cartwright, ed., Studies in Social Power (Ann Arbor, Mich.: Institute for Social Research, University of Michigan, 1959), pp. 150-165. Copyright © 1959 Institute for Social Research. Reprinted by permission.

forces operating at the moment. Change in an opinion, for example, may be determined jointly by a driving force induced by another person, a restraining force corresponding to anchorage in a group opinion, and an own force stemming from the person's needs.

SOCIAL INFLUENCE

Our theory of social influence and power is limited to influence on the person, P, produced by a social agent, O, where O can be either another person, a role, a norm, a group or a part of a group. We do not consider social influence exerted on a group.

The influence of O on system a in the life space of P is defined as the resultant force on system a which has its source in an act of O. This resultant force induced by O consists of two components: a force to change the system in the direction induced by O and an opposing resistance set up by the same act of O.

By this definition the influence of O does not include P's own forces nor the forces induced by other social agents. Accordingly the "influence" of O must be clearly distinguished from O's "control" of P. O may be able to induce strong forces on P to carry out an activity (i.e., O exerts strong influence on P); but if the opposing forces induced by another person or by P's own needs are stronger, then P will locomote in an opposite direction (i.e., O does not have control over P). Thus psychological change in P can be taken as an operational definition of the social influence of O on P only when the effects of other forces have been eliminated.

It is assumed that any system is interdependent with other parts of the life space so that a change in one may produce changes in others. However, this theory focuses on the primary changes in a system which are produced directly by social influence; it is less concerned with secondary changes which are indirectly effected in the other systems or with primary changes produced by nonsocial influences.

Commonly social influence takes place through an intentional act on the part of O. However, we do not want to limit our definition of "act" to such conscious behavior. Indeed, influence might result from the passive presence of O, with no evidence of speech or overt movement. A policeman's standing on a corner may be considered an act of an agent for the speeding motorist. Such acts of the inducing agent will vary in strength, for O may not always utilize all of his power. The policeman, for example, may merely stand and watch or act more strongly by blowing his whistle at the motorist.

The influence exerted by an act need not be in the direction intended by O. The direction of the resultant force on P will depend on the relative magnitude of the induced force set up by the act of O and the resisting force in the opposite direction which is generated by that same act. In cases where O intends to influence P in a given direction, a resultant force in the same direction may be termed positive influence whereas a resultant force in the opposite direction may be termed negative influence.

If O produces the intended change, he has exerted positive control; but if he produces a change in the opposite direction, as for example in the negativism of young children or in the phenomena of negative reference groups, he has exerted negative control.

SOCIAL POWER

The strength of power of O/P in some system a is defined as the maximum potential ability of O to influence P in a.

By this definition influence is kinetic power, just as power is potential influence. It is assumed that O is capable of various acts which, because of some more or less enduring relation to P, are able to exert influence on P.[4] O's power is measured by his maximum possible influence, though he may often choose to exert less than his full power.

An equivalent definition of power may be stated in terms of the resultant of two forces set up by the act of O: one in the direction of O's influence attempt and another resisting force in the opposite direction. Power is the maximum resultant of these two forces:

$$\text{Power of O/P(a)} = (f_{a,x} - f_{\overline{a},x})^{max}$$

where the source of both forces is an act of O.

Thus the power of O with respect to system a of P is equal to the maximum resultant force of two forces set up by any possible act of O: (a) the force which O can set up on the system a to change in the direction x, (b) the resisting force[5] in the opposite direction. Whenever the first component force is greater than the second, positive power exists; but if the second component force is greater than the first, then O has negative power over P.

It is necessary to define power with respect to a specified system because the power of O/P may vary greatly from one system to another. O may have great power to control the behavior of P but little power to control his opinions. Of course a high power of O/P does not imply a low power of P/O; the two variables are conceptually independent.

For certain purposes it is convenient to define the range of power as the set of all systems within which O has power of strength greater than zero. A husband may have a broad range of power over his wife, but a narrow range of power over his employer. We shall use the term "magnitude of power" to denote the summation of O's power over P in all systems of his range.

THE DEPENDENCE OF s(a) ON O

Several investigators have been concerned with differences between superficial conformity and "deeper" changes produced by social influence.[6] The kinds of systems which are changed and the stability of these changes have been handled by distinctions such as "public vs. private attitudes," "overt vs. covert behavior," "compliance vs. internalization," and "own vs. induced forces." Though stated as dichotomies, all of these distinctions suggest an underlying dimension of the degree of dependence of the state of a system on O.

We assume that any change in the state of a system is produced by a change in some factor upon which it is functionally dependent. The state of an opinion, for example, may change because of a change either in some internal factor such as a need or in some external factor such as the arguments of O. Likewise the maintenance of the same state of a system is produced by the stability or lack of change in the internal and external factors. In general, then, psychological change and stability can be conceptualized in terms of dynamic dependence. Our interest is focused on the special case of dependence on an external agent, O.[7]

In many cases the initial state of the system has the character of a quasi-stationary equilibrium with a central force held around $s_1(a)$.[8] In such cases we may derive a tendency toward retrogression to the original state as soon as the force induced by O is removed.[9] Let us suppose that O exerts influence producing a new state of the system, $s_2(a)$. Is $s_2(a)$ now dependent on the continued presence of O? In principle we could answer this question by removing any traces of O from the life space of P and by observing the consequent state of the system at time 3. If $s_3(a)$ retrogresses completely back to $s_1(a)$, then we may conclude that maintenance of $s_2(a)$ was completely dependent on O; but if $s_3(a)$ equals $s_2(a)$, this lack of change shows that $s_2(a)$ has become completely independent of O. In general the degree of dependence of $s_2(a)$ on O, following O's influence, may be defined as equal to the amount of retrogression following the removal of O from the life space of P:

Degree of dependence of $s_2(a)$ on $O =$
$$s_2(a) - s_3(a).$$

A given degree of dependence at time 2 may later change, for example, through the gradual weakening of O's influence. At this later time, the degree of dependence of $s_4(a)$ on O, would still be equal to the amount of retrogression toward the initial state of equilibrium $s_1(a)$. Operational measures of the degree of dependence on O will, of course, have to be taken under conditions where all other factors are held constant.

Consider the example of three separated employees who have been working at the same steady level of production despite normal, small fluctuations in the work environment. The supervisor orders each to increase his production, and the level of each goes up from 100 to 115 pieces per day. After a week of producing at the new rate of 115 pieces per day, the supervisor is removed for a week. The production of employee A immediately returns to 100 but B and C return to only 110 pieces per day. Other things being equal, we can infer that A's new rate was completely dependent on his supervisor whereas the new rate of B and C was dependent on the supervisor only to the extent of 5 pieces. Let us further assume that when the supervisor returned, the production of B and of C returned to 115 without further orders from the supervisor. Now another month goes by during which B and C maintain a steady 115 pieces per day. However, there is a difference between them: B's level of production still depends on O to the extent of 5 pieces whereas C has come to rely on his own sense of obligation to obey the order of his legitimate supervisor rather than on the supervisor's external pressure for the maintenance of his 115 pieces per day. Accordingly, the next time the supervisor departs, B's production again drops to 110 but C's remains at 115

pieces per day. In cases like employee B, the degree of dependence is contingent on the perceived probability that O will observe the state of the system and note P's conformity.[10] The level of observability will in turn depend on both the nature of the system (e.g., the difference between a covert opinion and overt behavior) and on the environmental barriers to observation (e.g., O is too far away from P). In other cases, for example that of employee C, the new behavior pattern is highly dependent on his supervisor, but the degree of dependence of the new state will be related not to the level of observability but rather to factors inside P, in this case a sense of duty to perform an act legitimately prescribed by O. The internalization of social norms is a related process of decreasing degree of dependence of behavior on an external O and increasing dependence on an internal value; it is usually assumed that internalization is accompanied by a decrease in the effects of level of observability.[11]

The concepts "dependence of a system on O" and "observability as a basis for dependence" will be useful in understanding the stability of conformity. In the next section we shall discuss various types of power and the types of conformity which they are likely to produce.

THE BASES OF POWER

By the basis of power we mean the relationship between O and P which is the source of that power. It is rare that we can say with certainty that a given empirical case of power is limited to one source. Normally, the relation between O and P will be characterized by several qualitatively different variables which are bases of power.[12] Although there are undoubtedly many possible bases of power which may be distinguished, we shall here define five which seem especially common and important. These five bases of O's power are:

(1) reward power, based on P's perception that O has the ability to mediate rewards for him; (2) coercive power, based on P's perception that O has the ability to mediate punishments for him; (3) legitimate power, based on the perception by P that O has a legitimate right to prescribe behavior for him; (4) referent power, based on P's identification with O; (5) expert power, based on the perception that O has some special knowledge or expertness.

Our first concern is to define the bases which give rise to a given type of power. Next, we describe each type of power according to its strength, range, and the degree of dependence of the new state of the system which is most likely to occur with each type of power. We shall also examine the other effects which the exercise of a given type of power may have upon P and his relationship to O. Finally, we shall point out the interrelationships between different types of power, and the effects of use of one type of power by O upon other bases of power which he might have over P. Thus we shall both define a set of concepts and propose a series of hypotheses. Most of these hypotheses have not been systematically tested, although there is a good deal of evidence in favor of several. No attempt will be made to summarize that evidence here.

REWARD POWER

Reward power is defined as power whose basis is the ability to reward. The strength of the reward power of O/P increases with the magnitude of the rewards which P perceives that O can mediate for him. Reward power depends on O's ability to administer positive valences and to remove or decrease negative valences. The strength of reward power also depends upon the probability that O can mediate the reward, as perceived by P. A common example of reward power is the addition of piece-work rate in the factory as an incentive to increase production.

The new state of the system induced by a promise of reward (for example the factory worker's increased level of production) will be highly dependent on O. Since O mediates the reward, he controls the probability that P will receive it. Thus P's new rate of production will be dependent on his subjective probability that O will reward him for conformity minus his subjective probability that O will reward him even if he returns to his old level. Both probabilities will be greatly affected by the level of observability of P's behavior. Incidentally, a piece rate often seems to have more effect on production than a merit rating system because it yields a higher probability of reward for conformity and a much lower probability of reward for nonconformity.

The utilization of actual rewards (instead of promises) by O will tend over time to increase the attraction of P toward O and therefore the referent power of O over P. As we shall note later, such referent power will permit O to induce changes which are relatively independent. Neither rewards nor promises will arouse resistance in P, provided P considers it legitimate for O to offer rewards.

The range of reward power is specific to those regions within which O can reward P for conforming. The use of rewards to change systems within the range of reward power tends to increase reward power by increasing the probability attached to future promises. However, unsuccessful attempts to exert reward power outside the range of power would tend to decrease the power; for example if O offers to reward P for performing an impossible act, this will reduce for P the probability of receiving future rewards promised by O.

COERCIVE POWER

Coercive power is similar to reward power in that it also involves O's ability to manipulate the attainment of valences. Coercive power of O/P stems from the expectation on the part of P that he will be punished by O if he fails to conform to the influence attempt. Thus negative valences will exist in given regions of P's life space, corresponding to the threatened punishment by O. The strength of coercive power depends on the magnitude of the negative valence of the threatened punishment multiplied by the perceived probability that P can avoid the punishment by conformity, i.e., the probability of punishment for nonconformity minus the probability of punishment for conformity.[13] Just as an offer of a piece-rate bonus in a factory can serve as a basis for reward power, so the ability to fire a worker if he falls below a given level of production will result in coercive power.

Coercive power leads to dependent change also; and the degree of dependence varies with the level of observability of P's conformity. An excellent illustration of coercive power leading to dependent change is provided by a clothes presser in a factory observed by Coch and French.[14] As her efficiency rating climbed above average for the group the other workers began to "scapegoat" her. That the resulting plateau in her production was not independent of the group was evident once she was removed from the presence of the other workers. Her production immediately climbed to new heights.[15]

At times, there is some difficulty in distinguishing between reward power and coercive power. Is the withholding of a reward really equivalent to a punishment? Is the withdrawal of punishment equivalent to a reward? The answer must be a psychological one—it depends upon the situation as it exists for P. But ordinarily we would answer these questions in the affirmative; for P, receiving a reward is a positive valence as is the relief of suffering. There is some evidence that conformity to group norms in order to gain acceptance (reward power) should be distinguished from conformity as a means of

forestalling rejection (coercive power).[16]

The distinction between these two types of power is important because the dynamics are different. The concept of "sanctions" sometimes lumps the two together despite their opposite effects. While reward power may eventually result in an independent system, the effects of coercive power will continue to be dependent. Reward power will tend to increase the attraction of P toward O; coercive power will decrease this attraction.[17] The valence of the region of behavior will become more negative, acquiring some negative valence from the threatened punishment. The negative valence of punishment would also spread to other regions of the life space. Lewin has pointed out this distinction between the effects of rewards and punishment.[18] In the case of threatened punishment, there will be a resultant force on P to leave the field entirely. Thus, to achieve conformity, O must not only place a strong negative valence in certain regions through threat of punishment, but O must also introduce restraining forces, or other strong valences, so as to prevent P from withdrawing completely from O's range of coercive power. Otherwise the probability of receiving the punishment, if P does not conform, will be too low to be effective.

LEGITIMATE POWER

Legitimate power is probably the most complex of those treated here, embodying notions from the structural sociologist, the group-norm and role oriented social psychologist, and the clinical psychologist.

There has been considerable investigation and speculation about socially prescribed behavior, particularly that which is specified to a given role or position. Linton distinguishes group norms according to whether they are universals for everyone in the culture, alternatives (the individual having a choice as to whether or not to accept them), or specialties (specific to given positions).[19] Whether we speak of internalized norms, role prescriptions and expectations,[20] or internalized pressures,[21] the fact remains that each individual sees certain regions toward which he should locomote, some regions toward which he should not locomote, and some regions toward which he may locomote if they are generally attractive for him. This applies to specific behaviors in which he may, should, or should not engage; it applies to certain attitudes or beliefs which he may, should, or should not hold. The feeling of "oughtness" may be an internalization from his parents, from his teachers, from his religion, or may have been logically developed from some idiosyncratic system of ethics. He will speak of such behaviors with expressions like "should" "ought to," or "has a right to." In many cases, the original source of the requirement is not recalled.

Though we have oversimplified such evaluations of behavior with a positive-neutral-negative trichotomy, the evaluation of behaviors by the person is really more one of degree. This dimension of evaluation, we shall call "legitimacy." Conceptually, we may think of legitimacy as a valence in a region which is induced by some internalized norm or value. This value has the same conceptual property as power, namely an ability to induce force fields.[22] It may or may not be correct that values (or the super-ego) are internalized parents, but at least they can set up force fields which have a phenomenal "oughtness" similar to a parent's prescription. Like a value, a need can also induce valences (i.e., force fields) in P's psychological environment, but these valences have more the phenomenal character of noxious or attractive properties of the object or activity. When a need induces a valence in P, for example, when a need makes an object attractive to P, this attraction applies to P but not to other persons.

When a value induces a valence, on the other hand, it not only sets up forces on P to engage in the activity, but P may feel that all others ought to behave in the same way. Among other things, this evaluation applies to the legitimate right of some other individual or group to prescribe behavior or beliefs for a person even though the other cannot apply sanctions.

Legitimate power of O/P is here defined as that power which stems from internalized values in P which dictate that O has a legitimate right to influence P and that P has an obligation to accept this influence. We note that legitimate power is very similar to the notion of legitimacy of authority which has long been explored by sociologists, particularly by Weber,[23] and more recently by Goldhammer and Shils.[24] However, legitimate power is not always a role relation: P may accept an induction from O simply because he had previously promised to help O and he values his work too much to break the promise. In all cases, the notion of legitimacy involves some sort of code or standard, accepted by the individual, by virtue of which the external agent can assert his power. We shall attempt to describe a few of these values here.

• *Bases for legitimate power.* Cultural values constitute one common basis for the legitimate power of one individual over another. O has characteristics which are specified by the culture as giving him the right to prescribe behavior for P, who may not have these characteristics. These bases, which Weber has called the authority of the "eternal yesterday," include such things as age, intelligence, caste, and physical characteristics.[25] In some cultures, the aged are granted the right to prescribe behavior for others in practically all behavior areas. In most cultures, there are certain areas of behavior in which a person of one sex is granted the right to prescribe behavior for the other sex.

Acceptance of the social structure is

another basis for legitimate power. If P accepts as right the social structure of his group, organization, or society, especially the social structure involving a hierarchy of authority, P will accept the legitimate authority of O who occupies a superior office in the hierarchy. Thus legitimate power in a formal organization is largely a relationship between offices rather than between persons. And the acceptance of an office as *right* is a basis for legitimate power—a judge has a right to levy fines, a foreman should assign work, a priest is justified in prescribing religious beliefs, and it is the management's prerogative to make certain decisions.[26] However, legitimate power also involves the perceived right of the person to hold the office.

Designation by a legitimizing agent is a third basis for legitimate power. An influencer O may be seen as legitimate in prescribing behavior for P because he has been granted such power by a legitimizing agent whom P accepts. Thus a department head may accept the authority of his vice-president in a certain area because that authority has been specifically delegated by the president. An election is perhaps the most common example of a group's serving to legitimize the authority of one individual or office for other individuals in the group. The success of such legitimizing depends upon the acceptance of the legitimizing agent and procedure. In this case it depends ultimately on certain democratic values concerning election procedures. The election process is one of legitimizing a person's right to an office which already has a legitimate range of power associated with it.

● *Range of legitimate power of O/P.* The areas in which legitimate power may be exercised are generally specified along with the designation of that power. A job description, for example, usually specifies supervisory activities and also designates the person

to whom the job-holder is responsible for the duties described. Some bases for legitimate authority carry with them a very broad range. Culturally derived bases for legitimate power are often especially broad. It is not uncommon to find cultures in which a member of a given caste can legitimately prescribe behavior for all members of lower castes in practically all regions. More common, however, are instances of legitimate power where the range is specifically and narrowly prescribed. A sergeant in the army is given a specific set of regions within which he can legitimately prescribe behavior for his men.

The attempted use of legitimate power which is outside of the range of legitimate power will decrease the legitimate power of the authority figure. Such use of power which is not legitimate will also decrease the attractiveness of O.[27]

● *Legitimate power and influence.* The new state of the system which results from legitimate power usually has high dependence on O though it may become independent. Here, however, the degree of dependence is not related to the level of observability. Since legitimate power is based on P's values, the source of the forces induced by O include both these internal values and O. O's induction serves to activate the values and to relate them to the system which is influenced, but thereafter the new state of the system may become directly dependent on the values with no mediation by O. Accordingly this new state will be relatively stable and consistent across varying environmental situations since P's values are more stable than his psychological environment.

We have used the term legitimate not only as a basis for the power of an agent, but also to describe the general behaviors of a person. Thus, the individual P may also consider the legitimacy of the attempts to use other types of power by O. In certain cases, P will consider that O has a legitimate right to threaten punishment for nonconformity; in other cases, such use of coercion would not be seen as legitimate. P might change in response to coercive power of O, but it will make a considerable difference in his attitude and conformity if O is not seen as having a legitimate right to use such coercion. In such cases, the attraction of P for O will be particularly diminished, and the influence attempt will arouse more resistance.[28] Similarly the utilization of reward power may vary in legitimacy; the word "bribe," for example, denotes an illegitimate reward.

REFERENT POWER

The referent power of O/P has its basis in the identification of P with O. By identification, we mean a feeling of oneness of P with O, or a desire for such an identity. If O is a person toward whom P is highly attracted, P will have a desire to become closely associated with O. If O is an attractive group, P will have a feeling of membership or a desire to join. If P is already closely associated with O he will want to maintain this relationship.[29] P's identification with O can be established or maintained if P behaves, believes, and perceives as O does. Accordingly O has the ability to influence P, even though P may be unaware of this referent power. A verbalization of such power by P might be, "I am like O, and therefore I shall behave or believe as O does," or "I want to be like O, and I will be more like O if I behave or believe as O does." The stronger the identification of P with O the greater the referent power of O/P.

Similar types of power have already been investigated under a number of different formulations. Festinger points out that in an ambiguous situation, the individual seeks some sort of "social reality" and may adopt the cognitive structure of the individual or group with which he identifies.[30] In such a case, the lack of clear structure may be threaten-ing to the individual and the agreement of his beliefs with those of a reference group will both satisfy his need for structure and give him added security through increased identification with his group.[31]

We must try to distinguish between referent power and other types of power which might be operative at the same time. If a member is attracted to a group and he conforms to its norms only because he fears ridicule or expulsion from the group for nonconformity, we would call this coercive power. On the other hand if he conforms in order to obtain praise for conformity, it is a case of reward power. The basic criterion for distinguishing referent power from both coercive and reward power is the mediation of the punishment and the reward by O: to the extent that O mediates the sanctions (i.e., has means control over P) we are dealing with coercive and reward power; but to the extent that P avoids discomfort or gains satisfaction by conformity based on identification, regardless of O's responses, we are dealing with referent power. Conformity with majority opinion is sometimes based on a respect for the collective wisdom of the group, in which case it is expert power. It is important to distinguish these phenomena, all grouped together elsewhere as "pressures toward uniformity," since the type of change which occurs will be different for different bases of power.

The concepts of "reference group"[32] and "prestige suggestion" may be treated as instances of referent power. In this case, O, the prestigeful person or group, is valued by P; because P desires to be associated or identified with O, he will assume attitudes or beliefs held by O. Similarly a negative reference group which O dislikes and evaluates negatively may exert negative influence on P as a result of negative referent power.

It has been demonstrated that the power which we designate as referent power is especially great when P is attracted to O.[33] In our terms, this would mean that the greater the attraction, the greater the identification, and consequently the greater the referent power. In some cases, attraction or prestige may have a specific basis, and the range of referent power will be limited accordingly: a group of campers may have great referent power over a member regarding campcraft, but considerably less effect on other regions.[34] However, we hypothesize that the greater the attraction of P toward O, the broader the range of referent power of O/P.

The new state of a system produced by referent power may be dependent on or independent of O; but the degree of dependence is not affected by the level of observability to O.[35] In fact, P is often not consciously aware of the referent power which O exerts over him. There is probably a tendency for some of these dependent changes to become independent of O quite rapidly.

EXPERT POWER

The strength of the expert power of O/P varies with the extent of the knowledge or perception which P attributes to O within a given area. Probably P evaluates O's expertness in relation to his own knowledge as well as against an absolute standard. In any case expert power results in primary social influence on P's cognitive structure and probably not on other types of systems. Of course changes in the cognitive structure can change the direction of forces and hence of locomotion, but such a change of behavior is secondary social influence. Expert power has been demonstrated experimentally.[36] Accepting an attorney's advice in legal matters is a common example of expert influence; but there are many instances based on much less knowledge, such as the acceptance by a stranger of directions given by a native villager.

Expert power, where O need not be a member of P's group, is called "informational power" by Deutsch and Gerard.[37] This type of expert power must be distinguished from influence based on the content of communication as described by Hovland et al.[38] The influence of the content of a communication upon an opinion is presumably a secondary influence produced after the *primary* influence (i.e., the acceptance of the information). Since power is here defined in terms of the primary changes, the influence of the content on a related opinion is not a case of expert power as we have defined it, but the initial acceptance of the validity of the content does seem to be based on expert power or referent power. In other cases, however, so-called facts may be accepted as self-evident because they fit into P's cognitive structure; if this impersonal acceptance of the truth of the fact is independent of the more or less enduring relationship between O and P, then P's acceptance of the fact is not an actualization of expert power. Thus we distinguish between expert power based on the credibility of O and informational influence which is based on characteristics of the stimulus such as the logic of the argument or the "self-evident facts."

Wherever expert influence occurs it seems to be necessary both for P to think that O knows and for P to trust that O is telling the truth (rather than trying to deceive him).

Expert power will produce a new cognitive structure which is initially relatively dependent on O, but informational influence will produce a more independent structure. The former is likely to become more independent with the passage of time. In both cases the degree of dependence on O is not affected by the level of observability.

The "sleeper effect"[39] is an interesting case of a change in the degree of dependence of an opinion on O. An unreliable O (who probably had negative referent power but some positive expert power) presented "facts" which were accepted by the subjects and which would normally produce secondary influence on their opinions and beliefs. However, the negative referent power aroused resistance and resulted in negative social influence on their beliefs (*i.e.*, set up a force in the direction opposite to the influence attempt), so that there was little change in the subjects' opinions. With the passage of time, however, the subjects tended to forget the identity of the negative communicator faster than they forgot the contents of his communication, so there was a weakening of the negative referent influence and a consequent delayed positive change in the subjects' beliefs in the direction of the influence attempt ("sleeper effect"). Later, when the identity of the negative communicator was experimentally reinstated, these resisting forces were reinstated, and there was another negative change in belief in a direction opposite to the influence attempt.[40]

The range of expert power, we assume, is more delimited than that of referent power. Not only is it restricted to cognitive systems but the expert is seen as having superior knowledge or ability in very specific areas, and his power will be limited to these areas, though some "halo effect" might occur. Recently, some of our renowned physical scientists have found quite painfully that their expert power in physical sciences does not extend to regions involving international politics. Indeed, there is some evidence that the attempted exertion of expert power outside of the range of expert power will reduce that expert power. An undermining of confidence seems to take place.

SUMMARY

We have distinguished five types of power: referent power, expert power, reward power, coercive power, and legitimate power. These distinctions led to the following hypotheses:

1. For all five types, the stronger the basis of power the greater the power.

2. For any type of power the size of the range may vary greatly, but in general referent power will have the broadest range.

3. Any attempt to utilize power outside the range of power will tend to reduce the power.

4. A new state of a system produced by reward power or coercive power will be highly dependent on O, and the more observable P's conformity the more dependent the state. For the other three types of power, the new state is usually dependent, at least in the beginning, but in any case the level of observability has no effect on the degree of dependence.

5. Coercion results in decreased attraction of P toward O and high resistance; reward power results in increased attraction and low resistance.

6. The more legitimate the coercion the less it will produce resistance and decreased attraction.

NOTES

1. S. E. Asch, *Social Psychology* (New York: Prentice-Hall, 1952). L. Festinger, "An Analysis of Compliant Behavior," in *Group Relations at the Crossroads*, eds. M. Sherif and M. O. Wilson (New York: Harper, 1953), pp. 232-56. H. Goldhammer and E. A. Shils, "Types of Power and Status," *Amer. J. Sociol.*, Vol. 45 (1939): 171-78. M. Jahoda, "Psychological Issues in Civil Liberties," *Amer. Psychologist*, Vol. 11 (1956): 234-40. H. Kelman, "Three Processes of Acceptance of Social Influence: Compliance, Identification and Internalization" (Paper read at the meetings of the American Psychological Association, August 1956). R. Linton, *The Cultural Background of Personality* (New York: Appleton-Century-Crofts, 1945). R. Lippitt et al., "The Dynamics of Power," *Hum. Relat.*, Vol. 5 (1952): 37-64. B. Russell, *Power: A New Social Analysis* (New York: Norton, 1938). E. P. Torrance and R. Mason, "Instructor Effort to Influence: An Experimental Evaluation of Six Approaches" (Paper presented at USAF-NRC Symposium on Personnel, Training, and Human Engineering, Washington, D.C., 1956).

2. The word "system" is here used to refer to a whole or to a part of the whole.

3. K. Lewin, *Field Theory in Social Science* (New York: Harper, 1951).

4. The concept of power has the conceptual property of *potentiality*; but it seems useful to restrict this potential influence to more or less enduring power relations between O and P by excluding from the definition of power those cases where the potential influence is so momentary or so changing that it cannot be predicted from the existing relationship. Power is a useful concept for describing social structure only if it has a certain stability over time; it is useless if every momentary social stimulus is viewed as actualizing social power.

5. We define resistance to an attempted induction as a force in the opposite direction which is set up by the same act of O. It must be distinguished from opposition which is defined as existing opposing forces which do not have their source in the same act of O. For example, a boy might resist his mother's order to eat spinach because of the manner of the induction attempt, and at the same time he might oppose it because he didn't like spinach.

6. Asch, *op. cit.* J. E. Dittes and H. H. Kelley, "Effects of Different Conditions of Acceptance upon Conformity to Group Norms,"*J. Abnorm. Soc. Psychol.,* Vol. 53 (1956): 100-07. Festinger, "An Analysis . . . ," *op. cit.* J. R. P. French, Jr., G. Levinger, and H. W. Morrison, "The Legitimacy of Coercive Power" (In preparation). J. R. P. French, Jr. and B. H. Raven, "An Experiment in Legitimate and Coercive Power" (In preparation). Jahoda, *op. cit.* D. Katz and R. L. Schank, *Social Psychology* (New York: Wiley, 1938). H. H. Kelley and E. H. Volkart, "The Resistance to Change of Group-Anchored Attitudes," *Amer. Soc. Rev.,* Vol. 17 (1952): 453-65. Kelman, *op. cit.* Lewin, *Field . . . , op. cit.* B. H. Raven and J. R. P. French, Jr., "Group Support, Legitimate Power, and Social Influence," *J. Person.,* Vol. 26 (1958): 400-09. R. Rommetveit, *Social Norms and Roles* (Minneapolis: University of Minnesota Press, 1953).

7. J. G. March, "An Introduction to the Theory and Measurement of Influence," *Amer. Polit. Sci. Rev.,* Vol. 49 (1955): 431-51.

8. Lewin, *Field . . . , op. cit.,* p. 106.

9. J. G. Miller, "Toward a General Theory for the Behavioral Sciences," *Amer. Psychologist,* Vol. 10 (1955): 513-31 assumes that all living systems have this character. However, it may be that some systems in the life space do not have this elasticity.

10. Dittes and Kelley, *op. cit.* Festinger, "An Analysis . . . ," *op. cit.* French, Levinger, and Morrison, *op. cit.* French and Raven, *op. cit.* Kelman, *op. cit.*

11. Rommetveit, *op. cit.*

12. Lippitt *et al., op. cit.,* chapter 11.

13. French, Levinger, and Morrison, *op. cit.*

14. L. Coch and J. R. P. French, Jr., "Overcoming Resistance to Change," *Hum. Relat.,* Vol. 1 (1948): 512-32.

15. Though the primary influence of coercive power is dependent, it often produces secondary changes which are independent. Brainwashing, for example, utilizes coercive power to produce many primary changes in the life space of the prisoner, but these dependent changes can lead to identification with the aggressor and hence to secondary changes in ideology which are independent.

16. Dittes and Kelley, *op. cit.*

17. French, Levinger, and Morrison, *op. cit.* French and Raven, *op. cit.*

18. K. Lewin, *Dynamic Theory of Personality* (New York: McGraw-Hill, 1935), pp. 114-70.

19. Linton, *op. cit.*

20. T. M. Newcomb, *Social Psychology* (New York: Dryden, 1950).

21. P. G. Herbst, "Analysis and Measurement of a Situation," *Hum. Relat.,* Vol. 2 (1953): 113-40.

22. Lewin, *Field . . . , op. cit,* pp. 40-41.

23. M. Weber, *The Theory of Social and Economic Organization* (Oxford: Oxford University Press, 1947).

24. Goldhammer and Shils, *op. cit.*

25. Weber, *op. cit.*

26. J. R. P. French, Jr., Joachim Israel, and Dagfinn Ås, "Arbeidernes Medvirkning i Industribedriften. En Eksperimentell Undersøkelse." Oslo, Norway: Institute for Social Research, 1957).

27. French, Levinger, and Morrison, *op. cit.* French and Raven, *op. cit.* Raven and French, *op. cit.*

28. French, Levinger, and Morrison, *op. cit.*

29. E. Stotland *et al.,* "Studies on the Effects of Identification" (Forthcoming, University of Michigan, Institute for Social Research). Torrance and Mason, *op. cit.*

30. L. Festinger, "Informal Social Communication," *Psychol. Rev.*, Vol. 57 (1950): 271-82.

31. G. M. Hochbaum, "Self-Confidence and Reactions to Group Pressures," *Amer. Soc. Rev.*, Vol. 19 (1954): 678-87. J. M. Jackson and H. D. Saltzstein, "The Effect of Person-Group Relationships on Conformity Processes," *J. Abnorm. Soc. Psychol.*, Vol. 57 (1958): 17-24.

32. G. E. Swanson, T. M. Newcomb, and E. L. Hartley, *Readings in Social Psychology* (New York: Henry Holt, 1952).

33. K. W. Back, "Influence through Social Communication," *J. Abnorm. Soc. Psychol.*, Vol. 46 (1951): 9-23. Festinger, *op. cit.* L. Festinger et al., "The Influence Process in the Presence of Extreme Deviates," *Hum. Relat.*, Vol. 5 (1952): 327-46. L. Festinger, S. Schachter, and K. Back, "The Operation of Group Standards," in *Group Dynamics: Research and Theory*, eds. D. Cartwright and A. Zander (Evanston, Ill.: Row, Peterson, 1953), pp. 204-23. H. B. Gerard, "The Anchorage of Opinions in Face-to-Face Groups," *Hum. Relat.*, Vol. 7 (1954): 313-25. Kelman, *op. cit.* Lippitt, et al., *op. cit.*

34. Lippitt et al., *op. cit.*

35. Festinger, "An Analysis . . . ," *op. cit.* Kelman, *op. cit.*

36. Festinger et al., *op. cit.* H. T. Moore, "The Comparative Influence of Majority and Expert Opinion," *Amer. J. Psychol.*, Vol. 32 (1921): 16-20.

37. M. Deutsch and H. B. Gerard, "A Study of Normative and Informational Influences upon Individual Judgment," *J. Abnorm. Soc. Psychol.*, Vol. 51 (1955): 629-36.

38. C. I. Hovland, A. A. Lumsdaine, and F. D. Sheffield, *Experiments on Mass Communication* (Princeton, N.J.: Princeton University Press, 1949). C. I. Hovland and W. Weiss, "The Influence of Source Credibility on Communication Effectiveness," *Publ. Opin. Quart.*, Vol. 15 (1951): 635-50. Kelman, *op. cit.* H. Kelman and C. I. Hovland, "'Reinstatement' of the Communicator in Delayed Measurement of Opinion Change," *J. Abnorm. Soc. Psychol.*, Vol. 48 (1953): 327-35.

39. Hovland and Weiss, *op. cit.* Kelman and Hovland, *op. cit.*

40. Kelmen and Hovland, *op. cit.*

18. Style or Circumstance: The Leadership Enigma*

FRED E. FIEDLER

What is it that makes a person an effective leader?

We take it for granted that good leadership is essential to business, to government and to all the myriad groups and organizations that shape the way we live, work and play.

We spend at least several billions of dollars a year on leadership development and executive recruitment in the United States. Leaders are paid 10, 20 and 30 times the salary of ordinary workers. Thousands of books and articles on leadership have been published. Yet, we still know relatively little about the factors that determine a leader's success or failure.

Psychologists have been concerned with two major questions in their research on leadership: How does a man become a leader? What kind of personality traits or behavior makes a person an *effective* leader? For the past 15 years, my own work at the University of Illinois Group-Effectiveness Research Laboratory has concentrated on the latter question.

Psychologists used to think that special personality traits would distinguish leaders from followers. Several hundred research studies have been conducted to identify these special traits. But the search has been futile.

People who become leaders tend to be somewhat more intelligent, bigger, more assertive, more talkative than other members of their group. But these traits are far less important than most people think. What most frequently distinguished the leader from his co-workers is that he knows more about the group task or that he can do it better. A bowling team is likely to choose its captain from good rather than poor bowlers, and the foreman of a machine shop is more likely to be a good machinist than a poor one.

In many organizations, one only has to live long in order to gain experience and seniority, and with these a position of leadership.

In business and industry today, the men who attain a leadership position must have the requisite education and talent. Of course, as W. Lloyd Warner and James C. Abegglen of the University of Chicago have shown, it has been most useful to come from or marry into a family that owns a large slice of the company's stock.

Becoming a leader, then, depends on personality only to a limited extent. A person can become a leader by happenstance, simply by being in the right place at the right time, or because of such various factors as age, education, experience, family background and wealth.

Almost any person in a group may be capable of rising to a leadership position if he is rewarded for actively participating in the group discussion, as Alex Bavelas and his colleagues at Stanford University have demonstrated. They used light signals to reward low-status group members for supposedly

*Source: From *Psychology Today Magazine* (March 1969), pp. 38-43. Copyright © 1969 Ziff-Davis Publishing Company.

"doing the right thing." However, unknown to the people being encouraged, the light signal was turned on and off at random. Rewarded in this unspecified, undefined manner, the low-status member came to regard himself as a leader and the rest of the group accepted him in his new position.

It is commonly observed that personality and circumstances interact to determine whether a person will become a leader. While this statement is undoubtedly true, its usefulness is rather limited unless one also can specify how a personality trait will interact with a specific situation. We are as yet unable to make such predictions.

Having become a leader, how does one get to be an effective leader? Given a dozen or more similar groups and tasks, what makes one leader succeed and another fail? The answer to this question is likely to determine the philosophy of leader-training programs and the way in which men are selected for executive positions.

There are a limited number of ways in which one person can influence others to work together toward a common goal. He can coerce them or he can coax them. He can tell people what to do and how to do it, or he can share the decision-making and concentrate on his relationship with his men rather than on the execution of the job.

Of course, these two types of leadership behavior are gross oversimplifications. Most research by psychologists on leadership has focused on two clusters of behavior and attitudes, one labeled autocratic, authoritarian and task-oriented, and the other as democratic, equalitarian, permissive and group-oriented.

The first type of leadership behavior, frequently advocated in conventional supervisory and military systems, has its philosophical roots in Frederick W. Taylor's *Principles of Scientific Management* and other early 20th Century industrial engineering studies. The authoritarian, task-oriented leader takes all responsibility for making decisions and directing the group members. His rationale is simple: "I do the thinking and you carry out the orders."

The second type of leadership is typical of the "New Look" method of management advocated by men like Douglas McGregor of M.I.T. and Rensis Likert of the University of Michigan. The democratic, group-oriented leader provides general rather than close supervision and his concern is the effective use of human resources through participation. In the late 1940s, a related method of leadership training was developed based on confrontation in unstructured group situations where each participant can explore his own motivations and reactions. Some excellent studies on this method, called T-group, sensitivity or laboratory training, have been made by Chris Argyris of Yale, Warren Bennis of State University of New York at Buffalo and Edgar Schein of M.I.T.

Experiments comparing the performance of both types of leaders have shown that each is successful in some situations and not in others. No one has been able to show that one kind of leader is always superior or more effective.

A number of researchers point out that different tasks require different kinds of leadership. But what kind of situation requires what kind of leader? To answer this question, I shall present a theory of leadership effectiveness that spells out the specific circumstances under which various leadership styles are most effective.

We must first of all distinguish between leadership style and leader behavior. Leader behavior refers to the specific acts in which a leader engages while directing or coordinating the work of his group. For example, the leader can praise or criticize, make helpful suggestions, show consideration for the welfare and feelings of members of his group.

Leadership style refers to the underlying needs of the leader that motivate his behavior. In other words, in addition to performing the task, what personal needs is the leader attempting to satisfy? We have found that a leader's actions or behavior sometimes does change as the situation or group changes, but his basic needs appear to remain constant.

To classify leadership styles, my colleagues and I have developed a simple questionnaire that asks the leader to describe the person with whom he can work least well:

LPC—Least-Preferred Co-worker

Think of the person with whom you can work least well. He may be someone you work with now, or he may be someone you knew in the past. Use an X to describe this person as he appears to you.

helpful :_:_:_:_:_:_:_: frustrating
        8 7 6 5 4 3 2 1

unen-   :_:_:_:_:_:_:_: enthusiastic
thusiastic 1 2 3 4 5 6 7 8

efficient :_:_:_:_:_:_:_: inefficient
        8 7 6 5 4 3 2 1

From the replies, a Least-Preferred Co-worker (LPC) score is obtained by simply summing the item scores. The LPC score does not measure perceptual accuracy, but rather reveals a person's emotional reaction to the people with whom he cannot work well.

In general, the high-scoring leader describes his least-preferred co-worker in favorable terms. The high-LPC leader tends to be "relationship-oriented." He gets his major satisfaction from establishing close personal relations with his group members. He uses the group task to gain the position of prominence he seeks.

The leader with a low score describes his least-preferred co-worker in unfavorable terms. The low-LPC leader is primarily "task-oriented." He obtains his major satisfaction by successfully completing the task, even at the risk of poor interpersonal relations with his workers.

Since a leader cannot function with-

out a group, we must also know something about the group that the leader directs. There are many types of groups, for example, social groups which promote the enjoyment of individuals and "counteracting" groups such as labor and management at the negotiating table. But here we shall concentrate on groups that exist for the purpose of performing a task.

From our research, my associates and I have identified three major factors that can be used to classify group situations: (1) position power of the leader, (2) task structure, and (3) leader-member personal relationships. Basically, these classifications measure the kind of power and influence the group gives its leader.

We ranked group situations according to their favorableness for the leader. Favorableness here is defined as the degree to which the situation enables the leader to exert influence over the group.

Based on several studies, leader-member relations emerged as the most important factor in determining the leader's influence over the group. Task structure is rated as second in importance, and position power is third. *(See Figure 18-1.)*

Under most circumstances, the leader who is liked by his group and has a clear-cut task and high position power obviously has everything in his favor. The leader who has poor relationships with his group members, an unstructured task and weak position power likely will be unable to exert much influence over the group.

The personal relationships that the leader established with his group members depend at least in part upon the leader's personality. The leader who is loved, admired and trusted can influence the group regardless of his position power. The leader who is not liked or trusted cannot influence the group except through his vested authority. It should be noted that a leader's assessment of how much he is liked often differs markedly from the group's evaluation.

Task structure refers to the degree the group's assignment can be programmed and specified in a step-by-step fashion. A highly structured task does not need a leader with much position power because the leader's role is detailed by the job specifications. With a highly structured task, the leader clearly knows what to do and how to do it, and the organization can back him up at each step. Unstructured tasks tend to have more than one correct solution that may be reached by any of a variety of methods. Since there is no step-by-step method that can be programmed in advance, the leader cannot influence the group's success by ordering them to vote "right" or be creative. Tasks of committees, creative groups and policy-making groups are typically unstructured.

Position power is the authority vested in the leader's position. It can be readily measured in most situations. An army general obviously has more power than a lieutenant, just as a department head has more power than an office manager. But our concern here is the effect this position has on group performance. Although one would think that a leader with great power will get better performance from his group, our studies do not bear out this assumption.

However, it must be emphasized that in some situations position power may supersede task structure (the military). Or a very highly structured task (launching a moon probe) may outweigh the effects of interpersonal relations. The organization determines both the task structure and the position power of the leader.

In our search for the most effective leadership style, we went back to the studies that we had been conducting for more than a decade. These studies investigated a wide variety of groups and leadership situations, including basketball teams, business management, military units, boards of directors, creative groups and scientists engaged in pure research. In all of these studies, we could determine the groups that had performed their tasks successfully or unsuccessfully and then correlated the effectiveness of group performance with leadership style.

Now by plotting these correlations of leadership style against our scale of group situations, we could, for the first time, find what leadership style works best in each situation. When we connected the median points on each column, the result was a bell-shaped curve. (See Figure 18-1.)

The results show that a task-oriented leader performs best in situations at both extremes—those in which he has a great deal of influence and power, and also in situations where he has no influence and power over the group members.

Relationship-oriented leaders tend to perform best in mixed situations where they have only moderate influence over the group. A number of subsequent studies by us and others have confirmed these findings.

The results show that we cannot talk about simply good leaders or poor leaders. A leader who is effective in one situation may or may not be effective in another. Therefore, we must specify the situations in which a leader performs well or badly.

This theory of leadership effectiveness by and large fits our everyday experience. Group situations in which the leader is liked, where he has a clearly defined task and a powerful position, may make attempts at nondirective, democratic leadership detrimental or superfluous. For example, the captain of an airliner can hardly call a committee meeting of the crew to share in the decision-making during a difficult landing approach. On the other hand, the chairman of a voluntary committee cannot ask with impunity that the group members vote or act according to his instructions.

Figure 18-1

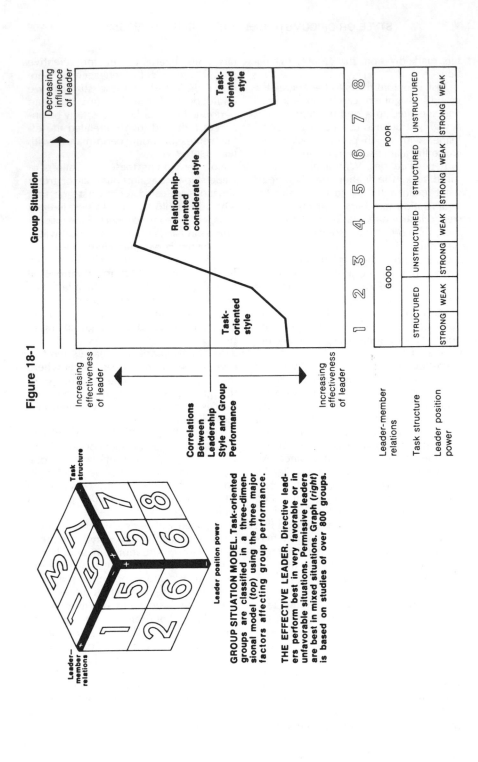

Group Situation

Decreasing influence of leader

Increasing effectiveness of leader

Increasing effectiveness of leader

Correlations Between Leadership Style and Group Performance

Task-oriented style

Relationship-oriented considerate style

Task-oriented style

	GOOD				POOR		
Leader-member relations							
Task structure	STRUCTURED	UNSTRUCTURED			STRUCTURED		UNSTRUCTURED
Leader position power	STRONG	WEAK	STRONG	WEAK	STRONG	WEAK	STRONG	WEAK

Task structure

Leader position power

Leader–member relations

GROUP SITUATION MODEL. Task-oriented groups are classified in a three-dimensional model (top) using the three major factors affecting group performance.

THE EFFECTIVE LEADER. Directive leaders perform best in very favorable or in unfavorable situations. Permissive leaders are best in mixed situations. Graph (right) is based on studies of over 800 groups.

Our studies also have shown that factors such as group-member abilities, cultural heterogeneity and stressfulness of the task affect the degree to which the leader can influence members of the group. But the important finding and the consistent finding in these studies has been that mixed situations require relationship-oriented leadership while very favorable and very unfavorable job situations require task-oriented leaders.

Perhaps the most important implication of this theory of leadership is that the organization for which the leader works is as responsible for his success or failure as is the leader himself.

The chances are that *anyone* who wants to become a leader can become one if he carefully chooses the situations that are favorable to his leadership style.

The notion that a man is a "born" leader, capable of leading in all circumstances, appears to be nothing more than a myth. If there are leaders who excel under all conditions, I have not found them in my 18 years of research.

When we think of improving leadership performance, we tend to think first of training the leader. Personnel psychologists and managers typically view the executive's position as fixed and unchangeable and the applicant as highly plastic and trainable. A man's basic style of leadership depends upon his personality. Changing a man's leadership style means trying to change his personality. As we know from experiences in psycho-therapy, it may take from one to several years to effect lasting changes in a personality structure. A leader's personality is not likely to change because of a few lectures or even a few weeks of intensive training.

It is doubtful that intensive training techniques can change an individual's style of leadership. However, training programs could be designed to provide the opportunity for a leader to learn in which situations he can perform well and in which he is likely to fail. Laboratory training also may provide the leader with some insights into his personal relationships with group members.

Our theory of leadership effectiveness predicts that a leader's performance can be improved by engineering or fitting the job to the leader. This is based, at least in part, on the belief that it is almost always easier to change a leader's work environment than to change his personality. The leader's authority, his task and even his interpersonal relations within his group members can be altered, sometimes without making the leader aware that this has been done.

For example, we can change the leader's position power in either direction. He can be given a higher rank if this seems necessary. Or he can be given subordinates who are equal or nearly equal to him in rank. His assistants can be two or three ranks below him, or we can assign him men who are expert in their specialties. The leader can have sole authority for a job, or he may be required to consult with his group. All communications to group members may be channeled through the leader, making him the source of all the inside information, or all members of the group can be given the information directly, thus reducing the leader's influence.

The task structure also can be changed to suit the leader's style. Depending upon the group situation, we can give the leader explicit instructions or we can deliberately give him a vague and nebulous goal.

Finally, we can change the leader–member relations. In some situations it may be desirable to improve leader–member relations by making the group homogeneous in culture and language or in technical and educational background. Interdisciplinary groups are notoriously difficult to handle, and it is even more difficult to lead a group that is racially or culturally mixed. Likewise, we can affect leader-member relations by giving a leader subordinates who get along well with their supervisor or assign a leader to a group with a history of trouble or conflict.

It may seem that often we are proposing the sabotaging of the leader's influence over his group. Although common sense might make it seem that weakening the leader's influence will lower performance, in actuality our studies show that this rarely happens. The average group performance (in other words, the leader's effectiveness) correlates poorly with the degree of the leader's influence over the group.

In fact, the findings from several studies suggest that a particular leader's effectiveness may be improved even though the situation is made less favorable for him.

The leader himself can be taught to recognize the situations that best fit his style. A man who is able to avoid situations in which he is likely to fail, and seek out situations that fit his leadership style, will probably become a highly successful and effective leader. Also, if he is aware of his strengths and weaknesses, the leader can try to change his group situation to match his leadership style.

However, we must remember that good leadership performance depends as much upon the organization as it does upon the leader. This means that we must learn not only how to train men to be leaders, but how to build organizations in which specific types of leaders can perform well.

In view of the increasing scarcity of competent executives, it is to an organization's advantage to design jobs to fit leaders instead of attempting merely to fit a leader to the job.

19. How to Choose a Leadership Pattern*

ROBERT TANNENBAUM

WARREN H. SCHMIDT

• I put most problems into my group's hands and leave it to them to carry the ball from there. I serve merely as a catalyst, mirroring back the people's thoughts and feelings so that they can better understand them.

• It's foolish to make decisions oneself on matters that affect people. I always talk things over with my subordinates, but I make it clear to them that I'm the one who has to have the final say.

• Once I have decided on a course of action, I do my best to sell my ideas to my employees.

• I'm being paid to lead. If I let a lot of other people make the decisions I should be making, then I'm not worth my salt.

• I believe in getting things done. I can't waste time calling meetings. Someone has to call the shots around here, and I think it should be me.

Each of these statements represents a point of view about "good leadership." Considerable experience, factual data, and theoretical principles could be cited to support each statement, even though they seem to be inconsistent when placed together. Such contradictions point up the dilemma in which the modern manager frequently finds himself.

NEW PROBLEM

The problem of how the modern manager can be "democratic" in his relations with subordinates and at the same time maintain the necessary au-

thority and control in the organization for which he is responsible has come into focus increasingly in recent years.

Earlier in the century this problem was not so acutely felt. The successful executive was generally pictured as possessing intelligence, imagination, initiative, the capacity to make rapid (and generally wise) decisions, and the ability to inspire subordinates. People tended to think of the world as being divided into "leaders" and "followers."

NEW FOCUS

Gradually, however, from the social sciences emerged the concept of "group dynamics" with its focus on *members* of the group rather than solely on the leader. Research efforts of social scientists underscored the importance of employee involvement and participation in decision making. Evidence began to challenge the efficiency of highly directive leadership, and increasing attention was paid to problems of motivation and human relations.

Through training laboratories in group development that sprang up across the country, many of the newer notions of leadership began to exert an impact. These training laboratories were carefully designed to give people a first-hand experience in full participation and decision making. The designated "leaders" deliberately attempted to reduce their own power and to make group members as responsible as possible for setting their own goals and methods within the laboratory experience.

It was perhaps inevitable that some of the people who attended the training laboratories regarded this kind of leadership as being truly "democratic" and went home with the determination to build fully participative decision making into their own organizations. Whenever their bosses made a decision without convening a staff meeting, they tended to perceive this as authoritarian behavior. The true symbol of democratic leadership to some was the meeting —and the less directed from the top, the more democratic it was.

Some of the more enthusiastic alumni of these training laboratories began to get the habit of categorizing leader behavior as "democratic" or "authoritarian." The boss who made too many decisions himself was thought of as an authoritarian, and his directive behavior was often attributed solely to his personality.

NEW NEED

The net result of the research findings and of the human relations training based upon them has been to call into question the stereotype of an effective leader. Consequently, the modern manager often finds himself in an uncomfortable state of mind.

Often he is not quite sure how to behave; there are times when he is torn between exerting "strong" leadership and "permissive" leadership. Sometimes new knowledge pushes him in one direction ("I should really get the group to help make this decision"), but at the same time his experience pushes him in another direction ("I really understand the problem better than the group and therefore I should make the decision"). He is not sure when a group decision is really appropriate or when holding a staff meeting serves merely as a device for avoiding his own decision-making responsibility.

The purpose of our article is to suggest a framework which managers may find useful in grappling with this dilemma. First, we shall look at the different patterns of leadership behavior that the manager can choose from in relating himself to his subordinates. Then, we shall turn to some of the questions suggested by this range of patterns. For instance, how important is it for a manager's subordinates to know what type of leadership he is using in a situation? What factors should he consider in deciding on a leadership pattern? What difference do his long-run objectives make as compared to his immediate objectives?

RANGE OF BEHAVIOR

Exhibit 19-1 presents the continuum or range of possible leadership behavior available to a manager. Each type of action is related to the degree of authority used by the boss and to the amount of freedom available to his subordinates in reaching decisions. The actions seen on the extreme left characterize the manager who maintains a high degree of control while those seen on the extreme right characterize the manager who releases a high degree of control. Neither extreme is absolute; authority and freedom are never without their limitations.

Now let us look more closely at each of the behavior points occurring along this continuum.

THE MANAGER MAKES THE DECISION AND ANNOUNCES IT

In this case the boss identifies a problem, considers alternative solutions, chooses one of them, and then reports this decision to his subordinates for implementation. He may or may not give consideration to what he believes his subordinates will think or feel about his decision; in any case, he provides no opportunity for them to participate directly in the decision-making process. Coercion may or may not be used or implied.

Exhibit 19-1

CONTINUUM OF LEADERSHIP BEHAVIOR

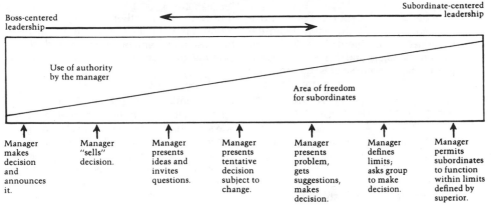

THE MANAGER "SELLS" HIS DECISION

Here the manager, as before, takes responsibility for identifying the problem and arriving at a decision. However, rather than simply announcing it, he takes the additional step of persuading his subordinates to accept it. In doing so, he recognizes the possibility of some resistance among those who will be faced with the decision, and seeks to reduce this resistance by indicating, for example, what the employees have to gain from his decision.

THE MANAGER PRESENTS HIS IDEAS, INVITES QUESTIONS

Here the boss who has arrived at a decision and who seeks acceptance of his ideas provides an opportunity for his subordinates to get a fuller explanation of his thinking and his intentions. After presenting the ideas, he invites questions so that his associates can better understand what he is trying to accomplish. This "give and take" also enables the manager and the subordinates to explore more fully the implications of the decision.

THE MANAGER PRESENTS A TENTATIVE DECISION SUBJECT TO CHANGE

This kind of behavior permits the subordinates to exert some influence on the decision. The initiative for identifying and diagnosing the problem remains with the boss. Before meeting with his staff, he has thought the problem through and arrived at a decision—but only a tentative one. Before finalizing it, he presents his proposed solution for the reaction of those who will be affected by it. He says in effect, "I'd like to hear what you have to say about this plan that I have developed. I'll appreciate your frank reactions, but will reserve for myself the final decision."

THE MANAGER PRESENTS THE PROBLEM, GETS SUGGESTIONS, AND THEN MAKES HIS DECISION

Up to this point the boss has come before the group with a solution of his own. Not so in this case. The subordinates now get the first chance to suggest solutions. The manager's initial role involves identifying the problem. He might, for example, say something of this sort: "We are faced with a number of complaints from newspapers and the general public on our service policy. What is wrong here? What ideas do you have for coming to grips with this problem?"

The function of the group becomes

one of increasing the manager's reper-
tory of possible solutions to the problem. The purpose is to capitalize on the
knowledge and experience of those
who are on the "firing line." From the
expanded list of alternatives developed
by the manager and his subordinates,
the manager then selects the solution
that he regards as most promising.[1]

THE MANAGER DEFINES THE LIMITS AND REQUESTS THE GROUP TO MAKE A DECISION

At this point the manager passes to the
group (possibly including himself as a
member) the right to make decisions.
Before doing so, however, he defines
the problem to be solved and the
boundaries within which the decision
must be made.

An example might be the handling of
a parking problem at a plant. The boss
decides that this is something that
should be worked on by the people involved, so he calls them together and
points up the existence of the problem.
Then he tells them:

> There is the open field just north of the
> main plant which has been designated for
> additional employee parking. We can
> build underground or surface multilevel
> facilities as long as the cost does not ex-
> ceed $100,000. Within these limits we are
> free to work out whatever solution makes
> sense to us. After we decide on a specific
> plan, the company will spend the available
> money in whatever way we indicate.

THE MANAGER PERMITS THE GROUP TO MAKE DECISIONS WITHIN PRESCRIBED LIMITS

This represents an extreme degree of
group freedom only occasionally encountered in formal organizations, as,
for instance, in many research groups.
Here the team of managers or engineers
undertakes the identification and diagnosis of the problem, develops alternative procedures for solving it, and
decides on one or more of these alternative solutions. The only limits directly
imposed on the group by the organization are those specified by the superior

of the team's boss. If the boss participates in the decision-making process,
he attempts to do so with no more authority than any other member of the
group. He commits himself in advance
to assist in implementing whatever decision the group makes.

KEY QUESTIONS

As the continuum in *Exhibit 19-1* demonstrates, there are a number of alternative
ways in which a manager can relate himself to the group or individuals he is supervising. At the extreme left of the range, the
emphasis is on the manager—on what *he*
is interested in, how *he* sees things, how
he feels about them. As we move toward
the subordinate-centered end of the continuum, however, the focus is increasingly
on the subordinates—on what *they* are
interested in, how *they* look at things, how
they feel about them.

When business leadership is regarded
in this way, a number of questions arise.
Let us take four of especial importance:

● *Can a boss ever relinquish his responsibility by delegating it to someone
else?* Our view is that the manager must
expect to be held responsible by his
superior for the quality of the decisions
made, even though operationally these
decisions may have been made on a
group basis. He should, therefore, be
ready to accept whatever risk is involved whenever he delegates
decision-making power to his subordinates. Delegation is not a way of "passing the buck." Also, it should be emphasized that the amount of freedom
the boss gives to his subordinates cannot be greater than the freedom which
he himself has been given by his own
superior.

● *Should the manager participate
with his subordinates once he has delegated responsibility to them?* The manager should carefully think over this
question and decide on his role prior to
involving the subordinate group. He
should ask if his presence will inhibit or

Exhibit 19-2

CONTINUUM OF MANAGER-NONMANAGER BEHAVIOR

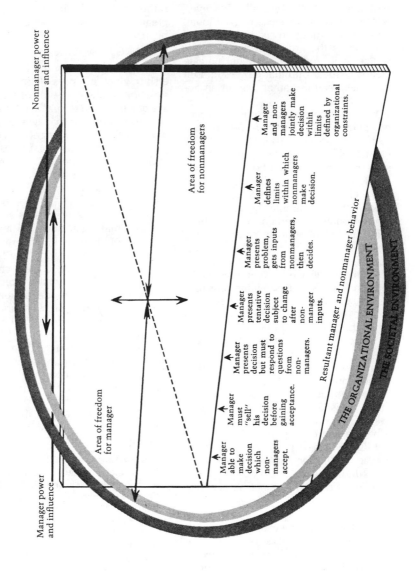

facilitate the problem-solving process. There may be some instances when he should leave the group to let it solve the problem for itself. Typically, however, the boss has useful ideas to contribute, and should function as an additional member of the group. In the latter instance, it is important that he indicate clearly to the group that he sees himself in a *member* role rather than in an authority role.

• *How important is it for the group to recognize what kind of leadership behavior the boss is using?* It makes a great deal of difference. Many relationship problems between boss and subordinate occur because the boss fails to make clear how he plans to use his authority. If, for example, he actually intends to make a certain decision himself, but the subordinate group gets the impression that he has delegated this authority, considerable confusion and resentment are likely to follow. Problems may also occur when the boss uses a "democratic" facade to conceal the fact that he has already made a decision which he hopes the group will accept as its own. The attempt to "make them think it was their idea in the first place" is a risky one. We believe that it is highly important for the manager to be honest and clear in describing what authority he is keeping and what role he is asking his subordinates to assume in solving a particular problem.

• *Can you tell how "democratic" a manager is by the number of decisions his subordinates make?* The sheer *number* of decisions is not an accurate index of the amount of freedom that subordinate group enjoys. More important is the *significance* of the decisions which the boss entrusts to his subordinates. Obviously a decision on how to arrange desks is of an entirely different order from a decision involving the introduction of new electronic data-processing equipment. Even though the widest possible limits are given in dealing with the first issue, the group will

sense no particular degree of responsibility. For a boss to permit the group to decide equipment policy, even within rather narrow limits, would reflect a greater degree of confidence in them on his part.

DECIDING HOW TO LEAD

Now let us turn from the types of leadership which are possible in a company situation to the question of what types are *practical* and *desirable*. What factors or forces should a manager consider in deciding how to manage? Three are of particular importance: forces in the manager, forces in the subordinates, and forces in the situation.

We should like briefly to describe these elements and indicate how they might influence a manager's action in a decision-making situation.[2] The strength of each of them will, of course, vary from instance to instance, but the manager who is sensitive to them can better assess the problems which face him and determine which mode of leadership behavior is most appropriate for him.

• *Forces in the manager.* The manager's behavior in any given instance will be influenced greatly by the many forces operating within his own personality. He will, of course, perceive his leadership problems in a unique way on the basis of his background knowledge, and experience. Among the important internal forces affecting him will be the following:

1. *His value system.* How strongly does he feel that individuals should have a share in making the decisions which affect them? Or, how convinced is he that the official who is paid to assume responsibility should personally carry the burden of decision making? The strength of his convictions on questions like these will tend to move the manager to one end or the other of the continuum shown in Exhibit 19-1. His behavior will also be influenced by the relative importance that he attaches to organizational efficiency, personal growth of subordinates, and company profits.[3]

2. *His confidence in his subordinates.*

Managers differ greatly in the amount of trust they have in other people generally, and this carries over to the particular employees they supervise at a given time. In viewing his particular group of subordinates, the manager is likely to consider their knowledge and competence with respect to the problem. A central question he might ask himself is: "Who is best qualified to deal with this problem?" Often he may, justifiably or not, have more confidence in his own capabilities than in those of his subordinates.

3. *His own leadership inclinations.* There are some managers who seem to function more comfortably and naturally as highly directive leaders. Resolving problems and issuing orders come easily to them. Other managers seem to operate more comfortably in a team role, where they are continually sharing many of their functions with their subordinates.

4. *His feelings of security in an uncertain situation.* The manager who releases control over the decision-making process thereby reduces the predictability of the outcome. Some managers have a greater need than others for predictability and stability in their environment. This "tolerance for ambiguity" is being viewed increasingly by psychologists as a key variable in a person's manner of dealing with problems.

The manager brings these and other highly personal variables to each situation he faces. If he can see them as forces which, consciously or unconsciously, influence his behavior, he can better understand what makes him prefer to act in a given way. And understanding this, he can often make himself more effective.

● *Forces in the subordinate.* Before deciding how to lead a certain group, the manager will also want to consider a number of forces affecting his subordinates' behavior. He will want to remember that each employee, like himself, is influenced by many personality variables. In addition, each subordinate has a set of expectations about how the boss should act in relation to him (the phrase "expected behavior" is one we

hear more and more often these days at discussions of leadership and teaching). The better the manager understands these factors, the more accurately he can determine what kind of behavior on his part will enable his subordinates to act most effectively.

Generally speaking, the manager can permit his subordinates greater freedom if the following essential conditions exist:

● If the subordinates have relatively high needs for independence. (As we all know, people differ greatly in the amount of direction that they desire.)

● If the subordinates have a readiness to assume responsibility for decision making. (Some see additional responsibility as a tribute to their ability; others see it as "passing the buck.")

● If they have a relatively high tolerance for ambiguity. (Some employees prefer to have clear-cut directives given to them; others prefer a wider area of freedom.)

● If they are interested in the problem and feel that it is important.

● If they understand and identify with the goals of the organization.

● If they have the necessary knowledge and experience to deal with the problem.

● If they have learned to expect to share in decision making. (Persons who have come to expect strong leadership and are then suddenly confronted with the request to share more fully in decision making are often upset by this new experience. On the other hand, persons who have enjoyed a considerable amount of freedom resent the boss who begins to make all the decisions himself.)

The manager will probably tend to make fuller use of his own authority if the above conditions do *not* exist; at times there may be no realistic alternative to running a "one-man show."

The restrictive effect of many of the forces will, of course, be greatly modified by the general feeling of confidence which subordinates have in the boss. Where they have learned to respect and trust him, he is free to vary his behavior. He will feel certain that he will not be perceived as an authoritarian boss on those occasions when he makes decisions by himself. Similarly, he will not be seen as using staff meetings to avoid his decision-making responsibility. In a climate of mutual confidence and respect, people tend to feel less threatened by deviations from normal practice, which in turn makes possible a higher degree of flexibility in the whole relationship.

● *Forces in the situation.* In addition to the forces which exist in the manager himself and in his subordinates, certain characteristics of the general situation will also affect the manager's behavior. Among the more critical environmental pressures that surround him are those which stem from the organization, the work group, the nature of the problem, and the pressures of time. Let us look briefly at each of these:

1. *Type of organization.* Like individuals, organizations have values and traditions which inevitably influence the behavior of the people who work in them. The manager who is a newcomer to a company quickly discovers that certain kinds of behavior are approved while others are not. He also discovers that to deviate radically from what is generally accepted is likely to create problems for him.

These values and traditions are communicated in numerous ways—through job descriptions, policy pronouncements, and public statements by top executives. Some organizations, for example, hold to the notion that the desirable executive is one who is dynamic, imaginative, decisive, and persuasive. Other organizations put more emphasis upon the importance of the executive's ability to work effectively with people—his human relations skills. The fact that his superiors have a defined concept of what the good executive should be will very likely push the manager toward one end or the other of the behavioral range.

In addition to the above, the amount of employee participation is influenced by such variables as the size of the working units, their geographical distribution, and the degree of inter- and intra-organizational security required to attain company goals. For example, the wide geographical dispersion of an organization may preclude a practical system of participative decision making, even though this would otherwise be desirable. Similarly, the size of the working units or the need for keeping plans confidential may make it necessary for the boss to exercise more control than would otherwise be the case. Factors like these may limit considerably the manager's ability to function flexibly on the continuum.

2. *Group effectiveness.* Before turning decision-making responsibility over to a subordinate group, the boss should consider how effectively its members work together as a unit.

One of the relevant factors here is the experience the group has had in working together. It can generally be expected that a group which has functioned for some time will have developed habits of cooperation and thus be able to tackle a problem more effectively than a new group. It can also be expected that a group of people with similar backgrounds and interests will work more quickly and easily than people with dissimilar backgrounds, because the communication problems are likely to be less complex.

The degree of confidence that the members have in their ability to solve problems as a group is also a key consideration. Finally, such group variables as cohesiveness, permissiveness, mutual acceptance, and commonality of purpose will exert subtle but powerful influence on the group's functioning.

3. *The problem itself.* The nature of the problem may determine what degree of authority should be delegated by the manager to his subordinates. Obviously he will ask himself whether they have the kind of knowledge which is needed. It is possible to do them a real disservice by assigning a problem that their experience does not equip them to handle.

Since the problems faced in large or growing industries increasingly require knowledge of specialists from many different fields, it might be inferred that the more complex a problem, the more anxious a manager will be to get some assistance in solving it. However, this is not always the case. There will be times when the very complexity of the problem calls for one person to work it out. For example, if the manager has most of the background and factual data relevant to a given issue, it may be easier for him to think it through himself than to take the time to fill in his staff on all the pertinent background information.

The key question to ask, of course, is: "Have I heard the ideas of everyone who has the necessary knowledge to make a significant contribution to the solution of this problem?"

4. *The pressure of time*. This is perhaps the most clearly felt pressure on the manager (in spite of the fact that it may sometimes be imagined). The more that he feels the need for an immediate decision, the more difficult it is to involve other people. In organizations which are in a constant state of "crisis" and "crash programming" one is likely to find managers personally using a high degree of authority with relatively little delegation to subordinates. When the time pressure is less intense, however, it becomes much more possible to bring subordinates in on the decision-making process.

These, then, are the principal forces that impinge on the manager in any given instance and that tend to determine his tactical behavior in relation to his subordinates. In each case his behavior ideally will be that which makes possible the most effective attainment of his immediate goal within the limits facing him.

LONG-RUN STRATEGY

As the manager works with his organization on the problems that come up day by day, his choice of a leadership pattern is usually limited. He must take account of the forces just described and, within the restrictions they impose on him, do the best that he can. But as he looks ahead months or even years, he can shift his thinking from tactic to large-scale strategy. No longer need he be fettered by all of the forces mentioned, for he can view many of them as variables over which he has some control. He can, for example, gain new in-

sights or skills for himself, supply training for individual subordinates, and provide participative experiences for his employee group.

In trying to bring about a change in these variables, however, he is faced with a challenging question: At which point along the continuum should he act? The answer depends largely on what he wants to accomplish. Let us suppose that he is interested in the same objectives that most modern managers seek to attain when they can shift their attention from the pressure of immediate assignments:

1. To raise the level of employee motivation.

2. To increase the readiness of subordinates to accept change.

3. To improve the quality of all managerial decisions.

4. To develop teamwork and morale.

5. To further the individual development of employees.

In recent years the manager has been deluged with a flow of advice on how best to achieve these longer-run objectives. It is little wonder that he is often both bewildered and annoyed. However, there are some guidelines which he can usefully follow in making a decision.

Most research and much of the experience of recent years give a strong factual basis to the theory that a fairly high degree of subordinate-centered behavior is associated with the accomplishment of the five purposes mentioned.[4] This does not mean that a manager should always leave all decisions to his assistants. To provide the individual or the group with greater freedom than they are ready for at any given time may very well tend to generate anxieties and therefore inhibit rather than facilitate the attainment of desired objectives. But this should not keep the manager from making a continuing effort to confront his subordinates with the challenge of freedom.

CONCLUSION

In summary, there are two implications in the basic thesis that we have been developing. The first is that the successful leader is one who is keenly aware of those forces which are most relevant to his behavior at any given time. He accurately understands himself, the individuals and group he is dealing with, and the company and broader social environment in which he operates. And certainly he is able to assess the present readiness for growth of his subordinates.

But this sensitivity or understanding is not enough, which brings us to the second implication. The successful leader is one who is able to behave appropriately in the light of these perceptions. If direction is in order, he is able to direct; if considerable participative freedom is called for, he is able to provide such freedom.

Thus, the successful manager of men can be primarily characterized neither as a strong leader nor as a permissive one. Rather, he is one who maintains a high batting average in accurately assessing the forces that determine what his most appropriate behavior at any given time should be and in actually being able to behave accordingly. Being both insightful and flexible, he is less likely to see the problems of leadership as a dilemma.

NOTES

1. For a fuller explanation of this approach, see Leo Moore, "Too Much Management, Too Little Change," *Harvard Business Review* (January-February 1956), p. 41.

2. See also Robert Tannenbaum and Fred Massarik, "Participation by Subordinates in the Managerial Decision-Making Process," *Canadian Journal of Economics and Political Science* (August 1950), p. 413.

3. See Chris Argyris, "Top Management Dilemma: Company Needs vs. Individual Development," *Personnel* (September 1955), pp. 123-134.

4. For example, see Warren H. Schmidt and Paul C. Buchanan, *Techniques That Produce Teamwork* (New London: Arthur C. Croft Publications, 1954) and Morris S. Viteles, *Motivation and Morale in Industry* (New York: W. W. Norton & Company, Inc., 1953).

20. Path-Goal Theory of Leadership*

ROBERT J. HOUSE

TERENCE R. MITCHELL

An integrated body of conjecture by students of leadership, referred to as the "Path-Goal Theory of Leadership," is currently emerging. According to this theory, leaders are effective because of their impact on subordinates' motivation, ability to perform effectively and satisfactions. The theory is called Path-Goal because its major concern is how the leader influences the subordinates' perceptions of their work goals, personal goals and paths to goal attainment. The theory suggests that a leader's behavior is motivating or satisfying to the degree that the behavior increases subordinate goal attainment and clarifies the paths to these goals.

HISTORICAL FOUNDATIONS

The path-goal approach has its roots in a more general motivational theory called expectancy theory.[1] Briefly, expectancy theory states that an individual's attitudes (e.g., satisfaction with supervision or job satisfaction) or behavior (e.g., leader behavior or job effort) can be predicted from: (1) the degree to which the job, or behavior, is seen as leading to various outcomes (expectancy) and (2) the evaluation of these outcomes (valences). Thus, people are satisfied with their job if they think it leads to things that are highly valued, and they work hard if they believe that effort leads to things that are highly valued. This type of theoretical rationale can be used to predict a variety of phenomena related to leadership, such as why leaders behave the way they do, or how leader behavior influences subordinate motivation.[2]

This latter approach is the primary concern of this article. The implication for leadership is that subordinates are motivated by leader behavior to the extent that this behavior influences expectancies, e.g., goal paths and valences, e.g., goal attractiveness.

Several writers have advanced specific hypotheses concerning how the leader affects the paths and the goals of subordinates.[3] These writers focused on two issues: (1) how the leader affects subordinates' expectations that effort will lead to effective performance and valued rewards, and (2) how this expectation affects motivation to work hard and perform well.

While the state of theorizing about leadership in terms of subordinates' paths and goals is in its infancy, we believe it is promising for two reasons. First, it suggests effects of leader behavior that have not yet been investigated but which appear to be fruitful areas of inquiry. And, second, it suggests with some precision the situational factors on which the effects of leader behavior are contingent.

The initial theoretical work by Evans asserts that leaders will be effective by making rewards available to subordinates and by making these rewards contingent on the subordinate's accomplishment of specific goals.[4] Evans

*Source: From *Journal of Contemporary Business* (Autumn 1974), pp. 81-97. Copyright © 1974 University of Washington. Reprinted by permission.

argued that one of the strategic functions of the leader is to clarify for subordinates the kind of behavior that leads to goal accomplishment and valued rewards. This function might be referred to as path clarification. Evans also argued that the leader increases the rewards available to subordinates by being supportive toward subordinates, *i.e.*, by being concerned about their status, welfare and comfort. Leader supportiveness is in itself a reward that the leader has at his or her disposal, and the judicious use of this reward increases the motivation of subordinates.

Evans studied the relationship between the behavior of leaders and the subordinates' expectations that effort leads to rewards and also studied the resulting impact on ratings of the subordinates' performance. He found that when subordinates viewed leaders as being supportive (considerate of their needs) and when these superiors provided directions and guidance to the subordinates, there was a positive relationship between leader behavior and subordinates' performance ratings.

However, leader behavior was only related to subordinates' performance when the leader's behavior also was related to the subordinates' expectations that their effort would result in desired rewards. Thus, Evans' findings suggest that the major impact of a leader on the performance of subordinates is clarifying the path to desired rewards and making such rewards contingent on effective performance.

Stimulated by this line of reasoning, House, and House and Dessler advanced a more complex theory of the effects of leader behavior on the motivation of subordinates.[5] The theory intends to explain the effects of four specific kinds of leader behavior on the following three subordinate attitudes or expectations: (1) the satisfaction of subordinates, (2) the subordinates' acceptance of the leader and (3) the expectations of subordinates that effort will result in effective performance and that effective performance is the path to rewards. The four kinds of leader behavior included in the theory are: (1) directive leadership, (2) supportive leadership, (3) participative leadership and (4) achievement-oriented leadership. Directive leadership is characterized by a leader who lets subordinates know what is expected of them, gives specific guidance as to what should be done and how it should be done, makes his or her part in the group understood, schedules work to be done, maintains definite standards of performance and asks that group members follow standard rules and regulations. Supportive leadership is characterized by a friendly and approachable leader who shows concern for the status, well-being and needs of subordinates. Such a leader does little things to make the work more pleasant, treats members as equals and is friendly and approachable. Participative leadership is characterized by a leader who consults with subordinates, solicits their suggestions and takes these suggestions seriously into consideration before making a decision. An achievement-oriented leader sets challenging goals, expects subordinates to perform at their highest level, continuously seeks improvement in performance *and* shows a high degree of confidence that the subordinates will assume responsibility, put forth effort and accomplish challenging goals. This kind of leader constantly emphasizes excellence in performance and simultaneously displays confidence that subordinates will meet high standards of excellence.

A number of studies suggest that these different leadership styles can be shown by the same leader in various situations.[6] For example, a leader may show directiveness toward subordinates in some instances and be participative or supportive in other instances.[7] Thus, the traditional method of characterizing a leader as either highly participative and supportive *or* highly directive is invalid;

rather, it can be concluded that leaders vary in the particular fashion employed for supervising their subordinates. Also, the theory, in its present stage, is a tentative explanation of the effects of leader behavior—it is incomplete because it does not explain other kinds of leader behavior and does not explain the effects of the leader on factors other than subordinates' acceptance, satisfaction and expectations. However, the theory is stated so that additional variables may be included in it as new knowledge is made available.

PATH-GOAL THEORY

GENERAL PROPOSITIONS

The first proposition of path-goal theory is that leader behavior is acceptable and satisfying to subordinates to the extent that the subordinates see such behavior as either an immediate source of satisfaction or as instrumental to future satisfaction.

The second proposition of this theory is that the leader's behavior will be motivational, *i.e.,* increase effort, to the extent that (1) such behavior makes satisfaction of subordinate's needs contingent on effective performance and (2) such behavior complements the environment of subordinates by providing the coaching, guidance, support and rewards necessary for effective performance.

These two propositions suggest that the leader's strategic functions are to enhance subordinates' motivation to perform, satisfaction with the job and acceptance of the leader. From previous research on expectancy theory of motivation, it can be inferred that the strategic functions of the leader consists of: (1) recognizing and/or arousing subordinates' needs for outcomes over which the leader has some control, (2) increasing personal payoffs to subordinates for work-goal attainment, (3) making the path to those payoffs easier to travel by coaching and direction, (4)

helping subordinates clarify expectancies, (5) reducing frustrating barriers and (6) increasing the opportunities for personal satisfaction contingent on effective performance.

Stated less formally, the motivational functions of the leader consist of increasing the number and kinds of personal payoffs to subordinates for work-goal attainment and making paths to these payoffs easier to travel by clarifying the paths, reducing road blocks and pitfalls, and increasing the opportunities for personal satisfaction en route.

CONTINGENCY FACTORS

Two classes of situational variables are asserted to be contingency factors. A contingency factor is a variable which moderates the relationship between two other variables such as leader behavior and subordinate satisfaction. For example, we might suggest that the degree of structure in the task moderates the relationship between leaders' directive behavior and subordinates' job satisfaction. Figure 20-1 shows how such a relationship might look. Thus, subordinates are satisfied with directive behavior in an unstructured task and are satisfied with nondirective behavior in a structured task. Therefore, we say that the relationship between leader directiveness and subordinate satisfaction is contingent upon the structure of the task.

The two contingency variables are (a) personal characteristics of the subordinates and (b) the environmental pressures and demands with which subordinates must cope in order to accomplish the work goals and to satisfy their needs. While other situational factors also may operate to determine the effects of leader behavior, they are not presently known.

With respect to the first class of contingency factors, the characteristics of subordinates, path-goal theory asserts that leader behavior will be acceptable to subordinates to the extent that the subordinates see such behavior as either an immediate source of satisfaction or as instrumental to future satisfaction. Subordinates' characteristics are hypothesized to partially determine this perception. For example, Runyon[8] and Mitchell[9] show that the subordinate's source on a measure called Locus of Control moderates the relationship between participative leadership style and subordinate satisfaction. The Locus-of-Control measure reflects the degree to which an individual sees the environment as systematically responding to his or her behavior. People who believe that what happens to them occurs because of their behavior are called internals; people who believe that what happens to them occurs because of luck or chance are called externals. Mitchell's findings suggest that internals are more satisfied with a participative leadership style and externals are more satisfied with a directive style.

A second characteristic of subordinates on which the effects of leader behavior are contingent is subordinates' perception of their own ability with respect to their assigned tasks. The higher the degree of perceived ability relative to task demands, the less the subordinate will view leader directiveness and coaching behavior as acceptable. Where the subordinate's perceived ability is high, such behavior is likely to have little positive effect on the motivation of the subordinate and to be perceived as excessively close control. Thus, the acceptability of the leader's behavior is determined in part by the characteristics of the subordinates.

The second aspect of the situation, the environment of the subordinate, consists of those factors that are not within the control of the subordinate but which are important to need satisfaction or to ability to perform effectively. The theory asserts that effects of the leader's behavior on the psychological states of subordinates are contingent on other parts of the subordinates' environment that are relevant to subordinate motivation. Three broad classifications of con-

tingency factors in the environment are: the subordinates' tasks, the formal authority system of the organization, and the primary work group.

Assessment of the environmental conditions makes it possible to predict the kind and amount of influence that specific leader behaviors will have on the motivation of subordinates. Any of the three environmental factors could act upon the subordinate in any of three ways: first, to serve as stimuli that motivate and direct the subordinate to perform necessary task operations; second, to constrain variability in behavior. Constraints may help the subordinate by clarifying expectancies that effort leads to rewards or by preventing the subordinates from experiencing conflict and confusion. Constraints also may be counterproductive to the extent that they restrict initiative or prevent increases in effort from being associated positively with rewards. Third, environmental factors may serve as rewards for achieving desired performance, e.g., it is possible for the subordinate to receive the necessary cues to do the job and the needed rewards for satisfaction from sources other than the leader, e.g., co-workers in the primary work group. Thus, the effect of the leader on subordinates' motivation will be a function of how deficient the environment is with respect to motivational stimuli, constraints or rewards.

With respect to the environment, path-goal theory asserts that when goals and paths to desired goals are apparent because of the routine nature of the task, clear group norms or objective controls of the formal authority systems, attempts by the leader to clarify paths and goals will be both redundant and seen by subordinates as imposing unnecessary, close control. Although such control may increase performance by preventing soldiering or malingering, it also will result in decreased satisfaction (see Figure 20-1). Also with respect to the work environment, the theory asserts that the more dis-

Figure 20-1

HYPOTHETICAL RELATIONSHIP BETWEEN DIRECTIVE LEADERSHIP AND
SUBORDINATE SATISFACTION WITH TASK STRUCTURE AS A
CONTINGENCY FACTOR

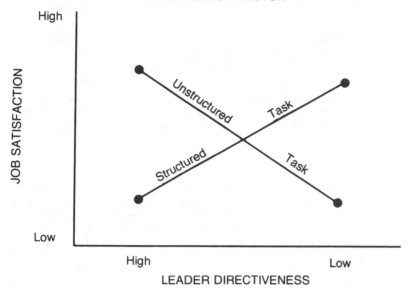

satisfying the task, the more the subordinates will resent leader behavior directed at increasing productivity or enforcing compliance to organizational rules and procedures.

Finally, with respect to environmental variables the theory states that leader behavior will be motivational to the extent that it helps subordinates cope with environmental uncertainties, threats from others or sources of frustration. Such leader behavior is predicted to increase subordinates' satisfaction with the job context and to be motivational to the extent that it increases the subordinates' expectations that their effort will lead to valued rewards.

These propositions and specification of situational contingencies provide a heuristic framework on which to base future research. Hopefully, this will lead to a more fully developed, explicitly formal theory of leadership.

Figure 20-2 presents a summary of the theory. It is hoped that these propositions, while admittedly tentative, will provide managers with some insights concerning the effects of their own leader behavior and that of others.

EMPIRICAL SUPPORT

The theory has been tested in a limited number of studies which have generated considerable empirical support for our ideas and also suggest areas in which the theory requires revision. A brief review of these studies follows.

LEADER DIRECTIVENESS

Leader directiveness has a positive correlation with satisfaction and expectancies of subordinates who are engaged in ambiguous tasks and has a negative correlation with satisfaction and expectancies of subordinates engaged in clear tasks. These findings were predicted by

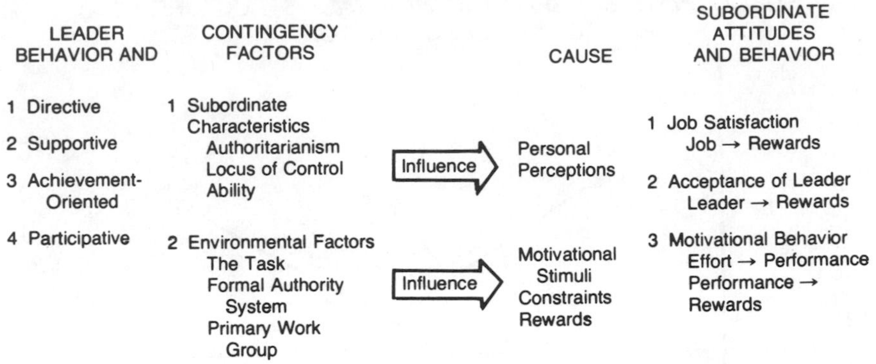

Figure 20-2

SUMMARY OF PATH-GOAL RELATIONSHIPS

			SUBORDINATE
LEADER	CONTINGENCY		ATTITUDES
BEHAVIOR AND	FACTORS	CAUSE	AND BEHAVIOR

1 Directive   1 Subordinate
                   Characteristics   1 Job Satisfaction

2 Supportive   Authoritarianism   Personal   Job → Rewards
                   Locus of Control   [Influence]   Perceptions

3 Achievement-   Ability   2 Acceptance of Leader
   Oriented   Leader → Rewards

4 Participative   2 Environmental Factors   3 Motivational Behavior
                   The Task   Motivational   Effort → Performance
                   Formal Authority   [Influence]   Stimuli   Performance →
                   System   Constraints   Rewards
                   Primary Work   Rewards
                   Group

the theory and have been replicated in seven organizations. They suggest that when task demands are ambiguous or when the organization procedures, rules and policies are not clear, a leader behaving in a directive manner complements the tasks and the organization by providing the necessary guidance and psychological structure for subordinates.[10] However, when task demands are clear to subordinates, leader directiveness is seen more as a hindrance.

However, other studies have failed to confirm these findings.[11] A study by Dessler[12] suggests a resolution to these conflicting findings—he found that for subordinates at the lower organizational levels of a manufacturing firm who were doing routine, repetitive, unambiguous tasks, directive leadership was preferred by closed-minded, dogmatic, authoritarian subordinates and nondirective leadership was preferred by nonauthoritarian, open-minded subordinates. However, for subordinates at higher organizational levels doing nonroutine, ambiguous tasks, directive leadership was preferred for both authoritarian and nonauthoritarian subordinates. Thus, Dessler found that two contingency factors appear to operate simultaneously: subordinate task ambiguity and degree of subordinate authoritarianism.

When measured in combination, the findings are as predicted by the theory; however, when the subordinate's personality is not taken into account, task ambiguity does not always operate as a contingency variable as predicted by the theory. House, Burill and Dessler recently found a similar interaction between subordinate authoritarianism and task abmiguity in a second manufacturing firm, thus adding confidence in Dessler's original findings.[13]

SUPPORTIVE LEADERSHIP

The theory hypothesizes that supportive leadership will have its most positive effect on subordinate satisfaction for subordinates who work on stressful, frustrating or dissatisfying tasks. This hypothesis has been tested in 10 samples of employees,[14] and in only one of these studies was the hypothesis disconfirmed.[15] Despite some inconsistency in research on supportive leadership, the evidence is sufficiently positive to suggest that managers should be alert to the critical need for supportive leadership under conditions where tasks are dissatisfying, frustrating or stressful to subordinates.

ACHIEVEMENT-ORIENTED LEADERSHIP

The theory hypothesizes that achievement-oriented leadership will cause subordinates to strive for higher standards of performance and to have more confidence in the ability to meet challenging goals. A recent study by House, Valency, and Van der Krabben provides a partial test on this hypothesis among white collar employees in service organizations.[16] For subordinates performing ambiguous, nonrepetitive tasks, they found a positive relationship between the amount of achievement orientation of the leader and subordinates' expectancy that their effort would result in effective performance. Stated less technically, for subordinates performing ambiguous, nonrepetitive tasks, the higher the achievement orientation of the leader, the more the subordinates were confident that their efforts would pay off in effective performance. For subordinates performing moderately unambiguous, repetitive tasks, there was no significant relationship between achievement-oriented leadership and subordinate expectancies that their effort would lead to effective performance. This finding held in four separate organizations.

Two plausible interpretations may be used to explain these data. First, people who select ambiguous, nonrepetitive tasks may be different in personality from those who select a repetitive job and may, therefore, be more responsive to an achievement-oriented leader. A second explanation is that achievement orientation only affects expectancies in ambiguous situations because there is more flexibility and autonomy in such tasks. Therefore, subordinates in such tasks are more likely to be able to change in response to such leadership style. Neither of the above interpretations have been tested to date; however, additional research is currently under way to investigate these relationships.

PARTICIPATIVE LEADERSHIP

In theorizing about the effects of participative leadership it is necessary to ask about the specific characteristics of both the subordinates and their situation that would cause participative leadership to be viewed as satisfying and instrumental to effective performance.

Mitchell recently described at least four ways in which a participative leadership style would impact on subordinate attitudes and behavior as predicted by expectancy theory.[17] First, a participative climate should increase the clarity of organizational contingencies. Through participation in decision making, subordinates should learn what leads to what. From a path-goal viewpoint participation would lead to greater clarity of the paths to various goals. A second impact of participation would be that subordinates, hopefully, should select goals they highly value. If one participates in decisions about various goals, it makes sense that this individual would select goals he or she wants. Thus, participation would increase the correspondence between organization and subordinate goals. Third, we can see how participation would increase the control the individual has over what happens on the job. If our motivation is higher (based on the preceding two points), then having greater autonomy and ability to carry out our intentions should lead to increased effort and performance. Finally, under a participative system, pressure towards high performance should come from sources other than the leader or the organization. More specifically, when people participate in the decision process they become more ego-involved; the decisions made are in some part their own. Also, their peers know what is expected and the social pressure has a greater impact. Thus, motivation to perform well stems from internal and social factors as well as formal external ones.

A number of investigations prior to the above formulation supported the idea that participation appears to be helpful,[18] and Mitchell presents a number of recent studies that support the above four points.[19] However, it is also true that we would expect the relationship between a participative style and subordinate behavior to be moderated by both the personality characteristics of the subordinate and the situational demands. Studies by Tannenbaum and Alport and Vroom have shown that subordinates who prefer autonomy and self-control respond more positively to participative leadership in terms of both satisfaction and performance than subordinates who do not have such preferences.[20] Also, the studies mentioned by Runyon[21] and Mitchell[22] showed that subordinates who were external in orientation were less satisfied with a participative style of leadership than were internal subordinates.

House also has reviewed these studies in an attempt to explain the ways in which the situation or environment moderates the relationship between participation and subordinate attitudes and behavior.[23] His analysis suggests that where participative leadership is positively related to satisfaction, regardless of the predispositions of subordinates, the task of the subjects appear to be ambiguous and ego-involving. In the studies in which the subjects' personalities or predispositions moderate the effect of participative leadership, the tasks of the subjects are inferred to be highly routine and/or nonego-involving.

House reasoned from this analysis that the task may have an overriding effect on the relationship between leader participation and subordinate responses, and that individual predispositions or personality characteristics of subordinates may have an effect only under some tasks. It was assumed that when task demands are ambiguous, subordinates will have a need to reduce the ambiguity. Further, it was assumed that when task demands are ambiguous, participative problem solving between the leader and the subordinate will result in more effective decisions than when the task demands are unambiguous. Finally,

it was assumed that when the subordinates are ego-involved in their tasks they are more likely to want to have a say in the decisions that affect them. Given these assumptions, the following hypotheses were formulated to account for the conflicting findings reviewed above:

• When subjects are highly ego-involved in a decision or a task and the decision or task demands are ambiguous, participative leadership will have a positive effect on the satisfaction and motivation of the subordinate, *regardless* of the subordinate's predisposition toward self-control, authoritarianism or need for independence.

• When subordinates are not ego-involved in their tasks and when task demands are clear, subordinates who are not authoritarian and who have high needs for independence and self-control will respond favorably to leader participation and their opposite personality types will respond less favorably.

These hypotheses were derived on the basis of path-goal theorizing; *i.e.*, the rationale guiding the analysis of prior studies was that both task characteristics and characteristics of subordinates interact to determine the effect of a specific kind of leader behavior on the satisfaction, expectancies and performance of subordinates. To date, one major investigation has supported some of these predictions[24] in which personality variables, amount of participative leadership, task ambiguity and job satisfaction were assessed for 324 employees of an industrial manufacturing organization. As expected, in nonrepetitive, ego-involving tasks, employees (regardless of their personality) were more satisfied under a participative style than a nonparticipative style. However, in repetitive tasks which were less ego-involving the amount of authoritarianism of subordinates moderated the relationship between leadership style and satisfaction. Specifically, low authoritarian subordinates were *more satisfied* under a participative style. These findings are exactly as the theory would predict; thus, it has promise in reconciling a set of confusing and contradictory findings with respect to participative leadership.

SUMMARY AND CONCLUSIONS

We have attempted to describe what we believe is a useful theoretical framework for understanding the effect of leadership behavior on subordinate satisfaction and motivation. Most theorists today have moved away from the simplistic notions that all effective leaders have a certain set of personality traits or that the situation completely determines performance. Some researchers have presented rather complex attempts at matching certain types of leaders with certain types of situations, e.g., the articles written by Vroom and Fiedler in this issue. But, we believe that a path-goal approach goes one step further. It not only suggests what type of style may be most effective in a given situation—it also attempts to explain *why* it is most effective.

We are optimistic about the future outlook of leadership research. With the guidance of path-goal theorizing, future research is expected to unravel many confusing puzzles about the reasons for and effects of leader behavior that have, heretofore, not been solved. However, we add a word of caution: the theory, and the research on it, are relatively new to the literature of organizational behavior. Consequently, path-goal theory is offered more as a tool for directing research and stimulating insight than as a proven guide for managerial action.

NOTES

1. T. R. Mitchell, "Expectancy Model of Job Satisfaction, Occupational Preference and Effort: A Theoretical, Methodological and Empirical Appraisal," *Psychological Bulletin* (1974, in press).

2. D. M. Nebeker and T. R. Mitchell, "Leader Behavior: An Expectancy Theory Approach," *Organization Behavior and Human Performance,* Vol. 11(1974), pp. 355-367.

3. M.G.Evans,"The Effects of Supervisory Behavior on the Path-Goal Relationship," *Organization Behavior and Human Performance,* Vol. 55 (1970), pp. 277-298; T. H. Hammer and H. T. Dachler, "The Process of Supervision in the Context of Motivation Theory," Research Report No. 3 (University of Maryland, 1973); F. Dansereau, Jr., J. Cashman and G. Graen, "Instrumentality Theory and Equity Theory as Complementary Approaches in Predicting the Relationship of Leadership and Turnover Among Managers," *Organization Behavior and Human Performance,* Vol. 10 (1973), pp. 184-200; R. J. House, "A Path-Goal Theory of Leader Effectiveness, *Administrative Science Quarterly,* Vol. 16, No. 3 (September 1971), pp. 321-338; T. R. Mitchell, "Motivation and Participation: An Integration," *Academy of Management Journal,* Vol. 16, No. 4 (1973), pp. 160-179; G. Graen, F. Dansereau, Jr., and T. Minami, "Dysfunctional Leadership Styles," *Organization Behavior and Human Performance,* Vol. 7 (1972), pp. 216-236; _____, "An Empirical Test of the Man-in-the-Middle Hypothesis Among Executives in a Hierarchical Organization Employing a Unit Analysis," *Organization Behavior and Human Performance,* Vol. 8 (1972), pp. 262-285; R. J. House and G. Dessler, "The Path-Goal Theory of Leadership: Some Post Hoc and A Priori Tests," to appear in J. G. Hunt, ed., *Contingency Approaches to Leadership* (Carbondale, Ill.: Southern Illinois University Press, 1974).

4. M. G. Evans, "Effects of Supervisory Behavior"; _____, "Extensions of a Path-Goal Theory of Motivation," *Journal of Applied Psychology,* Vol. 59(1974), pp. 172-178.

5. R. J. House, "A Path-Goal Theory"; R. J. House and G. Dessler, "Path-Goal Theory of Leadership."

6. R. J. House and G. Dessler, "Path-Goal Theory of Leadership"; R. M. Stogdill, *Managers, Employees, Organization* (Ohio State University, Bureau of Business Research, 1965); R. J. House, A. Valency and R. Van der Krabben, "Some Tests and Extensions of the Path-Goal Theory of Leadership" (in preparation).

7. W. A. Hill and D. Hughes, "Variations

in Leader Behavior As a Function of Task Type," *Organization Behavior and Human Performance* (1974, in press).

8. K. E. Runyon, "Some Interactions Between Personality Variables and Management Styles," *Journal of Applied Psychology,* Vol. 57, No. 3(1973), pp. 288-294; T. R. Mitchell, C. R. Smyser and S. E. Weed, "Locus of Control: Supervision and Work Satisfaction," *Academy of Management Journal* (in press).

9. T. R. Mitchell, "Locus of Control."

10. R. J. House, "A Path-Goal Theory"; _____ and G. Dessler, "Path-Goal Theory of Leadership"; A. D. Szalagyi and H. P. Sims, "An Exploration of the Path-Goal Theory of Leadership in a Health Care Environment," *Academy of Management Journal* (in press); J. D. Dermer, "Supervisory Behavior and Budget Motivation" (Cambridge, Mass.: unpublished, MIT, Sloan School of Management, 1974); R. W. Smetana, "The Relationship Between Managerial Behavior and Subordinate Attitudes and Motivation: A Contribution to a Behavioral Theory of Leadership" (Ph.D. diss, Wayne State University, 1974).

11. S. E. Weed, T. R. Mitchell and C. R. Smyser, "A Test of House's Path-Goal Theory of Leadership in an Organizational Setting" (paper presented at Western Psychological Assoc., 1974); J. D. Dermer and J. P. Siegel, "A Test of Path-Goal Theory: Disconfirming Evidence and a Critique" (unpublished, University of Toronto, Faculty of Management Studies, 1973); R. S. Schuler, "A Path-Goal Theory of Leadership: An Empirical Investigation" (Ph.D. diss, Michigan State University, 1973); H. K. Downey, J. E. Sheridan and J. W. Slocum, Jr., "Analysis of Relationships Among Leader Behavior, Subordinate Job Performance and Satisfaction: A Path-Goal Approach" (unpublished mimeograph, 1974); J. E. Stinson and T. W. Johnson, "The Path-Goal Theory of Leadership: A Partial Test and Suggested Refinement," *Proceedings* (Kent, Ohio: 7th Annual Conference of the Midwest Academy of Management, April 1974), pp. 18-36.

12. G. Dessler, "An Investigation of the Path-Goal Theory of Leadership" (Ph.D. diss, City University of New York, Bernard M. Baruch College, 1973).

13. R. J. House, D. Burrill and G. Dessler, "Tests and Extensions of Path-Goal Theory of Leadership, I" (unpublished, in process).

14. R. J. House, "A Path-Goal Theory"; _____ and G. Dessler, "Path-Goal Theory of Leadership"; A. D. Szalagyi and H. P. Sims, "Exploration of Path-Goal"; J. E. Stinson and T. W. Johnson, *Proceedings*; R. S. Schuler, "Path-Goal: Investigation"; H. K. Downey, J. E. Sheridan and J. W. Slocum, Jr., "Analysis of Relationships"; S. E. Weed, T. R. Mitchell and C. R. Smyser, "Test of House's Path-Goal."

15. A. D. Szalagyi and H. P. Sims, "Exploration of Path-Goal."

16. R. J. House, A. Valency and R. Van der Krabben, "Tests and Extensions of Path-Goal Theory of Leadership, II" (unpublished, in process).

17. T. R. Mitchell, "Motivation and Participation."

18. H. Tosi, "A Reexamination of Personality as a Determinant of the Effects of Participation," *Personnel Psychology,* Vol. 23 (1970), pp. 91-99; J. Sadler "Leadership Style, Confidence in Management and Job Satisfaction," *Journal of Applied Behavioral Sciences,* Vol. 6 (1970), pp. 3-19; K. N. Wexley, J. P. Singh and J. A. Yukl, "Subordinate Personality as a Moderator of the Effects of Participation in Three Types of Appraisal Interviews," *Journal of Applied Psychology,* Vol. 83 (1973), pp. 54-59.

19. T. R. Mitchell, "Motivation and Participation."

20. A. S. Tannenbaum and F. H. Allport, "Personality Structure and Group Structure: An Interpretive Study of Their Relationship Through an Event-Structure Hypothesis," *Journal of Abnormal and Social Psychology,* Vol. 53 (1956), pp. 272-280; V. H. Vroom, "Some Personality Determinants of the Effects of Participation," *Journal of Abnormal and Social Psychology,* Vol. 59 (1959), pp. 322-327.

21. K. E. Runyon, "Some Interactions Between Personality Variables and Management Styles," *Journal of Applied Psychology,* Vol. 57, No. 3 (1973), pp. 288-294.

22. T. R. Mitchell, C. R. Smyser and S. E. Weed, "Locus of Control."

23. R. J. House, "Notes on the Path-Goal Theory of Leadership" (University of Toronto, Faculty of Management Studies, May 1974).

24. R. S. Schuler, "Leader Participation, Task-Structure and Subordinate Authoritarianism" (unpublished mimeograph, Cleveland State University, 1974).

21. Who Gets Power—
and How They Hold on to It*

GERALD R. SALANCIK

JEFFREY PFEFFER

Power is held by many people to be a dirty word or, as Warren Bennis has said, "It is the organization's last dirty secret."

This article will argue that traditional "political" power, far from being a dirty business, is, in its most naked form, one of the few mechanisms available for aligning an organization with its own reality. However, institutionalized forms of power—what we prefer to call the cleaner forms of power: authority, legitimization, centralized control, regulations, and the more modern "management information systems"—tend to buffer the organization from reality and obscure the demands of its environment. Most great states and institutions declined, not because they played politics, but because they failed to accommodate to the political realities they faced. Political processes, rather than being mechanisms for unfair and unjust allocations and appointments, tend toward the realistic resolution of conflicts among interests. And power, while it eludes definition, is easy enough to recognize by its consequences—the ability of those who possess power to bring about the outcomes they desire.

The model of power we advance is an elaboration of what has been called strategic-contingency theory, a view that sees power as something that accrues to organizational subunits (individuals, departments) that cope with critical organizational problems. Power is used by subunits, indeed, used by all who have it,
to enhance their own survival through control of scarce critical resources, through the placement of allies in key positions, and through the definition of organizational problems and policies. Because of the processes by which power develops and is used, organizations become both more aligned and more misaligned with their environments. This contradiction is the most interesting aspect of organizational power, and one that makes administration one of the most precarious of occupations.

WHAT IS ORGANIZATIONAL POWER?

You can walk into most organizations and ask without fear of being misunderstood, "Which are the powerful groups or people in this organization?" Although many organizational informants may be *unwilling* to tell you, it is unlikely they will be *unable* to tell you. Most people do not require explicit definitions to know what power is.

Power is simply the ability to get things done the way one wants them to be done. For a manager who wants an increased budget to launch a project that he thinks is important, his power is measured by his ability to get that budget. For an executive vice-president who wants to be chairman, his power is evidenced by his advancement toward his goal.

People in organizations not only know

what you are talking about when you ask who is influential but they are likely to agree with one another to an amazing extent. Recently, we had a chance to observe this in a regional office of an insurance company. The office had 21 department managers; we asked ten of these managers to rank all 21 according to the influence each one had in the organization. Despite the fact that ranking 21 things is a difficult task, the managers sat down and began arranging the names of their colleagues and themselves in a column. Only one person bothered to ask, "What do you mean by influence?" When told "power," he responded, "Oh," and went on. We compared the rankings of all ten managers and found virtually no disagreement among them in the managers ranked among the top five or the bottom five. Differences in the rankings came from department heads claiming more influence for themselves than their colleagues attributed to them.

Such agreement on those who have influence, and those who do not, was not unique to this insurance company. So far we have studied over 20 very different organizations—universities, research firms, factories, banks, retailers, to name a few. In each one we found individuals able to rate themselves and their peers on a scale of influence or power. We have done this both for specific decisions and for general impact on organizational policies. Their agreement was unusually high, which suggests that distributions of influence exist well enough in everyone's mind to be referred to with ease—and, we assume, with accuracy.

WHERE DOES ORGANIZATIONAL POWER COME FROM?

Earlier we stated that power helps organizations become aligned with their realities. This hopeful prospect follows from what we have dubbed the strategic-contingencies theory of organizational power. Briefly, those subunits most able to cope with the organization's critical

problems and uncertainties acquire power. In its simplest form, the strategic-contingencies theory implies that when an organization faces a number of lawsuits that threaten its existence, the legal department will gain power and influence over organizational decisions. Somehow other organizational interest groups will recognize its critical importance and confer upon it a status and power never before enjoyed. This influence may extend beyond handling legal matters and into decisions about product design, advertising production, and so on. Such extensions undoubtedly would be accompanied by appropriate, or acceptable, verbal justifications. In time, the head of the legal department may become the head of the corporation, just as in times past the vice-president for marketing had become the president when market shares were a worrisome problem and, before him, the chief engineer, who had made the production line run as smooth as silk.

Stated in this way, the strategic-contingencies theory of power paints an appealing picture of power. To the extent that power is determined by the critical uncertainties and problems facing the organization and, in turn, influences decisions in the organization, the organization is aligned with the realities it faces. In short, power facilitates the organization's adaptation to its environment—or its problems.

We can cite many illustrations of how influence derives from a subunit's ability to deal with critical contingencies. Michael Crozier described a French cigarette factory in which the maintenance engineers had a considerable say in the plantwide operation. After some probing he discovered that the group possessed the solution to one of the major problems faced by the company, that of troubleshooting the elaborate, expensive, and irrascible automated machines that kept breaking down and dumbfounding everyone else. It was the one problem that the plant manager could in no way control.

The production workers, while troublesome from time to time, created no insurmountable problems; the manager could reasonably predict their absenteeism or replace them when necessary. Production scheduling was something he could deal with since, by watching inventories and sales, the demand for cigarettes was known long in advance. Changes in demand could be accommodated by slowing down or speeding up the line. Supplies of tobacco and paper were also easily dealt with through stockpiles and advance orders.

The one thing that management could neither control nor accommodate to, however, was the seemingly happenstance breakdowns. And the foreman couldn't instruct the workers what to do when emergencies developed since the maintenance department kept its records of problems and solutions locked up in a cabinet or in its members' heads. The breakdowns were, in truth, a critical source of uncertainty for the organization, and the maintenance engineers were the only ones who could cope with the problem.

The engineers' strategic role in coping with breakdowns afforded them a considerable say on plant decisions. Schedules and production quotas were set in consultation with them. And the plant manager, while formally their boss, accepted their decisions about personnel in their operation. His submission was to his credit, for without their cooperation he would have had an even more difficult time in running the plant.

IGNORING CRITICAL CONSEQUENCES

In this cigarette factory, sharing influence with the maintenance workers reflected the plant manager's awareness of the critical contingencies. However, when organizational members are not aware of the critical contingencies they face, and do not share influence accordingly, the failure to do so can create havoc. In one case, an insurance company's regional office was having problems with the performance of one of its departments, the coding depart-

ment. From the outside, the department looked like a disaster area. The clerks who worked in it were somewhat dissatisfied; their supervisors paid little attention to them, and they resented the hard work. Several other departments were critical of this manager, claiming that she was inconsistent in meeting deadlines. The person most critical was the claims manager. He resented having to wait for work that was handled by her department, claiming that it held up his claims adjusters. Having heard the rumors about dissatisfaction among her subordinates, he attributed the situation to poor supervision. He was second in command in the office and therefore took up the issue with her immediate boss, the head of administrative services. They consulted with the personnel manager and the three of them concluded that the manager needed leadership training to improve her relations with her subordinates. The coding manager objected, saying it was a waste of time, but agreed to go along with the training and also agreed to give more priority to the claims department's work. Within a week after the training, the results showed that her workers were happier but that the performance of her department had decreased, save for the people serving the claims department.

About this time, we began, quite independently, a study of influence in this organization. We asked the administrative services director to draw up flow charts of how the work of one department moved on to the next department. In the course of the interview, we noticed that the coding department began or interceded in the work flow of most of the other departments and casually mentioned to him, "The coding manager must be very influential." He said, "No, not really. Why would you think so?" Before we could reply he recounted the story of her leadership training and the fact that things were worse. We then told him that it seemed obvious that the coding department would be influential from the fact that all the other departments depended on it. It was also clear why productivity had fallen. The coding manager took the training seriously and began spending more time raising her workers' spirits than she did worrying about the problems of all the departments that depended on her. Giving priority to the claims area only exaggerated the problem, for their work was getting done at the expense of the work of the other departments. Eventually the company hired a few more clerks to relieve the pressure in the coding department and performance returned to a more satisfactory level.

Originally we got involved with this insurance company to examine how the influence of each manager evolved from his or her department's handling of critical organizational contingencies. We reasoned that one of the most important contingencies faced by all profit-making organizations was that of generating income. Thus we expected managers would be influential to the extent to which they contributed to this function. Such was the case. The underwriting managers, who wrote the policies that committed the premiums, were the most influential; the claims managers, who kept a lid on the funds flowing out, were a close second. Least influential were the managers of functions unrelated to revenue, such as mailroom and payroll managers. And contrary to what the administrative services manager believed, the third most powerful department head (out of 21) was the woman in charge of the coding function, which consisted of rating, recording, and keeping track of the codes of all policy applications and contracts. Her peers attributed more influence to her than could have been inferred from her place on the organization chart. And it was not surprising, since they all depended on her department. The coding department's records, their accuracy and the speed with which they could be retrieved, affected virtually every other operating department in the insurance office. The underwriters depended on them in getting the contracts straight; the typing department depended

on them in preparing the formal contract document; the claims department depended on them in adjusting claims; and accounting depended on them for billing. Unfortunately, the "bosses" were not aware of these dependences, for unlike the cigarette factory, there were no massive breakdowns that made them obvious, while the coding manager, who was a hard-working but quiet person, did little to announce her importance.

The cases of this plant and office illustrate nicely a basic point about the source of power in organizations. The basis for power in an organization derives from the ability of a person or subunit to take or not take actions that are desired by others. The coding manager was seen as influential by those who depended on her department, but not by the people at the top. The engineers were influential because of their role in keeping the plant operating. The two cases differ in these respects: The coding supervisor's source of power was not as widely recognized as that of the maintenance engineers, and she did not use her source of power to influence decisions; the maintenance engineers did. Whether power is used to influence anything is a separate issue. We should not confuse this issue with the fact that power derives from a social situation in which one person has a capacity to do something and another person does not, but wants it done.

POWER SHARING
IN ORGANIZATIONS

Power is shared in organizations; and it is shared out of necessity more than out of concern for principles of organizational development or participatory democracy. Power is shared because no one person controls all the desired activities in the organization. While the factory owner may hire people to operate his noisy machines, once hired they have some control over the use of the machinery. And thus they have power over him in the same way he has power over them. Who has more power over whom is a mooter point than that of recognizing the inherent nature of organizing as a sharing of power.

Let's expand on the concept that power derives from the activities desired in an organization. A major way of managing influence in organizations is through the designation of activities. In a bank we studied, we saw this principle in action. This bank was planning to install a computer system for routine credit evaluation. The bank, rather progressive-minded, was concerned that the change would have adverse effects on employees and therefore surveyed their attitudes.

The principal opposition to the new system came, interestingly, not from the employees who performed the routine credit checks, some of whom would be relocated because of the change, but from the manager of the credit department. His reason was quite simple. The manager's primary function was to give official approval to the applications, catch any employee mistakes before giving approval, and arbitrate any difficulties the clerks had in deciding what to do. As a consequence of his role, others in the organization, including his superiors, subordinates, and colleagues, attributed considerable importance to him. He, in turn, for example, could point to the low proportion of credit approvals, compared with other financial institutions, that resulted in bad debts. Now, to his mind, a wretched machine threatened to transfer his role to a computer programmer, a man who knew nothing of finance and who, in addition, had ten years less seniority. The credit manager eventually quit for a position at a smaller firm with lower pay, but one in which he would have more influence than his redefined job would have left him with.

Because power derives from activities rather than individuals, an individual's or subgroup's power is never absolute and derives ultimately from the context of the situation. The amount of power an individual has at any one time depends, not only on the activities he or she con-

trols, but also on the existence of other persons or means by which the activities can be achieved and on those who determine what ends are desired and, hence, on what activities are desired and critical for the organization. One's own power always depends on other people for these two reasons. Other people, or groups or organizations, can determine the definition of what is a critical contingency for the organization and can also undercut the uniqueness of the individual's personal contribution to the critical contingencies of the organization.

Perhaps one can best appreciate how situationally dependent power is by examining how it is distributed. In most societies, power organizes around scarce and critical resources. Rarely does power organize around abundant resources. In the United States, a person doesn't become powerful because he or she can drive a car. There are simply too many others who can drive with equal facility. In certain villages in Mexico, on the other hand, a person with a car is accredited with enormous social status and plays a key role in the community. In addition to scarcity, power is also limited by the need for one's capacities in a social system. While a racer's ability to drive a car around a 90° turn at 80 mph may be sparsely distributed in a society, it is not likely to lend the driver much power in the society. The ability simply does not play a central role in the activities of the society.

The fact that power revolves around scarce and critical activities, of course, makes the control and organization of those activities a major battleground in struggles for power. Even relatively abundant or trivial resources can become the bases for power if one can organize and control their allocation and the definition of what is critical. Many occupational and professional groups attempt to do just this in modern economies. Lawyers organize themselves into associations, regulate the entrance requirements for novitiates, and then get laws passed specifying situations that require the services of an attorney.

Workers had little power in the conduct of industrial affairs until they organized themselves into closed and controlled systems. In recent years, women and blacks have tried to define themselves as important and critical to the social system, using law to reify their status.

In organizations there are obviously opportunities for defining certain activities as more critical than others. Indeed, the growth of managerial thinking to include defining organizational objectives and goals has done much to foster these opportunities. One sure way to liquidate the power of groups in the organization is to define the need for their services out of existence. David Halberstam presents a description of how just such a thing happened to the group of correspondents that evolved around Edward R. Murrow, the brilliant journalist, interviewer, and war correspondent of CBS News. A close friend of CBS chairman and controllng stockholder William S. Paley, Murrow, and the news department he directed, were endowed with freedom to do what they felt was right. He used it to create some of the best documentaries and commentaries ever seen on television. Unfortunately, television became too large, too powerful, and too suspect in the eyes of the federal government that licensed it. It thus became, or at least the top executives believed it had become, too dangerous to have in-depth, probing commentary on the news. Crisp, dry uneditorializing headliners were considered safer. Murrow was out and Walter Cronkite was in.

The power to define what is critical in an organization is no small power. Moreover, it is the key to understanding why organizations are either aligned with their environments or misaligned. If an organization defines certain activities as critical when in fact they are not critical, given the flow of resources coming into the organization, it is not likely to survive, at least in its present form.

Most organizations manage to evolve a distribution of power and influence that is aligned with the critical realities they face in the environment. The environment, in turn, includes both the internal environment, the shifting situational contexts in which particular decisions get made, and the external environment that it can hope to influence but is unlikely to control.

THE CRITICAL CONTINGENCIES

The critical contingencies facing most organizations derive from the environmental context within which they operate. This determines the available needed resources and thus determines the problems to be dealt with. That power organizes around handling these problems suggests an important mechanism by which organizations keep in tune with their external environments. The strategic-contingencies model implies that subunits that contribute to the critical resources of the organization will gain influence in the organization. Their influence presumably is then used to bend the organization's activities to the contingencies that determine its resources. This idea may strike one as obvious. But its obviousness in no way diminishes its importance. Indeed, despite its obviousness, it escapes the notice of many organizational analysts and managers, who all too frequently think of the organization in terms of a descending pyramid, in which all the departments in one tier hold equal power and status. This presumption denies the reality that departments differ in the contributions they are believed to make to the overall organization's resources, as well as to the fact that some are more equal than others.

Because of the importance of this idea to organizational effectiveness, we decided to examine it carefully in a large midwestern university. A university offers an excellent site for studying power. It is composed of departments with nominally equal power and is administered by a central executive structure much like other bureaucracies. However, at the same time it is a situation in which the departments have clearly defined identities and face diverse external environments. Each department has its own bodies of knowledge, its own institutions, its own sources of prestige and resources. Because the departments operate in different external environments, they are likely to contribute differentially to the resources of the overall organization. Thus a physics department with close ties to NASA may contribute substantially to the funds of the university; and a history department with a renowned historian in residence may contribute to the intellectual credibility or prestige of the whole university. Such variations permit one to examine how these various contributions lead to obtaining power within the university.

We analyzed the influence of 29 university departments throughout an 18-month period in their history. Our chief interest was to determine whether departments that brought more critical resources to the university would be more powerful than departments that contributed fewer or less critical resources.

To identify the critical resources each department contributed, the heads of all departments were interviewed about the importance of seven different resources to the university's success. The seven included undergraduate students (the factor determining size of the state allocations by the university), national prestige, administrative expertise, and so on. The most critical resource was found to be contract and grant monies received by a department's faculty for research or consulting services. At this university, contract and grants contributed somewhat less than 50 percent of the overall budget, with the remainder primarily coming from state appropriations. The importance attributed to contract and grant monies, and the rather minor importance of undergraduate students, was not surprising for this particular university. The university was a major center for graduate education; many of its departments ranked in the top ten of their respective fields. Grant and contract monies were the primary source of discretionary funding available for maintaining these programs of graduate educ-

ation, and hence for maintaining the university's prestige. The prestige of the university itself was critical both in recruiting able students and attracting top-notch faculty.

From university records it was determined what relative contributions each of the 29 departments made to the various needs of the university (national prestige, outside grants, teaching). Thus, for instance, one department may have contributed to the university by teaching 7 percent of the instructional units, bringing in 2 percent of the outside contracts and grants, and having a national ranking of 20. Another department, on the other hand, may have taught 1 percent of the instructional units, contributed 12 percent to the grants, and be ranked the third best department in its field within the country.

The question was: Do these different contributions determine the relative power of the departments within the university? Power was measured in several ways; but regardless of how measured, the answer was Yes. Those three resources together accounted for about 70 percent of the variance in subunit power in the university.

But the most important predictor of departmental power was the department's contribution to the contracts and grants of the university. Sixty percent of the variance in power was due to this one factor, suggesting that the power of departments derived primarily from the dollars they provided for graduate education, the activity believed to be the most important for the organization.

THE IMPACT OF ORGANIZATIONAL POWER ON DECISION MAKING

The measure of power we used in studying this university was an analysis of the responses of the department heads we interviewed. While such perceptions of power might be of interest in their own right, they contribute little to our understanding of how the distribution of power might serve to align an organization with its critical realities. For this we must look to how power actually influences the decisions and policies of organizations.

While it is perhaps not absolutely valid, we can generally gauge the relative importance of a department of an organization by the size of the budget allocated to it relative to other departments. Clearly it is of importance to the administrators of those departments whether they get squeezed in a budget crunch or are given more funds to strike out after new opportunities. And it should also be clear that when those decisions are made and one department can go ahead and try new approaches while another must cut back on the old, then the deployment of the resources of the organization in meeting its problem is most directly affected.

Thus our study of the university led us to ask the following question: Does power lead to influence in the organization? To answer this question, we found it useful first to ask another one, namely: Why should department heads try to influence organizational decisions to favor their own departments to the exclusion of other departments? While this second question may seem a bit naive to anyone who has witnessed the political realities of organizations, we posed it in a context of research on organizations that sees power as an illegitimate threat to the neater rational authority of modern bureaucracies. In this context, decisions are not believed to be made because of the dirty business of politics but because of the overall goals and purposes of the organization. In a university, one reasonable basis for decision making is the teaching workload of departments and the demands that follow from that workload. We would expect, therefore, that departments with heavy student demands for courses would be able to obtain funds for teaching. Another reasonable basis for decision making is quality. We would expect, for that reason, that departments with esteemed reputations would be able to obtain funds both because their quality suggests they might use such funds

effectively and because such funds would allow them to maintain their quality. A rational model of bureaucracy intimates, then, that the organizational decisions taken would favor those who perform the stated purposes of the organization—teaching undergraduates and training professional and scientific talent—well.

The problem with rational models of decision making, however, is that what is rational to one person may strike another as irrational. For most departments, resources are a question of survival. While teaching undergraduates may seem to be a major goal for some members of the university, developing knowledge may seem so to others; and to still others, advising governments and other institutions about policies may seem to be the crucial business. Everyone has his own idea of the proper priorities in a just world. Thus goals rather than being clearly defined and universally agreed upon are blurred and contested throughout the organization. If such is the case, then the decisions taken on behalf of the organization as a whole are likely to reflect the goals of those who prevail in political contests, namely, those with power in the organization.

Will organizational decisions always reflect the distribution of power in the organization? Probably not. Using power for influence requires a certain expenditure of effort, time, and resources. Prudent and judicious persons are not likely to use their power needlessly or wastefully. And it is likely that power will be used to influence organizational decisions primarily under circumstances that both require and favor its use. We have examined three conditions that are likely to affect the use of power in organizations: scarcity, criticality, and uncertainty. The first suggests that subunits will try to exert influence when the resources of the organization are scarce. If there is an abundance of resources, then a particular department or a particular individual has little need to attempt influence. With little effort, he can get all he wants anyway.

The second condition, criticality, suggests that a subunit will attempt to influence decisions to obtain resources that are critical to its own survival and activities. Criticality implies that one would not waste effort, or risk being labeled obstinate, by fighting over trivial decisions affecting one's operations.

An office manager would probably balk less about a threatened cutback in copying machine usage than about a reduction in typing staff. An advertising department head would probably worry less about losing his lettering artist than his illustrator. Criticality is difficult to define because what is critical depends on people's beliefs about what is critical. Such beliefs may or may not be based on experience and knowledge and may or may not be agreed upon by all. Scarcity, for instance, may itself affect conceptions of criticality. When slack resources drop off, cutbacks have to be made—those "hard decisions," as congressmen and resplendent administrators like to call them. Managers then find themselves scrapping projects they once held dear.

The third condition that we believe affects the use of power is uncertainty: When individuals do not agree about what the organization should do or how to do it, power and other social processes will affect decisions. The reason for this is simply that, if there are no clear-cut criteria available for resolving conflicts of interest, then the only means for resolution is some form of social process, including power, status, social ties, or some arbitrary process like flipping a coin or drawing straws. Under conditions of uncertainty, the powerful manager can argue his case on any grounds and usually win it. Since there is no real consensus, other contestants are not likely to develop counter arguments or amass sufficient opposition. Moreover, because of his power and their need for access to the resources he controls, they are more likely to defer to his arguments.

Although the evidence is slight, we have found that power will influence the allocations of scarce and critical resources. In the analysis of power in the university, for instance, one of the most critical resources needed by departments is the general budget. First granted by the state legislature, the general budget is later allocated to individual departments by the university administration in response to requests from the department heads. Our analysis of the factors that contribute to a department getting more or less of this budget indicated that subunit power was the major predictor, overriding such factors as student demand for courses, national reputations of departments, or even the size of a department's faculty. Moreover, other research has shown that when the general budget has been cut back or held below previous uninflated levels, leading to monies becoming more scarce, budget allocations mirror departmental powers even more closely.

Student enrollment and faculty size, of course, do themselves relate to budget allocations, as we would expect since they determine a department's need for resources, or at least offer visible testimony of needs. But departments are not always able to get what they need by the mere fact of needing. In one analysis it was found that high-power departments were able to obtain budget without regard to their teaching loads and, in some cases, actually in inverse relation to their teaching loads. In contrast, low-power departments could get increases in budget only when they could justify the increases by a recent growth in teaching load, and then only when it was far in excess of norms for other departments.

General budget is only one form of resource that is allocated to departments. There are others such as special grants for student fellowships or faculty research. These are critical to departments because they affect the ability to attract other resources, such as outstanding faculty or students. We examined how power influenced the allocations of four resources department heads had described as critical and scarce.

When the four resources were arrayed from the most to the least critical and scarce, we found that departmental power best predicted the allocations of the most critical and scarce resources. In other words, the analysis of how power influences organizational allocations leads to this conclusion: Those subunits most likely to survive in times of strife are those that are most critical to the organization. Their importance to the organization gives them power to influence resource allocations that enhance their own survival.

HOW EXTERNAL ENVIRONMENT INFLUENCES EXECUTIVE SELECTION

Power not only influences the survival of key groups in an organization, it also influences the selection of individuals to key leadership positions, and by such a process further aligns the organization with its environmental context.

We can illustrate this with a recent study of the selection and tenure of chief administrators in 57 hospitals in Illinois. We assumed that since the critical problems facing the organization would enhance the power of certain groups at the expense of others, then the leaders to emerge should be those most relevant to the context of the hospitals. To assess this we asked each chief administrator about his professional background and how long he had been in office. The replies were then related to the hospital's funding, ownership, and competitive conditions for patients and staff.

One aspect of a hospital's context is the source of its budget. Some hospitals, for instance, are run much like other businesses. They sell bed space, patient care, and treatment services. They charge fees sufficient both to cover their costs and to provide capital for expansion. The main source of both their operating and capital funds is patient billings. Increasingly, patient billings are paid for, not by patients, but by private insurance companies. Insurers like Blue Cross dominate and represent a potent interest group outside a hospital's control but critical to its income. The insurance companies, in order to limit their own costs, attempt to hold down the fees allowable to hospitals, which they do effectively from their positions on state rate boards. The squeeze on hospitals that results from fees increasing slowly while costs climb rapidly more and more demands the talents of cost accountants or people trained in the technical expertise of hospital administration.

By contrast, other hospitals operate more like social service institutions, either as government health-care units (Bellevue Hospital in New York City and Cook County Hospital in Chicago, for example) or as charitable institutions. These hospitals obtain a large proportion of their operating and capital funds, not from privately insured patients, but from government subsidies or private donations. Such institutions rather than requiring the talents of a technically efficient administrator are likely to require the savvy of someone who is well integrated into the social and political power structure of the community.

Not surprisingly, the characteristics of administrators predictably reflect the funding context of the hospitals with which they are associated. Those hospitals with larger proportions of their budget obtained from private insurance companies were most likely to have administrators with backgrounds in accounting and least likely to have administrators whose professions were business or medicine. In contrast, those hospitals with larger proportions of their budget derived from private donations and local governments were most likely to have administrators with business or professional backgrounds and least likely to have accountants. The same held for formal training in hospital management. Professional hospital administrators could easily be found in hospitals drawing their incomes from private insurance and rarely in hospitals dependent on donations or legislative appropriations.

As with the selection of administrators,

the context of organizations has also been found to affect the removal of executives. The environment, as a source of organizational problems, can make it more or less difficult for executives to demonstrate their value to the organization. In the hospitals we studied, long-term administrators came from hospitals with few problems. They enjoyed amicable and stable relations with their local business and social communities and suffered little competition for funding and staff. The small city hospital director who attended civic and Elks meetings while running the only hospital within a 100-mile radius, for example, had little difficulty holding on to his job. Turnover was highest in hospitals with the most problems, a phenomenon similar to that observed in a study of industrial organizations in which turnover was highest among executives in industries with competitive environments and unstable market conditions. The interesting thing is that instability characterized the industries rather than the individual firms in them. The troublesome conditions in the individual firms were attributed, or rather misattributed, to the executives themselves.

It takes more than problems, however, to terminate a manager's leadership. The problems themselves must be relevant and critical. This is clear from the way in which an administrator's tenure is affected by the status of the hospital's operating budget. Naively we might assume that all administrators would need to show a surplus. Not necessarily so. Again, we must distinguish between those hospitals that depend on private donations for funds and those that do not. Whether an endowed budget shows a surplus or deficit is less important than the hospital's relations with benefactors. On the other hand, with a budget dependent on patient billing, a surplus is almost essential; monies for new equipment or expansion must be drawn from it, and without them quality care becomes more difficult and patients scarcer. An administrator's tenure reflected just these considerations. For those hospitals dependent upon private donations, the length of an administrator's term depended not at all on the status of the operating budget but was fairly predictable from the hospital's relations with the business community. On the other hand, in hospitals dependent on the operating budget for capital financing, the greater the deficit the shorter was the tenure of the hospital's principal administrators.

CHANGING CONTINGENCIES AND ERODING POWER BASES

The critical contingencies facing the organization may change. When they do, it is reasonable to expect that the power of individuals and subgroups will change in turn. At times the shift can be swift and shattering, as it was recently for powerholders in New York City. A few years ago it was believed that David Rockefeller was one of the ten most powerful people in the city, as tallied by New York magazine, which annually sniffs out power for the delectation of its readers. But that was before it was revealed that the city was in financial trouble, before Rockefeller's Chase Manhattan Bank lost some of its own financial luster, and before brother Nelson lost some of his political influence in Washington. Obviously David Rockefeller was no longer as well positioned to help bail the city out. Another loser was an attorney with considerable personal connections to the political and religious leaders of the city. His talents were no longer in much demand. The persons with more influence were the bankers and union pension fund executors who fed money to the city; community leaders who represent blacks and Spanish-Americans, in contrast, witnessed the erosion of their power bases.

One implication of the idea that power shifts with changes in organizational environments is that the dominant coalition will tend to be that group that is most appropriate for the organization's environment, as also will the leaders of an organization. One can observe this historically in the top executives of industrial firms in the United States. Up until the early 1950s, many top corporations were headed by former production line managers or engineers who gained prominence because of their abilities to cope with the problems of production. Their success, however, only spelled their demise. As production became routinized and mechanized, the problem of most firms became one of selling all those goods they so efficiently produced. Marketing executives were more frequently found in corporate boardrooms. Success outdid itself again, for keeping markets and production steady and stable requires the kind of control that can only come from acquiring competitors and suppliers or the invention of more and more appealing products— ventures that typically require enormous amounts of capital. During the 1960s, financial executives assumed the seats of power. And they, too, will give way to others. Edging over the horizon are legal experts, as regulation and antitrust suits are becoming more and more frequent in the 1970s, suits that had their beginnings in the success of the expansion generated by prior executives. The more distant future, which is likely to be dominated by multinational corporations, may see former secretaries of state and their minions increasingly serving as corporate figureheads.

THE NONADAPTIVE CONSEQUENCES OF ADAPTATION

From what we have said thus far about power aligning the organization with its own realities, an intelligent person might react with a resounding ho-hum, for it all seems too obvious: Those with the ability to get the job done are given the job to do.

However, there are two aspects of power that make it more useful for understanding organizations and their effectiveness. First, the "job" to be done has a way of expanding itself until it becomes less and less clear what the job is. Napoleon

began by doing a job for France in the war with Austria and ended up emperor, convincing many that only he could keep the peace. Hitler began by promising an end to Germany's troubling postwar depression and ended up convincing more people than is comfortable to remember that he was destined to be the savior of the world. In short, power is a capacity for influence that extends far beyond the original bases that created it. Second, power tends to take on institutionalized forms that enable it to endure well beyond its usefulness to an organization.

There is an important contradiction in what we have observed about organizational power. On the one hand we have said that power derives from the contingencies facing an organization and that when those contingencies change so do the bases for power. On the other hand we have asserted that subunits will tend to use their power to influence organizational decisions in their own favor, particularly when their own survival is threatened by the scarcity of critical resources. The first statement implies that an organization will tend to be aligned with its environment since power will tend to bring to key positions those capabilities relevant to the context. The second implies that those in power will not give up their positions so easily; they will pursue policies that guarantee their continued domination. In short, change and stability operate through the same mechanism, and, as a result, the organization will never be completely in phase with its environment or its needs.

The study of hospital administrators illustrates how leadership can be out of phase with reality. We argued that privately funded hospitals needed trained technical administrators more so than did hospitals funded by donations. The need as we perceived it was matched in most hospitals, but by no means in all. Some organizations did not conform with our predictions. These deviations imply that some administrators were able to maintain their positions independent of their suitability for those positions. By dividing administrators into those with long and short terms of office, one finds that the characteristics of longer-termed administrators were virtually unrelated to the hospital's context. The shorter-termed chiefs, on the other hand, had characteristics more appropriate for the hospital's problems. For a hospital to have a recently appointed head implies that the previous administrator had been unable to endure by institutionalizing himself.

One obvious feature of hospitals that allowed some administrators to enjoy a long tenure was a hospital's ownership. Administrators were less entrenched when their hospitals were affiliated with and dependent upon larger organizations, such as governments or churches. Private hospitals offered more secure positions for administrators. Like private corporations, they tend to have more diffused ownership, leaving the administrator unopposed as he institutionalizes his reign. Thus he endures, sometimes at the expense of the performance of the organization. Other research has demonstrated that corporations with diffuse ownership have poorer earnings than those in which the control of the manager is checked by a dominant shareholder. Firms that overload their boardrooms with more insiders than are appropriate for their context have also been found to be less profitable.

A word of caution is required about our judgment of "appropriateness." When we argue some capabilities are more appropriate for one context than another, we do so from the perspective of an outsider and on the basis of reasonable assumptions as to the problems the organization will face and the capabilities they will need. The fact that we have been able to predict the distribution of influence and the characteristics of leaders suggests that our reasoning is not incorrect. However, we do not think that all organizations follow the same pattern. The fact that we have not been able to predict outcomes with 100 percent accuracy indicates they do not.

MISTAKING CRITICAL CONTINGENCIES

One thing that allows subunits to retain their power is their ability to name their functions as critical to the organization when they may not be. Consider again our discussion of power in the university. One might wonder why the most critical tasks were defined as graduate education and scholarly research, the effect of which was to lend power to those who brought in grants and contracts. Why not something else? The reason is that the most powerful departments argued for those criteria and won their case, partly because they were more powerful.

In another analysis of this university, we found that all departments advocate self-serving criteria for budget allocation. Thus a department with large undergraduate enrollments argued that enrollments should determine budget allocations, a department with a strong national reputation saw prestige as the most reasonable basis for distributing funds, and so on. We further found that advocating such self-serving criteria actually benefited a department's budget allotments but, also, it paid off more for departments that were already powerful.

Organizational needs are consistent with a current distribution of power also because of a human tendency to categorize problems in familiar ways. An accountant sees problems with organizational performance as cost accountancy problems or inventory flow problems. A sales manager sees them as problems with markets, promotional strategies, or just unaggressive salespeople. But what is the truth? Since it does not automatically announce itself, it is likely that those with prior credibility, or those with power, will be favored as the enlightened. This bias, while not intentionally self-serving, further concentrates power among those who already possess it, independent of changes in the organization's context.

INSTITUTIONALIZING POWER

A third reason for expecting organizational contingencies to be defined in familiar ways is that the current holders of power can structure the organization in ways that institutionalize themselves. By institutionalization we mean the establishment of relatively permanent structures and policies that favor the influence of a particular subunit. While in power, a dominant coalition has the ability to institute constitutions, rules, procedures, and information systems that limit the potential power of others while continuing their own.

The key to institutionalizing power always is to create a device that legitimates one's own authority and diminishes the legitimacy of others. When the "Divine Right of Kings" was envisioned centuries ago it was to provide an unquestionable foundation for the supremacy of royal authority. There is generally a need to root the exercise of authority in some higher power. Modern leaders are no less affected by this need. Richard Nixon, with the aid of John Dean, reified the concept of executive privilege, which meant in effect that what the president wished not to be discussed need not be discussed.

In its simpler form, institutionalization is achieved by designating positions or roles for organizational activities. The creation of a new post legitimizes a function and forces organization members to orient to it. By designating how this new post relates to older, more established posts, moreover, one can structure an organization to enhance the importance of the function in the organization. Equally, one can diminish the importance of traditional functions. This is what happened in the end with the insurance company we mentioned that was having trouble with its coding department. As the situation unfolded, the claims director continued to feel dissatisfied about the dependency of his functions on the coding manager. Thus he instituted a reorganization that resulted in two coding departments. In so doing, of course, he placed activities that affected his department under his direct control, presumably to make the operation more

effective. Similarly, consumer-product firms enhance the power of marketing by setting up a coordinating role to interface production and marketing functions and then appoint a marketing manager to fill the role.

The structures created by dominant powers sooner or later become fixed and unquestioned features of the organization. Eventually, this can be devastating. It is said that the battle of Jena in 1806 was lost by Frederick the Great, who died in 1786. Though the great Prussian leader had no direct hand in the disaster, his imprint on the army was so thorough, so embedded in its skeletal underpinnings, that the organization was inappropriate for others to lead in different times.

Another important source of institutionalized power lies in the ability to structure information systems. Setting up committees to investigate particular organizational issues and having them report only to particular individuals or groups facilitates their awareness of problems by members of those groups while limiting the awareness of problems by the members of other groups. Obviously, those who have information are in a better position to interpret the problems of an organization, regardless of how realistically they may, in fact, do so.

Still another way to institutionalize power is to distribute rewards and resources. The dominant group may quiet competing interest groups with small favors and rewards. The credit for this artful form of cooptation belongs to Louis XIV. To avoid usurpation of his power by the nobles of France and the Fronde that had so troubled his father's reign, he built the palace at Versailles to occupy them with hunting and gossip. Awed, the courtiers basked in the reflected glories of the "Sun King" and the overwhelming setting he had created for his court.

At this point, we have not systematically studied the institutionalization of power. But we suspect it is an important condition that mediates between the environment of the organization and the capabilities of the organization for dealing with that environment. The more institutionalized power is within an organization, the more likely an organization will be out of phase with the realities it faces. President Richard Nixon's structuring of his White House is one of the better documented illustrations. If we go back to newspaper and magazine descriptions of how he organized his office from the beginning in 1968, most of what occurred subsequently follows almost as an afterthought. Decisons flowed through virtually only the small White House staff; rewards, small presidential favors of recognition, and perquisites were distributed by this staff to the loyal; and information from the outside world—the press, Congress, the people on the streets—was filtered by the staff and passed along only if initialed "bh." Thus it was not surprising that when Nixon met war protestors in the early dawn, the only thing he could think to talk about was the latest football game, so insulated had he become from their grief and anger.

One of the more interesting implications of institutionalized power is that executive turnover among the executives who have structured the organization is likely to be a rare event that occurs only under the most pressing crisis. If a dominant coalition is able to structure the organization and interpret the meaning of ambiguous events like declining sales and profits or lawsuits, then the "real" problems to emerge will easily be incorporated into traditional modes of thinking and acting. If opposition is designed out of the organization, the interpretations will go unquestioned. Conditions will remain stable until a crisis develops, so overwhelming and visible that even the most adroit rhetorician would be silenced.

IMPLICATIONS FOR THE MANAGEMENT OF POWER IN ORGANIZATIONS

While we could derive numerous implications from this discussion of power, our selection would have to depend largely on whether one wanted to increase one's power, decrease the power of others, or merely maintain one's position. More important, the real implications depend on the particulars of an organizational situation. To understand power in an organization one must begin by looking outside it—into the environment—for those groups that mediate the organization's outcomes but are not themselves within its control.

Instead of ending with homilies, we will end with a reversal of where we began. Power, rather than being the dirty business it is often made out to be, is probably one of the few mechanisms for reality testing in organizations. And the cleaner forms of power, the institutional forms, rather than having the virtues they are often credited with, can lead the organization to become out of touch. The real trick to managing power in organizations is to ensure somehow that leaders cannot be unaware of the realities of their environments and cannot avoid changing to deal with those realities. That, however, would be like designing the "self-liquidating organization," an unlikely event since anyone capable of designing such an instrument would be obviously in control of the liquidations.

Management would do well to devote more attention to determining the critical contingencies of their environments. For if you conclude, as we do, that the environment sets most of the structure influencing organizational outcomes and problems, and that power derives from the organization's activities that deal with those contingencies, then it is the environment that needs managing, not power. The first step is to construct an accurate model of the environment, a process that is quite difficult for most organizations. We have recently started a project to aid administrators in systematically understanding their environments. From this experience, we have learned that the most critical blockage to perceiving an organization's reality accurately is a failure to incorporate those with the relevant expertise into the process. Most organizations have the requisite experts on hand but they are positioned so that they can be comfortably ignored.

One conclusion you can, and probably should, derive from our discussion is that power—because of the way it develops and the way it is used—will always result in the organization suboptimizing its performance. However, to this grim absolute, we add a comforting caveat: If any criteria other than power were the basis for determining an organization's decisions, the results would be even worse.

22. Situational Leadership and Power*

PAUL HERSEY

KENNETH H. BLANCHARD

WALTER E. NATEMEYER

The concepts of leadership and power have generated lively interest, debate, and occasionally confusion throughout the evolution of management thought. Leadership is typically defined as the process of influencing the activities of an individual or a group in efforts toward goal accomplishment. Power is well described as the leader's *influence potential:* it is the resource that enables a leader to induce compliance from or influence followers. Given this integral relationship between leadership and power, leaders must not only assess their leadership behavior in order to understand how they actually influence other people; they must also examine their possession and use of power. The purpose of this article is to integrate the concept of power with Situational Leadership by showing how the perception of a leader's power bases can affect the utilization of various leadership styles. The paper is divided into sections that include (1) a discussion of power and its sources, (2) an integration of the concept of power and Situational Leadership, and (3) conclusions.

BASES OF POWER

Since leadership is the process of attempting to influence the behavior of others, and power is the means by which the leader actually gains the compliance of the follower(s), the two concepts are inseparable. A leader cannot automatically influence other people; he or she must utilize power to succeed in any influence attempt.

A number of bases of power have been identified over the years as potential means of successfully influencing the behavior of others. Seven important power bases[1] are defined below:

Coercive power is based on fear. A leader high in coercive power is seen as inducing compliance because failure to comply will lead to punishment such as undesirable work assignments, reprimands, or dismissal.

Connection power is based on the leader's "connections" with influential or important persons inside or outside the organization. A leader high in connection power induces compliance from others because they aim at gaining the favor or avoiding the disfavor of the powerful connection.

Expert power is based on the leader's possession of expertise, skill, and knowledge, which, through respect, influence others. A leader high in expert power is seen as possessing the expertise to facilitate the work behavior of others. This respect leads to compliance with the leader's wishes.

Information power is based on the leader's possession of or access to information that is perceived as valuable to others. This power base influences others

*Source: Originally entitled "Situational Leadership, Perception, and the Impact of Power." From Group and Organization Studies, Vol. 4, No. 4 (December 1979), pp. 418-428. Copyright © 1979 by Center for Leadership Studies. Reprinted by permission. All rights reserved.

because they need this information or want to be "in on things."

Legitimate power is based on the position held by the leader. Normally, the higher the position, the higher the legitimate power tends to be. A leader high in legitimate power induces compliance or influences others because they feel that this person has the right, by virtue of position in the organization, to expect that suggestions will be followed.

Referent power is based on the leader's personal traits. A leader high in referent power is generally liked and admired by others because of personality. This liking for, admiration for, and identification with the leader influences others.

Reward power is based on the leader's ability to provide rewards for other people. They believe that their compliance will lead to gaining positive incentives such as pay, promotion, or recognition.

Given the wide variety of power bases available to the leader, which type of power should be emphasized in order to maximize effectiveness? Numerous studies[2] have attempted to examine the relationship between the leader's primary power base and the follower's performance, but the results suggest that the appropriate power base is largely affected by situational variables. In other words, a leader should vary the use of power depending on the circumstances.

POWER BASES AND
MATURITY LEVEL

There appears to be a direct relationship between the level of maturity of individuals and groups and the kind of power bases that have a high probability of gaining compliance from or influencing those people.

One way of looking at maturity[3] is in reference to the *ability* and *willingness* of individuals or groups to take responsibility for directing their own behavior in a particular area. Thus maturity is a task-specific concept, and people are considered to be more or less mature depending on what

the leader is attempting to accomplish through their efforts.

Ability is a person's skill. People who have ability in a certain area have the skill, knowledge, and experience to perform related tasks. Willingness refers to a person's motivation. People who are willing to perform tasks in a particular area think that area is important and are committed to those tasks and self-confident in their ability to perform them.

As people move from lower levels to higher levels of maturity, their competence and confidence to do things increase. The seven power bases appear to have significant impact on the behavior of people at various levels of maturity (Figure 22-1).

INTEGRATING POWER BASES, MATURITY LEVEL, AND LEADERSHIP STYLE THROUGH SITUATIONAL LEADERSHIP

Situational Leadership[4] can provide the basis for understanding the potential impact of each power base. It is our contention that the maturity of the follower not only dictates which style of leadership will have the highest probability of success, but that the maturity of the follower also determines the power base that the leader should use in order to induce compliance or influence behavior.

A REVIEW OF SITUATIONAL
LEADERSHIP

According to Situational Leadership, there

Figure 22-1

THE IMPACT OF POWER BASES
AT VARIOUS LEVELS OF MATURITY

Figure 22-2

SITUATIONAL LEADERSHIP—LEADERSHIP STYLES CORRELATED
WITH MATURITY LEVELS OF FOLLOWERS

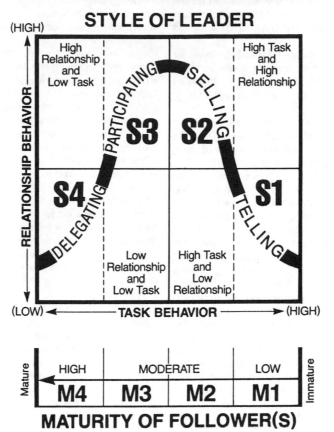

is no one "best" way to go about influencing people. Which leadership style a person should use with individuals or groups depends on the maturity level of the people the leader is attempting to influence. The "prescriptive curve" in Figure 22-2 shows the appropriate style directly above the corresponding level of maturity.

Each of the four styles—"telling," "selling," "participating," and "delegating"—in the "prescriptive curve" is a combination of task behavior and relationship behavior.[5] *Task behavior* is the extent to which a leader provides direction for people: telling them what to do, when to do it, where to do it, and how to do it. It means setting goals for them and defining their roles.

Relationship behavior is the extent to which a leader engages in two-way communication, which includes active listening and providing supportive and facilitating behaviors.

The maturity of followers is a question of degree. As can be seen in Figure 22-2, some benchmarks of maturity are provided for determining appropriate leadership style by dividing the maturity continuum below the leadership model into four levels: low (M1), low to moderate (M2), moderate to high (M3), and high (M4).

The appropriate leadership style for each of the four maturity levels includes the right combination of task behavior (direction) and relationship behavior (support).

"Telling" is for low maturity. People who are both *unable and unwilling* to take responsibility to do something need clear, specific directions and supervision. This style is called "telling" because it is characterized by the leader defining roles and telling people what, how, when, and where to do various tasks. It emphasizes directive behavior. Too much supportive behavior with people at this maturity level may be seen as permissive, easy, and, most importantly, as rewarding of poor performance. "Telling" involves high-task behavior and low-relationship behavior.

"Selling" is for low to moderate maturity. People who are *unable but willing* to take responsibility need directive behavior to reinforce their willingness and enthusiasm. This style is called "selling" because most of the direction is still provided by the leader. Yet through two-way communication and explanation of why certain things need to be done, the leader tries to get the followers psychologically to "buy into" desired behaviors. This style involves high-task behavior and high-relationship behavior.

"Participating" is for moderate to high maturity. Since the follower at this maturity level has the *ability* to do what the leader wants, but *lacks self-confidence or enthusiasm,* the leader needs to open the way for two-way communication and active listening to support the follower's efforts to use the ability that the follower already has. This style is called "participating" because the leader and follower share in decision making, with the main role of the leader being facilitating and com-

municating. This style involves high-relationship behavior and low-task behavior.

"Delegating" is for high maturity. Since people at this maturity level have both *ability and motivation,* little direction or support is needed from the leader. Followers are now permitted to "run the show" and decide on the how, when, and where. At the same time, they are psychologically mature and therefore do not need above-average amounts of two-way communication or supportive behavior. This style involves low-relationship behavior and low-task behavior.

The key to using Situational Leadership is to assess the maturity level of the follower and to behave as the model prescribes. Implicit in Situational Leadership is the idea that a leader should attempt to help followers grow in maturity as far as they are able and willing to go. This development of followers should be done by adjusting leadership behavior through the four styles along the "prescriptive curve" in Figure 22-2.

Situational Leadership contends that strong direction (task behavior) with immature followers is appropriate if they are to become productive. Similarly, it suggests that an increase in maturity on the part of people who are somewhat immature should be rewarded by increased positive reinforcement and socioemotional support (relationship behavior). Finally, as followers reach high levels of maturity, the leader should respond by not only continuing to decrease control over their activities, but also decreasing relationship behavior as well. With very mature people the need for socioemotional support is no longer as important as the need for autonomy. At this stage, one of the ways leaders can prove their confidence and trust in highly mature people is to leave them more and more on their own. It is not that there is less mutual trust and friendship between leader and follower; in fact, there is more, but it takes less direct effort on the leader's part to prove this to mature followers.

Regardless of the level of maturity of an individual or group, change may occur. Whenever a follower's performance begins to slip—for whatever reason—and motivation or ability decreases, the leader should reassess the maturity level of this follower and move backward through the "prescriptive curve," providing any appropriate socio-emotional support and direction.

THE SITUATIONAL USE OF POWER

Even if the leader is using the appropriate leadership style for a given maturity level, that style may not be maximizing the leader's probability of success if it does not reflect the appropriate power base. Therefore, just as an effective leader should vary leadership style according to the maturity level of the follower, it may be appropriate to vary the use of power similarly. The power bases that may influence people's behavior at various levels of maturity are pictured in Figure 22-3.[6]

Figure 22-3 shows a relationship only between power bases and maturity level. There also appears to be a direct relationship between the kind of power bases a person has and the corresponding leadership style that will be effective for that person in influencing the behavior of others at various maturity levels.

Coercive power.—A follower low in maturity generally needs strong directive behavior in order to become productive. To engage effectively in this *"telling"* style, coercive power is often necessary. The behavior of people at low levels of maturity seems to be influenced by the awareness that costs will be incurred if they do not learn and follow the "rules of the game." Thus, if people are *unable and unwilling,* sanctions—the perceived power to fire, transfer, demote, etc.—may be an important way that a leader can induce compliance from them. The leader's coercive power may motivate the followers to avoid the punishment or "cost" by doing what the leader tells them to do.

Connection power.—As a follower begins to move from *maturity level M1 to M2,* directive behavior is still needed, but increases in supportive behavior are also important. The *"telling"* and *"selling"* leadership styles appropriate for these levels of maturity may become more effective if the leader has connection power. The possession of this power base may induce compliance because a follower at this maturity level tends to aim at avoiding the punishments or gaining the rewards available through the powerful connection.

Reward power.—A follower at a low to moderate level of maturity often needs high amounts of supportive behavior and directive behavior. This *"selling"* style often is enhanced by reward power. Since individuals at this maturity level are *willing* to "try on" new behavior, the leader needs to be perceived as having access to

Figure 22-3

POWER BASES NECESSARY TO INFLUENCE PEOPLE'S BEHAVIOR AT VARIOUS LEVELS OF MATURITY

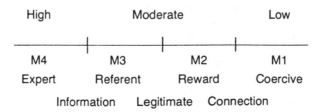

MATURITY LEVEL

High	Moderate	Low

| M4 | M3 | M2 | M1 |
| Expert | Referent | Reward | Coercive |

Information Legitimate Connection

rewards, in order to gain compliance and reinforce growth in the desired direction.

Legitimate power.—The leadership styles that tend to effectively influence those at both *moderate levels of maturity (M2 and M3)* are *"selling"* and *"participating."* To effectively engage in these styles legitimate power seems to be helpful. By the time a follower reaches these moderate levels of maturity, the power of the leader has become "legitimized." That is, the leader is able to induce compliance or influence behavior by virtue of his position in the organizational hierarchy.

Referent power.—A follower at a moderate to high level of maturity tends to need little direction but still requires a high level of communication and support from the leader. This *"participating"* style may be effectively utilized if the leader has referent power. This source of power is based on good personal relations with the follower. With people who are *able but unwilling or insecure,* this power base tends to be an important means of instilling confidence and providing encouragement, recognition, and other supportive behavior. When that occurs, followers will generally respond in a positive way, permitting the leader to influence them because they like, admire, or identify with the leader.

Information power.—The leadership styles that tend to effectively motivate followers at *above average maturity levels (M3 and M4)* are *"participating"* and *"delegating."* Information power seems to be helpful in using these two styles. People at these levels of maturity look to the leader for information to maintain or improve performance. The transition from moderate to high maturity may be facilitated if the follower knows the leader is available to clarify or explain issues and provide access to pertinent data, reports, and correspondence when needed. Through this information power the leader is able to influence these mature people.

Expert power.—A follower who develops to a high level of maturity often requires little direction or support. This follower is

able and willing to perform the tasks required and tends to respond most readily to a *"delegating"* leadership style and expert power. Thus a leader may gain respect from and influence most readily a person who has both competence and confidence by possessing expertise, skill, and knowledge that this follower recognizes as important.

An easy way to think about sources of power in terms of making diagnostic judgments is to draw a triangle, as shown in Figure 22-4, around the three power bases necessary to influence below-average, moderate, and above-average levels of maturity. It is important to stress here that with people of below-average maturity the emphasis is on compliance; with people of average maturity it is on compliance and influence; and with people of above-average maturity the emphasis is on influence.

A way to examine the high-probability power base for a specific maturity level is to draw inverted triangles as shown in Figure 22-5. Note that M1 and M4, the extreme maturity levels, include only two power bases instead of three.

DEVELOPING SOURCES OF POWER

While these seven power bases are potentially available to any leader as a means of inducing compliance or influencing the behavior of others, it is important to note that there is significant variance in the powers that leaders may actually possess. Some leaders have a great deal of power while others have very little. Part of the variance in actual power is due to the organization and the leader's position in the organization, and part is due to individual differences among the leaders themselves. The power bases that are most relevant at the below-average levels of maturity tend to be those that the organization or others can bestow upon the leader. On the other hand, the power bases that influence people who are above average in maturity must to a large degree be earned from the people the leader is attempting to influence. Therefore, we

Figure 22-4

POWER BASES NECESSARY TO INFLUENCE PEOPLE
AT VARIOUS MATURITY LEVELS

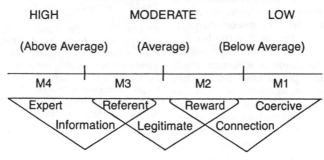

Figure 22-5

POWER BASES NECESSARY TO INFLUENCE PEOPLE'S BEHAVIOR
AT *SPECIFIC* LEVELS OF MATURITY

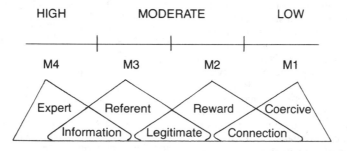

suggest that the word *"compliance"* is most descriptive with coercive, connection, and reward power bases, and that the word *"influence"* more accurately describes the effect on behavior from referent, information, and expert power. Legitimate power seems to be descriptive from both viewpoints—compliance and influence—depending on whether maturity is below average or above average. It should be remembered that these power bases together constitute an interaction-influence system. That is, power does not develop in a vacuum. Each power base tends to affect each of the other power bases.

THE PERCEPTION OF POWER

It is important to remember that truth and reality do not necessarily evoke behavior. It is perception or interpretation of reality that produces behavior. For example, when a couple has a fight it does not matter whether the cause is real or imagined—it is just as much of a fight.

It is the perception others hold about

a leader's power that gives that leader the ability to induce compliance or to influence their behavior. Therefore, power is like money in the bank. The ability of a person without identification to cash a check is dependent not only on the funds the person has deposited in the bank. It also depends on whether that person gives the impression of affluence. Thus, an individual's power base, like wealth, has to be known to others before it can effectively be used. Therefore, if leaders are to increase their probability of successfully influencing the behavior of others, they need information about the sources of power they are perceived as having by other people. Also, it is important for leaders to communicate to others the power they actually possess.

....

CONCLUSIONS

As has been emphasized throughout this article, whether a leader is maximizing effectiveness is not a question of style alone, but also a question of what power bases are available to that leader and whether these power bases are consistent with the maturity levels of the individual or group that the leader is trying to influence. As managers consider these relationships, it appears that dynamic and growing organizations gradually move away from reliance on power bases that emphasize compliance and toward the utilization of the power bases that aim at gaining influence with people. It is important to keep in mind that many times this change by necessity will be evolutionary rather than revolutionary.

_____

NOTES

1. Five of these descriptions of power bases (coercive, expert, legitimate, referent, and reward) have been adapted from the work of J. R. P. French, Jr., and B. Raven,

"The Bases of Social Power," in Dorwin Cartwright (ed.), _Studies in Social Power_ (Ann Arbor, Mich.: Institute for Social Research, The University of Michigan, 1959), pp. 150-167. One power base (information) was introduced by B. H. Raven and W. Kruglanski, "Conflict and Power," in P. G. Swingle (ed.), _The Structure of Conflict_ (New York: Academic Press, 1975), pp. 177-219. In addition to modifying some of these definitions, the authors added a seventh power base—connection power.

For further information on power, see also Amitai Etzioni, _A Comparative Analysis of Complex Organizations on Power, Involvement, and Their Correlates_ (New York: The Free Press, 1961).

2. As examples, see J. G. Bachman, D. G. Bowers, and P. M. Marcus, "Bases of Supervisory Power: A Comparative Study in Five Organizational Settings," in Arnold S. Tannenbaum, _Control in Organizations_ (New York: McGraw-Hill, 1968); J. M. Ivancevich and G. H. Donnelly, "Leader Influence and Performance," _Personnel Psychology_, 1970, 23(4): 539-549; R. J. Burke and D. S. Wilcox, "Bases of Supervisory and Subordinate Job Satisfactions," _Canadian Journal of Behavioral Science_, 1971; and D. W. Jamieson and K. W. Thomas, "Power and Conflict in the Student-Teacher Relationship," _Journal of Applied Behavioral Science_, 1974, 10(3).

3. For extensive discussions of the concept of maturity, see Chris Argyris, _Personality and Organization_ (New York: Harper & Row, 1957); _Interpersonal Competence and Organizational Effectiveness_ (Homewood, Ill: Dorsey, 1962); and _Integrating the Individual and the Organization_ (New York: Wiley, 1964); and Paul Hersey and Kenneth H. Blanchard, _Management of Organizational Behavior: Utilizing Human Resources_, 3rd ed. (Englewood Cliffs, N.J.: Prentice-Hall, 1977).

4. Situational Leadership is a management concept that Paul Hersey and Kenneth H. Blanchard have been developing together since 1967. The most extensive discussion of this concept can be found in their text, _Management of Organizational Behavior_ . . ., _op. cit._

5. Instruments to measure self-perception of leadership style (LEAD-Self) and the perception of others' leadership style (LEAD-Other) in terms of task behavior and rela-

tionship behavior have been developed by Paul Hersey and Kenneth H. Blanchard. These LEAD (Leader Effectiveness and Adaptability Description) instruments are published by the Center for Leadership Studies, Escondido, Calif., and are distributed by

Learning Resources Corporation, La Jolla, Calif.

6. This figure depicts only the maturity part of Situational Leadership and does not include the leadership-style portion of the model.

V

Organizational Change and Development

Introduction. In today's complex and dynamic environment, organizations must learn to continually adapt to new conditions if they are to remain viable and avoid organizational "future shock." Consequently, the process of organizational change and development has drawn increasing attention. Earlier chapters in this book commented on the importance of organizational adaptation and the consequences of failing to change. The selections presented in this section provide proven guidelines for organizations to follow as they seek to maintain stability and effectiveness in a turbulent world.

In the section's first selection, Lester Coch and John R. P. French, Jr., deal with a common problem associated with organizational change. Their article, "Overcoming Resistance to Change," addresses why people resist change and how this resistance is manifested in their behavior. As an example, they use their experiment with participative management at the Harwood Manufacturing Company, which had groups of workers involved in designing changes to be made in their jobs. The results show that the "rate of recovery" to changes in a job is directly proportional to the amount of worker participation and rates of turnover and aggression are inversely proportional to the amount of participation. Coch and French conclude by suggesting that it is possible for management to overcome resistance to change if the need for change is communicated effectively and if group participation is encouraged in planning for the change. This 1948 study is often considered to be one of the prime progenitors of the participative-management movement.

Rensis Likert, long one of the leading researchers and theorists in the field of management, is perhaps best known for his classification and discussion of Management Systems 1 through 4. "A Look at Management Systems," from Chapter 2 of Likert's well-known book *The Human Organization: Its Management and Value,* provides the reader with the opportunity to diagnose organizations using the Systems 1 through 4 framework. Likert contends that high-performing organizations typically possess System 4 characteristics, including a high level of trust, open communications, and motivation through participation and employee involvement.

Robert R. Blake and Jane S. Mouton's 1964 book, *The Managerial Grid*, contained the basis of their widely implemented, organization-development (OD) program. In a subsequent article, "Grid Organization Development," Blake and Mouton summarize their program and explain how it can be used to increase organizational effectiveness. OD is premised upon the notion that any organization wishing to survive must, from time to time, divest itself of those parts or characteristics contributing to its malaise. The process is usually associated with the idea that maximum effectiveness is to be found by integrating an individual's desire for personal growth with organizational goals. While there is no universal OD model that can be adapted for organizations, Blake and Mouton's Grid OD is one of the most famous.

Warren G. Bennis, in "Organizations of the Future," predicts the demise of bureaucracy as a viable organizational form. The major reasons for the vulnerability of bureaucracies are rapid and unexpected change, unprecedented growth in organizational size, the increasing complexity of modern technology, and the fundamental changes in the philosophical values underlying managerial controls and behavior. In the future, these trends are likely to continue, making bureaucracy even less effective as an organizational format. Bennis contends that organizations of the future must be more responsive, flexible, and humanistic, and, consequently, less rigid and bureaucratic. He concludes with a list of steps for organizations to follow as they adapt to the demands of the future.

In "Organization Development: Objectives, Assumptions and Strategies," Wendell French defines organization development as a long-range effort to improve an organization's problem-solving capabilities and its ability to adapt to changes in its environment. The article addresses the typical objectives, assumptions, attitudes, and strategies of OD programs. French contends that in order to maximize effectiveness, management must learn to adapt to changes in its environment. In order to accomplish this, an open and flexible organizational climate must be created to stimulate the growth and development of an organization's most important resource—its people.

In "Work Redesign," J. Richard Hackman and Greg R. Oldham are interested in studying which factors in "job enrichment" and "job enlargement" programs contribute to improved productivity and increased quality of work life for employees in organizations. The authors discuss four theoretical approaches to work redesign: motivation–hygiene theory, activation theory, socio-technical systems theory, and the Requisite Task Attributes Index, which analyzes the relationship between the nature of jobs and employees' reaction to them. The "job characteristics" model looks at how five "core" job dimensions (skill variety, task identity, task significance, autonomy, and feedback) affect three psychological states (meaningfulness, responsibility for outcomes, and knowledge of results of the work) which lead to beneficial personal and work outcomes (high motivation, quality performance, and job satisfaction).

23. Overcoming Resistance to Change*

LESTER COCH

JOHN R. P. FRENCH, JR.

INTRODUCTION

It has always been characteristic of American industry to change products and methods of doing jobs as often as competitive conditions or engineering progress dictates. This makes frequent changes in an individual's work necessary. In addition, the markedly greater turnover and absenteeism of recent years result in unbalanced production lines which again makes for frequent shifting of individuals from one job to another. One of the most serious production problems faced at the Harwood Manufacturing Corporation has been the resistance of production workers to the necessary changes in methods and jobs. This resistance expressed itself in several ways, such as grievances about the piece rates that went with the new methods, high turnover, very low efficiency, restriction of output, and marked aggression against management. Despite these undesirable effects, it was necessary that changes in methods and jobs continue.

Efforts were made to solve this serious problem by the use of a special monetary allowance for transfers, by trying to enlist the cooperation and aid of the union, by making necessary lay-offs on the basis of efficiency, etc. In all cases, these actions did little or nothing to overcome the resistance to change. On the basis of these data, it was felt that the pressing problem of resistance to change demanded further research for its solution. From the point of view of factory management, there were two purposes to the research: (1) Why do people resist change so strongly? and (2) What can be done to overcome this resistance?

Starting with a series of observations about the behavior of changed groups, the first step in the overall program was to devise a preliminary theory to account for the resistance to change. Then on the basis of the theory, a real life action experiment was devised and conducted within the context of the factory situation. Finally, the results of the experiment were interpreted in the light of the preliminary theory and the new data.

BACKGROUND

The main plant of the Harwood Manufacturing Corporation, where the present research was done, is located in the small town of Marion, Virginia. The plant produces pajamas and, like most sewing plants, employs mostly women. The plant's population is about 500 women and 100 men. The workers are recruited from the rural, mountainous areas surrounding the town, and are usually employed without previous industrial experience. The average age of the workers is 23; the average education is eight years of grammar school.

*Source: From *Human Relations* (August 1948), pp. 512-532. Copyright © 1948 Plenum Publishing Corporation. Reprinted by permission. Figure titles shortened by deletion of extraneous words.

The policies of the company in regard to labor relations are liberal and progressive. A high value has been placed on fair and open dealing with the employees and they are encouraged to take up any problems or grievances with the management at any time. Every effort is made to help foremen find effective solutions to their problems in human relations, using conferences and role-playing methods. Carefully planned orientation, designed to help overcome the discouragement and frustrations attending entrance upon the new and unfamiliar situation, is used. Plantwide votes are conducted where possible to resolve problems affecting the whole working population. The company has invested both time and money in employee services such as industrial music, health services, lunchroom, and recreation programs. In the same spirit, the management has been conscious of the importance of public relations in the local community; they have supported both financially and otherwise any activity which would build up good will for the company. As a result of these policies, the company has enjoyed good labor relations since the day it commenced operations.

Harwood employees work on an individual incentive system. Piece rates are set by time study and are expressed in terms of units. One unit is equal to one minute of standard work: 60 units per hour equal the standard efficiency rating. Thus, if on a particular operation the piece rate for one dozen is 10 units, the operator would have to produce 6 dozen per hour to achieve the standard efficiency rating of 60 units per hour. The skill required to reach 60 units per hour is great. On some jobs, an average trainee may take 34 weeks to reach the skill level necessary to perform at 60 units per hour. Her few weeks of work may be on an efficiency level of 5 to 20 units per hour.

The amount of pay received is directly proportional to the weekly average efficiency rating achieved. Thus, an operator with an average efficiency rating of 75 units per hour (25 percent more than standard) would receive 25 percent more than base pay. However, there are two minimum wages below which no operator may fall. The first is the plantwide minimum, the hiring-in wage; the second is a minimum wage based on six months' employment and is 22 percent higher than the plantwide minimum wage. Both minima are smaller than the base pay for 60 units per hour efficiency rating.

The rating of every piece worker is computed every day and the results are published in a daily record of production which is shown to every operator. This daily record of production for each production line carries the names of all the operators on that line arranged in rank order of efficiency rating, with the highest rating girl at the top of the list. The supervisors speak to each operator each day about her unit ratings. Because of the above procedures, many operators do not claim credit for all work done in a given day. Instead, they save a few of the piece rate tickets as a "cushion" against a rainy day when they may not feel well or may have a great amount of machine trouble.

When it is necessary to change an operator from one type of work to another, a transfer bonus is given. The bonus is so designed that the changed operator who relearns at an average rate will suffer no loss in earnings after the change. Despite this allowance, the general attitudes toward job changes in the factory are markedly negative. Such expressions as, "When you make your units (standard production), they change your job," are all too frequent. Many operators refuse to change, preferring to quit.

THE TRANSFER LEARNING CURVE

An analysis of the after-change relearning curves of several hundred experienced operators rating standard or better prior to change showed that 38 percent of the changed operators recovered to the standard unit rating of 60 units per hour. The other 62 percent either became chronically substandard operators or quit during the relearning period.

The average relearning curve for those who recover to standard production on the simplest type job in the plant *(see Figure 23-1)* is eight weeks long, and, when smoothed, provides the basis for the transfer bonus. The bonus is the percent difference between this expected efficiency rating and the standard of 60 units per hour. Progress is slow for the first two or three weeks, as the relearning curve shows, and then accelerates markedly to about 50 units per hour with an increase of 15 units in two weeks. Another slow progress area is encountered at 50 units per hour, the operator improving only 3 units in two weeks. The curve ends in a spurt of 10 units progress in one week, a marked goal gradient behavior. The individual curves, of course, vary widely in

Figure 23-1

LEARNING CURVE COMPARISON FOR NEW, INEXPERIENCED
EMPLOYEES WITH RELEARNING CURVE FOR ONLY THOSE TRANSFERS
(38 PERCENT) WHO EVENTUALLY RECOVER TO STANDARD PRODUCTION

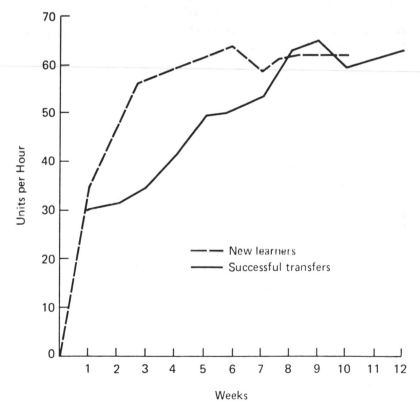

length according to the simplicity or difficulty of the job to be relearned; but in general, the successful curves are consistent with the average curve in form.

It is interesting to note in Figure 23-1 that the relearning period for an experienced operator is longer than the learning period for a new operator. This is true despite the fact that the majority of transfers—the failures, who never recover to standard—are omitted from the curve. However, changed operators rarely complain of "wanting to do it the old way," etc., after the first week or two of change; and time and motion studies show few false moves after the first week of change. From this evidence it is deduced that proactive inhibition or the interference of previous habits in learning the new skill is either nonexistent or very slight after the first two weeks of change.

Figure 23-2, which presents the relearning curves for 41 experienced operators who were changed to very difficult jobs, gives a comparison between the recovery rates for operators making standard or better prior to change, and those below standard prior to change. Both classes of operators dropped to a little below 30 units per hour and recovered at a very slow but similar rate. These curves show a general (though by no means universal) phenomenon: that the efficiency rating prior to change does not indicate a faster or slower recovery rate after change.

A PRELIMINARY THEORY OF RESISTANCE TO CHANGE

The fact that relearning after transfer to

Figure 23-2

DROP IN PRODUCTION AND RECOVERY RATE AFTER TRANSFER
(SKILLFUL AND SUBSTANDARD OPERATORS)

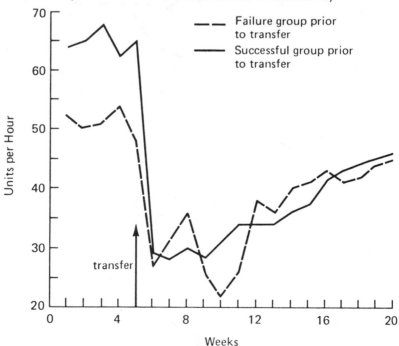

a new job is so often slower than initial learning on first entering the factory would indicate, on the face of it, that the resistance to change and the slow relearning is primarily a motivational problem. The similar recovery rates of the skilled and unskilled operators shown in Figure 23-2 tend to confirm the hypothesis that skill is a minor factor and motivation is the major determinant of the rate of recovery. Earlier experiments at Harwood by Alex Bavelas demonstrated this point conclusively. He found that the use of group decision techniques on operators who had just been transferred resulted in very marked increases in the rate of relearning, even though no skill training was given and there were no other changes in working conditions.[1]

Interviews with operators who have been transferred to a new job reveal a common pattern of feelings and attitudes which are distinctly different from those of successful nontransfers. In addition to resentment against the management for transferring them, the employees typically show feelings of frustration, loss of hope of ever regaining their former level of production and status in the factory, feelings of failure, and a very low level of aspiration. In this respect these transferred operators are similar to the chronically slow workers studied previously.

Earlier unpublished research at Harwood has shown that the nontransferred employees generally have an explicit goal of reaching and maintaining an efficiency rating of 60 units per hour. A questionnaire administered to several groups of operators indicated that a large majority of them accept as their goal the management's quota of 60 units per hour. This standard of production is the level of aspiration according to which the operators measure their own success or failure; and those who fall below standard lose status in the eyes of their fellow employees. Relatively few operators set a goal appreciably above 60 units per hour.

The actual production records confirm the effectiveness of this goal of standard production. The distribution of the total population of operators in accordance with their production levels is by no means a normal curve. Instead there is a very large number of operators who rate 60 to 63 units per hour and relatively few operators who rate just above or just below this range. Thus we may conclude that:

(1) **There is a force acting on the operator in the direction of achieving a production level of 60 units per hour or more. It is assumed that the strength of this driving force (acting on an operator below standard) increases as she gets nearer the goal—a typical goal gradient** (see Figure 23-1).

On the other hand restraining forces operate to hinder or prevent her from reaching this goal. These restraining forces consist among other things of the difficulty of the job in relation to the operator's level of skill. Other things being equal, the faster an operator is sewing the more difficult it is to increase her speed by a given amount. Thus we may conclude that:

(2) **The strength of the restraining force hindering higher production increases with increasing level of production.**

In line with previous studies, it is assumed that the conflict of these two opposing forces—the driving force corresponding to the goal of reaching 60 and the restraining force of the difficulty of the job—produces frustration. In such a conflict situation, the strength of frustration will depend on the strength of these forces. If the restraining force against increasing production is weak, then the frustration will be weak. But if the driving force toward higher production (i.e., the motivation) is weak, then the frustration will also be weak. Probably both of the conflicting forces must be above a certain minimum strength before any frustration is produced; for all goal-directed activity involves some degree of conflict of this type, yet a person is not usually frustrated so long as he is making satisfactory progress toward his goal. Consequently we assume that:

(3) **The strength of frustration is a function of the weaker of these two opposing forces, provided that the weaker force is stronger than a certain minimum necessary to produce frustration.**[2]

An analysis of the effects of such frustration in the factory showed that it resulted, among other things, in high turnover and absenteeism. The rate of turnover for successful operators with efficiency ratings above standard was much lower than for unsuccessful operators. Likewise, operators on the more difficult jobs quit more frequently than those on the easier jobs. Presumably the effect of being transferred is a severe frustration which should result in similar attempts to escape from the field.

In line with this theory of frustration and the finding that job turnover is one resultant of frustration, an analysis was made of the turnover rate of transferred operators as compared with the rate among operators who had not been transferred recently. For the year September 1946, to September 1947 there were 198 operators who had not been transferred recently, that is, within the 34-week period allowed for relearning after transfer. There was a second group of 85 operators who had been transferred recently, that is, within the time allowed for relearning the new job. Each of the two groups was divided into several classifications according to their unit rating at the time of quitting. For each classification the percent turnover per month, based on the total number of employees in that classification, was computed.

The results are given in Figure 23-3. Both the levels of turnover and the form of the curves are strikingly different for the two groups. Among operators who have not been transferred recently the average turnover per month is about 4.5 percent; among recent transfers the monthly turnover is nearly 12 percent. Consistent with the previous studies, both groups show a very marked drop in the turnover curve after an operator becomes a success reaching 60 units per hour or standard production. However, the form of curves at lower unit ratings is markedly different for the two groups. The nontransferred operators show a gradually increasing rate of turnover up to a rating of 55 to 59 units per hour. The transferred operators, on the other hand, show a high peak at the lowest unit rating of 30 to 34 units per hour, decreasing sharply to a low point at 45 to 49 units per hour. Since most changed operators drop to a unit rating of around 30 units per hour when changed and then drop no further, it is obvious that the rate of turnover was highest for these operators just after they were changed and again much later just before they reached standard. Why?

It is assumed that the strength of frustration for an operator who has *not* been transferred gradually increases because both the driving force towards the goal of reaching 60 and the restraining force of the difficulty of the job increase with increasing unit rating. This is in line with hypotheses (1), (2) and (3) above. For the transferred operator on the other hand the frustration is greatest immediately after transfer when the contrast of her present status with her former status is most evident. At this point the strength of the restraining forces is at a maximum because the difficulty is unusually great due to proactive inhibition. Then as she overcomes the interference effects between the two jobs and learns the new job, the difficulty and the frustration gradually decrease and the rate of turnover declines until the operator reaches 45–49 units per hour. Then at higher levels of production the difficulty starts to increase again and the transferred operator shows the same peak in frustration and turnover at 55–59 units per hour.

Though our theory of frustration explains the forms of the two turnover curves in Figure 23-3, it hardly seems ade-

Figure 23-3

RATE OF TURNOVER AT VARIOUS LEVELS OF PRODUCTION
(TRANSFERS COMPARED WITH NONTRANSFERS)

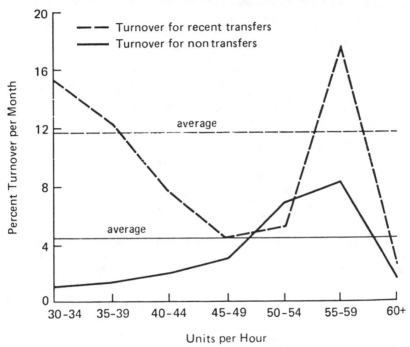

quate to account for the markedly higher level of turnover for transfers as compared to nontransfers. On the basis of the difficulty of the job, it is especially difficult to explain the higher rate of turnover at 55 59 units per hour for transfers. Evidently additional forces are operating.

Another factor which seems to affect recovery rates of changed operators is the amount of we-feeling. Observations seem to indicate that a strong psychological subgroup with negative attitudes toward management will display the strongest resistance to change. On the other hand, changed groups with high we-feeling and positive cooperative attitudes are the best relearners. Collections of individuals with little or no we-feeling display some resistance to change but not so strongly as the groups

with high we-feeling and negative attitudes toward management. However, turnover for the individual transfers is much higher than in the latter groups. This phenomenon of the relationship between we-feeling and resistance to change is so overt that for years the general policy of the management of the plant was never to change a group as a group but rather to scatter the individuals in different areas throughout the factory.

An analysis of turnover records for changed operators with high we-feeling showed a 4 percent turnover rate per month at 30 to 34 units per hour, not significantly higher than in unchanged operators but significantly lower than in changed operators with little or no we-feeling. However, the acts of aggression are far more numerous among operators with high we-feeling than among operators with little we-feeling. Since both types of operators experience the same frustration as individuals but react to it so differently, it is assumed that the effect on the in-group feeling is to set up a restraining force against leaving the group and perhaps even to set up driving forces toward staying in the group. In these circumstances, one would expect some alternative reaction to frustration rather than escape from the field. This alternative is aggression. Strong we-feeling provides strength so that members dare to express aggression which would otherwise be suppressed.

One common result in a subgroup with strong we-feeling is the setting of a group standard concerning production. Where the attitudes toward management are antagonistic, this group standard may take the form of a definite restriction of production to a given level. This phenomenon of restriction is particularly likely to happen in a group that has been transferred to a job where a new piece rate has been set; for they have some hope that if production never approaches the standard, the management may change the piece rate in their favor.

A group standard can exert extremely strong forces on an individual member of a small subgroup. That these forces can have a powerful effect on production is indicated in the production record of one presser during a period of 40 days.

For the first 20 days she was working in a group of other pressers who were producing at the rate of about 50 units per hour. Starting on the thirteenth day, when she reached standard production and exceeded the production of the other members, she became a scapegoat of the group. During this time her production decreased toward the level of the remaining members of the group. After 20 days the group had to be broken up and all the other members were

Table 23-1

Days	Production Per Day
In the Group	
1–3	46
4–6	52
7–9	53
10–12	56
Scapegoating Begins	
13–16	55
17–20	48
Becomes a Single Worker	
21–24	83
25–28	92
29–32	92
33–36	91
37–40	92

transferred to other jobs, leaving only the scapegoat operator. With the removal of the group, the group standard was no longer operative, and the production of the one remaining operator shot up from the level of about 45 to 96 units per hour in a period of 4 days. Her production stabilized at a level of about 92 and stayed there for the remainder of the 20 days. Thus it is clear that the motivational forces induced in the individual by a strong subgroup may be more powerful than those induced by management.

THE EXPERIMENT

On the basis of the preliminary theory that resistance to change is a combination of an individual reaction to frustration with strong group-induced forces it seemed that the most appropriate methods for overcoming the resistance to change would be group methods. Consequently an experiment was designed employing two variations of democratic procedure in handling groups to be transferred. The first variation involved participation through representation of the workers in designing the changes to be made in the jobs. The second variation consisted of total participation by all members of the group in designing the changes. A third control group was also used. Two experimental groups received the total participation treatment. The three experimental groups and the control group were roughly matched with respect to: (1) the efficiency ratings of the groups before transfer; (2) the degree of change involved in the transfer; (3) the amount of we-feeling observed in the groups.

In no case was more than a minor change in the work routines and time allowances made. The control group, the 18 hand pressers, had formerly stacked their work in one-half dozen lots on a flat piece of cardboard the size of the finished product. The new job called for stacking their work in one-half dozen lots in a box the size of the finished product. The box was located in the same place the cardboard had been. An additional two minutes per dozen was allowed (by the time study) for this new part of the job. This represented a total job change of 8.8 percent.

Experimental group 1, the 13 pajama folders, had formerly folded coats with prefolded pants. The new job called for the folding of coats with unfolded pants. An additional 1.8 minutes per dozen was allowed (by time study) for this new part of the job. This represented a total job change of 9.4 percent.

Experimental groups 2 and 3, consisting of 8 and 7 pajama examiners respectively, had formerly clipped threads from the entire garment and examined every seam. The new job called for pulling only certain threads off and examining every seam. An average of 1.2 minutes per dozen was subtracted (by time study) from the total time on these two jobs. This represented a total job change of 8 percent.

The control group of hand pressers went through the usual factory routine when they were changed. The production department modified the job, and a new piece rate was set. A group meeting was then held in which the control group was told that the change was necessary because of competitive conditions and that a new piece rate had been set. The new piece rate was thoroughly explained by the time study man, questions were answered, and the meeting dismissed.

Experimental group 1 was changed in a different manner. Before any changes took place, a group meeting was held with all the operators to be changed. The need for the change was presented as dramatically as possible, showing two identical garments produced in the factory; one was produced in 1946 and had sold for 100 percent more than its fellow in 1947. This demonstration effectively shared with the group the entire problem of the necessity of cost reduction. A general agreement was reached that a savings could be effected by removing the "frills" and "fancy" work from the garment without affecting the folders' opportunity to achieve a high efficiency rating. Management then presented a plan to set the new job and piece rate:

1. Make a check study of the job as it was being done.
2. Eliminate all unnecessary work.
3. Train several operators in the correct methods.
4. Set the piece rate by time studies on these specially trained operators.
5. Explain the new job and rate to all the operators.
6. Train all operators in the new method so they can reach a high rate of production within a short time.

The group approved this plan (though no formal group decision was reached) and chose the operators to be specially trained. A submeeting with the "special" operators was held immediately following the meeting with the entire group. They displayed a cooperative and interested attitude and immediately presented many good suggestions. This attitude carried over into the working out of the details of the new job; and when the new job and piece rates were set, the "special" operators referred to the resultants as "our job," "our rate," etc. The new job and piece rates were presented at a second group meeting to all the operators involved. The "special" operators served to train the other operators on the new job.

Experimental groups 2 and 3 went through much the same kind of change meetings. The groups were smaller than experimental group 1, and a more intimate atmosphere was established. The need for a change was once again made dramatically clear; the same plan was presented by management. However, since the groups were small, all operators were chosen as "special" operators; that is, all operators were to

participate directly in the designing of the new jobs and all operators would be studied by the time study man. It is interesting to note that in the meetings with these two groups, suggestions were immediately made in such quantity that the stenographer had great difficulty in recording them. The group approved of the plans, but again no formal group decision was reached.

RESULTS

The results of the experiment are summarized in graphic form in Figure 23-4. The gaps in the production curves occur because these groups were paid on a time-work basis for a day or two. The control group improved little beyond their early efficiency ratings. Resistance developed

Figure 23-4

EFFECTS OF PARTICIPATION THROUGH REPRESENTATION (GROUP 1) AND TOTAL PARTICIPATION (GROUPS 2 AND 3) ON RECOVERY AFTER AN EASY TRANSFER

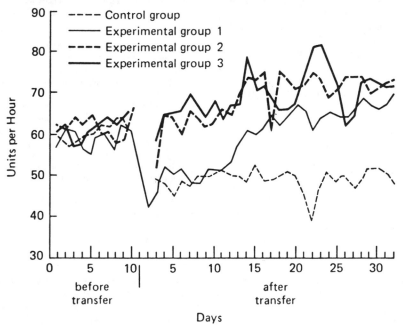

almost immediately after the change occurred. Marked expressions of aggression against management occurred, such as conflict with the methods engineer, expression of hostility against the supervisor, deliberate restriction of production, and lack of cooperation with the supervisor. There were 17 percent quits in the first 40 days. Grievances were filed about the piece rate, but when the rate was checked, it was found to be a little "loose."

Experimental group 1 showed an unusually good relearning curve. At the end of 14 days, the group averaged 61 units per hour. During the 14 days, the attitude was cooperative and permissive. They worked well with the methods engineer, the training staff, and the supervisor. (The supervisor was the same person in the cases of the control group and experimental group 1.) There were no quits in this group in the first 40 days. This group might have presented a better learning record if work had not been scarce during the first 7 days. There was one act of aggression against the supervisor recorded in the first 40 days. It is interesting to note that the three special representative operators in experimental group 1 recovered at about the same rate as the rest of their group.

Experimental groups 2 and 3 recovered faster than experimental group 1. After a slight drop on the first day of change, the efficiency ratings returned to a prechange level and showed sustained progress thereafter to a level about 14 percent higher than the prechange level. No additional training was provided them after the second day. They worked well with their supervisors and no indications of aggression were observed from these groups. There were no quits in either of these groups in the first 40 days.

A fourth experimental group, composed of only two sewing operators, was transferred by the total participation technique. Their new job was one of the most difficult jobs in the factory, in contrast to the easy jobs for the control group and the other three experimental groups. As expected, the total participation technique again resulted in an unusually fast recovery rate and a final level of production well above the level before transfer. Because of the difficulty of the new job, however, the rate of recovery was slower than for experimental groups 2 and 3, but faster than for experimental group 1.

In the first experiment, the control group made no progress after transfer for a period of 32 days. At the end of this period the group was broken up and the individuals were reassigned to new jobs scattered throughout the factory. Two and a half months after their dispersal, the 13 remaining members of the original control group were again brought together as a group for a second experiment.

This second experiment consisted of transferring the control group to a new job, using the total participation technique in meetings which were similar to those held with experimental groups 2 and 3. The new job was a pressing job of comparable difficulty to the new job in the first experiment. On the average it involved about the same degree of change. In the meetings no reference was made to the previous behavior of the group on being transferred.

The results of the second experiment were in sharp contrast to the first (see Figure 23-5). With the total participation technique, the same control group now recovered rapidly to their previous efficiency rating, and, like the other groups under this treatment, continued on beyond it to a new high level of production. There was no aggression or turnover in the group for 19 days after change, a marked modification of their previous behavior after transfer. Some anxiety concerning their seniority status was expressed, but this was resolved in a meeting of their elected delegate, the union business agent, and a management representative. It should be noted in Figure 23-5 that the prechange level on the second experiment is just above 60 units per hour; thus the individual transfers had progressed to just above standard during the two and a half months between the two experiments.

INTERPRETATION

The purpose of this section is to explain the drop in production resulting from transfer, the differential recovery rates of the control and the experimental groups, the increases beyond their former levels of production by the experimental groups, and the differential rates of turnover and aggression.

The first experiment showed that the rate of recovery is directly proportional to the amount of participation, and that the rates of turnover and aggression are inversely proportional to the amount of participation. The second experiment demonstrated more conclusively that the results obtained depended on the experimental treatment rather than on personality factors like skill or aggressiveness, for identical individuals yielded markedly different results in the control treatment as contrasted with the total participation treatment.

Apparently total participation has the same type of effect as participation through representation, but the former has a stronger influence. In regard to recovery rates, this difference is not unequivocal because the experiment was unfortunately confounded. Right after transfer, experimental group number 1 had insufficient material to work on for a period of seven days. Hence their slower recovery during this period is at least in part due to insufficient work. In succeeding days, however, there was an adequate supply of work and the dif-

Figure 23-5

COMPARISON OF THE EFFECT OF THE CONTROL PROCEDURE WITH
THE TOTAL PARTICIPATION PROCEDURE ON THE SAME GROUP

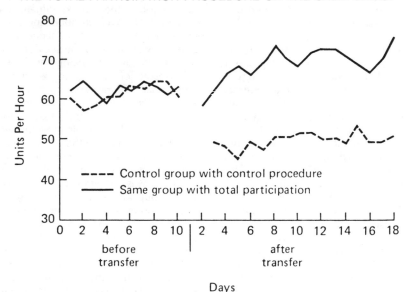

ferential recovery rate still persisted. Therefore we are inclined to believe that participation through representation results in slower recovery than does total participation.

Before discussing the details of why participation produces high morale, we will consider the nature of production levels. In examining the production records of hundreds of individuals and groups in this factory, one is struck by the constancy of the level of production. Though differences among individuals in efficiency rating are very large, nearly every experienced operator maintains a fairly steady level of production given constant physical conditions. Frequently the given level will be maintained despite rather large changes in technical working conditions.

As Lewin has pointed out, this type of production can be viewed as a quasi-stationary process—in the ongoing work the operator is forever sewing new garments, yet the level of the process remains relatively stationary. Thus there are constant characteristics of the production process permitting the establishment of general laws.

In studying production as a quasi-stationary equilibrium, we are concerned with two types of forces: (1) forces on production in a downward direction, (2) forces on production in an upward direction. In this situation we are dealing with a variety of both upward forces tending to increase the level of production and downward forces tending to decrease the level of production. However, in the present experiment we have no method of measuring independently all of the component forces either downward or upward. These various component forces upward are combined into one resultant force upward. Likewise the several downward component forces combine into one resultant force downward. We can infer a good deal about the relative strengths of these resultant forces.

Where we are dealing with a quasi-stationary equilibrium, the resultant forces upward and the forces downward are opposite in direction and equal in strength at the equilibrium level. Of course either resultant forces may fluctuate over a short period of time, so that the forces may not be equally balanced at a given moment. However over a longer period of time and on the average the forces balance out. Fluctuations from the average occur but there is a tendency to return to the average level.

Just before being transferred, all of the groups in both experiments had reached a stable equilibrium level at just above the standard production of 60 units per hour. This level was equal to the average efficiency rating for the entire factory during the period of the experiments. Since this production level remained constant, neither increasing nor decreasing, we may be sure that the strength of the resultant force upward was equal to the strength of the resultant force downward. This equilibrium of forces was maintained over the period of time when production was stationary at this level. But the forces changed markedly after transfer and these new constellations of forces were distinctly different for the control and the experimental groups.

For the control group the period after transfer is a quasi-stationary equilibrium at a lower level, and the forces do not change during the period of thirty days. The resultant force upward remains equal to the resultant force downward and the level of production remains constant. The force field for this group is represented schematically in Figure 23-6. Only the resultant forces are shown. The length of the vector represents the strength of the force; and the point of the arrow represents the point of application of the force, that is, the production level and the time at which the force applies. Thus the forces are equal and opposite only at the level of 50 units per hour. At higher levels of production the forces downward are greater than the forces upward; and at

Figure 23-6

SCHEMATIC DIAGRAM OF THE QUASI-STATIONARY EQUILIBRIUM
(CONTROL GROUP AFTER TRANSFER)

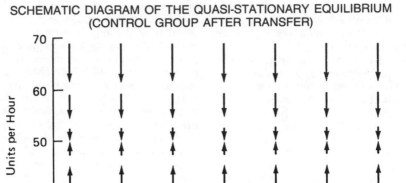

Days After Transfer

lower levels of production the forces upward are stronger than the forces downward. Thus there is a tendency for the equilibrium to be maintained at an efficiency rating of 50.

The situation for the experimental groups after transfer can be viewed as a quasi-stationary equilibrium of a different type. Figure 23-7 gives a schematic diagram of the resultant forces for the experimental groups. At any given level of production, such as 50 units per hour or 60 units per hour, both the resultant forces upward and the resultant forces downward change over the period of 30 days. During this time the point of equilibrium, which starts at 50 units per hour, gradually rises until it reaches a level of over 70 units per hour after 30 days. Yet here again the equilibrium level has the character of a "central force field" where at any point in the total field the resultant of the upward and the downward forces is in the direction of the equilibrium level.

To understand how the difference between the experimental and the control treatments produced the differences in force fields represented in Figures 23-6 and 23-7, it is not sufficient to consider only the resultant forces. We must also look at the component forces for each resultant force.

There are three main component forces influencing production in a downward direction: (1) the difficulty of the job . . . ; (2) a force corresponding to avoidance of strain; (3) a force corresponding to a group standard to restrict production to a given level. The resultant force upward in the direction of greater production is composed of three additional component forces: (1) the force corresponding to the goal of standard production . . . ; (2) a force corresponding to pressures induced by the management through supervision; (3) a force corresponding to a group standard of competition. Let us examine each of these six component forces.

Figure 23-7

SCHEMATIC DIAGRAM OF THE QUASI-STATIONARY EQUILIBRIUM
(EXPERIMENTAL GROUPS AFTER TRANSFER)

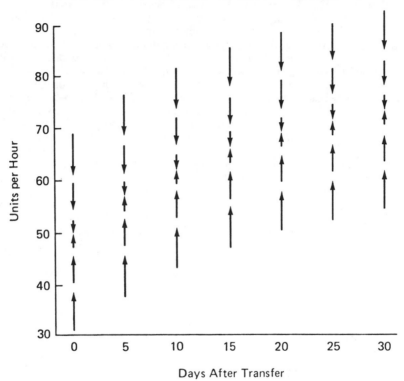

Days After Transfer

1. JOB DIFFICULTY

For all operators the difficulty of the job is one of the forces downward on production. The difficulty of the job, of course, is relative to the skill of the operator. The given job may be very difficult for an unskilled operator but relatively easy for a highly skilled one. In the case of a transfer a new element of difficulty enters. For some time the new job is much more difficult, for the operator is unskilled at that particular job. In addition to the difficulty experienced by any learner, the transfer often encounters the added difficulty of proactive inhibition. Where the new job is similar to the old job there will be a period of interference between the two similar but different skills required. For this reason a very efficient operator whose skills have become almost unconscious may suffer just as great a drop as a much less efficient operator *(see Figure 23-2).* Except for group 4, the difficulty of these easy jobs does not explain the differential recovery rate because both the initial difficulty and the amount of change were equated for these groups. The two operators in group 4 probably dropped further and recovered more slowly than any of the other three groups under total participation because of the greater difficulty of the job.

2. STRAIN AVOIDANCE

The force toward lower production corresponding to the difficulty of the job (or the lack of skill of the person) has the character of a restraining force—that is, it acts to prevent locomotion rather than as a driving force causing locomotion. However, in all production there is a closely related driving force toward lower production, namely "strain avoidance." We assume that working too hard and working too fast is an unpleasant strain; and corresponding to this negative valence there is a driving force in the opposite direction, namely towards taking it easy or working slower. The higher the level of production the greater will be the strain and other things being equal, the stronger will be the downward force of strain avoidance. Likewise, the greater the difficulty of the job the stronger will be the force corresponding to strain avoidance. But the greater the operator's skill the smaller will be the strain and the strength of the force of strain avoidance. Therefore:

(4) The strength of the force of strain avoidance =

$$\frac{\textbf{job difficulty} \times \textbf{production level}}{\textbf{skill of operator}}$$

The differential recovery rates of the control group in both experiments and the three experimental groups in Experiment I cannot be explained by strain avoidance because job difficulty, production level, and operator skill were matched at the time immediately following transfer. Later, however, when the experimental treatments had produced a much higher level of production, these groups were subjected to an increased downward force of strain avoidance which was stronger than in the control group in Experiment I. Evidently other forces were strong enough to overcome this force of strain avoidance.

3. THE GOAL OF STANDARD PRODUCTION

In considering the negative attitudes toward transfer and the resistance to being transferred, there are several important aspects on the complex goal of reaching and maintaining a level of 60 units per hour. For an operator producing below standard, this goal is attractive because it means success, high status in the eyes of her fellow employees, better pay, and job security. . . . On the other hand, there is a strong force against remaining below standard because this lower level means failure, low status, low pay, and the danger of being fired. Thus it is clear that the upward force corresponding to the goal of standard production will indeed be strong for the transfer who has dropped below standard.

It is equally clear why any operator, who accepts the stereotype about transfer, shows such strong resistance to being changed. She sees herself as becoming a failure and losing status, pay, and perhaps the job itself. The result is a lowered level of aspiration and a weakened force toward the goal of standard production.

Just such a weakening of the force toward 60 units per hour seems to have occurred in the control group in Experiment I. The participation treatments, on the other hand, seem to have involved the operators in designing the new job and setting the new piece rates in such a way that they did not lose hope of regaining the goal of standard production. Thus the participation resulted in a stronger force toward higher production. However, this force alone can hardly account for the large differences in recovery rate between the control group and the experimental groups; certainly it does not explain why the latter increased to a level so high above standard.

4. MANAGEMENT PRESSURE

On all operators below standard the management exerts a pressure for higher production. This pressure is no harsh and autocratic treatment involving threats. Rather it takes the form of persuasion and encouragement by the supervisors. They attempt to induce the low rating operator to improve her performance and to attain standard production.

Such an attempt to induce a psychological force on another person may have several results. In the first place the person may ignore the attempt of the inducing agent, in which case there is no induced force acting on the person. On the other hand, the attempt may succeed so that an induced force on the person exists. Other things being equal, whenever there is an induced force acting on a person, the person will locomote in the direction of the force. An induced force, which depends on the power field of an inducing agent—some other individual or group—will cease to exist when the inducing power field is withdrawn. In this report it is different from an "own" force which stems from a person's own needs and goals.

The reaction of a person to an effective induced force will vary depending, among other things, on the person's relation to the inducing agent. A force induced by a friend may be accepted in such a way that it acts more like an own force. An effective force induced by an enemy may be resisted and rejected so that the person complies unwillingly and shows signs of conflict and tension. Thus in addition to what might be called a "neutral" induced force, we also distinguish an *accepted* induced force and a *rejected* induced force. Naturally the acceptance and the rejection of an induced force can vary in degree from zero (*i.e.,* a neutral induced force) to very strong acceptance or rejection. To account for the difference in character between the acceptance and the rejection of an induced force, we make the following assumptions:

(5) The acceptance of an induced force sets up additional own forces in the same direction.

(6) The rejection of an induced force sets up additional own forces in the opposite direction.

The grievances, aggression, and tension in the control group in Experiment I indicate that they rejected the force toward higher production induced by the management. The group accepted the stereotype that transfer is a calamity, but the control procedure did not convince them that the change was necessary and they viewed the new job and the new piece rates set by management as arbitrary and unreasonable.

The experimental groups, on the contrary, participated in designing the changes and setting the piece rates so that they spoke of the new job as "our job" and the new piece rates as "our rates." Thus they accepted the new situation and accepted the management induced force toward higher production.

From the acceptance by the experimental groups and the rejection by the control group of the management induced forces, we may derive [by (5) and (6) above] that the former had additional own forces toward higher production whereas the latter had additional own forces toward lower production. This difference helps to explain the better recovery rate of experimental groups.

5. GROUP STANDARDS

Probably the most important force affecting the recovery under the control procedure was a group standard, set by the group restricting the level of production to 50 units per hour. Evidently this explicit agreement to restrict production is related to the group's rejection of the change and of the new job as arbitrary and unreasonable. Perhaps they had faint hopes of demonstrating that standard production could not be attained and thereby obtain a more favorable piece rate. In any case there was a definite group phenomenon which affected all the members of the group. We have already noted the striking example of the presser whose production was restricted in the group situation to about half the level she attained as an individual. . . . In the control group, too, we would expect the group to induce strong forces on the members. The more the member deviates above the standard the stronger would be the group induced force to conform to the standard, for such deviations both negate any possibility of management increasing the piece rate and at the same time expose the other members to increased pressure from management. Thus individual differences in levels of production should be sharply curtailed in the control group after transfer.

An analysis was made for all groups of the individual differences within the group in levels of production. In Experiment I the 40 days before change were compared with the 30 days after change; in Experiment II the 10 days before change were compared to the 17 days after change. As a measure of variability, the standard deviation was calculated each day for each group. The average daily standard deviations *before* and *after* change were as follows:

There is indeed a marked decrease in individual differences within the control group after their first transfer. In fact the restriction of production resulted in a lower variability than in any other group. Thus we may conclude that the group standard at 60 units per hour set up strong group-induced forces which were impor-

tant components in the central force field shown in Figure 23-6. It is now evident that for the control group the quasi-stationary equilibrium after transfer has a steep gradient around the equilibrium level of 50 units per hour—the strength of the forces increases rapidly above and below this level. It is also clear that the group standard to restrict production is a major reason for the lack of recovery in the control group.

The table of variability also shows that the experimental treatments markedly reduced variability in the other four groups after transfer. In experimental group 1 (participation by representation) this smallest reduction of variability was produced by a group standard of individual competition. Competition among members of the group was reported by the supervisor soon after transfer. This competition was a force toward higher production which resulted in good recovery to standard and continued progress beyond standard.

Experimental groups 2 and 3 showed a greater reduction in variability following transfer. These two groups under total participation were transferred on the same day. Group competition developed between the two groups. This group competition, which evidently resulted in stronger forces on the members than did the individual competition, was an effective group standard. The standard gradually moved to higher and higher levels of production with the result that the groups not only reached

Table 23-2

Group	Variability	
Experiment I	Before Change	After Change
Control group	9.8	1.9
Experimental 1	9.7	3.8
Experimental 2	10.3	2.7
Experimental 3	9.9	2.4
Experiment II		
Control group	12.7	2.9

but far exceeded their previous levels of production.

TURNOVER AND AGGRESSION

Returning now to our preliminary theory of frustration, we can see several revisions. The difficulty of the job and its relation to skill and strain avoidance has been clarified in proposition (4). It is now clear that the driving force toward 60 is a complex affair; it is partly a negative driving force corresponding to the negative valence of low pay, low status, failure, and job insecurity. Turnover results not only from the frustration produced by the conflict of these two forces, but also as a direct attempt to escape from the region of these negative valences. For the members of the control group, the group standard to restrict production prevented escape by increasing production, so that quitting their jobs was the only remaining escape. In the participation groups, on the contrary, both the group standards and the additional own forces resulting from the acceptance of management-induced forces combined to make increasing production the distinguished path of escape from this region of negative valence.

In considering turnover as a form of escape from the field, it is not enough to look only at the psychological present; one must also consider the psychological future. The employee's decision to quit the job is rarely made exclusively on the basis of a momentary frustration or an undesirable present situation; she usually quits when she also sees the future as equally hopeless. The operator transferred by the usual factory procedure (including the control group) has in fact a realistic view of the probability of continued failure because, as we have already noted, 62 percent of transfers do in fact fail to recover to standard production. Thus the higher rate of quitting for transfers as compared to non-

transfers results from a more pessimistic view of the future.

The control procedure had the effect for the members of setting up management as a hostile power field. They rejected the forces induced by this hostile power field, and group standards to restrict production developed within the group in opposition to management. In this conflict between the power field of management and the power field of the group, the control group attempted to reduce the strength of the hostile power field relative to the strength of their own power field. This change was accomplished in three ways: (1) the group increased its own power by developing a more cohesive and well-disciplined group, (2) they secured "allies" by getting the backing of the union in filing a formal grievance about the new piece rate, (3) they attacked the hostile power field directly in the form of aggression against the supervisor, the time study engineer, and the higher management. Thus the aggression was derived not only from individual frustration but also from the conflict between two groups. Furthermore, this situation of group conflict both helped to define management as the frustration agent and gave the members strength to express any aggressive impulses produced by frustration.

CONCLUSIONS

It is possible for management to modify greatly or to remove completely group resistance to changes in methods of work and the ensuing piece rates. This change can be accomplished by the use of group meetings in which management effectively communicates the need for change and stimulates group participation in planning the changes.

For Harwood's management, and presumably for managements of other industries using an incentive system, this experiment has important implications in the field of labor relations. A majority of all grievances presented at Harwood have always stemmed from a change situation. By preventing or greatly modifying group resistance to change, this concomitant to change may well be greatly reduced. The reduction of such costly phenomena as turn-over and slow relearning rates presents another distinct advantage.

Harwood's management has long felt that action research such as the present experiment is the only key to better labor-management relations. It is only by discovering the basic principles and applying them to the true causes of conflict that an intelligent, effective effort can be made to correct the undesirable effects of the conflict.

NOTES

1. John R. P. French, Jr., "The Behavior of Organized and Unorganized Groups under Conditions of Frustration and Fear, Studies in Topological and Vector Psychology, III," *University of Iowa Studies in Child Welfare*, Vol. 20 (1944), pp. 229-308.

2. Kurt Lewin, "Frontiers in Group Dynamics," *Human Relations*, Vol. 1, No. 1 (1947), pp. 5-41.

24. A Look at Management Systems*

RENSIS LIKERT

This article will be more interesting and more readily understood if a few minutes are taken now to complete the following form in accordance with these directions:

"Please think of the highest-producing department, division, or organization you have known well. Then place the letter H on the line under each organizational variable in the following table to show where this organization would fall. Treat each item as a continuous variable from the left extreme of System 1 to the right extreme of System 4."

Now that you have completed the form (Table 24-1) to describe the highest-producing department or unit you know well, please think of the *least* productive department, division, or organization you know well. Preferably it should be about the same size as your most productive unit and engaged in the same general kind of work. Then put the letter L on the line under each organizational variable in Table 24-1 to show where, in the light of your observations, you feel this least-productive organization falls on that item. As before, treat each item as a continuous variable from the left extreme of System 1 to the right extreme of System 4.

After you have completed Table 24-1 to describe both the most and the least productive departments you know well, compare the relative position of your two answers on each item. You are very likely to discover that on all items, or virtually all, your L's are to the left of your H's, i.e., that your high-producing department has a management system more to the right

in the table and your low-producing department is characterized by having a management system more to the left.

Many different groups of managers, totaling several hundred persons, have completed Table 24-1 describing both the highest- and lowest-producing departments which they knew well. They have varied in their descriptions of the most productive departments; some are quite far to the right, the H's being largely under System 4. For others, the most productive unit was largely under System 3. The striking fact, however, is that irrespective of where the H's describing the high-producing unit fall in the table, the L's for the low-producing department fall to the left. Quite consistently, the high-producing department is seen as toward the right end of the table.

For the vast majority of managers, this has been the pattern for every item in the table irrespective of the field of experience of the manager—production, sales, financial, office, etc.—and regardless of whether he occupies a staff or a line position. In about one case in twenty, a manager will place the low-producing unit to the right of the high on one or two items. But with very few exceptions, high-producing departments are seen as using management systems more to the right (toward System 4) and low-producing units as more to the left (toward System 1).

One would expect that such extraordinary consensus would lead managers to manage in ways consistent with it. When managers or nonsupervisory employees

Table 24-1

TABLE OF ORGANIZATIONAL AND PERFORMANCE CHARACTERISTICS
OF DIFFERENT MANAGEMENT SYSTEMS

Organizational variable	System 1	System 2	System 3	System 4
1. Leadership processes used				
Extent to which superiors have confidence and trust in *subordinates*	Have no confidence and trust in subordinates	Have condescending confidence and trust, such as master has to servant	Substantial but not complete confidence and trust; still wishes to keep control of decisions	Complete confidence and trust in all matters
Extent to which superiors behave so that subordinates feel free to discuss important things about their jobs with their immediate superior	Subordinates do not feel at all free to discuss things about the job with their superior	Subordinates do not feel very free to discuss things about the job with their superior	Subordinates feel rather free to discuss things about the job with their superior	Subordinates feel completely free to discuss things about the job with their superior
Extent to which immediate superior in solving job problems generally tries to get subordinates' ideas and opinions and make constructive use of them	Seldom gets ideas and opinions of subordinates in solving job problems	Sometimes gets ideas and opinions of subordinates in solving job problems	Usually gets ideas and opinions and usually tries to make constructive use of them	Always gets ideas and opinions and always tries to make constructive use of them

(Continued)

Table 24-1 (Continued)

Organizational variable	System 1	System 2	System 3	System 4
2. Character of motivational forces				
Manner in which motives are used	Fear, threats, punishment, and occasional rewards	Rewards and some actual or potential punishment	Rewards, occasional punishment, and some involvement	Economic rewards based on compensation system developed through participation; group participation and involvement in setting goals, improving methods, appraising progress toward goals, etc.
Amount of responsibility felt by each member of organization for achieving organization's goals	High levels of management feel responsibility; lower levels feel less; rank and file feel little and often welcome opportunity to behave in ways to defeat organization's goals	Managerial personnel usually feel responsibility; rank and file feel relatively little responsibility for achieving organization's goals	Substantial proportion of personnel, especially at high levels, feel responsibility and generally behave in ways to achieve the organization's goals	Personnel at all levels feel real responsibility for organization's goals and behave in ways to implement them
3. Character of communication process				
Amount of interaction and communication aimed at achieving organization's objectives	Very little	Little	Quite a bit	Much with both individuals and groups

(Continued)

Table 24-1 (Continued)

Organizational variable	System 1	System 2	System 3	System 4
Direction of information flow	Downward	Mostly downward	Down and up	Down, up, and with peers
Extent to which downward communications are accepted by subordinates	Viewed with great suspicion	May or may not be viewed with suspicion	Often accepted but at times viewed with suspicion; may or may not be openly questioned	Generally accepted, but if not, openly and candidly questioned
Accuracy of upward communication via line	Tends to be inaccurate	Information that boss wants to hear flows; other information is restricted and filtered	Information that boss wants to hear flows; other information may be limited or cautiously given	Accurate
Psychological closeness of superiors to subordinates (i.e., how well does superior know and understand problems faced by subordinates?)	Has no knowledge or understanding of problems of subordinates	Has some knowledge and understanding of problems of subordinates	Knows and understands problems of subordinates quite well	Knows and understands problems of subordinates very well

(Continued)

Table 24-1 (Continued)

Organizational variable	System 1	System 2	System 3	System 4
4. Character of interaction-influence process				
Amount and character of interaction	Little interaction and always with fear and distrust	Little interaction and usually with some condescension by superiors; fear and caution by subordinates	Moderate interaction, often with fair amount of confidence and trust	Extensive, friendly interaction with high degree of confidence and trust
Amount of cooperative teamwork present	None	Relatively little	A moderate amount	Very substantial amount throughout the organization
5. Character of decision-making process				
At what level in organization are decisions formally made?	Bulk of decisions at top of organization	Policy at top, many decisions within prescribed framework made at lower levels	Broad policy and general decisions at top, more specific decisions at lower levels	Decision making widely done throughout organization, although well integrated through linking process provided by overlapping groups
To what extent are decision makers aware of problems, particularly those at lower levels in the organization?	Often are unaware or only partially aware	Aware of some, unaware of others	Moderately aware of problems	Generally quite well aware of problems

(Continued)

Table 24-1 (Continued)

Organizational variable	System 1	System 2	System 3	System 4
Extent to which technical and professional knowledge is used in decision making	Used only if possessed at higher levels	Much of what is available in higher and middle levels is used	Much of what is available in higher, middle, and lower levels is used	Most of what is available anywhere within the organization is used
To what extent are subordinates involved in decisions related to their work?	Not at all	Never involved in decisions; occasionally consulted	Usually are consulted but ordinarily not involved in the decision making	Are involved fully in all decisions related to their work
Are decisions made at the best level in the organization so far as the motivational consequences (i.e., does the decision-making process help to create the necessary motivations in those persons who have to carry out the decisions?)	Decision making contributes little or nothing to the motivation to implement the decision, usually yields adverse motivation	Decision making contributes relatively little motivation	Some contribution by decision making to motivation to implement	Substantial contribution by decision-making processes to motivation to implement

(Continued)

Table 24-1 (Continued)

Organizational variable	System 1	System 2	System 3	System 4
6. Character of goal setting or ordering				
Manner in which usually done	Orders issued	Orders issued, opportunity to comment may or may not exist	Goals are set or orders issued after discussion(s) of problems and planned action	Except in emergencies, goals are usually established by means of group participation
Are there forces to accept, resist, or reject goals?	Goals are overtly accepted but are covertly resisted strongly	Goals are overtly accepted but often covertly resisted to at least a moderate degree	Goals are overtly accepted but at times with some covert resistance	Goals are fully accepted both overtly and covertly
7. Character of control processes				
Extent to which the review and control functions are concentrated	Highly concentrated in top management	Relatively highly concentrated, with some delegated control to middle and lower levels	Moderate downward delegation of review and control processes; lower as well as higher levels feel responsible	Quite widespread responsibility for review and control, with lower units at times imposing more rigorous reviews and tighter controls than top management

(Continued)

Table 24-1 (Continued)

Organizational variable	System 1	System 2	System 3	System 4
Extent to which there is an informal organization present and supporting or opposing goals of formal organization	Informal organization present and opposing goals of formal organization	Informal organization usually present and partially resisting goals	Informal organization may be present and may either support or partially resist goals of formal organization	Informal and formal organization are one and the same; hence all social forces support efforts to achieve organization's goals
Extent to which control data (e.g., accounting, productivity, cost, etc.) are used for self-guidance or group problem solving by managers and nonsupervisory employees; or used by superiors in a punitive, policing manner	Used for policing and in punitive manner	Used for policing coupled with reward and punishment, sometimes punitively; used somewhat for guidance but in accord with orders	Largely used for policing with emphasis usually on reward but with some punishment; used for guidance in accord with orders; some use also for self-guidance	Used for self-guidance and for coordinated problem solving and guidance; not used punitively

are asked, however, to use Table 24-1 to describe their own organization as they experience it, the answers obtained show that most organizations are being managed with systems appreciably more to the left than that which managers quite generally report is used by the highest-producing departments.

Parenthetically, some low-producing managers, although they display the same pattern of answers as other managers, believe that a manager should move toward System 4 *after* he has achieved high levels of productivity. They feel that the way to move from low to high productivity is to use a management system well toward the left (e.g., System 1 or 2) and move toward System 4 only after high productivity is achieved. Their view is essentially that of the supervisor of a low-producing unit who said: "This interest-in-people approach is all right, but it is a luxury. I've got to keep pressure on for production, and when I get production up, then I can afford to take time to show an interest in my employees and their problems." Research results show that managers who hold this view are not likely to achieve high productivity in their units.

The impressively consistent pattern of answers to Table 24-1 obtained from most managers poses important and perplexing questions: Why do managers use a system of management which they recognize is less productive than an alternate system which they can describe correctly and presumably could use? All these managers keenly want to achieve outstanding success. What keeps them from using the management system which they recognize yields the highest productivity, lowest costs, and best performance? There are two related questions which should be considered.

A significant finding emerges when experienced managers are asked the following: "In your experience what happens in a company when the senior officer becomes concerned about earnings and takes steps to cut costs, increase productivity, and improve profits? Does top management usually continue to use the management system it has been employing, or does it shift its operation to a management system more toward System 1 or more toward System 4?" Most managers report that, when top management seeks to reduce costs, it shifts its system more toward System 1, i.e., toward a system which they know from their own observations and experience yields poorer productivity and higher costs, on the average and over the long run, than does the existing management system of the company.

What causes the top management of a firm, when it wishes to reduce costs, to take steps which shift its management system in the direction which will actually increase costs over the long run rather than reduce them? What are the inadequacies in the accounting methods and in the financial reports which lead managers and boards of directors to believe that with the shift toward System 1 their costs and earnings are improving, when the actual facts are to the contrary? Why are not the reported increases in earnings shown for what they really are: cash income derived from what is usually an even greater liquidation of corporate human assets?

These are extremely important questions which affect the success or even the survival of companies.

25. Grid Organization Development*

ROBERT R. BLAKE

JANE S. MOUTON

Organizations are changing today, often dramatically. The changes are taking place in business organizations, in hospitals and institutions of various kinds, in local, state, and federal government bodies. Change in industrial organizations has been spurred by competition. New moves toward diversification of product lines have heightened change. Profit squeezes and steadily rising operating costs have stimulated it. Automation, computers, and improved methods of analysis have eroded the traditional ways of doing business. Efforts to capitalize on opportunities for moving into new forms of business have further energized change. In government, change has been spurred by the recognition of the need for efficiency in the use of tax dollars, by the emergence of new programs, and by demands for better management of programs. The public has demanded streamlining in government, the kind of change that makes for greater effectiveness.

All this has created new requirements for over-all effectiveness of organization. Yesterday's management practices are being challenged. New ways to achieve organization effectiveness are being pioneered and are having a wide impact on many segments of contemporary life.

BLUEPRINT FOR EFFECTIVENESS

Sound management can meet the challenge of change, even accelerate it. But a blueprint is needed to describe an organization so well managed that it can grasp opportunity from the challenge of change. What would such an organization be like?

1. *Its objectives would be sound, strong, and clear.* Its leaders would know where it was headed and how to get there. Its objectives would also be understood and embraced by all members of the management body. These persons would strive to contribute because the organization's objectives and their own goals would be consistent. There would be a high level of commitment to organization goals as well as to personal goals. Commitment would be based on understanding. To be understood, goals would be quite specific.

Every business has as an objective "profit." But this is too vague to motivate persons to greater effectiveness. Profit needs to be converted into concrete objectives. One might be, "To develop a position in the plastic industry which will service 20 percent of this market within the next 5 years." In a government organization, a specific objective might be "To establish six urban renewal demonstration projects distributed by regions and by city size within 10 months." Government objectives would be implemented through program planning and budgeting rather than the profit motive.

2. *Standards of excellence would be high.* Managers would be thoroughly acquainted with their areas of operation. A premium would be placed on knowledge and thorough analysis rather than on opinion and casual thought.

3. *The work culture would support the*

*Source: From Personnel Administration (January-February 1967). Copyright © 1967 International Personnel Management Association. Reprinted by permission of the International Personnel Management Association, 1617 Duke St., Arlington, VA 22314.

work. It would be an organization culture in which the members would be highly committed to achieving the goals of the organization, with accomplishment at the source of individual gratification.

4. *Teamwork would increase individual initiative.* There would be close cooperation within a work team, each supporting the others to get a job done. Teamwork would cut across department lines.

5. *Technical business knowledge needed for valid decision-making and problem-solving would come through coaching, developmental assignments, on-the-job training, and special courses.*

6. *Leadership would be evident.* With sound objectives, high standards of excellence, a culture characterized by high commitment, sound teamwork, and technical know-how, productivity would increase.

The way of life or culture of an organization can be a barrier to effectiveness. Barriers may stem from such elements of culture as the attitudes or traditions present in any unit of the organization. Culture both limits and guides the actions of the persons in the organization. Because of traditional ways and fear of change, an organization's leaders may be reluctant to apply modern management science. Yet, the need for change may be quite evident.

CRITERIA FOR CHANGE

A sound approach to introducing change and improvement is an Organization Development effort. It should:

1. *Involve the widest possible participation of executives, managers, and supervisors* to obtain a common set of concepts about how management can be improved.

2. *Be carried out by the organization itself.* The development of subordinates is recognized as part of the manager's job. When organization members from the line become the instructors, higher management's commitment, understanding, and support for on-the-job application and change are insured.

3. *Aim to improve the skills of executives and supervisors who must work together to improve management*—the skills of drawing on each other's knowledge and capacities, of making constructive use of disagreement, and of making sound deci-

sions to which members become committed.

4. *Aim to improve the ability of all managers to communicate better* so that genuine understanding can prevail.

5. *Clarify styles of management* so that managers learn how the elements of a formal management program (e.g., planned objectives, defined responsibilities, established policies) can be used without the organization's becoming overly formal and complex or unduly restricting personal freedom and needed individual initiative.

6. *Aid each manager to investigate his managerial style* to understand its impact and learn to make changes to improve it.

7. *Provide for examination of the organization's culture* to develop managers' understanding of the cultural barriers to effectiveness and how to eliminate them.

8. *Constantly encourage managers to plan and introduce improvements* based on their learnings and analysis of the organization.

ONE WAY TO GET THERE

Grid Organization Development is one way of increasing the effectiveness of an organization, whether it is a company, a public institution, or a government agency. The behavioral science concepts on which Organization Development is based reach back more than 50 years. Because Organization Development itself is only a decade or so old, those unfamiliar with its rationale may look upon it with doubt or skepticism, see it as a mystery or a package, a gimmick or a fad. Experience pinpoints which behavioral science concepts are tied to the struggle for a more effective organization. This has done much to help managers apply the pertinent concepts to everyday work.

There are several questions preceding the definition of Organization Development as it is applied to raise an organization's capacity to operate by using behavioral science concepts. One question is, "What is an organization?" Another is, "What is meant by development?'' Finally, ''What is it that Organization Development adds to the organization, that it lacks without it?''

SEVEN PROPERTIES OF AN ORGANIZATION

Because an organization is a complex entity, definitions often lap over into the abstract, becoming too vague to be useful. A meaningful way to define an organization is to list its properties. Seven properties of an organization are: purpose, structure, wherewithal, know-how, human interaction, culture, and results. If any are missing, the entity termed an organization probably cannot truly qualify as such.

PURPOSE

Purpose is the unifying principle around which human energy clusters in the organization. It defines direction. Any decision made can be tested against purpose to see if it makes the organization more effective or less so. Purpose is more complex than such simple statements as "to realize a fair return on investment" would suggest. Rarely is such a statement specific enough to help an organization improve. To be useful, a statement of purpose must be specific and operational, clearly understandable, and able to provide a direction. It must be realistic and practical, acceptable and meaningful to those running the organization. It must arouse the motivation to move forward.

STRUCTURE

Every member of the organization is not expected to do all the kinds of work required within it. Instead, there is a division of labor. Related work is lumped under organizational units. A way to coordinate efforts between the units is determined. The structure of a large organization is subdivided into regions or functional activities. It may be further subdivided within each of these into departments, divisions, sections, or units of various kinds. These vary widely from one organization to the next and depend to a great extent on purpose. Small organizations are likely to have more simple structures. All organizations, regardless of size, contain elements of structure.

FINANCIAL RESOURCES

Present in every organization is a financial system enabling it to invest in new efforts or withdraw its investments from less successful activities. Financial resources are important. Without them the organization would not be able to carry out its activities.

KNOW-HOW

To carry out the purposes of the organization its members supply technical skills and competence—know-how. No matter how clearly defined, how realistic, and how sound an organization's purposes may be, if its leaders are not competent to see that the purposes are obtained, the organization will flounder.

HUMAN INTERACTION

The human interaction property of the organization exists because the persons manning it must of necessity interact. They must exchange information, implement decisions made, and coordinate their efforts.

ORGANIZATION CULTURE

In any organization, over a period of time, a set of practices builds up. A way of organizational life becomes accepted. A climate is created; established practices become traditional. Everyone in the organization is expected to conform. Nonconformists may be punished. The punishment varies in kind as well as in degree. Sometimes it is very subtle. It may simply take the form of isolation of the person deviating from established practice, the cultural norm.

RESULTS

A seventh property of every organization is the generation of results that are in some way measurable in terms of organization purpose. If results show a loss, the major reason for sustaining the organization is absent and bankruptcy may be expected. Unless it provides a useful service that is in the public interest, in time the organization will go out of existence.

If the conglomeration of persons and equipment is truly an organization, it will have a realistic *purpose* clearly understood by all to provide a direction to their efforts; a *structure* that provides the necessary coordination of interlocking parts; access to *financial resources* needed to support decisions that enable it to obtain its purposes; the necessary technical skill and *know-how* among its personnel; a *human interaction process* supporting sound decision-making with a minimum of waste; a *culture* thoroughly understood and controlled which is an asset and not a liability; and, finally, an ability to achieve *results* so as to be effective within the free enterprise objective of realizing an acceptable return on investments. Results may also be in the form of a service that is in the public interest.

THE MEANING OF DEVELOPMENT

Once the meaning of "organization" is clear, "development" needs to be clarified. What characterizes an organization that is fully developed? The biggest task of an organization is integration. As used in relation to an organization, integration denotes the highest degree of attainment of these seven properties that can be achieved. Many fall short in development of one or more. They experience an endless parade of trials and troubles, ups and downs, low morale, resistance to needed change, and disregard by members of the problem of achieving results. Such organizations can be described as poorly integrated, for they have not achieved integration of the properties of organization.

The goal of Organization Development is to increase operational effectiveness by increasing the degree of integration of the seven properties of organization. Three of the seven properties are critical for development. They are purpose, human interaction, and organization culture. The others are more likely to be under managerial control and less likely to need attention through an Organization Development effort. It is not that one property is less important than the others, but that organizations usually insure the presence of the other four, whereas purpose, human interaction, and culture receive less attention.

It seems almost self-evident that everyone in an organization would have a clear idea of the *purpose* toward which its efforts were being directed. Yet this is seldom true. For many persons, an organization's purpose is fuzzy, unrealistic, and with little force as a motivator. A major Organization Development contribution is to clarify organization purposes and identify individual goals with them to increase efforts toward their attainment.[1,2]

As for the *human interaction* process, some styles of managing may decrease a person's desire to contribute to the organization's purpose. The kind of supervision exercised not only fails to make a subordinate feel "in" but even serves to make him feel "out." His efforts are alienated rather than integrated. This may hold true in the coordination of efforts between organized units. Relationships between divisions, for example, may deteriorate into the kind of disputes that can be reconciled only through arbitration by higher levels of management. At best, they are likely to encourage attitudes of appeasement and compromise.[3]

Finally, the organization's *culture*, its history, its traditions, its customs and habits which have evolved from earlier interaction and have become norms regulating human actions and conduct may be responsible for many of the organization's difficulties and a low degree of integration within it.

The basic theme of Organization Development is that the key to organization integration lies within the three organization properties, *purpose, human interaction process, and organization culture.* The executive who is trying to ferret out the source of problems in his organization may look at other properties. He may look to structure as preventing integration of effort and search for ways to change the organization chart. Organization structure far more often turns out to be a symptom of the integration problem than its cause. Or the executive may look at technical skills and know-how as the area of difficulty and search for better trained personnel. This area of technical competence often turns out to be a blind alley in which much effort is spent tracking down a problem. Second-rate human performance may be widespread but is not likely to be the cause of ineffectiveness. Competence is often present but poorly utilized. Finally, he may seize upon the absence of positive results as a difficulty and jump into finding ways to achieve greater earnings by cutting costs, meanwhile oblivious to the possibility that the organization's troubles might be in its culture or the interaction process. The concentration upon results may also be treating the symptom rather than finding the causes of the problem, which are probably rigidities of interaction, lack of clarity of purpose, and low morale of organization members who feel "out" rather than identified with the organization.

Organization Development deliberately shifts the emphasis away from the organization's structure, from human technical skill, from wherewithal and results per se as it diagnoses the organization's ills. Focusing on organization purpose, the human interaction process, and organization culture, it accepts these as the areas in which problems are preventing the fullest possible integration within the organization. Once an organization has moved to the point at which the three key properties are fully developed, the problems that originally seemed to be related to the others are more easily corrected.

SIX-PHASE APPROACH

How, specifically, does one go about Organization Development? The Managerial Grid is one way of achieving it. The six-phase approach provides the various methods and activities for doing so.

The Managerial Grid is a description of various approaches men use in managing. It is used to summarize management practices and compare them with behavioral science findings. It identifies five kinds of managerial behavior based on two key variables—concern for results and concern for people. *(See Exhibit 25-1.)*

Phase 1 of the six-phase approach involves study of *The Managerial Grid*. Managers learn the Grid concepts in seminars of a week's length.

These seminars are conducted both on a "public" and on an internal basis. They involve hard work. The program requires 30 or more hours of guided study before the beginning of the seminar week. A seminar usually begins Sunday afternoon, and participants work morning, afternoon, and evening through the following Friday.

The sessions include investigation by each man of his own managerial approach and alternative ways of managing which he is able to learn, experiment with, and apply. He measures and evaluates his team effectiveness in solving problems with others. He also studies methods of team action. A high point of Grid Seminar learning is when he receives a critique of his style of managerial thought and performance from other members of his team. The emphasis is on his style of managing, not on his character or personality traits. Another high point of the Grid Seminar

Exhibit 25-1

THE MANAGERIAL GRID

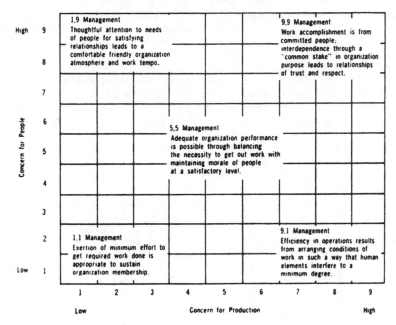

is when the manager critiques the style of his organization's culture—its traditions, precedents, and past practices—and begins to consider steps for increasing the effectiveness of the whole organization.

A participant in a Grid Seminar can expect to gain insight into his own and other managerial approaches and develop new ways to solve managerial problems. He can expect to improve his team effectiveness skills. He will on completion of Phase 1 have new standards of candor to bring to work activities and a greater awareness of the effects of his company's culture upon the regulation of work.

Comments are often heard to the effect, "The Grid has helped me to better understanding and is useful in many aspects of my life." But the vital question is in the use made of Phase 1 learning. The test for the manager is usefulness on the job. To direct this usefulness to the

work situation, and incidentally enhance it from a personal point of view, one proceeds to Phase 2.

Phase 2 is Work Team Development. As the title suggests, work team development is concerned with development of the individual and the work team. Phases 1 and 2 are often viewed as *management* development, while Phases 3 through 6 move into true *Organization* Development. The purpose of Phase 2 is to aid work team members to apply their Phase 1 learning directly to the operation of their team.

Individual effort is the raw material out of which sound teamwork is built. It cannot be had just for the asking. Barriers that prevent people from talking out their problems need to be overcome before their full potential can be realized.

Work Team Development starts with the key executive and those who report to him. It then moves down through the organization. Each supervisor sits down with his subordinates as a team. They study their barriers to work effectiveness and plan ways to overcome them.

An important result to be expected from the Phase 2 effort is teamwide agreement on ground rules for team operation. The team may also be expected to learn to use critique to improve teamwork on the job. Teamwork is increased through improving communication, control, and problem solving. Getting greater objectivity into work behavior is vital to improved teamwork. A team analysis of the team culture and operating practices precedes the setting of goals for improvement of the team operation along with a time schedule for achieving these goals. Tied into the goal-setting for the team is personal goal-setting by team members. This might be a goal for trying to change aspects of behavior so as to increase a member's contribution to teamwork. Setting standards for achieving excellence are involved throughout the process.

Phase 3 is Intergroup Development. It represents the first step in Grid OD that is applied to organization components rather than to individuals. Its purpose is to achieve *better problem-solving between groups through a closer integration of units that have working interrelationships.*

Managers examine and analyze these working relationships to strengthen and unify the organization across the board. Some dramatic examples of successful Phase 3 applications between labor and management groups are on record.[4] Other units that might appropriately be involved in Phase 3 would be a field unit and the headquarters group to whom it reports, or two sections within a division, or a region and its reporting parent group. It is the matter of coordination between such units that is the target of Phase 3. Problems of integration may be problems of function or merely problems in terms of level.

Management is inclined to solve the problem of functional coordination by setting up systems of reporting and centralized planning. Misunderstandings or disagreements between levels are often viewed as "a communications problem." Phase 3, in recognition that many problems are relationship problems, seeks closer integration of units through the exchange and comparison of group images as set forth by the members of two groups. Areas of misunderstanding are identified while conditions are created to reduce such intergroup problems and plan steps of operational coordination between the groups. Only groups that stand in a direct, problem-solving relationship with one another and share a need for improved coordination participate in Phase 3 intergroup development. And only those members with key responsibilities for solving the coordination problem are participants.

The activities of Phase 3 naturally follow Phase 2 because when there is conflict between working teams, if the teams themselves have already had the opportunity to solve their internal problems, they are prepared to engage in activities designed to solve their problem of working together. Phase 3 also can be expected to clear the decks for Phases 4 and 5. Any past intergroup problems that were barriers to coordinated effort are solved before the total Organization Development effort is launched in the latter phases. A successful Phase 3 will link groups vertically and horizontally and reduce intergroup blockages. This increases the problem-solving between departments, divisions, and other segments wherever coordination of effort is a vital necessity. Persons who have participated in Phase 3 report improved intergroup relationships and express appreciation of the team management concept, pointing out that it reverses the traditional procedure in which criticism flows from one level of management down to the next.

Phase 4 calls for the *Production of an*

Organization Blueprint. If Phases 1, 2, and 3 represent pruning the branches, Phase 4 gets at the root structure. A long-range blueprint is developed to insure that the basic strategies of the organization are "right." The immediate goal is to set up a model that is both realistic and obtainable for an organization's system for the future. How is this done? The existing corporate entity is momentarily set aside while an ideal concept is drawn up representing how it would be organized and operated if it were truly effective. The optimal organization blueprint is produced as a result of a policy diagnosis based on study of a model organization culture. The blueprint is drawn up by the top team and moves down through lower levels. The outcome is organization-wide understanding of the blueprint for the future.

It can be expected that as a result of Phase 4, the top team will have set a direction of performance goals to be achieved. Individuals and work teams will have developed understanding and commitment to both general and specific goals to be achieved.

Phase 5 is Blueprint Implementation. That is, Phase 5 is designed for the carrying out of the organizational plan through activities that change the organization from what it "is" to what it "should be." A Phase 5 may spread over several years, but as a result there comes about the effective realization of the goals that have been set in Phase 4 and specific accomplishments, depending on concrete issues facing the organization. During Phase 5, the members who are responsible for the organization achieve agreement and commitment to courses of action that represent steps to implement the Phase 4 blueprint for the future.

Phase 6 is stabilization. It is for reinforcing and making habitual the new patterns of management achieved in Phases 1 through 5. Organization members identify tendencies to slip back into the older and less effective patterns of work and take corrective action. Phase 6 involves an over-all critique of the state of the OD effort for the purpose of replanning for even greater effectiveness. It is not only to support and strengthen the changes achieved through earlier activities, but also to identify weaknesses and plan ways of eliminating them. By the time Phase 6 is under way, the stabilization of new communication, control, and problem-solving approaches should be evident. Moreover, there should be complete managerial confidence and competence in resisting the pressures to revert to old managerial habits.

NOTES

1. Robert R. Blake, Jane S. Mouton, L. B. Barnes, and L. E. Greiner, "Breakthrough in Organization Develpment," *Harvard Business Review.* Soldiers Field, Massachusetts; November-December 1964.

2. Bernard Portis, "Management Training for Organization Development," *The Business Quarterly.* London, Canada; Summer 1965.

3. Robert R. Blake, Herbert A. Shepard, and Jane S. Mouton, *Managing Intergroup Conflict in Industry.* Houston: Gulf Publishing Company; 1964.

4. Robert R. Blake, Jane S. Mouton, and R. L. Sloma, "The Union-Management Intergroup Laboratory," *Journal of Applied Behavioral Science.* January-March 1965.

26. Organizations of the Future*

WARREN G. BENNIS

Recently, I predicted that in the next 25 to 50 years we will participate in the end of bureaucracy as we know it and the rise of new social systems better suited to 20th Century demands of industrialization.[1] This forecast was based on the evolutionary principle that every age develops an organizational form appropriate to its genius and that the prevailing form of pyramidal-hierarchial organization, known by sociologists as "bureaucracy" and most businessmen as "that damn bureaucracy," was out of joint with contemporary realities.

I realize now that my prediction is already a distinct reality so that prediction is foreshadowed by practice.

I should like to make clear that by "bureaucracy" I mean the typical organizational structure that coordinates the business of most human organization we know of: industry, government, university, R & D labs, military, religious, voluntary, and so forth.

Bureaucracy, as I refer to it here, is a useful social invention, perfected during the Industrial Revolution to organize and direct the activities of the business firm. Max Weber, the German sociologist who developed the theory of bureaucracy around the turn of the century, once described bureaucracy as a social machine.

The bureaucratic "machine model" was developed as a reaction against the personal subjugation, nepotism, cruelty, and capricious and subjective judgments that often passed for managerial practices during the early days of the Industrial Revolution Bureaucracy emerged out of the need for more predictability, order, and precision. It was an organization ideally suited to the values and the demands of Victorian Empire. And just as bureaucracy emerged as a creative response to a radically new age, so today new organizational shapes and forms are surfacing before our eyes.

I shall try first to show why the conditions of our modern industrialized world will bring about the decline of bureaucracy and force a reconsideration of new organizational structures. Then, I will suggest a rough model of the organization of the future. Finally, I shall set forth the new tasks and challenges for the training and development manager.

WHY IS BUREAUCRACY VULNERABLE?

There are at least four relevant threats to bureaucracy. The first is a human, basically psychological one, which I shall return to later on, while the other three spring from extraordinary changes in our environment. The latter three are (1) rapid and unexpected change, (2) growth in size where volume of organization's traditional activities is not enough to sustain growth, and (3) complexity of modern technology where integration of activities and persons of very diverse, highly specialized competence is required.[2]

*Source: From Personnel Administration (September-October 1967). Copyright © 1967 International Personnel Management Association. Reprinted by permission of the International Personnel Management Association, 1617 Duke St., Arlington, VA 22314.

It might be useful to examine the extent to which these conditions exist *right now*.

RAPID AND UNEXPECTED CHANGE

It may be enough simply to cite the knowledge and population explosion. More revealing, however, are the statistics that demonstrate these events:

- Our productivity per man hour now doubles almost every 20 years rather than every 40 years, which was true before World War II.
- The federal government alone spent 16 billion in R&D activities in 1965 and will spend 35 billion by 1980.
- The time lag between a technical discovery and recognition of its commercial uses was 30 years before World War I, 16 years between the wars, and only 9 years since World War II.
- In 1946 only 30 cities in the world had populations of more than one million. Today there are 80. In 1930 there were 40 people for each square mile of the earth's land surface. Today, there are 63. By the year 2,000, there are expected to be 142.

GROWTH IN SIZE

Not only have more organizations grown larger, but they have become more complex and more international. Firms like Standard Oil of New Jersey (with 57 foreign affiliates), Socony Mobil, National Cash Register, Singer, Burroughs, and Colgate-Palmolive derive more than half their income or earnings from foreign sales. A long list of others, such as Eastman Kodak, Pfizer, Caterpillar Tractor, International Harvester, Corn Products, and Minnesota Mining and Manufacturing make from 30 to 50 percent of their sales abroad.[3] General Motors' sales are not only nine times those of Volkswagen, they are also bigger than the gross national product of The Netherlands and well over those of a hundred other countries. If we have seen the sun set on the British Empire, it will be a long time before it sets on the empires of General Motors, ITT, Royal Dutch/Shell and Unilever.

TODAY'S ACTIVITIES REQUIRE PERSONS OF VERY DIVERSE, HIGHLY SPECIALIZED COMPETENCE

Numerous dramatic examples can be drawn from studies of labor markets and job mobility. At some point during the past decade, the U.S. became the first nation in the world ever to employ more people in *service occupations* than in the production of tangible goods. Examples of this trend are:

- In the field of education, the *increase* in employment between 1950 and 1960 was greater than the total number employed in the steel, copper, and aluminum industries.
- In the field of health, the *increase* in employment between 1950 and 1960 was greater than the total number employed in automobile manufacturing in either year.
- In financial firms, the *increase* in employment between 1950 and 1960 was greater than total employment in mining in 1960.[4]

Rapid change, hurried growth, and increase in specialists: with these three logistical conditions we should expect bureaucracy to decline.

CHANGE IN MANAGERIAL BEHAVIOR

Earlier I mentioned a fourth factor which seemed to follow along with the others, though its exact magnitude, nature, and antecedents appear more obscure and shadowy due to the relative difficulty of assigning numbers to it. This factor stems from the personal observation that over the past decade there has been a fundamental change in the basic philosophy that underlies managerial behavior. The change in philosophy is reflected most of all in:

- A new concept of *Man*, based on increased knowledge of his complex and shifting needs, which replaces an oversimplified, innocent push-button idea of man.
- A new concept of *power*, based on col-

laboration and reason, which replaces a model of power based on coercion and threat.

- A new concept of *organization values*, based on humanistic-democratic ideals, which replaces the depersonalized mechanistic value system of bureaucracy.

These transformations of Man, power, and values have gained wide intellectual acceptance in management quarters. They have caused a terrific amount of rethinking on the part of many organizations. They have been used as a basis for policy formulation by many large-scale organizations. This philosophy is clearly not compatible with bureaucratic practices.

The primary cause of this shift in management philosophy stems not from the bookshelf but from the manager himself. Many of the behavioral scientists, like McGregor or Likert, have clarified and articulated—even legitimized—what managers have only half registered to themselves. I am convinced that the success of McGregor's *The Human Side of Enterprise* was based on a rare empathy for a vast audience of managers who were wistful for an alternative to a mechanistic conception of authority. It foresaw a vivid utopia of more authentic human relationships than most organizational practices allow. Furthermore, I suspect that the desire for relationships has little to do with a profit motive *per se*, though it is often rationalized as doing so.[5] The real push for these changes stems from some powerful needs, not only to humanize the organization, but to use the organization as a crucible of personal growth and development, for self-realization.[6]

CORE ORGANIZATION PROBLEMS

As a result of these changes affecting organizations of the future, new problems and tasks are emerging. They fall, I believe, into five major categories, which I visualize as the core tasks confronting organizations of the future.

1. *Integration* encompasses the entire range of issues having to do with the incentives, rewards, and motivation of the individual and how the organization succeeds or fails in adjusting to these needs. In other words, it is the ratio between individual needs and organizational demands that creates the transaction most satisfactory to both. The problem of *integration* grows out of our "consensual society," where personal attachments play a great part, where the individual is appreciated, in which there is concern for his well-being, not just in a veterinary-hygiene sense, but as a moral, integrated personality.

2. The problem of *social influence* is essentially the problem of power and how power is distributed. It is a complex issue and alive with controversy, partly because of an ethical component and partly because studies of leadership and power distribution can be interpreted in many ways, and almost always in ways which coincide with one's biases (including a cultural leaning toward democracy).

The problem of power has to be seriously reconsidered because of dramatic situational changes that make the possibility of one-man rule or the "Great Man" not necessarily "bad" but impractical. I am referring to changes in the role of top management. Peter Drucker, over 12 years ago, listed 41 major responsibilities of the chief executive and declared that "90 percent of the trouble we are having with the chief executive's job is rooted in our superstition of the one-man chief."[7] The broadening product base of industry, impact of new technology, the scope of international operations, make one-man control quaint, if not obsolete.

3. The problem of *collaboration* grows out of the very same social processes of conflict and stereotyping, and centrifugal forces that divide nations and communities. They also employ furtive,

Table 26-1

HUMAN PROBLEMS CONFRONTING CONTEMPORARY ORGANIZATIONS

Problem	Bureaucratic Solutions	New 20th Century Conditions
Integration. The problem of how to integrate individual needs and organizational goals.	No solution because of no problem. Individual vastly over-simplified, regarded as passive instrument. Tension between "personality" and role disregarded.	Emergence of human sciences and understanding of man's complexity. Rising aspirations. Humanistic-democratic ethos.
Social Influence. The problem of the distribution of power and sources of power and authority.	An explicit reliance on legal-rational power, but an implicit usage of coercive power. In any case, a confused, ambiguous shifting complex of competence, coercion, and legal code.	Separation of management from ownership. Rise of trade unions and general education. Negative and unintended effects of authoritarian rule.
Collaboration. The problem of producing mechanisms for the control of conflict.	The "rule of hierarchy" to resolve conflicts between ranks and the "rule of coordination" to resolve conflict between horizontal groups. "Loyalty."	Specialization and professionalization and increased need for interdependence. Leadership too complex for one-man rule or omniscience.
Adaptation. The problem of responding appropriately to changes induced by the environment.	Environment stable, simple, and predictable; tasks routine. Adapting to change occurs in haphazard and adventitious ways. Unanticipated consequences abound.	External environment of firm more "turbulent," less predictable. Unprecedented rate of technological change.
Revitalization. The problem of growth and decay.	Underlying assumption that the future will be certain and basically similar, if not more so, to the past.	Rapid changes in technologies, tasks, manpower, raw materials, norms and values of society, goals of enterprise and society all make constant attention to the process of revision imperative.

often fruitless, always crippling mechanisms of conflict resolution: avoidance or suppression, annihilation of the weaker party by the stronger, sterile compromises, and unstable collusions and coalitions. Particularly as organizations become more complex they fragment and divide, building tribal patterns and symbolic codes which often work to exclude others (secrets and noxious jargon, for example) and on occasion to exploit differences for inward (and always fragile) harmony. Some large organizations, in fact, can be understood only through an analysis of their cabals, cliques, and satellites, where a venture into adjacent spheres of interest is taken under cover of darkness and fear of ambush. Dysfunctional intergroup conflict is so easily stimulated, that one wonders if it is rooted in our archaic heritage when man struggled, with an imperfect symbolic code and early consciousness, for his territory. Robert R. Blake in his experiments has shown how simple it is to induce conflict, how difficult to arrest it.[8] Take two groups of people who have never been together before, and give them a task that will be judged by an impartial jury. In less than one hour, each group devolves into a tightly-knit band with all the symptoms of an "in-group." They regard their product as a "masterwork" and the other group's as "commonplace" at best. "Other" becomes "enemy"; "We are good; they are bad. We are right; they are wrong."[9]

Jaap Rabbie, conducting experiments on the antecedents of intergroup conflict at the University of Utrecht, has been amazed by the ease with which conflict and stereotype develop.[10] He brings into the experimental room two groups and distributes green name tags and green pens to one group and refers to it as the "green group." He distributes red pens and red name tags to the other group and refers to it as the "red group." The groups do not compete; they do not even interact. They are in sight of each other for only minutes while they silently complete a questionnaire. Only 10 minutes is needed to activate defensiveness and fear.

In a recent essay on animal behavior, Erikson develops the idea of "pseudo-species."[11] Pseudo-species act as if they were separate species created at the beginning of time by supernatural intent. He argues:

Man has evolved (by whatever kind of evolution and for whatever adaptive reasons) in pseudo-species, i.e., tribes, clans, classes, etc. Thus, each develops not only a *distinct sense of identity* but also a conviction of harboring the human identity, fortified against other pseudo-species by prejudices which mark them as extra-specific and inimical to "genuine" human endeavor. Paradoxically, however, newly born man is (to use Ernst Mayr's term) a generalist creature who could be made to fit into any number of pseudo-species and must, therefore, become "specialized" during a prolonged childhood. . . .

Modern organizations abound with pseudo-species, bands of specialists held together by the illusion of a unique identity and with a tendency to view other pseudo-species with suspicion and mistrust. Ways must be discovered to produce generalists and diplomats, and we must find more effective means of managing inevitable conflict and minimizing the pseudo-conflict. This is not to say that conflict is always avoidable and dysfunctional. Some types of conflict may lead to productive and creative ends.

4. The problem of *adaptation* is caused by our turbulent environment. The pyramidal structure of bureaucracy, where power was concentrated at the top, seemed perfect to "run a railroad." And undoubtedly for the routinized tasks of the nineteenth and early twentieth centuries, bureaucracy was and still is an eminently suitable social arrangement. However, rather than a placid and predictable environment, what predominates today is a dynamic and uncertain one in which there is a deepening interdependence among the economic and other facets of society.

5. Finally, the problem of *revitalization*. As Alfred North Whitehead says:

The art of free society consists first in the maintenance of the symbolic code, and secondly, in the fearlessness of revision. . . . Those societies which cannot combine reverence to their symbols with freedom of revision must ultimately decay . . .

Growth and decay emerge as the penultimate conditions of contemporary society. Organizations, as well as societies, must be concerned with those social structures that engender bouyancy, resilience, and a "fearlessness of revision."

I introduce the term "revitalization" to embrace all the social mechanisms that stagnate and regenerate and with the process of this cycle. The elements of revitalization are:

• An ability to learn from experience and to codify, store, and retrieve the relevant knowledge.
• An ability to "learn how to learn," that is, to develop methodologies for improving the learning process.
• An ability to acquire and use feedback mechanisms on performance, to develop a "process orientation," in short, to be self-analytical.
• An ability to direct one's own destiny.

These qualities have a good deal in common with what John Gardner calls "self-renewal." For the organization, it means conscious attention to its own evolution. Without a planned methodology and explicit direction, the enterprise will not realize its potential.

Integration, Distribution of Power, Collaboration, Adaptation, and Revitalization are the major human problems of the next 25 years. How organizations cope with and manage these tasks will undoubtedly determine the viability and growth of the enterprise.

ORGANIZATIONS
OF THE FUTURE[12]

Against this background I should like to set forth some of the conditions that will determine organizational life in the next two or three decades:

1. THE ENVIRONMENT

Rapid technological change and diversification will lead to interpenetration of the government with business.

Partnerships between government and business will be typical. It will be a truly mixed economy. Because of the immensity and expense of the projects, there will be fewer identical units competing for the same buyers and sellers. Organizations will become more interdependent.

The four main features of the environment are:

• Interdependence rather than competition.
• Turbulence and uncertainty rather than readiness and certainty.
• Large scale rather than small scale enterprises.
• Complex and multi-national rather than simple national enterprises.

2. POPULATION CHARACTERISTICS

The most distinctive characteristic of our society is, and will become even more so, education. Within 15 years, two-thirds of our population living in metropolitan areas will have attended college. Adult education is growing even faster, probably because of the rate of professional obsolescence. The Killian report showed that the average engineer required further education only 10 years after gaining his degree. It will become almost routine for the experienced physician, engineer, and executive to go back to school for advanced training every two or three years. Some 50 universities, in addition to a dozen large corporations, offer advanced management courses to successful men in the middle and upper ranks of business. Before World War II, only two such programs existed, both new, both struggling to get students.

All of this education is not just "nice," it is necessary. As Secretary of Labor Wirtz recently pointed out, computers can do the work of most high school graduates—cheaper and more effectively. Fifty years ago education was regarded as "nonwork" and intellectuals on the payroll were considered "overhead." Today the survival of the firm *depends* on the effective exploitation of brain power.

One other characteristic of the population which will aid our understanding of organizations of the future is increasing job mobility. The ease of transportation, coupled with the needs of a dynamic environment, change drastically the idea of "owning" a job—or "having roots." Already 20 percent of our population change their mailing address at least once a year.

3. WORK VALUES

The increased level of education and mobility will change the values we hold about work. People will be more intellectually committed to their *professional* careers and will probably require more involvement, participation, and autonomy.

Also, people will be more "other-directed," taking cues for their norms and values from their immediate environment rather than tradition. We will tend to rely more heavily on temporary social arrangements.[13] We will tend to have relationships rather than relatives.

4. TASKS AND GOALS

The tasks of the organization will be more technical, complicated, and unprogrammed. They will rely on intellect instead of muscle. And they will be too complicated for one person to comprehend, to say nothing of control. Essentially, they will call for the collaboration of specialists in a project or a team-form of organization.

There will be a complication of goals. Business will increasingly concern itself with its adaptive or innovative-creative capacity. In addition, meta-goals will have to be articulated; that is, supra-goals which shape and provide the foundation for the goal structure. For example, one meta-goal might be a system for detecting new and changing goals; another could be a system for deciding priorities among goals.

Finally, more conflict and contradiction can be expected from diverse standards of organizational effectiveness. One reason for this is that professionals tend to identify more with the goals of their profession than with those of their immediate employer. University professors can be used as a case in point. Within the University, there may be a conflict between teaching and research. Often, more of a professor's income derives from outside sources, such as foundations and consultant work. They tend not to be good "company men" because they divide their loyalty between their professional values and organizational goals.

5. ORGANIZATION

The social structure of organizations of the future will have some unique characteristics. The key word will be "temporary"; there will be adaptive, rapidly changing *temporary systems*. These will be "task forces" organized around problems-to-be-solved by groups of relative strangers who represent a diverse set of professional skills. The groups will be arranged on an organic rather than mechanical model; they will evolve in response to a problem rather than to programmed role expectations. The "executive" thus becomes a coordinator or "linking pin" between various task forces. He must be a man who can speak the diverse languages of research with skills to relay information and to mediate between groups. People will be evaluated not vertically according to rank and status, but flexibly and functionally according to skill and professional training. Organizational charts will consist of project groups rather than functional groups. This trend is already visible today in the aerospace and construction industries, as well as many professional and consulting firms.

Adaptive, problem-solving, temporary systems of diverse specialists, linked together by coordinating and task evaluating specialists in an organic flux—this is the organizational form that will gradually replace bureaucracy as we know it. As no catchy phrase comes to mind, I call this an organic-adaptive structure.

6. MOTIVATION

The organic-adaptive structure should increase motivation, and thereby effectiveness, because it enhances satisfactions intrinsic to the task. There is a harmony between the educated individual's need for meaningful, satisfactory, and creative tasks and a flexible organizational structure.

There will, however, also be reduced commitment to work groups, for these groups, as I have already mentioned, will be transient structures. I would predict that in the organic-adaptive system, people will learn to develop quick and intense relationships on the job, and learn to bear the loss of more enduring work relationships. Because of the added ambiguity of roles, time will have to be spent on continual rediscovery of the appropriate organizational mix.

The American experience of frontier neighbors, after all, prepares us for this, so I don't view "temporary systems" as such a grand departure. These "brief encounters" need not be more superficial than long and chronic ones. I have seen too many people, some occupying adjacent offices for many years, who have never really experienced or encountered each other. They look at each other with the same vacant stares as people do on buses and subways, and perhaps they are passengers waiting for their exit.

Europeans typically find this aspect of American life frustrating. One German expatriate told me of his disenchantment with "friendly Americans." At his first party in this country, he met a particularly sympathetic fellow and the two

of them fell into a warm conversation which went on for several hours. Finally, they had to leave to return to their homes, but like soul-mates, they couldn't part. They went down into the city street and walked round and round on this cold winter night, teeth chattering and arms bound. Finally, both stiff with cold, the American hailed a cab and went off with a wave. The European was stunned. He didn't know his new "friend's" name. He never saw or heard from him again. "That's your American friendship," he told me.

That is American friendship: intense, spontaneous, total involvement, unpredictable in length, impossible to control. They are happenings, simultaneously "on" and transitory and then "off" and then new lights and new happenings.

A Swiss woman in Max Frisch's *I'm Not Stiller* sums it up this way: "Apparently all these frank and easy-going people did not expect anything else from a human relationship. There was no need for this friendly relationship to go on growing."[14]

TRAINING REQUIREMENTS FOR ORGANIZATIONS OF THE FUTURE

How can we best plan for the organizational developments I forecast? And how can training and development directors influence and direct this destiny? One thing is clear: There will be a dramatically new role for the manager of training and development. Let us look at some of the new requirements.

1. TRAINING FOR CHANGE

The remarkable aspect of our generation is its commitment to change, in thought and action. Can training and development managers develop an educational process which:

• Helps us to identify with the adaptive process without fear of losing our identity?
• Increases our tolerance for ambiguity without fear of losing intellectual mastery?
• Increases our ability to collaborate with-

out fear of losing individuality?
• Develops a willingness to participate in our own social evolution while recognizing implacable forces?

Putting it differently, it seems to me that *we should be trained in an attitude toward inquiry and novelty rather than the particular content of a job;* training for change means developing "learning men."

2. SYSTEMS COUNSELING

It seems to me that management (and personnel departments) have failed to come to grips with the reality of *social systems*. It is embarrassing to state this after decades of research have been making the same point. We have proved that productivity can be modified by group norms, that training effects fade out and deteriorate if training goals are not compatible with the goals of the social system, that group cohesiveness is a powerful motivator, that intergroup conflict is a major problem facing modern organization, that individuals take many of their cues from their primary work group, that identification with the work group turns out to be the only stable predictor of productivity, and so on. Yet this evidence is so frequently ignored that I can only infer that there is something naturally preferable (almost an involuntary reflex) in locating the sources of all problems in the individual and diagnosing situations as functions of faulty individuals rather than as symptoms of malfunctioning social systems.

If this reflex is not arrested, it can have serious repercussions. In these new organizations, where roles will be constantly changing and certainly ambiguous, where changes in one sub-system will clearly affect other sub-systems, where diverse and multinational activities have to be coordinated and integrated, where individuals engage simultaneously in multiple roles and group memberships (and role conflict is endemic), a systems viewpoint

must be developed. Just as it is no longer possible to make any enduring change in a "problem child" without treating the entire family, it will not be possible to influence individual behavior without working with his particular sub-system. This means that our training and development managers of the future must perform the functions of *systems counselors.*

3. CHANGING MOTIVATION

The rate at which professional-technical-managerial types join organizations is higher than any other employment category. While it isn't fully clear what motivates them, two important factors emerge.

The first is a strong urge to "make it" professionally, to be respected by professional colleagues. Loyalty to an organization may increase if it encourages professional growth. Thus, the "good place to work" will resemble a super-graduate school, abounding with mature, senior colleagues, where the employee will work not only to satisfy organizational demands but, perhaps primarily, those of his profession.

The other factor involves the quest for self-realization, for personal growth which may not be task-related. That remark, I am well aware, questions four centuries of encrusted Protestant Ethic. And I feel uncertain as to how (or even *if*) these needs can be met by an organization. However, we must hope for social inventions to satisfy these new desires. Training needs to take more responsibility for attitudes about continuing education so that it is not considered a "retread" or a "repair factory" but a natural and inescapable aspect of work. The idea that education has a terminal point and that adults have somehow "finished" is old-fashioned. A "drop-out" should be redefined to mean anyone who *hasn't returned* to school.

However the problem of professional and personal growth is resolved, it is clear that many of our older forms of incentive, based on lower echelons of the need hierarchy, will have to be reconstituted.

4. SOCIALIZATION FOR ADULTS

In addition to continuing education, we have to face the problem of continuing socialization, or the institutional influences which society provides to create good citizens. Put simply, it means training in values, attitudes, ethics, and morals. We allot these responsibilities typically to the family, to church, to schools. We incorrectly assume that socialization stops when the individual comes of age. Most certainly, we are afraid of socialization for adults, as if it implies the dangers of a delayed childhood disease, like whooping cough.

Or to be more precise, we frown not on socialization, but on conscious and responsible control of it. In fact, our organizations are magnificent, if undeliberate, vehicles of socialization. They teach values, inculcate ethics, create norms, dictate right and wrong, influence attitudes necessary for success and all the rest. The men who succeed tend to be well socialized and the men who don't, are not: "Yeah, Jones was a marvelous worker, but he never fit in around here." And most universities grant tenure where their norms and values are most accepted, although this is rarely stated.

Taking conscious responsibility for the socialization process will become imperative in tomorrow's organization. And finding men with the right technical capability will not be nearly as difficult as finding men with the right set of values and attitudes. Of course, consciously guiding this process is a trying business, alive with problems, not the least being the ethical one: Do we have the right to shape attitudes and values? We really do not have a choice. Can we avoid it? How bosses lead and train subordinates, how individuals are treated, what and who gets rewarded,

the subtle cues transmitted and learned without seeming recognition, occur spontaneously. What we can choose are the mechanisms of socialization—how coercive we are, how much individual freedom we give, how we transmit values. What will be impermissible is a denial to recognize that we find some values more desirable and to accept responsibility for consciously and openly communicating them.

5. DEVELOPING PROBLEM-SOLVING TEAMS

One of the most difficult and important challenges for the training and development manager will be the task of promoting conditions for effective collaboration or building synergetic teams. Synergy is where individuals actually contribute more and perform better as a result of a collaborative and supportive environment. They play "over their heads," so to speak. The challenge I am referring to is the building of synergetic teams.

Of course, the job isn't an easy one. An easy way out is to adopt the "zero synergy" strategy. This means that the organization attempts to hire the best individuals it can and then permits them to "cultivate their own gardens." This is a strategy of isolation that can be observed in almost every university organization.

[Until universities take a serious look at their strategy of zero synergy, there is little hope that they will solve their vexing problems. The Berkeley protests were symptomatic of at least four self-contained, uncommunicating social systems (students, faculty, administration, trustees) without the trust, empathy, interaction (to say nothing of a tradition) to develop meaningful collaboration. To make matters even more difficult, if possible, academic types may, by nature (and endorsed by tradition) see themselves as "loners" and divergent to the majority. They all want to be independent together, so to speak. Academic narcissism goes a long way on the lecture platform but may be positively disruptive for developing a community.]

Another approach has the same effect but appears different. It is the pseudo-democratic style, in which a phony harmony and conflict-avoidance persists.

In addition to our lack of background and experience in building synergy (and our strong cultural biases against group efforts), teams take time to develop. They are like other highly complicated organisms and, just as we wouldn't expect a newborn to talk, we shouldn't expect a new team to work effectively from the start. Teams require trust and commitment and these ingredients require a period of gestation.

Expensive and time-consuming as it is, building synergetic and collaborative frameworks will become essential. The problems that confront us are too complex and diversified for one man or one discipline. They require a blending of skills, slants, and disciplines for their solution and only effective problem-solving *teams* will be able to get on with the job.

6. DEVELOPING SUPRA-ORGANIZATIONAL GOALS AND COMMITMENTS

The President of ABC (the fictitious name of a manufacturing company) was often quoted as saying:

"The trouble with ABC is that nobody aside from me ever gives one damn about the overall goals of this place. They're all seeing the world through the lenses of their departmental biases. What we need around here are people who wear the ABC hat, not the engineering hat or the sales hat or the production hat."

After he was heard muttering this rather typical president's dirge, a small group of individuals, who thought they could wear the ABC hat, formed a group they called the ABC HATS. They came from *various* departments and hierarchical levels and represented a

microcosm of the entire organization. The ABC HATS group has continued to meet over the past few years and has played a central role in influencing top policy.

It seems to me that training and development managers could affect the development of their organizations if they would encourage the formation of HATS groups. What worries me about the organization of the future, of specialized professionals and an international executive staff, is that their professional and regional outlook brings along with it only a relative truth and a distortion of reality. This type of organization is extremely vulnerable to the hardening of pseudo-species and a compartmentalized approach to problems.

Training and development can be helpful in a number of ways:

• They can identify and support those individuals who are "linking pins" individuals who have a facility for psychological and intellectual affinity with a number of diverse languages and cultures. These individuals will become the developers of problem-solving teams.
• They can perform the HATS function, which is another way of saying that training and development managers should be managers who keep over-all goals in mind and modulate the professional biases which are intrinsic to the specialists' work.
• They can work at the interfaces of the pseudo-species in order to create more inter-group understanding and interface articulation.

Today, we see each of the intellectual disciplines burrowing deeper into its own narrow sphere of interest. (Specialism, by definition, implies a peculiar slant, a segmented vision. A cloak and suit manufacturer went to Rome and managed to get an audience with His Holiness. Upon his return a friend asked him, "What did the Pope look like? The tailor answered, "A 41 Regular.") Yet, the most interesting problems turn up at the intersection between disciplines and it may take an outsider to identify these. Even more often, the separate disciplines go their crazy-quilt way and rely more and more on internal standards of evidence and competence. They dismiss the outsider as an amateur with a contemptuous shrug. The problem with intellectual effort today (and I include my own field of organization psychology) is that no one is developing the grand synthesis.

Organizations, too, require "philosophers," individuals who provide articulation between seemingly inimical interests, who break down the pseudospecies, and who transcend vested interests, regional ties, and professional biases in arriving at the solution to problems.

To summarize, I have suggested that the training and development director of the future has in store at least six new and different functions: (1) training for change, (2) systems counseling, (3) developing new incentives, (4) socializing adults, (5) building collaborative, problem-solving teams, and (6) developing supra-organizational goals and commitments. Undoubtedly there are others and some that cannot be anticipated. It is clear that they signify a fundamentally different role for personnel management from "putting out fires" and narrow maintenance functions. If training and development is to realize its true promise, its role and its image must change from maintenance to innovation.

I have seen this new role develop in a number of organizations, not easily or overnight, but pretty much in the way I have described it here. It might be useful to review briefly the conditions present in the cases I know about:

The personnel manager or some subsystem within personnel (it might be called "employee relations" or "industrial relations" or "career development") took an *active, innovative* role with respect to organizational goals and forcibly took responsibility for organizational growth and development.

Secondly, this group shifted its emphasis away from personnel functions *per se* (like compensation and selection) and toward organizational problems, like developing effective patterns of collaboration, or fostering an innovative atmosphere or reducing inter-group conflict, or organizational goal-setting and long-run planning.

Thirdly, this group developed a close working relationship to various subsystems in the organization, an organic, task-oriented relationship, not the frequently observed mechanical "line-staff" relationship.

Fourthly, they were viewed as full-fledged members of the management team, instead of the "head-shrinkers" or the "headquarters group." This was the hardest to establish in all cases, but turned out to be the most important. In fact, in one case, the man responsible for spearheading the organizational development effort has recently taken an important line job. The reverse happens too. Line management participates in so-called personnel activities, almost as if they are an adjunct to staff. Distinctions between line and staff blur in this context and an organic linkage develops, often serving as a prototype of a collaborative, problem-solving team.

One single factor stands out in retrospect over all others. There was always the conviction and the ability to make the training and development department the leading edge, the catalyst for organizational change and adaptability. Rather than performing the more traditional role, these groups became centers for innovation and organizational revitalization, and their leaders emerged as change-agents, the new managers of tomorrow's organizations.

I should now add another point in conclusion. It emerges from the previous points. They describe a far more autonomous, organizationally influential, self-directed role than trainers have been given or have asked for in the past.

If the training group is to be concerned with adult socialization, for example, it would be myopically irresponsible if not worse for them to define socialization in terms of momentary needs of the organization. Rather, they must take at least some of the responsibility for enunciating the goals and conditions of the enterprise. In a way, their systems counseling function is "organizational socialization." If they take responsibility for socializing both the members as people and the organization as a human system, then they must have values and standards which are somehow prior and outside both.

In fact, the emerging role I outline implies that the roles of the top management and training director become more inter-changeable than ever before.

NOTES

1. "The Decline of Bureaucracy and Organizations of the Future." Invited address presented to the Division of Industrial and Business Psychology at the American Psychological Association meeting, Los Angeles, Calif., Sept. 5, 1964.

2. A. H. Rubenstein and C. Haberstroh, *Some Theories of Organization* (Revised Edition). Irwin-Dorsey, Homewood, Ill., 1966.

3. Richard J. Barber, "American Business Goes Global." *The New Republic*. April 30, 1966, 14-18.

4. Victor R. Fuchs, "The First Service Economy." *The Public Interest*. Winter 1966, 7-17.

5. Chris Argyris, *Interpersonal Competence and Organizational Effectiveness*. Irwin-Dorsey, Homewood, Ill., 1962.

6. *The Varieties of Religious Experience*. The Modern Library, Random House, N. Y., 1902, 475-476.

7. D. Ron Daniel, "Team at the Top." *Harvard Business Review*, March-April 1965, 74-82.

8. Robert R. Blake, Herbert A. Shepard and Jane S. Mouton, *Managing Intergroup Conflict in Industry*, Gulf Publishing, Houston, Texas, 1964.

9. Carl Rogers, "Dealing with Psychological Tensions." *Journal of Applied Behavioral Sciences*, Jan.-Feb.-March 1965, 6-24.

10. Personal communication, Jan. 1966.

11. Erik Erikson, "Ontogeny of Ritualization." Paper presented to the Royal Society in June 1965.

12. Adapted from my earlier paper, "Beyond Bureaucracy," *Trans-Action*, July-August 1965.

13. "On Temporary Systems." In M. B. Miles (ed.), *Innovation in Education*, Bureau of Publications, Teachers College, Columbia University, N. Y., 1964, 437-490.

14. Penguin Books, Harmondsworth Middlesex. 1961, p. 244.

27. Organization Development: Objectives, Assumptions and Strategies*

WENDELL FRENCH

Organization development refers to a long-range effort to improve an organization's problem solving capabilities and its ability to cope with changes in its external environment with the help of external or internal behavioral-scientist consultants, or change agents, as they are sometimes called. Such efforts are relatively new but are becoming increasingly visible within the United States, England, Japan, Holland, Norway, Sweden, and perhaps in other countries. A few of the growing number of organizations which have embarked on organization development (OD) efforts to some degree are Union Carbide, Esso, TRW Systems, Humble Oil, Weyerhaeuser, and Imperial Chemical Industries Limited. Other kinds of institutions, including public school systems, churches, and hospitals, have also become involved.

Organization development activities appear to have originated about 1957 as an attempt to apply some of the values and insights of laboratory training to total organizations. The late Douglas McGregor, working with Union Carbide, is considered to have been one of the first behavioral scientists to talk systematically about and to implement an organization development program.[1] Other names associated with such early efforts are Herbert Shepard and Robert Blake who, in collaboration with the Employee Relations Department of the Esso Company, launched a program of laboratory training (sensitivity training) in the company's various refineries. This program emerged in 1957 after a headquarters human relations research division began to view itself as an internal consulting group offering services to field managers rather than as a research group developing reports for top management.[2]

OBJECTIVES OF TYPICAL OD PROGRAMS

Although the specific interpersonal and task objectives of organization development programs will vary according to each diagnosis of organizational problems, a number of objectives typically emerge. These objectives reflect problems which are very common in organizations:

1. To increase the level of trust and support among organizational members.
2. To increase the incidence of confrontation of organizational problems, both within groups and among groups, in contrast to "sweeping problems under the rug."
3. To create an environment in which authority of assigned role is augmented by authority based on knowledge and skill.
4. To increase the openness of communications laterally, vertically, and diagonally.

*Source: From California Management Review, Vol. 12, No. 2, pp. 23-34. Copyright © 1969 by the Regents of the University of California. Reprinted by permission of the Regents. Some subheadings shortened.

5. To increase the level of personal enthusiasm and satisfaction in the organization.

6. To find synergistic solutions[3] to problems with greater frequency. (Synergistic solutions are creative solutions in which 2 plus 2 equals more than 4, and through which all parties gain more through cooperation than through conflict.)

7. To increase the level of self and group responsibility in planning and implementation.[4]

DIFFICULTIES IN CATEGORIZING

Before describing some of the basic assumptions and strategies of organization development, it would be well to point out that one of the difficulties in writing about such a "movement" is that a wide variety of activities can be and are subsumed under this label. These activities have varied all the way from inappropriate application of some "canned" management development program to highly responsive and skillful joint efforts between behavioral scientists and client systems.

Thus, while labels are useful, they may gloss over a wide range of phenomena. The "human relations movement," for example, has been widely written about as though it were all bad or all good. To illustrate, some of the critics of the movement have accused it of being "soft" and a "handmaiden of the Establishment," of ignoring the technical and power systems of organizations, and of being too naively participative. Such criticisms were no doubt warranted in some circumstances, but in other situations may not have been at all appropriate. Paradoxically, some of the major insights of the human relations movement, e.g., that the organization can be viewed as a social system and that subordinates have substantial control over productivity have been assimilated by its critics.

In short, the problem is to distinguish between appropriate and inappropriate programs, between effectiveness and ineffectiveness, and between relevancy and irrelevancy. The discussion which follows will attempt to describe the "ideal" circumstances for organization development programs, as well as to point out some pitfalls and common mistakes in organization change efforts.

RELEVANCY TO DIFFERENT TECHNOLOGIES AND ORGANIZATION SUBUNITS

Research by Joan Woodward[5] suggests that organization development efforts might be more relevant to certain kinds of technologies and organizational levels, and perhaps to certain workforce characteristics, than to others. For example, OD efforts may be more appropriate for an organization devoted, to prototype manufacturing than for an automobile assembly plant. However, experiments in an organization like Texas Instruments suggest that some manufacturing efforts which appear to be inherently mechanistic may lend themselves to a more participative, open management style than is often assumed possible.[6]

However, assuming the constraints of a fairly narrow job structure at the rank-and-file level, organization development efforts may inherently be more productive and relevant at the managerial levels of the organization. Certainly OD efforts are most effective when they start at the top. Research and development units—particularly those involving a high degree of interdependency and joint creativity among group members—also appear to be appropriate for organization development activities, if group members are currently experiencing problems in communicating or interpersonal relationships.

BASIC ASSUMPTIONS

Some of the basic assumptions about

people which underlie organization development programs are similar to "Theory Y" assumptions[7] and will be repeated only briefly here. However, some of the assumptions about groups and total systems will be treated more extensively. The following assumptions appear to underlie organization development efforts.[8]

ABOUT PEOPLE

Most individuals have drives toward personal growth and development, and these are most likely to be actualized in an environment which is both supportive and challenging.

Most people desire to make, and are capable of making, a much higher level of contribution to the attainment of organization goals than most organizational environments will permit.

ABOUT PEOPLE IN GROUPS

Most people wish to be accepted and to interact cooperatively with at least one small reference group, and usually with more than one group, e.g., the work group, the family group.

One of the most psychologically relevant reference groups for most people is the work group, including peers and the superior.

Most people are capable of greatly increasing their effectiveness in helping their reference groups solve problems and in working effectively together.

For a group to optimize its effectiveness, the formal leader cannot perform all of the leadership functions in all circumstances at all times, and all group members must assist each other with effective leadership and member behavior.

ABOUT PEOPLE IN
ORGANIZATIONAL SYSTEMS

Organizations tend to be characterized by overlapping, interdependent work groups, and the "linking pin" function of supervisors and others needs to be understood and facilitated.[9]

What happens in the broader organization affects the small work group and vice versa.

What happens to one subsystem (social, technological, or administrative) will affect and be influenced by other parts of the system.

The culture in most organizations tends to suppress the expression of feelings which people have about each other and about where they and their organizations are heading.

Suppressed feelings adversely affect problem solving, personal growth, and job satisfaction.

The level of interpersonal trust, support, and cooperation is much lower in most organizations than is either necessary or desirable.

"Win-lose" strategies between people and groups, while realistic and appropriate in some situations, are not optimal in the long run to the solution of most organizational problems.

Synergistic solutions can be achieved with a much higher frequency than is actually the case in most organizations.

Viewing feelings as data important to the organization tends to open up many avenues for improved goal setting, leadership, communications, problem solving, intergroup collaboration, and morale.

Improved performance stemming from organization development efforts needs to be sustained by appropriate changes in the appraisal, compensation, training, staffing, and task-specialization subsystem—in short, in the total personnel system.

VALUE AND BELIEF SYSTEMS OF BEHAVIORAL SCIENTIST-CHANGE AGENTS

While scientific inquiry, ideally, is value-free, the applications of science are not value-free. Applied behavioral scientist-organization development consultants tend to subscribe to a comparable set of values, although we should avoid the trap of assuming that they constitute a completely homogenous group. They do not.

One value, to which many behavioral scientist-change agents tend to give high priority, is that the needs and aspirations of human beings are the reasons for organized effort in society. They tend, therefore, to be developmental in their outlook and concerned with the long-range opportunities for the personal growth of people in organizations.

A second value is that work and life can become richer and more meaningful, and organized effort more effective and enjoyable, if feelings and sentiments are permitted to be a more legitimate part of the culture. A third value is a commitment to an action role, along with a commitment to research, in an effort to improve the effectiveness of organizations.[10] A fourth value—or perhaps a belief—is that improved competency in interpersonal and intergroup relationship will result in more effective organizations.[11] A fifth value is that behavioral science research and an examination of behavioral science assumptions and values are relevant and important in considering organizational effectiveness. While many change agents are perhaps overly action-oriented in terms of the utilization of their time, nevertheless, as a group they are paying more and more attention to research and to the examination of ideas.[12]

The value placed on research and inquiry raises the question as to whether the assumptions stated earlier are values, theory, or "facts." In my judgment, a substantial body of knowledge, including research on leadership, suggests that there is considerable evidence for these assumptions. However, to conclude that these assumptions are facts, laws, or principles would be to contradict the value placed by behavioral scientists on continuous research and inquiry. Thus, I feel that they should be considered theoretical statements which are based on provisional data.

This also raises the paradox that the belief that people are important tends to result in their being important. The belief that people can grow and develop in terms of personal and organizational competency tends to produce this result. Thus, values and beliefs tend to be self-fulfilling, and the question becomes "What do you choose to want to believe?" While this position can become Pollyannaish in the sense of not seeing the real world, nevertheless, behavioral scientist-change agents, at least this one, tend to place a value on optimism. It is a kind of optimism that says people can do a better job of goal setting and facing up to and solving problems, not an optimism that says the number of problems is diminishing.

It should be added that it is important that the values and beliefs of each behavioral science-change agent be made visible both to himself and to the client. In the first place, neither can learn to adequately trust the other without such exposure—a hidden agenda handicaps both trust building and mutual learning. Second, and perhaps more pragmatically, organizational change efforts tend to fail if a prescription is applied unilaterally and without proper diagnosis.

STRATEGY IN OD:
AN ACTION RESEARCH MODEL

A frequent strategy in organization development programs is based on what behavioral scientists refer to as an "action research model." This model involves extensive collaboration between the consultant (whether an external or an internal change agent) and the client group, data gathering, data discussion, and planning. While descriptions of this model vary in detail and terminology from author to author, the dynamics are essentially the same.[13]

Figure 27-1 summarizes some of the essential phases of the action research model, using an emerging organization

Figure 27-1

AN ACTION RESEARCH MODEL FOR ORGANIZATION DEVELOPMENT

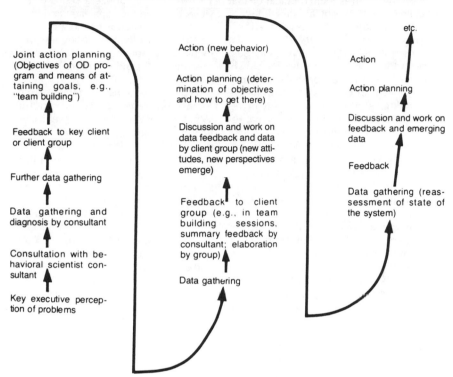

development program as an example. The key aspects of the model are diagnosis, data gathering, feedback to the client group, data discussion and work by the client group, action planning, and action. The sequence tends to be cyclical, with the focus on new or advanced problems as the client group learns to work more effectively together. Action research should also be considered a process, since, as William Foote Whyte says, it involves "a continuous gathering and analysis of human relations research data and the feeding of the findings into the organization in such a manner as to change behavior."[14] (Feedback we will define as nonjudgmental observations of behavior.)

Ideally, initial objectives and strategies of organization development efforts stem from a careful diagnosis of such matters as interpersonal and intergroup problems, decision-making processes, and communication flow which are currently being experienced by the client organization. As a preliminary step, the behavioral scientist and the key client (the president of a company, the vice president in charge of a division, the works manager or superintendent of a plant, a superintendent of schools, etc.), will make a joint initial assessment of the critical problems which need working on. Subordinates may also be interviewed in order to provide supplemental data. The diagnosis may very well indicate that the central problem is technological or that the key client is not at all willing or ready to examine the organization's problem-solving ability or his own managerial behavior.[15] Either could be a reason for postponing or moving slowly in the direction of organization development activities, although the technological problem may easily be related to deficiencies in interpersonal relationships or decision making. The diagnosis might also indicate the desirability of one or more additional specialists (in engineering, finance, or electronic data processing, for example) to simultaneously work with the organization.

This initial diagnosis, which focuses on the expressed needs of the client, is extremely critical. As discussed earlier, in the absence of a skilled diagnosis, the behavioral scientist-change agent would be imposing a set of assumptions and a set of objectives which may be hopelessly out of joint with either the current problems of the people in the organization or their willingness to learn new modes of behavior. In this regard, it is extremely important that the consultant hear and understand what the client is trying to tell him. This requires a high order of skill.[16]

Interviews are frequently used for data gathering in OD work for both initial diagnosis and subsequent planning sessions, since personal contact is important for building a cooperative relationship between the consultant and the client group. The interview is also important since the behavioral scientist-consultant is interested in spontaneity and in feelings that are expressed as well as cognitive matters. However, questionnaires are sometimes successfully used in the context of what is sometimes referred to as survey feedback, to supplement interview data.[17]

Data gathering typically goes through several phases. The first phase is related to diagnosing the state of the system and to making plans for organizational change. This phase may utilize a series of interviews between the consultant and the key client, or between a few key executives and the consultant. Subsequent phases focus on problems specific to the top executive team and to subordinate teams. *(See Figure 27-2.)*

Typical questions in data gathering or "problem sensing" would include: What problems do you see in your group, including problems between people, that are interfering with getting the job done the way you would like to see it done?; and what problems do you see in the broader organization? Such open-ended questions provide wide latitude on the part of the respondents and encourage a reporting of problems as the individual sees them. Such interviewing is usually conducted privately, with a commitment on the part of the consultant that the information will be used in such a way as to avoid unduly embarrassing anyone. The intent is to find out what common problems or themes emerge, with the data to be used constructively for both diagnostic and feedback purposes.

Two- or three-day offsite team-building or group problem-solving sessions typically become a major focal point in organization development programs. During these meetings the behavioral scientist frequently provides feedback to the group in terms of the themes which emerged in the problem-sensing interviews.[18] He may also encourage the group to determine which items or themes should have priority in terms of maximum utilization of time. These themes usually provide substantial and meaningful data for the group to begin work on. One-to-one interpersonal matters, both positive and negative, tend to emerge spontaneously as the participants gain confidence from the level of support sensed in the group.

Different consultants will vary in their mode of behavior in such sessions, but

Figure 27-2

ORGANIZATION DEVELOPMENT PHASES IN A
HYPOTHETICAL ORGANIZATION

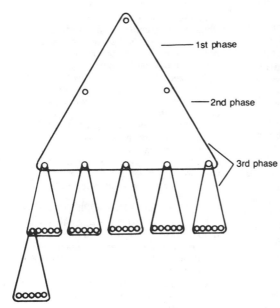

1st phase

2nd phase

3rd phase

1st phase. Data gathering, feedback and diagnosis—consultant and top executive only.

2nd phase. Data gathering, feedback, and revised diagnosis—consultant and two or more key staff or line people.

3rd phase. Data gathering and feedback to total top executive team in "team-building" laboratory, with or without key subordinates from level below.

4th and additional phases. Data gathering and team-building sessions with 2nd or 3rd level teams.
Subsequent phases. Data gathering, feedback, and interface problem-solving sessions across groups.
Simultaneous phases. Several managers may attend "stranger" T-Groups, courses in the management development program may supplement this learning.

will typically serve as "process" observers and as interpreters of the dynamics of the group interaction to the degree that the group expresses a readiness for such intervention. They also typically encourage people to take risks, a step at a time, and to experiment with new behavior in the context of the level of support in the group. Thus, the trainer-consultant(s) serves as a stimulant to new behavior but also as a protector. The climate which I try to build, for example, is: "Let's not tear down any more than we can build back together."[19] Further, the trainer-consultant typically works with the group to assist team members in improving their skills in diagnosing and facilitating group progress.[20]

It should be noted, however, that different groups will have different needs along a task-process continuum. For example, some groups have a need for intensive work on clarifying objectives; others may have the greatest need in the area of personal relationships. Further, the consultant or the chief consultant in a team of consultants involved in an organization development program will play a much broader role than serving as a T-group or team-building trainer. He will also play an important role in periodic data gathering and diagnosis and in joint long-range planning of the change efforts.[21]

LABORATORY TRAINING AND OD

Since organization development programs have largely emerged from T-group experience, theory, and research, and since laboratory training in one form or another tends to be an integral part of most such programs, it is

important to focus on laboratory training per se. As stated earlier, OD programs grew out of a perceived need to
relate laboratory training to the problems of ongoing organizations and a
recognition that optimum results could
only occur if major parts of the total social system of an organization were involved.

Laboratory training essentially
emerged around 1946, largely through a
growing recognition by Leland Bradford, Ronald Lippitt, Kenneth Benne,
and others, that human relations training which focused on the feelings and
concerns of the participants was frequently a much more powerful and viable form of education than the lecture
method. Some of the theoretical con-
structs and insights from which these
laboratory training pioneers drew
stemmed from earlier research by Lippitt, Kurt Lewin, and Ralph White. The
term "T-Group" emerged by 1949 as a
shortened label for "Basic Skill Training
Group"; these terms were used to identify the programs which began to
emerge in the newly formed National
Training Laboratory in Group Development (now NTL Institute for Applied
Behavioral Science).[22] "Sensitivity Training" is also a term frequently applied to
such training.

Ordinarily, laboratory training sessions have certain objectives in common. The following list, by two interna-
tionally known behavioral scientists,[23] is
probably highly consistent with the objectives of most programs:

SELF OBJECTIVES

Increased awareness of own feelings and
reactions, and own impact on others.

Increased awareness of feelings and
reactions of others, and their impact on
self.

Increased awareness of dynamics of
group action.

Changed attitudes toward self, others,
and groups, i.e., more respect for, tolerance for, and faith in self, others, and
groups.

Increased interpersonal competence,
i.e., skill in handling interpersonal and
group relationships toward more productive and satisfying relationships.

ROLE OBJECTIVES

Increased awareness of own organizational role, organizational dynamics, dynamics of larger social systems, and dynamics of the change process in self, small
groups, and organizations.

Changed attitudes toward own role, role
of others, and organizational relationships,
i.e., more respect for and willingness to
deal with others with whom one is interdependent, greater willingness to achieve
collaborative relationships with others
based on mutual trust.

Increased interpersonal competence in
handling organizational role relationships
with superiors, peers, and subordinates.

ORGANIZATIONAL OBJECTIVES

Increased awareness of, changed attitudes toward, and increased interpersonal
competence about specific organizational
problems existing in groups or units which
are interdependent.

Organizational improvement through
the training of relationships or groups
rather than isolated individuals.

Over the years, experimentation with
different laboratory designs has led to
diverse criteria for the selection of laboratory participants. Probably a majority
of NTL-IABS human relations laboratories are "stranger groups," i.e., involving participants who come from different organizations and who are not
likely to have met earlier. However, as
indicated by the organizational objectives above, the incidence of special
labs designed to increase the effectiveness of persons already working together appears to be growing. Thus
terms like "cousin labs," i.e., labs involving people from the same organization but not the same subunit, and
"family labs" or "team-building" sessions, i.e., involving a manager and all
of his subordinates, are becoming familiar. Participants in labs designed for organizational members not of the same

unit may be selected from the same rank level ("horizontal slice") or selected so as to constitute a heterogeneous grouping by rank ("diagonal slice"). Further, NTL-IABS is now encouraging at least two members from the same organization to attend NTL Management Work Conferences and Key Executive Conferences in order to maximize the impact of the learning in the back-home situation.[24]

In general, experienced trainers recommend that persons with severe emotional illness should not participate in laboratory training, with the exception of programs designed specifically for group therapy. Designers of programs make the assumptions, as Argyris states them,[25] that T-Group participants should have:

1. A relatively strong ego that is not overwhelmed by internal conflicts.
2. Defenses which are sufficiently low to allow the individual to hear what others say to him.
3. The ability to communicate thought and feelings with minimal distortion.

As a result of such screening, the incidence of breakdown during laboratory training is substantially less than that reported for organizations in general.[26] However, since the borderline between "normalcy" and illness is very indistinct, most professionally trained staff members are equipped to diagnose severe problems and to make referrals to psychiatrists and clinical psychologists when appropriate. Further, most are equipped to give adequate support and protection to participants whose ability to assimilate and learn from feedback is low. In addition, group members in T-Group situations tend to be sensitive to the emotional needs of the members and to be supportive when they sense a person experiencing pain. Such support is explicitly fostered in laboratory training.

The duration of laboratory training programs varies widely. "Micro-Labs," designed to give people a brief experience with sensitivity training, may last only one hour. Some labs are designed for a long weekend. Typically, however, basic human relations labs are of two weeks duration, with participants expected to meet mornings, afternoons, and evenings, with some time off for recreation. While NTL Management Work Conferences for middle managers and Key Executive Conferences run for one week, team-building labs, from my experience, typically are about three days in length. However, the latter are usually only a part of a broader organization development program involving problem sensing and diagnosis, and the planning of action steps and subsequent sessions. In addition, attendance at stranger labs for key managers is frequently a part of the total organization development effort.

Sensitivity training sessions typically start with the trainer making a few comments about his role—that he is there to be of help, that the group will have control of the agenda, that he will deliberately avoid a leadership role, but that he might become involved as both a leader and a member from time to time, etc. The following is an example of what the trainer might say:

This group will meet for many hours and will serve as a kind of laboratory where each individual can increase his understanding of the forces which influence individual behavior and the performance of groups and organizations. The data for learning will be our own behavior, feelings, and reactions. We begin with no definite structure or organization, no agreed-upon procedures, and no specific agenda. It will be up to us to fill the vacuum created by the lack of these familiar elements and to study our group as we evolve. My role will be to help the group to learn from its own experience, but not to act as a traditional chairman nor to suggest how we should organize, what our procedure should be, or exactly what our agenda will include. With these few comments, I think we are ready to begin in whatever way you feel will be most helpful.[27]

The trainer then lapses into silence. Group discomfort then precipitates a dialogue which, with skilled trainer assistance, is typically an intense but generally highly rewarding experience for group members. What goes on in the group becomes the data for the learning experience.

Interventions by the trainer will vary greatly depending upon the purpose of the lab and the state of learning on the part of the participants. A common intervention, however, is to encourage people to focus on and own up to their own feelings about what is going on in the group, rather than to make judgments about others. In this way, the participants begin to have more insight into their own feelings and to understand how their behavior affects the feelings of others.

While T-Group work tends to be the focal point in human relations laboratories, laboratory training typically includes theory sessions and frequently includes exercises such as role playing or management games.[28] Further, family labs of subunits of organizations will ordinarily devote more time to planning action steps for back on the job than will stranger labs.

Robert J. House has carefully reviewed the research literature on the impact of T-Group training and has concluded that the research shows mixed results. In particular, research on changes as reflected in personality inventories is seen as inconclusive. However, studies which examine the behavior of participants upon returning to the job are generally more positive.[29] House cites six studies, all of which utilized control groups, and concludes:

> All six studies revealed what appear to be important positive effects of T-Group training. Two of the studies report negative effects as well . . . all of the evidence is based on observations of the behavior of the participants in the actual job situations. No reliance is placed on participant response; rather, evidence is collected from those having frequent contact with the participant in his normal work activities.[30]

John P. Campbell and Marvin D. Dunnette,[31] on the other hand, while conceding that the research shows that T-Group training produces changes in behavior, point out that the usefulness of such training in terms of job performance has yet to be demonstrated. They urge research toward "forging the link between training-induced behavior changes and changes in job-performance effectiveness."[32] As a summary comment, they state:

> . . . the assumption that T-Group training has positive utility for organizations must necessarily rest on shaky ground. It has been neither confirmed nor disconfirmed. The authors wish to emphasize . . . that utility for the organization is not necessarily the same as utility for the individual.[33]

At least two major reasons may account for the inconclusiveness of research on the impact of T-Group training on job performance. One reason is simply that little research has been done. The other reason may center around a factor of cultural isolation. To oversimplify, a major part of what one learns in laboratory training, in my opinion, is how to work more effectively with others in group situations, particularly with others who have developed comparable skills. Unfortunately, most participants return from T-Group experiences to environments including colleagues and superiors who have not had the same affective (emotional, feeling) experiences, who are not familiar with the terminology and underlying theory, and who may have anxieties (usually unwarranted) about what might happen to them in a T-Group situation.

This cultural distance which laboratory training can produce is one of the reasons why many behavioral scientists are currently encouraging more than one person from the same organization to undergo T-Group training and, ideally, all of the members of a team and their superior to participate in some kind of laboratory training together. The latter assumes that a diagnosis of the organization indicates that the group is ready for such training and assumes such training is reasonably compatible with the broader culture of the total system.

CONDITIONS AND TECHNIQUES FOR SUCCESSFUL OD PROGRAMS

Theory, research, and experience to date suggest to me that successful OD programs tend to evolve in the following way and that they have some of these characteristics (these statements should be considered highly tentative, however):

• There is strong pressure for improvement from both outside the organization and from within.[34]

• An outside behavioral scientist-consultant is brought in for consultation with the top executives and to diagnose organizational problems.

• A preliminary diagnosis suggests that organization development efforts, designed in response to the expressed needs of the key executives, are warranted.

• A collaborative decision is made between the key client group and the consultant to try to change the culture of the organization, at least at the top initially. The specific goals may be to improve communications, to secure more effective participation from subordinates in problem solving, and to move in the direction of more openness, more feedback, and more support. In short, a decision is made to change the culture to help the company meet its organizational goals and to provide better avenues for initiative, creativity, and self-actualization on the part of organization members.

• Two or more top executives, including the chief executive, go to laboratory training sessions. (Frequently, attendance at labs is one of the facts which precipitates interest in bringing in the outside consultant.)

• Attendance in T-Group program is voluntary. While it is difficult to draw a line between persuasion and coercion, OD consultants and top management should be aware of the dysfunctional consequences of coercion (see the comments on authentic behavior below). While a major emphasis is on team-building laboratories, stranger labs are utilized both to supplement the training going on in the organization and to train managers new to the organization or those who are newly promoted.

• Team-building sessions are held with the top executive group (or at the highest point where the program is started). Ideally, the program is started at the top of the organization, but it can start at levels below the president as long as there is significant support from the chief executive, and preferably from other members of the top power structure as well.

• In a firm large enough to have a personnel executive, the personnel-industrial relations vice president becomes heavily involved at the outset.

• One of two organizational forms emerges to coordinate organization development efforts, either (a) a coordinator reporting to the personnel executive (the personnel executive himself may fill this role), or (b) a coordinator reporting to the chief executive. The management development director is frequently in an ideal position to coordinate OD activities with other management development activities.

• Ultimately, it is essential that the personnel-industrial relations group, including people in salary administration, be an integral part of the organization development program. Since OD groups have such potential for acting as catalysts in rapid organizational change, the temptation is great to see themselves as "good guys" and the other personnel people as "bad guys" or simply ineffective. Any conflicts between a separate organization development group and the personnel and industrial relations groups should be faced and resolved. Such tensions can be the "Achilles heel" for either program. In particular, however, the change agents in the organization development program need the support of the other people who are heavily involved in human resources administration and vice versa; what is done in the OD program needs to be compatible with what is done in selection, promotion, salary administration, appraisal, and vice versa. In terms of systems theory, it would seem imperative that one aspect of the human resources function such as any organization development program must be highly interdependent with the other human resources activities including selection, salary administration, etc. (TRW Systems is an example of an organization which involves top executives plus making the total personnel and industrial relations group an integral part of the OD program.[35])

• Team-building labs, at the request of the various respective executives, with laboratory designs based on careful data gathering and problem diagnosis, are conducted at successively lower levels of the organization with the help of outside consultants, plus the help of internal consultants whose expertise is gradually developed.

• Ideally, as the program matures, both members of the personnel staff and a few line executives are trained to do some organization development work in conjunction with the external and internal professionally trained behavioral scientists. In a sense, then, the external change agent tries to work himself out of a job by developing internal resources.

• The outside consultant(s) and the internal coordinator work very carefully together and periodically check on fears, threats, and anxieties which may be developing as the effort progresses. Issues need to be confronted as they emerge. Not only is the outside change agent needed for his skills, but the organization will need someone to act as a "governor"—to keep the program focused on real problems and to urge authenticity in contrast to gamesmanship. The danger always exists that the organization will begin to punish or reward involvement in T-Group kinds of activities per se, rather than focus on performance.

• The OD consultants constantly work on their own effectiveness in interpersonal relationships and their diagnostic skills so they are not in a position of "do as I say, but not as I do." Further, both consultant and client work together to optimize the consultant's knowledge of the organization's unique and evolving culture structure, and web of interpersonal relationships.

• There needs to be continuous audit of the results, both in terms of checking on the evolution of attitudes about what is going on and in terms of the extent to which problems which were identified at the outset by the key clients are being solved through the program.

• As implied above, the reward system and other personnel systems need to be readjusted to accommodate emerging changes in performance in the organization. Substantially improved performance on the part of individuals and groups is not likely to be sustained if financial and promotional rewards are not forthcoming. In short, management needs to have a "systems" point of view and to think through the interrelationships of the OD effort with the reward and staffing systems and the other aspects of the total human resources subsystem.

In the last analysis, the president and the "line" executives of the organization will evaluate the success of the OD effort in terms of the extent to which it assists the organization in meeting its human and economic objectives. For example, marked improvements on various indices from one plant, one division, one department, etc., will be important indicators of program success. While human resources administration indices are not yet perfected, some of the measuring devices being developed by Likert, Mann, and others show some promise.[36]

SUMMARY COMMENTS

Organization development efforts have emerged through attempts to apply laboratory training values and assumptions to total systems. Such efforts are organic in the sense that they emerge from and are guided by the problems being experienced by the people in the organization. The key to their viability (in contrast to becoming a passing fad) lies in an authentic focus on problems and concerns of the members of the organization and in their confrontation of issues and problems.

Organization development is based on assumptions and values similar to

"Theory Y" assumptions and values but includes additional assumptions about total systems and the nature of the client-consultant relationship. Intervention strategies of the behavioral scientist-change agent tend to be based on an action-research model and tend to be focused more on helping the people in an organization learn to solve problems rather than on prescriptions of how things should be done differently.

Laboratory training (or "sensitivity training") or modifications of T-group seminars typically are a part of the organizational change efforts, but the extent and format of such training will depend upon the evolving needs of the organization. Team-building seminars involving a superior and subordinates are being utilized more and more as a way of changing social systems rapidly and avoiding the cultural-distance problems which frequently emerge when individuals return from stranger labs. However, stranger labs can play a key role in change efforts when they are used as part of a broader organization development effort.

Research has indicated that sensitivity training generally produces positive results in terms of changed behavior on the job, but has not demonstrated the link between behavior changes and improved performance. Maximum benefits are probably derived from laboratory training when the organizational culture supports and reinforces the use of new skills in ongoing team situations.

Successful organization development efforts require skillful behavioral scientist interventions, a systems view, and top management support and involvement. In addition, changes stemming from organization development must be linked to changes in the total personnel subsystem. The viability of organization development efforts lies in the degree to which they accurately reflect the aspirations and concerns of the participating members.

In conclusion, successful organization development tends to be a total system effort; a process of planned change—not a program with a temporary quality; and aimed at developing the organization's internal resources for effective change in the future.

NOTES

1. Richard Beckhard, W. Warner Burke, and Fred I. Steele, "The Program for Specialists in Organization Training and Development," mimeographed, NTL Institute for Applied Behavioral Science, Dec. 1967, p. ii; and John Paul Jones, "What's Wrong With Work?" in *What's Wrong With Work?* (New York: National Association of Manufacturers, 1967), p. 8. For a history of NTL Institute for Applied Behavioral Science, with which Douglas McGregor was long associated in addition to his professorial appointment at M.I.T. and which has been a major factor in the history of organization development, see Leland P. Bradford, "Biography of an Institution," *Journal of Applied Behavioral Science*, III:2 (1967), 127-143. While we will use the word "program" from time to time, ideally organization development is a "process," not just another new program of temporary quality.

2. Harry D. Kolb, Introduction to *An Action Research Program for Organization Improvement* (Ann Arbor: Foundation for Research in Human Behavior, 1960), p. i.

3. Cattell defines synergy as "The sum total of the energy which a group can command." Daniel Katz and Robert L. Kahn, *The Social Psychology of Organizations* (New York: John Wiley and Sons, 1966), p. 33.

4. For a similar statement of objectives, see "What is OD?" *NTL Institute: News and Reports from NTL Institute for Applied Behavioral Science*, II (June 1968), 1-2. Whether OD programs increase the overall level of authority in contrast to redistributing authority is a debatable point. My hypothesis is that both a redistribution and an overall increase occur.

5. Joan Woodward, *Industrial Organization: Theory and Practice* (London: Oxford University Press, 1965).

6. See M. Scott Myers, "Every Employee

a Manager," *California Management Review,* X (Spring 1968), 9-20.

7. See Douglas McGregor, *The Human Side of Enterprise* (New York: McGraw-Hill Book Company, 1960), pp. 47-48.

8. In addition to influence from the writings of McGregor, Likert, Argyris, and others, this discussion has been influenced by "Some Assumptions About Change in Organizations," in notebook "Program for Specialists in Organization Training and Development," NTL Institute for Applied Behavioral Science, 1967; and by staff members who participated in that program.

9. For a discussion of the "linking pin" concept, see Rensis Likert, *New Patterns of Management* (New York: McGraw-Hill Book Company, 1961).

10. Warren G. Bennis sees three major approaches to planned organizational change, with the behavioral scientists associated with each all having "a deep concern with applying social science knowledge to create more viable social systems; a commitment to action, as well as to research . . . and a belief that improved interpersonal and group relationships will ultimately lead to better organizational performance." Bennis, "A New Role for the Behavioral Sciences: Effecting Organizational Change," *Administrative Science Quarterly,* VIII (Sept. 1963), 157-158; and Herbert A. Shepard, "An Action Research Model," in *An Action Research Program for Organization Improvement,* pp. 31-35.

11. Bennis, "A New Role for the Behavioral Sciences," 158.

12. For a discussion of some of the problems and dilemmas in behavioral science research, see Chris Argyris, "Creating Effective Relationships in Organizations," in Richard N. Adams and Jack J. Preiss, eds., *Human Organization Research* (Homewood, Ill.: The Dorsey Press, 1960), pp. 109-123; and Barbara A. Benedict, *et al.,* "The Clinical Experimental Approach to Assessing Organizational Change Efforts," *Journal of Applied Behavioral Science,* (Nov. 1967), 347-380.

13. For further discussion of action research, see Edgar H. Schein and Warren G. Bennis, *Personal and Organizational Change Through Group Methods* (New York: John Wiley and Sons, 1966), pp. 272-274.

14. William Foote Whyte and Edith Lentz Hamilton, *Action Research for Management* (Homewood, Ill.: Richard D. Irwin, 1964), p. 2.

15. Jeremiah J. O'Connell appropriately challenges the notion that there is "one best way" of organizational change and stresses that the consultant should choose his role and intervention strategies on the basis of "the conditions existing when he enters the client system" (*Managing Organizational Innovation* [Homewood, Ill.: Richard D. Irwin, 1968], pp. 10-11).

16. For further discussion of organization diagnosis, see Richard Beckhard, "An Organization Improvement Program in a Decentralized Organization," *Journal of Applied Behavioral Science,* II (Jan-March 1966), 3-4, "OD as a Process," in *What's Wrong with Work?,* pp. 12-13.

17. For example, see Floyd C. Mann, "Studying and Creating Change," in Timothy W. Costello and Sheldon S. Zalkind, eds., *Psychology in Administration—A Research Orientation* (Englewood Cliffs: Prentice-Hall, 1963), pp. 321-324. See also Delbert C. Miller, "Using Behavioral Science to Solve Organization Problems," *Personnel Administration,* XXXI (Jan.-Feb. 1968), 21-29.

18. For a description of feedback procedures used by the Survey Research Center, Univ. of Michigan, see Mann and Likert, "The Need for Research on the Communication of Research Results," in *Human Organization Research,* pp. 57-66.

19. This phrase probably came from a management workshop sponsored by NTL Institute for Applied Behavioral Science.

20. For a description of what goes on in team-building sessions, see Beckhard, "An Organizational Improvement Program," 9-13; and Newton Margulies and Anthony P. Raia, "People in Organizations—A Case for Team Training," *Training and Development Journal,* XXII (August 1968), 2-11. For a description of problem-solving sessions involving the total management group (about 70) of a company, see Beckhard, "The Confrontation Meeting," *Harvard Business Review,* XLV (March-April 1967), 149-155.

21. For a description of actual organization development programs, see Paul C. Buchanan, "Innovative Organizations—A Study in Organization Development," in *Applying Behavioral Science Research in Industry* (New York: Industrial Relations Counselors, 1964), pp. 87-107; Sheldon A. Davis, "An Organic Problem-Solving Method of Organizational Change," *Journal of Applied Behavioral Science,* III:1 (1967), 3-21; Cyril Sofer, *The Organization from Within*

(Chicago: Quadrangle Books, 1961); Alfred J. Marrow, David G. Bowers, and Stanley E. Seashore, *Management by Participation* (New York: Harper and Row, 1967); Robert R. Blake, Jane S. Mouton, Louis B. Barnes, and Larry E. Greiner, "Breakthrough in Organization Development," *Harvard Business Review*, XLII (Nov.-Dec. 1964), 133-155; Alton C. Bartlett, "Changing Behavior as a Means to Increased Efficiency," *Journal of Applied Behavioral Science*, III:3 (1967), 381-403; Larry E. Greiner, "Antecedents of Planned Organization Change," *ibid.*, III:1 (1967), 51-85; and Robert R. Blake and Jane Mouton, *Corporate Excellence Through Grid Organization Development* (Houston, Texas: Gulf Publishing Company, 1968).

22. From Bradford, "Biography of an Institution." See also Kenneth D. Benne, "History of the T Group in the Laboratory Setting," in Bradford, Jack R. Gibb, and Benne, eds., *T/Group Theory and Laboratory Method* (New York: John Wiley and Sons, 1964), pp. 80-135.

23. Schein and Bennis, p. 37.

24. For further discussion of group composition in laboratory training, see Schein and Bennis, pp. 63-69. NTL-LABS now include the Center for Organization Studies, the Center for the Development of Educational Leadership, the Center for Community Affairs, and the Center for International Training to serve a wide range of client populations and groups.

25. Chris Argyris, "T-Groups for Organizational Effectiveness," *Harvard Business Review*, XLII (March-April 1964), 60-74.

26. Based on discussions with NTL staff members. One estimate is that the incidence of "serious stress and mental disturbance" during laboratory training is less than one percent of participants and in almost all cases occurs in persons with a history of prior disturbance (Charles Seashore, "What Is Sensitivity Training," *NTL Institute News and Reports*, II [April 1968], 2).

27. *Ibid.*, 1.

28. For a description of what goes on in T-groups, see Schein and Bennis, pp. 10-27;

Bradford, Gibb, and Benne, pp. 55-67; Dorothy S. Whitaker, "A Case Study of a T-Group," in Galvin Whitaker, ed., T-Group Training: Group Dynamics in Management Education, A.T.M. Occasional Papers, (Oxford: Basil Blackwell, 1965), pp. 14-22; Irving R. Weschler and Jerome Reisel, *Inside a Sensitivity Training Group* (Berkeley: University of California, Institute of Industrial Relations, 1959); and William F. Glueck, "Reflections on a T-Group Experience," *Personnel Journal*, XLVII (July 1968), 501-504. For use of cases or exercises based on research results ("instrumented training") see Robert R. Blake and Jane S. Mouton, "The Instrumented Training Laboratory," in Irving R. Weschler and Edgar H. Schein, eds., *Five Issues in Training* (Washington: National Training Laboratories, 1962), pp. 61-76; and W. Warner Burke and Harvey A. Hornstein, "Conceptual vs. Experimental Management Training," *Training and Development Journal*, XXI (Dec. 1967), 12-17.

29. Robert J. House, "T-Group Education and Leadership Effectiveness: A Review of the Empiric Literature and a Critical Evaluation," *Personnel Psychology*, XX (Spring 1967), 1-32. See also Dorothy Stock, "A Survey of Research on T-Groups," in Bradford, Gibb, and Benne, pp. 395-441.

30. House, *ibid.*, pp. 18-19.

31. John P. Campbell and Marvin D. Dunnette, "Effectiveness of T-Group Experiences in Managerial Training and Development," *Psychological Bulletin*, LXX (August 1968), 73-104.

32. *Ibid.*, 100.

33. *Ibid.*, 101. See also the essays by Dunnette and Campbell and Chris Argyris in *Industrial Relations*, VIII (Oct. 1968), 1-45.

34. On this point, see Larry E. Greiner, "Patterns of Organization Change," *Harvard Business Review*, XLV (May-June 1967), 119-130.

35. See Sheldon A. Davis, "An Organic Problem-Solving Method."

36. See Rensis Likert, *The Human Organization: Its Management and Value* (New York: McGraw-Hill Book Company, 1967).

28. Work Redesign*

J. RICHARD HACKMAN

GREG R. OLDHAM

Work redesign is becoming increasingly prominent as a strategy for attempting to improve simultaneously the productivity and the quality of the work experience of employees in contemporary organizations. Although the benefits of work redesign (or "job enrichment" or "job enlargement") are widely touted in the management literature, in fact little is known about the reasons why "enriched" work sometimes leads to positive outcomes for workers and for their employing organizations. Even less is known about the relative effectiveness of various strategies for carrying out the redesign of work.[1]

One reason for this state of affairs is that existing theories of work redesign are not fully adequate to meet the problems encountered in their application. Especially troublesome is the paucity of conceptual tools that are directly useful in guiding the *implementation and evaluation* of work redesign projects. In the paragraphs to follow, we examine several existing theoretical approaches to work redesign, with a special eye toward the measurability of the concepts employed and the action implications of the theorizing.[2] We then propose a theory of work redesign that focuses specifically on how the characteristics of jobs and the characteristics of people interact to determine when an "enriched" job will lead to beneficial outcomes, and when it will not.

THEORETICAL APPROACHES TO WORK REDESIGN

Motivation–hygiene theory.—By far the most influential theory relevant to work redesign has been the Herzberg two-factor theory of satisfaction and motivation.[3] In essence, the theory proposes that the primary determinants of employee satisfaction are factors intrinsic to the work that is done (i.e., recognition, achievement, responsibility, advancement, personal growth in competence). These factors are called "motivators" because they are believed to be effective in motivating employees to superior effort and performance. Dissatisfaction, on the other hand, is seen as being caused by "hygiene factors" that are extrinsic to the work itself. Examples include company policies, supervisory practices, pay plans, working conditions, and so on. The Herzberg theory specifies that a job will enhance work motivation and satisfaction only to the degree that "motivators" are designed into the work itself. Changes that deal solely with "hygiene" factors should not lead to increases in employee motivation.

It is to the credit of the Herzberg theory that it has prompted a great deal of research, and inspired several successful change projects involving the redesign of work.[4] Yet there are difficulties with the theory that to some extent compromise its usefulness.

Source: From J. Richard Hackman and Greg R. Oldham, "Motivation Through the Design of Work: Test of a Theory," *Organizational Behavior and Human Performance,* Vol. 16 (1976), pp. 250-259. Copyright © 1976 by Academic Press, Inc. Reprinted by permission of Academic Press, Inc.

For one, a number of researchers have been unable to provide empirical support for the major tenets of the two-factor theory itself.[5] It appears that the original dichotomization of aspects of the workplace into "motivators" and "hygiene factors" may have been largely a function of methodological artifact, and the present conceptual status of the theory must be considered highly uncertain.

Moreover, the theory does not provide for differences among people in how responsive they are likely to be to "enriched" jobs. In the AT&T studies based on the theory,[6] for example, it was assumed that the motivating factors potentially could increase the work motivation of *all* employees. Yet it now appears that some individuals are much more likely to respond positively to an enriched, complex job than are others.[7] The theory provides no help in determining how such individual differences phenomena should be dealt with, either at the conceptual level or in the actual applications.

Finally, the theory in its present form does not specify how the presence or absence of motivating factors can be *measured* for existing jobs. At the least, this increases the difficulty of testing the theory in on-going organizations. It also limits the degree to which the theory can be used to diagnose jobs prior to planned change, or to evaluate the effects of work redesign activities after changes have been carried out.

Activation theory. While psychologists have for many years studied the antecedents and consequences of heightened and depressed levels of psychological and physiological activation in organisms,[8] only recently have attempts been made to use activation theory to understand the work behavior of individuals in organizations. Scott[9] has reviewed a number of studies that show how people react to chronic states of underactivation at work by engaging in arousal-enhancing behaviors, some of which have clearly dysfunctional consequences for work effectiveness. The findings Scott summarizes

suggest that activation theory may be of considerable use in understanding jobs that are highly repetitive—and in planning for task designs that minimize the dysfunctional consequences of underactivating work. Activation theorists have given relatively little attention to jobs that may be overstimulating, perhaps because few such jobs exist for rank-and-file workers in contemporary organizations.

While activation theory clearly has considerable relevance to both the theory and practice of job design, two thorny problems must be dealt with before the theory can be fully applied to real-world job design problems. First, means must be developed for measuring current levels of activation of individuals in actual work settings,[10] and for assessing the "optimal level" of activation for different individuals. Until such methodologies are developed, it will remain impractical to use activation theory in predicting or changing employee reactions to their jobs except in a very gross fashion; e.g., in situations where it is clear that most employees are enormously over- or understimulated by their jobs.

A second problem has to do with ambiguities regarding the processes by which individuals adapt to *changing* levels in stimulation. Individuals' levels of activation decrease markedly as a function of familiarity with a given stimulus situation. However, after a period of rest, re-presentation of the same stimulus situation will once again raise the level of activation.[11] More complete understanding of the waxing and waning of activation in various circumstances could have many implications for job design practices; for example, the practice of "job rotation." Those who advocate job rotation claim that work motivation can be kept reasonably high by rotating individuals through several different jobs, even though each of the jobs would become monotonous and boring if one were to remain on it for a long period of time. If future research can identify ways to maintain activation at near-optimal levels through planned stimulus change, then the theory can contribute substantially to increasing the usefulness of job rotation as a motivational technique. If, however, it turns out that there are general and inevitable decreases in activation over time regardless of how different tasks and rest periods are cycled, then the long-term usefulness of the technique would seem to be limited.

In either case, the potential for applying activation theory to the design of jobs may be limited mainly to those cases in which there are actively dysfunctional affective and behavioral outcomes associated with routine, repetitive jobs. The theory offers less guidance for the design of work that will elicit and maintain positive and self-reinforcing work motivation.

Socio-technical systems theory.—The socio-technical systems approach to work redesign provides significant insight into the interdependencies between technical aspects of the work itself and the broader social milieu in which the work is done.[12] The theory has evolved from (and has been used as an explanatory device for) numerous planned changes of work systems. Many of these experiments have provided vivid illustration of the interactions between the social and technical aspects of the workplace, and at the same time have proven successful as action projects—in that beneficial outcomes were obtained both for employees and for the organizations in which they worked.[13] Of special interest is the contribution of socio-technical systems theory in developing the notion of the "autonomous work group," in which members of a work team share among themselves much of the decision-making having to do with the planning and execution of the work.[14] Creation of autonomous work groups promises to become increasingly prominent and useful as a strategy for redesigning and improving work systems.

Yet for all its merit, the socio-technical systems approach provides few explicit specifications of how (and under what circumstances) the work itself and the social surroundings affect one another. It is,

therefore, difficult to test the adequacy of the theory *qua* theory. Moreover, the approach provides little specific guidance about how (and how not to) proceed in carrying out work redesign activities, other than the general dictum to attend to both the technical and social aspects of the work setting and the device of the autonomous work group. Absent from the approach, for example, are explicit means for diagnosing a work system prior to change (to ascertain what "should" be changed, and how), or for evaluating in systematic terms the outcomes of changes that have been completed.

For these reasons, the major value of socio-technical systems theory appears to be its considerable usefulness as a way of thinking about work systems and their redesign. In its present form, it has only limited use in generating new understanding through quantitative tests of theory-specified propositions, or in providing explicit and concrete guidance about what organizational changes to make under what circumstances.

Jobs and individual differences: An interactive approach.—Research on work design that focuses on the objective characteristics of jobs is rooted in the work of Turner and Lawrence.[15] These researchers developed measures of six "Requisite Task Attributes" that were predicted to relate positively to employee satisfaction and attendance. A summary measure, the Requisite Task Attributes Index (RTA Index) was derived from the six measures and used to test relationships between the nature of jobs and employee reactions to them.

Expected positive relationships between the RTA Index and employee satisfaction and attendance were found only for workers from factories located in small towns. For employees in urban work settings, satisfaction was inversely related to the scores of jobs on the RTA Index, and absenteeism was unrelated to the Index. The investigators concluded that reactions to jobs high on the RTA Index were moderated by differences in the cultural backgrounds of employees. Subsequent research by Blood and Hulin[16] provides support for the notion that subcultural factors moderate worker responses to the design of their jobs.

A study by Hackman and Lawler[17] provides further evidence that job characteristics can directly affect employee attitudes and behavior at work. These authors suggested that employees should react positively to four "core" dimensions adapted from those used previously by Turner and Lawrence (i.e., variety, task identity, autonomy, feedback). In addition, Hackman and Lawler proposed that individuals who were desirous of growth satisfactions at work should respond especially positively to jobs high on the core dimensions, since these individuals are most likely to value the kinds of opportunities and internal rewards that complex jobs offer.

Results of the study generally supported the hypothesis that employees who work on jobs high on the core dimensions show high work motivation, satisfaction, performance, and attendance. Also, Hackman and Lawler found that a number of dependent measures were moderated as predicted by growth need strength: That is, employees with high measured needs for growth responded more positively to complex jobs than did employees low in growth need strength.

The appropriate conceptualization and measurement of the differences among people that moderate how they respond to complex jobs has been the subject of a number of recent studies. Findings similar to those reported by Hackman and Lawler have been reported by Brief and Aldag[18] and by Sims and Szilagyi,[19] using a measure of growth need strength (although the Brief and Aldag study provided only partial replication). Supportive findings also have been obtained by Robey,[20] using as an individual difference measure "extrinsic" vs. "instrinsic" work values. Failures to obtain a moderating effect have been reported by Shepard[21] (using a measure of alienation from work) and by Stone[22] (using a measure of

employee endorsement of the Protestant work ethic). Wanous[23] directly compared the usefulness of (a) higher order need strength, (b) endorsement of the Protestant work ethic, and (c) urban vs. rural subcultural background as moderators of job effects. All three variables were found to be of some value as moderators, with the need strength measure strongest and the urban-rural measure weakest.

In sum, there is now substantial evidence that differences among people do moderate how they react to the complexity and challenge of their work, and studies using direct measures of individual needs seem to provide more consistent and strong support for this finding than do measures of subcultural background or of generalized work values.

THE JOB CHARACTERISTICS MODEL

The model presented in this paper is an attempt to extend, refine, and systematize the relationships described above between job characteristics and individual responses to the work. The basic job characteristics model is presented in Fig. 28-1. At the most general level, five "core" job dimensions are seen as prompting three psychological states which, in turn, lead to a number of beneficial personal and work outcomes. The links between the job dimensions and the psychological states, and between the psychological states and the outcomes, are shown as moderated by individual growth need strength. Each of the major classes of variables in the model is discussed in more detail below.

PSYCHOLOGICAL STATES

The three psychological states (experienced meaningfulness of the work, experienced responsibility for the outcomes of the work and knowledge of the results of the work activities) are the causal core of the model. Following Hackman and Lawler,[24] the model postulates that an individual experiences positive [e]ffect to

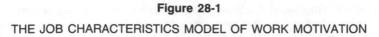

Figure 28-1

THE JOB CHARACTERISTICS MODEL OF WORK MOTIVATION

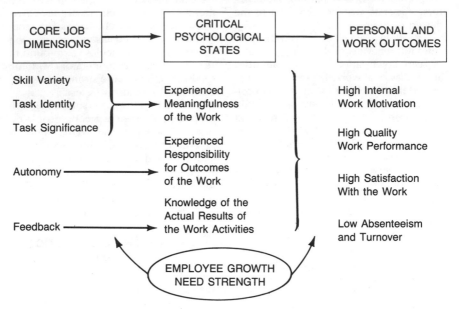

the extent that he *learns* (knowledge of results) that he *personally* (experienced responsibility) has performed well on a task that he *cares about* (experienced meaningfulness).

This positive [e]ffect is reinforcing to the individual, and serves as an incentive for him to continue to try to perform well in the future. When he does not perform well, he does not experience an internally reinforcing state of affairs, and he may elect to try harder in the future so as to regain the internal rewards that good performance brings. The net result is a self-perpetuating cycle of positive work motivation powered by self-generated rewards, that is predicted to continue until one or more of the three psychological states is no longer present, or until the individual no longer values the internal rewards that derive from good performance.

It should be noted that self-generated motivation should be highest when all three of the psychological states are present. If the performer feels fully responsible for work outcomes on a meaningful task, but never finds out how well he is performing, it is doubtful that he will experience the internal rewards that can prompt self-generated motivation. Similarly, if he has full knowledge of the results of the work, but experiences the task as trivial (or feels no personal responsibility for the results of the work), internal motivation will not be high.

The three psychological states are defined as follows:

Experienced Meaningfulness of the Work. The degree to which the individual experiences the job as one which is generally meaningful, valuable, and worthwhile;

Experienced Responsibility for Work Outcomes. The degree to which the individual feels personally accountable and responsible for the results of the work he or she does;

Knowledge of Results. The degree to which the individual knows and understands, on a continuous basis, how effectively he or she is performing the job.

JOB DIMENSIONS

Of the five characteristics of jobs shown in Fig. 28-1 as fostering the emergence of the psychological states, three contribute to the experienced meaningfulness of the work, and one each contributes to experienced responsibility and to knowledge of results.

Toward experienced meaningfulness.—Three job characteristics combine additively to determine the psychological meaningfulness of a job. They are:

(1) Skill Variety. The degree to which a job requires a variety of different activities in carrying out the work, which involve the use of a number of different skills and talents of the person.

When a task requires a person to engage in activities that challenge or stretch his skills and abilities, that task almost invariably is experienced as meaningful by the individual. Many parlor games, puzzles, and recreational activities, for example, achieve much of their fascination because they tap and test the intellective or motor skills of the people who do them. When a job draws upon several skills of an employee, that individual may find the job to be of enormous personal meaning—even if, in any absolute sense, it is not of great significance or importance.

(2) Task Identity. The degree to which the job requires completion of a "whole" and identifiable piece of work; that is, doing a job from beginning to end with a visible outcome.

If, for example, an employee assembles a complete product (or provides a complete unit of service) he should find the work more meaningful than would be the case if he were responsible for only a small part of the whole job, other things (such as skill variety) assumed equal.

(3) Task Significance. The degree to which the job has a substantial impact on the lives or work of other people, whether in the immediate organization or in the external environment.

When an individual understands that the results of his work may have a significant effect on the well-being of other people, the meaningfulness of that work usually is enhanced. Employees who tighten nuts on aircraft brake assemblies, for example, are much more likely to perceive their work as meaningful than are workers who fill small boxes with paper clips—again, even though the skill levels involved may be comparable.

Toward experienced responsibility.—The job characteristic predicted to prompt employee feelings of personal responsibility for the work outcomes is autonomy. To the extent that a job has high autonomy, the outcomes depend increasingly on the individual's *own* efforts, initiatives, and decisions rather than on the adequacy of instructions from the boss or on a manual of job procedures. In such circumstances, the individual should feel strong personal responsibility for the success and failures that occur on the job. Autonomy is defined as follows:

Autonomy. The degree to which the job provides substantial freedom, independence, and discretion to the individual in scheduling the work and in determining the procedures to be used in carrying it out.

Toward knowledge of results.—The job characteristic that fosters knowledge of results is feedback, which is defined as follows:

Feedback. The degree to which carrying out the work activities required by the job results in the individual obtaining direct and clear information about the effectiveness of his or her performance.

Summary: The overall "motivating potential" of a job.—According to the job characteristics model, the overall potential of a job to prompt internal work motivation on the part of job incumbents should be highest when all of the following are true: (a) the job is high on at least one (and hopefully more) of the three job dimensions that lead to experienced meaningfulness, (b) the job is high on autonomy, and (c) the job is high on feedback.

The Motivating Potential Score (MPS) is

$$\text{Motivating Potential Score (MPS)} = \left[\frac{\text{Skill Variety} + \text{Task Identity} + \text{Task Significance}}{3} \right] \times \text{Autonomy} \times \text{Feedback}$$

a measure of the degree to which the above conditions are met. MPS is computed by combining the scores of jobs on the five dimensions.

As can be seen from the formula, a near-zero score of a job on either autonomy or feedback will reduce the overall MPS to near-zero; whereas a near-zero score on one of the three job dimensions that contribute to experienced meaningfulness cannot, by itself, do so.

INDIVIDUAL GROWTH NEED STRENGTH

As noted earlier, there is now substantial evidence that differences among people moderate how they react to their work, and individual need strength appears to be a useful way to conceptualize and measure such differences. The basic prediction is that people who have high need for personal growth and development will respond more positively to a job high in motivating potential than people with low growth need strength.

There are two possible "sites" for this moderating effect in the motivational sequence shown in Figure 28-1: (a) at the link between the objective job dimensions and the psychological states, and (b) at the link between the psychological states and the outcome variables. The former would imply that high growth need people are more likely (or better able) to *experience* the psychological states when the objective job is good than are their low growth need counterparts. The latter allows the possibility that nearly everybody may experience the psychological states when job conditions are right, but that individuals with high growth needs

respond more positively to that experience. It may be, of course, that growth need strength moderates at *both* points in the sequence, as tentatively shown in Fig. 28-1.

OUTCOME VARIABLES

Also shown in Fig. 28-1 are several outcome variables that are predicted to be affected by the level of job-based motivation experienced by people at work. Especially critical to the theory is the measure of internal work motivation[25] because it taps directly the contingency between effective performance and self-administered affective rewards. Typical questionnaire items measuring internal work motivation include: (a) I feel a great sense of personal satisfaction when I do this job well; (b) I feel bad and unhappy when I discover that I have performed poorly on this job; and (c) My own feelings are *not* affected much one way or the other by how well I do on this job (reversed scoring).

Other outcomes listed in Fig. 28-1 are the quality of work performance, job satisfaction (especially satisfaction with opportunities for personal growth and development on the job), absenteeism, and turnover. All of these outcomes are expected to be more positive for jobs with high motivating potential than for jobs low in MPS. Causal priorities *among* the several outcome variables are not explicitly addressed by the model.

NOTES

1. J. R. Hackman, "On the Coming Demise of Job Enrichment," in E. L. Cass and F. G.

Zimmer (eds.), *Man and Work in Society* (New York: Van Nostrand–Reinhold, 1975).

2. L. W. Porter, E. E. Lawler, and J. R. Hackman, *Behavior in Organizations* (New York: McGraw-Hill, 1975), Ch. 10.

3. F. Herzberg, *Work and the Nature of Man* (Cleveland: World, 1966); F. Herzberg, B. Mausner, and B. Snyderman, *The Motivation to Work* (New York: Wiley, 1959).

4. R. N. Ford, *Motivation Through the Work Itself* (New York: American Management Association, 1969); W. J. Paul, Jr., K. B. Robertson, and F. Herzberg, "Job Enrichment Pays Off," *Harvard Business Review 47* (1969): 61-78.

5. See, for example, M. D. Dunnette, J. P. Campbell, and M. D. Hakel, "Factors Contributing to Job Satisfaction and Dissatisfaction in Six Occupational Groups," *Organizational Behavior and Human Performance 2* (1967): 143-174; B. L. Hinton, "An Empirical Investigation of the Herzberg Methodology and Two-Factor Theory," *Organizational Behavior and Human Performance 3* (1968): 286-309; N. A. King, "A Clarification and Evaluation of the Two-Factor Theory of Job Satisfaction," *Psychological Bulletin 74* (1970): 18-31. For analyses favorable to the theory, see Herzberg, *op. cit.;* D. A. Whitsett and E. K. Winslow, "An Analysis of Studies Critical of the Motivator-Hygiene Theory," *Personnel Psychology 20* (1967): 391-415.

6. Ford, *op. cit.*

7. C. L. Hulin, "Individual Differences and Job Enrichment," in J. R. Maher (ed.), *New Perspectives in Job Enrichment* (New York: Van Nostrand–Reinhold, 1971).

8. D. E. Berlyne, "Arousal and Reinforcement," *Nebraska Symposium on Motivation 15* (1967): 1-110.

9. W. E. Scott, "Activation Theory and Task Design," *Organizational Behavior and Human Performance 1* (1966): 3-30.

10. R. E. Thayer, "Measurement of Activation Through Self-report," *Psychological Reports 20* (1967): 663-678.

11. Scott, *op. cit.*

12. F. E. Emery and E. L. Trist, "Socio-technical Systems," in F. E. Emery (ed.), *Systems Thinking* (London: Penguin, 1969); E. L. Trist, G. W. Higgin, H. Murray, and A. B. Pollock, *Organizational Choice* (London: Tavistock, 1963).

13. L. E. Davis and E. L. Trist, "Improving the Quality of Work Life: Experience of the Socio-technical Approach" (Background paper commissioned by the U.S. Department

of Health, Education, and Welfare for the Work in America Project, June, 1972); A. K. Rice, *Productivity and Social Organization: The Ahmedabad Experiment* (London: Tavistock, 1958).

14. J. Gulowsen, "A Measure of Work Group Autonomy," in L. E. Davis and J. C. Taylor (eds.), *Design of Jobs* (Middlesex, England: Penguin, 1972); P. G. Herbst, *Autonomous Group Functioning* (London: Tavistock, 1962).

15. A. N. Turner and P. R. Lawrence, *Industrial Jobs and the Worker* (Boston: Harvard Graduate School of Business Administration, 1965).

16. M. R. Blood and C. L. Hulin, "Alienation, Environmental Characteristics, and Worker Responses," *Journal of Applied Psychology 51* (1967): 284-290; C. L. Hulin and M. R. Blood, "Job Enlargement, Individual Differences, and Worker Responses," *Psychological Bulletin 69* (1968): 41-55.

17. J. R. Hackman and E. E. Lawler, "Employee Reactions to Job Characteristics," *Journal of Applied Psychology Monograph 55* (1971): 259-286.

18. A. P. Brief and R. J. Aldag, "Employee Reactions to Job Characteristics: A Constructive Replication," *Journal of Applied Psychology 60* (1975): 182-186.

19. H. P. Sims and A. D. Szilagyi, "Individual Moderators of Job Characteristic Relationships" (Unpublished manuscript, Graduate School of Business, Indiana University, 1974).

20. D. Robey, "Task Design, Work Values, and Worker Response: An Experimental Test," *Organizational Behavior and Human Performance 12* (1974): 264-273.

21. J. M. Shepard, "Functional Specialization, Alienation, and Job Satisfaction," *Industrial and Labor Relations Review 23* (1970): 207-219.

22. E. F. Stone, "The Moderating Effect of Work-related Values on the Job Scope–Job Satisfaction Relationship," *Organizational Behavior and Human Performance 15* (1976): 147-179.

23. J. P. Wanous, "Individual Differences and Reactions to Job Characteristics," *Journal of Applied Psychology 59* (1974): 616-622.

24. Hackman and Lawler, *op. cit.*

25. E. E. Lawler and D. T. Hall, "The Relationship of Job Characteristics to Job Involvement, Satisfaction and Intrinsic Motivation," *Journal of Applied Psychology 54* (1970): 305-312; Hackman and Lawler, *op. cit.*

VI

Emerging Classics

Introduction. The 1980s are a sobering time for U.S. industry. Mega-problems such as the enormous national debt, huge trade deficits, ever-increasing foreign competition, turbulence in the stock market, instability in the currency markets, and the threat of unfriendly acquisition have made many managers realize that they must continuously strive for excellence if their organizations are to survive. In response to these threats, many organizations are making a concerted effort to get beyond lip-service and actually implement ideas set forth in these "classics" of organizational behavior. From the numerous publications in recent years which have addressed these crucial questions from an organizational perspective, a few management concepts have gained so much attention that they deserve recognition as "emerging classics."

The One Minute Manager, co-authored by Kenneth H. Blanchard and Spencer Johnson, became a best-seller with its common sense approach to managing people. The book reveals three "secrets" of effective management: One Minute Goal Setting, One Minute Praising, and One Minute Reprimands. *The One Minute Manager* clearly struck a responsive chord among practicing managers who have seen the problems associated with employees not knowing what they are supposed to do, failing to recognize people's positive contributions, and not holding employees accountable for their behavior. In the "One Minute Management" article, Blanchard describes how to put the three secrets to work.

In Search of Excellence, by Thomas J. Peters and Robert H. Waterman, Jr., rapidly became the all-time best-selling management book. Peters and Waterman argue that American business need not look to Japan to find solutions to the problems of poor performance. For years, top-performing American organizations have stood out as bright examples of how to create and sustain profitability and excellence. The summary presented here lists the key differentiating characteristics of these "excellent" companies, including their bias for action, concern for customers, people orientation, and emphasis on "sticking to their knitting." The authors' observations

337

can serve as a useful guide for managers interested in building managerial excellence within their organizations.

John Naisbitt's best-seller *Megatrends* describes 10 major changes transforming American society. The brief excerpt reprinted here is taken from the introductory and concluding chapters of the book in which Naisbitt lists 10 "megatrends," including the evolution toward an information society, the increased need for human "touch," the shift toward decentralization, and the transition from hierarchical power structures to networks. All of these changes have profound managerial implications. Naisbitt's insights support the common theme that in order to remain viable, organizations must stay attuned to changes in their environment and respond quickly to the new demands.

The final "emerging classic" is from the last chapter of *The Change Masters,* by Rosabeth Moss Kanter. This reading provides specific guidelines for arousing potential entrepreneurs within our organizations and creating an organizational climate in which innovation can flourish. Included among Kanter's suggestions are the need to develop a culture of pride, improve organizational communication, and reduce unnecessary layers of management. This article is a fitting end to *Classics of Organizational Behavior,* 2nd ed., for it reinforces the common theme that the way to long-term success is the effective utilization of the human potential that exists within our organizations.

29. One Minute Management*

KENNETH H. BLANCHARD

While managers all over the world feel the three secrets of One Minute Management are common sense, they are quick to admit that they are not common practice. Recognizing that fact, I make the following suggestions and comments about putting the three secrets—One Minute Goal Setting, One Minute Praising, and One Minute Reprimands—to work.

ONE MINUTE GOAL SETTING

The first secret to being a One Minute Manager is One Minute Goal Setting. This involves making sure that everyone of your staff is clear on two things: what they [sic] are being asked to do (areas of accountability) and what good behavior looks like (performance standards).

In our organization, we do a great deal of diagnostic work. And when we go into companies to help improve productivity, we begin by asking people to tell us what they do. Next we go to their managers and ask them to tell us what their people do. When we compare the responses, we often find two different lists, particularly if we ask these people to prioritize their duties.

One of the biggest obstacles to productivity improvement is that people who are most closely tied to a productivity issue do not even know it is their responsibility. For example, we once worked with a group of restaurant managers who were concerned about sales. We asked the managers, "Who is responsible for generating sales?" They replied, "The waiters." But when we asked the waiters what their job was, they said, "Serving food and taking orders." I was in one of these restaurants recently and the menu said, "Soup of the day." I asked the waiter what the soup of the day was, and he said, "Lentil, but it looks awful!"

Again, the first part of effective One Minute Goal Setting is to make sure people know what they are being asked to do. The second part is letting people know what doing a good job means.

We ask people, "Are you doing a good job?" Most people say, "Yes, I think so." Then we ask the tough question: "How do you know?" The primary response we receive is, "I haven't been chewed out lately by my boss," as if the number one motivator of people was non-punishment. That is not very motivating. And it leads to the most commonly used management style in America. When our people perform well we do nothing, but if they "screw up" we hit them. We call this the "leave-alone-zap" style of management. And believe me, it's not a very motivating style.

A number of years ago, researchers conducted a study to find out what unmotivated workers do in their free time. They assumed that unmotivated workers would also be unmotivated after work, but upon observation, soon found that was not true. In fact, they were amazed at how motivated these workers got at 5:00 P.M. when they headed out the door to hunt, fish, golf, coach, construct, sew, or cook. What is different about what people do at work versus after work that makes such a motivational difference? I once heard

*Source: Originally entitled "Have a Minute? Become an Effective Manager." From Executive Excellence (June 1984), pp. 7-8. Copyright © 1984 Executive Excellence. Reprinted by permission.

Scott Myers, a top management consultant, use an example of bowling to give the answer. Imagine an unmotivated worker bowling. What do you think this person would do when he or she threw a strike? Jump up and down and yell like anyone else. If that's true, then why aren't people jumping up and yelling in your company? Why don't your kids come down to breakfast in the morning yelling, "I cleaned up my room again—all right!"

logical example

The reason people are not yelling in organizations, following our bowling example, is that when they approach the alley, they notice there are no pins at the other end. How long would you want to bowl without any pins? And yet every day in the world of work people are literally bowling without any pins—they don't know what their goals are. That is why we work hard to get managers to set goals with their people. Without any "pins," people cannot get any feedback on performance. And the number one motivator of people is feedback on performance. In fact, the One Minute Manager has a saying that is worth remembering: "Feedback is the Breakfast of Champions." And you obtain feedback through information on performance.

goal setting theory

I think it's vital to put information on the performance of people into the hands of managers. Many organizations have elaborate systems for getting information to accountants and top executives, but never to anyone who can use it on a day-to-day basis. Managers need information—it's the most important tool they have. How can they know what to do if they don't know how well they are doing? Can you imagine training for the Olympics and not knowing how fast you ran or how high you jumped?

The first secret of the One Minute Manager is setting clear goals that are observable and measurable. Be careful, though, not to set too many goals. People can handle three to five goals at a time. Before you fill notebooks with goals, remember the 80/20 rule: 80 percent of the results you want to obtain from people comes from 20 percent of their activities. Therefore, you want to set goals toward accomplishing the few key activities that will yield the 80 percent of the desired result.

ONE MINUTE PRAISING

Reinforcement Theory

Once you make your people clear on what you are asking them to do and what good behavior looks like, you are ready for the second secret: One Minute Praising. Sneak around your organization and see if you can catch people doing anything right. When you do, give them a One Minute Praising. In order for your praising to be effective, you must be specific. Tell people what they did right. Say, "You submitted your report on time Friday and it was well written; in fact, I used it in a meeting today, and that report made you and me and our whole department look good."

After you praise people, tell them how you feel about what they did. Don't intellectualize. People want to know your gut feelings. "Let me tell you how I feel about that," you begin. "I feel super. You know I was so proud at the meeting that I want you to know I really feel good about you being on our team. Thanks a lot." Did that take very long? No. But did it last? Yes. People love it, and they remember it.

To help managers in catching their people doing things right, I often suggest that they schedule at least two hours each week for praising. But I warn them to do their homework *first* before they begin to wander around and praise people; otherwise, they will get themselves into trouble. For instance, one manager called me and said, "I'm doing what you told me to do—praising people from 1:30 to 2:30 on Wednesdays and Fridays—but it's not working." I said, "Why not?" He said, "I don't know." So I went over and had lunch with him one Wednesday. At 1:30 he said, "It's praising time." The moment he went out among his people I knew why it wasn't working. He was going up to people and saying things like, "Appreciate your efforts; thank you very much; I don't know what I'd do without you; keep up the good work." His staff thought he was running for political office.

Instead of praising people at random, first find out what they have done right. Use examples like, "I see productivity in your department is up ten percent; or, your report helped us win the contract with the Jones Company." To be effective, praisings must be specific.

Praising is the most powerful asset a manager has. In fact, it is the key to training people and making "winners" of everyone working for you. When you can't find winners—people who have proven that they can do the job, who have a good track record—you have to find potential winners and train them.

There are five steps to this training: 1) tell them what to do; 2) show them what to do; 3) let them try; 4) observe their performance (don't disappear and leave them alone); 5) praise progress and go back to show and tell again. You'll notice there is no mention of punishment here. Yelling at people does not teach them skills. Forget punishment as a training technique. Punishing people who are not yet winners will only immobilize them or teach them to avoid the punisher. If you do not see any progress, you cannot praise the person, but neither should you punish the performance. Go back to show and tell and redirect. If no progress is made after a while, you should talk to the person about career planning.

ONE MINUTE REPRIMAND

At this point people often say One Minute Management is not a tough enough management system. They say, "In the real world you have to be tough." Well, the third secret usually satisfies those people. It is called the One Minute Reprimand.

The "secret" is to reprimand only those people who know how to do the job, who have the skills, and you only reprimand them so they will start using their skills again.

There are four things to remember about a reprimand. First, do it immediately. Don't be one of those great "gunnysack" managers who see people doing something wrong but don't say anything; instead, they store up their feelings of disappointment or anger in an imaginary sack until one dark day, they dump their full load on a person. They let him "have it," telling him everything he has done wrong in the last six months. Second, be specific. Let people know exactly why you are angry or disappointed in them. Third, show and tell them how you feel about what they did wrong. Remember you have thoughts in your head but feelings in your stomach; what people really want to know is what you feel about what they did wrong. After you tell them how you feel, take a deep breath and give them the fourth part of the reprimand, which is the most important. End the reprimand with a praise. "Let me tell you one other thing. You are good, you are one of my best people. That is why I am annoyed with you. Normally, you get your reports in on time—this isn't anything like you. I want to tell you I am not going to let you get away with it because I count on you; you are one of my best people." I praise at the end of the reprimand for an important reason. When we part ways, I want them thinking about what they did wrong, not how I treated them.

Let me explain the difference between reprimanding someone who is good and redirecting someone who is learning. This example involves two college basketball players—Roger and John—whom I coached when I was in graduate school.

Roger could do it all. He could jump, shoot, rebound, and run like a deer. He was one of the best players the school had recruited in ten years, but he only wanted to play one end of the court—offense. Again and again, we asked him why he wouldn't play defense, but nothing seemed to work. Finally, we hauled the kid out of the game, put our nose against his nose, and screamed and yelled at him how we felt about his not playing defense. The first time we did this he said, "Why are you always yelling at me?" We yelled back, "Because you are good. You are the best player we've recruited in ten years." Then we put him back in the game.

Now John was a different story. If we put him in the game and he caught the ball, it was progress. If we were to treat him the same way when he made a mistake it would destroy him—or he would destroy us—because it would be unfair. So we would bench him and talk with him carefully. We had to teach him, and we could not teach him by yelling at him every time he made a mistake. The same reprimand behavior that was effective with Roger was ineffective with John.

So. remember to set clear goals in the beginning and then praise and reprimand according to peoples' performance and skills. If people do something right, praise them. If they make a mistake and they know better, give them a reprimand. When you reprimand, though, show them you are angry or disappointed with their behavior, but reaffirm their value as a person.

When you apply these three "secrets" to your work, let your staff know what you are trying to do. If you try practicing this without involving them, they will think you are out of your mind. But once they know the three steps too, they will help you become a One Minute Manager.

Delivering Feedback - behavior -

30. In Search of Excellence*

THOMAS J. PETERS

ROBERT H. WATERMAN, JR.

I. GOOD NEWS FOR AMERICAN BUSINESS: THE EXCELLENT COMPANIES

American industry rose to world dominance between 1920 and 1970. Guided by a belief in the principles of "scientific management" and the power of vast economies of scale, it was, until recently, the most productive, economic force the world had known.

Today, business performance in the United States is at an all-time low. America no longer makes the best or most reliable products, and seldom does it make them for less than foreign competitors. The symptoms of an economic impasse, even a decline, are everywhere.

The American business community has blamed a variety of factors for its troubles: costly safety and environmental regulation, government deficits, inadequate capital formation, a decline in research and development, and, of course, OPEC. Yet none of these external factors is the real cause. (The Japanese and Western Europeans have, after all, successfully coped with the same—and even more burdensome—restrictions.) The troubles are the direct result of the principles and methods employed by its own management. Once the envy of the world, American management is now the subject of pointed criticism.

FIVE CRITICISMS OF AMERICAN MANAGEMENT

1. American business schools are turning out MBA's skilled in quantitative analysis, but unable to cope with the nitty-gritty world of business decision-making.

2. Top management lacks a "gut feeling" for the "gestalt" of their [sic] business. As a result, it often fails to make a profit and get things done.

3. The typical manager does not "love the product" and lacks a hands-on knowledge of the company's technologies, customers, suppliers.

4. Managers don't treat their people as their most important resource, the key to productivity.

5. Top management analyzes and plans, but fails to act.

While many managers are looking to Japanese-style management as an antidote to poor performance, there is no reason to go so far afield. For years, top-performing American companies such as IBM, 3M, Johnson & Johnson, Caterpillar and others have stood as shining examples of how to create and sustain effective, profitable organizations. What do these excellent companies know that other American companies do not? We studied them to find out.

SOFT IS HARD

Our research yielded several broad observations.

1. People, values, quality, customer satisfaction, and other "soft" factors that are often dismissed by management as "vague" or "irrational" *can* be managed logically and sensibly.

2. Both "hard" (quantifiable) *and* "soft"

factors are essential to a company's economic health.

3. The excellent companies have been consistently successful largely *because* they are *intensely* concerned with the management of the "soft" aspects of their business.

4. This intense involvement reflects, at bottom, a deep respect for the individual—his potential and limitations—and a recognition that the individual's efforts and enthusiasm are the "bread and butter" of a healthy company.

While most companies pay lip service to things like "productivity through people," "values," and "service," the excellent companies actually *live* these concerns with unmatched intensity—and they experience direct bottom-line benefits as a result. They understand that soft *is* hard. Unfortunately, few American companies have profited from these management lessons. Here's why.

II. THE RISE AND FALL OF THE RATIONAL MODEL

Over the past 25 years, "professional management" has been equated with "hard-headed rationality." The ideal manager is supposed to be detached, analytical. He seeks quantitative justification for all decisions, and feels that his finely honed analytical skills qualify him to manage *all* types of businesses or organizations equally well.

Rational management techniques, introduced after World War II, were a necessary corrective to the seat-of-the-pants managment style then prevalent. They contributed to the post-war productivity boom. And they were well-suited to an economy in which there was tremendous pent-up demand for products, an absence of tough international competition, and a highly motivated, post-depression work force.

Today we face new foreign competitors, new products, new manufacturing processes, and the opening up of new global markets. American management has attempted to gain control over this new

economic complexity by developing equally complex, "matrix" management structures. New layers of staff have also been added to devise the rules, procedures, and systems of performance appraisal needed to clear up the conflicts and confusion created by these complex organizations.

The distance between top management and line workers has grown significantly, forcing top management to base its decision-making on "hard," yet abstract, data (rules and numbers) rather than on the concrete, everyday realities of producing and selling products and services. The result: rigid organizational structures that are divorced from the realities of the marketplace and unable to respond to—or profit from—shifts in the economic environment. The principles of scientific management that once brought prosperity are now sapping the vitality of American industry.

THE WRONG-HEADEDNESS OF HARD-HEADED RATIONALITY

Rational thought is useful in weeding out dumb options and pointing a business in the right direction. But an over-emphasis on a *narrow* view of rationality can be fatal. The hallmarks of this narrow view are:

— Big is necessarily better because you achieve economies of scale.

— Cost is the most important criterion when judging a product's viability.

— Analyze. Plan. Forecast. Set "hard" targets even when the future is inherently unpredictable.

— Get rid of "fanatical champions" who disrupt long-range planning.

— Implementation is of secondary importance to balancing the portfolio and buying into the right industries.

— Control everything by writing long job descriptions and creating complex, matrix structures. People are only factors of production.

— Get the incentives right for the top performers, weed out the 30 to 40 percent dead wood, and productivity will follow.

— Inspect to control quality. Workers need to be kept on their toes.

— If you can read the financial statements, you can manage anything.

— If the balance sheet and income statement look good, you don't have to worry about the marketplace.

— Buy into industries you don't understand if you must to maintain growth.

What are the shortcomings of the narrow view?

1. Narrow rationality reduces the *scope* of analysis. Important issues are left untouched. Cost reduction becomes a higher priority than revenue enhancement. The value of product duplication or the overkill of a charged-up sales force is missed.

2. The living element is left out of situations which cannot be accurately understood without it (e.g., "productivity through people").

3. Narrow rationality ignores insight based on experience.

4. Narrow rationality does not value experimentation, abhors mistakes and leads to inflexibility. This anti-experimental bias can force a company to bet on "super products" that *must* work. This is deadly in an era of rapid change.

5. The overly rational approach excludes informality.

6. The rational model denigrates *values.* Major decisions in the excellent companies are not shaped through analysis but by *values.* Values create a broad, uplifting, shared culture within which charged-up people make extraordinary contributions.

III. MAN WAITING
FOR MOTIVATION

Studies show that each of us wants to feel like a winner—even when we are not. The excellent companies allow the ordinary person to feel like a winner by, for example, establishing sales targets that almost all their salespeople can reach (IBM). Or by letting teams set their own objectives (TI and Tupperware). The achievement of these goals is then celebrated with lots of hoopla. When you call a person a winner, he starts acting like one.

LEFT BRAIN/RIGHT BRAIN

The excellent companies recognize that people have two sides to them: a rational, left-brained side, and an emotional, right-brained side. They provide contexts in which right-brain needs can be met: the desire to be on a winning team, the need for small group camaraderie, the need to stand out and celebrate outstanding achievement.

Excellent companies foster the intuitive, creative side of a person. "Trusting his gut" helps the manager in the excellent companies cope with the complexities of making business decisions in today's world.

KISS: KEEP IT SIMPLE, STUPID!

The excellent companies understand that human beings are not good at processing large streams of new information. They have developed devices for cutting through complexity and information overload. They keep staffs small. They focus on a few key values and objectives to let people know what is important and cut down on the need for daily instructions. They insist on 1-page memos. They ignore economies of scale to avoid having to coordinate unwieldy oganizations. They trust ingrained patterns of experience, instead of relying on voluminous studies or reports.

POSITIVE REINFORCEMENT

The excellent companies know that *positive* reinforcement—rewards for a job well-done—is more effective than negative reinforcement in changing behavior. Instead of attacking unwanted behavior head-on (a ploy that often has unpredictable consequences), the excellent company displaces it by positively reinforcing desired behavior.

Peer review—knowing how one is doing relative to others—is an important ingredient in positive reinforcement. Intrinsic motivation—knowing that a task is inherently worthwhile—is also essential.

DOING THINGS

Actions speak louder than words. If a manager can get his people to start acting the way he wants them to—even in a small way—they will come to believe in what they are doing. By labeling, and publicly praising these small wins along the way, a manager can garner commitment to a new strategic direction. Excellent companies act their way into strategies, not vice-versa.

MEANING

A dominant and coherent culture focussed on external market realities (e.g., service, customers, quality) gives meaning, security and direction to people. It obviates the need for policy manuals, organization charts, detailed procedures and other encumbrances of organizational life. Cultural values make clear what is important, and what each person should be doing. The external orientation keeps companies sensitive and adaptive to changes in the marketplace.

SELF-CONTROL

Because they are decentralized and authority is delegated far down the line, the excellent companies give their people a chance to stand out.

TRANSFORMING LEADERSHIP

The excellent companies have been blessed, usually at their founding, with a "transformer leader"—one who, by example and by teaching, instills purpose in his followers. Transforming leaders seldom wield naked power. Rather, they enlist the innate desire of human beings for meaning. Thus they transform unremarkable men and women into enthusiasts committed to particular sets of enduring values. For the individual, the institution becomes not just a place of work but a valued source of personal satisfaction.

Managing the irrational (as well as the rational) needs of his people is the *practical* thing for a manager to do. After all, human nature is largely irrational.

IV. MANAGING AMBIGUITY AND PARADOX

New management theory is needed to explain the performance of the excellent companies and provide guidance for tomorrow's managers. Old management theories were attractive because they were straightforward, without ambiguity or paradox. They leaned heavily on military metaphors: "chain of command," "attack," "discipline," "sending for reinforcements" and the like. Military metaphors are no longer functional; the economic environment is no longer straightforward. They hamper creative thinking by allowing only a narrow range of solutions to problems. New, more appropriate metaphors are: sailing, playfulness, foolishness, seesaws, space stations, garbage cans. They go a long way toward explaining the success of the excellent companies.

TOWARD A NEW MANAGEMENT THEORY

Our research into the excellent companies has shed light on some management concepts which may form the basis of a new, yet-to-be-formulated theory of business management.

Any new theory must recognize the limits of rationality, as well as the value of irrational needs. Like:

1. the need for meaning;
2. the need for control over one's destiny;
3. the need to feel like a winner;
4. the need to act before one believes.

In addition to these points, the new theory must treat companies as distinctive cultures and recognize that managed, unpredictable evolution is the key to keeping a culture adaptive.

CULTURE

Culture is *not* a luxury. Companies whose only articulated goals are financial do not do nearly as well *financially* as the excellent companies—which manage to integrate *within their cultures* the importance of fiscal health and values.

Though traditional management theory hardly touches upon culture, the excellent companies often credit their success to it. A manager's key role within these companies is *shaping cultural values*. He does not merely set up structures and goals; he uses the symbols, beliefs and rituals of his culture to *convince* his people that the articulated goals are *correct* and worthy of adherence. A strong, positive culture sets out the values that count, but gives individuals room to be innovative in putting them into practice. *Cultural management draws out the individual's creative potential.*

MANAGED EVOLUTION: "BUZZING, BOOMING ENVIRONMENTS"

To survive in a changing marketplace, a company must remain adaptive, must evolve. Traditional theory—and corporate practice—is both too rigid and too loose. It underplays the stabilizing role of rigidly shared values and culture; it overemphasizes the importance of rules and planning in adapting to change.

The excellent companies know that adaptation is too complex to manage by rules. They let their culture keep them stable, and then make sure there are always enough good experiments going on to satisfy the laws of probability. They are *learning organizations*. By dividing themselves into competing products and teams, they discover what works and what doesn't *before* the market overtakes them. Lots of rapid action and quick learning from experiments, both successful and not, help the excellent companies to evolve. Managers do not assume that productive change results from orders given and mechanically followed. Rather, they select successful experiments *that are already going on,* and then label them as "new strategic directions."

These companies also benefit from a rich flow of information—both internally and with their customers—that spurs new ideas. The small, buzzing, booming environments are not tidy: their rampant duplication of effort flies in the face of conventional wisdom about economies of scale and learning curves, yet they are highly efficient—as the excellent companies have proven.

V. EIGHT THINGS THE EXCELLENT COMPANIES DO RIGHT

1. THEY GET THINGS DONE

The excellent companies have developed a wide range of action devices that cut through complexity and help them get things done.

Organizational fluidity: MBWA.—The excellent companies have vast, informal communications networks. These insure that the right people are in regular contact with each other. Management-By-Wandering-Around (MBWA) insures that management is part of this network. Physical configurations (e.g., escalators instead of elevators, lots of small conference rooms, no doors) help these connections along. Regular, positive peer review and comparison is also a tremendous spur to action. Witness Tupperware's "Rally." More communication leads to more experiments, leads to more learning, leads to a company that is on top of changes in the marketplace.

Chunking.—Solving a problem is often a matter of breaking it down into manageable parts. "Chunking," or dividing into small groups, ad hoc task forces or project teams, gives the excellent companies flexibility to swiftly bring problem-solving resources—people and money—to bear on a given problem. To be effective, however, the social context, attitudes and culture must support the seemingly chaotic behavior that is part and parcel of chunking.

Some facts about *successful* small groups and task forces:

— They usually have ten members or less.

— The seniority of members is proportionate to the importance of the problem.

— They last for only a short time.

— Membership is voluntary; and goals are set from within.
— They are pulled together when needed and without a charter.
— Their conclusions are followed up swiftly.
— No staff is assigned to them.
— Documentation is informal and scant.

Experimental bias.—The excellent companies are willing to try out new product ideas on a low-cost, limited basis. It often costs less to build a prototype and run tests with it than it does to do lengthy market studies. Users/customers are almost always key participants in these experiments. If an experiment should fail, the company gets out early without losing too much.

Leaky systems.—Getting money and manpower for an experiment from outside the corporate mainstream (often called "bootlegging" or "scrounging") is an honored tradition at the excellent companies.

Experimental context.—Experimentation won't take hold unless management is tolerant of leaky systems, mistakes, failures, and the unexpected.

Simple systems.—Fluidity, chunking, and experimenting are enhanced by a simple organizational structure. Small staffs. A few, clear, action-oriented objectives (as opposed to a lot of financial ones). One-page memos. Simple revenue reports. It takes persistence to get the balance right between simplicity and complexity. It took Proctor and Gamble 150 years to perfect the 1-page memo.

2. THEY STAY CLOSE TO THE CUSTOMER

The customer is king. He intrudes into every aspect of the business: sales, manufacturing, research and accounting. The excellent companies are driven by what is, from a cost-analysis point of view, an unjustifiable, *over*-commitment to quality, reliability and service.

The service obsession: "You have to remember who pays the bills."—Whatever their basic business—high tech or hamburgers—the excellent companies define themselves as *service businesses.* This is evident in three ways:

— Top management treats service problems as "real time" issues. They meet frequently with junior sales staff, and are highly visible to customers either in person or by mail or both. Top execs all make sales calls and personally monitor customer satisfaction.
— A strong people orientation. Service objectives (rather than financial ones) are meaningful to people and inspire accountability far down the line. "Each one of us *is* the company."
— A high intensity of measurement and feedback. New rewards and incentive programs (training, hoopla) are in continuous preparation.

The quality obsession: "Doing it right is the only way."—Quality zealotry pervades the *entire* structure of excellent companies. Quality objectives are built into all MBO's. Cat's 48-hour parts delivery guarantee shows how certain Cat is that its machines work. In strict economic terms, this overachievement doesn't add up—until you look at Cat's revenue sheet.

Quality and reliability are always prized above technical wizardry. The excellent companies are often "second to the market" not because they aren't technically advanced but because they choose to make technology that works reliably for the customer.

Nichemanship.—The excellent companies divide their customer base into segments to provide them with tailored products and services. Here are 5 attributes of companies that stay close to the customer through niche strategies:

— They develop advanced technology for "lead users" that is subsequently marketed to more average users.
— They get into a market early; charge a lot for tailored products and then get out when the competition underbids them.
— They understand how to appeal to different market segments.
— Their sales people are customer problem-solvers.

— They are willing to spend on such things as market testing and merchandising.

Listening to the customer.—The excellent companies are better listeners than other companies. Most of their innovations come from listening. Bloomingdales gave Levi-Strauss the idea for faded jeans. Proctor and Gamble was the first company to put an 800 number on their packaging. In the first year, they got 200,000 calls and responded to every one.

The excellent companies are more concerned with staying close to the customer than by any other factor, including cost or technical wizardry. They innovate better because they innovate in response to market needs and involve potential users in the development of new products or services.

3. THEY ENCOURAGE AUTONOMY AND ENTREPRENEURSHIP

The excellent companies continue to innovate because, though big, they act small. They divide themselves into smaller working units and push autonomy far down the line to encourage the entrepreneurial spirit. Dana's "store managers" and 3M's "venture teams" are examples of this. They make a purposeful trade-off between the messiness, lack of coordination, internal competition and chaos of decentralization and the regular innovation that comes from entrepreneurial activity in the ranks.

The champion.—A champion is not a blue-sky dreamer or creative genius, but one who fanatically believes in an innovative product idea or service and doggedly persists in pursuing its implementation, however irrational or unpromising it might seem. The champion is the catalyst for all innovation. Because he does not fit the corporate mold, he is seldom hired or promoted, but the excellent companies have created social environments and devised incentives that encourage champions to come forward out of the ranks of "ordinary" men and women.

The championing system.—In addition to the champion, there is the executive champion, generally an ex-champion himself, who has been through the product development mill and can protect the champion from the nay-saying forces inherent in most organizations. The "godfather," often a founder whose life and deeds have taken on mythological proportions, serves as a role model for the champion. The champion is willing to take a risk because the godfather's legend tells him that doing so leads to success.

How the excellent companies innovate.—

• Innovation success is a numbers game. The odds of success with one experiment are small, but they are high with lots of experiments going on. The excellent companies have more experimenting champions than other companies do.

• The excellent companies have informal structures that support the champion's efforts. "Skunk works" or "limited autonomy positions" are leaks in the system that allow scrounging champions the money and people they need to get something done. The champion's autonomy, however, is not absolute; he is constrained by cultural values that spell out his responsibility as a champion to the corporation.

• The excellent companies substitute internal competition for formal, rule- and committee-driven product development. Competition between would-be product ideas is often decided by procedures such as "performance shoot-outs." The costs of duplication, cannibalization, overlapping products and divisions, and lost development dollars when the sales force won't "buy" a new idea are high, but the benefits are great in terms of commitment, innovation and revenue generation.

• Easy communication, an absence of barriers, is essential to innovation. Communication at the excellent companies is intense, but informal. There are physical supports for it (e.g., blackboards everywhere at IBM, many small conference rooms at HP). Communication spurs new ideas, but also acts as a control because people are always looking in to "see how things are going."

• Without a tolerance for failure, there's no learning and no innovation. Constant communication softens the impact of failure because projects just can't go wrong for long without someone noticing and calling a halt.

• Champions are the key to innovation. They don't emerge automatically, but given a supportive environment, the would-be champion population is much greater than a handful of creative geniuses.

4. THEY "LIVE" A PEOPLE ORIENTATION

Treat people as adults, as partners, as the company's *most important resource*—and productivity and profit will follow. At most companies, "people issues" are paid lip service, or addressed by adopting the latest human relations fad (e.g., quality circles). But at the excellent companies, "respect for the individual" pervades the structural fiber of the organization top to bottom.

Respect for the individual is evident in the depth and intensity of the training. At IBM, particularly. Dana U at Dana and Hamburger U at McDonald's are also good examples. Training is treated as a socialization process. Fast-trackers are started off in the "hands dirty" jobs to help them develop an instinct for the business. Bechtel's "A Fine Feel for the Doable" reflects this practice.

Information on performance and goals is shared throughout the organization to let people know how they are doing and compared to whom. While performance is measured, the numbers are not used by management to browbeat employees, but as a basis for peer review and pressure. Peer expectations are often higher than management's and are more effective in helping to boost performance. Non-monetary rewards (hoopla) are also potent incentives.

5. THEY ARE HANDS-ON, VALUE-DRIVEN

The excellent companies stand for a particular set of values. Through personal attention, persistence, and direct intervention in day-to-day operations, their managers shape and inculcate these values throughout the organization. Values are also communicated by means of stories, legends and myths. Frito-Lay tells service stories. Johnson & Johnson tells quality stories. 3M tells innovation stories.

Less well-performing companies have either no coherent values, or only sets of quantifiable objectives, usually financial. Financial goals, however, do not have much power to inspire the tens of thousands of people who make, sell and service the product. Values like quality, service, reliability do.

While each excellent company adheres to a different set of values (often determined by the industry they are part of), there are common attributes:

1. Values are stated in *qualitative* terms.
2. Values inspire the person at the bottom, the person with only average talent.
3. Values include:
— a belief in being the best
— a belief in taking care of the details of execution
— a belief in the importance of people as individuals
— a belief in providing superior quality and service
— a belief in people as innovators and a willingness to tolerate failure
— a belief in the importance of informality and communication
— a belief in the importance of economic growth

Clarifying and breathing life into a value system takes the persistence of a "hands-on" manager. It is the most important job he has.

6. THEY STICK TO THEIR KNITTING

Most acquisitions go awry. The predicted synergies seldom materialize. The executives of the acquired company often leave, despite assurances that the subsidiary will be run independently. The acquisition process draws management's attention away from the mainline business. The acquired company has a different culture and tends to dilute the parent company's values. Management loses its "feel" for the business, and its credibility as experienced, hands-on leadership.

How do the excellent companies avoid these problems? When they branch out (either internally or through acquisition), they acquire in small, manageable steps to contain the risk. They experiment; and if they don't succeed, they get out quickly. They diversify around a single skill or product line: 3M stays close to coating and bonding technology. "Never acquire a business you don't know how to run" (Robert Wood, founder of Johnson & Johnson). They only acquire small businesses that don't threaten the character of the parent organization.

7. THEY HAVE SIMPLE FORMS AND LEAN STAFFS

When a company owns many businesses, the simple, functional structure of finance, sales, manufacturing is no longer adequate and it must choose an alternate structure. It might organize around product groups, market segments or geographic locations where it has offices. However, if it tries to combine all these dimensions in one, formal, 4-dimensional matrix structure, the result is a logistic mess. Since everything is connected to everything else, everything is equally important. Priorities are diluted and action stops.

People need clear-cut priorities and allegiances to function effectively. The excellent companies provide a single, unchanging form—often the product division—to help people sort through daily complexities and pick out important matters. With one underlying form, the excellent companies can make flexible use of small divisions and units like task forces

to address problems that suddenly arise. (The excellent companies *appear* to be constantly reorganizing.)

The cultural supports that make the simple, product-division structure work are:

— Divisional integrity. All the main functions—product development, finance and personnel—are in each division.
— Constant "hiving off" of new divisions and rewards for doing so. (Most companies reward empire builders.)
— Guidelines that define when a new product line automatically becomes an independent division.
— A willingness to shift people and product lines regularly among divisions.

Staff at the excellent companies is lean, and tends to be out in the field most of the time solving problems rather than in the home office. Most of the traditional functions of the head office—personnel, finance, purchasing—are decentralized to the product division.

A "form" for the future.—There are at least 5 organizational forms.

— the functional form, typical of old-line consumer products firms
— the divisional form exemplified by GM
— the matrix form, a response to economic complexities through multi-dimensional structures
— the adhocracy, a way of responding to complexity without erecting a permanent bureaucracy
— the "missionary form" (McDonald's), a way of providing stability through values *instead* of structure.

We propose a hybrid form of all 5, a "structure for the 80's" that is built on 3 pillars. (See Figure 30-1.) Each pillar is a response to a primary need of business organizations.

The Stability Pillar responds to the need for efficient handling of the basics. It specifies the maintenance of a simple, consistent, underlying form and the development and maintenance of broad yet flexible values. The product-based division is our choice for the appropriate form. Values are included here under structure because "structure," most

Figure 30-1

THE THREE PILLARS OF THE "STRUCTURE OF THE EIGHTIES"

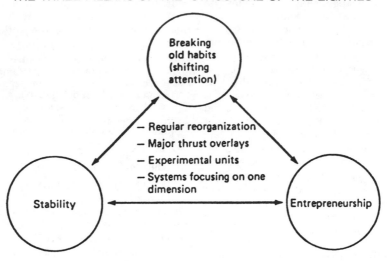

— Simple, basic underlying
   form

— Dominating values
   (superordinate goals)

— Minimizing/simplifying
   interfaces

— Entrepreneurial, "small is
   beautiful," units

— Cabals, other problem-solving
   implementation groups

— Measurement systems based on
   amount of entrepreneurship,
   implementation

broadly defined, means communications patterns.

The Entrepreneurial Pillar responds to the need for regular innovation. Keeping things small by hiving off new divisons is *the* key to keeping an organization adaptive. Divisions should possess their own support staff.

The Habit-Breaking Pillar helps to remain flexible and avoid calcification. A willingness to reorganize on a temporary basis to attack specific problems is essential. Hiving off new divisions, shifting product lines to different divisions to take advantage of managerial talents, bringing top talent together on project teams to solve central organizational problems are all part of this general willingness to reshuffle the boxes *within* a central form. Habit-breaking devices are good ways of

responding to shifting economic currents *without* setting up huge, permanent, integrating committee devices of the matrix form.

Taken together, these three pillars match closely the management systems of many of the excellent companies.

8. THEY LIVE BY THE
   DISCIPLINE OF VALUES

The excellent companies live according to the loose-tight principle: the co-existence of firm, central direction and a loose structure that affords maximum individual autonomy. They achieve this balance through their "faith" in values. To the excellent company, values like quality, service, innovation, and people productivity are the only things that count. Values are both loose *and* tight: the *discipline* of adhering to shared values provides a framework of stable expectations in which autonomy can take place. Peer pressure and attention to the customer are two of the "tightest" values.

The discipline of shared values dissolves many apparent contradictions. The "quality v. cost" trade-off is not a trade-off because attention to quality reduces waste and enhances innovation and productivity. The "efficiency v. effectiveness" contradiction dissolves because the small facility, with its turned-on worker in communication with his peers, is more efficient than the big plant. The "external v. internal" contradiction disappears because the excellent companies are externally focussed on service, quality, and innovation, and, *as a result,* internally focussed on things like employee-initiated quality control, internal competition, communication and, of course, people.

The dumb-smart rule, however, does still hold. The "smart" MBA-trained manager, skilled at producing 500-page reports, is too "smart" to see the value of what his "dumb" counterpart insists upon: personalized service for every customer. The highest quality products every time. Regular innovation from ordinary men and women. The MBA would label these attitudes simplistic. There are always practical, reasonable, justifiable reasons to compromise occasionally on quality or service. Yet largely because the excellent companies have remained simplistic about the important things, they have continued to prosper.

31. Megatrends*

JOHN NAISBITT

As a society, we have been moving from the old to the new. And we are still in motion. Caught between eras, we experience turbulence. Yet, amid the sometimes painful and uncertain present, the restructuring of America proceeds unrelentingly.

Megatrends is about a new American society that is not yet fully evolved. Nevertheless, the restructuring of America is already changing our inner and outer lives. Each of its ten chapters examines one of these critical restructurings [boldface added in following list]:

1. Although we continue to think we live in an industrial society, we have in fact changed to an economy based on the creation and distribution of information.

2. We are moving in the dual directions of high tech/high touch, matching each new technology with a compensatory human response.

3. No longer do we have the luxury of operating within an isolated, self-sufficient, national economic system; we now must acknowledge that we are part of a global economy. We have begun to let go of the idea that the United States is and must remain the world's industrial leader as we move on to other tasks.

4. We are restructuring from a society run by short-term considerations and rewards in favor of dealing with things in much longer-term time frames.

5. In cities and states, in small organizations and subdivisions, we have rediscovered the ability to act innovatively and to achieve results—from the bottom up.

6. We are shifting from institutional help to more self-reliance in all aspects of our lives.

7. We are discovering that the framework of representative democracy has become obsolete in an era of instantaneously shared information.

8. We are giving up our dependence on hierarchical structures in favor of informal networks. This will be especially important to the business community.

9. More Americans are living in the South and West, leaving behind the old industrial cities of the North.

10. From a narrow either/or society with a limited range of personal choices, we are exploding into a free-wheeling multiple-option society.

These larger patterns are not always clear. Helped by the news media, especially television, we seem to be a society of events, just moving from one incident—sometimes, even crisis—to the next, rarely pausing (or caring) to notice the process going on underneath. Yet only by understanding the larger patterns, or restructurings, do the individual events begin to make sense.

This book focuses on the megatrends or broad outlines that will define the new society. No one can predict the shape of that new world. Attempts to describe it in detail are the stuff of science fiction and futuristic guessing games that often prove inaccurate and annoying.

The most reliable way to anticipate the future is by understanding the present.

That is the premise of *Megatrends*.

For the past twelve years, I have been working with major American corporations to try to understand what is really happening in the United States by monitoring local events and behavior, because

*Source: From John Naisbitt, *Megatrends*, pp. 1-2, 249-252. Copyright © 1982 by John Naisbitt. Reprinted with permission of Warner Books, Inc.

collectively what is going on locally is what is going on in America.

. . . .

We are living in the *time of the parenthesis,* the time between eras. It is as though we have bracketed off the present from both the past and the future, for we are neither here nor there. We have not quite left behind the either/or America of the past—centralized, industrialized, and economically self-contained. With one foot in the old world where we lived mostly in the Northeast, relied on institutional help, built hierarchies, and elected representatives, we approached problems with an eye toward the high-tech, short-term solutions.

But we have not embraced the future either. We have done the human thing: We are clinging to the known past in fear of the unknown future. This book outlines one interpretation of that future in order to make it more real, more knowable. Those who are willing to handle the ambiguity of this in-between period and to anticipate the new era will be a quantum leap ahead of those who hold on to the past. The time of the parenthesis is a time of change and questioning.

As we move from an industrial to an information society, we will use our brainpower to create instead of our physical power, and the technology of the day will extend and enhance our mental ability. As we take advantage of the opportunity for job growth and investment in all the sunrise industries, we must not lose sight of the need to balance the human element in the face of all that technology.

Yet, the most formidable challenge will be to train people to work in the information society. Jobs will become available, but who will possess the high-tech skills to fill them? Not today's graduates who cannot manage simple arithmetic or write basic English. And certainly not the unskilled, unemployed dropouts who cannot even find work in the old sunset industries.

Farmer, laborer, clerk. The next transition may well be to technician. But that is a major jump in skill level.

As Third World countries take over many industrial tasks, the United States must be prepared to take the lead in the innovative new tasks of the future—or face the prospect of being a Great Britain, whose steel and automobile companies are merely disguised widespread-employment programs. All the while, as we tread water, unwilling to choose the winning businesses of the future and unable to let go of the losers, Japan and the "new Japans" of the Third World are free to eclipse our lead in electronics, biotechnology, and the other sunrise sectors.

But do we have the courage to abandon our traditional industries, industries that other countries can now do better. Do we have the innovative ability to venture forward into the future?

One good sign is that some American businesses appear to have discovered the advantages of the long-term approach and the appropriate reward systems, have developed the capacity to change the direction of a business as the world changes, and have recognized the opportunities inherent in being the world's leading provider of information, knowledge, and expertise.

Even while we think globally, the place to make a difference politically is at the local rather than the national level. Whether the issue is energy, politics, community self-help, entrepreneurship, the consumer movement, or wholistic health, the new creed is one of self-reliance and local initiative. In this new era of geographic diversity and decentralization, the conformity of mass society is a thing of the past. The divestiture of AT&T's local companies and the shift of responsibility from Washington back to the States could not have taken place twenty years ago. These prominent decentralist actions represent the culmination of a long process that has been evolving since the 1960s.

The political notion of governance is being completely redefined. Today's well-educated, well-informed citizen is capable and desirous of participating in political decisions to a greater extent than the present representative system permits. Hence the growth in referenda, initiatives, and recalls during the 1970s. Despite occasional outcries to the contrary, we do not want strong leadership in national affairs because we are basically self-governing. And we are gradually extending the ideal of democracy into corporations, where we are demanding a greater voice as consumers, shareholders, outside directors, and (most importantly) employees.

This newly evolving world will require its own structures. We are beginning to abandon the hierarchies that worked well in the centralized, industrial era. In their place, we are substituting the network model of organization and communication, which has its roots in the natural, egalitarian, and spontaneous formation of groups among like-minded people. Networks restructure the power and communication flow within an organization from vertical to horizontal. One network form, the quality control circle, will help revitalize worker participation and productivity in American business. A network management style is already in place in several young, successful computer firms. And the computer itself will be what actually smashes the hierarchical pyramid: With the computer to keep track of people and business information, it is no longer necessary for organizations to be organized into hierarchies. No one knows this better than the new-age computer companies.

The computer will smash the pyramid: We created the hierarchical, pyramidal, managerial system because we needed it to keep track of people and things people did; with the computer to keep track, we can restructure our institutions horizontally.

Amid all the other restructurings, America is engaged in a massive migration from the Northeast and Midwest to the Southwest (and to Florida). That population shift came about in large part as a response to three megashifts discussed in this book: (1) People are moving away from the thickly settled Northeast, where industrial society flourished earlier in this century, but where dying industries are leaving behind abandoned factories and jobless people; (2) the foreign competition we experience, especially in automobile and steel, as part of an interdependent world economy is forcing many of the old industries to close; and (3) the decentralization of business and the search for new energy sources are enabling people to find a job in an area where they would like to live (large numbers of young people, for example, have moved to the Rocky Mountain states).

Each of the ten cities of opportunity has recently attracted one or more new facilities in the new information industries. The North-South shift is irreversible in our lifetime. What is unclear is how the country will adjust to the changes. These are the questions for which local and regional planners must find innovative solutions. Are there ways to adaptively reuse the valuable infrastructure being left behind in the North? Ways to meet the growing demand for instant infrastructure in the Southwest? The burden falls most heavily on the cities where change is greatest, such as Detroit and Houston.

Although the North-South shift sounds like an either/or choice, it is not. Even geography can be multiple option because we have diversified into a society where almost anything is possible. The wide range of choices in work arrangements, the new definitions of family, the enormous diversity in the arts, the dazzling array of newly promoted specialty foods, are only some of the reflections of a society that is exploding with diversity. One measure is the way we have responded to the new wave of immigrants in recent years: We have finally abandoned the myth of the melting pot and learned to celebrate ethnic diversity. The new languages, ethnic food and restaurants, and the additional layer of foreign cultures all around us seem to fit the multiple-option mood. This new openness enriches us all.

Such is the time of the parenthesis, its challenges, its possibilities, and its questions.

Although the time between eras is uncertain, it is a great and yeasty time, filled with opportunity. If we can learn to make uncertainty our friend, we can achieve much more than in stable eras.

In stable eras, everything has a name and everything knows its place, and we can leverage very little.

But in the time of the parenthesis we have extraordinary leverage and influence—individually, professionally, and institutionally—if we can only get a clear sense, a clear conception, a clear vision, of the road ahead.

My God, what a fantastic time to be alive!

32. The Change Masters*

ROSABETH MOSS KANTER

Rip van Winkle went to sleep for twenty years. When he awakened, the American landscape had changed dramatically, and his bones creaked with age. The world around him was no longer one he understood or in which he could function well.

Will history someday see that classic story as a parable for much of corporate America today—falling asleep in the 1960s and waking up too old, too tired in the 1980s? Or can more organizations learn to operate in the integrative and highly people-centered ways of the innovating companies I have identified?

If American organizations use this opportunity to arouse the potential entrepreneurs in their midst—the people at all levels with new ideas to contribute—then, unlike Rip van Winkle, they could be renewed, refreshed, and readied for a changed world. The spirit of enterprise could thus be reborn, heralding a kind of Renaissance for corporate America.

The first question about a "corporate Renaissance" is its feasibility, especially for older, troubled industries. Doubters wonder whether the existence of more corporate entrepreneurs would really make much of a difference for them. They question whether the success of high-technology firms is really due to better management rather than to growing markets that will absorb virtually anything. In short, are practices characteristic of companies like Hewlett-Packard, "Chipco," and high-tech sectors of GE really transferrable to matured corporate giants?

At extremes of market conditions, of course, the quality of the organization probably does not matter much. Having the right product in a world hungry for it masks a large number of organizational sins: the company can get away with being poorly managed and still do well financially. At the other extreme, where the product is clearly the wrong thing at the wrong time, then no amount of organizational change by itself is likely to guarantee success.

We would search in vain for the organizational alchemy to transform a smokestack industry into a high-technology firm; and attempts to effect a "transmutation" via divestitures and acquisitions deflect important managerial attention from improving the quality of internal operations. Companies take on their shape, and in part become locked into it, from their industry and their history. More recently founded companies can adapt practices from a more modern era and can support more change while their basic systems are still being developed, making it more likely that computer and electronics companies will indeed have more innovation-stimulating practices, while industries with ample time to experience hardening-of-the-organizational-arteries, such as autos and insurance, will have fewer.

Yet despite these broad tendencies, individual firms even within the same industry still vary, and there is a range of differences with respect to investment in people and the encouragement of employees' participation in innovative problem solving. In my comparative study, those firms with early and progressive

*Source: From Rosabeth Moss Kanter, The Change Masters, pp. 352-370. Copyright © 1983 by Rosabeth Moss Kanter. Reprinted with permission of Simon & Schuster, Inc.

human-resource practices, when compared with a similar company in the *same industry*, had been significantly more profitable over the last twenty years.

Similarly, it is not only high-technology firms that are characterized by the kinds of practices that keep innovation alive for long periods of time. Procter and Gamble operates within one of the oldest industries, but has continued to break new ground in product introductions as well as workplace practices. (Indeed, the company considers information about its team-oriented manufacturing facilities "proprietary.") Cummins Engine, well known for its quality-of-work–life programs, occupies a spot in one of the so-called declining industries, but has performed consistently better than other diesel-engine manufacturers. And an even more striking illustration of the potential for transformation of older industries is the speed with which many banks are trying to reorient and develop new products and services as the rules governing financial institutions change. If banks, long considered among the most traditionbound of American corporations, can do it, then so can other industries.

Constraints and environmental conditions count; they make it more or less difficult to carry out organizational objectives, and they present leaders with problems as well as opportunities. It would be naive to fail to recognize this. But within those boundaries, it is the capacity to engage and use human energies effectively that sorts successes from failures, in the long run if not always in the short. Innovations such as new products or market applications, as well as effective organizational problem solving at all levels, depend on people—and the need for these competitive advantages grows with environmental turbulence and a less expansive economy.

Today more than ever, because of profound transformations in the economic and social environment for American business, it should be a national priority to release and support the skills of men and

women who can envision and push innovations. This requires, in turn, corporations that operate integratively, that help individuals make the connections and get the tools to move beyond preestablished limits and break new ground, working through coalitions and teams. Making the power available to people at all levels of organizations to take action to introduce or experiment with new strategies and practices, often seen as a luxury of rich times, is in fact a *necessity* for survival and success in difficult times.

"Corporate entrepreneurs" are often the authors not of the grand gesture but of the quiet innovation. They are the ones who translate strategy—set at the top—into actual practice, and by doing so, shape what strategy turns out to mean. Top leaders' general directives to open a new market, improve quality, or cut costs mean nothing without the ability of relevant managers and professionals to design the systems to carry them out or redirect their staffs' activities accordingly. So the meaning of change and the extent to which it can significantly affect an organization can be, in many cases, determined almost exclusively by the initiative and enterprise of people at middle levels and below, who themselves design new ways of carrying out their routine operations that may quickly or eventually add up to an altered state for the organization.

Indeed, without sufficient flexibility to permit random creativity in unexpected— and nonpreferred—places in the organization, many companies would not have developed new programs, new products, or new systems that were eventually adopted as organizationwide initiatives, to the great benefit of the whole. Because innovators have their finger on the pulse of operations, they can see, suggest, and set in motion new possibilities that top strategists may not have considered—until a crisis or galvanizing event makes them search for a successful departure from tradition in the company's own experience.

In short, individuals do not have to be doing "big things" in order to have their cumulative accomplishments eventually result in big performance for the company.

It is in this sense that individuals in the right circumstances are the keys to innovation. They are only rarely the inventors of the "breakthrough" system. They are only rarely doing something that is totally unique or that no one, in any organization, ever thought of before. Instead, they are often applying ideas that have proved themselves elsewhere, or they are rearranging parts to create a better result, or they are noting a potential problem before it turns into a catastrophe and mobilizing the actions to anticipate and solve it.

By being able to get the power to act, individuals are helping the organization stay ahead of change.

The environment—e.g., industry conditions—and history—e.g., a company's past investments—constrain the *arenas* in which corporate entrepreneurs can maneuver, but they do not eliminate the *possibility* for productive innovations in *some* arena.

If the physical or product side of the organization cannot be quickly modified, for example, owing to capital investment and other heavy sunk costs, there is still room for innovation in the organization itself—in modifying production methods, in changing product details to be more responsive to customers, in identifying novel uses, in improving quality, or in taking advantage of the knowledge of the organization's people to respond better and more quickly to the environment— to improve service, to improve relationships, to reduce labor conflict or other forms of costly friction in the company. Repeated studies of innovation in American companies make clear that it need not decline as the company ages or as a product matures but that the domain shifts away from rapid technical changes to changes in method or form of organization.

Even so, one should not rule out the possibility of a dramatic breakthrough in product form or use itself. It is when a company stops believing that it can always do better, regardless of the domain in which excellence is sought, that innovation is stifled.

Thus, the innovating organization needs the people ready to see and act on these possibilities. It needs the people capable of adapting as circumstances change because they already have a broader base of skills, of organizational knowledge, and of relationships in advance of any demand for change. They are flexible and deployable, with restraining time reduced.

In short, a company can make itself adaptable by removing more of the barriers to major changes in *advance* of external crisis or threat. It can have people familiar with problem solving and with working through others in teams, who will be ready to step forward as innovators when they see a need and a possibility. These skills are less necessary in routine operations, of course, where segmentalism can work—units separated from each other, levels working independently, individuals pursuing defined-in-advance jobs without looking for or thinking about improvements other than incremental ones. But under circumstances demanding change, demanding new responses, then an adaptable, cooperative, and even entrepreneurial work force is required.

It is in this sense that modifications in organization design and improvements in human-resource systems constitute innovation-promoting innovations. They make the organization ready to both stimulate and take advantage of unprogrammed innovations that come from participating teams at the bottom and entrepreneurial managers in the middle and higher.

What is important to note about the "failures" of older companies with respect to innovation is not the utter impossibility of change, but rather, how easily it *could* have been done. In both the smaller example of the "Petrocorp" Marketing Services Department and the larger example of General Motors, the pieces are there for transforming changes—toward a more integrative form—with the potential to solve major problems for the company. But if the organization's leaders do not recognize this, and do not put the pieces together, then the potential for innovation-enhancing innovations is lost. If there is any "failure" in these accounts, it is not in the impossibility of transforming change but in the lack of ability on the part of those guiding the systems to understand the change process sufficiently well to take advantage of the innovation in their midst. Maybe these isolated instances of microchanges would not, one by one, "save" the company—but they might change the odds; they might tip the balance.

The true "tragedy" for most declining American companies struggling to keep afloat in this environment is not how far they are from the potential for transformation but rather how close they might come and not know it. How many quiet corporate entrepreneurs have put foward the seeds of ideas for major improvements? How many of them have silently improved their own operations, or slightly shifted production methods, or raised quality standards, or involved their workers in problem-solving teams, and gained in the process an important kind of learning for the company, if leaders had only known? How many quality-of-work-life programs have shown so much potential and yet been limited in their application and spread? How many people *know* that they could contribute more but feel that their company does not care about their efforts?

All any company has to do to explore its own potential to become a more innovating organization is to see what happens when employees and managers are brought together and given a significant problem to tackle, along with the power tools—the resources, information, and support—to help them meet the challenge. The energy and excitement that are unleashed, the ideas that come bubbling forth, the zest for work that suddenly appears in employees who had looked like "deadwood" are just a few of the indications that there is more "entrepreneurial spirit" to be tapped in most organizations, more willingness to cooperate in solving problems when the roadblocks stemming from segmentalism are removed.

Many executives who are otherwise hard-boiled and tough-minded evaluate the impact of their innovation-stimulating organizational change efforts in just such qualitative terms. When I push them for measures, they counter with intuitive yardsticks. For example: "All I have to do is walk through the factory and I know it feels different around here. People say hello in a different way. They smile. They are tackling their work with energy. They push back. I hear from them. There are ideas bubbling up from the bottom. . . . I used to avoid walking through the plant if I could help it, but now it's a pleasure."

The executive who spoke those words was clear that there would be a payoff in both productivity and innovation to his support for a more integrative participative organization, and it would clearly show up in financial results. But he did not feel that he had to justify the creation of an energetic organization merely on the basis of bottom-line results. After all, that would defeat one of the purposes of his new style of organization: to begin to treat people as contributing individuals rather than an anonymous mass whose primary purpose was fitting into the slots the company had made available.

Thus, if there is a realm where economic and human interests coincide, it is here, in the creation of innovating organizations. Reporting the impact only in terms of numbers is to deny a very important part of the reality of these kinds of changes. After all, as people, we live out our work lives not only through abstractions like numbers but rather through the numerous daily encounters that give us opportunities for contributing—or not—as the organization's structure and culture allow.

HOW TO BEGIN

Obviously, not everybody in an organization should be involved in innovation and change all, or even much, of the time. Even while considering change, companies have to manage a wide range of ongoing operations where efficiencies may require repetitive and routinized tasks, tightly bounded jobs, and clearly defined authority. Specialization of organization segments and limited contact between them can be an excellent strategy where no change is required, where repeating what is known *works* because both the demands and the activities to meet them are predictable. So innovation is not the *only* task of a successful company; the structure must also allow for maintenance of ongoing routines.

When trying to visualize the kind of organization that has *both* an array of routine jobs and opportunities for innovation, I am reminded of a common magician's trick using a set of large "magic rings." To set the stage, the magician hands five separate rings perhaps 8 to 10 inches in diameter to a volunteer from the audience for inspection. The rings each appear perfectly smooth and unbroken, and try as he or she might, the volunteer cannot get the rings to connect. Then the magician takes the rings back and tosses them into the air, and they immediately interlock. For the next few minutes, the magician dazzles the audience with displays of all the possible configurations and interlocking rings.

This provides an intriguing metaphor for the innovating organization. For a large part of its ongoing operations, an innovating organization may look on the surface just like a segmented one. It has a clear structure; its organization charts may show a differentiation into departments or functional units, there may be stated reporting relationships, and people may occupy specific jobs with specific job descriptions and bounded responsibilities. Just like the magic rings, the parts can be separated and, for routine purposes, dealt with separately. But with the toss of a problem,

across segments become clear: executive teams considering decisions together; "dotted line" reporting relationships to another area or more; multidisciplinary project teams; regular meetings of councils representing several areas; crosscutting task forces; territories shared by more than one function; teams of employees pulling together to improve performance; the additional connections between and networks of peers who exchange information and support each other's projects.

It is the possibility that the separate rings can indeed be easily connected, when the need arises, that gives the organization its potential for innovation.

Integrative, participative mechanisms do not *replace* the differentiation of definable segments that carry out clear and limited tasks; they supplement it. They prevent the existence of segments from turning into segmentalism. This is the idea behind a "parallel" organization presented earlier, a second organization that links the separate rings of the maintenance-oriented organization in flexible and shifting ways to solve problems and guide changes. There is a clear structure for routine operations overlaid with vehicles for participation. There is a predictable routine punctuated by episodes of high involvement in change efforts.

Top executives, whose mandate is to define the organization's structure, are the appropriate "magicians" in this case. They are the ones who can allow the tossing of the rings to connect people in new ways, across segment boundaries, so that they can participate in solving problems.

The idea behind having a second, or parallel, organization alongside routine operations only makes explicit what is already implicit in an integrative, innovating company: the capacity to work together cooperatively regardless of field or level to tackle the unknown, the uncertain. In a formal, explicit parallel organization, this is not left to happenstance but is guided—managed—to get the best results for both the company and the people involved.

Note that the parallel organization is not itself another specific "program" to temporarily solve an immediate local problem (isolating bits and pieces of problems from each other in segmentalist fashion and not allowing solutions to affect the whole system) but rather a means for managing innovation, participation, and change to ensure a *continuing* adaptive organization and an adaptive population within it. But under the leadership of the parallel organization may be any number of specific "programs," improvements, R&D efforts, and problem-solving groups. Its steering committee may manage an array of integrative vehicles—from standing committees linking parts of the organization on issues of major policy concern to temporary problem-solving groups or teams to innovative projects initiated by corporate entrepreneurs.

As the issues and problems change, so does the configuration of the "rings" making up the parallel organization. The steering committee, as manager of this flexible and responsive system, makes the links among the rings, creating new links in new circumstances—and connects the parallel organization to ongoing operations. This connection is important, in both directions. It helps make the problem-solving efforts responsive to the needs of the rest of the system, and it helps ensure that they in turn can take full advantage of the innovations derived from parallel-organization efforts.

There is a parallel organization guiding change at the divisions making up Honeywell's Defense and Marine Systems Group, for example. There the steering committee is chaired by each division general manager and consists of all his direct reports plus other key operations heads. At different times, the steering committee is managing different projects; in mid-1982 they included an advisory committee monitoring the implementation of a new performance communication system it had designed; a standing committee on community relations; nine task teams on major employee concerns; a study group considering how to involve the union on the steering committee; and a number of individuals to whom division-wide tasks had been assigned. At the same time, the steering committee continued to take a broad view of policy and to examine long-range goals.

What is striking about Honeywell's participative activities is their careful *management*. The steering committee, with its staff, was watching over budgets, writing guidelines for proposals, establishing accountabilities, communicating to the rest of the organization, and generally handling all the logistics needed to make the parallel organization function effectively. In short, the parallel organization at Honeywell is a coherent vehicle for ensuring that the conditions supporting innovation and productive change are present in the division. (People still do their regular jobs in the routine hierarchy, but they also have a second way to contribute, through teams and task forces, above and beyond the limits of their job.) It is not surprising that Richard Boyle, the division general manager leading this activity, is known as an "entrepreneur" around Honeywell. For him the division's outstanding financial results, well above plan, and its future projections are inextricably connected to the commitment to participative management; besides, "it saves us [the executives] time when we can get more of the organization involved in helping us get ready for the future."

Thus, an appropriate place to begin replacing segmentalism with the integrative approaches that support innovation is with the creation of a second structure, a structure for change, parallel to and connected with the company's ongoing structure for doing business as it has already learned how to do. Building a steering committee to guide this structure for change is itself an integrative step: the team at the top working cooperatively across functional lines to view their territory as a whole and combine data about needed changes from many perspectives—problem seeking as well as problem solving. This group can look for and reward innovations that already exist—the departures from tradition that suggest new options—as well as stimulate and encourage other innovations. It can set broad guidelines that give direction to action, channeling the entrepreneurial instincts of innovators in productive directions. And it can decide whether and how to change the way ongoing activities are handled.

Top management has many options for stimulating more innovation. It can assure that a portion of each job definition is loose, that roles and interests overlap enough to force people to work together across disciplinary or hierarchical boundaries, through multiple connections fostering cross-segment initiatives and teamwork. It can support and coordinate the actions of innovators, providing legitimacy, information, and resources to potential corporate entrepreneurs. By seeing the connection of decisions to one another, and encouraging and supporting coalitions, it can avoid segmentalism and make changes that will help support valuable initiative so that it does not slide away. It can make sure that all kinds of people and all kinds of levels in the organization feel included in an integrated whole, with the chance to participate in making a difference for the organization.

And then, the new approach can cascade downward. Teamwork to guide a parallel organization at the top can be matched by similar teams at the head of each major operation, serving integrative functions on more local levels, and moving downward to create integrative mechanisms for middle management, across level, across function, across barriers of race, sex, or employment category. When this occurs, the opportunity for lower echelons to participate in improvement-oriented teams (such as quality circles or committees or task forces or simply staff meetings) can be related appropriately to a consistent organizational culture and coherent strategic directions—not detached pieces handled segmentally but integrated groups connected to an organizational style that begins at the top and that supports local flexibility and initiative.

With my findings about innovating organizations in mind, it is not hard to imagine an action program to remove roadblocks to innovation. These would be among the important elements to be managed by the executive team or its designated steering committee:

Encouragement of a culture of pride.—Highlight the achievements of the company's own people, through visible awards, through applying an innovation from one area to the problems of another—and letting the experienced innovators serve as "consultants."

Enlarged access to power tools for innovative problem solving.—Provide vehicles (a council? an R&D committee? direct access to the steering committee?) for supporting proposals for experiments and innovations—especially those involving teams or collaborators across areas.

Improvement of lateral communication.—Bring departments together. Encourage cross-fertilization through exchange of people, mobility across areas. Create cross-functional links, and perhaps even overlaps. Bring together teams of people from different areas who share responsibility for some aspect of the same end product.

Reduction of unnecessary layers of hierarchy.—Eliminate barriers to resource access. Make it possible for people to go directly after what they need. Push decisional authority downward. Create "diagonal" slices cutting across the hierarchy to share information, provide quick intelligence about external and internal affairs.

Increased—and earlier—information about company plans.—Where possible, reduce secretiveness. Avoid surprises. Increase security by making future plans known in advance, making it possible, in turn, for those below to make their plans. Give people at lower levels a chance to contribute to the shape of change before decisions are made at the top. Empower and involve them at an earlier point—e.g., through task forces and problem-solving groups or through more open-ended, change-oriented assignments, with more room left for the *person* to define the approach.

Before these kinds of organizational changes can be made, of course, corporate leaders must make a personal commitment to do what is needed to support innovation. They must believe that times are different, understand that the transforming nature of our era requires a different set of responses. They need a sense of sufficient power themselves that they can be expansive about sharing it. They need a commitment to longer-term objectives and longer-term measures. And they as individuals must think in integrative rather than segmentalist ways, making connections between problems, pulling together ideas across disciplines, viewing issues from many perspectives. In short, top executives need at least some of the qualities of corporate entrepreneurs in order to support his capacity at lower levels in the organization.

If there is any domain over which top executives have control, it is organizational culture and structure, the setting of the context for others around and below them. Even if ideas bubble up, organizational style bubbles down. Even the most effective of corporate entrepreneurs soon reach the limit of their own ability to push innovative improvement when the environment set at the top does not support their activities for the use of their results. Indeed, until corporate leaders see the nature of this environment in its full-blown implications, they are doomed to make segmental, and therefore ultimately less effective, responses.

Instead of continuing to think that they can run the organization from the top, effective leaders will be those who know how to take advantage of the capacity of those below. They will be those who appreciate the fundamental transformation in the way organizations and the people in them must work to fit the economic and social challenges of our time. And thus, they can help contribute to a resurgence of the entrepreneurial spirit even within large organizations, a virtual Renaissance for corporate America.

THE AMERICAN WAY TO A CORPORATE RENAISSANCE

The models for the innovating organization are not particularly new, although they have received greater public attention and legitimacy in just the last few years, when the news reached us that certain of our successful foreign competitors might be beating us because of more people-conscious, commitment-producing workplaces. During the last twenty years, a large number of tools have been made available to American companies to stimulate the highest performance from their employees and managers, from more meritocratic performance-appraisal systems that reward individual achievement to cross-level problem-solving teams.

The tools are there—if we care to use them.

To me, that is the central issue: not inventing still another fancy new management system with its own acronym or alphabet label, but using what we already have. The issue is to create the conditions that enable companies to take advantage of the good ideas which already exist, by taking better advantage of the talents of their people. By encouraging innovation and entrepreneurship at all levels, by building an environment in which more people feel included, involved, and empowered to take initiative, companies as well as individuals can be the masters of change instead of its victims.

New ideas will "save the American economy." New ideas will provide our competitive advantage.

The source of new ideas is people.

That's why an organization's way of educating and involving people, distributing them among assignments, and rewarding their efforts are so critical in its ability to innovate. Selecting "good" people, certainly. But there are not enough creative geniuses to go around. And there are too many problems in most American companies in this era for them to be able to afford to have only a handful of people thinking about solutions.

Individuals make a difference. That's the positive side of "American individualism"—entrepreneurs not afraid to break the mold in seeking to break a record or competing to win a game. In organizations, this initiative is best expressed through teamwork, and thus we saw that managerial entrepreneurs with innovative accomplishments were most likely to have participative/collaborative styles, to involve a team of others to bring their idea to fruition. Innovation and participation are linked. Strong individuals, along with a tradition of teamwork, bring productive accomplishments into being. It is hard to mention "teams" or "participation" anymore without someone's labeling them "Japanese-style management." In the first place, this is faintly ridiculous, because it is just as American to use teams, and when American companies do it, they are doing it as Americans, out of their own organizational priorities and images. But if we stopped there, with the idea of participation, we might indeed be missing a distinctively American strength: the initiative of individuals. Innovating companies emphasize teamwork, but they also reward individuals, and they give internal entrepreneurs free rein to pioneer—as long as they can also work with the team. So "American-style" participation does not and should not mean the dominance of committees over individuals, the submergence of the individual in the group, or the swallowing of the person by the team, but rather *the mechanism for giving more people at more levels a piece of the entrepreneurial action.*

Thus, companies need to be encouraged to *invest* in people rather than paying them off—that is, to channel more of their "rewards" into budgets for projects or new ventures and less into after-the-fact bonuses for executives. Tax incentives could help; e.g., by a combination of deferred compensation for individuals and write-offs for the company, pools of working capital could be made available to support innovative projects inside a corporation.

Indeed, Harry Olson, a former senior executive of American Express, has proposed that severance pay for personnel laid off during a recession could be treated this way, as "venture capital" rather than a payoff to the individuals terminated. He argued that the company could use the same amount of money that would otherwise be paid directly to the individuals to set each of them up in a business; this in turn might create long-term gain for the company. Even if only a small proportion of the businesses paid off, the company would be no worse off than it is by the present system of cash payments that are not reinvested for its benefit. A similar reasoning is behind the efforts of companies like 3M and Levi-Strauss to set up internal venture-capital banks to fund new ventures developed by internal entrepreneurs.

Investment in internal human-resource systems is also related to the encouragement of corporate entrepreneurship in the interests of productivity and innovation. To the extent that innovation and change can save jobs through better company performance, and to the extent that an investment in human resources creates a better labor pool not only for the current company but also for the society at large should people change companies, then it is in the public interest as well as the company's interest to support investments in these areas. There could be tax credits, for example, for the development of training programs or other internal educational efforts meeting certain standards—in part a way of acknowledging the important educational role increasingly played by major corporations in today's society.

While not all aspects of a company's human-resource practices are reducible to concrete manifestations that could be supported in this fashion, a surprising number would lend themselves to this: e.g., the start-up costs of improving labor-management cooperation or beginning a joint labor-management committee; the R&D costs of a program to encourage more innovation in manufacturing methods; the retraining costs of shifting workers from one manufacturing sector to another or giving them skills to be more adaptable in the face of the changing technical environment. (It is striking to contemplate what kinds of changes could be encouraged by this method. For the most part, government interventions in the human-resource realm, e.g., safety and affirmative action, have been negative—threatening companies with punishment if they do not comply with regulations but not providing any rewards for quick compliance and creative change.)

If more companies are encouraged to increase their investment in their people, following the lead of the innovating companies I have described by replacing segmentation with integration, then this could in fact turn out to be a transforming era—one that might even be termed an American "corporate Renaissance" because of its humanistic as well as economic benefits.

In an American corporate Renaissance, we could see the reawakening of a dormant spirit of enterprise at all levels of organizations, among all kinds of workers. Entrepreneurship and initiative would be rewarded in large as well as small companies, and there would be a sense of shared purpose—almost a missionary zeal— with which people approached their work. The humanistic thrust inherent in the idea of a Renaissance would be manifested in corporate attention toward ending the "miseries" of earlier corporate work systems, integrating quality-of-life concerns with productivity. The potential for doing this

already exists, in countless offices and factories all over America beginning to see the virtues of a more participative workplace.

The Renaissance analogy suggests a growing "intellectuality" surrounding the American corporation. No longer the mindless machine, the corporation could be the instrument for meaningful intellectual exploration. There is already a growing trend toward self-conscious corporate examination of purpose and philosophy, sometimes expressed in the narrower and more technical idea of a corporate "mission" but increasingly being expressed in more philosophical statements of operating principles that stress human concerns. I have participated in the drafting of several such statements by groups of executives, including phrases such as "work life and home life have interacting needs that will be recognized." What is striking is not the mechanics of producing such statements (talk is cheap, after all) but the self-reflective discussions that take place among corporate leaders who are now participating in perhaps their first chance to examine their own and others' values. I am not suggesting that such statements of philosophy always result in immediate action or solve all of the workplace problems to which they are addressed, but they are an important starting point for a corporate Renaissance.

This growing concern with corporate purpose and long-term responsibilities would be aided by a quest for leaders characterized by long-range, integrative thinking. And by their encouragement to operate, once in executive office, toward long-term objectives. Perhaps it would even be possible to build these encouragements into corporate charters, the very framework for the corporation itself.

Corporate governance—e.g., the shape and composition of the Board of Directors and the officer group has been much discussed over the last few decades as a means to ensure that the public interest, as well as that of key groups such as employees, is reflected in corporate decisions. But there has been practically no discussion of the use of such mechanisms to encourage investment in the long term, including in its traditional form of R&D expenditures. But what if, for example, there were tax incentives, or even requirements, for publicly chartered firms to withhold a proportion of an officer's or a director's compensation until five years after retirement? Would this decrease the tendency to manage against stock price or quarterly income statements and encourage investment in activities that might not payoff until after the executive's term? Would this encourage more careful succession planning and development of successors?

 At this point, of course, such suggestions seem fanciful, and we can only speculate about their likely results, But consider that entrepreneurs who *found* companies often have to be willing to wait years for a return, trying to build a long-term capacity rather than just make a quick killing. Why shouldn't corporate executives too have to wait for rewards until the ultimate results of their actions are known?

A long-term view and concern with corporate philosophy and mission is only one part of a Renaissance-style intellectual awakening. The intellectual dimension of a possible corporate Renaissance is represented in more mundane ways by the increasing numbers of "knowledge workers" whose task performance is linked to the quality of their intellect, a rapid growth in "intellectual" staff functions such as planning departments, and a general increase in the amount of education carried on by and within corporations. There are even some companies hiring historians and cultural anthropologists to help them grasp ineffable dimensions of the corporate experience.

We could see a potential Renaissance in the flowering of literature highlighting the drama and excitement of activities within the new-style innovating corporations. Most great literature about business in the past seemed to fall into one of two camps: muckraking treatments of the corporation as oppressor of the human spirit, or cynical accounts of how someone beat the system. But otherwise, great art has not come out of the corporate sector; only dull monotony and Babbitry. (The great executive/poet Wallace Stevens did not write about his insurance company.) Between Horatio Alger and the recent past, we have only Willy Loman and the man in the gray flannel suit—and stories about the smothering of creativity. But today business stories are beginning to be told for their dramatic qualities as well as their immediate news value. The corporation is being seen as a human arena, and thus one out of which great tragedy and great comedy might be crafted—or gripping adventure stories like *The Soul of a New Machine*, about the design of a new computer.

There is drama in innovation and change that does not exist in a segmentalist environment. Out of the new high-tech companies in the Silicon Valley and Route 128, populated by the generation that gave us beads and plumage, has come a more colorful and expressive kind of existence, full of Friday parties-by-the-company-pool, tales of legendary heroes who found important companies but occupy the smallest office, and rituals like a "boot camp" to teach new managers about company culture. Thus, business life in an innovating company may be seen not only as a necessity, but as *interesting*—a life through which people can express themselves.

This Renaissance could also be signaled by the beginning of an end of a "Dark Ages" of insularity, closed boundaries, and chauvinism of all kinds. The potential for this is clear, though we still have a distance to go. With awareness and acknowledgment of the successes of foreign competition, American companies have become less smug and insular, willing to learn from other countries and other companies, integrating their overseas operations into the domestic mainstream—but respecting the differences of other cultures, and not automatically assuming American superiority. A greater sense of community and social responsibilities would also bring about a corporate Renaissance. Indeed, I nominate Minneapolis as the capital city for the corporate Renaissance because of the pioneering efforts of companies like Dayton-Hudson, General Mills, Honeywell, Control Data, and others to break down boundaries between company and community, behave responsibly, develop new work systems, and join together to promote these values.

Other forms of chauvinism and insularity would have to be overcome to warrant the Renaissance label, of course: assumptions of managerial superiority, male superiority, white superiority. But companies *could* do it—we have models of successful work systems that are more integrative environments—if they chose to put a commitment into the effort. Models exist.

Finally the potential for an American corporate Renaissance would be enhanced by the kinds of people developed and rewarded in leading-edge innovating companies: broader-gauged, more able to move across specialist boundaries, comfortable working in teams that may include many disciplines, knowledgeable about how to manage ambiguous assignments and webs of interdependencies. In short, Renaissance people—men and women of skill and cultivation who could function simultaneously in several organizational worlds.

The style of thought and problem-solving capacity associated with such Renaissance people are encouraged by a strong, affordable educational system that combats narrow vocationalism and permits people the luxury of studying a variety of fields before becoming too specialized. *Affordable* is the key word. When a liberal-arts education is not only priced out of the reach of most middle-income families but also appears to be a frill in a job-hungry society where there is no public assistance for either job finding or translation of a general education into a specific entry credential, then we encourage single-skilled people unable to function on the kinds of cross-disciplinary teams that produce innovation—and less adaptable when circumstances change. Thus, the potential for a corporate Renaissance would be enhanced by public—and really, federal—financing of higher education, particularly in the liberal arts.

Clearly we will always require a large number of specialists, particularly technically trained personnel skilled in the newest technologies. But if their education is balanced by a general education giving them a broader view and an ability to make intellectual and interpersonal connections with people in other fields, then the potential innovative capacity of the organizations that employ them is expanded. Some of those who become general managers in the most innovative high-technology firms have minimal technical competence but are well educated in an integrative discipline—including lawyers or personnel experts I met who had risen to head divisions in engineering-based companies. Purely technical experts are often unable to put all the pieces together to manage a business in a demanding, rapidly changing environment; Renaissance people are required.

If we were to have a corporate Renaissance, the organization itself would be the arena in which its great achievements would take place: new products, markets, policies, structures, methods, and philosophies. The excitement of change, the drama of invention captures the imagination in a way that routine, everyday work in a defined job does not. Being part of a team designing a new program for the company can give people a heightened sense of importance and involvement, an experience of creation that punctuates the rest of their ongoing work experience. Changing a part of an organization, inventing its shape can be fun, can be uplifting. And thus, some of the more deadening aspects of work in segmented systems could be alleviated by the opportunity to move beyond or outside of the job to innovate.

Of course, the organization itself can be the arena for innovation only if corporate leaders are focused on their own operations as the realm for investment, rather than seeking financial gains by manipulating assets—merging, acquiring, and divesting bundles of capacity rather than putting resources into increasing or redirecting that capacity itself.

As the recent Bendix debacle has made clear, attempts at mergers and acquisitions that serve no productive purposes are made possible in part by the ability of companies to write off certain of the costs involved against their taxes—in essence, a public subsidy of such activity. But it would be more clearly in the public interest to encourage companies like Bendix to reinvest their profits (or gains from the sale of assets) in the development of their own businesses, as Edgar Bronfman, chairman of Seagram's and himself a player in a large takeover battle with Du Pont, suggested in a column in *The New York Times*. To the extent that the marriage metaphor applies to a merger—whether it is a "shotgun romance" or a "courtship"—we can also see that our present system encourages companies to increase the "divorce" rate by "trading in spouses" rather than working on improving the quality of existing marriages. Under these circumstances, less attention is paid to internal innovation and fewer resources are made available to invest in it. But internal investment is what creates the climate for the innovations allowing companies to stay ahead in a changing environment.

In a corporate Renaissance, in short, companies would be more like "families" making long-term commitments to the development, health, and prosperity of each of their members, and looking to all of them for productive new ideas.

The potential exists for an American corporate Renaissance, with its implied return to greatness. Because recent economic conditions have been so unfavorable for American business, leaders should be motivated to search for new solutions — and to engage their entire work force in the search. I argue that innovation is the key. Individuals can make a difference, but they need the tools and the opportunity to use them. They need to work in settings where they are valued and supported, their intelligence given a chance to blossom. They need to have the power to be able to take the initiative to innovate.

Whether the promise of this corporate Renaissance is fulfilled depends on how fully corporate leaders understand this need and decide to act on it. It depends on whether we can come to embrace change, to see it as an opportunity, and thus to stimulate the people in our organizations to take action to master it.

As a nation, we can no longer afford to do otherwise.